Wissenschaftliche Untersuchungen
zum Neuen Testament · 2. Reihe

Herausgeber / Editor
Jörg Frey (Zürich)

Mitherausgeber/Associate Editors
Markus Bockmuehl (Oxford) · James A. Kelhoffer (Uppsala)
Tobias Nicklas (Regensburg) · Janet Spittler (Charlottesville, VA)
J. Ross Wagner (Durham, NC)

509

Matthew L. Walsh

Angels Associated with Israel in the Dead Sea Scrolls

Angelology and Sectarian Identity at Qumran

Mohr Siebeck

MATTHEW L. WALSH, born 1978; 2016 PhD in Religious Studies (Second Temple Period Judaism and Early Christianity) from McMaster University in Hamilton, Ontario, Canada; since 2016 Assistant Professor of Biblical Studies, Acadia Divinity College in Wolfville, Nova Scotia, Canada.

ISBN 978-3-16-155303-5 / eISBN 978-3-16-155304-2
DOI 10.1628/978-3-16-155304-2

ISSN 0340-9570 / eISSN 2568-7484 (Wissenschaftliche Untersuchungen zum Neuen Testament, 2. Reihe)

The Deutsche Nationalbibliothek lists this publication in the Deutsche Nationalbibliographie; detailed bibliographic data are available on the Internet at *http://dnb.dnb.de*.

The book was printed by Laupp & Göbel in Gomaringen on non-aging paper and bound by Buchbinderei Nädele in Nehren.

Printed in Germany.

For Christine, Elijah, Joseph,
Sarah, and Oliver

Preface

This study is a revision of my doctoral dissertation, which was defended on 24 June 2016 at McMaster University in Hamilton, Ontario. A dissertation/book may be written by one person, but without the wisdom, assistance, and diligence of numerous individuals, it would not have seen the light of day.

First, I am profoundly grateful for the astute and consistent supervision of Eileen Schuller, whose knowledge and scholarly acumen are only surpassed by the concern she has for her students. Though I am responsible for any shortcomings, this project is unquestionably stronger because of her excellent guidance. I also owe a tremendous debt of gratitude to Daniel Machiela and Stephen Westerholm, whose expertise and meticulous interaction with my work are greatly appreciated. Special thanks are due to Dana Hollander, who served as the internal-external reader for the defense, and Joseph Angel of Yeshiva University, who served as the external reader. Their questions and suggestions prompted invaluable insights that have sharpened my research. Additionally, my time at McMaster was supported by a doctoral fellowship from the Social Sciences and Humanities Research Council of Canada. On this point, a word of thanks is due to the unsung hero of the McMaster Religious Studies department, Doreen Drew, who tirelessly organizes scholarship applications for the graduate students.

Second, I experienced a wonderful sense of camaraderie at McMaster, and I am thankful for my fellow former occupants of the University Hall basement offices, particularly: Miriam DeCock, Michael Johnson, Andrew Krause, Nick Meyer, Eric Montgomery, and Andy Perrin. I would also like to thank the faculty and students who participated in the annual Dead Sea Scrolls conferences jointly organized by McMaster and the University of Toronto.

Third, there are a host of people who have indirectly contributed to this project. For introducing me to the academic discipline of biblical studies, I am indebted to my former Acadia University professors, Timothy Ashley, Allison Trites, Craig Evans, and Glenn Wooden. For moral support, I am grateful for my parents, Barrie and Alice Walsh, and my in-laws, Ray and Marilyn Monette. For their listening ears and friendship over the years, I thank Andrew Boone, Tammy Giffen, Matt Leyennar, Greg Monette, Danny Zacharias, and my brother, Peter Walsh. For granting me time to write in 2015, I am thankful for the congregation of West End Baptist Church, particularly Lynn and Glenn

Anderson, Suzanne and Jonathan Trites, and especially David Watt, who is an exemplary pastor, mentor, and friend. I would also be remiss not to thank my supportive colleagues, the faculty and staff of Acadia Divinity College, including our recently retired boss, Harry Gardner.

Jörg Frey, editor of the WUNT 2 series, accepted my work for publication, and both Henning Ziebritzki and Matthias Spitzner at Mohr Siebeck were helpful and patient as I prepared the manuscript. I thank the three of them for this opportunity.

Most of all, I am grateful for my wife, Christine, and our children, Elijah, Joseph, Sarah, and Oliver, who exude love and understanding on a daily basis. They have been a constant source of encouragement, and it is with joy that I dedicate this study to them.

Matthew L. Walsh
Fall River, Nova Scotia
4 November 2019

Table of Contents

Chapter 3: Angels Associated with Israel in Second Temple Period Qumran Texts of a Non-Sectarian Provenance 56

Abbreviations

AB	Anchor Bible
ABD	*Anchor Bible Dictionary*. Edited by David Noel Freedman. 6 vols. New York: Doubleday, 1992.
ABRL	Anchor Bible Reference Library
AGJU	Arbeiten zur Geschichte des antiken Judentums und des Urchristentums
AJEC	Ancient Judaism and Early Christianity
ANET	*Ancient Near Eastern Texts Relating to the Old Testament*. Edited by James B. Pritchard. 3rd ed. Princeton: Princeton University Press, 1969.
ANYAS	Annals of the New York Academy of Sciences
ArBib	The Aramaic Bible
ASORMS	American Schools of Oriental Research Monograph Series
ATANT	Abhandlungen zur Theologie des Alten und Neuen Testaments
ATDan	Acta Theologica Danica
ATSAT	Arbeiten zu Text und Sprache im Alten Testament
AUSDDS	Andrews University Seminary Doctoral Dissertation Series
BA	*Biblical Archaeologist*
BAR	*Biblical Archaeology Review*
BBR	*Bulletin for Biblical Research*
BCOTWP	Baker Commentary on the Old Testament Wisdom and Psalms
BETL	Bibliotheca ephemeridum theologicarum lovaniensium
Bib	*Biblica*
BibInt	Biblical Interpretation Series
BRLJ	Brill Reference Library of Judaism
BSac	*Bibliotheca Sacra*
BT	*The Bible Translator*
BZAW	Beihefte zur Zeitschrift für die alttestamentliche Wissenschaft
BZRGG	Beihefte zur Zeitschrift für Religions – und Geistesgeschichte
CBQ	*Catholic Biblical Quarterly*
CBQMS	Catholic Biblical Quarterly Monograph Series
CurBR	*Currents in Biblical Research*
CDSSE	*The Complete Dead Sea Scrolls in English: Revised Edition*. Géza Vermes. New York: Penguin Books, 2011.
CEJL	Commentaries on Early Jewish Literature
CJAS	Christianity and Judaism in Antiquity Series

CQS	Companion to the Qumran Scrolls
CSCO	Corpus Scriptorum Christianorum Orientalium
CTA	*Corpus des tablettes en cuneiforms alphabetiques découvertes à Ras Shamra-Ugarit de 1929 à 1939.* Edited by Andrée Herdner. Paris: Geuthner, 1963.
CTU	*The Cuneiform Alphabetic Texts from Ugarit, Ras Ibn Hani, and Other Places.* Edited by Manfried Dietrich, Oswald Loretz, and Joaquin Sanmartin. Münster: Ugarit-Verlag, 1995.
DCLS	Deuterocanonical and Cognate Literature Studies
DCLY	Deuterocanonical and Cognate Literature Yearbook
DDD	*Dictionary of Deities and Demons in the Bible.* Edited by Karel van der Toorn, Bob Becking, and Pieter W. van der Horst. Leiden: Brill, 1995. 2nd rev. ed. Grand Rapids: Eerdmans, 1999.
DJD	Discoveries in the Judaean Desert
DSD	*Dead Sea Discoveries*
DSSANT	*The Dead Sea Scrolls: A New Translation.* Michael O. Wise, Martin G. Abegg, Jr., and Edward M. Cook. New York: Harper Collins, 1996.
DSSSE	*The Dead Sea Scrolls Study Edition.* Florentino García Martínez and Eibert J. C. Tigchelaar. 2 vols. Leiden: Brill. Grand Rapids: Eerdmans, 1997–98.
ECDSS	Eerdmans Commentaries on the Dead Sea Scrolls
EDSS	*Encyclopedia of the Dead Sea Scrolls.* Edited by Lawrence H. Schiffman and James C. VanderKam. 2 vols. New York: Oxford University Press, 2000.
EJL	Early Judaism and its Literature
EPRO	Etudes préliminaires aux religions orientals dans l'empire romain
ETL	*Ephemerides Theologicae Lovanienses*
FAT	Forschungen zum Alten Testament
FO	*Folia Orientalia*
FOTL	Forms of the Old Testament Literature
GAP	Guides to the Apocrypha and Pseudepigrapha
HALOT	*The Hebrew and Aramaic Lexicon of the Old Testament.* Ludwig Koehler, Walter Baumgartner, and Johann J. Stamm. Translated and edited under the supervision of Mervyn E. J. Richardson. 4 vols. Leiden: Brill, 1994–1999.
HAR	*Hebrew Annual Review*
HBAI	*Hebrew Bible and Ancient Israel*
HdO	Handbuch der Orientalistik
Hen	*Henoch*
HSM	Harvard Semitic Monographs
HSS	Harvard Semitic Studies
HTR	*Harvard Theological Review*
HTS	Harvard Theological Studies

HUCA	*Hebrew Union College Annual*
ICC	International Critical Commentary
IEJ	*Israel Exploration Journal*
Imm	*Immanuel*
Int	*Interpretation*
IOS	*Israel Oriental Studies*
JAAJ	*Judaïsme Ancien – Ancient Judaism*
JAJ	*Journal of Ancient Judaism*
JAJSup	Journal of Ancient Judaism Supplements
JBL	*Journal of Biblical Literature*
JBS	*Journal of Biblical Studies*
JCTC	Jewish and Christian Texts in Context and Related Studies
JESOT	*Journal for the Evangelical Study of the Old Testament*
JHebS	*Journal of Hebrew Scriptures*
JJS	*Journal of Jewish Studies*
JNES	*Journal of Near Eastern Studies*
JPSTC	Jewish Publication Society Torah Commentary
JQR	*Jewish Quarterly Review*
JSJ	*Journal for the Study of Judaism in the Persian, Hellenistic, and Roman Periods*
JSJSup	Supplements to the Journal for the Study of Judaism
JSOT	*Journal for the Study of the Old Testament*
JSOTSup	Journal for the Study of the Old Testament Supplement Series
JSP	*Journal for the Study of the Pseudepigrapha*
JSPSup	Journal for the Study of the Pseudepigrapha Supplement Series
JSS	*Journal of Semitic Studies*
JTS	*Journal of Theological Studies*
KTU	*Die keilalphabetischen Texte aus Ugarit.* Edited by Manfried Dietrich, Oswald Loretz, and Joaquin Sanmartin. Münster: Ugarit-Verlag, 2013.
LHBOTS	Library of Hebrew Bible/Old Testament Studies
LNTS	Library of New Testament Studies
LSTS	Library of Second Temple Studies
MT	Masoretic Text
NICOT	New International Commentary on the Old Testament
NovTSup	Supplements to Novum Testamentum
NRSV	New Revised Standard Version
NTL	New Testament Library
NTS	*New Testaments Studies*
OTL	Old Testament Library
OTP	*The Old Testament Pseudepigrapha.* Edited by James H. Charlesworth. 2 vols. New York: Doubleday, 1983, 1985.
OTS	Old Testament Studies
OtSt	*Oudtestamentische Studiën*

PTSDSSP	Princeton Theological Seminary Dead Sea Scrolls Project
PVTG	Pseudepigrapha Veteris Testamenti Graece
RB	*Revue biblique*
RBL	*Review of Biblical Literature*
RevQ	*Revue de Qumrân*
RHR	*Revue de l'histoire des religions*
SB	Sources biblique
SBLDS	Society of Biblical Literature Dissertation Series
SBLMS	Society of Biblical Literature Monograph Series
SBLSP	Society of Biblical Literature Seminar Papers
SBLSymS	Society of Biblical Literature Symposium Series
SBT	Studies in Biblical Theology
ScrHier	Scripta Hierosolymitana
SCS	Septuagint and Cognate Studies
SDSSRL	Studies in the Dead Sea Scrolls and Related Literature
SJLA	Studies in Judaism in Late Antiquity
SMSR	*Studi e materiali di storia delle religioni*
SNTSMS	Society for New Testament Studies Monograph Series
SSN	Studia Semitica Neerlandica
SSU	Studia Semitica Upsaliensia
STAC	Studien und Texte zu Antike und Christentum
StBibLit	Studies in Biblical Literature (Lang)
STDJ	Studies on the Texts of the Desert of Judah
SubBi	Subsidia Biblica
SUNT	Studien zur Umwelt des Neuen Testaments
SVTG	Septuaginta Vetus Testamentum Graecum
SVTP	Studia in Veteris Testamenti Pseudepigraphica
TBN	Themes in Biblical Narrative
TDNT	*Theological Dictionary of the New Testament*. Edited by Gerhard Kittel and Gerhard Friedrich. Translated by Geoffrey W. Bromiley. 10 vols. Grand Rapids: Eerdmans, 1964–1976.
TDOT	*Theological Dictionary of the Old Testament*. Edited by G. Johannes Boatterweck, Helmer Ringgren, and Heinz-Josef Fabry. Translated by David E. Green and Douglas W. Scott. 16 vols. Grand Rapids: Eerdmans, 1974–2018.
TLOT	*Theological Lexicon of the Old Testament*. Edited by Ernst Jenni and Claus Westermann. Translated by M. E. Biddle. 3 vols. Peabody: Hendrickson, 1997.
TSAJ	Texte und Studien zum antiken Judentum
TSK	*Theologische Studien und Kritiken*
TWOT	*Theological Wordbook of the Old Testament*. Edited by R. Laird Harris, Gleason L. Archer, Jr., and Bruce K. Waltke. 2 vols. Chicago: The Moody Bible Institute, 1980.

TynBul	*Tyndale Bulletin*
VT	*Vetus Testamentum*
VTSup	Supplements to Vetus Testamentum
WBC	Word Biblical Commentary
WLAW	Wisdom Literature from the Ancient World
WMANT	Wissenschaftliche Monographien zum Alten und Neuen Testament
WUNT	Wissenschaftliche Untersuchungen zum Neuen Testament
ZAW	*Zeitschrift für die alttestamentliche Wissenschaft*
ZKT	*Zeitschrift für katholische Theologie*
ZNW	*Zeitschrift für neutestamentliche Wissenschaft und die Kunde der älteren Kirche*
ZTK	*Zeitschrift für Theologie und Kirche*

Chapter 1

General Introduction, History of Research, and Objectives and Plan of Study

A. General Introduction

Angelic beings are depicted in a variety of ways in the Hebrew Bible: as messengers, as military commanders, and as protectors of the faithful, but for the most part they are unnamed and relatively undeveloped as characters. It is not until the middle of the Second Temple Period that we begin to witness heightened interest in angels. Many developments stem from reflection upon biblical themes and categories, as angels are creatively assigned names, ranks, and duties with ever-increasing specificity.[1]

An aspect of Hebrew Bible angelology[2] that was the subject of considerable speculation in the Second Temple Period – and a main concern of the present study – was the concept that certain angels were closely associated with Israel. These angels are cast as having at least two vocations, though not infrequently there is overlap between them. 1.) Angels who served as the guardians of God's people: while angelic assistance or support for Israel in times of trouble or war has considerable biblical precedent (e.g., Exod 14:19; Josh 5:13–15; 2 Kgs 19:35), the early Jewish expansion of this concept includes the notions that certain angels were warriors who strived against the angels associated with Israel's enemies in the celestial realm and/or were granted a prominent role in the eschatological deliverance of God's people.[3]

---

[1] On this development, see Larry W. Hurtado, "Monotheism, Principal Angels, and the Background of Christology," in *The Oxford Handbook of the Dead Sea Scrolls* (eds., Timothy H. Lim and John J. Collins; Oxford: Oxford University Press, 2010), 550–551.

[2] Kevin P. Sullivan, *Wrestling with Angels: A Study of the Relationship between Angels and Humans in Ancient Jewish Literature and the New Testament* (AJEC 55; Leiden: Brill, 2004), 7, echoes the oft-noted warning that the term "angelology" be used with caution as it can misleadingly suggest that a given text or corpus is systematic in its presentation of angelic beings. I use "angelology" here and elsewhere mindful of the diversity with which angels are portrayed both in the Hebrew Bible and in the literature of the Second Temple Period.

[3] For an introduction, see Darrell D. Hannah, "Guardian Angels and Angelic National Patrons in Second Temple Judaism and Early Christianity," in *Angels: The Concept of Celestial Beings – Origins, Development and Reception* (eds., Friedrich V. Reiterer, Tobias Nicklas, and Karen Schöpflin; DCLY; New York: de Gruyter, 2007), 413–435.

2.) Angels who served as priests: a notion that is implicit at best in the Hebrew Bible yet a topic of interest in the Second Temple period literature is that there were angelic priests who ministered in a heavenly temple. In this scenario, the celestial sanctuary and its celebrants seemed to have been understood as the archetypes for Israel's sanctuary and priesthood.[4] A crucial component of the presentation of both angelic guardians and priests was that they were envisioned within apocalyptic worldviews that assumed that "earthly realities reflect and mirror heavenly ones,"[5] and a related development was that there was thought to be some kind of connection, correspondence, or parallel relationship between the realms. While angels associated with Israel could be a named or titled individual, another development – and one often found side-by-side with the notion of an angelic leader-figure – was that the existence, actions, and fates of the angelic host collectively were connected to the Jewish people on earth.

Certain texts will be key to my discussion and will form the basis of much of the analysis in subsequent chapters. Deuteronomy 32:8–9 is an obvious starting point, as according to this text Yhwh has assigned celestial beings a guardian-like role over other nations, but he rules Israel directly. In contrast, the Enochic *Book of Watchers* suggests that, at least by the 3rd cent. BCE, there were those who thought there were named angels in heaven such as Michael, who is said to have a special relationship with God's people (cf. 1 En. 20:5). Similarly, the Book of Daniel (2nd cent. BCE) portrays Michael as exemplary among the angelic host, whose struggles and victories in the heavenly realm are paralleled in the lives of God's people on earth (cf. Dan 10:13, 21; 12:1). While Jubilees (also 2nd cent. BCE) contains no angels with proper names,[6] a titled angelic class – "the angels of the presence" – and its eponymous leader are clearly marked as Israel's heavenly counterparts and serve as priests before God (cf. Jub. 2:2–30; 6:18; 15:27–28; 30:18; 31:14).[7]

But a parallel relationship between the realms does not sufficiently explain some of the claims of the Qumran texts, which speak of eschatological and even present interaction or communion between angels and humans. As I will discuss at length in later chapters, the Qumran movement[8] anticipated that they would fight in conjunction with the angels at the eschaton, as the

---

[4] On the concept of heaven as a temple and suggestions for this development, see Martha Himmelfarb, *A Kingdom of Priests: Ancestry and Merit in Ancient Judaism* (Philadelphia: University of Pennsylvania Press, 2006), 19–20, who comments that in early Jewish literature heaven is depicted as the "the true temple, of which the Jerusalem temple is merely a copy."

[5] Hannah, "Guardian Angels and Angelic National Patrons," 420.

[6] The exception is the wicked Mastema. Cf. O. S. Wintermute, "Jubilees," *OTP* 2:47.

[7] "The angels of presence" and "the angels of holiness" are created circumcised, keep the Sabbath, and celebrate Shavuot; see Chapter 3, below.

[8] I will review how scholars refer to the group(s) associated with the Dead Sea Scrolls later in this chapter.

War Scroll predicts that Michael would lead an angel-human coterie known as the "Sons of Light" or "God's lot," and together they would take their stand against the "Sons of Darkness" at the great eschatological battle (cf. 1QM XVII, 4–9). Scholars have also suggested that the *Songs of the Sabbath Sacrifice* were employed liturgically by the sect to achieve fellowship with angelic priests in the present time, a feat celebrated in the sectarian hymns (cf. 1QH^a XI, 20–24; XIX, 13–17; 1QS XI, 7–9).

However, the designations scholars have coined to express this relationship between heaven and earth can be employed without technical precision. For example, an individual angelic leader charged with the guardianship of a people or nation is often called a "patron."[9] Given that figures such as Michael wage war against the angels of other nations and have a role in securing eschatological salvation for the people of God, "patron" is not an inappropriate classificatory term. "Counterpart" is also used in reference to individual angelic guardians,[10] and though this term is quite helpful in that it expresses the thought that the people have a chief angelic complement in the heavenly realm, it is not without difficulties. First, "counterpart" may be less apt than "patron" to convey that the referenced angel is a benefactor, let alone one who leads the angelic host, protects God's people, and fights with them and on their behalf. Second, the plural, "counterparts," is often used as a descriptor for the collective angelic host associated with Israel, be it "the angels of the presence" and "the angels of holiness," who according to Jubilees bear the marks of the covenant and carry out priestly roles in the heavenly sanctuary,[11] or the Danielic "holy ones of the Most High," whose fates are closely intertwined with "the *people* of the holy ones of the Most High."[12] As with the singular, scholars use the plural "patrons" interchangeably with "counter-

---

[9] E.g., Michael is referred to as a "patron" by Hannah, "Guardian Angels and Angelic National Patrons," 420; George W. E. Nickelsburg, *1 Enoch 1: A Commentary on the Book of 1 Enoch, Chapters 1–36, 81–108* (Hermeneia; Minneapolis: Fortress Press, 2001), 295; John J. Collins, *The Apocalyptic Imagination: An Introduction to Jewish Apocalyptic Literature* (2nd ed.; Grand Rapids: Eerdmans, 1998), 103.

[10] John J. Collins, *Daniel: A Commentary on the Book of Daniel* (Hermeneia; Minneapolis: Fortress, 1993), 310, 317, dubs Michael the "heavenly counterpart of Israel," and similarly refers to the angel-like benefactor of the *Similitudes of Enoch*, "that Son of Man," as both the people's "patron" and their "counterpart."

[11] E.g., Devorah Dimant, "Men as Angels: The Self-Image of the Qumran Community," in *Religion and Politics in the Ancient Near East* (ed., Adele Berlin; Bethesda: University of Maryland Press, 1996), 99, who writes, "the angels of presence and angels of holiness … were created circumcised (cf. *Jub.* 15:27–28). A sign of the divine covenant, it marks them as partakers of this covenant, and as heavenly counterparts of earthly Israel." Cf. R. M. M. Tuschling, *Angels and Orthodoxy: A Study of the Development in Syria and Palestine from the Qumran Texts to Ephrem the Syrian* (STAC 40; Tübingen: Mohr Siebeck, 2007), 119.

[12] E.g., Collins, *Daniel*, 318, in a discussion of Dan 7: "There is … a synergism between the faithful Israelites on earth and their angelic counterparts in heaven … ."

parts,"[13] and it is therefore important to specify the function of the counter-parts under discussion. Another term that has been used by scholars to refer to a chief angel figure is "Doppelgänger,"[14] in the sense that Israel has a heavenly "double," whose exaltation and power in heaven will ultimately mean salvation for the suffering community this figure represents. Not surprisingly, the designation angelic "representatives"[15] is also used, and in light of the fact that the English word "representative(s)" can convey the concepts of "standing for" or "defending" someone (as per the role of angelic guardians) and "epitomizing" or "corresponding to" someone (as per the role of priestly angels) it is not an inappropriate term.

While I will make careful use of the above terms, the general designation I prefer is *angels associated with Israel*. Moreover, I will highlight whether these angels serve as Israel's guardians, who were expected to defend God's people against the nation's aggressors (angelic and human), or as priests in the heavenly temple, though it needs to be reiterated that angels are sometimes portrayed as fulfilling more than one vocation or role.

Thus, angels associated with Israel and the worldviews which envisioned these angels as connected to the people of God are the primary foci of this study. In short, I will examine the relevant Dead Sea Scrolls widely considered to be of a non-sectarian provenance (i.e., works not composed by the Qumran movement). I will also examine sectarian writings, and I will endeavor to show that the well-known angelic fellowship assertions of the sect made a significant contribution to how it viewed itself vis-à-vis other Jews. To provide a rationale for this study and to frame it in the context of modern critical scholarship, I will now present a brief history of research, which will be primarily focused on the intersection of angelology and Qumran studies.

---

[13] Collins, *Daniel*, 318, again in reference to "the holy ones of the Most High," writes, "to the pious Jews of the Maccabean era, who had a lively belief in supernatural beings, nothing could be more relevant than that their angelic patrons should 'receive the kingdom.'"

[14] John J. Collins, "The Heavenly Representative: The 'Son of Man' in the Similitudes of Enoch," in *Ideal Figures in Ancient Judaism: Profiles and Paradigms* (eds., George W. E. Nickelsburg and John J. Collins; SCS 12; Missoula: Scholars Press, 1980), 116, applies the term to the "Son of Man" of the *Similitudes of Enoch*.

[15] E.g., I. P. Culianu, "The Angels of the Nations and the Origins of Gnostic Dualism," in *Studies in Gnosticism and Hellenistic Religions: Presented to Gilles Quispel on the occasion of His 65th Birthday* (eds., R. van den Broek and M. J. Vermaseren; Leiden: Brill, 1981), 186. Also see, George Caird, *Principalities and Powers: A Study in Pauline Theology* (Oxford: Claredon Press, 1956), 16–17, whose discussion rightly implies that to the ancient mind, humans could also be considered the earthly representatives of heavenly realities.

B. History of Research

Studies of early Jewish angelology have often been conducted in the course of investigating other topics, and it has been relatively rare for Second Temple Period angelology to be studied for its own sake.[16] Recent monographs and compilations have begun to address this void and rightly take into account the prominence of angels in the Dead Sea Scrolls. But angels associated with Israel and the worldviews within which these angels are presented have still not received the attention they deserve, especially as it pertains to investigating the religious identity of the Qumran movement. In this section, I will review relevant scholarship according to topic; I will then summarize the significance of this research for investigating angels associated with Israel in the Dead Sea Scrolls.

I. Angelology and Christology

Much angelological research has taken shape within New Testament scholarship on Christology. The intersection of angelology and Christology was, initially, an area of interest for German scholarship. Lueken's study appeared at the end of the 19th cent. and was followed by an intensified interest in the topic in the early 1940s.[17] These German works were the beginnings of research into "angel Christology" and "angelmorphic Christology," which have been the subjects of numerous studies in the last twenty-five years.

That ancient Judaism provided the earliest followers of Jesus with traditions of divine agency – the idea that the God of Israel, while maintaining his uniqueness, granted to a heavenly figure the role of chief vizier or agent – is central to the Christological thesis of Hurtado.[18] The diversity of Greco-

---

[16] Cf. Aleksander R. Michalak, *Angels as Warriors in Late Second Temple Period Literature* (WUNT 2/330; Tübingen: Mohr Siebeck, 2012), 4, who observes that angelology often functions as a "springboard" for other scholarly pursuits.

[17] Wilhelm Lueken, *Michael: Eine Darstellung und Vergleichung der jüdischen und der morgenländisch-christlichen Tradition vom Erzenglel Michael* (Göttingen: Vandenhoeck & Ruprecht, 1898). The earlier German research was continued and expanded by Joseph Barbel, *Christos Angelos: Die Anschauung von Christus als Bote und Engel in der gelehrten und volkstümlichen Literatur des christlichen Altertums* (Bonn: Hanstien, 1941), 1. Cf. Martin Werner, *Die Entstehung des christlichen Dogma* (Tübingen: Katzmann, 1941); Wilhelm Michaelis, *Zur Engelchristologie im Urchristentum: Abbau der Konstruktion Martin Werners* (Basel: Heinrich Majer, 1942).

[18] Larry W. Hurtado, *One God, One Lord: Early Christian Devotion and Ancient Jewish Monotheism* (2nd ed.; Edinburgh: T & T Clark, 1998), 12, 39. Examples include Michael (Dan 7–12) and Melchizedek (11Q13), who are pictured as having heavenly origins, exalted in heaven, and/or attributed with power and authority that approximate divine prerogatives. Thus, Hurtado argues that principal angel figures have more in common with the status ac-

Roman Judaism ensured that this chief agent could be envisioned in a variety of ways including that of a "principal angel,"[19] and the conclusion of Hurtado and others is that the elevated profiles of these divine agents did not compromise Jewish monotheism. Moreover, since the existence and even veneration[20] of these heavenly agents of mediation[21] and protection[22] did not impinge on the kind of devotion that was due God alone, early Christians found the language used to honour angels helpful in formulating their worship of Jesus, an act which the Church insisted did not contradict the oneness of the God of Israel.[23] The worship of Jesus should thus be seen as a distinctive modification or mutation of Jewish divine agency traditions.[24] As I will point out, it is not only true that Jewish monotheism was generally considered uncompromised by high-profile angelic leader-figures:[25] it was also considered a defining characteristic of God's people to have the support of these angels.

II. Angelology and Anthropology

A second area in which angelological investigation has taken place is the study of early Jewish anthropology, which includes attempts to explain hu-

---

corded the risen Jesus by the early Church than earthly agents of God such as prophets, priests, kings, and messiahs.

[19] Hurtado, *One God*, 17–18, 71–92.

[20] So Loren T. Stuckenbruck, "'Angels' and 'God': Exploring the Limits of Early Jewish Monotheism," in *Early Jewish and Christian Monotheism* (eds., idem and Wendy E. S. North; JSNTSup 263; London: T & T Clark, 2005), 69–70, who points out that while some early Jewish sources "could tolerate language of prayer and praise as directed towards angels" (e.g., Tob 11:14; 4Q418 [=*4QIntstruction*] 81 1–15; T. Levi 5:5–6; Jos. Asen. 11–12), … "even where the venerative language towards angelic beings is allowed, the authors ensure that it does not come at the price of reflection and focus on God. The logical tension remains, but the uniqueness of God continues to be asserted against any other possibility." Also see idem, *Angel Veneration and Christology: A Study in Early Judaism and in the Christology of the Apocalypse of John* (WUNT 2/70; Tübingen: Mohr Siebeck, 1995). Cf. Peter R. Carrell, *Jesus and the Angels: Angelology and the Christology of the Apocalypse of John* (SNTSMS 95; New York: Cambridge University Press, 1997).

[21] Philip G. Davis, "Divine Agents, Mediators, and New Testament Christology," *JTS* 45 (1994): 479–503, emphasizes the influence divine agency traditions had on the Church's understanding of the mediatorial role of Christ.

[22] Darrell D. Hannah, *Michael and Christ: Michael Traditions and Angel Christology in Early Christianity* (WUNT 2/109; Tübingen: Mohr Siebeck, 1999), 218, explores the connections between Michael and Christology, concluding that the early Church "utilized Michael traditions to illustrate the heavenly significance of Christ, particularly his protection of and intercession for Christians."

[23] Stuckenbruck, "'Angels' and 'God,'" 70.

[24] So Hurtado, *One God*, 12, 93–124.

[25] As Hannah, *Michael and Christ*, 217, observes: Michael traditions had more Christological usefulness than other principal angel traditions because "they were the most pervasive and the most multifarious" in the Second Temple Period.

mans with an exalted status. While many scholars have insisted on maintaining a distinction between angels and humans,[26] the most ardent proponent of the juxtaposition of angelology and anthropology is Fletcher-Louis, who has claimed the original and eschatological-redeemed state of humanity envisioned by the Qumran sect included an exalted anthropology, which he describes as "divine (and/or angelic)."[27] The Qumran movement attained this true humanity through their worship, which transcended not only time and space but also human ontology. The notion of angelic humanity traditions has been criticized, however, for seeing an ontological ambiguity between angels and humans when the evidence suggests only the "possibility of crossing the boundary between the earthly and heavenly sphere, especially by angels and on rare occasions by very righteous humans."[28] Fletcher-Louis has clarified and supplemented his approach,[29] and I will briefly return to some of his more controversial assertions in subsequent chapters. But it needs to be said here that the present study is, in part, a response to his observation that there is a need for more detailed investigations of the intersection of angelology and the sectarian identity of the Qumran movement.[30]

---

[26] So, e.g., Sullivan, *Wrestling with Angels*.

[27] Crispin H. T. Fletcher-Louis, *All the Glory of Adam: Liturgical Anthropology in the Dead Sea Scrolls* (STDJ 42; Leiden: Brill, 2003). Cf. idem, *Luke-Acts: Angels, Christology, and Soteriology* (Tübingen: Mohr Siebeck, 1997). Also see Charles A. Gieschen, *Angelmorphic Christology: Antecedents and Early Evidence* (AGJU 42; Leiden: Brill, 1998), 152–183. For a classic investigation of seven Pseudepigrapha, which are either later than the Second Temple Period or are notoriously difficult to date, see James H. Charlesworth, "The Portrayal of Righteous as an Angel," in *Ideal Figures in Ancient Judaism: Profiles and Paradigms* (eds., George W. E. Nickelsburg and John J. Collins; SCS 12; Chico: Scholars Press, 1980), 135–151.

[28] Sullivan, *Wrestling with Angels*, 232. Cf. J. O'Neill, review of Crispin H. T. Fletcher-Louis, *Luke-Acts: Angels, Christology, and Soteriology*, JTS 50 (1999), 225–230; Carol A. Newsom, review of Crispin H. T. Fletcher-Louis, *All the Glory of Adam: Liturgical Anthropology in the Dead Sea Scrolls*, DSD 10 (2003): 431–435.

[29] Crispin H. T. Fletcher-Louis, "Further Reflections on a Divine and Angelic Humanity in the Dead Sea Scrolls," in *New Perspectives on Old Texts: Proceedings of the Tenth International Symposium of the Orion Center for the Study of the Dead Sea Scrolls and Associated Literature, 9–11 January, 2005* (eds., Esther G. Chazon, Betsy Halpern-Amaru, and Ruth A. Clements; STDJ 88; Leiden: Brill, 2010), 183–198, here 197, has sought to explain his "divine and/or angelic" anthropology thesis by further recourse to the *War Scroll*, which he sees as espousing a "thoroughgoing image-of-God-in-humanity theology." For example, the standards of Israel's army, which were dedicated to the people of God, Israel, Aaron, and the twelve tribes (cf. 1QM III, 13–14), were not promoting idolatry but countering the idolatrous military equipment of the Romans, whose standards made use of zoomorphic images. Thus, Fletcher-Louis argues that the sectarians were convinced of the following: "[I]n order to cleanse the world of idolatrous man-made images and gods who are no gods, God intends to use his true image, Adam-in-Israel, to fill creation with his Glory."

[30] Fletcher-Louis, *All the Glory*, 88–89.

III. Angelology and Mysticism

Given the fascination with the heavenly realm in mystical texts, angelological investigation has also occurred in studies of mysticism. A particular focus of recent scholarship is the attempt to trace the development of Jewish and Christian mysticism, and often included in these investigations is a survey of the apocalyptic literature of the Second Temple Period, as this addresses a perceived weakness of the foundational work of Scholem,[31] who could only allude to the significance of the Dead Sea Scrolls given their slow publication process.   Access to the complete Qumran corpus has, not surprisingly, prompted explorations of the relationship between the Scrolls and the later *Merkavah* and *Hekhalot* literature.[32] A particularly ambitious and controversial monograph is that of Elior,[33] and though her work has been criticized for positing a centuries-spanning continuum of priestly ideology and for implying that the diverse texts of the Second Temple Period are univocal on a number of issues, she draws attention to an important theme in the early Jewish literature: the correspondence between heaven and earth, particularly the correlation between angels and the priests.[34] Texts like Jubilees and *Songs of the Sabbath Sacrifice* testify to the belief that the priesthood has angelic ori-

---

[31] Cf. Gershom G. Scholem, *Major Trends in Jewish Mysticism* (New York: Schocken Books, 1954); idem, *Jewish Gnosticism, Merkavah Mysticism, and Talmudic Tradition* (New York: Jewish Theological Seminary, 1960).

[32] E.g., Michael D. Swartz, "The Dead Sea Scrolls and Later Jewish Magic and Mysticism," *DSD* 8 (2001): 182–190; Ra'anan Abusch, "Sevenfold Hymns in the Songs of the Sabbath Sacrifice and the Hekhalot Literature: Formalism, Hierarchy and the Limits of Human Participation," in *The Dead Sea Scrolls as Background to Postbiblical Judaism and Early Christianity: Papers from an International Conference at St. Andrews in 2001* (ed., James R. Davila; STDJ 46; Leiden: Brill, 2003), 220–247; Elisabeth Hamacher, "Die Sabbatopferlieder im Streit um Ursrung und Anfänge der jüdischen Mystik," *JJS* 27 (1996): 119–154.

[33] Rachel Elior, *The Three Temples: On the Emergence of Jewish Mysticism* (Oxford: Littman Library of Jewish Civilization, 2004).

[34] See the chapter entitled "Priests and Angels" in Elior, *The Three Temples*, 165–200. But even on this point, see the critique of Martha Himmelfarb, "Merkavah Mysticism since Scholem: Rachel Elior's *The Three Temples*," in *Mystical Approaches to God: Judaism, Christianity, Islam* (ed., Peter Schäfer; München: R. Oldenbourg Verlag, 2006), 24–30, 34–36, who suggests that Elior either does not pay sufficient attention to the important differences between texts or obscures significant details. For example, in an effort to bolster her claim that mystical traditions were valued and transmitted in priestly circles, Elior obscures a key claim of Jubilees: *all* Israel (i.e., not just the priests) are represented by the priestly angels. Cf. eadem, "The Book of Jubilees and Early Jewish Mysticism," in *Enoch and Mosaic Torah: The Evidence of Jubilees* (eds., Gabriele Boccaccini and Giovanni Ibba; Grand Rapids: Eerdmans, 2009), 389–390.

gins, and thus the angelic priesthood served as both a role model and a source of heavenly validity for the earthly priesthood.[35]

Key features of mysticism for which the Dead Sea Scrolls are studied are the goal of the mystic and how mystical experience was achieved. Schäfer contends that ascent was the means by which the mystic bridged the gap between heaven and earth, an experience resulting in a vision of God on his throne and communion – not union[36] – with the divine, and that the *Self-Glorification Hymn* and the *Songs of the Sabbath Sacrifice* were used to achieve this communion.[37] Schäfer also makes the important observation that mystical ascent was, with few exceptions, not an end in itself but the experience of a worthy individual for the sake of his community.[38]

In addition to situating the Dead Sea Scrolls in the history of Jewish and Christian mysticism, Alexander wrestles with two issues: how to define "mysticism" and whether mysticism was present at Qumran.[39] In so doing, Alexander articulates an undercurrent in many discussions of mysticism and the Scrolls: there is no universally accepted definition of mysticism, and it is therefore a "hugely contested" term, a consequence of which is that the *Songs of the Sabbath Sacrifice* become a lightning rod of sorts.[40] Alexander con-

---

[35] Elior, *The Three Temples*, 173, 180. Cf. Christopher Rowland, *The Open Heaven: A Study of Apocalyptic in Judaism and Early Christianity* (London: SPCK, 1982), 444–447, who makes the general observation that a connection with the "world beyond" as found in the apocalyptic literature was not just a source of future hope but also assurance in midst of present circumstances.

[36] Peter Schäfer, *The Origins of Jewish Mysticism* (Tübingen: Mohr Siebeck, 2009), 349–350, 353, stresses the distinction between "*communion* with God" (i.e., experiencing nearness to God in some sense) and "*union* with God" (i.e., "*absorption into God*" or "*deification*"). According to Schäfer, Jewish mysticism testifies to the former and not the latter.

[37] Schäfer, *The Origins of Jewish Mysticism*, 151–152.

[38] Schäfer, *The Origins of Jewish Mysticism*, 345, 353–354.

[39] Philip S. Alexander, *Mystical Texts: Songs of the Sabbath Sacrifice and Related Manuscripts* (LSTS 61; CQS 7; London: T & T Clark, 2006). Cf. idem, "Qumran and the Genealogy of Western Mysticism," in *New Perspectives on Old Texts*, 213–245, in which the author expands aspects of his earlier work.

[40] Alexander, "Qumran and the Genealogy," 219. Cf. Bilhah Nitzan, "Harmonic and Mystical Characteristics in Poetic and Liturgical Writings from Qumran," *JQR* 85 (1994): 183, who posits that the *Songs of the Sabbath Sacrifice* "may have been considered as a medium for creating an experience of *mystic communion* [emphasis added] between the earthly and the heavenly worshippers, each one of which kept the Sabbath law in their respective dwellings." However, Eliott Wolfson, "Mysticism and the Poetic-Liturgical Compositions from Qumran: A Response to Bilhah Nitzan," *JQR* 85 (1994): 201, argues that unless ascension and enthronement of the mystic occur, a text should not be considered "mystical." Thus, as per Schäfer, *The Origins of Jewish Mysticism*, 153, 349, the only proper mystical text from Qumran is the *Self-Glorification Hymn*. Cf. Esther G. Chazon, "Human and Angelic Prayer in Light of the Dead Sea Scrolls," in *Liturgical Perspectives: Prayer and Poetry in Dead Sea Scrolls. Proceedings of the Fifth International Symposium of the Orion Center for the Study*

cludes that mysticism was indeed present at Qumran and defines it as the longing for a closer relationship with a transcendent presence.[41] The transcendent presence longed for at Qumran was, of course, the God of Israel. But as Alexander notes, "the closest relationship to God which the texts envisage the mystic attaining is that enjoyed by the angels in heaven, who perpetually offer to him worship and adoration in the celestial Temple. … The Qumran mystics long to join the angels in their liturgy, to form with them one worshipping community."[42] An indispensable component of Alexander's understanding of "mysticism" is *praxis*: a *via mystica* is always necessary.[43] It is for this reason that the *Songs of Sabbath Sacrifice* is a key text, since many scholars consider it to be liturgical: the chanting of the *Songs* within the context of worship likely brought about a "communal ascent"[44] and communion with the angelic host for which the sectarians longed.

In sum, this brief discussion of angelology and mysticism has highlighted an important point to which I will return in Chapter 5: though scholars disagree as to the appropriateness of labeling the *Songs of the Sabbath Sacrifice* and other documents as "mystical," they are in general agreement that certain texts were used by the Qumran movement in the context of worship to facilitate communion with the angels.

IV. Studies Focused on Angels

As noted above, recent scholarship has begun to take into consideration the prominence of angels in the Qumran literature. In 1950, Bietenhard did not have the luxury of incorporating the Dead Sea Scrolls into his study,[45] but his

---

of the Dead Sea Scrolls and Associated Literature (ed., eadem; STDJ 48; Leiden: Brill, 2003), 36, who cites Wolfson in her reluctance to use the term "mystic."

[41] Alexander, "Qumran and the Genealogy," 220.

[42] Though Alexander, "Qumran and the Genealogy," 220–221, uses the term *unio mystica* to describe the consummation of relationship to God envisaged by the texts, he suggests that a more appropriate term for theistic systems is *communion*. However, Alexander also contends that "the *language* of union" is common in theistic systems, a claim that appears to be a justification for using *unio mystica* to describe mystical experiences of the Qumran texts. Cf. idem, *Mystical Texts*, 101–110. Schäfer, *The Origins of Jewish Mysticism*, 349–350, would prefer that Alexander use "communion" and "union" more carefully.

[43] Alexander, *Mystical Texts*, 110–122; idem, "Qumran and the Genealogy," 226.

[44] Alexander, *Mystical Texts*, 119; idem, "Qumran and the Genealogy," 226 n. 23, concedes that the language of later "ascents" is not found in the *Songs* (cf. Schäfer, *The Origins of Jewish Mysticism*, 144; Wolfson, "Mysticism and the Poetic-Liturgical," 194; Nitzan, "Harmonic and Mystical Characteristics," 183). Alexander claims that the lack of ascent language is "probably less significant than some have supposed" because mystical texts do not universally use the language of ascents, and because he is using *ascent*, not in a technical sense, but as a "useful shorthand" for mystical communion with the angels.

[45] Hans Bietenhard, *Die himmlische Welt im Urchristentum und Spätjudentum* (WUNT 2; Tübingen: Mohr Siebeck, 1951).

monograph is nonetheless similar to later studies in that it covers a wide variety of topics rather than providing detailed treatments of individual issues or concepts, including angels associated with Israel and the worldviews in which they are depicted.

Numerous scholars have pointed out that nationally associated angels are related to the ancient Near Eastern concept of the divine council,[46] a topic that has been the focus of the work of Heiser.[47] Among other issues, Heiser has been a vocal critic of readings championed by Smith that post-exilic Judaism was characterized by a shift from polytheism to "intolerant" monotheism[48] and its alleged results: the collapse of the hierarchy of the divine council in the Second Temple Period and a lack of distinction between higher-ranking "gods" (אלוהים or אלים) and lower-tier "angels" (מלאכים). While Heiser's calls to recognize the prevalence of a fulsome divine council in the Second Temple Period and to be more terminologically precise may in some cases be warranted, in others instances he arguably overstates the significance of the presence (or lack thereof) of certain designations, and I will interact with his work throughout this study. For now, it is sufficient to state that, as per widespread scholarly practice, I will employ the term "angels" to refer to various spiritual beings – including "gods" – yet without necessarily implying an equation with/subordination to other beings in the celestial hierarchy.

As I will outline in the following chapter, an important example of the biblical tradition's incorporation of the divine council is found in Deut 32:8–9, where members of Yhwh's assembly have been appointed as the heavenly

---

[46] The classic treatments of the divine council include Frank Moore Cross, *Canaanite Myth and Hebrew Epic: Essays in the History of the Religion of Israel* (Cambridge: Harvard University Press, 1973); Conrad E. L'Heureux, *Rank Among the Canaanite Gods: El, Baal, and the Rephaim* (HSM 21: Missoula: Scholars Press, 1979); E. Theodore Mullen, Jr., *The Assembly of the Gods: The Divine Council in Canaanite and Early Hebrew Literature* (HSM 24; Chico: Scholars Press, 1980), 175–201; Lowell K. Handy, *Among the Host of Heaven: The Syro-Palestinian Pantheon as Bureaucracy* (Winona Lake: Eisenbrauns, 1994). For a more recent discussion, see Ellen White, *Yahweh's Council: Its Structure and Membership* (FAT 2/65; Tübingen: Mohr Siebeck, 2014).

[47] Cf. Michael S. Heiser, "The Divine Council in Late Canonical and Non-Canonical Second Temple Jewish Literature (Ph.D. diss., University of Wisconsin–Madison, 2004); idem, "Monotheism, Polytheism, Monolatry, or Henotheism? Toward an Assessment of Divine Plurality in the Hebrew Bible," *BBR* 18 (2008): 1–30; idem, "Should אלהים (Elohim) with Plural Predication be Translated 'Gods'?" *BT* 61 (2010): 123–136; idem, "Does Divine Plurality in the Hebrew Bible Demonstrate an Evolution from Polytheism to Monotheism in Israelite Religion?" *JESOT* 1 (2012): 1–24; idem, "Monotheism and the Language of Divine Plurality in the Hebrew Bible and the Dead Sea Scrolls," *TynBul* 65 (2014): 85–100.

[48] E.g., Mark S. Smith, *The Origins of Biblical Monotheism: Israel's Polytheistic Background and the Ugaritic Texts* (New York: Oxford University Press, 2000); idem, *The Early History of God: Yahweh and the Other Deities in Ancient Israel* (2nd ed.; Grand Rapids: Eerdmans, 2002).

beings associated with the Gentile nations.[49] A not infrequently overlooked text for the study of angels associated with Israel is Dan 7 (not least because it seemingly departs from the sentiment of Deut 32:8–9), and Collins has defended two controversial interpretations of this key passage: 1.) that the unnamed "one like a son of man" (cf. Dan 7:13–14) is Michael, the heavenly guardian of the Jews and the leader of the angelic host; and 2.) that "the holy ones of the Most High" (cf. Dan 7:18, 22, 25) are the collective angelic representatives of the Jews and should be distinguished from "the *people* of the Holy Ones of the Most High" (cf. Dan 7:27), who are Jews on earth.[50] In a discussion of Daniel and 1 Enoch,[51] Collins cites Eliade, who points out that to the ancient mind "reality [was] a function of the imitation of the celestial archetype."[52] Similarly, Collins argues that national angels were viewed as both "more real" than and prior to the people with whom they were associated.[53] But as Collins also points out, the opposite is true from the perspective of a modern critic; "it is," in the words of Lacocque, "a question of men before it is a question of angels."[54] The angels associated with Israel thus symbolize the present ideals and anticipated destinies of the people of God.[55]

A comparison of the depictions of angels in the sections of 1 Enoch extant at Qumran with the angelologies of the sectarian texts is the subject of Davidson's study.[56] While it is an invaluable starting point, it is far from exhaustive,[57] as not all the pertinent texts were available when this book was published in the early 1990s. Most importantly and as previously noted, there is a need to move beyond observation and comparison to analysis with the aim of gaining a better understanding of the contribution angelological convictions made to the religious identity of the Qumran movement. Analogous

---

[49] Cf. Culianu, "The Angels of the Nations," 78–91, who largely focuses on texts beyond the scope of this study but briefly draws attention to Isa 24:21–23, which is discussed in Chapter 2, below.

[50] Collins, *Daniel:* 305–323. Cf. idem, "The Son of Man and the Saints of the Most High in the Book of Daniel," *JBL* 93 (1973): 50–66.

[51] Collins, *The Apocalyptic Imagination*, 110–112, 185–187.

[52] Mircea Eliade, *The Myth of the Eternal Return or, Cosmos and History* (Princeton: Princeton University Press, 1974), 3–11, here 5.

[53] Collins, *The Apocalyptic Imagination*, 187.

[54] André Lacocque, *The Book of Daniel* (trans. by David Pellauer; Atlanta: John Knox Press, 1979), 131.

[55] Collins, *The Apocalyptic Imagination*, 187.

[56] Maxwell J. Davidson, *Angels at Qumran: A Comparative Study of 1 Enoch 1–36, 72–108 and Sectarian Writings from Qumran* (JSPSup 11; Sheffield: JSOT Press, 1992).

[57] Davidson *Angels at Qumran*, 323, concedes that "it would prove profitable to consider the angelology of the canonical book of Daniel in relation to those of the Enochic and other related books from the period of Second Temple Judaism."

comments can be or have been made concerning the helpful but even wider-ranging contributions of Mach[58] and Olyan.[59]

In addition to a collection of short angelological essays in the 2007 *DCL Yearbook*,[60] an especially pertinent study is that of Michalak, who investigates the martial function of angels in the late Second Temple Period. I will interact with Michalak's insights in subsequent chapters, including the important observations that angels of high rank have "no independent power to initiate their own missions,"[61] and that there are, generally speaking, two traditions: those in which earthly wars had heavenly equivalents[62] and those in which soldiers could anticipate angelic assistance on the earthly battlefield.

Another study with which I will interact extensively is the recent monograph of Angel, who addresses the themes of the heavenly priesthood and

---

[58] Michael Mach, *Entwicklungsstadien des jüdischen Engelglaubens in vorrabbinischer Zeit* (TSAJ 34; Tübingen: Mohr Siebeck, 1992), provides one of the most comprehensive studies of Jewish angelology ever written. His topics include angel traditions in the Hebrew Bible, Greek terminology for angels, and a lengthy discussion of the angels in the early Jewish literature. However, it has been said that Mach's "impressive breadth and comprehensiveness are attained at the cost of a somewhat superficial treatment"; see John J. Collins, review of Michael Mach, *Entwicklungsstadien des jüdischen Engelglaubens in vorrabbinsicher Zeit*, *JBL* 119 (1994): 140–141.

[59] Saul M. Olyan, *A Thousand Thousands Served Him: Exegesis and the Naming of Angels in Ancient Judaism* (TSAJ 36; Tübingen: Mohr Siebeck, 1993), looks into the exegetical foundations of the naming and organization of the angelic host. He highlights that many names for angels in the Second Temple Period and beyond stem from interpretive reflection on either specific words of the Hebrew Bible such as *hapax legomena* occurring in a theophanic or angelphanic context. Focused as it is on the exegetical origins of nomenclature, Olyan's study precludes detailed discussion of the characteristics and functions of the various angels and the contributions they make to the texts in which they are found.

[60] Friedrich V. Reiterer, Tobias Nicklas, and Karen Schöpflin eds., *Angels: The Concept of Celestial Beings: Origins, Development and Reception* (DCLY; New York: de Gruyter, 2007). Among the most relevant essays are those of Jacques T. A. G. M. van Ruiten, "Angels and Demons in the Book of Jubilees," 585–609, who touches on Jubilees' use of Deut 32:8–9 traditions; and the aforementioned contribution of Hannah, "Guardian Angels and Angelic National Patrons," 413–435, which by his own admission is "a brief overview." Also see Cecilia Wassén, "Angels in the Dead Sea Scrolls,"499–523, who provides discussions of angelic terminology, the nature and function of angels, and fellowship with angels.

[61] Michalak, *Angels as Warriors*, 243.

[62] Cf. James R. Davila, "Melchizedek, Michael, and War in Heaven," *SBL Seminar Papers, 1996* (SBLSP 35; Atlanta: Scholars Press, 1996), 259–272, who traces the origins of the eschatological battle between the forces of good and evil to Canaanite and Israelite mythological traditions regarding the conquest of Leviathan and the astral deity revolt (e.g., Isa 14:12–20); Davila contends that at some point Michael and, less frequently, Melchizedek replaced Yhwh in both myths. On the development of the figure of Melchizedek, see idem, "Melchizedek: King, Priest, and God," in *The Seductiveness of Jewish Myth: Challenge or Response?* (ed., S. Daniel Breslauer; Albany: State University of New York, 1997), 217–234.

eschatological priestly leadership in the Dead Sea Scrolls.[63] I will especially focus on the first of these topics. His conclusion that the heavenly priesthood and the sect's liturgical communion with it were "an innovative expression of confidence inasmuch as it argues that the community no longer has a need for the Jerusalem temple"[64] is significant and will serve as a key point for my own analysis. Furthermore, Angel's cautious approach as far as history is concerned is one I will share: influenced by Kugler, who has warned against pressing the Scrolls too hard for socio-historical realities, especially in relation to the priestly origins of the Qumran community,[65] Angel makes it clear that his study "largely abandons ... historical inquiry in favor of investigation of the imagined constructs of the priesthood in the Scrolls corpus."[66] As Angel contends, this is not the same as saying that historical information cannot be gleaned from Qumran texts, but it is to say that the texts tell us more about how the authors envisioned reality than reality itself.[67]

It was noted at the outset of this section – and highlighted throughout – that angelolgical studies are often broad in scope and/or give little attention to the concept of angels associated with Israel and their corresponding worldviews. But as Collins contends, even if angels associated with Israel tend to be "superfluous to modern critics, ... they are an integral and important part of the symbolic universe of [the mid to late Second Temple Period]."[68] Yet even those studies which examine aspects of angelology in the Dead Sea Scrolls have not fully explored the relationship between angels associated with Israel and the self-identity of the sectarians. Thus, in order to provide further rationale and a framework for the present study, the last sections of this history of research will survey scholarship on the notions of non-sectarian and sectarian texts and religious identity at Qumran.

V. "Non-Sectarian" and "Sectarian" Texts

In the last thirty years, discussions concerning the identification of both those responsible for producing and preserving the Qumran texts and their oppo-

---

[63] Joseph L. Angel, *Otherworldly and Eschatological Priesthood in the Dead Sea Scrolls* (STDJ 86; Leiden: Brill, 2010). Similar subject matter is treated in Tobias Nicklas et al., eds., *Other Worlds and Their Relation to This World: Early Jewish and Ancient Christian Traditions* (JSJSup 143; Leiden: Brill, 2010).

[64] Angel, *Otherworldly*, 305.

[65] Robert A. Kugler, "Priesthood at Qumran," in *The Dead Sea Scrolls After Fifty Years: A Comprehensive Assessment, Volume 2* (eds., Peter W. Flint and James C. VanderKam; Leiden: Brill, 1999), 114, writes, "we have for too long asked the Scrolls to give us evidence of social realities where the literature more often seems to convey imagined realities instead." For further discussion of this point, see below.

[66] Angel, *Otherworldly*, 15.

[67] Angel, *Otherworldly*, 13–16.

[68] Collins, *Daniel*, 319.

nents have become increasingly complex as the validity of earlier consensuses have been questioned. Therefore, exactly to whom one is referring when using terms such as the Qumran "community" or "sect" and whether certain texts can justifiably be classified as "sectarian" and "non-sectarian" have become contentious issues in Qumran scholarship. Here, I can only provide a concise overview, so I will establish and draw out the aspects of the debate most relevant to the present study.

When the first group of documents from Cave 1 came to light in the late 1940s, similarities between the content of the texts and what the classical sources – Josephus, Philo, and Pliny (cf. Josephus, *B.J.* 2:119–161; *Ant.* 18:18–22; Philo, *Prob.* 75–91; Pliny, *Nat.* 5.17.4 [73]) – say about a Jewish sect called the "Essenes" were immediately noticed, and within a decade, a virtual consensus emerged which identified the authors of the texts as Essenes.[69] Though scholars who accept this general identification do not agree on all the particulars,[70] the umbrella term, "Essene Hypothesis" (henceforth, EH), is often used to describe their views.[71] According to the EH, texts such as the *Damascus Document* and the *pesharim* recount events directly related to the emergence of the sect, events which were precipitated by the political and religious turbulence of the 170s and 160s BCE. When the non-Zadokite Hasmoneans usurped the high-priesthood in the wake of the Maccabean revolt in 152 BCE, this was not acceptable to a figure called "the Teacher of Righteousness," who may have been a prominent Zadokite priest, perhaps even the high priest.[72] As tensions over *halakhic*, calendrical, and moral issues surfaced, this "Teacher" was forced to flee from his Hasmonean adversary, villainized in the *pesharim* as "the Wicked Priest" (cf. 1QpHab I, 13; VIII, 8; IX, 9; XI, 4; XII, 2, 8; 4Q171 IV, 8).[73] Eventually, "the Teacher" and

---

[69] Cf. Geza Vermes, *Les manuscrits du desert de Juda* (Paris: Desclée, 1954); Frank Moore Cross, *The Ancient Library of Qumran: Revised and Expanded Edition* (Minneapolis: Fortress, 2004); Józef T. Milik, *Ten Years of Discovery in the Wilderness of Judaea* (SBT 26; London: SCM, 1959).

[70] E.g., some contend that the Essenes originated in Babylon with the Qumran Essenes distancing themselves from the larger Essene movement shortly after they returned to Palestine, during Jonathan's tenure as high-priest; see Jerome Murphy-O'Connor, "The Essenes and their History," *RB* 81 (1974): 224–225. Another view is that Essenes emerged from a 2nd cent. BCE group about which little is known, the *Hasidim* (cf. 1 Macc 2:42; 7:13; 2 Macc 14:6).

[71] E.g., the section entitled, "The Case for the Essene Hypothesis," in James C. VanderKam, *The Dead Sea Scrolls Today* (2nd ed.; Grand Rapids: Eerdmans, 2010), 97–113.

[72] On the identity of this figure, see Michael Knibb, "Teacher of Righteousness," *EDSS* 2:918–921. Also see the discussion of John J. Collins, *Beyond the Qumran Community: The Sectarian Movement of the Dead Sea Scrolls* (Grand Rapids: Eerdmans, 2010), 95–99.

[73] Proponents of the EH usually identify "the Wicked Priest" as Jonathan or Simon (cf. CD I, 1–11; XX, 32; 1QpHab I, 13; II, 2; V, 10; VII, 4; VIII, 3; XI, 5; 4Q165 1–2, 3; 4Q171 III, 15; IV, 27).

his followers ended up at Qumran, a location in close proximity to the caves where the texts were found. The Scrolls, therefore, were seen as the library of the Qumran Essenes.

In recent years, however, the EH has come under scrutiny. In addition to the objections of those who would caution that the cryptic or utopian nature of the sources means that they should not be pressed for historical realities,[74] the archaeological conclusions of de Vaux, who proposed a mid 2nd cent. BCE occupation of Qumran,[75] have been challenged. In an influential study, Magness contends that the site was in use in the early or mid 1st cent. BCE, and that there is little to support de Vaux's conclusion of a 2nd cent. BCE occupation.[76] It is, therefore, problematic to conclude that the "Teacher" had an acrimonious relationship with Jonathan (152–143 BCE) or Simon (143–135 BCE) and subsequently led his followers to Qumran.[77]

Another reason the EH has come under scrutiny is the objection that the similarities between the Qumran texts and what the classical sources say about Essenes have been exaggerated;[78] that is, the differences are too significant to label the Qumranites "Essenes,"[79] at least without qualification. The

---

[74] See the comments of Angel and Kugler, above. Cf. Charlotte Hempel, *The Qumran Rule Texts: Collected Essays* (TSAJ 154; Tübingen: Mohr Seibeck, 2013), 4–7; George J. Brooke, "The Pesharim and the Origins of the Dead Sea Scrolls," in *Methods of Investigation of the Dead Sea Scrolls and the Khirbet Qumran Site: Present Realities and Future Prospects* (eds., Michael O. Wise et al.; ANYAS 722; New York: The New York Academy of Sciences, 1994), 34–43; Philip Davies, "Redaction and Sectarianism in the Qumran Scrolls," in *The Scriptures and the Scrolls: Studies in Honour of A. S. van der Woude on the Occasion of his 65th Birthday* (eds., Florentino García-Martínez, Anthony Hilhorst, and C. J. Labuschagne; VTSup 49; Leiden: Brill, 1992), 152–163.

[75] Roland de Vaux, *Archaeology and the Dead Sea Scrolls* (London: Oxford University Press, 1973).

[76] Jodi Magness, *The Archaeology of Qumran and the Dead Sea Scrolls* (SDSSRL; Grand Rapids: Eerdmans, 2002).

[77] A modified version of the EH deals with this issue by claiming that 1st cent. BCE followers of the now deceased "Teacher" (cf. CD XX, 13–15, which may refer to his death) made their way to Qumran to devote themselves to the proper study of Israel's scriptures (cf. 1QS VIII, 12–16); see VanderKam, *The Dead Sea Scrolls Today*, 132–133.

[78] E.g., the well-known objections of Norman Golb, "Who Hid the Dead Scrolls?" *BA* 48 (1985): 68–82; cf. idem, *Who Wrote the Dead Sea Scrolls? The Search for the Secret of Qumran* (New York: Scribner, 1995), who claims there is insufficient evidence to connect the Dead Sea Scrolls to the Essenes as depicted in the classical sources; he also is a vocal proponent of the view of that the Scrolls were hidden in the caves by those fleeing Jerusalem at the time of the first Jewish war (66–70 CE).

[79] Martin Goodman, "A Note on the Qumran Sectarians, the Essenes and Josephus," *JJS* 46 (1995): 161–166, argues that it would be incorrect to assume that the literary sources mention all of the Palestinian Jewish groups of the Second Temple Period and that these groups would have had many characteristics in common. Moreover, there are too many differences to label the Qumran group as Essene. Cf. Albert I. Baumgarten, "Who Cares and Why Does it Matter? Qumran and the Essenes Once Again!" *DSD* 11 (2004): 174–190.

"Groningen Hypothesis" (henceforth, GH) attempts to account for these dis-crepancies by "making a clear distinction between the origins of the Essene movement and those of the Qumran group."[80] According to the GH, the Es-senes emerged from the apocalyptic traditions of Palestinian Judaism in the 3rd or early 2nd cent. BCE, and, in turn, the Qumran group – those loyal to the "Teacher" – resulted from a break with the parent Essene movement.[81] Thus, texts that resemble what the classical sources say about Essenism belonged to the parent Essenes; texts with more nuanced views were the product of the sect at various stages of its existence.[82] A hypothesis offered by Boccaccini has affinities with the GH in that it sees the Essenes as part of a non-conformist priestly movement best described as "Enochic Judaism" (hence-forth, EJ),[83] the texts of which were found at Qumran.[84] The EJ theory ech-oes the GH in that the Qumran group is a radicalized minority of Essenes (= Enochians) led by the "Teacher."

A different approach has been advocated by those who question the appro-priateness of using terms such as *the* "Qumran community."[85] Given that 1.) there are different rule texts,[86] 2.) there are different and sometimes contra-

---

[80] Florentino García Martínez, "Qumran Origins and Early History: A Groningen Hypoth-esis," *FO* 25 (1988): 113–136, here 113. Cf. idem and A. S. van der Woude, "A 'Groningen' Hypothesis of Qumran Origins and Early History," *RevQ* 14 (1990): 521–541; idem, "The Groningen Hypothesis Revisited," in *The Dead Sea Scrolls and Contemporary Culture: Pro-ceedings of the International Conference at the Israel Museum, July 6–8, 2008* (eds., Adolfo D. Roitman, Lawrence H. Schiffman, and Shani Tzoref; STDJ 93; Leiden: Brill, 2011), 17–30.

[81] García Martínez, "Qumran Origins and Early History," 113.

[82] The GH has four classifications of texts: i.) "common heritage" texts of the apocalyptic tradition from which the Essenes came; ii.) "Essene" works resembling the classical sources; iii.) "formative period" works, which evidence the Qumran group distancing itself from its Essene parents; iv.) "sectarian" texts reflecting the most developed thoughts of the Qumran group; see García Martínez, "Qumran Origins and Early History," 116.

[83] Gabriele Boccaccini, *Beyond the Essene Hypothesis: The Parting of the Ways between Qumran and Enochic Judaism* (Grand Rapids: Eerdmans, 1998).

[84] The "Enochic chain of documents" includes the i.) foundational texts of EJ (e.g., *Book of Watchers, Astronomical Book, Aramaic Levi Document*), ii.) texts reflecting the various communities of EJ in the post-Maccabean revolt period (e.g., Jubilees, *Temple Scroll*, 4QMMT), and iii.) sectarian texts of the Qumran group; see Boccaccini, *Beyond the Essene Hypothesis*, 160–162. Cf. Eckhard J. Schnabel, review of Gabriele Boccaccini *Beyond the Essene Hypothesis*, *RBL* (2000).

[85] Collins, *Beyond the Qumran Community*, 10.

[86] The main rule texts are the *Damascus Document* and the *Community Rule*. A well-known difference between the two is that the former assumes that some if not most of its addressees were married with children while the latter does not mention family matters, prompting some to suggest that the *Community Rule* assumes the celibacy of those who ad-here to it; see Collins, *Beyond the Qumran Community*, 4–5.

dictory recensions of the rule texts,[87] and 3.) the *Community Rule* assumes the existence of more than one place of residence (cf. 1QS VI, 1–8),[88] Collins has proposed that "the different forms of the text served different communities within the broader association, and that they were only taken to Qumran and hidden there secondarily, in a time of crisis."[89] Collins has convincingly argued that the sectarians who made their way to Qumran should be viewed then, not as acrimoniously splitting from this broader association, but as separating from it amicably in order to pursue a higher degree of purity and holiness.[90] In his words, "since both rules continued to be copied, it would seem that the kind of family-based movement envisioned in the *Damascus Rule* was not simply superseded, but continued to exist in tandem with the more intensive communities of the *Yahad*."[91] It with this proposal in mind that I use the designation "the Qumran movement."

Since alternatives to the EH just surveyed propose that the Qumran sectarians were born from a split with its parent movement – whether acrimoniously or amicably – some have questioned whether the designations "nonsectarian" texts and "sectarian" texts are still helpful.[92] But this traditional distinction, which is supported here, has been defended by Dimant, who regards these categories as "indispensable for understanding the true nature of

---

[87] The *Damascus Document* is represented by CD (the medieval copy from the Cairo Genizah) and the Cave 4 manuscripts (4Q266–273); the *Community Rule* is represented by manuscripts from Cave 1 (1QS) and Cave 4 (4Q255–264); for a discussion of the differences in the recensions of both documents, see Collins, *Beyond the Qumran Community*, 3–4.

[88] Also see Philo, *Apologia pro Iudaies*, as quoted in Eusebius, *Praep. evang.* 8.6–7; Josephus, *B.J.* 2:122.

[89] Collins, *Beyond the Qumran Community*, 3. Cf. Allison Schofield, *From Qumran to the Yahad: A New Paradigm of Textual Development for The Community Rule* (STDJ 77; Leiden: Brill, 2009).

[90] Collins, *Beyond the Qumran Community*, 6, 155–156, 209, cautiously identifies both the broader association and the Qumranites as "Essene," with the two groups respectively corresponding to Josephus' characterization of Essenes as either marrying, as per the *Damascus Document*, or celibate, as per the *Community Rule*.

[91] Collins, *Beyond the Qumran Community*, 79.

[92] E.g., Florentino García Martínez, "Aramaica Qumranica Apocalyptica?" in *Aramaica Qumranica: Proceedings of the Conference on the Aramaic texts from Qumran at Aix-en-Provence, 30 June–2 July 2008* (eds., Katell Berthelot and Daniel Stökl Ben Ezra; STDJ 94; Leiden: Brill, 2010), 441, who has posited that the appropriation of texts – *not* a given text's origin – is what is important. He proposes that the non-sectarian/sectarian discussion can be informed by scholarship on the so-called "biblical," "para-biblical" and "re-written scripture" scrolls. He points out that scholars of these texts, in order to avoid anachronistic notions of canon, "refer to the study of the different authority-conferring strategies used in the various writings." García Martínez, has also suggested that appropriation and authority mean that questions of origin are "no longer relevant." Cf. idem, "¿Sectario, no-sectario, o qué? Problems de una taxonomía correcta de los textos qumránicos," *RevQ* 23 (2008): 383–394.

the Qumran collection,"[93] and she argues that to neglect these designations is to ignore the "distinct style, vocabulary and terminology displayed by the sectarian texts, and not shared by other Qumran manuscripts."[94] To be sure, texts such as 1 Enoch and Jubilees demonstrate some affinities with the perspectives of certain sectarian texts, but it goes beyond the evidence to classify them as such. It is more accurate to conclude that these earlier compositions likely emerged in a stream of Judaism that was similar to the Qumran sect and even exerted considerable influence upon it.[95] Recognizing the distinction between sectarian and non-sectarian texts enables scholars to understand how broader Jewish themes were interpreted, emphasized, or refined by the Qumran movement.[96] A goal of this study, of course, is to better appreciate how the Qumran movement put its own stamp on common angelological convictions.

---

[93] Devorah Dimant, "Sectarian and Non-Sectarian Texts from Qumran: The Pertinence and Usage of a Taxonomy," *RevQ* 24 (2009): 7–18, here 8.

[94] Dimant, "Sectarian and Non-Sectarian Texts," 8 n. 4, who is directly responding to García Martínez; see also Dimant's earlier work on the same topic: eadem, "The Qumran Manuscripts: Contents and Significance," in *Time to Prepare a Way in the Wilderness: Papers on the Qumran Scrolls by Fellows of the Institute for Advanced Studies of the Hebrew University, Jerusalem, 1989–1990* (eds., eadem and Lawrence H. Schiffman; STDJ 16; Leiden: Brill, 1995), 23–58, a study which she compares to the well-known essay of Carol A. Newsom, "'Sectually Explicit' Literature from Qumran," in *The Hebrew Bible and Its Interpreters* (eds., William H. Propp, Baruch Halpern, and David Noel Freedman; Winona Lake: Eisenbrauns, 1990), 179–185. Specifically, Dimant highlights the unique lexical characteristics of the *Community Rule*, the *Rule of the Congregation*, the *Rule of Benedictions*, the *Damascus Document*, the *War Scroll*, the *Pesharim*, and the *Hodayot*, which include 1.) the community's organization (e.g., היחד, a self-designation for the community; 2.) locutions alluding to historical events often in the form of cryptic epithets (e.g., מורה הצדק, "the Teacher of Righteousness,") and 3.) terms reflecting religious ideas (e.g., בני אור, "the Sons of Light"). While the first two categories *only* occur in sectarian texts, theological terms similar to those found in sectarian texts may be present in non-sectarian compositions (e.g., dualistic thought is found in the sectarian *War Scroll* as well as the non-sectarian *Visions of Amram*).

[95] See Collins, *Beyond the Qumran Community*, 41–43, 50–51.

[96] Despite the differences between non-sectarian and sectarian texts, Dimant, "The Qumran Manuscripts," 32–33, is surely correct that the Qumran material is not "a haphazard assemblage" but an "intentional" collection. On the related notion of the Scrolls as a sectarian "library," see Sidnie White Crawford and Cecilia Wassén, eds., *The Dead Sea Scrolls at Qumran and the Concept of a Library* (STDJ 116; Leiden: Brill, 2015). On a proposed third category of texts (i.e., one that is "between" sectarian and non-sectarian), see Devorah Dimant, "Between Sectarian and non-Sectarian: The Case of the Apocryphon of Joshua," in *Reworking the Bible: Apocryphal and Related Texts at Qumran: Proceedings of a Joint Symposium by the Orion Center for the Study of the Dead Sea Scrolls and Associated Literature and the Hebrew University Institute for Advanced Studies Research Group on Qumran, 15–17 January, 2002* (eds., Esther G. Chazon, Devorah Dimant, and Ruth A. Clements; STDJ 58; Leiden: Brill, 2005), 105–134.

Another facet of the sectarian and non-sectarian discussion concerns the texts composed in Aramaic.[97] In the past, the differentiation of the themes of the Aramaic Scrolls received little attention, but scholars are now beginning to note the salient characteristics of the Aramaic texts as a corpus, including the focus on the investiture of the Levitical priestly line and its connection to the angelic realm.[98] The scholarly consensus is that the Aramaic texts are non-sectarian in origin, which is the viewpoint from which I will proceed.[99]

---

[97] The Aramaic texts amount to approximately 120 manuscripts; see Florentino García Martínez, "Scribal Practices in the Aramaic Literary Texts from Qumran," in *Myths, Martyrs, and Modernity: Studies in the History of Religion in Honour of Jan N. Bremmer* (eds., Jitse Dijkstra et al.; Leiden: Brill, 2010), 330. For a listing of the Aramaic texts, see Emmanuel Tov et al., *The Texts from the Judaean Desert: Indices and an Introduction to the Discoveries in the Judaean Desert Series* (DJD 39; Oxford: Clarendon, 2002), 27–114.

[98] See Devorah Dimant, "The Qumran Aramaic Texts and the Qumran Community," in *Flores Florentino: Dead Sea Scrolls and Other Early Jewish Studies in Honour of Florentino García Martínez* (eds., Anthony Hilhorst, Emile Puech, and Eibert J. C. Tigchelaar; JSJSup 122; Leiden: Brill, 2007), 197–205, who also points out that a thematic focus of the Aramaic texts is the eastern Diaspora (e.g., the Babylonian setting of Dan 2–6). On the apocalyptic character of many of the Aramaic texts, see Daniel A. Machiela, "Situating the Qumran Aramaic Texts: Reconsidering their Language and Socio-Historical Settings," in *Apocalyptic Thinking in Early Judaism: Engaging with John Collins' The Apocalyptic Imagination* (eds., Sidnie White Crawford and Cecilia Wassén; JSJSup 183; Leiden: Brill, 2017), 88–109; idem, "Aramaic Writings of the Second Temple Period and the Growth of Apocalyptic Thought," *JAAJ* 2 (2014): 113–134. On the Aramaic texts more generally, see idem and Andrew B. Perrin, "Tobit and the Genesis Apocryphon: Towards a Family Portrait," *JBL* 133 (2014): 112–113; Florentino García Martínez, "Scribal Practices in the Aramaic Literary Texts," 334; Eibert J. C. Tigchelaar, "The Imaginal Context and the Visionary of the Aramaic New Jerusalem," in *Flores Florentino*, 257–270.

[99] It has been argued that the Aramaic literature largely pre-dates Qumran, as the nationalist sentiments of the Hasmonean era resulted in a resurgence in Hebrew as the language of composition for religious literature. On the 3rd or early 2nd cent. BCE dating of the Aramaic texts, see Ben Zion Wacholder, "The Ancient Judaeo-Aramaic Literature (500–164 BCE): A Classification of Pre-Qumranic Texts," in *Archaeology and History in the Dead Sea Scrolls: The New York University Conference in Memory of Yigael Yadin* (ed., Lawrence H. Schiffman; JSOT/ASORMS 2; JSPSup 8; Sheffield: JSOT Press, 1990), 273–275. Cf. Elias J. Bickerman, "Aramaic Literature," in idem, *The Jews in the Greek Age* (Cambridge: Harvard University Press, 1988), 51–65. For discussion and further bibliography, see Eibert J. C. Tigchelaar, "Aramaic Texts from Qumran the Authoritativeness of the Hebrew Scriptures: Preliminary Observations," in *Authoritative Scriptures in Ancient Judaism* (ed., Mladen Popovic; JSJSup 141; Leiden: Brill, 2010), 155–171. *Contra* García Martínez, "Scribal Practices in the Aramaic Literary Texts," 336, who argues that a text composed in Aramaic should not, *a priori*, "exclude the possibility" that it was written at Qumran, though elsewhere he concedes that Hebrew was the "preferred language of the group when penning their own compositions … "; see idem, "Aramaica Qumranica," 439–440. Lastly, even if as Dimant, "The Qumran Aramaic Texts," 199, observes, the Aramaic texts are largely void of sectarian terminology, it does not necessitate that the Aramaic texts were a neglected holding of the

VI. Sectarian Identity at Qumran

The study of sectarian identity in the Dead Sea Scrolls has become a central
question in recent scholarship, and in her exploration of how identity was
constructed at Qumran, Newsom writes:

> [T]hough the Qumran community was a sectarian group, its discourse cannot be thought of
> as a sort of mumbling to itself. Nothing that was said at Qumran can be understood with-
> out reference to the larger discursive context of Second Temple Period Judaism. This is
> true not only for the obviously polemical statements in Qumran texts but also for every
> utterance. The words they used, the forms of speech, the content of their prayers, and the
> claims they made about themselves were always in part replies, responses, and counter-
> claims to utterances made by others within a broader cultural context.[100]

Similarly, Jokiranta notes that "identity" is a concept often employed in the
study of the Scrolls but warns that it is not exhausted by understanding the
unique beliefs and practices of those responsible for producing and preserving the texts. What is frequently overlooked is that "identity is defined in
relations to others."[101] Jokiranta thus understands a "sect" as "a religious
movement that is at the high-tension end on a continuum that reflects the relationship of the religious group to the wider socio-cultural movement, ...
[and] it is vital that the member categorize himself in terms of the shared social identity of the group."[102] A particularly powerful way to label outsiders
is the polemical use of shared traditions such as the scriptures.[103]

   That the sectarian texts make assertions – even in works or passages that
are not overtly polemical[104] – vis-à-vis the claims found in other Second
Temple Period literature is an invaluable insight that will inform the present
study. As Dimant suggests, it is important to ask how those responsible for
the Qumran texts framed their existence: "What was the essential, basic idea

---

sect. As Wacholder, "The Ancient Judaeo-Aramaic," 257–281, here 271, points out, these
texts anticipated sectarian thought and were part of its "ancestral patrimony."

   [100] Carol A. Newsom, *The Self As Symbolic Space: Constructing Identity at Qumran*
(STDJ 52; Leiden: Brill, 2004), 3.

   [101] Jutta Jokiranta, *Social Identity and Sectarianism in the Qumran Movement* (STDJ 105;
Leiden: Brill, 2013), 1. How the Qumran movement viewed itself in relation to "others" is a
burgeoning area of interest in Qumran scholarship. E.g., see Florentino García Martínez and
Mladen Popovic, eds., *Defining Identities: We, You, and the Other in the Dead Sea Scrolls:
Proceedings of the Fifth Meeting of the IOQS in Groningen* (STDJ 70; Leiden: Brill, 2008).

   [102] Jokiranta, *Social Identity and Sectarianism*, 215–216.

   [103] Jokiranta, *Social Identity and Sectarianism*, 217–218, highlights the importance of the
(shared) base-text of the *pesharim*: "what the *pesharim* do is to make the listener/reader see
the world in a new light. ... [A] powerful way of labeling outsiders is to use a shared tradition, describing the enemy as wicked within that tradition [e.g., the Book of Habakkuk] that
the enemy itself acknowledged."

   [104] So Carol A. Newsom, "Constructing 'We, You, and Others' through Non-Polemical
Discourse," in *Defining Identities*, 13–22.

which held together the entire system, and what was the self-image underlying it?"[105] Dimant's response to her own question begins to provide a helpful framework for understanding the contribution the sect's angelological convictions made to their identity: an integral part of the sectarians' self-image was that they viewed themselves as "an angel-like priestly community."[106] Highlighting the analogy between angels and Israel in Jubilees (cf. Jub. 1:26–33; 2:31–32; 31:14), Dimant notes that Jubilees and the *Songs of the Sabbath Sacrifice* – both of which were texts of apparent significance at Qumran – share a concern for priestly angels.[107] Also noteworthy is that the detailed depictions of angelic priests in the *Songs of the Sabbath Sacrifice* "reveal a striking resemblance" to the main activities of the sect.[108] In light of these similarities, Dimant suggests that sectarian communion with the angels, best known from passages such as 1QH^a XI, 20–24, XIX, 13–17, and 1QS XI, 7–9, should be understood as a "communion by analogy rather than an actual one";[109] that is, the members of the Qumran movement were connected to the angels because they emulated them. A different reading is offered by Tuschling, who claims that the sectarians thought of themselves as the earthly counterparts to the priestly angels, and that use of the *Songs of the Sabbath Sacrifice* at Qumran evoked the heavenly angel worship on earth. In her words, "earth and heaven are thus interpenetrated."[110] Angelic fellowship or communion was intimately connected to the community's priestly character, the roots of which lie in Jubilees (cf. Jub. 31:13–17; 1QSb III, 22–IV, 28).[111] Tuschling, then, states that angelic communion is

more than simply a sharing of worship; it is a *communion of identity*. When functioning liturgically, the priestly member of the community becomes the same as angels. In fact, by doing what angels do, living the angelic life, they actually become angels, in the limited liturgical context [emphasis mine].[112]

Tuschling is thereby contrasting her "communion of identity"[113] with Dimant's analogical understanding. Yet another understanding of angelic fel-

---

[105] Dimant, "Men as Angels," 95.

[106] Dimant, "Men as Angels," 95.

[107] Dimant, "Men as Angels," 99–100.

[108] Dimant, "Men as Angels," 100–101, provides a helpful chart comparing the actions ascribed to angels (as per the *Songs*) and the actions of the community (as per CD, 1QS, etc.): e.g., a covenant with God, offering of bloodless sacrifices, existing in perfect purity, praising of God, and teaching. For further, see Chapter 5, below.

[109] Dimant, "Men as Angels," 101.

[110] Tuschling, *Angels and Orthodoxy*, 119.

[111] Tuschling, *Angels and Orthodoxy*, 117–119.

[112] Tuschling, *Angels and Orthodoxy*, 118.

[113] Though Tuschling, *Angels and Orthodoxy*, 118–119, uses the helpful "communion of identity" to articulate her understanding, it is rendered somewhat ambiguous when followed

lowship is articulated by those who argue that the promises of angelic fellowship after death in some texts (cf. Dan 12:3; 1 En. 104:2–6) were considered a *present reality* for sect members who have joined the angels in heaven via ascent experience in the context of worship.[114] Moreover, Schäfer highlights that there are various forms of angelic fellowship including the martial fellowship at eschaton envisioned by the *War Scroll* as well as the present liturgical communion referred to in the *Hodayot*.[115]

As Schuller has observed – and as the preceding paragraph confirms – "there is little agreement on what exactly is being claimed"[116] when scholars refer to the sectarian notion of angelic fellowship. I would suggest that a helpful way forward lies in another proposal of Tuschling, namely, that angelic communion be understood within the overarching belief that the Qumran movement belonged to the lot of the righteous, which was headed by the principal angel variously called "Michael," "the Prince of Light(s)," etc. She describes these beliefs as

part of the mapping of the whole cosmos in terms of the influence of angelic and demonic armies. This is most clearly seen in the *Treatise on the Two Spirits*. The sphere of the Prince of Lights and the Angel of Darkness find their equivalent within each human soul, the spirits of truth and of deceit (1QS III, 18f).[117]

Tuschling is thus calling for angelic fellowship to be considered within the framework of the dualistic divide, the respective sides of which are angel-led. Recent scholarship has tended to view the dualistic material in some of the sectarian texts – including cosmic or angelic dualism – as secondarily adopted "to provide a theological explanation"[118] for the separation from other Jews that occurred primarily for *halakhic* and social reasons. That non-sectarian texts reveal such features lends credence to the possibility that angelic dualism was later borrowed and developed by the sect to bolster legal, interpretive, or other arguments.

---

by the (loftier) claims that sect members "become the same as angels" or "actually become angels."

[114] See John J. Collins, "The Angelic Life," in *Metamorphoses: Resurrection, Body, and Transformative Practices in Early Christianity* (eds., Turid Karlsen Seim and Jorunn Økland; Berlin: de Gruyter, 2009), 291–296. Cf. Chazon, "Human & Angelic Prayer," 43–45; Alexander, *The Mystical Texts*, 118–119; Angel, *Otherworldly*, 84.

[115] Schäfer, *The Origins of Jewish Mysticism*, 151–152.

[116] Eileen M. Schuller, "Recent Scholarship on the Hodayot," *CurBR* 10 (2011): 151.

[117] Tuschling, *Angels and Orthodoxy*, 115, 136.

[118] E.g., the dualism of the "Treatise on the Two Spirits" (cf. 1QS III, 13–IV, 26) referenced by Tuschling; see John J. Collins, *The Scriptures and Sectarianism: Essays on the Dead Sea Scrolls* (WUNT 332; Tübingen: Mohr Siebeck, 2014), 193–194. For a recent collection of essays, see Géza G. Xeravits, ed., *Dualism in Qumran* (LSTS 76; London: T & T Clark, 2010). I will address the dualism of the *Treatise* in Chapter 4, below.

The union between heaven and earth assumed by the sect's angelic fellow-ship claims also reflects the conviction that access to the heavenly temple was, at least in part, a substitute for the Jerusalem temple, which they rejected as defiled.[119] Thus, angel-human interaction meant that issues of moral and ritual purity were of paramount concern at Qumran (cf. 1QSa II, 3–9).[120] As Harrington points out, the ritual impurity of outsiders – both Gentiles and non-sectarian Jews – "was primarily a label which preserved group identity as a 'holy house for Aaron and Israel' by reinforcing the barrier between member and non-member."[121] Though some scholars do not find evidence of the belief that Gentiles were considered ritually impure by the sect,[122] there are strong indications that outsiders, due to both ritual and moral impurity, were viewed in very negative terms at Qumran, with designations like "holy house for Aaron and Israel" and "an eternal planting" rightly viewed as ex-clusivist claims that the sect considered itself alone to be the true Israel.[123]

VII. Summary and Points of Departure

As this history of research has indicated, there is a need to move beyond de-scription and observation and, to that end, to investigate more fully the inter-section of angelology and sectarian identity in the Dead Sea Scrolls. The notions of principal angelic guardian figures and angelic priests were im-portant features of Second Temple Period angelological speculation, and even in non-sectarian texts these angelic guardians and priests are envisioned as having some sort of connection or correspondence to the people of God, thereby justifying my descriptor, angels associated with Israel. And if Se-cond Temple Period Jews considered angels associated with Israel as arche-

---

[119] Collins, "The Angelic Life," 298. On the issue of separation from the Jerusalem tem-ple, see Beate Ego, et al., eds., *Gemeinde ohne Temple: zur Substituierung und Transfor-mation des Jerusalemer Temples und seines Kults im Alten Testament, antiken Judentum und frühen Christentum* (WUNT 118; Tübingen: Mohr Siebeck, 1999).

[120] See Collins, "The Angelic Life," 301.

[121] Hannah K. Harrington, "Keeping Outsiders Out: Impurity at Qumran," in *Defining Identities*, 203.

[122] So, e.g., Christine E. Hayes, *Gentile Impurities and Jewish Identities: Intermarriage and Conversion from the Bible to the Talmud* (Oxford: Oxford University Press, 2002), 65. Cf. Harrington, "Keeping Outsiders Out," 187. On the notion of proselytes at Qumran, see Carmen Palmer, *Converts in the Dead Sea Scrolls: Gēr and Mutable Ethnicity* (STDJ 126; Leiden: Brill, 2018).

[123] E.g., Paul Swarup, *The Self-Understanding of the Dead Sea Scrolls Community: An Eternal Planting, A House of Holiness* (LSTS 59; London: T & T Clark, 2006), 193–202. On the sect as "Israel," see especially John J. Collins, "The Construction of Israel in the Sectarian Rule Books," in *Judaism in Late Antiquity, Part 5: The Judaisms of Qumran: A Systematic Reading of the Dead Sea Scrolls, Vol. 1: Theory of Israel* (eds., Alan J. Avery-Peck, Jacob Neusner, and Bruce D. Chilton; HdO 58; Leiden: Brill, 2001), 25–42. Cf. Harrington, Har-rington, "Keeping Outsiders Out," 203.

typal and "more real"[124] than themselves, this association would have been highly valued and is therefore worthy of investigation, especially as it pertains to how a relationship with these angels was viewed to be a mark of the true people of God.

While there is some uncertainty as to what exactly is indicated by sectarian angelic fellowship claims, this phenomenon seems to be related to but qualitatively greater than a connection or correspondence with the angels. Moreover, Tuschling's call to view sectarian angelic fellowship within the framework of an angel-led dualistic divide will be fruitful, especially if it is remembered that to be a sect member – and thus on the righteous side of the dualistic divide – is, by definition, to be part of the true Israel. That is, if sectarian membership includes not just a connection/correspondence but also fellowship with both angelic guardian figures and the priestly angels of whom the sectarians claim to be earthly counterparts, then to be part of true Israel is to have fellowship with these angels associated with Israel. Boasts of angelic communion would have thus constituted a powerful assertion vis-à-vis the claims of other Jews, and, indeed, far more than the sect "mumbling to itself"[125] – especially as it pertains to who constitutes the legitimate embodiment of "Israel." Said another way, it is not merely the sect's standing in the proper dualistic camp that is at stake: given its claims to be the correct interpreters of Torah, peerless when it comes to *halakhic* matters, and the recipients of unique and timely heavenly insights, the Qumran movement's boasts of fellowship with angels associated with Israel would have greatly strengthened assertions that they were the true and faithful people of God. Schuller has suggested that a comparison of angelic fellowship passages in the sectarian literature may highlight "what all these texts share in common";[126] I am convinced that sectarian attempts to assert themselves as the true Israel is one such commonality. In order to gain the fullest possible appreciation of sectarian angelic fellowship claims, it is necessary to differentiate them from the wider idea of an angelic connection/correspondence. Thus, the Second Temple Period Jewish texts not composed by the Qumran movement – works that apparently had broad(er) appeal – will have to be compared with those texts deemed to have been penned by the sectarians themselves.

---

[124] So Collins, *The Apocalyptic Imagination*, 187.
[125] Cf. Newsom, *The Self as Symbolic Space*, 3, cited earlier.
[126] Schuller, "Recent Scholarship on the Hodayot," 152.

C. Objectives and Plan of Study

In view of the preceding history of research, the primary objectives of this study are to determine the contributions angels associated with Israel make to mid and late Second Temple Period compositions extant among the Dead Sea Scrolls. The depictions of a relationship between these angels and faithful Jews on earth in non-sectarian texts will be carefully examined and compared to the presentations of angels associated with Israel in sectarian writings, with special attention granted to the notion of angelic fellowship at Qumran. A key component of my discussions of all texts will be to highlight the relationship between these angels and a given work's understanding or definition of Israel, thereby setting the stage to discuss the intersection of angelology and the Qumran movement's conviction that its ranks alone constituted the true Israel. The present study is justified in that it will move beyond the descriptive and observational approaches that have characterized many angelological treatments; and it will do so by utilizing the concept of angels associated with Israel to gain a better understanding of how the Qumran movement adapted shared traditions to shape its religious identity vis-à-vis other Jews.

The organization will be as follows: Chapter 2 will briefly explore the conceptual backgrounds of angels associated with Israel, both in the Canaanite literature and in pre-exilic, exilic, and early post-exilic passages of the Hebrew Bible, with Chapters 3–5 comprising the main body of the study. Specifically, Chapter 3 will examine both angelic guardians and priests associated with Israel in mid and late Second Temple Period compositions of a non-sectarian provenance, whereas Chapters 4 and 5 will be devoted to the sectarian texts: angelic guardians will be investigated in Chapter 4; and angelic priests will be the focus of Chapter 5. The conclusions of the study and brief suggestions for expanding the scope of research are found in Chapter 6. Unless otherwise stated, English translations of the Hebrew Bible and Deuterocanonical books are from the NRSV.[127]

---

[127] Harold W. Attridge, ed., *The HarperCollins Study Bible, Fully Revised and Updated, New Revised Standard Version, Including the Apocryphal/Deuterocanonical Books with Concordance* (New York: HarperCollins, 2006).

Chapter 2

Angels Associated with Israel:
Conceptual Foundations

A. Introduction

This study of angels associated with Israel includes the angelic vocations of guardians and priests, and, as such, the most important sections of this chapter will highlight the conceptual foundations of the angels who serve in these capacities in pre-exilic, exilic, and early post-exilic passages of the Hebrew Bible. This is important because focused interest in these celestial beings only arose as part of the angelological developments of early Judaism, which means that the notion that Israel had a celestial guardian other than Yhwh is relatively undeveloped in the Hebrew Bible prior to the Book of Daniel.[1]

As I will highlight, the belief that God provided Israel with celestial guardianship in figures like Michael, Melchizedek, and the Prince of Light is indebted not only to earlier figures such as the Angel of Yhwh but also to the concept of national deities, that is, the idea that certain divine beings watch over other nations as Yhwh watches over Israel. I will thus examine three biblical texts showcasing gods of the nations that are essential for understanding both angels associated with Israel and the worldviews within which they were envisioned. In the Hebrew Bible, national deities are, in turn, connected to the ancient Near Eastern concept of the divine council or assembly, and I will therefore begin this chapter with a brief overview of the assembly in the Canaanite texts.[2]

B. The Canaanite Divine Assembly

Broadly conceived, the divine assembly is the royal court of the highest god and comprised of subordinate deities who had various ranks and roles. Inves-

---

[1] The evidence for the belief in angelic priests before the mid Second Temple Period is even more sparse; I will address this subject in the last section of the present chapter.

[2] There are, of course, relevant parallels in other ancient Near Eastern texts, but there is an especially close relationship between the ancient Canaanites and Israelites, who were both West Semitic peoples. For an overview, see Smith, *The Early History of God*, 19–31.

tigation of the Canaanite council involves several complex issues, including how the relationship between the assembly members should be understood and who should be identified as highest the god of the pantheon.

I. Who is the High God of the Canaanite Pantheon?

The only extant indigenous texts for studying the Canaanite divine council are the tablets of the ancient city of Ugarit, found in 1928. Among other myths, these 14th cent. BCE texts contain what has become known as the "Baal Cycle,"[3] which is centered on the battles of the storm god, Baal, to attain kingship of the cosmos.[4] But it is precisely the issue of Baal's kingship that poses a crux for interpreters. Scholars have understood the prominence of Baal differently, and there are two main conclusions: while some see the kingship of Baal in the Ugaritic texts as parallel yet subordinate to the reign of El, who is considered the highest god, others understand Baal to be the supreme ruler over the gods, El included. The issue is not just that there are those who conclude that Baal became the power-broker of the Canaanite pantheon as the status of El diminished over time; some have also made the more drastic claim that Baal's kingship was established after a conflict between El and Baal from which the latter emerged victorious.[5]

In short, I find neither the external evidence[6] nor the witness of the Canaanite texts themselves supportive of the view that Baal violently usurped

---

[3] Cf. Mark S. Smith, *The Ugaritic Baal Cycle: Volume I: Introduction with Texts, Translation and Commentary of KTU 1.1–1.2* (VTSup 55; Leiden: Brill, 1994); idem and Wayne T. Pitard, *The Ugaritic Baal Cycle: Volume II: Introduction with Text, Translation and Commentary of KTU 1.3–1.4* (VTSup 114; Leiden: Brill, 2009).

[4] While there have been numerous attempts to provide a comprehensive interpretation of the Baal cycle, Smith, *Ugaritic Baal Cycle*, 1:59–60, notes that, despite the differences in opinion on the specifics, there has been a virtual consensus in recognizing the text as a conflict-resolution story which is royal in nature: Baal's kingship – secured by his victories over Yamm and Mot – represent and are celebrations of life overcoming chaos/destruction and death. In one sense, the exclamation of the goddess, Athirat, in *KTU* 1.4 IV 43–44 captures well the thrust of the texts: "Our King is Mightiest Baal, Our ruler, with none above him."

[5] Cf. Ulf Oldenburg, *The Conflict Between El and Baal in Canaanite Religion* (Leiden: Brill, 1969), who most ardently defends the view that Baal violently usurped El's throne.

[6] I.e., comparison of the Ugaritic texts with other ancient documents has been said to support the view that Baal triumphed over El. For example, Eusebius of Caesarea, in his *Praeparatio evangelica* (ca. 315 CE), includes excerpts of the *Phoenician History* by a certain Sanchuniathon, whose work was translated into Greek by Philo of Byblos (ca. 100 CE) (for text and commentary, see Harold W. Attridge and Robert A. Oden, Jr., *Philo of Byblos the Phoenician History: Introduction, Critical Text, Translation, Notes* [CBQMS 9; Washington: Catholic Biblical Association of America, 1981]; Albert I. Baumgartner, *The Phoenician History of Philo of Byblos: A Commentary* [EPRO; Leiden: Brill, 1981]). Though it is clear that i.) Philo used a source which was genuinely familiar with Canaanite

El's sovereignty over the Canaanite pantheon.[7] Moreover, it is likely correct that "El's battles are not extant in the Ugaritic texts and that his theogonic wars lie in the distant past."[8] But just because El was not an active participant in the kingship battles of the younger gods does not mean that he was envisioned as weak or otiose at Ugarit,[9] and the bravado of the younger gods has not universally been interpreted as evidence of a low view of El[10] and should not obscure the fact that Yamm, Baal, and others could not undertake significant action without first securing the permission of El, particularly as it

---

thought; and ii.) the *Phoenician History* identifies Kronos as El of the Canaanite pantheon (i.e., Kronos is the father of large family of gods, the names and actions of whom are similar, at times, to the gods of the Ugaritic texts; cf. Eusebius, *Praep. evang.*, 1.10.29; see Mullen, *Assembly of the Gods*, 32 n. 55; Patrick D. Miller, Jr., *The Divine Warrior in Early Israel* [HSM 5; Cambridge: Harvard University Press, 1973], 9, 62), it is equally obvious that Philo describes the Kronos-El figure as a mighty warrior whose kingship is unambiguously connected to his prowess in combat, and the resulting picture is that Kronos-El, no less than other deities, is a warrior who battles against his enemies. Conversely, it is far from evident that El's primary function is that of a warrior or that his kingly status is attributable to military exploits. This discrepancy has led some scholars to suggest that the Ugaritic texts envision El as a weak, otiose king, whose rule had been, at the very least, seriously undermined by the kingship of Baal by the time the Ugaritic texts were written. That El's status had in some sense waned by the time of the Ugaritic texts was first proposed by R. G. Roggia, "Alcune osservationioni sul culto di El a Ras-Samra," *Aevum* 15 (1941): 559–575. Cf. Marvin H. Pope, *El in the Ugaritic Texts* (VTSup 2; Leiden: Brill, 1955), 29; Oldenburg, *The Conflict Between El and Baal*, 101–116. It should be noted, however, that the *Phoenician History* states that the kingship of Zeus-Hadad over the gods came about not by the storm god's violent disposition of his father but rather with Kronos' *permission*: "Zeus Demarous who is Hada, king of the gods, reigned over the place with the consent of Kronos" (cf. Eusebius, *Praep. evang.* 1.10.31); see Attridge and Oden, *Philo of Byblos*, 54–55, 91. For detailed analyses and rebuttal of the supposed lowly status of El, see L'Heureux, *Rank Among the Canaanite Gods*, 3–70; Mullen, *Assembly of the Gods*, 92–110; Smith, *Ugaritic Baal Cycle*, 1:88–96, 296.

[7] For discussion of passages frequently cited as examples of El's low status and/or conflict between El and Baal, see, e.g., L'Heureux, *Rank Among the Canaanite Gods*, 3–28. For challenges to the view that the Ugaritic texts depict El as banished, see Richard J. Clifford, *The Cosmic Mountain in Canaan and the Old Testament* (HSM 4; Cambridge: Harvard University Press, 1972), 35–57; Smith, *Ugaritic Baal Myth*, 1:225–230.

[8] Smith, *The Origins*, 220. Cf. Cross, *Canaanite Myth*, 43.

[9] As noted by Mullen, *Assembly of the Gods*, 10, 45.

[10] In reference to the divine council's response (i.e., lowering their heads) to Yamm's messengers (*KTU* 1.2 I 23–24), Smith, *Ugaritic Baal Cycle*, 1:299–300, notes that in other ANE council scenes, raising the head indicates one's desire or willingness to act; thus, its opposite – lowering – would suggest a desire *not* to act. Therefore, even if El is to be included with those who "lower their heads" at the sight of Yamm's emissaries, it may not be that El and the council are afraid; it may simply be that the gods are making known their prerogative: that they did not wish to act against Yamm's messengers, who were charged to remove Baal from the assembly.

pertained to matters of kingship.[11] Additionally, though the Ugaritic texts exalt Baal as king of the cosmos, Baal's exaltation and reign are not portrayed as absolute but limited and fragile,[12] as the storm god often requires the assistance of the other deities, especially El.[13] A helpful way to conceptualize the role of El, then, is as high king of the pantheon, which includes the management of the kingships of the younger gods.[14] In other words, El reigned supreme over the pantheon, but the younger gods – the sons of El – were permitted to vie with each other for rule of the cosmos.[15] Understanding El as both high king *and* manager of kingships not only accounts for the lofty royal epithets applied to his sons, but it also suggests that the reigns of El and Baal were relatively harmonious, an assertion which finds support in a text explicitly noting the relationship between El and Baal: "El sat enthroned with Astarte; El judged with Haddu, his shepherd."[16]

II. The Organization of the Divine Assembly

Given his preeminent status, it comes as no surprise that the Ugaritic texts depict El as the head of the pantheon's social structure, which is referred to as the council or assembly. Table 1 lists the assembly's tiers, which are derived from various passages (cf. *KTU* 1.2 I; 1.4 III; 1.15 II):

---

[11] E.g., despite their boldness, Yamm's emissaries could not simply take Baal from the assembly without El's consent (cf. *KTU* 1.2 I 11–39); it is only by the decree of El that a palace could be built for Yamm (cf. *KTU* 1.1 IV 17–20) and Baal (cf. *KTU* 1.4 IV 54–V 63). See Smith, *Ugaritic Baal Cycle*, 1:105.

[12] Smith, *Ugaritic Baal Cycle*, 1:96–114, discusses the possibility that Baal's limited power reflects political frustrations at Ugarit. The limited and fragile power of Baal stands in stark contrast to the absolute power of Baal's Mesopotamian counterpart, Marduk, in the *Enuma Elish*.

[13] As Smith, *Ugaritic Baal Cycle*, 1:296, observes, "El emerges as a figure more fully invested with power in the Baal Cycle precisely because Baal is not predominant throughout so much of the plot. [In numerous situations, o]nly when El gives his authority for the palace does [El] recede into the background of the plot.

[14] Cf. Mullen, *Assembly of the Gods*, 37–38, who refers to El as the "dispenser" of kingships.

[15] J. D. Scholen, "The Exile of Disinherited Kin in *KTU* 1.12 and *KTU* 1.23," *JNES* 52 (1993): 209–220, has observed that conflict seems to be patrilateral in nature; i.e., there are indications that Baal was adopted into family of El and that sibling rivalries with Yamm and Mot are the source of the conflict. Cf. Smith, *Ugaritic Baal Cycle*, 94.

[16] Jean Nougayrol et al., eds., *Ugaritica V* (Paris: Imprimerie Nationale, 1968), 2.2b–3a. Cf. Collins, *Daniel*, 287, who notes Baal's "harmonious subordination to El" in the text. The picture is similar to that of Kronos and Zeus in the *Phoenician History*; see Smith, *Ugaritic Baal Cycle*, 1:296–297; Cross, *Canaanite Myth*, 37 n. 147.

Table 1: The Four Tiers of the Divine Assembly[17]

Tier	Gods and Goddesses	Characteristics of Tier
Highest	El and his consort, Athirat	High kingship, management of pantheon
Second	Baal, Yamm, Mot, Anath	Kingship, royal children, combat, nature assoc.
Third	Kothar wa-Hasis	Service of higher tiers (e.g., craftsmanship)
Fourth	Minor deities	Messengers, part of retinues of higher-tier gods

The highest tier of the assembly is that of El, and his consort, Athirat, who influenced his decisions.[18] That ultimate authority in the pantheon belonged to El has already been highlighted, and one of the ways the Ugaritic texts emphasize El's supremacy is the non-democratic nature of the council; that is, the decree of El is tantamount to the decree of the council.[19] The gods and goddesses of the second tier are associated with forces of nature:[20] as noted above, Yamm is the god of the sea, Mot is the god of death, and Baal the god of the storm/rain. Baal's victory over Yamm and Mot are, in part, celebrations of life overcoming chaos and death, but the associations with natural forces complement and emphasize the combative nature of the deities of this tier.[21] The third tier of the assembly has sparse representation in the Ugaritic

---

[17] So Smith, *The Origins of Biblical Monotheism*, 45–46. Cf. Handy, *Among the Host*, 169–177, who subscribes to the same tiers but with different nomenclature. Despite the fact that Smith views the entire pantheon as coterminous with the assembly and Handy does not, White, *Yahweh's Council*, 5–10, points out the affinities between their readings.

[18] E.g., After Anath's request that a palace be built for Baal was denied, it was Athirat's petition that persuaded El (cf. *KTU* 1.4 IV–V); see Smith, *The Origins,* 45.

[19] I.e., even when the mighty Baal is presented as part of the assembly, he must act within the strictures of the El's decree. Smith, *Ugaritic Baal Cycle*, 1:315–316, suggests that *KTU* 1.2 I is an example of the Baal cycle using yet undermining the ANE type-scene of the council's selection of a hero to fight on its behalf: rather than being the chosen champion of the assembly, Baal does not have the support of the assembly and is declared by El to be Yamm's vassal. Once again, Baal's portrayal in the Ugaritic texts stands in sharp contrast with the council-supported hero of Mesopotamian mythology, Markduk.

[20] There is also evidence (iconographical and textual) that the family of El was considered to be astral in nature; e.g., the parallelism of *KTU* 1.10 I 35: sons of El/assembly of the stars/circle of those of heaven. For discussion of the names and characteristics of specific deities, see Smith, *The Origins,* 61–66.

[21] Iconographic and textual evidence suggests that Baal was considered the warrior-patron of Ugarit and its king, and it has been posited that the rise and struggles of the storm god in the Baal Cycle were a reflection of the rise and struggles of the Niqumaddu line at Ugarit in the Middle and Late Bronze Age. For bibliography, see Smith, *Ugaritic Baal Cycle*, 1:90, 106–114. Cf. Handy, *Among the Host*, 102: "the role of Baal as the patron deity of Ugarit [was] decidedly more political ... than merely controlling rain."

texts,[22] but the fourth and lowest tier of the assembly is well-represented, even if this level consists of servant gods, who were often the non-individuated[23] *bn qdsh,* "sons of the Holy One/Holiness" (cf. *KTU* 1.2 I 21, 38) or *phr bn 'ilm,* "assembly of the sons of El" (cf. *KTU* 1.4 III 14).[24] Deities of this tier served as messengers and in their superiors' retinues, military or otherwise.[25]

In sum, the concept of the divine assembly in the Ugaritic texts appears to have had multiple distinct tiers, which likely mirrored similar levels of ancient society. As I will highlight, the Canaanite conception of the divine assembly is relevant to this study in multiple ways, not least being the El-like manner in which Yhwh is depicted as sitting at the head of the council in Deut 32 and Ps 82, which I will discuss in this chapter.

There is, however, an important difference between these texts and the Canaanite material: a facet of the biblical tradition's incorporation of the divine assembly not explicitly evident in the Ugaritic texts is the way council members are appointed as gods of the nations. As Tigay explains,

the idea that God distributed the nations among the [gods] is unique to the bible. Elsewhere we hear of the major gods dividing the regions of the universe among themselves by lot [*Atrahasis* I, 11–18; *Iliad* 15:184–193], or of a chief deity distributing cities, lands, and regions to other gods [cf. Eusebius, *Praep. Evang.,* 1.10.32–39]. These myths are concerned with the allotment of residences and cult centers to the gods, *not with relationship of the gods to the people of these places. In the bible, the motif serves to express God's relationship to humanity and his election of Israel* [emphasis mine].[26]

Again, an aim of this chapter is to underscore that the concept of national deities contributed to the Second Temple Period portrayals of Israel's celestial guardians. I will, thus, begin my examination of the Hebrew Bible by discussing three texts which best elucidate the later concept of angels associated with Israel and the worldviews within which these beings were envisioned, namely, that the actions of heavenly beings tangibly impact humanity.

---

[22] The exemplar of this level is Kothar wa-Hasis, who provides craftsmanship and wise counsel to the gods; see Smith, *The Origins,* 46; Handy, *Among the Host,* 131–147. Cf. Heiser, "The Divine Council," §2.3, who reviews the evidence for this tier in the Ugaritic texts, deeming it "speculative."

[23] Mullen, *Assembly of the Gods,* 177. Cf. Handy, *Among the Host,* 149.

[24] For discussion of these terms, see Miller, *The Divine Warrior,* 14–15; Smith, *Ugaritic Baal Cycle,* 1:266–267, 294–295; idem and Pitard, *Ugaritic Baal Cycle,* 2:62, 462.

[25] Smith, *The Origins,* 46; Mullen, *Assembly of the Gods,* 175–201. Cf. Handy, *Among the Host,* 157–159.

[26] Jeffrey Tigay, *Deuteronomy: The Traditional Hebrew Text with the New JPS Translation* (JPSTC; Philadelphia: Jewish Publication Society, 1996), 515, 546 n. 12–13. Cf. Clifford, *The Cosmic Mountain,* 47; Mullen, *Assembly of the Gods,* 202–205.

C. The Biblical Background of Angels Associated with Israel
Part I: Angelic Guardians

I. Deuteronomy 32:8–9

Part of the so-called "Song of Moses,"[27] Deut 32:8–9 has been referred to as the "standard or charter for the topic of the deities of the other nations."[28] In addition to its impact on later tradition,[29] a main reason why this is such an important text is that it is the most explicit statement in the Hebrew Bible regarding not only the existence of the gods of the nations but also the nature of the relationship of these national deities to Yhwh and Israel. The MT[30] of Deut 32:8–9 reads as follows:

8 בְּהַנְחֵל עֶלְיוֹן גּוֹיִם בְּהַפְרִידוֹ בְּנֵי אָדָם יַצֵּב גְּבֻלֹת עַמִּים לְמִסְפַּר בְּנֵי יִשְׂרָאֵל
9 כִּי חֵלֶק יְהוָה עַמּוֹ יַעֲקֹב חֶבֶל נַחֲלָתוֹ

8 When the Most High apportioned the nations, when he divided humankind, he fixed the boundaries of the peoples according to the number of the sons of Israel.
9 Yhwh's own portion was his people, Jacob his allotted share.

The end of verse 8 has well-known textual variants.[31] Specifically, the LXX[32] and the Dead Sea Scrolls[33] do not have the "sons of Israel," a phrase which has perplexed interpreters.

---

[27] The "Song of Moses" is found in Deut 32:1–43, the first section of which (vv. 1–14) emphasizes Yhwh's past kindness to Israel and the nation's consequent obligation to serve God faithfully. Its archaic poetic features have persuaded many scholars that it originally was an independent composition that pre-dates the bulk of Deuteronomy, even if there is no consensus on its precise date and provenance. For an overview, see Paul Sanders, *The Provenance of Deuteronomy 32* (OTS 37; Leiden: Brill, 1996). Classic studies that date the Song to the 11th cent. BCE include Otto Eissfeldt, *Das Lied Moses, Deutermomomium 32:1–43 und das Lehrgedicht Asaphs samt einer Analyse der Umgebung des Mose-Liedes* (Berlin, Akademie-Verlag, 1958); William F. Albright, "Some Remarks on the Song of Moses," *VT* 9 (1959): 339–346. Tigay, *Deuteronomy*, 512–513, rightly cautions that the inconsistent occurrences of archaic poetic features may indicate that the poem was written and/or revised either during a period of transition when old and new forms were used interchangeably or perhaps at a later time in conscious but inconsistent imitation of the older tradition. His instructive conclusion, "that [the Song] is older than Deuteronomy 1–31 and 34, perhaps considerably older," will be provisionally accepted here. For additional discussion, see Mark S. Smith, *God in Translation: Deities in Cross-Cultural Discourse in the Biblical Word* (Grand Rapids: Eerdmans, 2008), 139–141.

[28] Smith, *God in Translation*, 210.

[29] For a brief discussion of the reception of Deut 32:8–9 in Second Temple Period Judaism, see Smith, *God in Translation*, 208–210.

[30] Hebrew Bible text is from Karl Elliger, William Rudolph, and H. P. Rüger, eds., *Biblia Hebraica Stuttgartensia* (Stuttgart: Deutsche Bibelgesellschaft, 1984).

[31] Helpful overviews of the textual witnesses are provided by Michael S. Heiser, "Deuteronomy 32 and the Sons of God," *BSac* 158 (2001): 52–54; Smith, *God in Translation*, 139–140.

Table 2: Textual Variants of Deut 32:8

Source	Variant	Translation
MT	בְּנֵי יִשְׂרָאֵל	sons of Israel
Dead Sea Scrolls (4QDeutʲ)	בני אלוהים	sons of god
LXX (some manuscripts)	υἱῶν θεοῦ	sons of god
LXX (most manuscripts)	ἀγγέλων θεοῦ	angels of god

The discovery of the Qumran Cave 4 manuscripts has all but confirmed the long-held scholarly suspicion that the LXX was dependent on a Hebrew *Vorlage* similar to that of 4QDeutʲ and that this tradition pre-dated that reflected in the MT. The critical consensus on the variants of verse 8, then, is that the MT's "sons of Israel" – despite its illogic[34] – was a deliberate emendation of בני אלוהים by later scribes who may have been uncomfortable with the polytheistic implications of the verse.[35] The text is thus corrected by critical

---

[32] John William Wevers, ed., *Deuteronomium* (SVTG 3/2; Göttingen: Vandenhoeck and Ruprecht, 1977), 347.

[33] Julie Ann Duncan, "37. 4QDeutʲ," in *Qumran Cave 4. IX: Deuteronomy, Joshua, Judges, Kings* (eds., E. Ulrich et al.; DJD 14; Oxford: Claredon Press, 1995), 90.

[34] S. R. Driver, *Deuteronomy* (3rd ed.; ICC; Edinburgh: T & T Clark, 1973), 355–356, whose commentary was first published in 1895 – well before the discoveries at Qumran – suggests that Deut 32:8–9 is intelligible in light of Gen 10 and 46:27: i.e., as per Tg. Ps.-J., Driver argues that "a correspondence was intended between [the 70 nations descended from the sons of Noah] and the 70 souls of Gen 46:27." Thus, God divided the nations according to the number of Jacob's sons who went down to Egypt. But as Heiser, "Deuteronomy 32 and the Sons of God," 53–54, points out, even if one presupposes an intended connection between the separation (פרד) of the nations in Gen 10–11 and their separation (פרד) in Deut 32:8–9, "What possible point would there be behind connecting the pagan Gentile nations numerically with the Israelites?" Cf. Tigay, *Deuteronomy*, 302.

[35] Smith, *God in Translation*, 141, 197–201. Cf. Emmanuel Tov, *Textual Criticism of the Hebrew Bible* (3rd ed.; Minneapolis: Augsburg Fortress Press, 2012), 269. A. van der Kooij, "Ancient Emendations in MT," in *L'Ecrit et L'Esprit: Etudes d'histoire du texte et de théologie biblique en homage à Adrian Schenker* (eds., Dieter Böhler, I. Imbaza, P. Hugo; Göttingen: Vandenhoeck & Ruprecht, 2005), 152–159, has proposed that the scribal emendation dates to 2nd cent. BCE priestly circles, though Heiser, "The Divine Council," §§1.4; 3.1, suggests a 100 CE date, largely because he does not consider the Second Temple Period to have been nearly as "intolerantly monotheistic" as is sometimes suggested. Cf. idem, "Monotheism and the Language," 85–100. It should also be noted that an emendation similar to that of verse 8 was likely carried out at the end of the Song of Moses: while the LXX and Qumran manuscripts of Deut 32:43 preserve, respectively, two and four-line imperatives for the heavenly beings to worship Yhwh, the MT emends and truncates this. For discussion of LXX and MT Deut 32:8–9 and 43 vis-à-vis the Qumran manuscripts, see Tigay, *Deuteronomy*, 516–518, who does not specify a date for the emendations, other than to suggest that they occurred before the Rabbinic period. Cf. Alexander Rofé, "The End of the Song of Moses (Deuteronomy 32:43)," in *Liebe und Gebot: Studien zum Deuteronomium* (eds., Reinhard G. Kratz and Hermann Spiekermann; Göttingen:

commentators and some modern translations to reflect the Qumran and LXX witnesses,[36] and the thrust of Deut 32:8–9 is understood as follows: the God of Israel assigned or sub-contracted the subordinate beings of his assembly a guardian-like role over the other nations, but such an arrangement was not established for Israel, who is privileged to be ruled directly by Yhwh.[37]

In a series of related studies,[38] Smith has championed and developed the view that a fuller understanding of Deut 32:8–9 and related passages is more complex than the brief sketch provided in the preceding paragraph, even if it is ultimately correct. Smith's work is concerned with the notion of "translatability," which he defines as "a worldview that could recognize other national gods as valid for Israel's neighbors just as Yhwh was for Israel."[39] Contrary to claims that Israelite religion exhibited a lack of translatability due to its "Mosaic distinction,"[40] Smith contends that there is, indeed, evidence of translatability in monarchic Israel, and that certain texts "are not nearly as monotheistic as they have been interpreted."[41] While Smith claims that translatability *began* to wane when the Assyrians and Babylonians rose to power, he claims that a "Mosaic distinction" cannot truly be maintained until the late biblical period and post-biblical reception of the Hebrew Bible.[42] Perhaps the

---

Vandenhoeck & Ruprecht, 2000), 164–172, who articulates the general scholarly consensus: "theological correction lies at the bottom of the textual manipulations that ensued."

[36] E.g., the NRSV translates the end of verse 8 as "gods."

[37] Cf. Alexander Rofé, *Angels in the Bible: Israelite Belief as Evidence by Biblical Traditions* (2nd. ed.; Jerusalem: Carmel, 2012), xii; Peter C. Craigie, *Deuteronomy* (NICOT; Grand Rapids: Eerdmans, 1976), 379–380; Mullen, *Assembly of the Gods*, 202–205; Tigay, *Deuteronomy*, 302–304; Heiser, "Deuteronomy 32 and the Sons of God," 52–74; Christenson, *Deuteronomy 21:10 34:12*, 796. The idea that God has allotted divine beings to the other nations is not limited to the Song of Moses, as Deut 4:19–20 and 29:25–26 attest.

[38] Cf. Smith's previously cited monographs, *The Early History of God, The Origins*, and *God in Translation*.

[39] Smith, *God in Translation*, 10.

[40] Smith, *God in Translation*, 1–9, 103, is clear that his research is primarily a critique and development of the work of Assmann and Hendel. E.g., Jan Assmann, *Moses the Egyptian: The Memory of Egypt in Western Monotheism* (Cambridge: Harvard University Press, 1997), claims that the distinctive feature of Mosaic religion stems from it being "'counter religion' because it rejects and repudiates everything that went before and what is outside itself as 'paganism.' ... Whereas polytheism ... rendered different cultures mutually transparent or compatible, the new counter-religion blocked inter-cultural translatability. False gods cannot be translated." Cf. idem, *Die Mosaische Unterscheidung: Oder der Preis des Monotheismus* (München: C. Hanser, 2003); Ronald Hendel, *Remembering Abraham: Culture Memory, and the History of the Hebrew Bible* (Oxford: Oxford University Press, 2005).

[41] Smith, *God in Translation*, 129, highlights how texts such as Gen 31:43–53, Num 23:9, Judg 11:24, and 1 Kgs 20:23–28 "reflect various forms of translatability largely involving the recognition of the class of national military gods across cultural boundaries."

[42] Smith, *God in Translation*, 10.

most relevant aspect of Smith's work for the present study is his proposal that the move from translatability to non-translatability in ancient Israel involved a sophisticated process of development "that retained older formulations of translatability within expressions of non-translatability and monotheism."[43] According to Smith, Deut 32:8–9 is an example of a text that preserves vestiges of an older translatable worldview even as it rejects that same worldview. Smith addresses two aspects of the passage: the textual variants of verse 8 and "Elyon," an epithet associated with El (cf. Gen 14:18–20).

Not only has the long-recognized existence of separate traditions – a "southern" Yhwh tradition and a Canaanite El tradition[44] – prompted Smith to suggest that the identification of these gods occurred secondarily; Smith is also a proponent of what is arguably now the consensus view, that Deut 32:8–9 actually points to a past distinction and translatability between El and Yhwh.[45] In other words, "the passage says how Jacob (i.e., Israel) became Yhwh's allotment"; that is, "Yhwh is one of the gods who receives his inheritance from (El) Elyon."[46] Smith is adamant, however, that the translatability

---

[43] Smith, *God in Translation*, 10.

[44] Cf. Cross, *Canaanite Myth*, 60–75; Johannes C. De Moor, *The Rise of Yahwism* (2nd ed.; BETL 91; Leuven: Leuven University Press, 1997), 310–369; Meindert Dijkstra, "El, Yhwh and their Asherah: On Continuity and Discountinuity in Canaanite and Ancient Israelite Religion," in *Ugarit: Ein ostmediterranes Kulturzentrum im Alten Orient. Ergebnisse und Perspektiven der Forschung. Band I: Ugarit und seine altorientalische Umwelt* (eds., Manfred Dietrich and Oswald Loretz; ALASP 7; Münster: Ugarit, 1995), 43–74; Klaus Koch, *Der Gott Israels und die Götter des Orients* (Göttingen: Vandenhoeck & Ruprecht, 2006), 13–20, 171–209. For discussion, see Smith, *God in Translation*, 98.

[45] The view that the Canaanite, El, and the southern God, Yhwh, were originally distinct is often associated with the well-known article of Otto Eissfeldt, "El and Yhwh," *JSS* 1 (1956): 25–37. For discussion and additional bibliography see Smith, *God in Translation*, 96–98; John Day, *Yahweh and the Gods and Goddesses of Canaan* (JSOTSup 265; Sheffield: Sheffield Academic Press, 2000), 13–17. For a hypothetical three-stages process by which Yhwh and El came to be identified, see Smith, *The Origins,* 143–145.

[46] Smith, *God in Translation*, 139, 196. Such a reading has profound implications for understanding the divine assembly in ancient Israel: if the passage has vestiges of Yhwh's past subordination to (El) Elyon, it may suggest that Yhwh was initially envisioned in Israel as belonging to a lower tier of the divine assembly; that is, Yhwh may not always have been equated with (El) Elyon but rather was a named son of El; see idem, *The Origins*, 49. A similar reading has been offered by White, *Yahweh's Council*, 16, 34–39, who views Deut 32:8–9 as referring to a council "not under the leadership of Yhwh" and prefers the interpretation that "each of the nations of the Earth received their territory and their national god from עליון and Israel was given Yhwh." Also note the comments of Ronnie Goldstein, "A New Look at Deuteronomy 32:8–9 and 43 in Light of Akkadian Sources," *Tarbiz* 79 (2009): 5–21 [Hebrew], who proposes that parallels with Akkadian hymnic texts suggest that the original import of Deut 32:8–9 was to celebrate that Yhwh – likely as one of the sons of El – had ascended to the position of the main god and that Israel was given to him as part of his new role. Cf. Day, *Yahweh and Gods and Goddesses*, 14, who notes that Yhwh has similarities not only with El, who is portrayed as benevolent, but also the

of Deut 32:8–9 is vestigial,[47] and that the composer/compiler of Deut 32:1–43 did not intend to produce a polytheistic picture since the poem's numerous monoaltrous assertions[48] indicate that Elyon was understood as a title of Yhwh.[49]

There have been vigorous objections to such readings,[50] with Smith himself conceding that this interpretation of Deut 32:8–9 cannot be established with certainty.[51] In fact, whether an eventual equation of Yhwh with (El) Elyon in Israel effectively collapsed the notion of a Canaanite-like, multi-tiered assembly,[52] or whether (El) Elyon was an epithet applied to Yhwh, who was always considered to be the unrivaled head of an assembly (i.e., even in the earliest stages of Israelite religion),[53] the end result is the same: reinforced by their placement in the Song of Moses and, indeed, the rest of the Book of

---

warrior Baal, who is a god of the second tier of the Canaanite assembly and associated with the storm (e.g., Judg 5:4–5). For detailed discussions of how the language and imagery of both El and Baal are applied to Yhwh, see Smith, *The Early History of God*, 32–47; 65–107.

[47] Smith, *God in Translation*, 202. Cf. idem, *The Origins,* 78.

[48] E.g., verse 17: "They sacrificed to demons, not God, to deities they had never known, to new ones recently arrived, whom your ancestors had not feared" (cf. vv. 21, 39, 43).

[49] See Smith, *God in Translation*, 142.

[50] E.g., Michael S. Heiser, "Are Yahweh and El Distinct Deities in Deut. 32:8–9 and Psalm 82?" *HIPHIL* 3 (2006): 1–9, https://see-j.net/index.php/hiphil/article/view/29/26. Cf. idem, "The Divine Council," §3.4.

[51] Smith, *God in Translation*, 98. Cf. Collins, *Daniel*, 292: "Whether [Deut 32:8–9] understands Yhwh as subordinate to Elyon is questionable."

[52] On the possibility that Israel's notion of the assembly was initially similar to the Canaanite conception, Smith, *The Origins,* 48, suggests that international politics may have played a role: " … [T]he neo-Assyrian empire presented a new world order. Only after this alternation of the world scene did Israel require a different 'world theology' that not only advanced Yhwh to the top but eventually eliminated the second tier altogether insofar as it treated all other gods as either non-entities or expressions of Yhwh's power."

[53] Smith, *God in Translation*, 11–15, 211, here 211, writes, "What we have in Deut 32:8–9 is a notion of minor divinities, who serve the absolute divine King; these are, relatively speaking, so powerless compared to Yhwh that for the composer, they do not truly constitute gods like Yhwh. They are perhaps like the *'elim* of the Qumran Songs of the Sabbath Sacrifices, minor 'divinities,' actually angels, but hardly gods in the modern conventional sense." Cf. Heiser, "The Divine Council," §§1.4; 2.4–5; 7.0–8.1; idem, "Monotheism and the Language," 91, who, as noted, argues that there is no evidence that the Hebrew Bible and Qumran sectarian texts consider higher-tier "gods" (אלוהים and אלים) to be merely lower-tier "angels" (מלאכים), even if a.) אלוהים and אלים could act *functionally* as a מלאך (e.g., the "Angel of Yhwh"; see below); and b.) non-sectarian Second Temple Period compositions could use מלאך and its translations to refer to beings of any rank. I will address some of the implications of Heiser's assertions at various points throughout this study.

Deuteronomy, verses 8–9 assert that Yhwh's stature and authority are incomparable, making (El) Elyon an appropriate designation for Yhwh.[54]

Even if these "sons of god" were considered vastly inferior to Yhwh, an open question concerns their status – ontological and otherwise – in the mind of the composer,[55] and on this issue, a few comments are required. First, despite the monolatrous assertions of the poem, the existence of בני אלוהים does not appear to have been problematic for the composer of Deut 32:1–43. That is, even if the poem is working with an inherited polytheistic trope[56] and has effaced this polytheism "by combining it with statements that express divinity in more exclusive terms,"[57] the effacement is implicit not explicit.[58] In fact, Deut 32:8–9 and other passages suggest a measure of translatability or "division in religious devotion":[59] Yhwh is the god for the Israelites and the "sons of god" are the "gods" for the nations (cf. Deut 4:19–20; 29:25).[60] Moreover, while it is correct that the "sons of god" are not envisioned to be gods in the same sense that Yhwh is,[61] Tigay points out that the expectation that the nations will one day forsake idolatry and devote themselves exclusively to Yhwh is not unambiguously expressed in the Hebrew Bible before

---

[54] Tigay, *Deuteronomy*, 303, writes, "'Most High' is an ideal epithet for God. In [Deut 32:8] it emphasizes His supremacy over the other divine beings, and since it does not have exclusively Israelite associations it suits the context of God's organizing the human race as a whole. Cf. Craigie, *Deuteronomy*, 379: "The title emphasizes God's sovereignty and authority over all nations, whereas in relation to [Israel] he is called Yhwh or Lord (v. 9)."

[55] Smith, *God in Translation*, 211.

[56] Smith, *God in Translation*, 142, 197, suggests that multiple "sons of god" was likely deemed by the composer to be an inherited trope as per the seventy divine sons of El and Athirat in the Ugaritic texts (cf. *KTU* 1.4 IV 44–46).

[57] I.e., the language of "no gods" in Deut 32:17, 21, 39; see Smith, *God in Translation*, 197. On this "denial language," see Heiser, "Does Divine Plurality in the Hebrew Bible," 7–9, who argues that, while such statements are often understood to indicate the *non-existence* of other gods (particularly in later texts such as Second Isaiah), they are better interpreted as commenting on Yhwh's *incomparability* vis-à-vis the gods of the nations. Cf. idem, "Monotheism, Polytheism, Monolatry, 13–18; idem, "The Divine Council," §§4.1–3.

[58] Smith, *God in Translation*, 142.

[59] Smith, *God in Translation*, 204–205, argues that Deut 4:19–20 and 29:25 are dependent on Deut 32:8–9. For an overview of these passages, see Tigay, *Deuteronomy*, 435–436; Smith, *God in Translation*, 203–208. On Deut 4:19–20 and 29:25–26 as components of exilic or post-exilic additions to Deuteronomy, see Moshe Weinfeld, *Deuteronomy 1–11: A New Translation with Introduction and Commentary* (AB; New York: Doubleday, 1995), 228–229, 234–235; Gerhard von Rad, *Deuteronomy* (2nd rev. ed.; OTL; Atlanta: Westminster, 1966), 55.

[60] Smith, *The Origins*, 49. Cf. Heiser, "The Divine Council," §1.3.

[61] Smith, *God in Translation*, 204. Cf. Heiser, "Monotheism, Polytheism, Monolatry," 29: "In the briefest terms, the statements in the canonical text (poetic or otherwise) inform the reader that, for the biblical writer, Yhwh was an אֱלֹהִים, but no other אֱלֹהִים was Yhwh – *and never could be* [emphasis retained]."

the time of the prophets (e.g., Jer 50:35–39).[62] Smith suggests, therefore, that Deuteronomy captures a tension between the expression of inherited polytheistic motifs and language, on the one hand, and ancient Israel's assertion of the matchless stature and authority of Yhwh, on the other hand.[63]

However, an understated component of this tension may be the moral character of the "sons of god." If, as Smith suggests, the composer(s) only implicitly effaced the inherited polytheism in the poem, Smith seems to place a greater emphasis on the *effacement* of the polytheism and less stress on what the implications of the *implicitness* of this effacement might be, in particular, the relative moral neutrality with which these beings are portrayed in Deuteronomy.[64] Numerous scholars have placed Ps 82:1–8 – a text that will be examined more closely in the next section of this chapter – in the same tradition as Deut 32:8–9 in that it, too, has vestiges of an older translatable worldview even as it rallies against that same worldview. Smith contends that the psalm may have served to clarify any ambiguity regarding the ontology of figures such as the בני אלוהים of Deut 32:8–9, precisely because the אֱלֹהִים and בְּנֵי עֶלְיוֹן of Ps 82 will "die like mortals."[65] But the gods of Ps 82:1–8 are also judged for being unjust (vv. 6–7). Thus, if Smith is right to suggest that Ps 82:1–8 "contributes to our understanding of the larger hermeneutical shift that informs the textual censorship operative in Deut 32:8–9,"[66] then it is plausible that the tradition deemed it necessary to make a definite pronouncement not only on the ontology of the gods of the nations but also in reference to their morality.[67] Indeed, Ps 82:1–8 seems to be revoking the

---

[62] See Tigay, *Deuteronomy*, 435, who writes: "In the Torah, the nations are held guilty for what they do in the name of their religion, such as child sacrifice, but not for what they worship." E.g., Deut 12:29–31; 18:9–12; 20:18. It is, of course, a primary concern of Deuteronomy that Israel's only option is to love and serve Yhwh (e.g., Deut 6:4–5).

[63] The existence of this tension describes, *in nuce*, Smith's discussion of Deut 4:19–20 and 29:25 vis-à-vis Deut 32:8–9; see *God in Translation*, 203–208.

[64] See Smith, *God in Translation*, 197, 203.

[65] Smith, *God in Translation*, 210.

[66] According to Smith, *God in Translation*, 211, just as various forms of censorship in Deut 32:8–9 sought to rid the text of any vestiges of translatability (e.g., the identification of Elyon and Yhwh, the later emending of "sons of god" to "sons of Israel," or the less dramatic censorship of most LXX witnesses, which translate בני אלוהים as ἀγγέλων θεοῦ), Ps 82 explicitly censors the possibility of equating the divinity of the gods of the nations with that of Yhwh by declaring the mortality of the former.

[67] On the connection between divinity and morality, John E. Goldingay, *Psalms: Volume 2: Psalms 42–89* (BCOTWP; Grand Rapids: Baker, 2007), 568, writes: "Realizing the morally incompetent way the gods are governing the world has made the suppliant [of the psalm] realize that they cannot be offspring of the Most High, and that in two senses. It cannot be so because surely they would then show more of a family resemblance. God does not tolerate the neglect or oppression of the poor, so how can God's offspring collude with it? But also it cannot be so because the suppliant knows that God will take the same action against the gods as God takes against human oppressors. God puts them down.

"good opinion of the אלהים so far held,"[68] and given that Deut 32:8–9 "admits"[69] that the God of Israel has assigned the other nations to the "sons of god,"[70] it is difficult to see how the original composer/hearers of Deut 32:1–43 could have concluded that they were evil or unjust *per se.*

Thus, for the purposes of understanding the trajectory of Israelite tradition, the implicit effacement of the ontology of the gods, which is seemingly present in the Song of Moses, needs to be differentiated from the explicit ontological and moral judgments of the gods of the nations, which are unambiguously articulated in Ps 82. This distinction is important, and I will return to its significance, below.

II. Psalm 82:1–8

The topics discussed in this chapter thus far – Deut 32:8–9 and the divine assembly – are important for understanding Ps 82, which not only refers to the gods of the nations but also makes use of the Canaanite type-scene of the high god El presiding over the assembly.[71] Almost every conceivable time period has been proposed for the date of composition, though it seems likely that Ps 82 evokes Deut 32:8–9 and is, therefore, later than it:[72]

They will lose their lives. And if that is a possibility, this too shows they cannot really be God's offspring. They do not share in God's eternity." Cf. Frank-Lothar Hossfeld and Erich Zenger, *Psalms 2: A Commentary on Psalms 51–100* (Hermeneia; Minneapolis: Fortress, 2005), 333: "While in ancient Near Eastern texts the obligation to protect orphans, widows and the dispossessed rested only on individual 'law deities,' our psalm makes this obligation of protection the crucial mark of the divinity of all deities, and thus the essential characteristic of divinity pure and simple."

[68] So Hans-Joachim Kraus, *Psalms 60–150* (CC; Minneapolis: Augsburg, 1993), 157.

[69] So Rofé, *Angels in the Bible*, xii.

[70] Tigay, *Deuteronomy*, 435–436, in a short excursus devoted to "The Biblical View of the Origin of Polytheism," deems the attempts of the LXX and the Rabbis to downplay the other-gods-for-other-nations thrust of Deut 4:19–20 and 32:8–9 "unlikely." I.e., early in Israel's history, the conception that Yhwh had granted gods to the Gentiles was acceptable, in theory, so long as Israel did not worship these deities.

[71] Hossfeld and Zengler, *Psalms 2*, 329, point out that there are three mythological concepts brought together in Psalm 82: i.) the hierarchy of the divine assembly; ii.) the notion of national gods as per Deut 32:8–9; and iii.) the rise to power within the pantheon (cf. Baal's rise to power in the Canaanite texts and Marduk's ascension in the Babylonian literature). Also see Kraus, *Psalm 60–151*, 155; Smith, *God in Translation*, 135.

[72] Goldingay, *Psalms*, 2:560, provides a helpful summary of the options. For a pre/early monarchic period date, see Mitchell J. Dahood, *Psalms 2* (AB 17; Garden City: Doubleday, 1964), 269; Samuel Terrien, *The Psalms* (Grand Rapids: Eerdmans, 2002), 591. For a late monarchic period date, see David Qimchi, *Tehillim* in *Miqraot Gedolot* (repr., with partial English trans. in A. J. Rosenberg, *Psalms* [3 vols. New York: Judaica, 1991]). For an exilic period date, see A. Gonzales, "Le Psaume lxxxii," *VT* 13 (1969), 78–80. For an early post-exilic period date, see Zoltan Rokay, "Vom Stadttor zu den Verhöfen," *ZKT* 116 (1994): 457–63; Julian Morgenstern, "The Mythological Background of

1 אֱלֹהִים נִצָּב בַּעֲדַת־אֵל בְּקֶרֶב אֱלֹהִים יִשְׁפֹּט
2 עַד־מָתַי תִּשְׁפְּטוּ־עָוֶל וּפְנֵי רְשָׁעִים תִּשְׂאוּ־סֶלָה
3 שִׁפְטוּ־דַל וְיָתוֹם עָנִי וָרָשׁ הַצְדִּיקוּ
4 פַּלְּטוּ־דַל וְאֶבְיוֹן מִיַּד רְשָׁעִים הַצִּילוּ
5 לֹא יָדְעוּ וְלֹא יָבִינוּ בַּחֲשֵׁכָה יִתְהַלָּכוּ יִמּוֹטוּ כָּל־מוֹסְדֵי אָרֶץ
6 אֲנִי־אָמַרְתִּי אֱלֹהִים אַתֶּם וּבְנֵי עֶלְיוֹן כֻּלְּכֶם
7 אָכֵן כְּאָדָם תְּמוּתוּן וּכְאַחַד הַשָּׂרִים תִּפֹּלוּ
8 קוּמָה אֱלֹהִים שָׁפְטָה הָאָרֶץ כִּי־אַתָּה תִנְחַל בְּכָל־הַגּוֹיִם

1 God has taken his place in the divine council; in the midst of the gods he holds judgment:
2 "How long will you judge unjustly and show partiality to the wicked? Selah
3 Give justice to the weak and the orphan; maintain the right of the lowly and the destitute.
4 Rescue the weak and the needy; deliver them from the hand of the wicked."
5 They have neither knowledge nor understanding, they walk around in darkness;
all the foundations of the earth are shaken.
6 I say, "You are gods, children [lit.: sons] of the Most High, all of you;
7 nevertheless, you shall die like mortals, and fall like any prince."
8 Rise up, O God, judge the earth; for all the nations belong to you!

The first occurrence of אֱלֹהִים in verse 1 refers to Yhwh,[73] who stands[74] in the "assembly of El/in the midst of the gods" in order to judge the immorality of

---

Psalm 82," *HUCA* 14 (1939): 119–121. For the development of the psalm over a long period of time, see Oswald Loretz, *Psalmstudien* (BZAW 309; Berlin: de Gruyter, 2002), 268–273. Lastly, the similarities with Daniel (see below) may suggest a very late date. Given that there is a similar lack of agreement on the date of composition of the Song of Moses, caution is warranted (i.e., it is possible that Deut 32:1–43 and Ps 82 are contemporaneous and simply contain competing viewpoints). However, since Ps 82 refers to the gods as "sons of Elyon" (cf. Deut 32:8 where Yhwh is referred to as "Elyon") and states that all nations "belong" (נחל) to the God of Israel (cf. Deut 32:9, where Israel alone is Yhwh's נַחֲלָה), the psalm seems to be clarifying, updating, or even criticizing the claims of Deut 32:8–9 in that gods of the nation have been deposed and that the authority and jurisdiction of the God of Israel are unlimited in scope. Thus, Ps 82 may have been a later, direct response to Deut 32:8–9 (so Sanders, *The Provenance of Deuteronomy 32*, 370–371), though how much later is uncertain.

[73] In the so-called "Elohistic Psalter" (Pss 42–83), יְהוָה can be read for אֱלֹהִים, and doing so helps to distinguish between the first and second occurrences of אֱלֹהִים in Ps 82:1 (i.e., as a proper name and as a reference to subordinate heavenly beings, respectively); see Goldingay, *Psalms*, 2:561; Kraus, *Psalm 60–150*, 154. Commenting on the characteristics of the Elohistic Psalter, Hossfeld and Zenger, *Psalms 2*, 5, note that "there is preference for speaking of Elohim when God's universality is to be underscored," which is an apt description of the thrust of Ps 82.

[74] For a detailed discussion of the verb נצב, see Smith, *God in Translation*, 133 n. 4. Hossfeld and Zenger, *Psalms 2*, 333, observe that נצב emphasizes Yhwh's prosecutorial role. Thus, the Canaanite type-scene is modified in that Yhwh is not only the assembly's presider/judge (so Klaus Seybold, *Das Gebet des Kranken im Alten Testament: Untersuchungen zur Bestimmung und Zuordnung der Krankheits – und Heilungspsalmen* [BWANT 19; Stuttgart: Kohlhammer, 1973], 325) but also the prosecutor/accuser. Cf.

the assembly members, called "gods" and "sons of Elyon" in verse 6. The God of Israel occupies the role of El at the head of the assembly,[75] and since there also seems to be reference to "gods" who (used to) rule the nations as Yhwh rules Israel, Smith contends that the psalm, as noted above, is another example of a text having vestiges of translatability; Ps 82, however, is more explicit than Deut 32:8–9 in its rejection of translatability.[76] Indeed, Yhwh is depicted as having "exclusive divine competency."[77]

Most relevant to the present study, however, is how Ps 82 declares Yhwh's universal reign. While some commentators have interpreted[78] the psalm as an

---

Hans-Jochen Boecker, *Redeformen des Rechtslebens im Alten Testament* (2nd ed.; WMANT 14; Neukirchen-Vluyn: Neukirchenser Verlag, 1970), 85.

[75] E.g., *KTU* 1.2 I. Ps 82:6–7 declares that the "gods" are corrupt, and that these "sons of Elyon" will die like humans for their injustice. Smith, *The Origins,* 49, notes that, if the notion of a multi-leveled, Canaanite-like assembly in which Yhwh was a second-tier deity was ever part of the mythology of ancient Israel, Ps 82 is even clearer than Deut 32:8–9 in stating that such an understanding of the divine hierarchy had collapsed. Cf. Hossfeld and Zenger, *Psalms 2,* 333: "[N]othing is said about El, the president of the gods, as an independent figure. The psalm is not concerned that the God of Israel takes over the role of El by ascending to the position of chief of the pantheon (as has repeatedly been said in interpretations of this psalm), but rather that 'all the gods' (cf. v. 6b) are condemned to death by the God of Israel, and he himself becomes the God of the whole earth and all the nations."

[76] In fact, Smith *God in Translation,* 139, claims that Ps 82 is a decisive call to end translatability. *Contra* Heiser, "The Divine Council," §3.2–3, who argues that reading Yhwh's universal sovereignty in Ps 82 as "new" disregards the witness of texts such as Exod 15:18, Pss 24 and 29, which are not infrequently dated to the 12th–10th cent. BCE. Cf. Goldingay, *Psalms,* 2:562 n. 18, who rightly notes that even if, in an earlier stage of the history of the scene/material, El was conceived as the head of the assembly and Yhwh as a (subordinate) assembly member, such a scenario "cannot be the meaning of the psalm," either in the context of the Psalter, in general, or Psalm 82, in particular. Also see White, *Yahweh's Council,* 33, who, in remarks similar to those she makes regarding Deut 32:8–9, proposes that "while Yhwh is a character in this divine council type-scene, he is not the head of it (El is) until possibly the end of the psalm when he takes over the position of the council. So this scene cannot truly be considered a Council of Yhwh type-scene, but it could represent a transition from a more ancient form of type-scene towards the Council of Yhwh type-scene corpus." For an additional reading of this text, see Michael Segal, "Who is the 'Son of God' in 4Q246? An Overlooked Example of Early Biblical Interpretation," *DSD* 21 (2014): 295, who, though he views Ps 82 as a "direct development" of Deut 32:8–9, is supportive of the proposal of David Frankel, "El as the Speaking Voice in Ps 82:6–7," *JHebS* 10 (2010): 1–24, who argues that verse 8 is not a petition penned by the psalmist but rather the words of El directed to his subordinate, Yhwh. Frankel's reading means that the Canaanite heritage of Ps 82 is still very much in the foreground of the psalm. Segal, in turn, applies Frankel's interpretation to Dan 7, a reading to which I will briefly return in Chapter 3.

[77] Hossfeld and Zenger, *Psalms 2,* 328.

[78] For a brief discussion of the interpretive options, see Hossfeld and Zenger, *Psalms 2,* 330–332.

indictment of the gods of the nations, and others have understood it as a judgment of human rulers who are described in exalted language,[79] a third option – and the view accepted here – is that the first two interpretations are not mutually exclusive, and that Ps 82 posits a connection between the gods and human beings.[80] The question of the second verse presupposes the ANE notion that the gods have judicial responsibilities in heaven with real implications on earth.[81] I have already noted that a hallmark of Ps 82 is the explicit denunciation of the gods in verse 7 for their immorality. But an equally significant conceptual contribution of this psalm is that it posits a connection between the behaviour of the gods and the actions of people on earth. Goldingay summarizes this worldview as follows:

[T]he gods are expected to identify with the principles that Yhwh believes in and expect human beings to live by. The presupposition is that the gods share in responsibility for the proper supervision of life in the world, under God but above earthly authorities. ... They are to exercise authority for the faithful and elevate them and to see that earthly authorities do so.[82]

However, the gods have favoured the רְשָׁעִים, and the poor are oppressed as a result.[83]

An important question concerns the sense in which the gods of Ps 82 were thought to be aiding the wicked and failing to exercise authority for those on the margins of society.[84] While it is possible that the psalm is claiming that the poor in Israel suffer because of Israel's collusion with other nations who are, in turn, inspired by their unjust gods,[85] in light of frequent biblical ad-

---

[79] See Alfons Deissler, *Die Psalmen* (Düsseldorf: Patmos, 1964), 319–320, who highlights that the psalm is similar to prophetic texts in which Yhwh judges Israel's rulers (cf Isa 1:17; 3:13–26; Mic 3:9–12). In this reading, the עֲדַת־אֵל in verse 1, then, refers to the עַם יהוה, Israel's general populace (e.g., Num 27:17; Josh 22:16–17), and אֱלֹהִים is a mytho-poetic way of referring to Israel's ruling officials. Heiser, "Deuteronomy 32:8 and the Sons of God," 62, notes that, as early as the 1930s, identifying the "gods" of Ps 82 with human rulers was criticized as an attempt to guard the text from polytheism. Cf. Cyrus H. Gordon, "אלהים in Its Reputed Meaning of Rulers, Judges," *JBL* 54 (1935): 139–144.

[80] So Herbert Niehr, "Götter oder Menschen – eine falsche Alternative: Bemerkungen zu Ps 82," *ZAW* 99 (1987) 94–98. Hossfeld and Zenger, *Psalms 2*, 330–331, agree with Niehr that it is a false dichotomy to choose between humans *or* gods as the objects of God's judgment in Ps 82, but rightly emphasize Yhwh's indictment of the gods, who were the realities behind the unjust systems and rulers on earth. For similar interpretations, see Kraus, *Psalms 60–150*, 153–158; Goldingay, *Psalms*, 2:558–570; Heiser, "Deuteronomy 32:8 and the Sons of God," 62; Mullen, *Assembly of the Gods*, 228.

[81] Cf. Kraus, *Psalm 60–150*, 156; Hossfeld and Zenger, *Psalms 2*, 333.

[82] Goldingay, *Psalms*, 2:563.

[83] So Kraus, *Psalm 60–150*, 156.

[84] Goldingay, *Psalms*, 2:565.

[85] See Goldingay, *Psalms*, 2:565: "The gods do not have responsibility for relationships within the Israelite community; that is Yhwh's business. But the Israelites were often

monishments of Israel for idolatry, the psalm may also imply the following charge: Israel had made the gods of the nations their *de facto* objects of worship,[86] and as per the analogous relationship between heaven and earth presupposed by the psalm, the injustice of Israel's *de facto* gods was somehow paralleled or mirrored in Israel. The emphasis on the judgment of the gods (rather than the culpability of Israel) may serve, then, not only to assert the authority and stature of Yhwh vis-à-vis the gods of the nations but also to underscore the folly of idolatry by highlighting the corruption and impotence of Israel's *de facto* gods.

In any case, it would seem that the psalmist considers the injustice of the gods to have such dramatic, earth-impacting consequences[87] that any ambiguity regarding the moral and ontological status of the gods of the nations needed to be addressed with an unequivocal statement: their actions and resultant punishment – death – reveal that these אֱלֹהִים are inferior in every way to Yhwh. In verse 8, the God of Israel is, thus, implored to judge the earth, which, in light of the worldview of the psalm, means that "God will act as the one who holds power in the world and can govern it in the way it needs."[88] Hossfeld and Zenger claim that the petition of verse 8 "looks back to Deut 32:8–9" in that it calls on the God of Israel "*to become* the God he, as the God of the exodus, really is [emphasis retained]."[89] However, it may be more

---

suffering because of the attacks of other peoples (see Psalm 83), for which these people's gods could then be held responsible [so Michael D. Goulder, *The Psalms of Asaph and the Pentateuch* (JSOTSup 20; Sheffield: Sheffield Academic Press, 1996), 163–164] ... . Might the psalm be protesting the way the gods collude in or inspire the oppression of the vulnerable within the nations they oversee (cf. the critiques in Amos 1:3–2:3)?"

[86] In the preceding psalm (cf. Ps 81:7–16), Israel is rebuked for failing to listen to God's command not to have "strange" and "foreign" gods among them. The placement/succession of Pss 81–82 may suggest that early readers understood Ps 82 as reinforcing the polemic against idolatry by pointing out the dangerous reality behind it.

[87] Hence, verse 5: "They have neither knowledge nor understanding, they walk around in darkness; all the foundations of the earth are shaken." Cf. Kraus, *Psalm 60–150*, 157, who points out that elsewhere in the Hebrew Bible (e.g., Ps 96:10; Isa 28:16–17) justice is portrayed as foundational to the created order.

[88] Goldingay, *Psalms*, 2:568, follows others in highlighting not only the importance of the verb שׁפט to the psalm but also its nuances. Cf. Kenneth M. Craig, "Psalm 82," *Int* 49 (1995): 281–284. Also see Smith, *God in Translation*, 134 n. 6: "[שׁפט] in this psalm does not refer to ruling the divine council itself. In verse 1 it characterizes the divine indictment of the other deities, while in verses 2–3 and [8] it denotes proper rule or adjudication within in a god's divine realm."

[89] Hossfeld and Zenger, *Psalms 2*, 335, do not elaborate on their comment, but as noted above, the use of the title "Elyon" in the context of Deut 32:8–9 conveys the sense of Yhwh's authority over all people and gods. Whereas in Deut 32:8–9 Yhwh uses his authority to delegate, the psalmist implores the God of Israel to exercise that same authority in a more comprehensive, hands-on manner so the world can be governed as it ought and needs to be governed (see preceding footnote).

accurate to view verse 8 as looking back to Deut 32:8–9[90] *in order to reeval-*
uate its claims, especially in light of verses 6–7, the overarching import of
which is clear: optimism or ambivalence concerning the gods of the nations
may have been acceptable in the past, but such a nonchalant attitude is dangerous because they have proven themselves unworthy of their delegated responsibilities to the detriment of people on earth.[91]

III. Isaiah 24:21–23

A text with a worldview similar to that of Ps 82 is Isa 24:21–23:[92]

21 וְהָיָה בַּיּוֹם הַהוּא יִפְקֹד יְהוָה עַל־צְבָא הַמָּרוֹם בַּמָּרוֹם וְעַל־מַלְכֵי הָאֲדָמָה עַל־הָאֲדָמָה

22 וְאֻסְּפוּ אֲסֵפָה אַסִּיר עַל־בּוֹר וְסֻגְּרוּ עַל־מַסְגֵּר וּמֵרֹב יָמִים יִפָּקֵדוּ

23 וְחָפְרָה הַלְּבָנָה וּבוֹשָׁה הַחַמָּה כִּי־מָלַךְ יְהוָה צְבָאוֹת בְּהַר צִיּוֹן וּבִירוּשָׁלַם וְנֶגֶד זְקֵנָיו כָּבוֹד

21 On that day Yhwh will punish the host of heaven in heaven, and on earth the kings of
the earth.
22 They will be gathered together like prisoners in a pit; they will be shut up in a prison,
and after many days they will be punished.
23 Then the moon will be abashed, and the sun ashamed; for Yhwh of hosts will reign on
Mount Zion and in Jerusalem, and before his elders he will manifest his glory.

The most pertinent line for the present study is verse 21, which, in light of the
eschatological outlook of the passage that precedes it,[93] announces what will

---

[90] Echoing the comments I made above, White, *Yahweh's Council*, 38, speaks of the
"evolution" of the Hebrew Bible divine council passages, placing Deut 32:8–9 and Ps 82 in
the first and second positions, respectively.

[91] Although discussions have ensued concerning both the identity of the speaker in
verses 6–7 (i.e., Yhwh or the psalmist) and the nuance of the antithetical relationship between אֲנִי־אָמַרְתִּי and אָכֵן, the denunciation of the gods is apparent, despite indications that
they were formerly held in higher esteem; see especially, Matitiahu Tsevat, "God and the
Gods in Assembly," *HUCA* 40–41 (1969–70): 129–130: "The poem presents two views of
the gods, an earlier one and a later one." Cf. Heiser, "Deuteronomy 32 and the Sons of
God," 64; Cyrus H. Gordon, "History of Religion in Psalm 82," in *Biblical and Near Eastern Studies: Essays in Honor of William Sanford LaSor* (ed., Gary A. Tuttle; Grand Rapids: Eerdmans, 1978), 129–131; Goldingay, *Psalms*, 2:567; Kraus, *Psalm 60–150*, 157.

[92] These verses are situated in the so-called "Apocalypse of Isaiah" (Isa 24–27), which
is widely considered to be a post-exilic redactional addition to First Isaiah. On the post-
exilic date of Isa 24–27, see Christopher R. Seitz and Richard J. Clifford, "Isaiah, Book of"
in *ABD* 3:472–506; Hans Wildberger, *Isaiah 13–27* (CC; Minneapolis: Fortress Press,
1997), 445–451, 462–467; Otto Kaiser, *Isaiah 13–39: A Commentary* (OTL; Philadelphia:
Westminster, 1974), 173–179. For defense of an eighth century date, see John N. Oswalt,
Isaiah 1–39 (NICOT; Grand Rapids: Eerdmans, 1986), 441–444. Understandably, referring to this section as an *apocalypse* has generated a great deal of scholarly discussion, and
though Isaiah 24–27 is missing some of features of later apocalyptic literature, the summary of Wildberger, *Isaiah 13–27*, 602, is helpful: "[Isa 24–27] is not an apocalypse, but
the beginnings of an apocalyptic understanding of the world and an awareness of history
are there." Cf. Collins, *The Apocalyptic Imagination*, 24–25.

be included when "that day" of eschatological judgment arrives (cf. 24:16b–20).[94] The parallelism of the bicolon is revealing and will serve as the point of departure for my discussion.

Table 3: Parallelism of Isa 24:21

colon 1	עַל־צְבָא הַמָּרוֹם בַּמָּרוֹם	וְהָיָה בַּיּוֹם הַהוּא יִפְקֹד יְהוָה
colon 2	וְעַל־מַלְכֵי הָאֲדָמָה עַל־הָאֲדָמָה	

Isa 24:21 envisions an eschatological battle in which Yhwh will decisively contend with the forces of evil. But as the poetry suggests, this conflict will not be fought on the earthly battlefield alone but simultaneously "in the heaven/height" against "the host." Mention of the heavenly battle before its earthy counterpart may not only suggest that a relationship between the realms was envisioned but also that what transpires in the heavenly realm is primary; that is, the decisive battle would occur on the heavenly stage and what happens on the earthly stage corresponds to and is dependent on what happens on the heavenly stage.[95] Additionally, commentators have wrestled with the identity of "the host of heaven" who correspond to the "kings of the earth." Elsewhere in the Hebrew Bible, the host (צָבָא) can constitute the army/entourage of Yhwh,[96] but since the passage is clear that the host will face judgment, they cannot be faithful servants of the God of Israel. Given that the host of verse 21 appear to be synonymous with the sun and moon of verse 23, scholars have proposed the following: the gods – identified here as the heavenly bodies[97] – have rebelled against Yhwh and will be punished for their insubordination.[98]

Thus, Isa 24:21–23 seems to present a worldview analogous to that found in Ps 82 insofar as what happens on earth is a connected to heavenly realities. Moreover, Isa 24:21–23 leaves no doubt that its author considered the gods of the nations and their corresponding human devotees to be hostile to Yhwh, and that both the celestial and humans enemies would be the recipients of divine wrath at the eschaton for their insubordination.

---

[93] As Kaiser, *Isaiah 13–27*, notes, the prophet/redactor "loosely attaches his promise [of vv. 21–23] to the preceding scene of horror."

[94] Wildberger, *Isaiah 13–27*, 505.

[95] So Wildberger, *Isaiah 13–27*, 506.

[96] Cf. "צָבָא," *HALOT* 3:995. Also see Kaiser, *Isaiah 13–39*, 194. Moreover, the God of Israel is commonly referred to as יְהוָה צְבָאוֹת (e.g., Ps 33.6; Isa 40:26; Neh 9:6).

[97] The Hebrew Bible frequently identifies the gods of the nations with the heavenly bodies (e.g., Deut 4:19; Zeph 1:5; Jer 19:13; 2 Chr 33:5; see also Job 38:7, where the faithful sons of god – who, via the poetic parallelism, are identified with "the stars" – give praise to God; cf. *CTA* 10 I 3–5). See Michalak, *Angels as Warriors*, 44.

[98] See Kaiser, *Isaiah 13–39*, 194; Wildberger, *Isaiah 13–27*, 506–507.

IV. Summary, A Curious Tension, and Israel's Guardians

The following points summarize the most pertinent aspects of the texts examined in this section. First, Deut 32:8–9 portrays the gods of the nations as ontologically distinct from and vastly inferior to Yhwh but in a relatively neutral light, morally speaking (cf. Deut 4:19–20; 29:25–26). Second, if there was any lingering ambiguity concerning the ontological or moral status of the gods of the nations, Ps 82 and Isa 24:21–23 are clear: these gods are unjust and insubordinate to Yhwh, and they will be punished for their malevolence and dereliction. Third, the same passages suggest that the actions of the gods of the nations impact humanity, and the worldviews of the texts reveal that what happens on earth mirrors or corresponds to what happens in heaven, though the precise mechanics of this analogy are never delineated. Taken together, these points indicate that the *hostile opponents* of the celestial beings we will encounter in the following chapters are conceptually indebted to the corrupt gods of the nations as depicted in the Hebrew Bible texts just surveyed. This is particularly obvious as it pertains to the angelic "princes" of Greece and Persia in Dan 10,[99] but wicked, trans-national, angelic opponents like Mastema, Belial, and the Angel of Darkness are also reminiscent of the denounced national deities.

More significant to note for my purposes, however, is that a curious tension emerges when these biblical texts are compared to the mid and late Second Temple Period compositions that will be examined in subsequent chapters: whereas hostile national or trans-national angels can be understood as a development of the thought of certain passages of the Hebrew Bible, the existence and function of *principal angel figures who contend on Israel's behalf* – Michael, Melchizedek, and the Prince of Light(s), for example – stand in a degree of tension with the idea that Yhwh is Israel's guardian, a notion found

---

[99] It is frequently pointed out that the gods of the nations as depicted in Ps 82 and Isa 24 are both a development of the thought of Deut 32:8–9 and a precursor to national angelic guardians as presented in the early Jewish literature, especially in the Book of Daniel. For example, John E. Goldingay, *Daniel* (WBC 30; Dallas: Word Books, 1989), 286, after observing that "there is no Persian equivalent to the idea of heavenly beings identified with particular peoples," notes that the angelic princes of Persia and Greece in Dan 10–12 are "likely a development of ... Deut 32:8–9." Similarly, Duane L. Christensen, *Deuteronomy 21:10–34:12* (WBC 6B; Nashville: Thomas Nelson, 2002), 796, comments that the divine beings of Deut 32:8 "anticipate the later doctrine of guardian angels watching over the nations in Dan 10:13, 20–21, 12:1." Also note Kaiser, *Isaiah 13–39*, 194, in his discussion on Isa 24:21–24, says the following about Deut 4:19–20, which, as previously noted, is similar to (and often considered to be dependent on) Deut 32:8–9: "We find the strange conception that Yhwh has allotted the stars to the other nations to worship. From this it was only one further step to seeing in the army of heaven, or of the height [in Isa 24:21–23], the astral angels of other nations which we meet [in Daniel]."

not only in Deut 32:8–9 but possibly in other passages.[100] As Collins summarizes, "In the Hebrew Bible prior to Daniel, the Lord serves as ruler of Israel, a role given to Michael [in Daniel]."[101]

At the same time, this tension could easily be overstated, as it is important to recognize that Israel is portrayed as the beneficiary of celestial assistance long before the time of the Qumran covenanters and their contemporaries, and it is virtually certain that the following characters and motifs contributed to the development of the Second Temple Period concept of angelic guardians of Israel.[102] Judg 5:19–22 seems to envision a cosmic dimension to Israel's battles in which the stars – Yhwh's foot soldiers – fight against the Canaanite enemy.[103] Moreover, the Hebrew Bible has numerous references to the מַלְאַךְ יְהוָה (cf. Gen 22:11–19; Exod 3:2; Num 22:22–35; Judg 13:3; 2 Kgs 1:1–16; Isa 37:36; Zech 3:1–7; Ps 34:8)[104] and מַלְאַךְ הָאֱלֹהִים (cf. Exod 14:19; 23:20–23; 32:34), who are portrayed as Israel's protectors.[105] Outside of the Book of Daniel,[106] the closest the Hebrew Bible comes to presenting a celestial guardian of Israel akin to Second Temple Period figures is found in Josh 5:13–15:

---

[100] E.g., Isa 63:9, which may reflect the same idea; see below. Cf. Jub 15:31–32; Sir 17:17.

[101] This observation comes at the end of a comment suggesting that the conceptual foundation for the angelic princes of Greece and Persia is to be found in Deut 32:8–9; see Collins, *Daniel*, 374–375. Intriguingly, later Rabbinic interpretation included the proposal that, after the Golden calf incident, Israel lost the privilege of being led by Yhwh directly and was subsequently led by an angel (cf. Exod. Rab. 32:7). See Hannah, "Guardian Angels and National Angelic Patrons," 432–433; Michalak, *Angels as Warriors*, 102 n. 23.

[102] E.g., Michalak, *Angels as Warriors*, 100, who reiterates the frequent suggestion that Michael is indebted to exegetical reflection upon the celestial figures referenced in Exodus and Joshua; see further, below.

[103] The imagery is enigmatic, but as Susan Niditch, *Judges: A Commentary* (OTL; Louisville: Westminster John Knox, 2008), 80, comments, "Human and meta-human adversaries collide and operate, and the primordial Kishon, as personified, alternates with the sound of stampeding horses; the sight and sounds of battle encompass both." Cf. Josh 10:10–12 and Hab 3:3–6, which as Michalak, *Angels as Warriors*, 50, puts it, may also envision the heavenly luminaries as soldiers "under God's orders." Also see Cross, *Canaanite Myth*, 70–71.

[104] The "Angel of Yhwh" appears approximately 50x in the Hebrew Bible. For a recent discussion on this figure, especially his military/guardianship role, see Michalak, *Angels as Warriors*, 35–40, who mentions the long-recognized observation that there is a significant evolution in this character from being nearly indistinguishable from Yhwh himself (e.g., Judg 6) to being more independent, though still a faithful servant of God (e.g., Zech 3). Cf. S. A. Meier, "Angel of Yahweh מלאך יהוה," *DDD* 53–59.

[105] On the מַלְאַךְ יְהוָה and מַלְאַךְ הָאֱלֹהִים as the same figure, see Michael S. Heiser, "Co-regency in Ancient Israel's Divine Council as the Conceptual Backdrop to Ancient Jewish Binitarian Monotheism," *BBR* 26 (2015): 219.

[106] For my treatment of the Book of Daniel, see Chapter 3.

13 וַיְהִי בִּהְיוֹת יְהוֹשֻׁעַ בִּירִיחוֹ וַיִּשָּׂא עֵינָיו וַיַּרְא וְהִנֵּה־אִישׁ עֹמֵד לְנֶגְדּוֹ וְחַרְבּוֹ שְׁלוּפָה בְּיָדוֹ וַיֵּלֶךְ יְהוֹשֻׁעַ אֵלָיו וַיֹּאמֶר לוֹ הֲלָנוּ אַתָּה אִם־לְצָרֵינוּ:

14 וַיֹּאמֶר לֹא כִּי אֲנִי שַׂר־צְבָא־יְהוָה עַתָּה בָאתִי וַיִּפֹּל יְהוֹשֻׁעַ אֶל־פָּנָיו אַרְצָה וַיִּשְׁתָּחוּ וַיֹּאמֶר לוֹ מָה אֲדֹנִי מְדַבֵּר אֶל־עַבְדּוֹ:

15 וַיֹּאמֶר שַׂר־צְבָא יְהוָה אֶל־יְהוֹשֻׁעַ שַׁל־נַעַלְךָ מֵעַל רַגְלֶךָ כִּי הַמָּקוֹם אֲשֶׁר אַתָּה עֹמֵד עָלָיו קֹדֶשׁ הוּא וַיַּעַשׂ יְהוֹשֻׁעַ כֵּן:

13 Once when Joshua was by Jericho, he looked up and saw a man standing before him with a drawn sword in his hand. Joshua went to him and said to him, "Are you one of us, or one of our adversaries?"
14 He replied, "Neither; but as commander of the army of Yhwh I have now come." And Joshua fell on his face to the earth and worshiped, and he said to him, "What do you command your servant, my lord?"
15 The commander of the army of Yhwh said to Joshua, "Remove the sandals from your feet, for the place where you stand is holy." And Joshua did so.

Cross describes the שַׂר־צְבָא־יְהוָה as "Joshua's cosmic counterpart,"[107] and the scene indicates that Yhwh's "heavenly armies, led by their commander, would assist those of Israel."[108] In fact, Heiser has championed the view that the מַלְאַךְ הָאֱלֹהִים, מַלְאַךְ יְהוָה, שַׂר־צְבָא־יְהוָה, and other celestial protectors refer to the same principal angel, who should be identified as the "vice-regent" of the divine council, second in rank only to Yhwh himself.[109] However, the overarching picture of the pre-Danielic books of the Hebrew Bible – and the picture likely operative even in a passage like Josh 5:11–13 – is that the God of Israel is a warrior (cf. Exod 15:3; Ps 24:8), who, as יְהוָה צְבָאוֹת, has a direct or "hands-on" leadership role in Israel's conflicts, despite the fact that he does not fight alone (e.g., Deut 33:2).[110]

Conversely, numerous texts from Qumran are witnesses to the Second Temple Period angelological development briefly introduced above: now Israel has elite celestial warriors to whom Yhwh has delegated great power and authority, which seemingly includes, in comparison to earlier biblical texts, a more individuated role as it pertains to the guardianship of Israel.

---

[107] Cross, *Canaanite Myth*, 70.

[108] Michalak, *Angels as Warriors*, 43. Cf. J. Alberto Soggin, "The Conquest of Jericho through Battle," *EI* 16 (1982): 216.

[109] Cf. Heiser, "The Divine Council," esp. §§2.5–6, who echoes some of the comments made above: "The vice-regent in Israelite religion was a divine being considered an extension of Yhwh himself. ... This 'personal extension' dynamic is in operation in the Hebrew Bible's portrayal of the relationship between מלאך יהוה and Yhwh. This special agent of Yhwh and Yhwh himself are at times virtually indistinguishable, yet the מלאך יהוה is not Yhwh." For recent discussion of the topic with a helpful bibliography, see idem, "Co-regency in Ancient Israel's Divine Council," 195–225.

[110] On the biblical depiction of Yhwh as a warrior, see the classic study of Miller, *The Divine Warrior*, 64–165. Cf. idem, "The Divine Council and the Prophetic Call to War," *VT* 18 (1968): 100–107; Cross, *Canaanite Myth*, 60–144; Mullen, *Assembly of the Gods*, 189–201; Michalak, *Angels as Warriors*, 13–54.

Indeed, *just as the wicked gods of the nations, though inferior to Yhwh, are cast in the Hebrew Bible as beings with great freedom and power and whose actions impact humanity, so too, Israel's righteous angelic guardians in mid and late Second Temple Period texts.*

Although the complexities of why angels rather than Yhwh were increasingly portrayed as fighting for/protecting Israel are beyond the parameters of this study, major factors are often said to be the perceived transcendence of God and the reevaluation of a (simplistic) Deuteronomistic worldview in the aftermath of the exile, as well as the subsequent rise of apocalypticism.[111] Michalak connects the transfer of some of Yhwh's martial prerogatives to his angels to the perception of God as "more distant,"[112] and it may have been that the angelic/heavenly struggle – especially when the forces of evil momentarily had the upper hand and humanity was thereby negatively impacted – was perceived as God's inaction/indifference or helped to explain it.[113]

Not to be overlooked, however, is an important observation made by Hurtado, who points out that early Jewish fascination with the angelic realm may not be indicative of a lack of confidence in God's power and proximity, but that the opposite conclusion may actually be more plausible, insofar as the envisioning of detailed angelic hierarchies and the dispatching of the foremost of their ranks functioned to emphasize God as "the true king [...] in the sphere of ultimate reality – the heavenlies."[114] In other words, the shift in focus to the angelic host and its high-profile exemplars who are charged with what were previously the guardianship prerogatives of Yhwh does not detract from God's grandeur but underscores the fact that God, as guardian-in-chief, has celestial subordinates who obediently fulfill their mandates. The God-ordained victory of these angels over their wicked opponents – even in the context of a heavenly battle – is mysteriously connected to Israel's victory and the cessation of their hardships on earth. Belief in angelic guardians of Israel was thus far from speculative esoterica but was considered eminently practical and relevant. But before we turn to the Second Temple Period texts

---

[111] See the comments of D. S. Russell, *The Method and Message of Jewish Apocalyptic: 200 BC–100 AD* (OTL; Louisville: Westminster, 1964), 237–240. Cf. Cross, *Canaanite Myth*, 343–346; Mullen, *Assembly of the Gods*, 278; Mach, *Entwicklungsstadien*, 115–116; Collins, *The Apocalyptic Imagination*, 1–42.

[112] Michalak, *Angels as Warriors*, 14, 32, 56, and passim. Cf. Davila, "Melchizedek, Michael, and War in Heaven," 259–272, esp. 270.

[113] I will briefly return to these themes in Chapter 3.

[114] Hurtado, *One God*, 26. Cf. Stefan Beyerle, "The 'God of Heaven' in the Persian and Hellenistic Periods," in *Other Worlds and Their Relation to This World*, 17–36, who argues that the authority and legitimacy emphasized by having God reside in heaven does not mean he is transcendent or unattainable. As will be addressed below, the question becomes who is able or worthy to approach God in heaven.

that showcase these angelic guardians, we need to review the Hebrew Bible foundations of another group of angels associated with Israel: angelic priests.

D. The Biblical Background of Angels Associated with Israel
Part II: Angelic Priests

The biblical evidence for the notion of a heavenly temple served by angelic priests who constitute the models for Israel's sanctuary and its priesthood are even more ambiguous than that for the concept of angelic guardians of Israel. My discussion will therefore be brief, and it will be helpful to look at the alleged background of a heavenly temple and angelic priests separately. I will begin with the former.

I. Archetypal Celestial Sanctuary: Original Intention or Later Interpretation?

The Second Temple Period idea of a heavenly temple served by angelic priests is ultimately indebted to the ancient Near Eastern religious concept of the divine council or court, which, as just discussed, has clearly left its mark on the Hebrew Bible. The progression from council to temple has been described as follows:

> If God dwells in a celestial palace [surrounded by his council], it is only natural that his earthly residence, the temple, should also be conceived as a divine palace. Indeed, in the Hebrew Bible the word היכל refers not only to the temple but also to the king's palace. However, in the Second Temple Period, there is increasing evidence of the reverse assumption – a shift to a conceptualization of God's royal court as a celestial temple and his councilors as supernatural priests.[115]

However, the pre-exilic, exilic, and early post-exilic Hebrew Bible passages often cited as primitive indications of the belief in a heavenly temple and priesthood are debated.

On the one hand, there are hints that God was envisioned as enthroned in a heavenly temple (cf. Deut 26:15; 1 Kgs 22:19–21; Isa 6:1–13; Jer 25:30; Ezek 1:1–28; Ps 11:4; 2 Chr 30:27), which suggests that the notion that a god's heavenly dwelling was the inspiration for an earthly counterpart[116] was

---

[115] Angel, *Otherworldly*, 24. Cf. Martha Himmelfarb, *Ascent to Heaven in Jewish and Christian Apocalypses* (New York: Oxford University Press, 1993), 14–20.

[116] E.g., after Baal defeats Yamm, the storm god announces his desire for a palace – the ancient Near Eastern symbol of kingship – in order to legitimize his reign; see Smith and Pitard, *The Ugaritic Baal Cycle: Volume II*, 282, 324. In the Babylonian Creation Epic, Marduk has an earthly "counterpart" to his "luxurious" heavenly temple (cf. *Enuma Elish* V 119ff); see *ANET*, 501–503.

an idea that influenced the biblical tradition at a relatively early point.[117]   On
the other hand, there has been much discussion concerning the interpretation
of the noun תַּבְנִית (cf. Exod 25:9, 40; 26:30; 27:8; 1 Chr 28:19).[118]   Though
some scholars argue that the word includes the idea of an archetypal heavenly
temple,[119] others stress that it connotes only the divine "plan" or "blueprint"
for the earthly sanctuary, a concept which finds its biblical zenith in the eschatological temple of Ezek 40–48.[120]   For example, Klawans is right to insist
that the notion of a heavenly blueprint for an earthly temple is "vastly different ... from the idea that there is *ongoing angelic worship of God in a permanent heavenly temple* [emphasis retained]"[121] – and thus one should not
presume an inherent linkage between the two concepts. But in light of ANE
precedent, it may be overly cautious not to give due consideration to the possibility that 1.) the Hebrew Bible occurrences of תַּבְנִית refer to an archetypal
temple in heaven, or 2.) later, creative reflection on תַּבְנִית is at least partially

---

[117] For discussion, see Johann Maier, *Vom Kultus zur Gnosis* (Salzburg: Otto Müller,
1964), 106–148; David Noel Freedman, "A Temple Without Hands," in *Temples and High
Places in Biblical Times: Proceedings of the Colloquium in Honor of the Centennial of
Hebrew Union College-Jewish Institute of Religion, Jerusalem, 14–16 March 1977* (ed.,
Avraham Biran; Jerusalem: Hebrew Union College-Jewish Institute of Religion, 1981),
21–30; Himmelfarb, *A Kingdom of Priests*, 19–21. Cf. Margaret Barker, *The Gate of Heav-
en: The History and Symbolism of the Temple in Jerusalem* (Sheffield: Sheffield Phoenix
Press, 2008); Dan Lioy, *Axis of Glory: A Biblical and Theological Analysis of the Temple
Motif in Scripture* (StBibLit 138; New York: Peter Lang, 2010). Given that the New Testament Epistle of Hebrews (ca. late 1st cent. CE) employs the notion of a heavenly tem-
ple/priesthood in the service of Christology, a helpful excursus on the background of this
thought is provided by Harold W. Attridge, *The Epistle to the Hebrews: A Commentary on
the Epistle to the Hebrews* (Hermeneia; Philadelphia: Fortress Press, 1989), 222–224.

[118] For helpful treatments, see Himmelfarb, *Ascent to Heaven*, 118; Attridge, *The Epistle to the Hebrews*, 222; James R. Davila, "The Macrocosmic Temple, Scriptural Exegesis,
and Songs of the Sabbath Sacrifice," *DSD* 9 (2002): 1–19.

[119] So, e.g., Carol Meyers, *Exodus* (NCBC; Cambridge: Cambridge University Press,
2005), 227. Cf. Eliade, *The Myth of the Eternal Return*, 3–11, who cites Exod 25:9, 40; 1
Chr 28:19, and Ezek 40–48 as support, and then argues for the importance of "archetypes
of territories, temples and cities" in the Hebrew Bible, which also reveals Jerusalem as
having a "celestial archetype." Also see L. Goppelt, "τύπος," *TDNT* 8:256–257.

[120] So, e.g., Jonathan Klawans, *Purity, Sacrifice, and the Temple: Symbolism and Supersessionism in the Study of Ancient Judaism* (New York: Oxford University Press, 2006),
128–129, who highlights the similar comments of George Buchanan Gray, *Sacrifice in the
Old Testament: Its Theory and Practice* (2nd ed.; New York: KTAV Publishing House,
1971), 153–157. Cf. Sara Japhet, *I & II Chronicles* (OTL; Louisville: Westminster John
Knox Press, 1993), 493–498, who refers only to the "plan" sense of תַּבְנִית in 1 Chr 28:1–
21.

[121] Klawans, *Purity, Sacrifice, and the Temple*, 129.

responsible for Second Temple Period presentations of heaven as a sanctuary.[122]

II. Hints of an Angelic Priesthood?

When it comes to the notion of heavenly priests, the Hebrew Bible is similarly ambiguous. Though there are references to celestial beings whose descriptions may be indicative of priestly attire,[123] there is no mention of cultic activity in heaven nor are angels ever specifically referred to as כֹּהֲנִים. However, Mal 2:4–7, a passage that addresses God's covenant with Levi and the teaching role of the priesthood, may have been suggestive to early Jewish interpreters:

4 וִידַעְתֶּם כִּי שִׁלַּחְתִּי אֲלֵיכֶם אֵת הַמִּצְוָה הַזֹּאת לִהְיוֹת בְּרִיתִי אֶת־לֵוִי אָמַר יְהוָה צְבָאוֹת:

5 בְּרִיתִי הָיְתָה אִתּוֹ הַחַיִּים וְהַשָּׁלוֹם וָאֶתְּנֵם־לוֹ מוֹרָא וַיִּירָאֵנִי וּמִפְּנֵי שְׁמִי נִחַת הוּא:

6 תּוֹרַת אֱמֶת הָיְתָה בְּפִיהוּ וְעַוְלָה לֹא־נִמְצָא בִשְׂפָתָיו בְּשָׁלוֹם וּבְמִישׁוֹר הָלַךְ אִתִּי וְרַבִּים הֵשִׁיב מֵעָוֹן:

7 כִּי־שִׂפְתֵי כֹהֵן יִשְׁמְרוּ־דַעַת וְתוֹרָה יְבַקְשׁוּ מִפִּיהוּ כִּי מַלְאַךְ יְהוָה־צְבָאוֹת הוּא:

4 Know, then, that I have sent this command to you, that my covenant with Levi may hold, says Yhwh of hosts.
5 My covenant with him was a covenant of life and well-being, which I gave him; this called for reverence, and he revered me and stood in awe of my name.
6 True instruction was in his mouth, and no wrong was found on his lips. He walked with me in integrity and uprightness, and he turned many from iniquity.
7 For the lips of a priest should guard knowledge, and people should seek instruction from his mouth, for he is the messenger of Yhwh of hosts.

As will be noted in Chapter 3, these verses were instrumental in the creative exegesis that arose concerning the patriarch Levi, his heavenly ascent, and his sacerdotal investiture by the angelic priesthood. Moreover, though in the context of the Book of Malachi it is virtually certain that מַלְאַךְ means (human) "messenger,"[124] Newsom points out that the ambiguity of the word "may have provided grounds for speculation about the angelic priesthood," who are elsewhere characterized by knowledge (e.g., 4Q400 1 I, 17).[125]

---

[122] Especially relevant here is Heb 8:1–6, which links the idea of a heavenly temple with the divine blueprint for an earthly one – and quotes Exod 25:40 to do so (cf. Wis 9:8; Acts 7:44). For comment, see Attridge, *The Epistle to the Hebrews*, 219–221. The two most important early Jewish texts as it pertains to the heavenly temple and an angelic priesthood, are 1 En. 14:8–23 and *Songs of the Sabbath Sacrifice*, which will be discussed in Chapters 3 and 5, respectively.

[123] Note the "linen" (בַּד) garb of the angels in Ezek 9:2–10:7, which is comparable to the descriptions of priestly vestments elsewhere in the Hebrew Bible (e.g., Exod 39:28; Lev 6:10; 16:4–34); see Angel, *Otherworldly*, 24.

[124] See Heiser, "The Divine Council," §2.4.

[125] Carol A. Newsom, *Songs of the Sabbath Sacrifice: A Critical Edition* (HSM 27; Atlanta: Scholars Press, 1985), 105. Cf. Angel, *Otherworldly*, 96.

Another noteworthy passage is Isa 63:8–9, which speaks of God's past saving actions. The MT reads as follows with the pertinent part of the translation italicized:

8 וַיֹּאמֶר אַךְ־עַמִּי הֵמָּה בָּנִים לֹא יְשַׁקֵּרוּ וַיְהִי לָהֶם לְמוֹשִׁיעַ׃

9 בְּכָל־צָרָתָם לֹא צָר וּמַלְאַךְ פָּנָיו הוֹשִׁיעָם בְּאַהֲבָתוֹ וּבְחֶמְלָתוֹ הוּא גְאָלָם וַיְנַטְּלֵם וַיְנַשְּׂאֵם כָּל־יְמֵי עוֹלָם׃

8 For he said, "Surely they are my people, children who will not deal falsely"; and he became their savior
9 in all their distress. *It was no messenger or angel but his presence that saved them*; in his love and in his pity he redeemed them; he lifted them up and carried them all the days of old.

As VanderKam notes, some modern interpreters have understood the verse as per the LXX,[126] which has seemingly taken צר as צִיר, "messenger,[127] resulting in translations like that of the NRSV, which is cited. This rendering complements verse 8, which suggests that God himself was Israel's guardian (cf. Deut 32:8–9), but it is not the only way Isa 63:9 has been interpreted. Specifically, while the *Ketiv* in verse 9 is לֹא, the *Qere* is לוֹ, and if the first part of the line is treated as if it is the beginning of a new sentence, there is an important nuance to God's assistance:

In all their troubles, He was troubled [lit.: it was trouble to Him], and *the angel of His Presence* delivered them.[128]

Instead of reading צר as צִיר, the word is understood to be צָר, "anxiety/trouble," which, when read in conjunction with the *Qere* (לוֹ) and what precedes it, asserts that Yhwh's compassionate response to Israel's desert hardships was to dispatch מַלְאַךְ פָּנָיו, "the angel of his presence."[129] Indeed, 1QIsaᵃ attests to the sequence of מלאך פניו הושיעם and may have been "quite suggestive to an ancient reader."[130] At the very least, מלאך פניו seems to have been an impetus for the so-named class of angels, who are later depicted as among the most privileged priests of the celestial temple and as the heavenly counterparts to Israel (cf. Jub. 1:27, 29; 2:1–2, 18, 30; 6:18; 15:27; 30:18; 31:14; 1QHᵃ XIV, 16; 1QSb IV, 25–26; also see T. Levi 3:7; T. Jud.

---

[126] The pertinent section of LXX Isa 63:9 = οὐ πρέσβυς οὐδὲ ἄγγελος, ἀλλ᾽ αὐτὸς κύριος ἔσωσεν αὐτούς. See Joseph Ziegler, ed., *Isaias* (SVTG 14; Göttingen: Vandenhoeck & Ruprecht, 1983), 335.

[127] James C. VanderKam, "The Angel of the Presence in the Book of Jubilees," *DSD* 7 (2000): 383.

[128] E.g., *Tanakh: The Holy Scriptures: The New JPS Translation According to the Tradition Hebrew Text* (Philadelphia: Jewish Publication Society, 1985).

[129] Note the reading of Tg. Isa. = "an angel sent from him saved them." See Bruce D. Chilton, *The Targum of Isaiah* (ArBib 11; Wilmington: Michael Glazier, 1987), 121. Cf. VanderKam, "The Angel of the Presence," 383.

[130] See VanderKam, "The Angel of the Presence," 383. For further on the interpretation of the verse, see Olyan, *A Thousand Thousands*, 105–109.

25:2; Matt 18:11). It may also have been that the figurative representation of God's presence/face (cf. Exod 33:14–15; Deut 4:37), in conjunction with the four-faced attendants of God's throne in Ezekiel's vision (cf. Ezek 1:6), contributed conceptually to this designation.[131]

III. Summary

In short, it is uncertain as to whether these pre-exilic, exilic, and early post-exilic biblical passages were originally intended to convey a belief in the existence of an archetypal heavenly temple serviced by an angelic priesthood. More certain is that they were later interpreted as such and were influential in the depictions and naming of the priestly angels who have prestigious roles in the mid and late Second Temple Period texts to be discussed in subsequent chapters. My investigations will reveal that these celestial celebrants make vital contributions to the works in which they are found, and that, together with angelic guardians, angelic priests were believed to have important connection to Israel and were a source of significant hope.

---

[131] Cf. C. L. Seow, "Face פנים," *DDD* 322–325; VanderKam, "The Angel of the Presence," 383.

Chapter 3

Angels Associated with Israel
in Second Temple Period Qumran Texts
of a Non-Sectarian Provenance

A. Introduction

This chapter will examine angelic guardians and priests associated with Israel in mid and late Second Temple Period compositions extant at Qumran of a non-sectarian provenance. Several diverse texts will form the basis of my discussion. Since Dan 7–12 is the clearest non-sectarian exemplar of Israel having angelic guardians whose struggles in heaven are intimately related to those of the nation on earth, I will open the chapter by looking at this section of the Book of Daniel.[1] Next, I will consider three of the traditions of 1 Enoch: the *Book of Watchers*, the *Animal Apocalypse*, and the *Epistle of Enoch*; the first of these is especially important as it is often thought to preserve the earliest presentation of heaven as a temple and angels as priests. I will then turn my attention to the *Aramaic Levi Document* and *Visions of Amram*, texts which may suggest that Israel's priestly line had a privileged connection to heaven, and that ideal sacerdotal service on earth is informed by the priests' link with the angelic priesthood. Following this will be treatments of Tobit and Jubilees, which may hint that at least some angels were envisioned as both guardians and priests, and *4QInstruction*, which has affinities with Qumran sectarian compositions, including the notion that the faithful share a "lot" with the angels. I will round out the chapter by looking at the enigmatic *Son of God Text*, the most recent interpretations of which warrant its inclusion here.

In addition to noting how angelic guardians and priests make important contributions to the works in which they are found, a key component of my discussions will be to highlight the relationship between these angels and a given work's understanding or definition of Israel, thereby setting the stage for a comparison with the Qumran sectarian texts in subsequent chapters.

---

[1] The scholarly consensus is that the Book of Daniel in its final form is a late Second Temple Period composition, so I place my treatment of Dan 7–12 here rather than in the previous chapter.

B. Daniel 7–12

Angels associated with Israel are central to the worldview of Dan 7–12, as these chapters reveal that the persecutions of the Jews at the hands of Antiochus IV Epiphanes are only part of a larger reality: the evil that is transpiring on earth is parallel to a battle in heaven, with the outcome of the earthly conflict determined by events in the heavenly realm. The severity of the situation is highlighted by descriptions of the oppression of the angelic host, who are defended by their leader, Michael. This section will include a chapter-by-chapter discussion of the Book of Daniel's presentation of these angels, but I will begin by addressing interrelated historical, structural, and linguistic issues that are integral to the interpretation of Dan 7–12.

I. The History, Structure, and Languages of Daniel 7–12

The bilingual composition of Daniel,[2] the different genres of the book, and the various scholarly viewpoints on its redactional history render any division of the book a complicated endeavor. A comprehensive discussion of the issues is not required here,[3] but a few comments will serve to highlight the challenges. First, a virtual consensus of modern critical scholarship is that Dan 7 bears the marks of the Maccabean crisis. Second, it is clear that chapters 2–7 have a concentric literary structure, including the corresponding four-kingdom schemas of chapters 2 and 7.[4] Scholars are divided, however, on the provenance of chapter 7. The concentric arrangement of chapters 2–7, as well as the fact that chapter 7, like chapters 2–6, was composed in Aramaic, have led some to conclude that chapters 2–7 once circulated as an independent Aramaic book.[5] Moreover, many consider the court tales of chapters 2–6 to be earlier than the 2nd cent. BCE.[6] Thus, if chapters 2–7 at one time stood independently, and if chapter 7 (in its final form) refers to the persecutions of Antiochus Epiphanes and the Maccabean crisis, it necessarily follows

---

[2] The Aramaic section of Daniel is 2:4b–7:28; the Hebrew sections are 1:1–2:4a and 8:1–12:13.

[3] For detailed discussions, see Collins, *Daniel*, 12–38; 277–280. Cf. Rainer Albertz, "The Social Setting of the Aramaic and Hebrew Book of Daniel" in *The Book of Daniel: Composition and Reception* (eds., John J. Collins and Peter W. Flint; VTSup 83.1; Leiden: Brill, 2001), 171–204.

[4] On the concentric arrangement of chapters 2–7, see the influential article of Adrien Lenglet, "La Structure littéraire de Daniel 2–7," *Bib* 53 (1972): 169–190.

[5] For a thorough history of scholarship, see Collins, *Daniel*, 26–38, who points out this view is indebted to the proposals of Johannes Meinhold, *Die Composition des Buches Daniel* (Greifswald: Abel, 1884); Gustav Hölscher, "Die Entstehung des Buches Daniel," *TSK* 92 (1919): 113–138.

[6] E.g., Wacholder, "The Ancient Judaeo-Aramaic Literature," 268–269; Bickerman, "Aramaic Literature," in idem, *The Jews in the Greek Age*, 63.

that chapter 7 had a pre-Maccabean core to which the Antiochus references were later added.[7]

But the view that chapter 7 is a redacted work is far from unanimous. Detractors point to the lack of a consensus among proponents as to precisely what verses were part of a pre-Maccabean core;[8] it has also been countered that the supposed additions to chapter 7 – the allusions to Antiochus Epiphanes, the "little horn" (cf. 7:8, 20–21, 24–26) – are not peripheral to the vision but integral to it.[9] Moreover, while it is true that chapter 7 forms a concentric pattern with chapters 2–6, a number of features bind chapter 7 to chapters 8–12, including a first-person perspective, a new chronological sequence, and perhaps most significantly, shared themes within an apocalyptic framework.[10] It has been proposed, therefore, that chapter 7 was written – as a conclusion to chapters 2–6 – early in the Maccabean crisis.[11] In this scenario, chapters 2–7 could have briefly constituted an independent Aramaic book to which the Hebrew sections of Daniel were subsequently written and appended with chapter 7 in mind.[12]

---

[7] I.e., specific verses are deemed to have come from different authorial or redactional hands. This view has been particularly (though not exclusively) championed in German scholarship; cf., e.g., Hölscher, "Die Entstehung des Buches Daniel," 113–138; Reinhard G. Kratz, *Translatio Imperii: Untersuchungen zu den aramäischen Danielerzählungen und ihrem theologiegeschichtlichen Umfeld* (WMANT 63; Neukrichen-Vluyn: Neukirchener Verlag, 1991), 6–42; Louis F. Hartman and Alexander A. DiLella, *The Book of Daniel* (AB 23; Garden City: Doubleday, 1978), 208–210. For additional discussion and bibliography, see Collins, *Daniel*, 26–29, 277–280.

[8] Collins, *Daniel*, 278: "[V]irtually every study is distinguished by some original variation." Cf. Klaus Koch, *Das Buch Daniel* (Darmstad: Wissenschaftliche Buchgesellschaft, 1980), 70.

[9] Collins, *Daniel*, 35.

[10] On the parallelism of the visions, see John J. Collins, *The Apocalyptic Vision of the Book of Daniel* (HSM 16; Missoula: Scholars Press, 1977), 132–147. There is a particularly close relationship between chapters 7 and 8; see Collins, *Daniel*, 34. Cf. Paul A. Porter, *Metaphors and Monsters: A Literary-Critical Study of Daniel 7 and 8* (CB; Lund: C. W. K. Gleerup, 1983).

[11] This is the proposal of Otto Eissfeldt, *The Old Testament: An Introduction* (Oxford: Blackwell, 1964), 518, who is followed by Collins, "The Son of Man and the Saints of the Most High," 54 n. 27; cf. idem, *Daniel*, 294.

[12] A proposal that attempts to mitigate some of these issues is that of Ralph J. Korner, "The 'Exilic' Prophecy of Daniel 7: Does it Reflect Late Pre-Maccabean or Early Hellenistic Historiography?" in *Prophets, Prophecy, and Ancient Israelite Historiography* (eds., Mark J. Boda and Lissa M. Wray Beal; Winona Lake: Eisenbrauns, 2013), 333–353, who argues that the little horn of the fourth beast should be identified, not as the Seleucid ruler, Antiochus IV Epiphanes, but as the Ptolemaic ruler, Ptolemy I Soter (ca. 323–282 BCE). If correct, this identification would allow for an earlier date for the final form of chapter 7 and provide more time for chapters 2–7 to have circulated as an independent Aramaic work before the Hebrew sections were added to it in the 160s BCE. However, given that

Since my primary concern is the concept of angels associated with Israel in the Scrolls, the present study will examine Daniel thematically rather than divide it on linguistic grounds. Moreover, Flint notes that the Daniel scrolls found at Qumran "reveal no major disagreements against the Masoretic text ... ."[13] Thus, Dan 7 should be read as part of a completed work, regardless of what an early form of chapter 7 may have meant or what its content/shape was originally. Indeed, chapters 7–12 *as a unit* reveal the centrality of angels associated with Israel in the mind of its composer and/or editor:

What we find in the visions [of Dan 7–12] is not just a reaction to the events of the Maccabean period but a way of perceiving those events that is quite different from what we find in the books of Maccabees. ... Behind the wars of the Hellenistic princes lies the heavenly combat between the angelic princes. While the language is imaginative and symbolic, it points to a dimension of reality that is crucial for Daniel. The first objective of the book is to persuade its readers of the reality of this supernatural dimension. The struggle is not ultimately between human powers or within human control. ... The beast from the sea will be destroyed, and Michael will prevail in the heavenly combat. The very fact that the situation is beyond human control is, in the end, reassuring, for it is in the hand of God, the holy ones, and the angelic prince, Michael.[14]

As will be highlighted below, the themes of chapter 7 complement and are complemented by those of chapters 8–12.[15]

II. Daniel 7

Any study of Dan 7 must address the enigmatic "one like a son of man," who appears at the climax of Daniel's initial vision:

Korner's conclusion is the somewhat modest claim that "Daniel 7 correlates as well with the reign of Ptolemy I Soter as it does with Antiochus," a stronger argument will likely have to be made for Ptolemy I to shift the consensus opinion that the little horn is Antiochus Epiphanes, especially given the strong affinities the little horn has with what is known of the career of Antiochus.

[13] The eight fragments of Daniel extant among the Scrolls are designated as 1QDan[a–b], 4QDan[a–e], and 6QpapDan; see Peter W. Flint, "The Daniel Tradition at Qumran," in *The Book of Daniel: Composition and Reception* (eds., John J. Collins et al.; VTSup 83.2; Leiden: Brill, 2001), 331. Cf. Eugene Ulrich, "The Text of Daniel in the Qumran Scrolls," in *The Book of Daniel: Composition and Reception*, 2:573–585.

[14] Collins, *Daniel*, 61.

[15] In his comments on the formation of the Book of Daniel, Michael Segal, "Monotheism and Angelology in Daniel," in *One God – One Cult – One Nation: Archaeology and Biblical Perspectives* (eds., Reinhard G. Kratz and Hermann Spieckmann; BZAW 405; Berlin: de Gruyter, 2010), 419, argues that chapter 7 provided the "theological underpinnings of the national [angelic] princes" found in chapters 10 and 12. This is an important observation, as it suggests that Dan 7 was the impetus for the (more explicit) portrayal of Israel's angelic guardians in chapters 10 and 12.

13 חָזֵה הֲוֵית בְּחֶזְוֵי לֵילְיָא וַאֲרוּ עִם־עֲנָנֵי שְׁמַיָּא כְּבַר אֱנָשׁ אָתֵה הֲוָה וְעַד־עַתִּיק יוֹמַיָּא מְטָה
וּקְדָמוֹהִי הַקְרְבוּהִי
14 וְלֵהּ יְהִיב שָׁלְטָן וִיקָר וּמַלְכוּ וְכֹל עַמְמַיָּא אֻמַּיָּא וְלִשָּׁנַיָּא לֵהּ יִפְלְחוּן שָׁלְטָנֵהּ שָׁלְטָן עָלַם
דִּי־לָא יֶעְדֵּה וּמַלְכוּתֵהּ דִּי־לָא תִתְחַבַּל

13 As I watched in the night visions, I saw one like a human being coming with the clouds of heaven. And he came to the Ancient One [or Ancient of Days] and was presented before him.
14 To him was given dominion and glory and kingship that all peoples, nations, and languages should serve him. His dominion is an everlasting dominion that shall not pass away, and his kingship is one that shall never be destroyed.

The identity of this figure is debated, and only compounding the matter is that its interpretation is tied to another exegetical crux: the identification of "the holy ones (or saints) of the Most High." The views adopted here are that the "one like a son of man" is a highly exalted heavenly being, the chief angelic guardian of God's people, perhaps Michael,[16] though some consider this figure to be angel that outranks Michael,[17] and that "the holy ones of the Most

---

[16] Collins, *Daniel*, 318 (cf. idem, *The Apocalyptic Imagination*, 101–106; idem, "The Son of Man and the Saints of the Most High," 50–68) has championed the "one like a son of man" as Michael, but the view was first put forward by N. Schmidt, "The Son of Man in the Book of Daniel," *JBL* 19 (1900): 22–28. Cf. John A. Emerton, "The Origins of the Son of Man Imagery," *JTS* 9 (1958): 225–242; 242; Ulrich B. Müller, *Messias und Menschensohn in jüdischen Apokalypsen und in der Offen barung des Johannes* (SNT 6; Gütersloh: Mohn, 1972), 28; Lacocque, *Daniel*, 133–134; Rowland, *The Open Heaven*, 182. Some scholars have supported the angelic interpretation of Dan 7:13–14 but rather than identify the "one like a son of man" as Michael have proposed that the figure is an unnamed angelic leader (e.g., Arthur J. Ferch, *The Apocalyptic Son of Man in Daniel 7* [AUSDDS 6; Berrien Springs: Andrews University Press, 1979], 105), or perhaps Gabriel (e.g., Ziony Zevit, "The Structure and Individual elements of Daniel 7," *ZAW* 80 [1960]: 394–396; cf. idem, "The Exegetical Implications of Daniel viii 1, ix 21," *VT* 28 [1978]: 488–492). If the composer(s) of Dan 8–12 are to be distinguished from the composer(s) of chapter 7, it would seem that the former interpreted the "one like a son of man" as Michael, especially given the prominence of angels, in general, and Michael more specifically, in Dan 8–12. As noted above, Segal, "Monotheism and Angelology," 405–420, has recently argued that that final form of Dan 10–12 is the product of different authors, and that while he considers the references to Michael in chapter 10 and 12 to be secondary, he argues that these additions were actually influenced by readings of Dan 7:13–14. Cf. John Day, *God's Conflict with the Sea: Echoes of a Canaanite Myth in the Old Testament* (Cambridge: Cambridge University Press, 1985), 173: "It is certainly justified to correlate the figure of the one like a son of man of Dan 7 with the angel Michael in Dan 12:1, since, even if those are right who maintain that Dan. 2:4b–7:28 and 8–12 come from different authors, … Dan 8–12 forms a kind of midrash on Dan. 7, so that it may be argued that the overall redactor of the book of Daniel wished to equate the one like a son of man with the angel Michael."

[17] E.g., Heiser, "The Divine Council," §§6.2–3; 7.4, contends that the "one like a son of man" should identified with various other Second Temple Period principal angels whom he considers to be presentations of God's "vice-regent," a figure who ranks second in the

High" are best understood as the collective angelic host. These interpretations have been proposed and defended at length elsewhere,[18] but it is worth highlighting why the angelic interpretations of the "one like a son of man" and "the holy ones of the Most High" are persuasive.

In the last century, a majority of critical scholars have interpreted the "one like a son of man" in one of two ways: as either a collective symbol for the Jewish people, or an individual heavenly being closely associated with the Jewish people.[19] Both interpretations are dependent, at least in part, on the structure of chapter 7, which includes Daniel's vision report (vv. 2b–14), the interpretation of the vision (vv. 15–18), and an additional clarification of the vision (vv. 19–27).[20] As Collins has observed, it is not unreasonable to assume that "because the 'one like a son of man' receives dominion after the death of the fourth beast, ... he has in some way triumphed over it."[21] But when Daniel inquires as to the meaning of his vision, the interpretation offered by the angelic attendant is puzzling: "As for these four great beasts, four kings shall arise out of the earth. But the holy ones of the Most High shall receive the kingdom and possess the kingdom forever – forever and ever" (v. 18). The first aspect of the interpretation – the revelation that the four beasts are four kings – is relatively straightforward, but the second is

---

hierarchy of the divine council (see Chapter 2, above). Michael, however, is to be differentiated from this chief angelic lieutenant, a conclusion partially drawn from the weight Heiser places on the fact that Michael's portrayal is allegedly not as lofty as other celestial beings nor is he ever explicitly referred to as an אלהים, a designation which Heiser contends is reserved for higher-ranking figures. For a similar interpretation, see Gillian Bampfylde, "The Prince of the Host in the Book of Daniel and the Dead Sea Scrolls," *JSJ* 14 (1983): 129–134. As I will highlight, below, such readings may underestimate Michael's role in Daniel, especially Dan 12:1.

[18] For a survey of scholarship, see Collins, *Daniel*, 304–311; 313–317; cf. idem, "The Son of Man and the Saints of the Most High," 50–68.

[19] Collins, "The Son of Man and the Saints of the Most High," 50. A minority of modern scholars have understood the "one like a son of man" as a messianic figure, but there is nothing in Dan 7 to indicate that a messiah is in view. In the words of Hartman and DiLella, *Daniel*, 219, "In Daniel 7, the symbolic manlike figure has no messianic meaning except perhaps as connected with messianism in the broad sense, i.e., with God's plan of salvation for his chosen People." It seems, however, that a messianic interpretation of Dan 7:13 arose rather quickly in the reception history of the passage; see especially William Horbury, "Messianic Associations of the Son of Man," *JTS* 36 (1985): 34–55. Cf. Loren T. Stuckenbruck, "'One like a Son of Man as the Ancient of Days' in the Old Greek Recension of Daniel 7, 13: Scribal Error or Theological Translation?" *ZNW* 86 (1995): 268–276; H. Daniel Zacharias, "Old Greek Daniel 7:13–14 and Matthew's Son of Man," *BBR* 21 (2011): 453–461.

[20] The outlines of chapter 7 proposed by scholars may vary in their minutiae, but there seems to be a consensus as to the general structure; the three sections mentioned are preceded by an introduction (vv. 1–2a) and a concluding statement (v. 28).

[21] Collins, *Daniel*, 291. Cf. Day, *God's Conflict*, 162.

ambiguous, as there is no reference to the "one like a son of man," who is the recipient of the kingdom according to the initial vision report; instead, the attendant reveals that it is "the holy ones of the Most High" who will possess the kingdom forever. When Daniel requests further clarification of his vision, he is informed that the fourth beast is a kingdom,[22] and that the horn of this beast represents a particularly violent and arrogant king who will emerge from this kingdom. But despite the brutal reign of this ruler, dominion and kingship will be granted to "the *people* of the Holy Ones of the Most High" (Dan 7:27). There is, therefore, a degree of correspondence between the "one like a son of man," "the holy ones of the Most High," and "the people of the holy ones of the Most High," all of whom are said to be granted dominion. The precise nature of this correspondence, however, is the subject of debate.

Since the beasts seem to function as allegorical symbols for kings/kingdoms,[23] many have suggested that the "one like a son of man" should be understood in the same way; in other words, "[the 'one like a son of man'] is a pure symbol, ... not a real being who exists outside Daniel's dream."[24] Moreover, given that "the holy ones" and "the people of the holy ones" – without distinction between them – have often been interpreted as references to the Jewish people,[25] it is understandable that the antecedent

---

[22] But as noted, v. 17 states that the four beasts are four kings; there appears, then, to be some fluidity between "king" and "kingdom" in chapter 7, a point which will be addressed, below.

[23] Collins, *Daniel*, 305. For a discussion of allegorical symbolism in apocalyptic literature, see idem, *The Apocalyptic Vision*, 112–114.

[24] Maurice Casey, *Son of Man: The Interpretation and Influence of Daniel 7* (London: SPCK, 1979), 24–25, continues by providing two main reasons for viewing the "one like a son of man" as a collective symbol as opposed to a figure existing outside of the vision: i.) "In the first place, the author provided an interpretation of the symbolism of this dream, which reaches a climax with the full description of the triumph of the people of the Saints of the Most in v. 27. This triumph was very important to the author, and it corresponds precisely to what is said of the man-like figure in vs. 14, but it does not mention him. If the author had viewed him as a real being who would lead or deliver the Saints, he must have mentioned him here." ii.) "The second reason is that on this view the basic structure of the symbolism is consistent. The first four kingdoms are presented by beast-like figures, the fifth by a man-like figure. It is not suggested that the beast-like figures really existed somewhere; we only attribute consistency to the symbolism by concluding that the man-like figure was not a real being either." Cf. Mathias Delcor, *Le Livre de Daniel* (SB; Paris: Gabalda, 1971), 155; Hartman and DiLella, *Daniel*, 91–92; James D. G. Dunn, "'Son of God' as 'Son of Man' in the Dead Sea Scrolls? A Response to John Collins on 4Q246," in *The Scrolls and the Scriptures: Qumran Fifty Years After* (eds., Stanley E. Porter and Craig A. Evans; JSPSup 26; Sheffield: Sheffield Academic Press, 1997), 198–210. Also see the discussion of Collins, *Daniel*, 305 n. 253. For responses to the symbolic interpretation, see below.

[25] Proponents of this view include C. W. Brekelmans, "The Saints of the Most High and Their Kingdom," *OtSt* 14 (1965): 305–329; Robert Hanhart, "Die Heiligen des Höchsten,"

"one like a son of man" has been interpreted as symbolic of Israel, who will be granted dominion and kingship, despite the dire situation caused by an oppressive foreign ruler. Others have countered that while the impulse to connect the "one like a son of man" with the Jewish people is correct as far as it goes, the figure should be viewed as more than a symbolic reference to the people of God.[26] A key point in this fuller understanding of the "one like a son of man" stems from the recognition that the initial section of chapter 7, Daniel's vision report (vv. 2b–14), contains two distinct yet complementary parts: the succession of four increasingly terrifying beasts (vv. 2b–8) and the arrival of the "one like a son of man" before "the Ancient of Days" (vv. 9–14).[27] "The Ancient of Days" has been described as a representation of a different order than the four beasts, as this figure seems to be a "mythic-realistic symbol for God,[28] ... who is assumed to exist outside of the

---

in *Hebräische Wortforschung* (VTSup 16; Leiden: Brill, 1967), 90–101; Matthias Delcor, *Le Livre de Daniel*, 155–156; Vern S. Poythress, "The Holy Ones of the Most High in Daniel VII," *VT* 26 (1976): 208–213. Cf. Goldingay, *Daniel*, 176–178, who is sympathetic to the view that "the holy ones of the Most High" refers to humans, even if he considers it "marginally more likely to denote celestial beings."

[26] Collins, *Daniel*, 309, writes: "There is no doubt that the exaltation of the "one like a son of man" represents in some way the triumph of the Jewish people. The question is whether the collective interpretation does justice to the fullness of the apocalyptic symbolism with which this triumph is portrayed."

[27] In contrast to the narrative-like description of the beasts in vv. 2b–8, numerous scholars have noted how vv. 9–10 describe "the Ancient of Days" in a quasi-poetic fashion (BHS marks these lines as poetry); cf. Susan Niditch, *The Symbolic Vision in Biblical Tradition* (HSM 30; Chico: Scholars Press, 1983), 195–199; James A. Montgomery, *A Critical and Exegetical Commentary on the Book of Daniel* (ICC; Edinburgh: Clark, 1927), 296. Also see Collins, *Daniel*, 300, who adds that the recognition that the vision contains two distinct parts does not "undermine the unity of the vision."

[28] The imagery of thrones being set up, a fiery throne (chariot) with wheels of fire, white hair/clothes, thousands standing before him, the courts convened in his presence, and the open books, make it clear that the Ancient of Days is the God of Israel. In the words of Cross, *Canaanite Myth*, 17: "[T]he identity of the Ancient One is transparent" (cf. Ps 122:5 1 Kgs 22:1; Isa 6:1–5; Ezek 1:1–28). Similar imagery is found in the 3rd cent. BCE *Book of Watchers* (cf. 1 En. 14:8–23; to be discussed, below) and a scene from the mid 2nd cent. BCE *Book of Giants* (cf. 4Q530), which is a narrative re-telling of 1 En. 6–16 written from the perspective of the offspring of the fallen watchers. These strong affinities have resulted in numerous proposals regarding the traditions involved and the direction of dependence. A sampling of viewpoints will be sufficient, here: Emerton, "The Origin," 225–242, has argued that Dan 7:9–10 and 1 En. 14:8–23 developed independently of one another and that their similarities can be attributed to biblical passages such as Gen 5:24, 2 Kgs 2:1, and Ezek 8:3. Ryan E. Stokes, "The Throne Visions of Daniel 7, *1 Enoch* 14, and the Qumran *Book of Giants* (4Q530): An Analysis of their Literary Relationship," *DSD* 15 (2008): 340–358, has proposed that 1 En. 14:18–23 modified the tradition preserved in Dan 7:9–10 and *The Book of Giants* in order to assert God's sovereignty more strongly (e.g., by removing the reference to plural thrones of judgment). Loren T. Stuckenbruck,

dream."[29] Moreover, neither "the Ancient of Days" nor the "one like a son of man" are interpreted by the attending angel, and as Rowland comments, "if the Son of Man figure had merely been a symbol of the Saints of the Most High, we might have expected to find the same kind of identification between the Son of Man and the saints which we find in respect of the beasts and the kings in v. 19, but this is lacking."[30] Given that humans frequently represent angels or angel-like beings, both in the Book of Daniel (cf. Dan 3:25; 8:15; 9:21;10:5; 12:5–7) and in visionary and apocalyptic literature, more broadly (cf. Josh 5:13; Judg 13:6–16; Ezek 8–10; Zech 1:8; 2:5; 1 En. 87:2; 89:1–9, 36; 90:14–22), the interpretation of the "one like a son of man" as an angel

---

"Daniel and Early Enoch Traditions in the Dead Sea Scrolls," in *The Book of Daniel: Composition and Reception*, 2:382–384, is a proponent of the view that Dan 7:9–10 has abbreviated the more lengthy scene in 1 En. 14:8–23, while *The Book of Giants* is the most primitive of the three texts because the number of angelic attendants is less (i.e., it is likely the grandeur of the scene was increased by adding to the number of angels). Finally, the position provisionally accepted here is that articulated by Jonathan R. Trotter, "The Tradition of the Throne Vision in the Second Temple Period: Daniel 7:9–10, *1 Enoch* 14:18–23, and the *Book of Giants* (4Q530)," *RevQ* 25 (2012): 451–466, who posits independent use of a common oral tradition, a view which accounts well for both the similarities and discrepancies between the passages. Similarly, Joseph L. Angel, "The Divine Courtroom Scenes of Daniel 7 and the Qumran Book of Giants: A Textual and Contextual Comparison," in *The Divine Courtroom in Comparative Perspective* (eds., Ari Mermelstein and Shalom E. Holtz; Leiden: Brill, 2014), 25–48, emphasizes the use of shared divine courtroom traditions but also notes that the discrepancies suggest different social milieus. The affinities these three texts share with another passage, 1 En. 90:20, is noted by Carol A. Newsom with Brennan W. Breed, *Daniel: A Commentary* (OTL; Louisville: Westminster John Knox Press, 2014), 227–228, who also argues that since 1 En. 90:20 and *The Book of Giants* take place on earth, so too Dan 7:9–10, which specifies that thrones were "set up" (i.e., such "furniture" would already be arranged in heaven). I am not convinced, however, that the other features of the passage – particularly the imagery of the divine council – support an earthly setting, and as Newsom concedes, "the details of the scene in Daniel thus combine two traditions *about heaven*: the myriad attendants represent the worship of God, while the seated court foregrounds the judicial function)" [emphasis mine]. Most recently, see Amanda M. Davis Bledsoe, "Throne Theophanies, Dream Visions, and Righteous(?) Seers: Daniel, the Book of Giants, and 1 Enoch Reconsidered," in *Ancient Tales of Giants from Qumran and Turfan: Contexts, Traditions, and Influences* (eds., Matthew Goff, Loren T. Stuckenbruck, and Enrico Morano; WUNT 360; Tübingen: Mohr Siebeck, 2016), 81–96, who argues that the evidence is too scant to determine the direction of dependence.

[29] Collins, *Daniel*, 305.

[30] Rowland, *The Open Heaven*, 180. *Contra* Casey, *Son of Man*, 25, who, as noted above, has claimed that if the "one like a son of man" was more than a symbol for God's people, he would have been mentioned later in the chapter. However, Casey does not mention why "the Ancient of Days" is not identified; see Collins, *Daniel*, 305 n. 254. It should also be noted that the interpretation of the four beasts as four kings/kingdoms likely does not exhaust the meaning of the beasts; see below.

has merit. Furthermore, early Jewish and Christian interpretations of Dan 7:13 that indicate that the "one like a son of man" was understood as an angel-like figure are all the more intelligible if the Danielic "one like a son of man" was originally intended to be viewed as such.[31]

Additional support for understanding the "one like a son of man" as an angel is related to the observation that a differentiation should be made between קַדִּישֵׁי עֶלְיוֹנִין, "the holy ones of the Most High" and עַם קַדִּישֵׁי עֶלְיוֹנִין, "the people of the holy ones of the Most High."[32] In the Hebrew Bible, virtually every occurrence of the substantive form of קדושים refers to heavenly beings,[33] a usage mirrored elsewhere in Daniel,[34] as well as in the ANE literature and in the Qumran texts (cf. *CTA* 2 I 21, 28; 17 I 4; 1QapGen II, 1; 1QM XV, 14.).[35] To be sure, the Scrolls highlight that the Qumran movement could include themselves – that is, the human sect members – in their use of קדושים; it is likely, however, that such usage reflects, at least in part, the self-identity of the sect as an angel-like community, which embraced the belief

---

[31] Collins, "The Son of Man and the Saints of the Most High," 64. Scholars have often noted the influence of Dan 7:13–14 on the latest section of 1 Enoch, the *Similitudes* (cf. 1 En. 46:1; 48:10; 52:4); see further, below. Angelic interpretations of Dan 7:13–14 are also found in 1st cent. CE texts such as 4 Ezra 13:26 and Rev 14:14. In addition, New Testament scholars have occasionally understood certain references to Dan 7:13–14 in the Gospels as reflecting Jesus' belief in a heavenly figure other than himself who would have a role at the impending eschaton (cf. Mark 13:26, Matt 24:44 et al.); see Adella Yarbro Collins, "The Influence of Daniel on the New Testament," in Collins, *Daniel*, 93.

[32] According to this understanding (= the consensus), קַדִּישֵׁי is a construct plural form of קַדִּישִׁין, with עֶלְיוֹנִין functioning as a *pluralis excellentiae*, leading to the translation, "holy ones of the Most High"; Dan 7:18, 22, and 25 have been listed as examples of this use of the plural. See E. Kautzsch, ed., *Gesenius' Hebrew Grammar* (trans., A. E. Cowley; Mineola: Dover Publications, 2006) §124. It has also been proposed that the phrase is adjectival or epexegetical and should be translated "holy ones on high"; see Goldingay, *Daniel*, 146 n. 18a; cf. idem, "Holy Ones on High," *JBL* 107 (1988): 495–497. Alternatively, Michael Segal, *Dreams, Riddles, and Visions: Textual, Contextual, and Intertextual Approaches to the Book of Daniel* (BZAW 455; Berlin: DeGruyter, 2016), 132–154, suggests that the entire phrase קַדִּישֵׁי עֶלְיוֹנִין be read as both a *pluralis excellentiae* and a reference to Yhwh. Segal also considers the "one like a son of man" to be Yhwh, who receives dominion from his superior, the Ancient of Days; see further, below.

[33] קדושים is the Hebrew equivalent of the Aramaic קַדִּישִׁין, the construct form of which, as mentioned in the preceding footnote, is found in Dan 7 (cf., e.g., Ps 89:6–8; Job 5:1; 15:15). For passages that may refer to humans, see Deut 33:2; Pss 16:3; 34:10. On the human vs. angelic use of קדושים, see Collins, *Daniel*, 314 n. 326.

[34] Cf. Dan 4:14, where the Aramaic קַדִּישִׁין refers to heavenly beings.

[35] A particularly influential article for understanding "the holy ones" of Dan 7 to be angelic beings as opposed to humans/Israel was written by Martin Noth, "The Holy Ones of the Most High," in idem, *The Laws in the Pentateuch and Other Essays* (London: Oliver and Boyd; 1966; repr., London: SCM, 1984), 215–228. For a thorough defense of the angelic interpretation with discussion of the pertinent early Jewish literature, see the excursus, "Holy Ones," in Collins, *Daniel*, 313–317.

that sect members enjoyed fellowship in the present-time with the angelic host (cf. 1QHᵃ XI, 20–24; XIX, 13–17; 1QS XI, 7–9), a phenomenon that is a distinctly post-mortem privilege according to the Book of Daniel (cf. 12:2–3).[36]

In light of these points, and in light of the prevalence of angels in Dan 8–12, the evidence suggests that the קַדִּישֵׁי עֶלְיוֹנִין of chapter 7 are not people, especially given the qualified phrase of Dan 7:27, עַם קַדִּישֵׁי עֶלְיוֹנִין, which is almost certainly a reference to humans.[37] "The holy ones of the Most High," then, are the angelic host, whereas "the people of the holy ones of the Most High" are the Jewish people, who belong or pertain to the angelic host in a tutelary relationship.[38] In other words, Dan 7 reflects the belief that Israel on earth corresponds to and is represented and protected by angels in heaven. As for the identity of the "one like a son of man," Collins argues,

The conclusion that the holy ones are angelic beings strongly supports the view that the 'one like a human being' should be identified with … the leader of the heavenly host. The specification of an individual angel does justice to the symbolism of the human figure in the vision. That the kingdom is variously given to an individual, to the holy ones, or to the people of the holy ones is analogous to the vacillation that we find between kings and kingdom in the interpretation of the beasts. … [T]he references to the giving of the kingdom are nicely complementary. The first, in v. 13, refers to the leader of the host, the second and third to the host itself (vv 18, 22), and the final reference to the people on earth.[39]

Furthermore, given that Dan 10 states that it is Michael who contends against the angelic representatives of Persia and Greece (10:2–21), and that Dan 12 suggests that it is the rule and superiority of Michael in heaven that "makes possible the dominion of Israel on earth" (v. 1),[40] the proposal that the "one like a son of man" should be identified as Michael, the leader of the angelic host,[41] warrants serious consideration. Indeed, the exaltation of Michael in

---

[36] I will discuss the Qumran movement's practice of referring to sect members using what is normally angelic terminology (and *vice versa*) in Chapter 5, below; see also Collins, *Daniel*, 314; idem, "The Angelic Life," 291–310; Dimant, "Men as Angels," 99–103.

[37] Citing 1QHᵃ XI, 22–23 for support, Noth, "The Holy Ones of the Most High," 220–224, contended that עַם is a reference to the angelic host. However, numerous commentators have pointed out that in the case of 1QHᵃ, עַם is the preposition עִם and should be translated "with." Cf. Day, *God's Conflict with the Dragon*, 170; Hartmut Stegemann, Eileen M. Schuller, and Carol A. Newsom, eds., *1QHodayotᵃ: With Incorporation of 1QHodayotᵇ and 4QHodayotᵃ⁻ᶠ* (DJD 40; Oxford: Clarendon, 2009), 155.

[38] A possessive, genitival, or tutelary relationship between the angels (holy ones) and Israel (people of the holy ones) is proposed by L. Dequeker, "The Saints of the Most High," *OtSt* 18 (1973): 155–156, 179–187; followed by Collins, *Daniel*, 315–316. Similar language is found in the War Scroll (1QM); see Chapter 4, below.

[39] Collins, *Daniel*, 318.

[40] Collins, *Daniel*, 319.

[41] Collins, *Daniel*, 318; cf. idem, *The Apocalyptic Imagination*, 101–106.

Dan 12:1 supports such a conclusion and is perhaps the most difficult obstacle to readings of the text that understand the "one like a son of man" or other figures from Dan 7–12 as outranking Michael.[42]

Excursus: The Mythological Imagery of Daniel 7

Additional support for the "one like a son of man" as the leader of the angelic host is arguably found in the imagery of the chapter. The origins of the mythology used in Dan 7 has been a topic of intense scholarly interest, with various backgrounds being proposed. However, it is widely held that the imagery has the closest affinities to the Baal cycle,[43] and as such, my earlier review of the relationship between El and Baal in the Ugaritic texts will be useful. The most significant parallels between the Canaanite literature and Dan 7 concern the protagonists of the vision, "the Ancient of Days" (Yhwh) and the "one like a son of man," and can be summarized as follows:[44] 1.) both El and "the Ancient of Days" – are described as aged judges;[45] 2.) both El and "the

---

[42] As previously noted, a subordinate Michael interpretation has been championed by Heiser, "The Divine Council," §§6.2–3; 7.4. Cf. Bampfylde, "The Prince of the Host," 129–134.

[43] Impetus for the scholarly investigations into the imagery of Dan 7 is due in large part to the work of Hermann Gunkel (in particular, his monograph *Schöpfung und Chaos in Urzeit und Endzeit: Eine religionsgeschichtliche Untersuchung über Gen 1 und Ap Joh 12* [Göttingen: Vadenhooeck & Ruprecht, 1895], 323–335), who argued for a Babylonian background for the imagery of Dan 7. A detailed argument for a Canaanite background of the imagery was first proposed by Emerton, "The Origin," 225–242. For an evaluation of the various proposals of the religious-historical background of chapter 7 and support of the Canaanite proposal, see especially Day, *God's Conflict*; 151–177; Collins, *Daniel*, 280–294; idem, "Stirring Up the Great Sea: The Religio-Historical Background of Daniel 7," in *The Book of Daniel in the Light of New Findings* (ed., Adam S. van der Woude; BETL 106; Leuven: Leuven University Press, 1993), 121–136; André Lacocque, "Allusions to Creation in Daniel 7," in *The Book of Daniel: Composition and Reception*, 1:114–131. Also see the recent essay of Carol A. Newsom, "The Reuse of Ugaritic Mythology in Daniel 7: An Optical Illusion?" in *Biblical Essays in Honor of Daniel J. Harrington, S. J., and Richard J. Clifford, S. J.: Opportunity for No Little Instruction* (eds., Christopher G. Frechette and Christopher R. Matthews; New York: Paulist Press, 2014), 86, who, while wary of the manner in which the Canaanite mythology has been used to interpret Dan 7, acknowledges that its influence "is widely accepted and might appropriately be described as the consensus view." I will return to Newsom's analysis, below.

[44] For discussion and bibliography of the following points, see Day, *God's Conflict*, 161–167; Collins, *Daniel*, 290–291; Lacocque, "Allusions to Creation in Daniel 7," 114–124.

[45] There has been much debate regarding the Ugaritic phrase '*ab shnm*, "Father of Years," and its similarity to עַתִּיק יוֹמַיָּא, "the Ancient of Days." Regardless, both the Ugaritic texts and Daniel depict El and Yhwh, respectively, as aged judges. While the description of Yhwh as a judge is widespread, as Collins, *Daniel*, 290, notes, this depiction of

Ancient of Days" are pictured as surrounded by the divine assembly (cf. *KTU* 1.2 I 21; Dan 7:10b); 3.) the "one like a son of man" is depicted as "coming with the clouds of heaven," which is reminiscent of Baal's epithet, "rider of the clouds" (cf. *KTU* 1.2 IV 29; Dan 7:13); 4.) both Baal and the "one like a son of man" are granted everlasting dominion (cf. *KTU* 1.2 IV 10; Dan 7:14); 5.) the "one like a son of man" is victorious despite the violent and chaos-wreaking beasts that emerge from the sea, which is analogous to Baal's victory over the chaotic power of Yamm/Sea and Mot/Death; 6.) as was emphasized above, Baal is El's powerful yet subordinate co-regent, which approximates the relationship between the "one like a son of man" and "the Ancient of Days." Traditionally, some scholars have been hesitant to embrace the idea that a pious Jewish author would have employed Canaanite imagery in a religious text.[46] In response, it has been argued that the recognition of parallels between Dan 7 and ANE mythology is not tantamount to saying that there is a one-to-one correspondence between the texts.[47]

It is precisely the degree of correspondence between the texts that has prompted Newsom to question the way scholars have used the Canaanite imagery to understand Dan 7. In a recent essay, she cautions against over-interpreting the Canaanite mythological imagery, since the motifs may have been stock imagery with which the author was familiar. In her words, scholars need to "distinguish between mere points of correlation and a truly formational force of a mythic pattern."[48] After surveying various alleged points of comparison[49] – and stressing that these points are indeed better described as correlations rather than the preservation of a mythic pattern – Newsom then addresses the relationship between "the Ancient of Days" and the "one like a son of man," which Collins and others have claimed is analogous to the supe-

---

God (i.e., with white hair) is unique to Daniel among the books of the Hebrew Bible (cf. *KTU* 1.1 III 24; 1.4 IV 24; 1.4 V 65–66; 1.6 I 36; *Ug. V.* 2b–3a; Dan 7:9–10).

[46] See the overview of Collins, *Daniel*, 280–281.

[47] I.e., the thrust of chapter 7 is not that the "one like a son of man" *is* Baal, as the use of mythology is clearly not a wholesale representation, adoption, or endorsement of Canaanite figures, concepts, and practices; see, e.g., Markus Zehnder, "Why the Danielic 'Son of Man' Is a Divine Being," *BBR* 24 (2014): 331–347, who marshals the use of Baal imagery as one of the evidences that the son of man is divine "as opposed to having only symbolic, human, or angelic status." As Collins, *Daniel*, 281, has argued, the issue "is not holistic correspondence but that the use of a particular image be rendered intelligible by analogy with the proposed prototype."

[48] Newsom, "The Reuse of Ugaritic Mythology," 87, 90, also describes the differentiation for which she is arguing as distinguishing between "historical authorial intertextuality" and "modern, scholarly readers' intertextuality"; i.e., Newsom is suggesting that critical scholars have equated the former with the latter, and the result has been to see the *pattern* of the Ugaritic material in Dan 7 when there are only *similarities*.

[49] Newsom, "The Reuse of Ugaritic Mythology," 87–90.

rior-subordinate relationship between El and Baal in the Ugaritic texts.[50]
Though conceding that the similarities are "striking," Newsom suggests that
the author of chapter 7 likely did not intend for the *pattern* of the El-Baal
relationship to inform the relationship between "the Ancient of Days" and the
"one like a son of man" and that any resemblance is "accidental."[51] To be
sure, Newsom's judicious observations deserve more discussion – especially
in light of the proposal of Segal, who suggests that not less but an even greater
degree of correspondence between the Ugaritic texts and Dan 7 may have been
operative.[52] For now, I cautiously accept that the burgeoning apocalypticism
and angelology of early Judaism may have found the ancient Canaanite pattern
a useful and perhaps even traditional[53] vehicle to convey that Yhwh ("the An-

---

[50] See Chapter 2, above; cf. Collins, *Daniel*, 286–287.

[51] Newsom, "The Reuse of Ugaritic Mythology," 96.

[52] Segal, "Who is the 'Son of God' in 4Q246?" 295–296; idem, *Dreams, Riddles, and Visions*, 152, has argued, not only for the translatability of Deut 32:8–9 and Ps 82 to the extent that Second Temple Period readers of these texts would have recognized El as granting authority to Yhwh (cf. Frankel, "El as the Speaking Voice," 1–24), but also that such an interpretation "finds its natural continuation in the apocalypse of Dan 7, in which a senior deity (the Ancient of Days) convicts subordinate divine characters (the four beasts) to death, while granting dominion over all the nations of the world to a divine character of special status, the one like a man." Segal thus interprets the "one like a son of man" (and קַדִּישֵׁי עֶלְיוֹנִין) as Yhwh, and concludes that it was only "subsequent interpretations [that] transformed this theological-cosmological picture, promoting Yhwh … and equating him with the Ancient of Days. This promotion, however, created a vacuum for the identification of the one like a man … and opened up the possibility of a new character, a divine second-in-command over Israel, a notion that is developed in subsequent chapters of Daniel [cf. Michael in Dan 10:13, 21; 12:1]." While Segal offers the caveats that "rather than presenting the religious worldview [of Dan 7's author], it may be the result of his dependence upon the ancient myths of the division of the world expressed in Deut 32 and Ps 82" and that "the author of Dan 7 intended for his audience to identify and be aware of these earlier sources passages," his fascinating reading presses the persistence and correspondence of the Canaanite imagery in the late Second Temple Period to a level that is, in my opinion, questionable. For a brief response, see John J. Collins, "The Legacy of Canaan in Ancient Israel and Early Christianity," in *Opportunity for No Little Instruction*, 79–81.

[53] As Paul D. Hansen, *The Dawn of Apocalyptic: The Historical and Sociological Roots of Jewish Apocalyptic Eschatology* (rev. ed; Philadelphia: Fortress Press, 1979), 6, 17, has noted, "the apocalyptic literature of the second century and after is the result of a long development reaching back to pre-exilic times and beyond, and not the new baby of second century foreign parents," and he continues by observing that "the earlier one goes in Israel's religious history, the more powerful the untranslated visionary element becomes, as illustrated by many of the archaic traditions … (e.g., Exodus 15, Judges 5, Joshua 10). This pattern suggests that Israel did not enter nationhood with a fully developed historiography; for that nation emerged from a mixture of peoples, many embracing worldviews which would not have contrasted sharply with mythopoeic view which can be seen, for example, in the literature of ancient Ugarit. The move toward a more mythopoeic view of reality which is discernable in early apocalyptic is thus not an unexpected adventure into uncharted territory; it is a return to some of Israel's most ancient roots." Cf. John J. Col-

cient of Days") had an active and formidable celestial subordinate (the "one like a son of man"), who played an integral role in the struggles of the angelic host and the people of God.

Turning to the subject of the beasts of chapter 7, it was noted above that the interpretations provided by the angelic attendant are brief: the four beasts represent four kings/kingdoms. Given the internal evidence of chapter 7, as well as the witness of chapters 7–12 as a unit, viewing the beasts as symbols for earthly kings and kingdoms likely does not exhaust their meaning. More specifically, it has been argued that a "beast," according to chapter 7, functions not only as a symbol but also as a dynamic, multivalent concept. Caragounis describes the complexity of imagery:

[T]he term "beasts" does not stand for any particular king, but for the whole series of kings involved in each kingdom. Moreover – and this is of extreme importance – the beast is not quite identical with this totality of kings. The oscillation between king and kingdom observable in the text, obtains also between the king on the one hand and the entity that is conceived of as being the core in the concept of "Beast" on the other. The recognition of the dynamic nature of the text is of crucial importance for understanding the nature of the concept of 'Beast.' ... *Our author is grappling with his problem on a two dimensional basis. While cogitating on human affairs the author goes beyond what is observable in the empirical realm. He introduces his readers to another plane, the plane of vision, where earthly phenomena are seen to have their invisible counterparts to 'events' beyond the world of sense.* More than this, there is a causal connection between the invisible and the visible worlds. *Earthly events are not simply the result of the whim of earthly potentates; they are to be explained by reference to realties in the invisible world.* It is this double dimension in the author's perspective which renders the concept of 'Beast' a complex concept of ambivalent nature. Therefore, in the author's way of thinking the 'Beast's' essential character is neither the state nor the king. What is perhaps only implicit as yet in chapter 7 become quite explicit in [chapter 10]. Here, two of the beasts/kingdoms, Persia and Greece, are described as having a 'prince,' ... who tries to thwart God's purpose by opposing the angelic emissary. That these 'princes' cannot possibly refer to ... human

---

lins, *The Scepter and the Star: Messianism in Light of the Dead Sea Scrolls* (2nd ed.; Grand Rapids: Eerdmans, 2010), 193–194, who makes the following observation regarding Daniel 7: "This imagery had long been adapted in Israelite religion, and had its *Sitz-im-Leben* in the royal cult in the preexilic period. We do not know precisely from what source Daniel derived it, but that is hardly surprising in the present state of our knowledge of Jewish religion prior to the Maccabean revolt." So, too, Lacocque, "Allusions to Creation in Daniel 7," 117: "[I]n spite of some 1200 years elapsing between the Ugaritic version of the myth (14th cent. BCE) and the book of Daniel (2nd cent. BCE), the Canaanite influence on Daniel 7 is, I believe, undeniable. A roughly contemporary text like Isa 27:1 (and Isaiah 24–27 in general) shows that God's fight with the Dragon or Mot was very much on the minds of second century Israelites. It is not utterly surprising to find a resurgence of mythological elements in the Isaiah apocalypse or in the book of Daniel. For, in contrast to the evolution of the mythic narrative toward systematic sapiential doctrine, the 'apocalypses' retain much more the narrative form of the older creation traditions."

kings is placed beyond reasonable doubt in verse 21 which in identical terms speaks of the angel Michael as the 'prince' of the Jews [emphasis mine].[54]

More will be said about this two-dimensional worldview, below. For now, it is sufficient to note that if the symbolism of the beasts includes the heavenly or angelic powers that lie behind the respective earthly kings/kingdoms represented by each beast,[55] then the angelic interpretation of the "one like a son of man" constitutes a powerful announcement: that dominion is granted to the leader of the angelic host means that, in the end, the celestial forces behind Antiochus will be defeated. And "to the pious Jews of the Maccabean era, who had a lively belief in supernatural beings, nothing could be more relevant"[56] than that their angelic guardians – and not the heavenly beings that stood behind their enemies – would "receive dominion and glory and kingship" (v. 14).

Chapter 7 is clear that the ultimate fortunes of the "one like a son of man" are the same as those of "the holy ones of the Most High," the angelic host, who will possess the kingdom forever (v. 18). But the chapter also mentions the hardships of "the holy ones," as verse 21 reads: "[the] horn made war with the holy ones and was prevailing over them." Elaborating upon this statement, verse 25 reveals that the horn is a king who, among other blasphemous acts, "shall speak words against the Most High, [and] attempt to wear out the holy ones of the Most High ... ." There have been questions concerning the precise meaning of the verb בלה, "to wear out,"[57] but the sense of the word seems to be the affliction of someone or something over time, with the result that the object is severely strained or taxed.[58] According to verse 22, this affliction is reversed by the judgment of "the Ancient of

---

[54] Chrys C. Caragounis, *The Son of Man: Vision and Interpretation* (WUNT 38; Tübingen: Mohr Siebeck, 1986), 69–70.

[55] Cf. Collins, *Daniel*, 312 n. 306, 320: "[T]he complexity of the beasts ... imply a spiritual power behind the kingdoms" ... and "The little horn here should not be understood in purely human terms."

[56] Collins, *Daniel*, 318.

[57] Noth, "The Holy Ones of the Most High," 226, even though he considers "the holy ones of the Most High" to be the angelic host, understood the abbreviated "holy ones" of v. 21 to be the Jewish people (see further, below). He was, however, uncertain as to whether בלה could take a human object, and therefore proposed that the word might be related to the Arabic verb, *bala*, "to offend." While Antiochus, the "horn," certainly offended Jews during the events of the 160s BCE, it has already been discussed why viewing "the holy ones" as the Jewish people is unsatisfactory.

[58] E.g., an article of clothing (cf. Josh 9:13; Neh 9:21); also see "בלה," *HALOT* 5:1834, which notes the REB's translation, "to wear down."

Days," a point that serves to reinforce the interconnected fates of "the holy ones of the Most High" and the "one like a son of man."[59]

The Jewish people are only mentioned in verse 27,[60] where it is said that "the people of the holy ones of the Most High" will be given "the kingship and dominion and the greatness of the kingdom under the whole heaven." As noted above, the epithet "the people of the holy ones" suggests a close association between the Jews and their angelic guardians and may even imply that the latter protect the former (or are supposed to do so).[61] Moreover, as with the "one like a son of man" and "the holy ones of the Most High," the fortunes of "the people of the holy ones" are dependent upon the judgment of the heavenly court (v. 26). As Lacocque observes, "the passage from the 'son of man' to his collective dimension, that is to those who, like him, receive 'the kingship, dominion, and grandeur of all the kingdoms under heaven' is the dominant theme in this chapter in its present form."[62]

Chapter 7 portrays this close relationship between heaven and earth in different ways. First, the symbolism of the chapter describes Antiochus afflicting "the holy ones" (vv. 21, 25). Collins explains the depiction of a human antagonist attacking a cosmic protagonist as follows: "the empirical data lie in the persecution of the Jews by Antiochus Epiphanes, but in the apocalyptic imagination of the author these events are understood as an assault on the heavenly host and ultimately on God himself."[63] But how exactly has Antiochus assaulted heaven? Kvanvig notes that there are essentially three interpretations of this description:[64] the offensive of Antiochus was envisioned as being against either people on earth,[65] the angels in heaven,[66] or both.[67]

---

[59] The coming of the "one like a son of man" in the visionary sequence (vv. 13–14) directly follows the judgment scene of the fourth beast and its horn (vv. 11–12) at which "the Ancient of Days" (vv. 9–10) presumably presides.

[60] While humans are not specifically mentioned elsewhere in chapter 7, it is obvious that the actions of the beasts impact earth, even if not exclusively so.

[61] Dequeker, "The Saints of the Most High," 186.

[62] Lacocque, *Daniel*, 154.

[63] Collins, *Daniel*, 320.

[64] Helge S. Kvanvig, *Roots of Apocalyptic: The Mesopotamian Background of the Enoch Figure and of the Son of Man* (WMANT 61; Neukirchen-Vluyn: Neukirchener Verlag, 1988), 579.

[65] So Brekelmans, "The Saints of the Most High," 305–329. As noted, even some supporters of the angelic interpretation of "the holy ones of the Most High" have opted to view the abbreviated designation of v. 21, "the holy ones," as a reference to the Jewish people, against whom the horn, Antiochus, was waging war, likely in an attempt to mitigate the presumed illogic of Antiochus attacking heaven; cf. Noth, "The Holy Ones of the Most High," 226; Kvanvig, *Roots of Apocalyptic*, 582–583.

[66] So Dequeker, "The Saints of the Most High," 155–156.

[67] So Collins, *Daniel*, 304–324; cf. idem, "The Son of Man and the Saints of the Most High," 50–66.

While Kvanvig attributes to Collins the view that the actions of Antiochus are against both heaven and earth, this view better describes Kvanvig's own understanding, which is dependent on the ANE concept of the "rebel king," who ascends to heaven and provokes God.[68] Collins' interpretation, while similar to Kvanvig's insofar as Antiochus' actions are understood to have impact in both realms, is different in that Collins does not posit an ascension of Antiochus; instead, he suggests that, as per Caragounis' reading of the beasts just mentioned, "the little horn should not be understood purely in human terms,"[69] especially since chapter 10 is explicit in its depiction of earthly struggles being a reflection or an out working of heavenly ones.[70] A second way the chapter accomplishes this concerns the intertwined fortunes of the Jewish people and the angels associated with them. For example, it is without question that the hostility of "the little horn" results in hardship for God's people on earth, even if, again, the earthly impact of the horn's actions does not exhaust the symbolism. However, the description of the action of the little horn *on earth* (v. 8) is followed by the judgment of the *heavenly* court; the horn is also said to be waging war against and wearing out the angelic host (vv. 9–14, 21–22). It is not until the end of the chapter 7 – that is, after judgment has twice been said to occur from heaven and for heavenly recipients – that "the people of the holy ones of the Most High" explicitly receive the same favorable judgment. Indeed, "the parallelism between the Jewish people and its heavenly counterpart extends to adversity. When things go badly on earth, it is supposedly because they are going badly in the heavenly battle too. When the Ancient of Days arrives in judgment, fortunes are reversed on both levels."[71]

III. Daniel 8

Daniel 8 covers much of the same historical ground as chapter 7, with many scholars suggesting that Dan 8, which marks the book's transition to Hebrew, is dependent on Dan 7.[72] The earthly and cosmic impact associated with the

---

[68] Kvanvig, *Roots of Apocalyptic*, 460–484, 581–583.

[69] Collins, *Daniel*, 320. Cf. Caragounis, *Son of Man*, 69–70.

[70] Collins, "Mythology of Holy War," 598.

[71] Collins, *Daniel*, 320. Cf. Kvanvig, *Roots of the Apocalyptic*, 583, who notes that chapter 7 deliberately portrays "the fate of the terrestrial and the celestial groups in parallel to each other. Both groups suffer under the attack of the demonic king (vv. 21, 25), and both receive justice and the kingdom at the end (vv. 22, 27)."

[72] Cf. Collins, *Daniel*, 342; Goldingay, *Daniel*, 201. On the use of animal metaphors in the two chapters, see Porter, *Metaphors and Monsters*, 121. On the use of scripture in chapter 8, including Isa 14, see Susan Niditch, *The Symbolic Vision in Biblical Tradition* (HSM 30; Missoula: Scholars Press, 1983), 228.

persecutions of Antiochus, who is again symbolized by a little horn,[73] are in focus, and the chapter ends with a brief yet hopeful statement indicating that the oppressor will meet his demise through divine intervention.[74] Broadly speaking, chapter 8 has two sections: a vision report (vv. 3–14) and its interpretation (vv. 15–26).

A possible reference to an angelic leader figure occurs at verse 11,[75] where it is said that the little horn acted arrogantly against שַׂר־הַצָּבָא, "the prince of the host." Given that verse 11 continues by mentioning that the horn "took the regular burnt offering away from *him* and overthrew the place of *his* sanctuary" – with the antecedent of the pronouns almost certainly referring to "the prince of the host" – the epithet is often understood as a description of the God of Israel; that the interpretation section seemingly refers to "the prince of the host" as שַׂר־שָׂרִים, "the prince of princes," (v. 25) is said to strengthen the identification.[76] This conclusion, however, while widespread, has not been the only option proposed. Early 20th century commentators argued that a high priest is in view.[77] Goldingay suggests that שַׂר־הַצָּבָא needs to be understood in light of the phrase צְבָא הַשָּׁמַיִם, "the host of heaven," in verse 10; taken together, the verses would then indicate that שַׂר־הַצָּבָא is "the leader of Israel's celestial equivalents."[78] While ultimately not favouring the reading

---

[73] In the words of Hartman and DiLella, *Daniel*, 235, "the name of Antiochus IV Epiphanes … is not mentioned anywhere in this chapter, but there is not the slightest doubt that he is the one meant in the description of the "[little] horn," whom the angel identifies as a king 'brazen-faced and skilled in trickery' (vv. 23–25)."

[74] As Goldingay, *Daniel*, 204, implies, the absence of any mention of divine intervention until the very end of the chapter highlights the severity of the persecutions of Antiochus. But also see the insightful observation of Newsom, *Daniel*, 272, who notes that Antiochus' demise is communicated with only three Hebrew words (וּבְאֶפֶס יָד יִשָּׁבֵר, "But he shall be broken, and not by human hands"; see 8:25) and thus summarizes: "The rhetorical economy of the text deflates Antiochus's massive pretentions."

[75] The angel Gabriel is mentioned in 8:16, but his role there is not as a guardian of God's people *per se* but as a revealer/messenger (cf. 9:21).

[76] Cf. Hartman and DiLella, *Daniel*, 236; Collins, *Daniel*, 333; Newsom, *Daniel*, 264. The translators of the NRSV apparently concur with this evaluation as is evidenced by the capitalization of the epithet (i.e., "Prince of princes"); note the parallel to Dan 8:11 = 11:36, "The king shall act as he pleases. He shall exalt himself and consider himself greater than any god, and shall speak horrendous things against the *God of gods*." See John J. Collins, "Prince שַׂר," *DDD* 662–664. If this interpretation is correct, Dan 8 is a rare instance of the use of שַׂר as an epithet for the God of Israel. The clearest use of the designation for Yhwh in early Jewish texts is 1QHᵃ XVIII, 10 (cf. 4Q417 2 I, 5; 4Q418 140 4).

[77] Cf. R. H. Charles, *A Critical and Exegetical Commentary on the Book of Daniel* (Oxford: Clarendon, 1929), 204; Martinus A. Beek, *Das Danielbuch: Sein Historischer Hintergrund und seine literarische Entwicklung* (Leiden: Bringsberg, 1935), 80. Proponents of this interpretation note that the word שַׂר can be used in priestly contexts (e.g., 1 Chr 16:5; 24:5; Ezra 8:24).

[78] Goldingay, *Daniel*, 210.

of this leader-figure as Michael,[79] Goldingay and others do not rule out this interpretation entirely,[80] due in part to the similarities between the epithet שַׂר־הַצָּבָא and that of the enigmatic angelic leader of Josh 5:13–15, who is called שַׂר־צְבָא־יְהוָה, though some scholars understand שַׂר־הַצָּבָא to be Michael's angelic superior.[81] Elsewhere in Daniel, the noun שַׂר refers to an angel (cf. 10:13, 20, 21; 12:1);[82] given that chapter 7 describes "the little horn" as waging war against the angelic host, it is certainly plausible that chapter 8, in the course of emphasizing the hubris of the horn,[83] would depict the horn as challenging even the leader of the host, which שַׂר־שָׂרִים would also signify.[84] In order to make sense of this scene, the important observation made regarding chapter 7 – that the little horn should not be considered solely in human terms – is also appropriate here.

Chapter 8 utilizes the ANE motif that the stars are gods or angelic beings.[85] As discussed in Chapter 2, the astral host could be envisioned as either for or against Yhwh, but it is obvious in verse 10 that the stars are the victims of the horn's aggression, and are, thus, "good"[86] angels:

10 וַתִּגְדַּל עַד־צְבָא הַשָּׁמָיִם וַתַּפֵּל אַרְצָה מִן־הַצָּבָא וּמִן־הַכּוֹכָבִים וַתִּרְמְסֵם:

10 "[The horn] grew as high as the host of heaven. It threw down to earth some of the host and some of the stars, and trampled on them.

The angelic "stars" and the trampling they endured from the horn is reminiscent of the war the horn waged against "the holy ones" in Dan 7 and serves to highlight the similarities between the two chapters, and together, they empha-

---

[79] Goldingay, *Daniel*, 210, prefers to identify שַׂר־הַצָּבָא as God.

[80] Michael was proposed by the medieval commentator, Ibn Ezra.

[81] E.g., Bampfylde, "The Prince of the Host," 129–134, who considers the שַׂר־הַצָּבָא to be the same figure as both the lofty angel mentioned in vv. 5–6, 21, 12:6, and the "one like a son of man" from 7:13–14; also see Hesier, "The Divine Council," §§6.2–6.3.

[82] Lacocque, *Daniel*, 162, is incorrect to state that the Book of Daniel "always" uses שַׂר in reference to an angel (cf. 1:7–11, 18; 9:6, 8; 11:5).

[83] Cf. Dan 8:25: "in his own mind he shall be great."

[84] So Lacocque, *Daniel*, 170–171. A recent suggestion of Segal, "Monotheism and Angelology," 19–20, should also be noted. In his discussion of the redaction-critical history of Daniel, he argues that the language of chapter 8 – specifically, the word שַׂר – influenced the Michael passages in Dan 10 and 12, which he considers to be secondary additions. While Segal interprets שַׂר־שָׂרִים and שַׂר־הַצָּבָא to be epithets of the God of Israel, he cautiously proposes that the scribe who added the Michael passages in Dan 10 and 12 mistakenly interpreted the designations to be references to a chief angel figure. However, Segal also allows for the possibility that שַׂר־שָׂרִים and שַׂר־הַצָּבָא were originally intended to refer to an angel, and that the Michael passages in chapters 10 and 12 thus correctly reflect the meaning of chapter 8.

[85] Alternatively, the stars were considered to be manifestations of divine beings, though the distinction is sometimes unclear; see Collins, *Daniel*, 331. Cf. Goldingay, *Daniel*, 209–210; Mullen, *Assembly of the Gods*, 194–196; Bietenhard, *Die himmlische Welt*, 16.

[86] Collins, *Daniel*, 332.

size the cosmic consequences associated with the assaults of Antiochus. That the host is said to be "given over"[87] to the horn (v. 11) continues the bleak description of the angelic host under attack.[88]

Daniel 8 emphasizes the correspondence between heaven and earth by alternating references to each realm in a manner similar to that witnessed in Dan 7. This oscillation can occur abruptly: after a rather lengthy description of the power of the goat and its horns (vv. 5–9), which symbolize events on earth (at least primarily), attention is suddenly given to the cosmic disturbances associated with the horn:

The small horn grows south, east, and toward Palestine (v. 9). This aggressive movement then moves onto a different plane, to reach to the celestial army and the commander of that army (vv. 10, 11). Alongside the references here to שמים ('heaven/the heavens,' vv. 8, 10) appear a number of references to הארץ ('the earth/ground,' vv 5, 7, 10, 12, 18): both are capable of referring both to the this-worldly plane and to movement between earth and heaven.[89]

Chapter 8 also exhibits this oscillation on a smaller scale, that is, within the same line; verse 12 reads as follows: "Because of wickedness, the host was given over to [the horn] together with the regular burnt offering." Admittedly, the text is problematic and various emendations have been proposed.[90] But if the above reading is to be accepted, in the same breath the impact of the horn is said to touch heaven and earth, and "here again, the empirical tribulation of the Jewish people is understood to have its counterpart in the heavenly battle."[91]

---

[87] The text is difficult here; see further, below.

[88] The interpretation section of chapter 8 is plagued by textual problems at v. 24, which may include a reference to the collective angelic host. In short, while the pertinent part of the verse reads, "He shall destroy the powerful and the people of the holy ones" (עַם־קְדֹשִׁים), it has been suggested that the original reading was simply "holy ones" (קְדוֹשִׁים). On the one hand, Collins, *Daniel*, 340–341, suggests that "holy ones" is the preferred reading, in part because it better anticipates the reference to the heavenly "prince of princes" in v. 25 and coheres with earlier references to "holy ones" (v. 13) and the "host" (v. 10). On the other hand, Lacocque, *Daniel*, 170–171, claims that an elaborate parallelism justifies reading "people of the holy ones" (a reading which would again emphasize the tutelary correspondence between the people and the angels as per 7:27). However one deciphers the textual issues, it is clear that the severity and scope of the persecutions of Antiochus are being emphasized.

[89] Goldingay, *Daniel*, 205.

[90] For a discussion of the options, see Collins, *Daniel*, 334–335.

[91] Collins, *Daniel*, 333–335. Lacocque, *Daniel*, 162, not only supports the interpretation that "the prince of the host" is Michael, but in keeping with the option briefly mentioned above he also sees the epithet as simultaneously referring to the high priest. While this view is quite speculative, it is likely an attempt to underscore what Collins describes as "the synergism between the heavenly and earthly worlds that is pervasive in these chapters."

IV. Daniel 9

Several features distinguish chapter 9 from the rest of Dan 7–12, not least of which is Daniel's lengthy penitential prayer. But the fact that the framework of the chapter is an angel-mediated revelation means that it is not out of place, here, and warrants brief discussion. To be sure, revealed knowledge is a multi-faceted subject,[92] and much of it is beyond the direct scope of the present study. However, I will highlight the possibility that there are priestly connotations to the role of Gabriel in Dan 9.

Numerous passages in the Hebrew Bible entrust Israel's priesthood with scriptural teaching (e.g., Lev 10:10–11; Deut 33:8–11; Ezek 44:23–24; Mal 2:4–7), and with this in mind, Gabriel's words to Daniel are intriguing. Verses 21–23 read as follows:

21 עוֹד אֲנִי מְדַבֵּר בַּתְּפִלָּה וְהָאִישׁ גַּבְרִיאֵל אֲשֶׁר רָאִיתִי בֶחָזוֹן בַּתְּחִלָּה מֻעָף בִּיעָף נֹגֵעַ אֵלַי כְּעֵת מִנְחַת־עָרֶב:
22 וַיָּבֶן וַיְדַבֵּר עִמִּי וַיֹּאמַר דָּנִיֵּאל עַתָּה יָצָאתִי לְהַשְׂכִּילְךָ בִינָה:
23 בִּתְחִלַּת תַּחֲנוּנֶיךָ יָצָא דָבָר וַאֲנִי בָּאתִי לְהַגִּיד כִּי חֲמוּדוֹת אָתָּה וּבִין בַּדָּבָר וְהָבֵן בַּמַּרְאֶה:

21 while I was speaking in prayer, the man Gabriel, who I had seen before in a vision, came to me in swift flight at the time of the evening sacrifice.
22 He came and said to me, "Daniel, I have now come out to give you wisdom and under-standing.
23 At the beginning of your supplications a word went out, and I have come to declare it, for you are greatly beloved. So consider the word and understand the vision …"

The revelation of Gabriel is a response to Daniel's pious prayer, which sug-gests that the angel was functioning, at least partially, in an intercessory ca-pacity. In and of itself, intercession is a priestly prerogative.[93] But it is also interesting that language used elsewhere to depict the teaching role of the priests and Levites is employed in verses 22–23 to describe the purpose of Gabriel's communication: to provide timely interpretation of scripture, name-ly, the prophecy of Jeremiah (cf. Dan 9:1–3; Jer 25:11–12; 29:10), which Daniel had misunderstood.[94] First, Dan 9:22 uses שׂכל and בִּינָה, whose cog-

---

[92] For a recent treatment of this topic, see Eric Montgomery, "A Stream from Eden: The Nature and Development of a Revelatory Tradition in the Dead Sea Scrolls" (Ph.D. diss; McMaster University, 2013).

[93] See, e.g., Angel, *Otherworldly*, 29 n. 21, who cites Exod 28:29 as a prime example of the intercessory role of priests in the Hebrew Bible: "So Aaron shall bear the names of the children of Israel on the breastpiece of judgment upon his heart whenever he enters the holy place as a continual memorial before the Lord."

[94] On the "mild irony" of Daniel claiming to perceive (בִּינֹתִי) Jeremiah's prophecy and subsequently being corrected by Gabriel's revelation, the purpose of which was to provide him with understanding (בִּינָה), see Newsom, *Daniel*, 290.

nates[95] are applied in other texts to the priests and Levites, specifically as it relates to their provision of insight and the correct interpretation of scripture (cf. Ezra 8:12–16; Neh 8:7–8; 2 Chr 30:22; 35:3). Daniel 9:23 also has the admittedly not-infrequent combination of נגד and דָּבָר, though it should be noted that the pairing is found in the injunction to heed the decision announced by the Levitical priests (cf. Deut 17:8–11).

While an analogy between the angels and those responsible for the Book of Daniel has been observed,[96] it is possible that an analogy between the angels and Israel's priesthood[97] is also intended. Thus, the Book of Daniel may not only be claiming that angels have information to disclose that is normally inaccessible to humans but also be hinting that the content of such teaching is reliable because the angel who reveals it is a priest and therefore one who presumably serves in closest proximity to God.[98] It must be conceded, however, that this is, at best, implicit in Dan 9.

V. Daniel 10–12

The final vision of the Book of Daniel encompasses chapters 10–12 and is comprised of an initial vision (10:1–11:1), which serves as an introduction for an angel-mediated audition or discourse containing what modern, critical scholars have concluded is an *ex eventu* prophecy of the history of the 4th–2nd cent. BCE (11:2–12:4); an epilogue (12:5–13) follows this discourse.[99] The introductory nature of the initial vision does not mean, however, that it is superfluous to the larger vision or that the real importance of Dan 10–12 lies in the historical details of the discourse. Indeed, the "retrospective"[100] of the

---

[95] On the use of the cognate word מבין in revelatory contexts, see Armin Lange, "Sages and Scribes in the Qumran Literature," in *Scribes, Sages, and Seers in the Eastern Mediterranean World* (ed., Leo G. Perdue; Göttingen: Vandenhoeck and Ruprecht, 2008), 274–275. Also see my discussion of *4QInstruction*, below.

[96] Insofar as both are presented as revealing divine knowledge; see Collins, *Daniel*, 352.

[97] See, e.g., Newsom, *Daniel*, 293–294, who proposes a high view of the (earthly) priesthood in chapter 9, which may assist in explaining the non-inclusion of priests in a list of critiqued figures in Daniel's penitential prayer. Cf. Goldingay, *Daniel*, 329: "[Daniel's] authors and audience seem to be people who feel ousted from power in their own community, which is divided into people who support the foreign government and people who oppose it. They are persecuted by these foreign overlords and puzzled at their God's failure to act in response to attacks on his sphere – his shrine, its priesthood, its worship, its people. They are people who attach particular importance to such cultic matters; the authors could have belonged to priestly circles, though their concern about the temple need not imply that."

[98] Of course, the stature of the angel in Dan 9 is additionally enhanced by the fact that it is cast an angel known in Jewish tradition to be an "archangel," though this term is not used in Daniel. I will return to the subject of archangels when I discuss 1 Enoch, below.

[99] For detailed outlines of Dan 10–12, see Goldingay, *Daniel*, 281–282; Collins, *Daniel*, 371–372.

[100] The designation of Lacocque, *Daniel*, 214.

discourse is meant to convey that history proceeds according to the pre-
determined plan of God. The vision of chapter 10 is foundational for understanding the prophecies of chapter 11, as the former elucidates the latter by
providing a glimpse of "what is really going on";[101] in other words, what is
somewhat cryptic in chapters 7–8 is explicit in chapter 10: the struggle of
God's people on earth mirrors the struggle of Israel's angelic guardians in
heaven. Chapters 10–12 are clear, however, that this struggle will end in victory for Michael which means victory for God's people.[102]

The linen garb of the angel(s) mentioned in 10:5 (cf. 12:6–7) may be indicative of a priestly status (cf. Ezek 9:2–10:7);[103] a priest-like intercessory
role may also be suggested by the descriptions of the unnamed angel in Dan
10:12, as it has been observed that Daniel's prayers were (temporarily) im-
peded by the angels associated with Greece and Persia.[104] The focus of chapter 10, however, is a battle between these hostile angels and those associated
with Israel. In Dan 10–12, Michael is three times referred to as a שַׂר,
"prince" (cf. 10:13, 21; 12:1), a designation indicating that his role corresponds to those of שַׂר פָּרַס, "the prince of Persia" (10:13, 20) and שַׂר־יָוָן,
"the prince of Greece" (10:21). Once again, the use of the term "prince" may
stem, in part, from reflection upon the שַׂר־צְבָא־יְהוָה of Josh 5:13–15, and in
the context of chapter 10 is likely meant to convey that Israel has an elite
angelic warrior-guardian who fights on her behalf.[105] But as previously noted, while Goldingay concedes that Michael has a "special relationship with
Israel parallel to that of other leaders with Persia or Greece," he also claims
that referring to Michael as the שַׂר־הַצָּבָא (8:11) or שַׂר־שָׂרִים (8:25) would
invest him with authority that "goes beyond that of Michael elsewhere: he is

---

[101] So Collins, *Daniel*, 61.

[102] As previously mentioned, Segal, "Monotheism and Angelology," 419, has argued
that the passages referring to angelic princes in Dan 10 and 12 (10.13, 20–21; 12:1) are
secondary, deliberately added to complement the picture of Dan 7 and 8, namely, that "the
Lord renders judgment on the nations of the world, including Israel. Each of these nations
is depicted by a supernatural being, and in the case of Israel, by a divine entity [i.e., Mi-
chael] second in rank only to God himself." Segal suggests that his analysis helps to make
sense of awkward "seams" in the text, e.g., the tribulation and arrival of Michael at 12:1–4
after the demise of Antiochus at the end of chapter 11. But whether original or added later
(though it could not have been much later), the result is the same: the author(s) was (were)
attempting to convey a worldview that envisioned a correspondence between heaven and
earth. Cf. Collins, *Daniel*, 390, who does not consider these passages secondary and notes
that the "at that time" of 12:1 refers to "the time of the king's invasion of Israel and his
death, which is in 'the time of the end' (11:40) and is the time of the decisive heavenly
intervention."

[103] See Angel, *Otherworldly*, 24.

[104] Robert E. Moses, "Tangible Prayer in Early Judaism and Christianity," *JSP* 25
(2015): 118–149, esp. 141–143.

[105] Hartman and DiLella, *Daniel*, 282–283. Cf. Michalak, *Angels as Warriors*, 105.

only one of the prominent [angelic] leaders (10:13)."[106]   While the points
adduced by Goldingay and others have perhaps not received the attention
they deserve, it is difficult to conclude that Michael has an angelic superior.

First, while it is true that chapter 10 describes Michael as אַחַד הַשָּׂרִים
הָרִאשֹׁנִים, "one of the chief princes" (v. 13), it is apparent that Michael is exemplary or even extraordinary among the angels. As verse 21 makes clear,
the unnamed angel[107] who requires Michael's assistance in the struggle
against the angelic princes of Persia and Greece has only Michael to rely on:
"There is no one with me who contends against these princes except Michael,
your prince." [108]   Second, the designation שַׂרְכֶם, "your prince," reveals more
than a "special relationship" to Israel. It is evidence of a more elaborate arrangement than that stated in Deut 32:8–9 (cf. Jub. 15:31–32; Sir 17:17), in
that an angelic being is singled-out as having a significant role in Yhwh's
prestigious prerogative: the guardianship of Israel.[109]   Third, as the historical
discourse ends, Michael's role is affirmed as central to the triumph of Israel
in the book's eschatological scenario; and it is the opening verse of chapter
12 that is most difficult to reconcile with the interpretation that Michael is
inferior to another angel:

1 וּבָעֵת הַהִיא יַעֲמֹד מִיכָאֵל הַשַּׂר הַגָּדוֹל הָעֹמֵד עַל־בְּנֵי עַמֶּךָ

1 At that time Michael, the great prince, the protector of your people, shall arise.

While the second occurrence of the verb עמד connotes protection,[110] the
meaning of the first occurrence is disputed,[111] with martial and judicial roles

---

[106] Goldingay, *Daniel*, 210. Cf. Bampfylde, "The Prince of the Host," 129–134; Heiser,
"The Divine Council," §6.2–3.

[107] Some scholars have identified this unnamed angel as Gabriel, given the similarities
between Dan 8:15–17 and 10:5–7 (also see 9:1, 20–21 and 11:1). If correct, it would seem
that, in addition to his revelatory charge, Gabriel has a guardianship role. On the militaristic role of Gabriel in Jewish literature, see Michalak, *Angels as Warriors*, 124–125. *Contra* Heiser, "The Divine Council," §6.3, who argues that this unnamed angel outranks Gabriel, not least because Dan 8:16 indicates that the former commands the latter.

[108] Though it should be highlighted that it is possible that the unnamed angel (speaking
in the first-person) mentions the assistance he provides Michael in Dan 11:1: "As for me,
in the first year of Darius the Mede, I stood up to support and strengthen him"; see Goldingay, *Daniel*, 293. On the "jumble of ideas" presented in Dan 10:20–11:2a and the resultant interpretive challenges, see Newsom, *Daniel*, 334–336.

[109] Cf. Collins, *Daniel*, 374–376, here 376: "The idea that Michael is prince of Israel
occurs here for the first time in the Bible, although a slightly earlier occurrence may be
found in 1 En. 20:5. It marks a departure from earlier tradition [i.e., Deut 32:8–9]." As
noted, however, this "departure" from tradition should not be overstated insofar as Israel is
frequently portrayed as the beneficiary of divinely-dispatched angelic assistance; see
Chapter 2.

[110] Followed by the preposition, עַל, the verb עמד means "to protect" or "to defend" (cf.
Esth 8:1; 9:6); see Hartman and DiLella, *Daniel*, 273.

being proposed. There is, however, no reason to pit these nuances against one another, as both are important to the Book of Daniel: whereas the central scene of chapter 7 (vv. 9–14) involves divine judgment, which includes dominion being granted to the "one like a son of man," who most likely should be understood as the leader of Israel's angelic host, chapter 10 (vv. 13, 21) is unambiguous in its description of the martial role of Michael.[112] Thus, even if one concludes that Michael, in theory, has an angelic superior, it can hardly be denied that the final form of the book celebrates Michael's victory, which secures the triumph of those he protects, namely, the people of Israel.

Although chapters 10–12 do not explicitly mention the collective angelic host, it is implied: as noted, Michael is portrayed as coming to the assistance of an unnamed angelic being, who reiterates on two occasions that Michael is his only recourse in the fight against the angelic princes of Persia and Greece. The suggestion, then, is that the other angels are either unwilling to help or, more likely, outmatched.[113] Given that chapters 7–8 describe the collective angelic host as being oppressed by the little horn, it would seem that chapter 10 is underscoring the severity of the persecution by reiterating that even God's angels – with the exception of the unnamed angel and Michael – are too weak to contend successfully against their cosmic enemies.[114]

Daniel 12 makes two important claims regarding the people of God, which serve as a fitting close not only to the last vision but also to the entire book. First, after announcing the role of the Michael at the end of the age, verse 1 states that "at that time your people shall be delivered, everyone who is found written in the book." That is, while the imagery of beasts and the behind-the-scenes glimpses into the heavenly world that dominate Dan 7–12 work together to reveal that history is progressing according to a divinely-ordained plan, verse 1 is clear that the goal of this plan is the deliverance of God's people. Second, verses 2–3 are important for what they say regarding the resurrected state:

2 וְרַבִּים מִיְּשֵׁנֵי אַדְמַת־עָפָר יָקִיצוּ אֵלֶּה לְחַיֵּי עוֹלָם וְאֵלֶּה לַחֲרָפוֹת לְדִרְאוֹן עוֹלָם:
3 וְהַמַּשְׂכִּלִים יַזְהִרוּ כְּזֹהַר הָרָקִיעַ וּמַצְדִּיקֵי הָרַבִּים כַּכּוֹכָבִים לְעוֹלָם וָעֶד:

2 Many of those who sleep in the dust of the earth shall awake, some to everlasting life, and some to shame and everlasting contempt.
3 Those who are wise shall shine like the brightness of the sky, and those who lead many to righteousness, like the stars forever and ever.

---

[111] For discussion of the word, see Collins, *Daniel*, 390.

[112] So Hannah, *Michael and Christ*, 105. Cf. Collins, *Daniel*, 390.

[113] Cf. Todd R. Hanneken, *The Subversion of the Apocalypses in the Book of Jubilees* (EJL 34; Atlanta: Society of Biblical Literature, 2012), 68–69, who argues that Dan 10 is an example of angelic "inefficiency" or "inefficacy" in apocalypses.

[114] Cf. Lacocque, *Daniel*, 213: "Only 'Michael, your prince' is faithful, but he will suffice."

Although well-known for being the only explicit reference to resurrection in the Hebrew Bible,[115] the value of these verses for the present study is in what they say regarding the resurrected state of at least some[116] of those who rise to eternal life. In light of the notion of the astral angelic host, verse 3 is asserting that the "wise" (literally, הַמַּשְׂכִּלִים) will become like angels in heaven at the resurrection. Goldingay suggests that the significance of this distinction is related to the connection between heaven and earth presupposed throughout Dan 7–12: the *Maskilim*, who demonstrate their faithfulness through wise teaching and suffering (cf. 11:33),[117] will be honoured by being granted the prestige and privileges of heaven and its inhabitants, the angels to whom the *Maskilim* correspond.[118] Despite their apparent privilege and distinct status, Collins observes that the orientation of the *Maskilim* – those responsible for the book[119] – is "outward" insofar as they continue to function "within the larger community" and are not antagonistic toward broader Judaism.[120] Such statements are supported by the solidarity Daniel shows with his fellow Jews when he says that he was "confessing my sin and the sin of my people Israel" (9:20).[121]

---

[115] Collins, *Daniel*, 392. Cf. George W. E. Nickelsburg, *Resurrection, Immortality and Eternal Life in Intertestamental Judaism* (HTS 26; Cambridge: Harvard University Press, 1972), 11–27, who notes that this is the earliest reference to resurrection in the Second Temple Period literature.

[116] Hartman and DiLella, *Daniel*, 310, stress that not everyone who is resurrected shines like the stars as this is reserved for the wise. Cf. Collins, *Daniel*, 392: "Only in the case of the wise *Maskilim* are we given any information about the resurrected state."

[117] Newsom, *Daniel*, 352–353, highlights that Dan 12:2–3 ("those who are *wise* ... those who lead *many* to righteousness") contains an intertextual allusion to Isaiah's Suffering Servant song (cf. Isa 52:13; 53:11–12) – but that this does not necessitate an opposition to the violent ways of the Maccabees as per Porphory's interpretation of the "little help" mentioned in Dan 11:34. Cf. Collins, *Daniel*, 386; Goldingay, *Daniel*, 303.

[118] Goldingay, *Daniel*, 308–309, notes that the correspondence between heaven and earth has various manifestations in the Hebrew Bible including the lofty status of the king (e.g., 1 Sam 29:9; 2 Sam 14:17, 20; Isa 9:5) and the prophets "who partake of the honour of a place in Yhwh's council." Thus, Goldingay seems to be saying that the resurrected state of the *Maskilim* will include the angel-like privileges that were associated with respected offices of Israel. Cf. Walter Wifall, "The Status of 'Man' as Resurrection," *ZAW* 90 (1978): 382–394; Nickelsburg, *Resurrection*, 26.

[119] As Nickelsburg, *1 Enoch 1*, 68, notes, the recipients of the book's dream-visions and revelations, as well as its fictional author, are a "stand-in for the real authors," the *Maskilim*. Cf. Collins, *Daniel*, 385.

[120] Collins, *The Apocalyptic Imagination*, 112, also points out that even if "[t]he commitment of the masses appears uncertain, ... [t]here is no evidence of separate organization, such as we find at Qumran. The temple and central institutions of the religion are evidently not rejected ..., although for the present they are defiled."

[121] Cf. Newsom, *Daniel*, 287, who observes that chapter 9 "focuses extensively on the relationship between YHWH and Israel – a topic absent from the other chapters."

VI. Summary

Dan 7–12 reveals the conviction that the happenings of the heavenly realm constituted "what was really going on." And despite the chaotic persecutions that seemingly overwhelmed much of the angelic host, God had decreed that victory would be granted to the angels and their leader, a verdict which rendered certain the deliverance of Israel on earth and the defeat of Antiochus and his forces. More specifically, the outlook of Dan 7–12 is that Yhwh has a high-ranking angelic lieutenant who could be envisioned as Israel's guardian and the leader of the larger angelic host, who, in a sense, constituted heavenly Israel, and whose fates were intimately tied to those of Israel on earth. While Dan 7–12 appears to set apart the *Maskilim* for a privileged, angel-like afterlife, the work as whole is not exclusivist: solidarity with wider Israel is emphasized and thus there is little to suggest that the hope of angelic guardianship or its results – which are ultimately dependent on God's decisive intervention – are reserved only for the pious Jews responsible for the book.

C. 1 Enoch

An amalgam of five traditions,[122] the work known as 1 Enoch is extant in its entirety only in an Ethiopic (Ge'ez) translation dated between the 4th and 6th cent. CE.[123] However, the discovery among the Scrolls[124] of all but one of these traditions has confirmed the long-held assumption that Aramaic was the language of composition of at least four sections of 1 Enoch.[125] Of the

---

[122] The traditions are: The *Book of Watchers* (chapters 1–36); *The Book of Parables or Similitudes* (chapters 37–71); *The Astronomical Book or Book of the Luminaries* (chapters 72–82); *The Book of Dreams* (chapters 83–90); *The Epistle of Enoch* (chapters 91–108). On the traditions and languages of 1 Enoch, see Nickelsburg, *1 Enoch 1*, 7–20.

[123] For the Ethiopic text, see Michael A. Knibb, *The Ethiopic Book of Enoch* (2 vols.; Oxford: Claredon, 1978).

[124] For the Qumran texts of 1 Enoch, see Józef T. Milik, *The Books of Enoch: Aramaic Fragments of Qumran Cave 4* (Oxford: Clarendon, 1976); Stephen J. Pfann et al., eds., *Cryptic Texts and Miscellanea, Part 1: Qumran Cave 4.XXVI* (DJD 36; Oxford: Clarendon, 2000). Also extant are fragments of a Greek translation (likely dating to the late 1st cent. CE), intermediate between the Aramaic original and the Ethiopic translation. For the Greek text, see Matthew Black, *Apocalypsis Henochi Graece* (PVTG 3; Leiden: Brill, 1970).

[125] Only the *Parables* were not found at Qumran, and scholars are thus unsure as to the language of composition of chapters 37–71 – though it is virtually certain that this section had a Semitic (i.e., Aramaic or Hebrew) original; see the discussions of R. H. Charles, *The Book of Enoch, or 1 Enoch* (Oxford: Clarendon, 1912), lxi–lxviii; Knibb, *The Ethiopic Book of Enoch*, 2:7; Nickelsburg, *1 Enoch 1*, 9. Since the *Parables* were not found among the Scrolls, they will not be discussed in detail, here; cf., e.g., Davidson, *Angels at Qum-*

Enochic traditions found at Qumran, parts of the *Book of Watchers*, the *Book of Dreams*, and the *Epistle of Enoch* are relevant to this study.

I. The Book of Watchers (1 Enoch 1–36)

The tradition with which 1 Enoch opens, the *Book of Watchers* (henceforth, *BW*) is widely held to have been completed in the 3rd cent. BCE.[126] The work is clearly enamored with Enoch,[127] taking as its point of departure the limited and cryptic biblical references to this ante-diluvian patriarch to whom the divine plan is revealed. Numerous angels and their functions are mentioned in *BW*, including the notion of a guardian tasked with watching over God's people. This is where I will begin my discussion.

Shortly after outlining how the celestial rebels, Shemihazah and Asael, wrought havoc on the inhabitants of earth (6:3–8:3), *BW* has the first of a number of important references to named angelic leaders who have remained faithful to God:

Then Michael and Sariel and Raphael and Gabriel looked down from the sanctuary of heaven upon the earth and saw much blood shed upon the earth. All the earth was filled with the godlessness and violence that had befallen it (9:1).[128]

---

ran, 20, 25–27. For a detailed discussion of the date of the *Parables*, see George W. E. Nickelsburg and James C. VanderKam, *1 Enoch 2: A Commentary on the Book of 1 Enoch Chapters 37–82* (Hermeneia; Minneapolis: Fortress, 2011), 58–63, who prefer a late 1st cent. BCE/early 1st cent. CE date of composition.

[126] It is thus one of the earliest extant apocalyptic texts, only *The Book of the Luminaries* likely being older; cf. Nickelsburg, *1 Enoch 1*, 7, 169–171; James C. VanderKam, *Enoch and the Growth of an Apocalyptic Tradition* (CBQMS 16; Washington: The Catholic Biblical Association of America, 1984), 111–114. *BW* is itself an amalgam of traditions; on this issue, see Collins, *The Apocalyptic Imagination*, 47.

[127] The biblical "career" of Enoch is as mysterious as it is brief. According to Gen 5:24, "Enoch walked with God; then he was no more, because God took him." As Schäfer, *The Origins of Jewish Mysticism*, 54, succinctly puts it, "these few enigmatic sentences in the Hebrew Bible became the springboard for much speculation in the postbiblical and (later) Christian literature." Moreover, Gen 5:24 serves as *BW*'s impetus: "... Enoch was taken; and none of the sons of men knew where he had been taken, or where he was, or what had happened to him. And his works were with the watchers, and with the holy ones were his days" (1 En. 12:1–2). It is important to note, however, that whereas Gen 5:24 is seemingly a reference to the disappearance of Enoch at the end of his earthly life, *BW* refers to a heavenly journey that precedes Enoch's final removal from earth; see the comments of VanderKam, *Enoch and the Growth*, 130–131; Nickelsburg, *1 Enoch 1*, 233; Angel, *Otherworldly*, 31. The role and significance of Enoch will be addressed, below.

[128] Unless otherwise noted, all translations of 1 Enoch are from Nickelsburg, *1 Enoch 1*; idem and VanderKam, *1 Enoch 2*.

Intriguingly, a list of seven rather than four archangels[129] is found in 1 En. 20:1–8, and it is here that we are informed of Michael's role as it pertains to the people:

These are the names of the holy angels who watch. ... Michael, one of the holy angels who has been put in charge of the good ones of the people (20:5).

These passages, in conjunction with the significance of his implied functions elsewhere in *BW*, provide several relevant items of discussion. First, the preface to the list of seven archangels in chapter 20 highlights the angelological terminology of *BW*. It has been proposed that "holy angels who watch" (20:1)[130] should be understood as a paraphrase of the more common double-designation, "watchers and holy ones."[131] That "holy ones" is a common designation for heavenly beings was discussed earlier in this chapter, but "watchers" is used less frequently in early Jewish texts (cf. Dan 4:10, 14, 20). The term is often considered to be derived from the root, עיר, "to be awake/watchful,"[132] carrying the sense of being alert for various commissioned tasks; in *BW*, angels are charged with the guardianship of heaven and earth.[133]

---

[129] "Archangel(s)" is the term often used by scholars to describe named heavenly leader figures, and it is the designation used in verse 8b of the Greek translation of the book (i.e., ἀρχαγγέλων). In an excursus entitled, "The Four – or Seven – Archangels in Jewish and Early Christian Literature," Nickelsburg, *1 Enoch 1*, 207, notes that the fact that there are four such beings is likely dependent on the four living creatures of Ezek 1–2. On the reception of Ezekiel's vision, see especially David J. Halperin, *The Faces of the Chariot: Early Jewish Responses to Ezekiel's Vision* (Tübingen: Mohr Siebeck, 1988). Other texts that have four archangel figures include the Qumran *War Scroll* (cf. 1QM IX, 15 16; see Chapter 4, below), the *Testament of Abraham* (cf. T. Ab. 12–14), and various Rabbinic texts (cf. Num. Rab. 2:10; Pesiq. Rab. 44; Pirqe R. El. 4). The expansion to seven archangels in 1 En. 20–36, and 81 is due, at least in part, to the necessity of there being an angel at each stop of Enoch's heavenly tour. The Book of Revelation seems to have incorporated both the four and the seven archangel traditions (cf. Rev 1:4; 4:5–8). On this topic, see also Christoph Berner, "The Four (or Seven) Archangels in the First Book of Enoch and Early Jewish Writings of the Second Temple Period," in *Angels: The Concept of Celestial Beings*, 395–409.

[130] So Nickelsburg, *1 Enoch 1*, 295.

[131] In his excursus, "The Watchers and Holy Ones," Nickelsburg, *1 Enoch 1*, 140–141, draws the following terminological conclusions from what he concedes is fragmentary evidence: i.) "watchers" is the angelological term used frequently in *BW* and can be employed as a general designation (i.e., for faithful or rebel angels); while ii.) the double-designation, "holy ones and watchers," is used for angels faithful to God, iii.) the translators used the Greek equivalent of "watchers," ἐγρήγοροι, as a special term for the angelic rebels.

[132] Hence the Greek translation, ἐγρήγορος (cf. LXX Lam 4:14).

[133] Robert P. R. Murray, "The Origin of the Aramaic *'ir*, angel," *Or* 53.2 (1984): 303–317 (cf. Mitchell Dahood, *Psalms I 1–50: A New Translation with Introduction and Com-

But like other texts, *BW* suggests that Israel has a guardian *par excellence* in Michael, who is specified among the archangels listed in chapter 20 for being "in charge of the good ones of the people." Though there is uncertainty on textual grounds as to whether Michael is envisioned here as the angelic protector of the entire nation or a righteous remnant thereof,[134] there is little rationale for limiting the purview of Michael's guardianship to those responsible for *BW*, at least in an overly strict fashion (see below). That *BW* describes Michael as the protector of Israel indicates that his association with a guardianship role pre-dates the Book of Daniel, and at least in his role as guardian of the people, Michael appears to be without angelic peer;[135] *BW* may even indicate that Michael outranks all other angels, as 24:6–25:7 not only mentions the archangel's special connection to the people (in that Michael is the interpreter who announces their glorious future)[136] but the passage also makes a statement on angelic hierarchy: "Then Michael answered me, one of the holy angels who was with me and was their leader ..." (24:6). There is ambiguity as to what exactly is being said of Michael's leadership here,[137] but it is clear that Michael is considered a ranking angel, perhaps the

---

mentary [AB 16; New York: Doubleday, 1966], 55), has argued that the use of עִיר in reference to angels is connected to the guardian deities of the Ugaritic pantheon. Whether or not one accepts Murray's suggestion that this usage of עִיר was suppressed in the Hebrew Bible due to its associations with Semitic guardian deities, it is apparent that the faithful angels of 1 Enoch have been charged with an attentive guardianship of various sorts (e.g., 6:7; 14:21–23; 20:1; cf. 39:12–13; 40:2; 61:12; 71:7); see the excursus of Nickelsburg, *1 Enoch 1*, 140. It is interesting to note that in Deut 32:11 – which immediately follows the statement of Deut 32:8–9 that heavenly beings watch over other nations but that Yhwh himself is Israel's guardian – the verb עִיר contributes to the description of Yhwh's guardianship of the nation: "as an eagle *stirs up* (יָעִיר) its nest, and hovers over its young; as it spreads its wings, takes them up, and bears them aloft on it pinions, Yhwh alone guided them ... ." See Murray, "The Origin," 307; Tigay, *Deuteronomy*, 304.

[134] See Nickelsburg, *1 Enoch 1*, 294–296, who notes that while λαός can be a technical term for Israel (cf. H. Strathamann, "λαός," *TDNT* 4:34–35), Michael's special relationship to the "righteous" and "chosen" in 25:4–5 may be a reference to a faithful remnant of the people. I will return to the subject of the identity of the "chosen"/"righteous," below.

[135] Even if the roles of various angels overlap to a certain extent; i.e., *BW* indicates that *other angels* have been tasked for roles that benefit the people of God (e.g., just as Michael is not the only angel to intercede on behalf of humanity [cf. 9:1; see below]), Raphael's charge to watch over the wicked souls awaiting eschatological judgment contributes to the future well-being of the faithful, albeit indirectly (cf. 20:3; 22:3, 6).

[136] On Michael's relatively infrequent role as an interpreter in early Judaism, see the brief discussion of Hannah, *Michael and Christ*, 47–48. The term used for "leader" in the Greek translation, ἡγέομαι, is the same word used in LXX Sir 17:17 to refer to the celestial guardians of the Gentile nations.

[137] Nickelsburg, *1 Enoch 1*, 314, points out that it is unclear whether Michael outranks the named archangels or whether he stands at the head of another group of angels under his command (i.e., his personal retinue).

highest.[138] Additionally, 9:1–11 states that the angels have an intercessory role: on account of the suffering wrought by the sin of the rebel watchers, Michael and the other angels hear the prayers of suffering humanity.[139] As noted above, intercession has priestly connotations (e.g., Exod 28:29; cf. Dan 9:22; 10:1–5), and the language of "approach" may support a sacerdotal reading of the text.[140] In turn, these observations align with an important facet of *BW*: the depiction of heaven as a temple. In fact, *BW* is often noted as a key example of an early Jewish text in which the Jerusalem temple is cast as the terrestrial reflection of an archetypal heavenly sanctuary.

While the text does not explicitly refer to heaven as a temple or angels as priests, both are strongly intimated in chapters 9–16, the centerpiece of which is the account of Enoch's ascent in 14:8–23.[141] More specifically, terms from the Hebrew Bible and LXX are used to describe the angels' posture[142] or their approach,[143] as well as language that emphasizes the holiness of God's dwelling place,[144] have prompted many scholars to conclude that the archetype/celestial equivalent of the earthly sanctuary is in view.[145] Heaven's

---

[138] In addition to calling Michael "one of the 'holy' angels," some Ethiopic manuscripts of 1 En. 24:6 add "and honoured"; see Nickelsburg, *1 Enoch 1*, 313.

[139] On Michael as a heavenly intercessor in early Judaism, see Moses, "Tangible Prayer," 140–141; Hannah, *Michael and Christ*, 42–45; Nickelsburg, *1 Enoch 1*, 208–210.

[140] On the cultic use of קרב and προσέρχομαι as well as the reconstruction of 9:4, see Nickelsburg, *1 Enoch 1*, 203, 211; cf. 1 En. 14:23, which is discussed, below.

[141] As noted earlier in this chapter, scholars have often observed the similarities between and 1 En. 14:8–23, Dan 7:9–14, and a scene from the *Book of Giants* (4Q530), but there is little consensus on the direction of dependence. Unlike the scene in the Book of Giants, the scenes in Daniel and *BW* take place in heaven. On the similarities between 1 En. 14 and the heavenly scene found in Isa 6, see Kelley Coblentz Bautch, "The Heavenly Temple, the Prison in the Void, and the Uninhabited Paradise: Otherworldly Sites in the Book of Watchers," in *Other Worlds and Their Relation to This World*, 40–41.

[142] E.g., στάσις (1 En. 12:4; cf. LXX 2 Chr 30:16; 35:10).

[143] E.g., ἐγγίζω (1 En. 14:23; cf. LXX Ezek 40:46; 42:13). Commenting on οἱ ἐγγίζοντες, George W. E. Nickelsburg, "Enoch, Levi, and Peter: Recipients of Revelation in Upper Galilee," *JBL* 100 (1981): 585 n. 37, observes that ἐγγίζω, which often translates קרב or נגש in the Hebrew Bible, can have "technical cultic connotations" (e.g., Ezek 44:13–16; 45:4); Nickelsburg also points out the priestly sentiment of being in the temple "day and night" (e.g., 1 Chr 23:3; Josephus, *Ant.* 7.363–367; Luke 2:37). In the context of 1 En. 12:4, it is likely that στάσις translates מעמד, which refers to the priestly "station" or "course" (e.g., 1 Chr 23:28); see Heinz-Wolfgang Kuhn, *Enderwartung und gegenwärtiges Heil: Untersuchungen zu den Gemeindeliedern von Qumran mit einem Anhang über Eschatologie und Gegenwart in der Verküngdigung Jesu* (SUNT 4; Göttingen: Vandenhoeck and Ruprecht, 1966), 70–72. Cf. Angel, *Otherworldly*, 28.

[144] E.g., קדשי שמיא (1 En. 9:1 = 4Q201 1 IV, 7; cf. Ps 134:2; Dan 8:13); ἁγίασμα (1 En. 12:4; cf. LXX Ezra 9:8; 2 Chr 20:8; 1 Macc 1:37).

[145] See the helpful overview of Nickelsburg, *1 Enoch 1*, 271. Cf. Angel, *Otherworldly*, 28–30, who summarizes as follows: "[T]he upper realm is described in terms which relate rather precisely to the three major architectural sections of the Jerusalem temple, the אולם

sanctuary is also the place which the rebel watchers forsook,[146] hence the severity of the watchers' sin (cf. 9:1; 12:4; 15:3).

This depiction of heaven as a temple, along with Michael's aforementioned intercessory role, are consistent with the proposal that his actions, including his binding of the rebel angels in order to cleanse the earth from impurity and wrongdoing, serve to portray Michael as a celestial high priest. More specifically, it has been posited that the role of the Michael-led angels in 10:11–11:2 is an etiological allegory for the *Yom Kippur* scapegoat ceremony found in Lev 16:1–34: that is, just as the high priest sends the sin-laden goat into the wilderness, Michael leads the way in rounding up, binding, and consigning the sinful watchers to their punishment.[147]   Therefore, Michael,

---

(1 Kgs 6:3; cf. Ezek 40:48), היכל (1 Kgs 6:17; cf. Ezek 41:1), and דביר/קדש הקדשים (1 Kgs 6:5, 16; cf. Ezek 41:4)"; also see Himmelfarb, *Ascent to Heaven*, 10–11; Schäfer, *The Origins of Jewish Mysticism*, 66. Most recently, see Philip Church, *Hebrews and the Temple: Attitudes to the Temple in Second Temple Judaism and in Hebrews* (NovTSup 171; Leiden: Brill, 2017), 151–156, who understands *BW's* heavenly temple "not so much as a reflection of the earthly temple [but] as a replacement of it." *Contra* Crispin H. T. Fletcher-Louis, "On Angels, Men and Priests (Ben Sira), the Qumran Sabbath Songs and the Yom Kippur Avodah)," in *Gottesdienst und Engel im antiken Judentum und frühen Christentum* (eds., Jörg Frey and Michael R. Jost; WUNT 2/446; Tübingen: Mohr Siebeck, 2017), 154, who denies that Enoch enters a macrocosmic heavenly temple but instead advocates a reading of *BW* that understands chapter 14 as referring to a microcosmic depiction of the Jerusalem temple, i.e., "a roofed sanctuary that equates to the roofed sanctuary of Israel's temple. ... There is no temple 'up there' synchronised to a temple 'down here' in *1 Enoch*." I will briefly return to Fletcher-Louis' interpretation in Chapter 5. Another recent study challenging the consensus interpretation is that of Philip F. Esler, *God's Court and Courtiers in the Book of Watchers: Re-Interpreting Heaven in 1 Enoch 1–36* (Eugene: Cascade Books, 2017), who has advocated that *BW* presents heaven not as a temple/sanctuary in which angelic priests minister but instead as a royal court serviced by angelic courtiers.

[146] In the words of Nickelsburg, *1 Enoch 1*, 269, "Sexual intercourse was given by God to the human race to assure the continuity of one's line. The watchers, being immortal, needed no such instrument. Nonetheless, they have lusted and acted like human beings and have defiled their heavenly and holy status through sexual contact with earthly women ... . The sin is compounded by the fact that watchers are priests in the heavenly sanctuary. Thus their holiness is not simply a special pure state that has been polluted. It is that state which allows them to draw near to God and minister to him. Since they have contaminated that state and violated God's order of creation, they are banished from his presence in heaven ... ."

[147] For this interpretation, see Paul D. Hanson, "Rebellion in Heaven, Azazel, and Euhemeristic Heroes in 1 Enoch 6–11," *JBL* 96 (1977): 220–226; Devorah Dimant, "1 Enoch 6–11: A Methodological Perspective," in *SBL Seminar Papers, 1978* (SBLSP 1; Missoula: Scholars Press, 1978), 326–327; Fletcher-Louis, *All the Glory*, 463; Nickelsburg, *1 Enoch 1*, 44; Angel, *Otherworldly*, 29. For later texts that specify a high-priestly role for Michael, see 3 Bar. 11–16; As. Mos. 10.2; T. Levi 2–5; T. Dan 6; b. Hag. 12b. On Michael's exceptional priestly prerogatives in *3 Baruch* as foreshadowed by *BW*, see the comment of Moses, "Tangible Prayer," 140–141.

though he is not specifically named, may be one of the angels permitted to approach God's throne in 14:23, and, if this interpretation is accepted, Michael's dual role in *BW* is that of guardian of God's people and celestial high priest.

If some angels in *BW* were envisioned as having a role analogous to the earthly high priest insofar as they were allowed to serve in closest proximity to God,[148] Enoch's vision of the heavenly temple may suggest that those not permitted to approach God were thought to be priests of a lower rank, thus explaining their non-access to the innermost part of the heavenly sanctuary. That is, even the language used to describe the angelic multitudes who could not come closest to God may still be indicative of cultic activity,[149] as 14:22 reads as follows: "[F]laming fire encircled him, and a great fire stood (παρειστήκει) by him; and none of those about him approached him. Ten thousand times ten thousand stood (ἐστήκασιν) before him; but he needed no counselor ... ." The parallelism of verse 22 can be seen in the following table:

Table 4: Parallelism of 1 En. 14:22[150]

... fire stood by him	none ... approached him
... ten thousands stood before him	he needed no counselor

Given that the "fire" is parallel to the "ten thousands times ten thousand," which is almost certainly a reference to angels, it is plausible that the former is angelic, as well.[151] Furthermore, the fire//ten thousands are apparently not in closest proximity to the divine throne, but they are nevertheless said to *stand* before God, with the verbs ἵστημι and especially παρίστημι being used in the LXX and elsewhere of priests and Levites in the earthly tabernacle/temple[152] or of angels in heaven[153] to describe acts of service and wor-

---

[148] Nickelsburg, *1 Enoch 1*, 265.

[149] Nickelsburg, *1 Enoch 1*, 265.

[150] Cf. Nickelsburg, *1 Enoch 1*, 265, who provides a similar table.

[151] It is interesting to note that another Aramaic text, *4QWords of Michael*, refers to the angelic host as גדודי נורא, "troops of fire" (4Q529 2). Alternatively, the description of the fire may be approximating *Songs of the Sabbath Sacrifice*'s depiction of the celestial sanctuary, which has been referred to as "animate"; see Chapter 5, below.

[152] E.g., ἵστημι (cf. 1 Chr 23:30; 2 Chr 29:11); παρίστημι (cf. Deut 10:8, 17:12; Judg 20:28).

[153] E.g., ἵστημι (cf. 2 Chr 18:18); παρίστημι (Job 1:6, 2:1; T. Sol. 5:9, 26:9; Apoc. Ab. 7:11; Luke 1:19). Additionally, Nickelsburg, *1 Enoch 1*, 265, points out that παρίστημι is used in LXX Dan 7:10 to describe the angelic myriads who stand before "the Ancient of Days."

ship.[154] Thus, the angelic priesthood of the heavenly temple as depicted in chapter 14 may be approximating the priesthood of the earthly sanctuary or other depictions of the heavenly sanctuary insofar as priestly leadership is tiered.[155]

As for why *BW* posits heaven as having angelic guardians and priests, it is commonly asserted that the text addresses events of the 3rd cent. BCE by transposing political and religious concerns to the "mythological plane"[156] in that the chaos imposed by warring foreign powers – specifically the *Diadochoi*[157] – and the immorality of (some of) the Jerusalem priests[158] are said to be allegorized in *BW* by the boundary-transgressing watchers, who have forsaken their priest-like duties in heaven. But despite the widespread recognition that *BW* is concerned with matters of a priestly nature, the extent to which the apocalyptic symbolism of the text can or should be pressed for historical realities is a matter of debate;[159] there is also disagreement as to what

---

[154] G. Bertram, "παρίστημι," *TDNT* 5:838, explains that in the LXX the word often carries the meaning of "respectful standing or service" before kings or superiors (e.g., 1 Kgs 10:8; 2 Kgs 5:25; Isa 60:10; Prov 22:29; 2 Chr 9:7), and that "only with the help of the particular relation of the servant to the king can one understand the religious and cultic use of [the word] ... ."

[155] The Jerusalem temple is served by, in ascending order of authority, Levites, priests, and the high priest. Furthermore, while *BW* suggests that some angels served in a priestly capacity, it is like other texts in that it is silent as to what percentage of the entire angelic host were so tasked; see the comments of Nickelsburg, *1 Enoch 1*, 44, 265.

[156] Collins, *The Apocalyptic Imagination*, 51–52.

[157] Nickelsburg, *1 Enoch 1*, 170, suggests that the fallen watchers represent the *Diadochoi*, the hubristic successors to Alexander the Great: "Such a context may allow a more specific definition of the myth's message and function. The image of divine begetting is reminiscent of the claims that some of the *Diadochoi* had gods as their fathers. If this similarity is to the point, the myth would be an answer to these claims in the form of a kind of parody. The author would be saying, 'Yes, their fathers were divine; however, they were not gods, but demons – angels who rebelled against the authority of God.'" Also see idem, "Apocalyptic and Myth in 1 Enoch 6–11," *JBL* 96 (1977): 383–405; Rüdiger Bartelmus, *Heroentum in Israel und seiner Umwelt* (AThANT 65; Zurich: Theologischer Verlag, 1979), 180–183. Most recently, see Loren T. Stuckenbruck, "Coping with Alienating Experience: Four Strategies in Second Temple Texts," in *Rejection: God's Refugees in Biblical and Contemporary Perspective* (ed., Stanley E. Porter; Eugene: Pickwick Publications, 2015), 61.

[158] See especially David Suter, "Fallen Angel, Fallen Priest: The Problem of Family Purity in 1 Enoch 6–16," *HUCA* 50 (1979): 119; also see Nickelsburg, "Enoch, Levi, and Peter," 575–600. There is debate concerning the specifics and extent of the priestly issues reflected in *BW*, and I will return to these, below.

[159] E.g., Annette Yoshiko Reed, *Fallen Angels and the History of Judaism and Christianity: The Reception of the Enochic Literature* (New York: Cambridge University Press, 2005) 63, is wary of Nickelsburg's fallen watchers = *Diadochoi* interpretation, in large part because she questions the assumption that *BW* is necessarily representative of a marginalized or oppressed group. She suggests instead that "it may be more heuristic to focus on

specific priestly sins may have provoked the ire of *BW*'s authors[160] and how strongly *BW* should be read as a critique of the Jerusalem temple.[161] While the *Diadochoi* and priestly concerns could have been motivating factors for the authors of *BW*, the non-specificity of the text serves an important purpose;[162] and so long as it is recognized that the heavenly realm was consid-

---

its continuities with broader trends in postexilic Judaism, viewing its appeal to the fallen angels in terms of the reemergence of ancient, mythic imagery in late biblical prophecy and understanding its interest in the origins of evil in terms of the concern for theodicy in Wisdom books like Job and Qohelet" (cf. Cross, *Canaanite Myth and Hebrew Epic*, 343–346). While Reed is right to caution against an overly explicit reading of the text, the possibility that historical referents – e.g., the *Diadochoi* – were at least partial impetuses for the presentation of the fallen watchers is not mutually exclusive of a reading that has also been shaped by the concerns and motifs operative in contemporaneous Jewish literature. Reed herself is open to the view that priestly concerns inform the myth.

[160] Insofar as the actions of the watchers are said to be an allegory for the sins of earthly priests, there is discussion as to what sins are in view. Whereas some have emphasized that the temple-polluting sin in question was that priests were marrying foreign women (e.g., Himmelfarb, *A Kingdom of Priests*, 21–25), others have suggested that authors were also concerned that the Jerusalem priests had sexual contact with women who were in a state of menstrual impurity (e.g., Suter, "Fallen Angel, Fallen Priest," 119; Nickelsburg, *1 Enoch 1*, 271–272).

[161] On the one hand, Nickelsburg, "Enoch, Levi, and Peter," 586, considers the tradition found in chapters 12–16 to be a statement that the Jerusalem temple and its priesthood were considered defiled and "therefore under the irrevocable judgment of God"; cf. Schäfer, *The Origins of Jewish Mysticism*, 66–67. On the other hand, Himmelfarb, *A Kingdom of Priests*, 20–21, argues that *BW*'s criticism of the Jerusalem temple is somewhat muted in comparison to the temple critiques of later texts: "The preference for the heavenly temple over the earthly in *1 Enoch* 12–16 suggests that the affairs of the temple were not being conducted in a manner that lived up to the author's standards. ... But chapters 12–16 report that all is not well in the heavenly temple either. Some of the priests of the heavenly temple have abandoned their posts; they have descended to earth, undertaken marriages unsuitable to them, and reveal secrets that should not have been made known, to devastating effect. ... But it is important to notice that according to *BW* many watchers remain in heaven performing their duties. Thus, the criticism of earthly priests that chapters 12–16 read in the story of the descent of the watchers is not directed at all priests, and thus it appears that in the view of the author of these chapters, the earthly temple, despite its problems, remains a viable temple – just like the heavenly temple." Cf. eadem, *Ascent to Heaven*, 15–22. In a similar vein, Reed, *Fallen Angels*, 63, is suspicious of an approach that equates the social settings and viewpoints of the various traditions of 1 Enoch; i.e., one should not assume that the nature and severity of the 2nd cent. BCE temple critiques of the *Animal Apocalypse* in the *Book of Dreams* or the *Apocalypse of Weeks* in the *Epistle of Enoch* are necessarily the same as those of a 3rd cent. BCE work like *BW*. Cf. Klawans, *Purity, Sacrifice, and the Temple*, 128–144, who highlights the scholarly tendency to exaggerate anti-Jerusalem temple sentiments in texts which speak of a heavenly sanctuary, including *BW*.

[162] Collins, *The Apocalyptic Imagination*, 51–52, who argues as follows: "By telling the story of the watchers rather than of the *Diadochoi* or the priesthood, *1 En.* 1–36 becomes a

ered the "truer, more real world"[163] – that is, the archetypal significance of
the heavenly realm is not unduly minimized by seeing it only in allegorical
terms – my own sense is that this transposition (and thereby aggrandizing) of
events to the mythical plane would have been effective in reassuring those for
whom *BW* was written. Specifically, the knowledge that Michael is carrying
out what would become his traditional role as Israel's patron[164] – in addition
to the fact that other righteous angels were incarcerating the celestial rebels
(10:4–15; 21:1–10) and would be part of God's decisive eschatological arrival (1:1–9)[165] – would have served to lessen the fears wrought by the watchers' malevolence. Similarly, if some Jerusalem priests had succumbed to
various temptations (that may or may not have been related to the warring
Diadochoi and other foreign influences),[166] the revelation of a pure, heavenly

---

paradigm which is not restricted to one historical situation but can be applied whenever an
analogous situation arises. ... The resolution of the ancient conflict generated by the
watchers emerges with an inevitability that guarantees a similar resolution of the conflicts
of the Hellenistic age. The superhuman status of the actors takes the action out of the
sphere of human control and places the immediate situation in a deterministic perspective
which also serves to relieve the anxiety."

[163] So Alexander, *Mystical Texts*, 61, whose descriptor I quote here in order to emphasize the primacy of the heavenly realm in the Second Temple Period worldview. Note, for
instance, the comment of Collins, *The Apocalyptic Imagination*, 48, who states that the
celestial realm "forms the *backdrop* of the human action [emphasis mine]" in *BW*. His
statement and the one quoted above are sound provided that they are not taken to mean that
BW's authors considered these angels in the same way modern scholars do. As Collins
says elsewhere (idem, *Daniel*, 318): "For the modern Western critic, only the human people are real. For the Jewish visionary, however, heavenly counterparts were not only real
but vital to human destiny." For additional comments on the reality of the heavenly realm
and a call not to minimize its importance and/or archetypal significance, see Angel, *Otherworldly*, 101–105; Stuckenbruck, "Coping with Alienating Experience," 61 n. 7; idem,
"Theological Anthropology and the Enochic Book of Watchers (1 En. 6–16)," in *Dust of
the Ground and Breath of Life (Gen 2:7) – The Problem of a Dualistic Anthropology in
Early Judaism and Christianity* (eds., Jacques T.A.G.M. van Ruiten and George H. van
Kooten; TBN 20; Leiden: Brill, 2016), 32, 34.

[164] So Nickelsburg, *1 Enoch 1*, 295.

[165] On the sufficiency of the revelation that the angelic rebels will be incarcerated until
the final judgment, see Collins, *The Apocalyptic Imagination*, 58–59. Cf. Davidson, *Angels at Qumran*, 321, who points out that the dualism of the Enochic texts should be differentiated from that found in the Qumran sectarian texts insofar as in the latter a prompt
incarceration follows the angelic rebellion, whereas in the former the wicked angels remain
in a state of rebellion until the eschaton.

[166] On this point, see George W. E. Nickelsburg, "The We and the Other in the
Worldview of 1 Enoch, the Dead Sea Scrolls, and Other Early Jewish Texts," in *The "Other" in Second Temple Judaism: Essays in Honour of John J. Collins* (eds., Daniel C. Harlow et al.; Grand Rapids: Eerdmans, 2011), 264, who remarks that "by attributing this
broad spectrum of evils to supernatural intervention, the myth asserts that these evils cannot be reduced to the sinful deeds of the humans who carry them out – generals and their

temple and its angelic priesthood would have served to encourage Jews that the actions of *some* rebellious priests on earth ultimately do not negate the efficacy of the heavenly temple or its terrestrial counterpart in Jerusalem.[167]

To appreciate fully these angelological features of *BW*, it is necessary to review additional facets of the text. First, whoever the "righteous" and "chosen" are, it is likely that they are the "recipients" of *BW's* revelation of the heavenly world.[168] Second, the importance and authority of this revealed knowledge is heightened by a.) the subtle yet noticeable downplaying of the Mosaic Torah vis-à-vis the content of the vision;[169] and b.) the pseudepigraphic attribution of the vision to the enigmatic Enoch, who is portrayed as

---

armies, sorcerers and prognosticators, craftsmen, and fornicators. They are the functions of a malevolent demonic realm that is bent on the destruction of God's creation and created order. In the wake of the wars waged by the Hellenistic kings and the penetration of Hellenistic culture, the poets who created these mythic materials experienced reality with an intensity that led them to posit a force qualitatively greater and other than the humans who perpetrated these evils."

[167] In short, I am sympathetic to readings of *BW* that do not see the Jerusalem temple as profaned and rejected, at least irrevocably so; e.g., Klawans, *Purity, Sacrifice, and the Temple*, 131–145, here 131, who advocates for an interpretation similar to what I am suggesting: "That *some* of God's own angels will fall into transgression certainly does not constitute a prediction that *all* earthly priests will inevitably fall short [emphasis retained]." He also rightly points out that, void of a specific critique of the Jerusalem temple, the notion of an archetypal heavenly sanctuary actually serves to bolster the efficacy (and thus, authority) of the earthly one.

[168] Nickelsburg, *1 Enoch 1*, 67, conjectures that *BW*'s writers may have been preeminent among the chosen/righteous but suggests this cautiously: "[W]ho [the authors of *BW*] were, and to what extent they were in any sense superiors of other colleagues, is a secret that is hidden behind their pseudepigraphic mask." On the same subject, Reed, *Fallen Angels*, 61–66, is also cautious.

[169] An indication that the authors of *BW* should be differentiated from other Jews is how the Torah is used. On the one hand, the language and imagery of Deut 33 – the so-called "blessing of Moses" – have been detected in the opening lines of *BW* (cf. 1:1–9); references to the blessings of God's people and a theophany at Sinai are common to both texts, and the presence of these features has led some scholars to the conclusion that the Sinai-revealed Torah would be the basis for the eschatological judgment described in these verses; cf. James C. VanderKam, "The Theophany of 1 Enoch 1:3b–7, 9," *VT* 23 (1973): 136–38; Lars Hartman, *Asking for a Meaning: A Study of 1 Enoch 1–5* (Lund: Gleerup, 1979), 42–44. But it has also been highlighted that the Mosaic covenant does not occupy center stage in *BW*. For example, whereas God comes *from* Sinai in Deut 33:2, God descends *to* Sinai in 1 En. 1:4; as Collins, *The Apocalyptic Imagination*, 48, points out, "this slight change is significant. Sinai has a place in Enoch's revelation, but it is not the ultimate source." Nickelsburg, *1 Enoch 1*, 52, summarizes this reading as follows: "[The authors] have leapfrogged Moses and identified Enoch as the primordial recipient of all heavenly wisdom. This devaluing of the character of Moses is evident at the very beginning of the corpus (1:1–9), which places in the mouth of Enoch a text that was modeled after the Blessing of Moses (Deut 33)." Cf. Davidson, *Angels at Qumran*, 321.

an exalted, angel-like priest,[170] and who likely, in some sense, represents *BW*'s authors.[171] Third, despite its focus on authoritative revelation, *BW* is not rigidly exclusivist. Nickelsburg describes the "righteous"/"chosen" as "the *true* Israel,"[172] but this may be too strong a characterization, especially if the same designation is used to refer to other, more stringent groups.[173] As

---

[170] Enoch is assigned two priestly privileges of note: access to the innermost part of the heavenly sanctuary and an intercessory role, which are captured in God's response to the patriarch in 15:2: "Go and say to the watchers of heaven, who sent you to petition in their behalf, 'You should petition in behalf of men, and not men in behalf of you.'" On Zech 3:7 as influential in priests gaining prophet-like access to the divine council in early Jewish texts, see Heiser, "The Divine Council," §5.3. VanderKam, *Enoch and the Growth*, 131, notes that Enoch not only associates with angels in *BW*, but his actions also imply that there are heavenly beings he outranks. Angel, *Otherworldly*, 31–32, suggests that Michael's intercessory role is (at least partially) taken up by Enoch (cf. 12:3–6; 14:4–7; 15:2–16:4) and that Enoch's access to the divine throne is all the more profound in light of the fact that some (most?) angels were not granted such privileges. Cf. Coblentz Bautch, "The Heavenly Temple, the Prison in the Void, and the Uninhabited Paradise," 38; Himmelfarb, *A Kingdom of Priests*, 18; Nickelsburg, "Enoch, Levi, and Peter," 576–587; Michael E. Stone, "Enoch and the Fall of the Angels," *DSD* 22 (2015): 342–357. The conclusion of Schäfer, *The Origins of Jewish Mysticism*, 62, that Enoch's status is indicative of *BW* being "anti-angelic," is an overstatement. On the possibility that Enoch's scribal activity (cf. 12:4; 13:6; 15:1) served to mitigate the tension that existed in early Judaism between the hereditary office of the priesthood and the non-hereditary scribal office, see Himmelfarb, *A Kingdom of Priests*, 30.

[171] Nickelsburg, *1 Enoch 1*, 67, states that in the same way the namesake of the Book of Daniel is a stand-in for the *Maskilim*, Enoch is a stand-in for *BW*'s authors. Rowland, *The Open Heaven*, 232–247, goes even further by suggesting that the thermal descriptions in 14:8–23 reflect the physical aspects of the visionary's ascent experience. Davidson, *Angels at Qumran*, 315, emphasizes the authority carried by the scene, but he does not offer a suggestion as to who might stand behind Enoch. Similarly, Schäfer, *The Origins of Jewish Mysticism*, 64–66, highlights the authority inherent in Enoch's ascent, the ultimate goal of which is to benefit Israel, but he does not allow that the details of the vision reflect the experience of a visionary. In short, I see no reason to drive a wedge between the authoritative benefit of casting Enoch as the recipient of the vision, and the possibility that Enoch is a stand-in for *BW*'s authors, who perhaps had visionary experiences of their own. On this point, Alexander, *Mystical Texts*, 90, is surely correct: "Ascent was not just something done by certain spiritual superheroes in the past (though their example was important in showing it was possible), but something that could still be achieved here and now." Given that *BW* envisions heaven as a temple, Enoch's role cannot be understated, as the privilege accorded the patriarch may be suggestive of the belief that the righteous could be granted that which was normally the prerogative of angelic priests. On the impact of Enoch's ascent in later Jewish Doppelgänger traditions, see Andrei A. Orlov, *The Greatest Mirror: Heavenly Counterparts in the Jewish Pseudepigrapha* (New York: SUNY, 2017) 8–11.

[172] So Nickelsburg, *1 Enoch 1*, 147; emphasis retained.

[173] I.e., the texts I will examine in Chapters 4–5 are more appropriately characterized as rigidly exclusivist or "sectarian," and I will use the designation "the true Israel" to refer to how the Qumran movement understood their reconstitution of Israel's covenant.

some have noted, even if the myth of the watchers reflects, in part, a priestly dispute among Second Temple Period Jews, the "party lines are not clearly drawn."[174] The epithet "plant of righteous" (10:16c) echoes biblical language for ethnic Israel (cf. Isa 60:21; 61:3),[175] and while it has been proposed that the use of this language was an elitist usurpation by *BW's* authors,[176] I see no reason to rule out that this "plant" was not ultimately envisioned as inclusive of other Jews,[177] who perhaps, it was hoped, would be stirred by the revealed knowledge and wisdom of the "chosen"/"righteous." Stuckenbruck has argued that use of the plant metaphor here does not appear to be as exclusivist as it is in another non-sectarian text, *4QInstruction.*[178] Verse 16 also declares that this plant "will become a blessing" (cf. Gen 12:1–3), which may be related to the remarkably inclusive statements that "all the sons of men will be-

---

[174] Collins, *The Apocalyptic Imagination*, 72. Cf. Nickelsburg, "The We and the Other," 264–265, who, even though elsewhere emphasizes what he considers to be the exclusivist nature of *BW*, acknowledges that the main antagonists of the text are the "nonhuman Other" (i.e., *not* other Jews or even Gentiles). I will return to this insight, below. Also see Luca Arcari, "'Minority' as a Self-Definition Discourse in Second Temple Judaism," *SMSR* 83 (2017): 350, who, though arguing for the polemical import of 1 Enoch, rightly questions if "the myth *always* questions ... the vision of the world professed by those who controlled the Temple of Jerusalem ... [emphasis retained]."

[175] On the background of the term in early Jewish texts, see Patrick A. Tiller, "The 'Eternal Planting' in the Dead Sea Scrolls," *DSD* 4 (1997): 312–335, esp. 315–319, which address its use in *BW*. Cf. Nickelsburg, *1 Enoch 1*, 444–445.

[176] E.g., Nickelsburg, *1 Enoch 1*, 226.

[177] See, e.g., Collins, *The Apocalyptic Imagination*, 72: "In *1 Enoch* 10:16 the plant of righteousness and truth is apparently Israel, and we are not told of any other offshoot." Cf. Torleif Elgvin, "The Mystery to Come: Early Essene Theology of Revelation," in *Qumran between the Old and New Testaments* (eds., Frederick H. Cryer and Thomas L. Thompson; JSOTSup 290; Sheffield: Sheffield Academic Press, 1998), 126–128, who comments on the use of the term in 1 Enoch and other texts: "the designation 'eternal planting' indicates that the community [represented by each text's author] is the nucleus of the future-restored Israel." Elgvin suggests that the "eternal plant" metaphor contributes to an exclusivist notion of "remnant" and compares the use in 1 Enoch to similar language in the writings of the Qumran movement (cf. 1QS VIII, 5–6; XI, 7–9). But referring to an author's community as the "nucleus" of Israel presupposes a measure of openness to outsiders, at least potentially.

[178] On the complex editing of 1 En. 10 and the relationship this has to the use of the "plant" metaphor, see Loren T. Stuckenbruck, "4QInstruction and the Possible Influence of Early Enochic Traditions: An Evaluation," in *The Wisdom Texts from Qumran and the Development of Sapiential Thought* (eds., Charlotte Hempel, Armin Lange, and Herman Lichtenberger; BETL 69; Leuven: Leuven University Press, 2002), 253–254, who suggests that "the scope of the community in *4QInstruction* seems to be narrower [than that envisioned in *BW*], if 'plant(ing)' [in *4QInstruction*] is strictly equivalent to a particular group within historical Israel." I will discuss *4QInstruction* later in this chapter.

come righteous" and that "all the people will worship [God]" (10:21).[179] Though a quick reading might suggest some tension with *BW's* judgment of wickedness, these verses reveal strong universalistic leanings.[180] Focusing on the anthropology of the text, such "openness" in *BW* has been explained as follows:

> For all its rejection of aberrant culture and of the oppression that comes through it, this story's essential mythic character imparts an extraordinary openness that holds the existence of a community of obedient Jews in tension with the existence of a human species which, though perhaps largely aligned with the demonic world, is nevertheless created by God and, in itself has not set the world down the wrong path. The Enochic tradition at this point may be lamenting the tyranny and coercive domination on the part of groups like the Seleucid overlords and their conduits in the Jewish priesthood. However, the text does not descend into reductionist demonization of these groups: they were and remain human beings, who though to be held responsible and punished for their activities, do not provide any warrant for a destruction of humanity as a whole. *1 Enoch* 6–16 does not, then, present a 'social dualism' that pits one group of humans against another; instead, it is the watchers who have breached the boundaries that distinguish the heavenly from the earthly sphere ... . The fundamental distinction between human nature ... , on the one hand, and the demonic (which by its very nature is a perversion of the created order), on the other, keeps humanity in principle and as a whole within the purview of divine purpose of redemption.[181]

Indeed, *BW's* emphasis is seemingly not on the demise of wicked people *per se*, but on the destruction of wicked "deeds" (10:16, 20).[182] Lastly, Reed has challenged the assumption that the ascent or otherworldly journey apocalypses are necessarily the product of small, isolated, antiestablishment groups, and instead points to an emphasis on "an apocalyptic epistemology that celebrates the didactic dimension of cosmological, geographical, and ouranographical knowledge."[183] In light of the fact that the fallen watchers have

---

[179] As Nickelsburg, *1 Enoch 1*, 226, observes, "The reference to the plant's becoming a blessing may well be an allusion to Gen 12:2 ... in which case the corresponding unit in [v. 21] may be construing that blessing in terms of the conversion of the nations, a motif that would accord well with Gen [12:3c]." Stuckenbruck, "Theological Anthropology," 34, is correct, however, when he notes that *how* the righteous might influence the nations is ambiguous insofar as *BW* "does not draw a direct line of continuity between 'the plant of righteous' and the deliverance of humanity from destruction ... ."

[180] Cf. Nickelsburg, "The We and the Other," 265; Collins, *The Apocalyptic Imagination*, 56.

[181] See Stuckenbruck, "Theological Anthropology," 32–33, who also notes how *BW* invokes the concepts of new beginnings and an openness to humankind in general (i.e., not just pious Jews) as per Isa 65–66 and Gen 6–9. For further on the Noahic background of the passage, see idem, "4QInstruction and the Possible Influence," 253–254.

[182] So Stuckenbruck, "Theological Anthropology," 32 n. 45.

[183] Reed, *Fallen Angels*, 62, whose comments here complement her insights cited earlier. For further on revealed wisdom as a hallmark of 1 Enoch, see especially, Nickelsburg, *1 Enoch 1*, 52–54. Cf. idem, "Revealed Wisdom as a Criterion for Inclusion and Exclu-

transgressed the very boundaries of the created order and have thus ignored the ontological distinctions inherent to creation's proper functioning, it is ironic that *BW* resolves this cataclysm through the supernatural revelation to humanity via "Enoch" that God and his faithful angels exist and act to bring vindication and peace to the entire created order.[184] Yet even the knowledge of these angels and the hope of assistance from them was, on its own, insufficient: not until God arrives with his angelic holy ones (cf. 1:1–9) will *BW's* envisioned future come to pass.

In short, these observations suggest that the import of *BW's* presentation of angels associated with Israel is found in the revelation of the existence of these righteous guardians and priests, who protect the people and intercede for them, rid the world of sin and its causes, and ostensibly serve as the model and validation of the earthly priesthood. Their actions are for the encouragement and benefit of the "plant of righteous," who are, firstly, the circle responsible for *BW*, but there is little to indicate that other Jews are necessarily excluded. In fact, it is said that this group will "become a blessing," which may be related to the assertion that "all the sons of men will become righteous," even if these universalistic hints appear to stand in tension with other aspects of the text. However, it was noted that the real enemies as far as the authors of *BW* are concerned are not humans but the non-human, boundary-transgressing watchers, who have caused humankind to suffer. Thus, the existence and counter-actions of the God-commissioned righteous angels are ultimately for the benefit of all of humanity. That this knowledge was revealed to the pious, ante-diluvian hero, Enoch, grants a measure of authority to both the vision itself and those for whom Enoch is a presumably a stand-in, *BW's* authors.

II. The Animal Apocalypse (1 Enoch 85–90)

The section of 1 Enoch known as *The Book of Dreams* has two major parts, both of which describe Enoch as conveying the content of supernatural revelations to his son, Methusaleh. But rather than depicting Enoch as ascending

---

sion: From Jewish Sectarianism to Early Christianity," in *To See Ourselves as Others See Us: Christians, Jews, and "Others" in Late Antiquity* (eds., Jacob Neusner and Ernest S. Frerichs; Chico: Scholars Press, 1985), 74–91; Randal A. Argall, *1 Enoch and Sirach: A Comparative Literary and Conceptual Analysis of the Themes of Revelation, Creation, and Judgment* (Atlanta: Scholars Press, 1995), 101–107.

[184] Nickelsburg, *1 Enoch 1*, 41. On the possibility that 1 Enoch 6–11, which neither refers to Enoch nor portrays heavenly revelation in a positive light, was "co-opted and surrounded by material (chapters 1–5 and 12–16) that hails Enoch as a legitimate conduit for heavenly knowledge," see Matthew J. Goff, "A Blessed Rage for Order: Apocalypticism, Esoteric Revelation, and the Cultural Politics of Knowledge in the Hellenistic Age," *HBAI* 5 (2016): 199.

to heaven, *The Book of Dreams* has the patriarch recounting two dream-visions,[185] the second of which is relevant to this study. Known as the *Animal Apocalypse* (henceforth, *AA*),[186] this composition has been understood to contain important references to angels associated with Israel.

AA is a retelling of Israelite/Jewish history in which time is divided into three distinct eras: the "remote past" (85:3–89:9), the "present" (89:9–90:27), and the "ideal future" (90:28–38).[187] The most distinctive feature of *AA*, however, is its allegorical representation of humans as animals,[188] hence the title given to the text by scholars; the allegory also includes the presentation of angels as humans.[189] In addition to contributing to the generic diversity of 1 Enoch[190] and giving the work a typical or timeless character,[191] *AA*'s allegorical treatment of history allows its author(s) to integrate the various players of Israel's cosmic drama onto a single stage:

> [*AA*] ... show[s] history as it really is, a great playing field where God, angels and demons compete for possession of and control over the humans that pass in and out of it. By means of the allegory, the author has been able to level this playing field so that he can imaginatively present the whole hierarchy of God, angels and demons, and humans as acting on the same playing field. The allegory bridges the cosmic dualism between heaven

---

[185] Cf. 1 En. 83:1: "And now, my son, Methusaleh, I will show you all the visions that I saw; before you I will recount (them). Two visions I saw before I took a wife ... ." For a recent examination of the genre of dream-visions in the Qumran Aramaic texts, see Andrew B. Perrin, *The Dynamics of Dream-Vision Revelation in the Aramaic Dead Sea Scrolls* (JAJSup 19; Göttingen: Vandenhoeck & Ruprecht, 2015).

[186] Specifically, *AA* is found in 85:1–90:42.

[187] As articulated by Patrick A. Tiller, *The Animal Apocalypse of 1 Enoch: A Commentary on the Animal Apocalypse of 1 Enoch* (EJL 4; Atlanta: Scholars Press, 1993), 3. Cf. Nickelsburg, *1 Enoch 1*, 354, who classifies these eras as "creation to the flood," "the renewal of creation to the great judgment," and "the second renewal into an open future." Also see Daniel C. Olson, *A New Reading of the Animal Apocalypse of 1 Enoch: 'All Nations Shall Be Blessed'* (SVTP 24; Leiden: Brill, 2013), 14, who emphasizes that the hallmark of *AA*'s envisioned future is the transformation of the nation of Israel, who will be a universal blessing as per Gen 12:1–3. For a recent discussion of *AA's* eras and their progression, see Antti Laato, "The Chronology in the Animal Apocalypse of *1 Enoch* 85–90," *JSP* 26 (2016): 3–19.

[188] Israelites/Jews are presented as kosher or clean animals; Gentiles are presented as unclean animals.

[189] On angels appearing as men in apocalyptic literature, cf. 1 En. 17:1; Dan 7:13–14; 8:15; 9:21; 10:5; see Tiller, *The Animal Apocalypse*, 245.

[190] Nickelsburg, *1 Enoch 1*, 360.

[191] Collins, *The Apocalyptic Imagination*, 70. Cf. Tiller, *The Animal Apocalypse*, 27: "[The] allegory serves admirably in any propaganda war since its basic function is to subvert normal language that has been traditionally pressed into service for the dominant party. Agents, objects, and ideals can be caricatured in new ways that may be more natural to the narrative fiction than to the reality it represents."

and earth, and the angels are seen as being as much a part of the life of Israel as a shepherd is a part of the life of a sheep.[192]

The angels associated with the Gentile nations are allegorized as seventy malevolent shepherds who have no small role as it relates to the fate of Israel throughout its history. The violence imposed by the seventy shepherds is great, and their rules are divided respectively into four reigns of 12, 23, 23, and 12 shepherds, which correspond approximately to the Babylonian, Persian, Ptolemaic, and Seleucid periods;[193] this violent chaos is thus limited within the strictures of divine order and providence.[194] Moreover, the archangel Michael has been interpreted as having a role in 90:13–14, a passage which corresponds to events of the Maccabean revolt; this section is used to date *AA* to the mid to late 160s BCE,[195] and angelic assistance was therefore considered part of the God-ordained plan that brought Israel another step closer to the ideal future anticipated by *AA*'s authors.

After *AA* relays its own account of the fall of the angelic rebels (86:1–6),[196] Enoch sees seven, white-clad figures who have the appearance of men (87:1–4). Since men signify angels in *AA*, it is thus widely accepted that the these seven "men" correspond to the seven archangels mentioned elsewhere in 1 Enoch:[197] three of the archangels transport or translate Enoch to an elevated location so he can best view what is going to transpire on Earth, and from this vantage point Enoch witnesses the remaining four archangels act as agents of judgment against the fallen watchers and the giant offspring fathered by them (87:1–88:3). While the fact that their raiment is white may suggest that the archangels have a priestly status,[198] there is no imagery or language of a heavenly temple as there is in *BW*, though *AA* does ascribe an intercessory role to the archangels (cf. 89:70–71, 76–77; 90:14, 17).[199]

Key references to nationally associated angels are found in relation to the dominant concept of the work noted above: that God has utilized seventy "shepherds" to rule successively over the "sheep," that is, Israel. In the con-

---

[192] Tiller, *The Animal Apocalypse*, 27–28.

[193] On the background of "seventy" as it relates to the shepherds, see Nickelsburg, *1 Enoch 1*, 391–393.

[194] Collins, *The Apocalyptic Imagination*, 69.

[195] For issues in the dating of *AA*, see Tiller, *The Animal Apocalypse*, 61–79; Nickelsburg, *1 Enoch 1*, 360–361; Olson, *A New Reading*, 216–218.

[196] These verses describe the fallen watchers as "stars," a designation that highlights yet again the astral-angelic association in ancient Judaism.

[197] Nickelsburg, *1 Enoch 1*, 374 summarizes the matter as follows: "The [archangels] are numbered in two groups. The four, who will be active in 88:1–89:1, correspond to the four in chap. 10 [= Sariel, Raphael, Gabriel, and Michael]. The other three fill the complement of seven mentioned in chap. 20 [= Uriel, Raguel, and Remiel] ... ."

[198] So Tiller, *The Animal Apocalypse*, 245.

[199] See Nickelsburg, *1 Enoch 1*, 374.

text of the apostasy of the pre-exilic monarchy, God charges the shepherds with the following bleak instructions in 89:59–60:

"Every one of you from now on shall pasture the sheep, and everything that I command you, do. I am handing them over to you duly numbered, and I will tell you which of them are to be destroyed. Destroy them." And [God] handed those sheep over to them.

There are many instances in the Hebrew Bible where God or the leaders of Israel are referred to as shepherds (cf. Pss 23:1–6; 80:2; 100:3; Isa 40:11), with Ezek 34 and Zech 11 constituting the most detailed negative examples of the metaphor.[200] In keeping with *AA*'s allegorical scheme, the shepherds – a human vocation – should be understood to be angels.[201] While these shepherds have been instructed by God to facilitate the punishment of disobedient Israel (cf. 89:58, 68),[202] it is clear that the shepherds have malevolently overstepped their mandate. Scholars have not missed the affinity these angelic shepherds have with Deut 32:8 and its "sons of god," whom the God of Israel has appointed to rule over the Gentiles; for this reason, the shepherds are widely identified as the gods or angels of the nations.[203] But as Nickelsburg rightly points out, the character of *AA*'s shepherds is more akin to the unambiguously unjust אלהים and בני עליון of Ps 82:6.[204] The divine response to the injustice of the shepherds is unexpected. Instead of intervening himself or sanctioning an immediate counter assault of righteous angelic forces, God instructs a scribe to record the actions of the shepherds; 89:61–64 states that

another he summoned and said to him, "Observe and see everything that the shepherds do against the sheep, for they will destroy more of them than I have commanded them. Every excess and destruction that is done by the shepherds, write down – how many they destroy at my command, and how many they destroy on their own. Every destruction by each individual shepherd, write down against them. And by number read them in my presence – how many they destroy, and how many they hand over to destruction, so that I may have

---

[200] See especially Nickelsburg, *1 Enoch 1*, 391, who has devoted an excursus to the topic: "The Biblical Sources of the Idea of the Negligent Shepherds."

[201] See Charles, *Enoch*, 200; Tiller, *The Animal Apocalypse*, 325.

[202] I will address the mechanics/worldview of this arrangement, below.

[203] So Charles, *The Book of Enoch*, 200. Cf. Black, *The Book of Enoch*, 200; Davidson, *Angels at Qumran*, 98, 108–109; Collins, *The Apocalyptic Imagination*, 68–69; Michalak, *Angels as Warriors*, 145. *Contra* Tiller, *The Animal Apocalypse*, 53–54, who views the shepherds as *Israel's* angelic patrons, whom God has turned against the nation. When the seventy shepherds are introduced in 89:59, it is interesting to note that they are not the only ones addressed by God: "And he said to the shepherds *and their subordinates* [emphasis mine] …" (cf. 89:69). As Tiller, *The Animal Apocalypse*, 325, notes, the Ethiopic word used is the (collective) singular *dammad*, meaning someone who is bound in service to another, thus his translation, "retinue"; in addition to Nickelsburg, *1 Enoch 1*, 387, who also translates the word as "subordinates," see Olson, *A New Reading*, 192, who prefers "associates"; E. Issac, "1 [Ethiopic Apocalypse of] Enoch," *OTP* 1:68, who translates it as "colleagues."

[204] Nickelsburg, *1 Enoch 1*, 391, 395. Deut 32:8 and Ps 82 were discussed in Chapter 2.

this testimony against them, that I may know every deed of the shepherds, that I may measure them and see what they are doing – whether they are acting according to the command that I gave them, or not. And do not let them know it, and do not show them or rebuke them. But write down every destruction by the shepherds, one by one, in his own time, and bring it all up to me" (cf. 89:70–71, 76–77; 90:14, 17, 22).

The consensus opinion is that this scribe is an angel: not only is the figure referred to as "another" in 89:61 – which should likely not be taken to mean that he is another malevolent shepherd but rather that the scribe is another angel[205] – *AA* also later announces that the scribe is "one of those seven white ones" (90:22) who acts as an agent of judgment against the excessive shepherds.[206]

A number of scholars have identified the angelic scribe more specifically as the archangel Michael.[207] In addition to the fact that the scribe-as-Michael interpretation is extant in the marginal notes of certain Ethiopic manuscripts,[208] it is widely held that *AA* refers to the events of 1 Macc 4:30–35 and its theological development in 2 Macc 11:6–12, where angelic assistance is highlighted.[209] The relevant verse is found at 90:14:

And I looked until that man came who wrote the names of the shepherds and brought (them) before the Lord of the sheep and he helped [that ram] and showed it everything; his help came down to that ram.

The ram with the great horn first introduced in 1 En. 90:9–10 is most often considered a reference to Judas Maccabeus;[210] that he receives assistance

---

[205] See Tiller, *The Animal Apocalypse*, 326, who, in addition to noting that the Ethiopic text is problematic at this point, states: "It is not entirely clear who this 'other' is. Surely, he is not another [malevolent] shepherd. Apparently, the allegory has faded and what is meant is another angel." Cf. Black, *The Book of Enoch*, 271.

[206] This verse refers to the seven, white-clad archangels first mentioned in *AA* at 87:2. Moreover, the angelic scribe serves as a heavenly witness and intercessor throughout chapters 88–90, roles which are in keeping with *BW*'s portrayal of the archangels.

[207] So Charles, *The Book of Enoch*, 201, 211–213; C. C. Torrey, "Alexander Jannaeus and the Archangel Michael," *VT* 4 (1954): 208–211; Russell, *The Method and Message*, 201; Davidson, *Angels at Qumran*, 109; Black, *The Book of Enoch*, 277; Nickelsburg, *1 Enoch 1*, 391; Hannah, *Michael and Christ*, 37; idem, "Guardian Angels and National Angelic Patrons," 421; Michalak, *Angels as Warriors*, 146; Olson, *A New Reading*, 218. Tiller, *The Animal Apocalypse*, 326, while conceding the similarities between the angelic scribe and Michael, questions the identification.

[208] Tiller, *The Animal Apocalypse*, 326.

[209] Hannah, *Michael and Christ*, 37.

[210] Cf., e.g., Tiller, *The Animal Apocalypse*, 62–63, 355; Nickelsburg, *1 Enoch 1*, 400; Michalak, *Angels as Warriors*, 146; Olson, *A New Reading*, 213. *Contra* Torrey, "Alexander Jannaeus and the Archangel Michael," 208–211, who has proposed that the horn was John Hyrcanus. Alternatively, Eyal Regev, "The Ram and Qumran: The Eschatological Character of the Ram in the Animal Apocalypse (1 En. 90:1–13)," in *Apocalyptic Thinking*

from the angel is clear enough. Since the scribe not only seems to be identified as one of the archangels but is also cast as Israel's guardian and assigned a role in the downfall of the shepherds (90:22), commentators have justifiably proposed that the angelic scribe is Michael.[211]

In order to put *AA's* envisioned angelic guardianship in perspective, it is important to note that the authors make no attempt to romanticize Israel's history. The nation or significant portions of it are often said to have "strayed" (89:33, 51) or have been "blinded" (89:41, 74), and the matter becomes acute during the divided monarchy, when *AA* states that the people "went astray in everything" (89:54). The divine response to this apostasy is to "abandon" (89:55) the sheep to various wild beasts, that is, Israel's enemies.[212] Yet despite Enoch's protestation to the devastation,[213] God remains silent and actually "rejoices" (89:58) in the Babylonian conquest.[214]

What happens next in the narrative – the commissioning of the seventy angelic shepherds – not only reinforces the bleak perspective of Israel's history held by *AA's* authors but also highlights an important aspect of the worldview operative in the text. In short, God's abandonment of the flock and the apostasy that prompted it are heightened by the handing over of the sheep to the shepherds:[215] no longer is the Lord of the sheep the subject of verbs of which the sheep are beneficiaries,[216] and God effectively distances himself from

---

in Early Judaism, 181–195, has stressed that this figure is not Judah but rather a future messiah.

[211] Hannah, *Michael and Christ*, 37, summarizes the interpretation as follows: "To begin with, it is more likely that this figure is one of the four named archangels whose missions parallel Michael's, Gabriel's, Raphael's, and Sariel's in *1 En.* 9–10 than one of the three who effect Enoch's translation, for the four appear to be more important to our author than the three. If the author of the *Animal Apocalypse* knew *1 En.* 20:5, which is not unlikely as he certainly knew and used other portions of the *Book of Watchers*, an identification with Michael would be certain, for this 'white man' acts as Israel's guardian and champion. Finally, and most importantly, a comparison of 88:3 and 90:22–25 suggests that both passages refer to the same angel. The fallen angels bound by Michael in 88:3 are in 90:24–25 judged along with the shepherds captured by this angelic figure. The action of this figure has resulted in the judgment of both the fallen angels and the shepherds."

[212] E.g., lions, leopards, wolves, etc. On the identification of the wild beasts with specific Gentile nations, see Nickelsburg, *1 Enoch 1*, 385.

[213] Cf. 89:57: "And I began to cry out with all my might and to call to the Lord of the sheep and to show him concerning the sheep, because they were devoured by all the wild beasts." Nickelsburg, *1 Enoch 1*, 385, remarks that "in the Enochic corpus, [Enoch's plea] functions like angelic intercession." For similar sentiments in *BW*, see 13:4–7; 22:12.

[214] On this point, see Tiller, *The Animal Apocalypse*, 322–323, who emphasizes *AA's* focus on waywardness in Israel's history and God's righteous prerogative to judge.

[215] Nickelsburg, *1 Enoch 1*, 389–390.

[216] As is the case numerous times from the Exodus onward (cf. 1 En. 89:28ff).

Israel when he hands over the sheep to the shepherds. Not to be missed, however, are the mechanics of this arrangement:

This scene takes place in heaven,[217] where the Lord of the sheep summons first the seventy shepherds and then an angelic scribe, who will be responsible to report to God in the heavenly courtroom. ... *The scenario is that God delivers the sheep to the shepherds and their associates* [89:58, 68], *and the shepherds hand over the sheep to the wild beasts and birds of prey for destruction.* In so doing, however, they deliver for destruction more than they should and thus act as negligent, malevolent, and disobedient shepherds. God is aware of this malfeasance of office before he delivers the sheep to the shepherds, but this foreknowledge is accompanied by God's determination to hold the shepherds responsible for their actions [emphasis mine].[218]

The wild beasts and birds of prey are, of course, Israel's enemies. Thus, in the commissioning of the angelic shepherds we have another example of earthly realities paralleling those of heaven.

As noted, the faithful counterpart to the malevolent shepherds, the angelic scribe, is not depicted as immediately influencing earthly realities, at least in the same way the shepherds do. While the scribe records, testifies, and intercedes for God's people,[219] there is no mention of this figure engaging the shepherds in a heavenly battle with earthly consequences. Scholars have suggested that the angelic scribe is Michael; and though it is true that the role of the angelic scribe in 90:13–22 has affinities with that of Michael as portrayed, for example, in Dan 7–12,[220] a distinction needs to be made: Michael's role in the Book of Daniel is largely a heavenly one with earthly import whereas the angelic scribe's activities, at least in his role as "Israel martial champion,"[221] take place on earth.[222]

An important observation is that the earthly actions of the angelic scribe are set within the context of what is a notable feature of *AA*'s depiction of

---

[217] There is debate as to when the heavenly commissioning of the shepherds occurs vis-à-vis events on earth. Most scholars see their malevolent rule as beginning during God's abandonment of the sheep as described in 89:55 (i.e., slightly before the shepherds' formal introduction in 89:59 = ca. 604–587 BCE), but some view it as beginning as early as the Assyrian conquest of the Northern Kingdom (ca. 722 BCE). See the excursus of Nickelsburg, *1 Enoch 1*, 391–393, entitled, "The Chronology of the Vision: Seventy Shepherds Ruling for Seventy Weeks of Years." Cf. Olson, *A New Reading*, 191–192.

[218] Nickelsburg, *1 Enoch 1*, 390.

[219] Nickelsburg, *1 Enoch 1*, 390; see above.

[220] As is frequently noted by commentators; cf., e.g., Hannah, "Guardian Angels and National Angelic Patrons," 421; Nickelsburg, *1 Enoch 1*, 391; Michalak, *Angels as Warriors*, 146; Olson, *A New Reading*, 218.

[221] Olson, *A New Reading*, 218.

[222] Even when God instructs the scribe to round up the shepherds for judgment in 90:20–27, this scene takes place on earth; see Nickelsburg, *1 Enoch 1*, 403. Moreover, the scribe's role on earth may be to counter what Olson, *A New Reading*, 218, calls the "surprising" mention of the angelic shepherds in the enemy coalition of 90:13.

Israel: a militant role for the people (cf. 90:6–34). While the rams who rally to fight alongside Judas have traditionally been identified as the *Hasidim* (90:10), recent scholarship has been more cautious on this point.[223] For the purposes of this study, it is sufficient to note that *AA* is among a group of 2nd and 1st cent. BCE texts that depict Israel's history – particularly the post-exilic period – in an unfavorable light.[224] This reality is especially evident at two points: 89:73–74, which mentions the blindness of the people and the pollution of the temple,[225] and 90:6–7, which reports the birth of lambs who "began to open their eyes and to see and to cry out to the flock." The latter verses refer to the emergence of enlightened reformers who were not content with the religious status quo, and it is possible this group represents the authors' own.[226] Whether *AA* and other texts testify to a singular reform movement or a series of such movements is debated,[227] though Regev makes the important observation that *AA's* authors "combine a religious elitism of knowing the truth or being close to God with an awareness of the destiny of the entire people of Israel *without* sectarian withdrawal and separation [emphasis mine]."[228] Moreover, it is clear that those responsible for *AA* support the Maccabean uprising as at least part of what would contribute to the reestablishment of "traditional religious observance";[229] the requested and received angelic intervention in 90:13–14 only lends theological warrant to this militant *modus operandi*.[230]

To bring together the various parts of this discussion, two additional points need to be made. First, angelic assistance on its own is not sufficient to usher in the eschaton as *AA* anticipates it: the theophanic scenes of 90:15–42 suggest that it will only be God's direct intervention and judgment that secures Israel's future. Second, it is clear that not all Gentiles and apostate Jews are

---

[223] So Olson, *A New Reading*, 214; Tiller, *The Animal Apocalypse*, 109–115, 356; Nickelsburg, *1 Enoch 1*, 363, 400.

[224] See the excursus of Nickelsburg, *1 Enoch 1*, 398–400, entitled, "Traditions about a Religious Awakening in the Hellenistic Period," which examines the similarities between *AA*, the *Apocalypse of Weeks*, the *Damascus Document*, etc. Common themes include criticism of the temple, cult, and priesthood.

[225] Nickelsburg, *1 Enoch 1*, 395: "Employing language possibly taken from Mal 1:7 and 12, the author asserts that from its inception the cult of the Second Temple did not follow correct laws of ritual purity."

[226] See the helpful historical summary of Olson, *A New Reading*, 210–211. Cf. Tiller, The *Animal Apocalypse*, 101.

[227] Nickelsburg, *1 Enoch 1*, 400, characterizes the movement(s) of these texts as having "an eschatological worldview that was authenticated by claims of revelation."

[228] Regev, "The Ram and Qumran," 192–193, specifically contrasts the posture of *AA* and other texts with those penned by the Qumran movement, who *did* withdrawal in a sectarian manner.

[229] Tiller, *The Animal Apocalypse*, 323.

[230] Cf. Collins, *The Apocalyptic Imagination*, 70.

destroyed in the final judgment since the pure and glorious future envisioned by *AA* includes the eradication of the blindness that formerly plagued the sheep, a new Jerusalem and new temple,[231] the resurrection and conversion of the judged wild beasts and birds of prey (i.e., Gentiles) that previously ravaged the flock and the total transformation of humanity to its "primordial righteousness and perfection" (cf. 90:20–36).[232] The snow-white bull which appears in 90:37–38 has been variously interpreted,[233] but its introduction immediately prior to the transformation of all creatures to snow-white cows suggests that this figure, at minimum, is the God-ordained catalyst which stands at the head of transformed humanity.

In short, the overall import of *AA* has similarities to what was witnessed in *BW*: the revelation that an angel provides intercession for Israel in the midst of chaotic circumstances would have served as an encouragement to those who viewed themselves as faithful to God; that this same angel responded to the prayers of the people by aiding the Maccabean warriors on the battlefield would have been all the more significant for those anticipating God's direct and decisive intervention (90:15–17).[234] But *AA* suggests that these angelic activities were ultimately part of a plan that was not just for the benefit of Israel but also in some sense inclusive of humankind more broadly, since the glorious future envisioned by the text is universalistic insofar as a significant number of apostate Jews and sinful Gentiles seemingly survive the final judgment to be part of a restored and transformed humanity.[235]

III. The Epistle of Enoch (1 Enoch 91–108)

The *Epistle of Enoch* (henceforth, *EE*), is comprised of a number of different traditions that have been brought together within a testament-like framework in which Enoch is presented as imparting revelation and wisdom to his entire family.[236] The most well-known portion of *EE* is the *Apocalypse of Weeks*

---

[231] Oliver Dyma, "Tempel, Raum, und Zeit in apokalyptischen Erwartungen," in *In memoriam Wolfgang Richter* (ed., Hans Rechenmacher; ATSAT 100; St. Ottilien: Eos Verlag Erzabtei St. Ottilien, 2016), 45, discusses proximity to God in the eschatological scenario of *AA* as a resolution of the tension prompted by a polluted Jerusalem temple, though admittedly there is debate as to whether the new Jerusalem ("the house") of this scene specifically refers to a temple. On the last point, see Nickelsburg, *1 Enoch 1*, 405.

[232] Nickelsburg, *1 Enoch 1*, 407.

[233] E.g., the messiah. For discussion and bibliography, see Nickelsburg, *1 Enoch 1*, 406–408, who points out that the transformation to white cows is a return to the one species from which all species came. Cf. Tiller, *The Animal Apocalypse*, 383–392.

[234] On the significance of 90:17, see the comments of Nickelsburg, *1 Enoch 1*, 361.

[235] As is also the case with *BW*; see Nickelsburg, "We and the Other," 266.

[236] *EE* includes the *Apocalypse of Weeks* (93:1–10; 91:11–17; see further below); an *Exhortation* (91:1–10, 18–19); the *Epistle* proper (from which the name of the larger section comes; 92:1–5; 93:11–105:2); the *Birth of Noah* (106:1–107:3); an *Eschatological*

(henceforth, *AW*),[237] a historical overview that divides history into ten periods or "weeks." *AW* has numerous affinities with *AA*, including the emergence of enlightened reformers – likely a reference to authors' own circle – who will take up arms against the wicked,[238] namely, those who have used their financial security and power to oppress others.[239] "The chosen" (93:10) therefore have a role in the advent of the righteous eschaton that will arrive in its fullness at the end of *AW*'s tenth and final week (cf. 9:17). *AW* thus connects thematically with the ethical exhortations that precede and follow it (cf. 91:18; 94:1–5);[240] indeed, *EE* is largely paraenetic in nature, encouraging the reader to walk in righteous paths and to avoid paths of violence and wickedness, especially oppression of the poor.[241] Most significant for this study is that *EE* refers to the roles angels have in securing not just the punishment of the wicked but also the glorious fate of the righteous.[242]

That being said, angels receive relatively limited attention in *AW*, a facet which may be due to the brevity of the work.[243] The first possible reference to angels associated with Israel occurs during *AW*'s fourth week

after this will arise a fourth week, and at its conclusion, visions of the holy and righteous will be seen; and a covenant for all generations and a tabernacle will be made in it (93:6).

This verse, the only reference to the Mosaic covenant in 1 Enoch,[244] describes the events of Sinai.[245] Though "the holy and righteous" may refer to pious

---

Admonition (108:1–15); see Loren T. Stuckenbruck, *1 Enoch 91–108* (CEJL; New York: de Gruyter, 2007), 1. Given that *EE* is this amalgam of traditions, issues of dating and provenance are difficult to determine with certainty. However, a 2nd cent. BCE composition of chapters 91–107 – and their subsequent editing into a collection – is likely. There was no extant evidence of chapter 108 among the Qumran manuscripts of *1 Enoch*, and it has been suggested this chapter was added to the tradition ca. 100 CE; cf. Milik, *The Books of Enoch*, 217; Nickelsburg, *1 Enoch 1*, 427–428, 554; Stuckenbruck, *1 Enoch 91–108*, 1, 691–694.

[237] It should be noted that a Qumran manuscript of *BD* (cf. 4QEn^g = 4Q212) has confirmed what scholars have long-suspected regarding *AW*: the Ethiopic tradition has misplaced the conclusion of the apocalypse so that *AW* is actually 93:3–10 followed by 91:11–17; see Nickelsburg, *1 Enoch 1*, 414–415.

[238] Other affinities with *AA* are the depiction of history and its anticipated future, which occur within the strictures of divine order and providence, and a negative view of the post-exilic period and its temple. For a detailed comparison of *AW* and *AA*, see Nickelsburg, *1 Enoch 1*, 398–399, 447.

[239] On the wicked in *EE* as "well-to-do" and oppressive of fellow Jews, see the helpful overview of Stuckenbruck, "Coping with Alienating Experience," 68–73.

[240] Nickelsburg, *1 Enoch 1*, 415, 454–456.

[241] Collins, *The Apocalyptic Imagination*, 66.

[242] Davidson, *Angels at Qumran*, 123.

[243] Davidson, *Angels at Qumran*, 119.

[244] Cf. Stuckenbruck, *1 Enoch 91–108*, 107; Nickelsburg, *1 Enoch 1*, 446.

[245] Stuckenbruck, *1 Enoch 91–108*, 103.

Israelites (cf. 100:5), it is better understood as a reference to angels in 93:6, even if the expression is an "unusual"[246] one for celestial beings.[247] Specifically, "the holy and righteous" have been understood to be the angels involved in the theophany at Sinai (cf. Josephus, *Ant.* 15.136; Acts 7:53; Gal 3:19; Heb 2:2). As Stuckenbruck explains, "The claim in Exodus 24:9–11 that Moses, Aaron, Nadab, Abihu, and the seventy elders saw 'the God of Israel' on the mountain could have been taken as a vision of the heavenly throne room, from which the notion of the presence of an angelic entourage is not remote."[248] When I discussed *BW*, it was observed that only certain angels were permitted to be in closest proximity to God. Thus, if the angelic interpretation of "the holy and righteous" of 93:6 is correct, the angels involved are plausibly the angelic priests who have access to the innermost part of the heavenly temple. Moreover, as in *BW* and *AA*, angels are charged with the priestly task of intercession, with 99:3 announcing the following:

> Then be prepared, O righteous, and present your petitions as a reminder; offer them as a testimony before the angels, that they may bring in the sins of the unrighteous before the Most High as a reminder.[249]

The righteous are thus comforted with the knowledge that prayers offered in the midst of persecution are heard – and that they have heavenly intercessors who will testify on their behalf at the eschatological judgment (cf. 97:6; 99:3; 100:10; 102:3; 104:1–8; 108:3, 7).[250]

It was noted above that "the chosen" are likely a reference to the authors' own group, but it seems that *AW's* authors hold the post-exilic period in even lower esteem than the authors of *AA*.[251] This perspective can be seen in the

---

[246] Nickelsburg, *1 Enoch 1*, 446.

[247] Stuckenbruck, *1 Enoch 91–108*, 104 n. 212, observes that the angelic interpretation is strengthened by the fact that an Ethiopic manuscript omits the "righteous"; i.e., the reading is the "holy [ones]."

[248] Stuckenbruck, *1 Enoch 91–108*, 105. Cf. Nickelsburg, *1 Enoch 1*, 446: "The author may be alluding to an exposition of Exod 24:9–11 that described a vision of the heavenly court like *1 Enoch* 14 or Daniel 7." As will be examined later in this chapter, Jubilees ascribes an important role to angels at Sinai.

[249] Likewise, 104:1 states that "the angels in heaven make mention of you for good before the glory of the Great One, and your names are written before the glory of the Great One."

[250] Nickelsburg, "The We and the Other," 268. Cf. Davidson, *Angels at Qumran*, 125–126, who notes that angels are not specifically mentioned as writing records of the sins of the unrighteous (committed against the righteous), but such activity is strongly intimated. Given the role of the angelic scribe in *AA*, this is a sound reading.

[251] Note the comments of Stuckenbruck, *1 Enoch 91–108*, 122: "Significantly, there is no mention of any return from exile and, with it, of the Second Temple. Instead, the scattering of Israel in the sixth week is seamlessly followed in the seventh by the rise of 'a wicked generation.' … The absence of any reference to the people's return to the land or

designation, "the chosen will be chosen, as witnesses of righteousness from the eternal plant of righteousness" (93:10; cf. 10:16), with the "chosen" designation, again, deemed deserved due in part to their status as the recipients of divine revelation.[252] The reference to Abraham earlier in the same chapter indicates that the "eternal plant" is Israel (cf. Isa 60:21; 61:3),[253] and the emergence *from* this plant gives the impression that the author's group is the faithful embodiment of the nation (cf. 99:2; 104:12).[254] It is important to note, however, that they are chosen to *testify* to righteousness,[255] and that they are effective in doing so is evident in 91:14, which exclaims that "all humankind will look to the path of eternal righteousness" (cf. 100:6; 105:1–2).[256] As with *BW* and *AA*, the references to judgment in *EE* render these verses almost paradoxical.[257] But the statements highlight the hope with which the three Enochic works examined here anticipate the eschaton. More specifical-

---

rebuilding of the Temple is striking. It is in stark contrast with references to making or building of '[the tabernacle]' in the fourth week (93:6) and to building of the 'house of glory' in the fifth (v. 7). ... [A]s far as [the author] and his community are concerned, the Second Temple is of no consequence in relation to God's plan for Israel. In this respect, he may be as, or even more radical than the *Animal Apocalypse*, in which the author, despite serious misgiving about the Second Temple, could nevertheless at least give Judas Maccabeus – and, by association, the cult – principled, though temporary, support ... ."

[252] I.e., the authors viewed themselves as an enlightened entity within Israel. Stuckenbruck, *1 Enoch 91–108*, 124–125, discusses the possible nature of the knowledge disclosed to "the chosen" and concludes that "of chief concern ... is the righteous community's identity as the definitive receptacle of divine disclosure."

[253] Cf. 93:5: "... a man will be chosen as the plant of righteous judgment, and after him will go forth the plant of righteousness forever and ever." On the "eternal plant" as a designation for the nation of Israel from which these "chosen" would emerge, see Tiller, "The Eternal Plant," 319–321; Nickelsburg, *1 Enoch 1*, 444–445; Stuckenbruck, *1 Enoch 91–108*, 124; idem, "4QInstruction and the Possible Influence," 255–257.

[254] On this point, see Stuckenbruck, *1 Enoch 91–108*, 124. As such, God would work through them to inaugurate the eschaton, an era that would begin with the violent destruction of the wicked and the construction of a new temple. 91:12–13 states that, "After this will arise an eighth week of righteousness, in which a sword will be given to all the righteous, to execute righteous judgment on the all the wicked, and they will be delivered into their hands. And at its conclusion, they will acquire possessions in righteousness; and the temple of the kingdom of the Great One will be built in the greatness of its glory for all the generations of eternity." The righteous thereby help to establish the conditions for the piety and righteousness that will characterize the eternal era that follows the tenth week (cf. 91:15–17).

[255] Cf. Nickelsburg, *1 Enoch 1*, 448: "The elect are chosen, first of all, to be the recipients of wisdom and knowledge. ... But the elect are not chosen simply to be the recipients of the salvation granted through this wisdom and knowledge; they are chosen for a mission, viz., to be witnesses of righteousness."

[256] For more detailed discussion of these sentiments and their background in Third Isaiah, see Nickelsburg, *1 Enoch 1*, 449–450.

[257] So Nickelsburg, "The We and the Other," 268.

ly, *EE's* envisioned future for the righteous includes a relationship with the angels whose intercession and assistance has helped them and will continue to do so. In a passage that contrasts present persecutions with a glorious future,[258] 104:2–6 reveals the following:

Take courage then; for formerly you were worn out by evils and tribulations, but now you will shine like the luminaries of heaven; you will shine and appear, and the portals of heaven will be opened for you. ... Take courage and do not abandon your hope, for you will have great joy like the angels of heaven. ... Fear not, O righteous, when you see the sinners growing strong and prospering, and do not be their companions; but stay far from all their iniquities, for you will be companions of the host of heaven (cf. 92:4).

These verses are making a comparison: upon death the righteous do not become angels; they are like angels.[259] The simile is akin to that found in Dan 12:3, but there is a clear distinction between the two texts: whereas Dan 12 suggests that only the *Maskilim* will shine like stars, the present verses seem to affirm that all righteous people will attain an angel-like afterlife.[260] Also, the exhortation to the righteous not to associate with sinners in the present is made with the eschatological incentive that the righteous will one day not only be like the angels but also have fellowship with the angels.[261] As such, the faithful need not fear the coming decisive judgment of God,[262] not least because he will arrive with an angelic entourage tasked with the in-gathering of human oppressors "in one place" for judgment (100:4). Significantly, the very next verse announces that God will "set a guard of the holy angels over all the righteous and holy and they will be kept as the apple of the eye, until evil and sin come to an end" (100:5). In other words, hostile spiritual beings can do no harm to the souls of the righteous dead, who are protected by their angelic guardians until the final judgment when they will receive angel-like exaltation, and guardianship will become fellowship.[263]

---

[258] Nickelsburg, *1 Enoch 1*, 529.

[259] Cf. Davidson, *Angels at Qumran*, 129; Stuckenbruck, *1 Enoch 91–108*, 573–574.

[260] Nickelsburg, *1 Enoch 1*, 529.

[261] In the words of Stuckenbruck, *1 Enoch 91–108*, 577: "Being associates with angelic beings is not a claim about what the author's community already are by virtue of their covenant faithfulness. Rather, the statement is promisorial ... ." Elsewhere Stuckenbruck mentions that *EE's* author is refuting the mistaken view of his readers, namely, that the flourishing of evildoers will continue. Instead, their respective lots will be reversed and the present suffering of the righteous will give way to the future reward of angelic fellowship; see idem, "The 'Otherworld' and the Epistle of Enoch," in *Other Worlds and Their Relation to This World*, 90. In the same volume, John J. Collins, "The Otherworld in the Dead Sea Scrolls," 97, observes that the "angelic afterlife" of 1 En. 104 complements the hope of a transformed earth in *AW*.

[262] So Nickelsburg, *1 Enoch 1*, 530.

[263] So Nickelsburg, *1 Enoch 1*, 500–501.

In closing, *EE* portrays angels as having an intercessory role, and while there are no explicit references to heaven as a temple or angels as priests, "the holy and righteous" of 93:6 are plausibly understood to be the angelic priests who serve in closest proximity to God. As with *AA*, the righteous – so deemed at least partially because they are the privileged recipients of divine revelation and knowledge – will take up arms against the wicked (cf. 91:12–13; 98:12–13). But here there is no explicit mention of martial angelic assistance on the battlefield or in heaven, for that matter; the only angelic guardianship activities are the protection of the righteous dead and the in-gathering of the sinful humanity for judgment, an event which will only occur at God's decisive eschatological arrival. Of the three Enochic texts examined in this chapter, *EE* may be the most exclusivist – yet it paradoxically shares the hopeful vision of the future of *BW* and *AA* that seemingly has some room for the redemption of wider humanity. The full, eschatological expression of this redemption is characterized by angel-like glory and even fellowship with the angels. Thus, the knowledge that the angelic guardians and priests associated with Israel exist and act for the benefit of humanity, though not occupying pride of place in *EE*, would have served to encourage those Jews responsible for the text that their present oppression did not go unnoticed and that the eschaton would bring a dramatic reversal of fortunes for themselves and even others.

D. Aramaic Levi Document

Found on seven fragmentary manuscripts from Qumran as well as being known from previously discovered texts,[264] the *Aramaic Levi Document* (henceforth, *ALD*) was likely composed in the late 3rd or early 2nd cent.

---

[264] The texts of the Qumran manuscripts of *ALD* have been published as follows: 1QLevi [= 1Q21]: Dominique Barthélemy and Józef T. Milik, eds., *Qumran Cave 1* (DJD 1; Oxford: Clarendon, 1955), 87–91; 4QLevi[a–f] [= 4Q213, 213a, 213b, 214, 214a, 214b]: M. E. Stone and J. C. Greenfield, "A. Aramaic Levi Document," in *Qumran Cave 4.XVII: Parabiblical Texts, Part 3* (eds., George Brooke et al.; DJD 22; Oxford: Clarendon, 1996), 1–72. The work is also known from fragments from the Cairo Geniza (designated as *Cambridge* Columns a–f; *Bodleian* Columns a–d), as well as a Greek translation interpolated into an 11th cent. text of *The Testament of the Twelve Patriarchs* from the Monastery of Koutloumous known as the Athos manuscript. See Jonas C. Greenfield, Michael E. Stone, and Esther Eshel, *The Aramaic Levi Document: Edition, Translation, Commentary* (SVTP 19; Leiden: Brill, 2004), 1–6. For an additional study with text, translation, and commentary, see Henryk Drawnel, *An Aramaic Wisdom Text from Qumran: A New Interpretation of the Levi Document* (JSJSup 86; Leiden: Brill, 2004).

BCE.[265]   An influential text, *ALD* is thought to have left its mark on *Visions of Amram,* Jubilees, and other texts found among the Dead Sea Scrolls, but it is best known for its affinities with BW[266] and, particularly, the Greek Testament of Levi (henceforth, T. Levi).[267]   The latter text, which dates to the 2nd cent. CE, is either a Christian composition outright or came to its present form through the influence of Christian interpolators.[268]   Nevertheless, it is widely held that T. Levi is, in some sense, indebted to *ALD,*[269] and I will thus refer to both documents.

T. Levi is concerned with the patriarch Levi and his priesthood, presenting both the person and his office in a lofty manner that far exceeds the biblical depictions.[270]   Levi's vision of heaven functions as his priestly investiture,

---

[265] See the discussions and bibliographies provided by Greenfield, Stone, and Eshel, *The Aramaic Levi Document,* 19–22; Drawnel, *An Aramaic Wisdom Text,* 63–79. The paleographic dates of the Qumran *ALD* manuscripts have been estimated as ranging from the mid 2nd cent. BCE to the mid 1st cent. BCE, and this factor, in conjunction with *ALD's* impact on other texts, suggests a 3rd cent. or early 2nd cent. date of composition. For a recent review and critique of the proposal that there are two clearly delineated recensions of *ALD,* see Andrew B. Perrin, "The Textual Forms of Aramaic Levi Document at Qumran," in *Reading the Bible in Ancient Traditions and Modern Editions: Studies in Memory of Peter W. Flint* (eds., idem, Kyung S. Baek, and Daniel K. Falk; EJL 47; Atlanta: SBL Press, 2017), 431–452.

[266] The affinities between *BW* and T. Levi (e.g., a patriarch being granted a vision of the celestial realm, and the notions of heaven as a temple and angels as priests, etc.; see Klawans, *Purity, Sacrifice, and the Temple,* 132; Nickelsburg, *1 Enoch 1,* 76) have led to proposals that *BW* and *ALD* (which was a source for T. Levi; see below) originated in the same circles. Cf., e.g., Nickelsburg, "Enoch, Levi, and Peter," 588–590; Michael E. Stone, "Enoch, Aramaic Levi, and Sectarian Origins," *JSJ* 19 (1988): 159–170.

[267] Greek T. Levi is part of a larger work known as the Testaments of the Twelve Patriarchs. For the critical text, see Marinus de Jonge, *The Testaments of the Twelve Patriarchs: A Critical Edition of the Greek Text* (PVTG 1; Leiden: Brill, 1978), which is cited here. For translation, see Harm W. Hollander and Marinus de Jonge, *The Testaments of the Twelve Patriarchs: A Commentary* (SVTP 8; Leiden: Brill, 1985).

[268] See the helpful summary of options provided by Robert A. Kugler, *The Testaments of the Twelve Patriarchs* (GAP; Sheffield: Sheffield Academic Press, 2001), 31–38.

[269] Evaluating the relationship between *ALD* and T. Levi is difficult and well beyond the purview of the present study. For discussion, see Kugler, *The Testaments,* 47–56. Cf. idem, *From Patriarch to Priest: The Levi-Priestly Tradition from Aramaic Levi to the Testament of Levi* (EJL 9; Atlanta: Scholars Press, 1996), 171–220; Marinus de Jonge, "The Testament of Levi and 'Aramaic Levi,'" *RevQ* 13 (1988): 376–385.

[270] E.g., the biblical portrait of Levi is absent of any kind of visionary or ascent experience. As Angel, *Otherworldly,* 58, summarizes the matter, *ALD* "elevates Levi to unprecedented heights, and attributes to his priesthood royal, sapiential, and other accolades." For a recent discussion of the biblical texts employed in *ALD's* exegetical development of the Levi tradition including Mal 2:4–7, see Perrin, *The Dynamics,* 149–157. Cf. James L. Kugel, "Levi's Elevation to the Priesthood in Second Temple Writings," *HTR* 86 (1993): 1–64.

and the commissioning import of the text is evident in the angel's opening declaration to the patriarch in chapter 2:

10 ... σὺ ἐγγὺς κυρίου στήσῃ, καὶ λειτουργὸς αὐτοῦ ἔσῃ, καὶ μυστήρια αὐτοῦ ἐξαγγελεῖς τοῖς ἀνθρώποις ...

10 ... you will stand close to the Lord, and you will be his servant, and you will announce his secrets to men ...[271]

This sacerdotal charge is conveyed elsewhere in T. Levi: not only is the patriarch adorned with priestly vestments (chapter 8) but his call is also confirmed by a vision of his father, Jacob (chapter 9). The clearest statement on the matter, however, is found in 4:2–5:2, which has an angel pronounce Levi as

4:2 ... θεράποντα καὶ λειτουργὸν τοῦ προσώπου αὐτοῦ
4:3 φῶς γνώσεως φωτεινὸν φωτιεῖς ἐν Ἰακώβ, καὶ ὡς ὁ ἥλιος ἔσῃ παντὶ σπέρματι Ἰσραήλ. ...
4:5 καὶ διὰ τοῦτο δέδοταί σοι βουλὴ καὶ σύνεσις, τοῦ συνετίσαι τοὺς υἱούς σου περὶ αὐτοῦ ...
5:2 καὶ εἶπέ μοι· Λευί, σοὶ δέδωκα τὰς εὐλογίας τῆς ἱερατείας ...

4:2 ... a servant and a minister of his presence.
4:3 You will cause the light of knowledge to shine in Jacob, and you will be like the sun to the whole seed of Israel. ...
4:5 Therefore wisdom and understanding have been given to you, so that you may instruct your sons ...
5:2 Then ... [the Most High] said to me: "Levi, I have given you the blessings of the priesthood ... .

Levi's priesthood is thus specified as having a teaching role (cf. Deut 33:10: Mal 2:4–7), which, as just mentioned, includes the disclosure of God's "secrets" (2:10). Levi is shown various tiers or levels of heaven,[272] the highest of which is God's dwelling place and is referred to as the "holy of holies." The correspondence between the Jerusalem sanctuary and that of heaven is obvious and is strengthened by a reference to sacrifices – though here described as "reasonable and bloodless" in nature[273] – and the angels who per-

---

[271] The uses of ἵστημι and ἐγγίζω (the verbal form of ἐγγύς) in priestly contexts were noted in my discussion of BW (cf. 1 En. 14:23; LXX 1 Chr 23:30; 2 Chr 18:18; 29:11; Ezek 44:13–16; 45:4; see Nickelsburg, "Enoch, Levi, and Peter," 585 n. 37); λειτουργὸς also has a priestly usage (cf. LXX Isa 61:6; Ezra 7:24; Neh 10:40; Sir 7:30; 50:14; and possibly Ps 102:21 [MT 103:21]; Ps 103:4 [MT 104:4]).

[272] It is clear that T. Levi's portrait of heaven is tiered; less certain is whether T. Levi originally envisioned three or seven levels of heaven. Due to its fragmentary condition, ALD's configuration of the celestial realm is also uncertain. For helpful discussions with bibliography, see Klawans, Purity, Sacrifice, and the Temple, 132–133; Kugler, From Patriarch to Priest, 181 n. 36; Angel, Otherworldly, 48 n. 104.

[273] The "sweet savor/aroma" language of the passage (3:6) is an allusion to the earthly cultic sacrifices (e.g., Exod 29:18, 25), but this has been understood in various ways. On "reasonable and bloodless" as a Christian gloss, which makes the notion of sacrifice "safe"

form them. Significantly, 3:7 styles these beings as ἀγγέλοις τοῦ προσώπου κυρίου, "angels of the Lord's presence" (cf. Isa 63:9), and the fact that Levi is dubbed with a similar title indicates that the priesthood in which he has been installed is modeled on and thus validated by the priesthood of heaven. As Klawans points out, 14:3[274] amounts to a statement that "earthy purity [specifically that of the Levites] is in emulation of heavenly purity."[275]

While the above references are from Greek T. Levi, it seems that its notion of a heaven-earth correspondence was inherited from *ALD*. For example, though references specifically to the angel of the presence and Levi's analogous description are not extant in the Aramaic text, 4Q213a 2 15–18 describes the patriarch's visionary experience, which refers to the heavenly realm and an angel:[276]

15 *vacat* אדין חזיון אחזית[ן
16 בחזית חזויא וחזית שמ[י]א
17 תחותי רם עד דבק לשמי[א
18 לי תרעי שמיא ומלאך ...

15 Then I was shown visions[
16 in the vision of visions, and I saw the heaven[s
17 beneath me, high until it reached to the heaven[s
18 to me the gates of heavens, and an angel ...

Though fragmentary, this passage has been noted for its affinities with not only the Levi's vision in T. Levi 2:5–6 but also the introductory section to Enoch's experience in 1 En. 13:7–9[277] and may suggest that Levi is "transported to heaven and sees an angel,"[278] possibly an *angelus intepres* (cf. Dan 7:16). *ALD* also refers to the patriarch as כהן לאל עליון, "a priest of/to the God Most High" (*Bodl.* col. b 5–6; cf. *Bodl.* col. a 20; 4Q213b 6).[279] The designation is the same as that applied to Melchizedek in Gen 14:10 (cf. 1QapGen XXII, 15), and given that other texts interpret this enigmatic human

---

for Christians as per Rom 12:1, see Hollander and de Jonge, *The Testaments*, 138. Cf. Klawans, *Purity, Sacrifice, and the Temple*, 132.

[274] The verse reads as follows: "For just as the sky is purer than the earth in the Lord's eyes, so are you [i.e., the Levitical priests] than all the nations."

[275] Klawans, *Purity, Sacrifice, and the Temple*, 132.

[276] Text and translation are from Stone and Greenfield, DJD 22, 30–31.

[277] Drawnel, *An Aramaic Wisdom Text*, 227.

[278] Kugel, "Levi's Elevation to the Priesthood," 10.

[279] While *Bodl.* col. b 6–7 has "God Most High," there is some ambiguity with *Bodl.* col. a 20, which seems to have עלמיא, "eternity," written over עליון. Cf. Drawnel, *An Aramaic Wisdom Text*, 117; Greenfield, Stone, and Eshel, *The Aramaic Levi Document*, 36–37; Collins, *The Scepter and the Star*, 97 n. 72. For the reading "God of eternity" in *ALD*, see the discussion of 4Q213b 6 in Stone and Greenfield, DJD 22, 38–39.

priest as an angelic warrior-priest,[280] it has been suggested that a Melchizedek connection would have been a way for *ALD* to establish a correspondence between the earthly priesthood of Levi and the angelic priesthood.[281]   Corroborating this idea – as well the reference to Levi's rapport with God in T. Levi 2:10 – is the pronouncement that the patriarch is "close (קריב) to God and close (קריב) to all his holy ones" (*Bodl.* col. b 21–22).[282]   As Drawnel explains, this proximity to God and his holy ones "is a response to Levi's request to be close [קרב] to God [in 4Q213a 1 18].   That would assume that Levi's life and liturgical service is parallel to the heavenly liturgy of the angels."[283]   Moreover, the reference to God as the "Lord of the heavens" (*Bodl.* col. b 6) likely functioned to undergird the idea that Levi has a "particular relationship with the heavenly realm."[284]

It may be that Levi's closeness to the angelic holy ones extends beyond priestly matters.   In his prayer, the use of the verb קרב has understandably prompted Drawnel to conclude that Levi's request has a "sacerdotal character."[285]   I am not convinced, however, that issues of the priesthood are the sole motivation for these words.   Earlier in his prayer, Levi petitions God with the imperative: "do not allow any *satan* (שׁטן) to rule over me" (4Q213a 1 17; cf. 11QPs^a XIX, 15–16).[286]   Thus, Levi is presumably requesting that

---

[280] On the Melchizedek tradition, proposals for how it developed, and on this figure's identification with Michael, see my discussion of *11QMelchizedek* in Chapter 4. On the possible references to Melchizedek as the ranking angelic priest in the *Songs of the Sabbath Sacrifice*, which may also cast him as a warrior, see Chapter 5. I will make additional comments on Melchizedek as it pertains to *ALD*, below.

[281] So Anders Aschim, "Melchizedek and Levi," in *The Dead Sea Scrolls Fifty Years After Their Discovery: Proceedings of the Jerusalem Congress, July 20–25, 1997* (eds., Lawrence H. Schiffman, Emmuanel Tov, James C. VanderKam; Jerusalem: Israel Exploration Society, 2000), 780. Cf. Perrin, *The Dynamics*, 168–169; Collins, *The Scepter and the Star*, 97; Greenfield, Stone, and Eshel, *The Aramaic Levi Document*, 155. Drawnel, *An Aramaic Wisdom Text*, 251, also notes: "Melchizedek was the first priest (כהן) ever mentioned in the Genesis account; in order then to enhance Levi's position as the first person to hold the priestly office, Melchizedek's title is ascribed to Levi."

[282] The translation is from Drawnel, *An Aramaic Wisdom Text*, 268. As mentioned above, the priestly import of T. Levi 2:10 includes the description of Levi as standing "close" (ἐγγὺς) to the Lord. It comes as no surprise, then, that the Athos manuscript renders the Aramaic קריב as ἐγγὺς. Cf. MT and LXX Ezek 45:4, which use a similar combination of words to describe the actions of priests.

[283] See Drawnel, *An Aramaic Wisdom Text*, 268, who also notes the similarities these ideas have with passages I have noted previously (cf. Zech 3:7) or will discuss later (cf. Jub. 30:18; 31:14; 1QSb IV, 24).

[284] So Drawnel, *An Aramaic Wisdom Text*, 260.

[285] Drawnel, *An Aramaic Wisdom Text*, 221.

[286] The translation is from Drawnel, *An Aramaic Wisdom Text*, 216. For discussion of Levi's prayer in *ALD* and its similarities to other texts, as well as the assertion that demon-

his connection to the holy ones include protection from the "darkness" of the hostile spiritual beings to which he refers (cf. 4Q213 4 6). The previously noted interpretation of Melchizedek as an angelic warrior-priest would make Melchizedek the ideal answer to Levi's prayer.[287] Also, T. Levi describes those who adorned Levi in his priestly vestments as "seven men in white clothing" (8:1), which is likely indicative of their status as both archangels[288] and priests.[289] If these are the same as the "seven" who depart from Levi in his dream in *ALD* (cf. 4Q213b 2; *Bodl.* col. a 9), it suggests that the Aramaic text had Levi's earthly priesthood legitimized by no less than the heavenly priesthood itself.[290]

---

ic beings rather than merely an evil inclination are in view, see Benjamin Wold, "Demonizing Sin? The Evil Inclination in 4QInstruction," in *Evil in Second Temple Judaism and Early Christianity* (eds., Chris Keith and Loren T. Stuckenbruck; WUNT 2/417; Tübingen: Mohr Siebeck, 2016), 37–38; Armin Lange, "Considerations Concerning the 'Spirits of Impurity' in Zech 13.2," in *Die Dämonen – Demons* (eds., Hermann Lichtenberger, Armin Lange, Diethard Römhelf; Tübingen: Mohr Seibeck 2003), 262.

[287] As Drawnel, *An Aramaic Wisdom Text*, 217, 347, observes, *4QVisions of Amram* "already has a full-blown division of the spiritual world between two classes of angelic beings represented by Melchizedek and Melchiresha," and that "[t]his composition ... evidently develops the ideas on the nature of the spiritual world already present in [*ALD*]." I will address *4QVisions of Amram* in the following section of this chapter.

[288] I.e., seven angels, which is almost certainly an allusion to the early Jewish tradition that there were seven – rather than four – archangels (cf. 1 En. 20:1–7). On this topic, see my discussion of *BW*, above.

[289] On white (or linen) clothing of angelic figures as possibly indicative of a priestly vocation, see Ezek 9:2–11; 10:2; cf. Dan 10:5; 12:6–7. It should also be remembered that seven white-clad angelic figures make an appearance in 1 En. 87:1–4, and it has been suggested that, there, these figures are heavenly priests; see Tiller, *The Animal Apocalypse*, 245. Cf. Angel, *Otherworldly*, 51, who summarizes as follows: "The garments of the angels in both Ezekiel and *T. Levi* recall those that the high priest is to wear once a year on the Day of Atonement when he enters the holy of holies (Lev 16:4). Thus, the white clothing of the angels in *T. Levi* 8 most likely identifies them as priests. Though the clothing of the seven is not described in the preserved portions of *ALD*, it is possible that *T. Levi* followed *ALD* in this case."

[290] As Himmelfarb, *Ascent to Heaven*, 30–46, notes, Levi's investiture as an earthly priest in T. Levi follows his ascent to heaven, which suggests that the latter legitimized the former. Angel, *Otherworldly*, 53, expounds on this idea by proposing that the collectedness exhibited by Levi during his vision of heaven in T. Levi 2–5 – in contrast to the dread of Enoch in *BW* (cf. 1 En. 14:14–15) – is indicative of the patriarch's elevated status "near to God and near to all his holy ones" (*Bodl.* col. b 21–22; cf. T. Levi 2:10), not of a transformed or perhaps diminished significance of the temple for later Christians, as some have argued (e.g., M. de Jonge, "Levi, the Sons of Levi and the Law in Testament of Levi X, XIV–XV and XVI," in *Jewish Eschatology, Early Christian Christology and the Testaments of the Twelve Patriarchs: Collected Essays of Marinus de Jonge* [NovTSup 63; Leiden: Brill, 1991], 180–190). Once again, extant *ALD* does not reveal the patriarch's composure during his visions of heaven, and as Angel surmises, "it is possible that Levi's

The following observations will assist in drawing my discussion of *ALD* to a close. I highlighted above that T. Levi posits a teaching role for Levi and his priesthood (cf. 2:10; 4:2–5:2). The didactic import of *ALD* is similarly evident, and here I cite a passage situated near the end of the composition. The reconstruction incorporates 4Q213 1 I, 9–11 and *Cambr.* col. e and has Levi conveying these words:[291]

9 ...   *vacat*   וכען בני ספר מוסר חכמה
10 אלפו לבניכן ותהוה חכמתא עמכן ליקר עלם די אלף חכמה יקר
11 הוא בה ודי שאט חכמתא לבסרון ולשיטו מתיהב ...

9 ... And now, my sons, teach scribal craft, instruction, wisdom
10 to your children and let wisdom be with you for eternal glory. For he who learns wisdom will (attain) glory
11 through her, but he who despises wisdom will become an object of disdain and scorn ...

Drawnel proposes that *ALD* reflects a family-based, Levitical education, which espouses the view that "the priestly class is to occupy the leading role in Israel – provided that it keeps the tradition of the forefathers and transmits it to the future priestly generations [since n]eglecting sapiential education leads to abandoning the way of truth and justice, and to the dominion of darkness over the sons of Levi."[292] Kugler argues for a more contentious context for the emergence of *ALD* in that he sees the text as stemming from

---

calmness in *T. Levi* reflects an older notion inherited from *ALD* – the notion that the earthly priesthood of Levi is analogous to and somehow participates in the nature of the angelic priesthood serving God in the celestial temple." It should also be noted that Levi's murderous vengeance against the Shechemites, which, in the biblical narrative is initially condemned (cf. Gen 34:1–31; 49:7), is elsewhere celebrated or affirmed as the kind of action apropos for those of priestly lineage (cf. Num 25:12–13; Deut 33:8–11). On Levi's Shechemite zealotry being affirmed in *ALD*/T. Levi, see *Cambr.* col. d 15–18. Cf. Drawnel, *An Aramaic Wisdom Text*, 263; Collins, *The Scepter and the Star*, 102; Perrin, *The Dynamics*, 149–150. I mention this here because other Aramaic texts depict the sin-purging/binding of perpetrators to be angelic prerogatives (cf. 1 En. 10:1–15; 90:22; 100:4), which may be yet another way Levi is associated with his priestly angelic counterparts.

[291] This is a simplified presentation of the reconstructed text and its translation, incorporating the treatments of Drawnel, *An Aramaic Wisdom Text*, 156–158, 194–195, 328–333; Stone, Greenfield, and Eshel, *The Aramaic Levi Document*, 102–103. On the significance of this passage for the Levitical family being portrayed as having both access to the divine will and the responsibility to disseminate it, see Hanna Tervanotko, "Visions, Otherworldly Journeys and Divine Beings," in *Crossing Imaginary Boundaries: The Dead Sea Scrolls in the Context of Second Temple Judaism* (eds., Mika Pajunen and Hanna Tervanotko; Helsinki: The Finnish Exegetical Society, 2015), 210–240, here 221.

[292] Drawnel, *An Aramaic Wisdom Text*, 78–85, 349–351, here 350.

competition-driven priestly disputes.[293] Given both the limited material with which scholars have to work and its fragmentary nature, any proposals for *ALD's* origins are tentative, though I am inclined to agree with those who are suspicious of overly polemical readings of the text.[294] As Machiela has observed, the "rather generous orthopraxy" of Aramaic compositions like *ALD* stand in contrast to the "more narrowly-focused sectarian works" composed by the Qumran movement.[295] Moreover, I would offer that a connection to heaven and its priests undergirds the hortatory import of the text: a heavenly link only heightens any pleas for Israel's priests to treat their office with utmost sanctity – a charge which also presupposes, in theory, a high view of the Jerusalem temple and the priestly office.[296] Lastly, it is obvious that the priesthood is a matter of utmost importance for *ALD's* author(s), and for my purposes, it is significant that one of the ways the text seems to assert that the priesthood should have "the leading role in Israel," is by connecting it to its angelic archetype and exemplar. This impulse reveals not only that the notion of a correspondence between heaven and earth was central but also that it was considered ideal for Israel's priests to emulate and to learn from the heavenly priests.[297] The juxtaposition of Levi's closeness to the holy ones and his request to be delivered from hostile spiritual forces indicates that

---

[293] Kugler, *From Patriarch to Priest*, 135–137, contends that *ALD* is a polemic against those who have rejected the ideal priesthood of Levi which emphasizes purity, sapiential matters, and education.

[294] E.g., Drawnel, *An Aramaic Wisdom Text*, 84–85.

[295] Of the "generally accepted norms" noted by Machiela, "Situating the Aramaic Texts," 92, *ALD* not only supports the Levitical priesthood but also endogamous marriage (cf. *Bodl.* col. b 14–21; *Cambr.* col. d 3–4). On the latter topic in *ALD*, see Andrew R Perrin, "Tobit's Contexts and Contacts in the Qumran Aramaic Anthology," *JSP* 25 (2015): 23–51, esp. 37.

[296] Cf. Klawans, *Purity, Sacrifice, and the Temple*, 132–134, whose comments pertain to T. Levi but arguably apply by extension to *ALD*.

[297] Cf. Machiela, "Situating the Aramaic Texts," 94–97, who explains Levi's sapiential exhortation to his children (e.g., 4Q213 1 I, 13–19, which is continuation of the passage just cited) as an example of what the Aramaic literature esteems as "following the divinely-bestowed ancestral traditions." Thus, the assertion that Israel's priesthood is modelled on and informed by heaven may be additional evidence for the idea that Jews viewed themselves as keeping these "divinely-bestowed" traditions. Machiela also asserts that the concomitant honour, peace, and respect that these traditions were thought to foster among non-Jews make good sense in the context of Hellenistic Judaism, a period marked by foreign oppression, uncertainty, and temptation. With this in view, a connection to the angels would have been invaluable, not least for the confidence it engendered in Israel's priestly calling and its Levitical lineage. On *ALD's* priestly lineage emphasis, see Donshing Don Chang, *Phinehas, The Sons of Zadok, and Melchizedek: Priestly Covenant in Late Second Temple Texts* (LSTS 90; London: Bloomsbury T & T Clark, 2016), 83, who puts it succinctly: "The Levites are the heirs of a ... priestly tradition that was written in books handed down to the later generations, which implies that they have authentic antiquity."

ALD's author(s) had a confident belief that the priesthood's connection to the angelic realm extended beyond sacerdotal matters to guardianship, perhaps in part because the sanctity of the priesthood warranted and necessitated such provision.

E. Visions of Amram

Seven fragmentary manuscripts from Cave 4 have been dubbed *Visions of Amram* (henceforth, *VA*),[298] so named from its incipit found in 4Q543 1 1–2 (which is reconstructed with parallels from 4Q545):[299]

פרשגן כתב מלי חזות עֹמֹרם בֹר[ן קהת בר לוי כול דין] 1
אחוי לבנוהי ודי פקֹד אֹנון ב[יום מותה ... 2

1 A copy of the document of the Vision of Amram, son[of Qahat, son of Levi: Everything which]
2 he revealed to his sons and which he appointed for them on[the day of his death ...

As the reference to Levi indicates, *VA* is concerned with Israel's priestly line, and, as such, has been classified as being part of a "series"[300] of Aramaic sacerdotal texts. Given *VA*'s proposed dependence on the oldest text in this series, *ALD*, it is estimated that *VA* was composed in the first half of the 2nd cent. BCE or slightly earlier.[301] In brief, it is the two angelic figures of Amram's vision that have particular relevance for this study.

---

[298] The *Visions of Amram* manuscripts (4Q543–549 [= *4QVisions of Amram*ᵃ⁻ᵍ]) have been published by Emile Puech, ed., *Qumran Grotte 4.XXII: Textes araméens, première partie: 4Q529–549* (DJD 31; Oxford: Claredon, 2001), 283–405. However, thematic elements and the absence of overlap with the other manuscripts indicate that 4Q548 and 4Q549 should not be considered *VA* witnesses; see Robert R. Duke, *The Social Location of the Visions of Amram (4Q543–547)* (StBibLit 135; New York: Peter Lang, 2010), 35–42.

[299] Hebrew text, sigla, and line numbering of *VA* are from Puech, DJD 31; translations are based on Duke, *The Social Location*.

[300] As Michael E. Stone, "Amram," *EDSS* 1:23–24, points out, *ALD*, *VA*, and another text, the *Testament of Qahat* (4Q542), form a "series of priestly instruction." On the thematic similarities of these and other Aramaic works, see Perrin, *The Dynamics*, 158–189. Cf. Hanna Tervanotko, "A Trilogy of Testaments? The Status of the Testament of Qahat Versus Texts Attributed to Levi and Amram," in *Old Testament Pseudepigrapha and the Scriptures* (ed., Eibert J. C. Tigchelaar; BETL 270; Leuven: Peeters, 2014), 41–59. The sacerdotal concerns of 4Q542 do not include the angelic realm, and it will therefore not be discussed.

[301] Paleographic analysis suggests a *terminus ante quem* of 125 BCE (see Puech, DJD 31, 285–288), but as noted in the previous section, *ALD* is dated to the 3rd or early 2nd cent. BCE. Given the likelihood that *VA* has developed the thought of *ALD*, a date of composition for *VA* no later than the first half of the 2nd cent. BCE is realistic.

According to 4Q544 1 10–11, Amram sees the two figures "judging" (דאנין) and having a "great quarrel" (תגר רב) concerning him. After Amram inquires as to what he has seen, the two confirm to the patriarch that they are "ruling (שליטין) over all the sons of men." It appears Amram is then asked by the figures something about their rule.[302] Amran's response has not been preserved, but he does relay a description of the appearance of the figures in lines 12–14 of the same fragment:

12 ... והא נטלת עיני וחזית[
13 די/וחד] מנהון חזוה חשל[ן כפ]תן [וכול]ל[ן ב]ו[ש]ה צבענין וחשיך חשור[ן אנפוהי
14 ואחרנא חזית]ו[ד]הֿאֿ [∘]ל[ן   ] בחזוה ואנפיוה העכן ו[מכסה ...

12 I raised my eyes and I saw.
13 And one from them his appearance [reading is debated; see below] all his clothes are colorful and dark is the darkness of [...]. And the other one
14 I saw and beho[ld ...] in his appearance and his face is smiling and he is covered ...

4Q544 2 13–14 suggests that the figure associated with darkness is named מלכי רשע, "Melchiresha," which means "(my) king of wickedness." An angelic identity for Melchiresha is suggested by the fact that elsewhere in the Scrolls he is portrayed as an evil spiritual being, who is cursed elsewhere (cf. 4Q280 1–7) in a manner reminiscent of the imprecations against Belial in the *Community Rule* (cf. 1QS II, 4–10).[303] The name of the righteous figure who stands opposite to Melchiresha is not extant, but Milik's proposal of Melchizedek has found widespread acceptance[304] and is only strengthened by the fact that the namesake of *11QMelchizedek* is often understood to be an angelic benefactor who contends against a wicked adversary (see Chapter 4); *VA* also

---

[302] It has been widely accepted/assumed that Amram is here asked to *choose* the figure with which he will align himself, a notion that stems from what has become the influential reconstruction of Józef T. Milik, "4QVisions d'Amram et une citation d'Origène," *RB* 79 (1972): 79–80, who introduced the verb בחר to line 12. For a recent defense of this reading, see Blake A. Jurgens, "Reassessing the Dream-Vision of the Vision of Amram (4Q543–547)," *JSP* 24 (2014): 3–42. However, Andrew B. Perrin, "Another Look at Dualism in *4QVisions of Amram*," *Hen* 36 (2014): 106–117, has challenged Milik's reconstruction, arguing that it is less certain than it is often assumed to be. I will return to this issue, below.

[303] For discussion of 4Q280, see Józef T. Milik, "Milkî-sedek et Milkî-resha' dans les anciens écrits juifs et chrétiens," *JJS* 23 (1972): 126–139; Paul J. Kobelski, *Melchizedek and Melchiresa* (CBQMS 10; Washington: Catholic Biblical Society of America, 1981), 38–42. The angelic identity of Melchiresha is further corroborated if the restoration of עירא, "watcher," is accepted in 4Q544 2 12; so Milik, "4QVisions d'Amram," 83. Cf. Puech, DJD 31, 327. Note, however, the caution of Davidson, *Angels at Qumran*, 265, who points out that there is scant evidence for this reading.

[304] Melchizedek (meaning "[my] king of righteousness") is, of course, the perfect counter to Melchiresha; see Milik, "4QVisions d'Amram," 85–86. Cf., e.g., Puech, DJD 31, 329; Davidson, *Angels at Qumran*, 266–268; Kobelski, *Melchizedek and Melchiresa*, 36.

indicates that each angel had "three names" (4Q544 3 1–2),[305] with these pairs often suggested: Melchiresha and Melchizedek, the Prince of Darkness and Prince of Light, and Belial and Michael.[306]

Two features of this angelic scenario are noteworthy for my purposes. First, the contrast between the menacing[307] description of Melchiresha and the reassuring countenance of his righteous adversary may suggest that Melchizedek was ideally envisioned as providing Amram and his descendants a measure of protection from his wicked counterpart. Whether Amram is prompted to align himself with one of the angels is, as noted above, not as certain as it is commonly assumed to be.[308] That being said, if *VA* is dependent on *ALD*,[309] the emphasis the latter places on the conditional nature of the priesthood's leadership[310] may suggest that in the former Amram was asked

---

[305] Line 2 reads: ואן[מֹ]ר לי תלתה שמה]ן, "And he s]aid to me, 'Three name[s …'." See Puech, DJD 31, 328.

[306] On the reconstruction of the three pairs of names, see Milik, "4QVisions d'Amram," 85–86; Kobelski, *Melchizedek and Melchiresha*, 33–36; John J. Collins, "Powers in Heaven: God, Gods, and Angels in the Dead Sea Scrolls," in *Religion in the Dead Sea Scrolls* (eds., John J. Collins and Robert A. Kugler; SDSSRL; Grand Rapids: Eerdmans, 2000), 18.

[307] There is debate over the reading of the first part of the description of Melchiresha's countenance (4Q544 1 13), which Duke leaves blank in his translation. Milik, "4QVision d'Amram," 79–80, influentially proposed that the angel's appearance is תן[כפ], "that of a snake," with Puech, DJD 31, 322–324, preserving and developing the serpentine imagery. *Contra* Perrin, "Another Look at Dualism," 112–116, who has expanded an unpublished suggestion of Edward M. Cook, making a strong case for a reading of דחיל ואימ]תן, "dreadful and terrifying," which is similar to Dan 7:7.

[308] Perrin, "Another Look at Dualism," 110–112.

[309] The evidence of which includes a possible Melchizedek connection and similar dualistic depictions of hostile *"satans"* or spiritual beings. As Drawnel, *An Aramaic Wisdom Text*, 347, observes, the "unique expression חשוך שטן proves that [*ALD's*] eschatology is related to the light-darkness opposition, characteristic of a dualistic view of the spiritual world. In *ALD* 1a v. 10 [= 4Q213a 1 17] Levi prays not to be misled by any *satan* from God's path, and, while his prayer is heard in his life, the contrary is true in the future of his sons. The term שטן denotes a spiritual being hostile to humanity. … His association with darkness in *ALD* 102 l. 6 [= 4Q213 4 6] recalls Melchiresha from the *Testament of Amram*. He is an angelic being whose dominion is darkness and who rules over humankind (see 4Q543 5–9 4–5; 4Q544 1 13; 2 12–15). Walking in the darkness of *satan* refers, therefore, to being under the power and dominion of spiritual beings hostile to light. Note that in the *Testament of Amram*, there appears another angelic being whose dominion is light and whose name is most probably Melchizedek (see 4Q542 5–9 6–8; 4Q544 1 14; 2 16). Levi, who prays not to be under the rule of satan and is evidently heard by God, is indirectly associated with the person of biblical Melchizedek." Additional evidence for *ALD's* influence on *VA* is noted by Perrin, *The Dynamics*, 162–165, who observes the similarities between the terms applied to Levi in *ALD* and Aaron in *VA*. Cf. Angel, *Otherworldly*, 55.

[310] Again, the import of *ALD* is captured by Drawnel, *An Aramaic Wisdom Text*, 350: "The priestly class is to occupy the leading role in Israel *provided that it keeps the tradition of the forefathers and transmits it to future priestly generations* [emphasis mine]."

to choose a side of the dualistic divide.[311] Regardless, *VA* appears to be an early witness to a dualism that has two angels standing at the heads of opposing sides of the dualistic divide.[312] The implication, therefore, is that Israel's priestly line has privileged angelic guardianship in Melchizedek.

The second noteworthy feature of *VA's* angelic scenario is related to the first: if Israel's priests have a connection to Melchizedek, it would only make sense that, like the possible connection in *ALD*, there is priestly significance to the relationship. In addition to what may be a reference to Aaron as a "holy priest [to God Most High ..." (4Q545 4 16),[313] it is significant that in the same line it may be Melchizedek who makes known to Aaron רז עובדה, "the mystery of his service." Perrin notes that a revelatory role for Melchizedek would emphasize that a component of this mystery is a "close connection"[314] with the celestial priesthood, which serves to link the earthly priests "into a chain of command that stretches upwards to the heavens, ultimately to the head of the priestly order, Melchizedek himself."[315]

Duke has argued that *VA* is the product of pre-Hasmonean, disenfranchised priests who were being oppressed by wealthy elites.[316] While this is an interesting proposal, my own sense is that the brevity and fragmentary condition of the text mean that specific proposals for the scribal context of the document need to be considered tentatively. Even if correct, there are no indications in the extant document that its authors desired to separate themselves from other Jews.[317] What is most significant for this study is the possibility

---

[311] Indeed, choice is strongly implied in the dualistic and sapiential language of 4Q548 1 12. Even in light of his recent call to reevaluate the certainty with which commentators have placed a question on the lips of the angels, Perrin, "Another Look at Dualism," 111, acknowledges that the words במן מננא (4Q544 1 12) are indicative that Melchizedek and Melchiresha said or asked *something* to/of Amram. On the relationship between the so-called "two-ways" tradition and dualism in *VA*, see Duke, *The Social Location*, 83–85.

[312] Duke, *The Social Location*, 80–83, highlights the important role that the "two-ways" and angels play in *VA*. Cf. Collins, "Powers in Heaven," 18. For further on the dualism of *VA*, see Liora Goldman, "Dualism in the Visions of Amram," *RevQ* 24 (2010): 421–432.

[313] Puech, DJD 31, 342, restores the end of line 16 as: כהן קדיש הוא לאל עליון... He does so due to similar language in *VA* (4Q543 22 2), *ALD* (*Bodl.* col. b 5–6), and the *Genesis Apocryphon* (1Q20 XXII, 16), and, if accepted, this reading may be functioning in a manner similar to that proposed for *ALD* insofar as it establishes a correspondence between the earthly priesthood of Aaron and that of Melchizedek, who in other texts is interpreted as an angelic-warrior priest; see Perrin, *The Dynamics*, 166–169.

[314] Perrin, *The Dynamics*, 188.

[315] See Perrin, *The Dynamics*, 166–170, here 170, who also provides a helpful discussion of the use of רז in the Dead Sea Scrolls.

[316] So Duke, *The Social Location*, 7, 110.

[317] Again, it is telling that *VA's* emphasizes "generally accepted norms" of ancient Judaism (e.g., endogamous marriage; cf. 4Q544 1 5–9; 4Q547 1–2) rather than the "narrowly-focused" concerns of the Qumran movement; see Machiela, "Situating the Aramaic Texts," 92, 95.

that *VA* stresses the following: that Israel's priestly line has a relationship to its heavenly counterparts, and that if these human priests are to serve as they ought, the basis for their actions must be the knowledge obtained from heaven's priests, of whom Melchizedek may have been envisioned as foremost.

F. Tobit

Six manuscripts of the Book of Tobit were found among the Dead Sea Scrolls – five in Aramaic and one in Hebrew[318] – and these discoveries have effectively ended the debate as to whether Tobit was composed in Greek or a Semitic language.[319] While there is still some disagreement over Hebrew or Aramaic as the language of composition, the growing consensus that opts for composition in Aramaic will be accepted here.[320] Though set in the Assyrian exile, the work was likely written in the 3rd or 2nd cent. BCE.[321]

Tobit has been called "a delightful story of the afflictions of a pious Israelite and the adventures of his dutiful son, who makes a journey in the company of a disguised angel and returns with a bride and the means to restore the father's health and wealth."[322] The book has also been described as an "ex-

---

[318] The Qumran manuscripts of Tobit are designated as follows: Aramaic: 4QpapTob[a] [= 4Q196]; 4QTob[b–d] [4Q497–499]; Schøyen Tobit [= 4Q196a]; and Hebrew: 4QTob[e] [= 4Q200]. Cf. Joseph A. Fitzmyer, "196–200. 4QpapTobit a ar, 4QTobit b–d ar, and 4QTobit e," in *Qumran Cave 4. XIV: Parabiblical Texts, Part 2* (eds., M. Broshi et al.; DJD 19; Oxford: Clarendon Press, 1995), 1–76; Michaela Hallermayer, *Text und Überlieferung des Buches Tobit* (DCLS 3; Berlin: de Gruyter, 2008); Torleif Elgvin, ed., *Gleanings from the Caves: Dead Sea Scrolls and Artifacts from the Schøyen Collection* (LSTS 71; London: Continuum, 2016). For the Greek text of Tobit, see Robert Hanhart, ed., *Tobit* (SVTG 8/5; Göttingen: Vandenhoeck & Ruprecht, 1983), which is the basis for text cited here.

[319] Carey A. Moore, *Tobit: A New Translation with Introduction and Commentary* (AB 40A; New York: Doubleday, 1996), 34.

[320] See the discussions and bibliographies provided by Moore, *Tobit*, 33–39; Joseph A. Fitzmyer, *Tobit* (CEJL; Berlin: de Gruyter, 2003), 18–28; Machiela and Perrin, "Tobit and the Genesis Apocryphon," 111–132, esp. 113 n. 6; Andrew B. Perrin, "An Almanac of Tobit Studies: 2000–2014," *CurBR* 13 (2014): 111–113; idem, "Tobit's Contexts and Contacts," 24 n. 1. On the translation of Tobit into Hebrew at Qumran, see Andrew B. Perrin, "From Lingua Franca to Lingua Sacra: The Scripuralization of Tobit in 4QTob[e]," *VT* 66 (2016): 117–132.

[321] For a discussion of the options, see Perrin, "An Almanac," 113. Cf. Moore, *Tobit*, 41–42; Fitzmyer, *Tobit*, 50–52.

[322] H. Neil Richardson, "The Book of Tobit," in *The Interpreter's One-Volume Commentary on the Bible* (ed., Charles M. Laymon; Nashville: Abingdon, 1971), 526, as quoted in Moore, *Tobit*, 3.

tended angelology,"[323] since the angel, Raphael, who disguises himself as a man until the end of the story, has a significant role in the narrative. Hannah describes Raphael as one of the earliest Jewish examples of the notion that individuals have a personal guardian angel,[324] and to the extent that Raphael assists and protects Tobit and his family members, Hannah's description is accurate. However, the notion of a *personal* guardian angel may not sufficiently capture Raphael's role. To put this in perspective, note the comments of Delcor on the objective of Tobit:

> The author is trying to convince his reader that God never abandons a pious [person] ... . Throughout the book the author exhorts his fellow countrymen to obey the law. For even if they live in the Diaspora, God will not fail to protect them, as long as, in spite of the difficulties of their peculiar position, they remain faithful to him.[325]

There is a sense, then, in which Raphael is more than a personal angelic guardian; he is also a national angelic guardian, a role often reserved for his archangelic compatriot, Michael. And Raphael's actions serve to emphasize the following: for the faithful and exiled Israelite,[326] the dispatch of an angel for special protection is not out of the question.

Highlighting some of the specifics of this angelic succor will bring it into sharper relief. First, Raphael (which means "God has healed") binds the demon, Asmodeus (8:3),[327] an act that is reminiscent of those attributed to Raphael and other angels in the Enochic tradition (cf. 1 En. 10:1–15; 90:22;

---

[323] So George W. E. Nickelsburg, *Jewish Literature Between the Bible and the Mishnah: A Historical and Literary Introduction* (Minneapolis: Fortress, 1981), 40 n. 41. Cf. Géza G. Xeravits, "The Angel's Self-Revelation in Tobit 12," in *Sibyls, Scriptures, and Scrolls: John Collins at Seventy* (eds., Joel Baden, Hindy Najman, and Eibert Tigchelaar; JSJSup 175; Leiden: Brill, 2016), 1399–1417, here 1399, who refers to the Book of Tobit (chapter 12, in particular) as "a kind of summary of the angelology of Palestinian Judaism of the last centuries BCE," insofar as it presents Raphael as a revealer of divine knowledge, a mediator, a being of prominent heavenly rank, yet simultaneously one who is subordinate to God.

[324] Hannah, "Guardian Angels and Angelic National Patrons," 423–424.

[325] Matthias Delcor, "The Apocrypha and Pseudepigrapha of the Hellenistic Period: Tobit," in *The Cambridge History of Judaism: Volume 2, The Hellenistic Age* (eds., W. D. Davies and Louis Finkelstein; Cambridge: Cambridge University Press, 1989), 474, as quoted in Moore, *Tobit*, 24.

[326] Though it is clear that Tobit and his family are portrayed as faithful and exemplary Israelites (cf. 1:15–2:5), it should be noted that scholars have grappled with what sense the book's author is "in exile"; i.e., the geographical location of Tobit's author is a highly contested issue, with virtually every conceivable location (either Diasporic or Judean) having been proposed. For discussion, see Perrin, "An Almanac," 115–116.

[327] On the role of Asmodeus, see J. Edward Owens, "Asmodeus: A Less Than Minor Character in the Book of Tobit: A Narrative-Critical Study," in *Angels: The Concept of Celestial Beings*, 277–290.

100:4).[328] While Raphael's binding of the jealous demon who had killed Sarah's previous husbands is a powerful statement, his earlier intervention
(6:16–17) facilitated the endogamous marriage of Tobias and Sarah, which is
said to be "in accordance with the decree in the book of Moses" (7:11–13).[329]
Thus, the implicit assertion is that those with the utmost regard for *halakhic*
matters and the correct (re)interpretation of Torah have access to angelic assistance,[330] a point reinforced by Raphael's incognito name, Azariah, which
means "Yhwh has helped." Third, we are introduced to Raphael because he
is "sent to heal" – a play on his angelic name – Tobit and Sarah from blindness and demon possession, respectively (3:17); Raphael's commissioning is
the direct result of the protagonists' prayers being heard "in the glorious
presence of God" (3:16). This sentiment, once again, has parallels in 1
Enoch, which, as we have seen, portrays angels as not only in proximity to
God's throne but also serving in priest-like, intercessory capacities (cf. 1 En.
8:4–10:22; 14:22; 93:6; 97:5; 99:3; 104:1).[331] When Raphael finally reveals
himself as an angel, he announces the following in 12:12–15:

---

[328] On the connections to 1 Enoch, see Moore, *Tobit*, 160. Cf. Devorah Dimant, "Tobit
and the Qumran Aramaic Texts," in *Is There a Text in This Cave? Studies in the Textuality
of the Dead Sea Scrolls in Honour of George J. Brooke* (eds., Ariel Feldman, Maria Cioată,
and Charlotte Hempel; STDJ 119; Leiden: Brill, 2017), 399–402, who highlights the "dualistic components" of the texts, including the notion of two spiritual beings "pitted against"
one another and the similarities this scenario has with other Aramaic texts like *Visions of
Amram*. I also suggested above that the notion of the Levitical priesthood having a close
association with its angelic counterparts may find support in *ALD*/T. Levi's affirmation of
the vengeance of Levi on the Shechemites, precisely because such sin-purging is what
angels are cast as doing in other texts.

[329] For discussion of this scene, see Perrin, "Tobit's Context and Contacts," 39–40, who
observes that Levitical marriage cannot be in view here (*contra* Robert J. Littman, *Tobit:
The Book of Tobit in Codex Sinaiticus* [Septuagint Commentary Series 9; Leiden: Brill,
2008], 121) because Tobias is not a brother of Sarah's previous husbands. Moreover,
Shaye J. D. Cohen, "From the Bible to the Talmud: The Prohibition of Intermarriage,"
HAR 7 (1983), 23–39, has noted that there is nothing in the Torah specifically prohibiting
marriage to Gentiles, prompting Perrin to suggest that in the same way Ezra considered the
breaking of exogamous marital unions to be in accordance with the Law of Moses (cf. Ezra
10:3), Tobit is referring to a *halakhic* expansion of Torah. On this phenomenon, see Hindy
Najman, *Seconding Sinai: The Development of Mosaic Discourse in Second Temple Judaism* (JSJSup, 77; Leiden: Brill, 2003).

[330] See George W. E. Nickelsburg, "Seeking the Origin of the Two Ways Tradition in
Jewish and Christian Ethical Texts," in *A Multiform Heritage: Studies on Early Judaism
and Christianity in Honor of Robert A. Kraft* (ed., Benjamin G. Wright; Atlanta: Scholars
Press, 1999), 96, who discusses Tobit as part of the "two-ways" tradition and that the "nat-
uralness of [its] imagery of angelic accompaniment" is a precursor to later texts such as
1QS III, 13–IV, 26. Cf. Duke, *The Social Location*, 84.

[331] So Moore, *Tobit*, 157.

12 καὶ νῦν ὅτε προσηύξω καὶ Σαρρα, ἐγὼ προσήγαγον τὸ μνημόσυνον τῆς προσευχῆς
ὑμῶν ἐνώπιον τῆς δόξης κυρίου· καὶ ὅτε ἔθαπτες τοὺς νεκρούς, ὡσαύτως·
13 καὶ ὅτε οὐκ ὤκνησας ἀναστῆναι καὶ καταλιπεῖν σου τὸ ἄριστον καὶ ᾤχου καὶ
περιέστειλες τὸν νεκρόν, τότε ἀπέσταλμαι ἐπὶ σὲ πειράσαι σε.
14 καὶ ἅμα ἀπέσταλκέν με ὁ θεὸς ἰάσασθαί σε καὶ Σαρραν τὴν νύμφην σου.
15 ἐγώ εἰμι Ραφαηλ, εἷς τῶν ἑπτὰ ἀγγέλων, οἳ παρεστήκασιν καὶ εἰσπορεύονται ἐνώπιον
τῆς δόξης κυρίου.

12 So now, when you and Sarah prayed, it was I who brought and read the record of your
prayer before the glory of the Lord, and likewise whenever you buried the dead.
13 And that time when you did not hesitate to get up and leave your dinner to go and bury
the dead,
14 I was sent to you to test you. And at the same time God sent me to heal you and Sarah
your daughter-in-law.
15 I am Raphael, one of the seven angels who stand ready and enter before the glory of the
Lord.

Though not stated outright, Raphael is seemingly envisioned as an angel of
the presence,[332] and the lofty description of Jerusalem in Tobit's hymn
(13:15–17) may suggest a celestial Jerusalem/temple,[333] presumably where
the prayers of the pious are heard and from which angelic assistance is dis-
patched.

---

[332] On the Isa 63:9-inspiried epithet "the angel of the presence," see Chapter 2. The
priestly connotations of Raphael's role are emphasized in part by the verb παρίστημι,
which is elsewhere used in sacerdotal contexts, and this is made more explicit in the so-
called shorter version of the Greek text of v. 15 which rehearses the revelation of v. 12:
ἐγώ εἰμι Ραφαηλ, εἷς ἐκ τῶν ἑπτὰ ἁγίων ἀγγέλων, οἳ προσαναφέρουσιν τὰς προσευχὰς
τῶν ἁγίων καὶ εἰσπορεύονται ἐνώπιον τῆς δόξης τοῦ ἁγίου, "I am Raphael, one of the
seven holy angels who present the prayers of the saints and enter into the glorious presence
of the Holy One." See Fitzmyer, *Tobit*, 295 whose translation of the shorter text is cited.
On Raphael as an angel of the presence, see, e.g., Davidson, *Angels at Qumran*, 195; Beate
Ego, "The Figure of the Angel Raphael According to His Farewell Address in Tob 12:6–
20," in *Angels: The Concept of Celestial Beings*, 244.

[333] Alexander, *Mystical Texts*, 55, notes that the language of 12:15 hints at a heavenly
temple. Cf. Stuckenbruck, "Coping with Alienating Experience," 66–67, who suggests
that the Jerusalem of Tobit's hymn "relates to the *heavenly* Jerusalem, not to Jerusalem as
it currently exists. ... The burden of 'exile' borne by Tobit and the other characters in the
book would initially seem to involve remoteness from the Jerusalem in the land of Israel.
However, when Jerusalem is envisioned as heavenly, this distance no longer applies in the
same way. Israelites everywhere, including Tobit in a place of exile, can through prayer
and thanksgiving engage in a form of hymnic worship (without the offering of sacrifices)
that, in effect, closes the gap ... . Rather than being placed at a disadvantage due to living
in the Diaspora, those who live out pious lives can engage authentically in the worship of
God by focusing on Jerusalem in its heavenly dimension. The text thus implies that this
Jerusalem above is what ultimately counts and that genuine piety is not exiled form this
reality [emphasis retained]."

Thus, what is implied at the beginning of Tobit is also reiterated near its conclusion: the assistance available to faithful and exiled Israelites is not from just any celestial being: it is provided by one of the elite angels who serve in closest proximity to God.

G. Jubilees

Extant in its entirety only in Ethiopic,[334] the Book of Jubilees is a 2nd cent. BCE work and one of the most important exemplars of the genre scholars have dubbed "Rewritten Bible."[335] Set at Mount Sinai and taking its cue from Exod 24:12–18, the framework of the book includes an angel dictating to Moses from heavenly tablets; the contents of the tablets cover the events from creation to the building of the sanctuary (Jub. 1:27) and are thus a creative

---

[334] For the Ethiopic text of Jubilees, see James C. VanderKam, *The Book of Jubilees: A Critical Text* (CSCO 510–511; Louvain: Peeters, 1989). The Ethiopic of Jubilees is based on a Greek translation, while the Dead Scrolls have confirmed that the language of composition was Hebrew. For the Qumran manuscripts of Jubilees and related texts, see Józef T. Milik, "1Q17–18" in *Qumran Cave I* (eds., Dominique Barthélemy et al.; DJD 1; Oxford: Clarendon, 1955), 82–84; Maurice Baillet, ed., "2Q19–20" and "3Q5" in *Les petites grottes de Qumran* (eds., Maurice Balliet et al.; DJD 3; Oxford: Clarendon, 1962), 77–79, 96–98; James C. VanderKam and Józef T. Milik, "216. 4QJubilees^a" thru "228. 4QText with a Citation of Jubilees," in *Qumran Cave 4.VIII: Parabiblical Texts, Part 1* (eds., Harold W. Attridge et al.; DJD 13; Oxford: Clarendon Press, 1994), 1–185; Florentino Garcia-Martinez and Eibert J. C. Tigchelaar, "11Q12" in *Qumran Cave 11.II: 11Q2–18, 11Q20–31* (eds., F. Garcia-Martinez et al.; DJD 23; Oxford Clarendon, 1998), 207–220. For an exhaustive, recent treatment of the composition, see James C. VanderKam, *Jubilees 1–21: A Commentary on the Book of Jubilees Chapters 1–21* (Hermeneia; Minneapolis: Fortress Press, 2018); and idem, *Jubilees 22–50: A Commentary on Jubilees Chapters 22–50* (Hermeneia; Minneapolis: Fortress, 2018). Also see James L. Kugel, *A Walk Through Jubilees: Studies in the Book of Jubilees and the World of its Creation* (JSJSup 156; Leiden: Brill, 2012).

[335] For commentary and bibliography on Jubilees as "rewritten Bible/Scripture," see Michael Segal, *The Book of Jubilees: Rewritten Bible, Redaction, Ideology, and Theology* (JSJSup 117; Leiden: Brill, 2007), 4–5. For a recent discussion of scholarship and terminology of the genre, see Daniel A. Machiela, "Once More, with Feeling: Rewritten Scripture in Ancient Judaism – A Review of Recent Developments," *JSJ* 51 (2010): 308. It is recognized, however, that Jubilees has elements of other genres including those of apocalyptic literature, not least of which is the revelation of heavenly knowledge to an ancient worthy by an angelic mediator; see Collins, *Apocalyptic Imagination*, 81, who refers to Jubilees as a "borderline case for the apocalyptic genre." On Jubilees as a work that "subverts" themes common to apocalyptic literature, see Hanneken, *The Subversion of the Apocalypses*.

retelling of Genesis and the first half of Exodus.[336] The large number of Jubilees manuscripts[337] found among the Scrolls suggests that it was a work held in high esteem at Qumran.[338] The feature of Jubilees that is particularly relevant to this study is the creation and description of angelic classes that are closely associated with Israel.

According to the opening chapter of Genesis, the sole action of God on the first day of creation was to bring light, and, thereby, day and night, into existence (Gen 1:3–5). But one of the first examples of Jubilees' interpretive expansion of its biblical base text is that day one of creation now includes the formation of the angelic world, thereby addressing the silence of Genesis on this matter; 2:2 states:[339]

---

[336] So described by James C. VanderKam, *The Book of Jubilees* (GAP; Sheffield: Sheffield Academic Press, 2001), 11. The recasting of the biblical narrative allows the author of Jubilees, as Himmelfarb, *A Kingdom of Priests*, 54, states, "to demonstrate that many of the laws of the Torah were observed by the Israelites even before they were revealed at Mount Sinai. This insistence on the eternal status of the laws of the Torah may be a response to a Hellenistic critique of Judaism that admired monotheism but viewed the ritual laws, which they saw as superstitious and misanthropic, as a later addition. The laws in question, according to Jubilees, could be found on heavenly tablets. These heavenly tablets are central to Jubilees' thought." Approaching the subject from a different yet complementary angle, Segal, *The Book of Jubilees*, 7, points out that the significance of Jubilees' heavenly tablets is to stress that God's covenant with Israel has its foundation at creation rather than Sinai. Thus, Israel's relationship with God is from the very beginning of time.

[337] Fourteen (possibly fifteen) manuscripts of Jubilees were found at Qumran, which means that only Psalms (36), Deuteronomy (29), Isaiah (21), Exodus (17), and perhaps Genesis (15) were found in greater numbers; see Angel, *Otherworldly*, 36. The oldest copy of Jubilees found at Qumran, 4Q216, has been dated on paleographic grounds to the last quarter of the 2nd cent. BCE (see VanderKam and Milik, DJD 13, 1–3), and in conjunction with the reference to Jubilees in the *Damascus Document* (the earliest copy of which, 4Q266, dates to the first half of the first century BCE), indicates a *terminus ante quem* of 100 BCE for Jubilees. A *terminus post quem* is more difficult to ascertain, but Jubilees' reliance upon the story of the watchers suggests it can't be earlier than the 3rd cent. BCE, and possible allusions to the Maccabean revolt (cf., e.g., Jub. 37–38; 1 Macc 5) may indicate a date of composition in the late 160s BCE. For discussion, see James C. VanderKam, *Textual and Historical Studies in the Book of Jubilees* (HSM 14; Missoula: Scholars Press, 1977), 207–285; idem, *Jubilees 1–21*, 25–37; Segal, *The Book of Jubilees*, 35–41.

[338] Jubilees' affinities with themes in the sectarian texts include support for a 364-day solar calendar (cf. 4Q252; 11QPs^a) and a date of 15/3 for *Shavuot*, which is the occasion of the sectarian covenant renewal ceremony (cf. 4Q266 XI, 17–18; 4Q270 7 II, 11–12; 1QS I, 16–III, 12). These and other similarities suggest that Jubilees was highly valued by the Qumran movement, even if it is widely considered to have had a non-sectarian provenance; see VanderKam, *The Book of Jubilees*, 145–146.

[339] As VanderKam, *The Book of Jubilees*, 29, comments: "Within day one the writer has included the contents of the introductory statements in Gen 1:1–2 (the heavens and the earth) and creation of the angels. The latter category solves the problem that Genesis,

For on the first day he created the heavens that are above, and the earth, the waters and all the spirits who serve before him, namely: the angels of the presence, and the angels of holiness ... ."[340]

The account continues with the creation of other angelic classes, specifically those who oversee various meteorological domains. Several factors suggest, however, that the author of Jubilees envisioned "the angels of the presence" and "the angels of holiness"[341] as not only occupying the highest angelic ranks but also having a special connection to Israel. First, Jubilees refers to the angels of the presence and the angels of holiness as the "two great kinds" (2:18).[342] Second, in the verse just quoted, these angels are said to minister before God, a priestly privilege already intimated by the words "presence" and "holiness."[343] A sacerdotal function for these two classes is all but confirmed later in Jubilees, first, when it is announced by the angel of the presence[344] in 30:18 that

Levi's descendants were chosen for the priesthood and as Levites to serve before the Lord *as we (do)* for all time [emphasis mine].

---

while it mentions angels several times (see 3:24), does not say when (or whether) they were created."

[340] Unless otherwise stated, translations of Jubilees are from VanderKam, *The Book of Jubilees*.

[341] 4Q216 suggests that the Hebrew titles for the angels of the presence and the angels of holiness were, respectively, מלאכי הפנים and מלאכי קודש, with the former sometimes translated as "the angels of sanctification"; see VanderKam and Milik, DJD 13, 13.

[342] The word "great," while present in the Ethiopic text, is missing from 4Q216; see VanderKam and Milik, DJD 13, 19–20. Segal, *The Book of Jubilees*, 9 n. 22, rightly points out that even if the adjective was added secondarily due to the influence of the phrase "a great sign" in 6:17, the rest of Jubilees is clear that these two classes of angels are extraordinary.

[343] While it is not certain that the qualifying phrase "serve/minister before him" in 2:2 should be restricted to "the angels of presence" and "the angels of holiness," commentators have, for good reason, taken it to mean this, since other texts portray the angels of presence in particular as having a privileged status: they are said to serve in God's presence, whereas other angels must ascend in order to offer their gifts (cf. T. Levi 3:7), and it is implied that these beings are subordinate only to God (cf. T. Judah 25:2). The *Similitudes* refer to four "faces/presences," who are none other than the archangels, Michael, Raphael, Gabriel, and Phanuel (1 En. 40:8; cf. Ezek 1:6); see VanderKam, "The Angel of the Presence," 385. Thus, on the role of the angels of the presence and angels of the holiness in Jubilees, Dimant, "Men as Angels," 99, writes, "These angels are clearly distinguished from the ones in charge of other cosmic domains. For them is reserved the task of serving before the Divine Throne in the innermost heavenly sanctuary ... ."

[344] As will be discussed below, the celestial being who dictates the heavenly tablets to Moses and serves as the narrator of Jubilees is *the* angel of the presence, a high-ranking figure who apparently stood at the head of an eponymous class of angels; see Hannah, *Michael and Christ*, 49 n. 109.

As Wintermute summarizes, "the 'we' refers to the host of angels who minister before the LORD continually. The Levites are to minister on earth as the angels do in heaven."[345] Shortly thereafter, in 31:14, the priestly vocation of the angels of the presence is similarly emphasized when Jacob blesses Levi:

> May the Lord give you and your descendants extremely great honor; may he make you and your descendants (alone) out of all humanity approach him to serve in his temple *like the angels of the presence and the holy ones.*[346] *The descendants of your sons will be like them in honour, greatness, and holiness,* may he make them great throughout all ages [emphasis mine]."

They are also said to keep the Sabbath (2:18, 30) and celebrate *Shavuot* in heaven until the days of Noah (6:18); and they are the only heavenly beings created circumcised (6:18; 15:25–27). Such characteristics mark the angels of the presence and the angels of holiness as "partakers of [the divine covenant], and as the heavenly counterparts of earthly Israel."[347] As Scott has observed, the progression from the angelic observance of the Sabbath in Jub. 2:18 to God's announcement to the angels that he would separate a people for himself to keep the Sabbath on earth constitutes an *imitatio angelorum* and serves as part of the book's "on earth as in heaven" motif.[348] In the context of a discussion of Jubilees' understanding of the Jewish people vis-à-vis the Gentiles, Angel elaborates upon the observation that certain celestial beings correspond to Israel, summarizing the matter as follows:

> The [angels] were ... created in a tripartite hierarchy, with the angels of presence at the top, followed by the angels of holiness, and finally by the angels of cosmic phenomena. Only the first two groups continue to play a role in the remainder of the book, while the third is not mentioned again. 2:18 reports that the top two tiers of angels are charged to celebrate the Sabbath. Of all the nations of the earth, only Israel is commanded to celebrate the Sabbath along with the angels and God. All the other nations, as well as the angels of cosmic phenomena, presumably continue to work on the seventh day due to their inferior state of holiness (2:19, 31). *In this way, Jubilees' picture of earth is modeled on its vision of celestial reality – there is a direct parallelism between the existence and actions of heavenly beings and those of their human counterparts on earth. Written into the very order of creation, Israel corresponds to the angels closest to God, while the Gentiles correlate to those farthest away. ... The fact that the angels [of the presence and the an-*

---

[345] Wintermute, "Jubilees," *OTP* 2:113.

[346] Charles, *APOT* 2:60, suggested that "the holy ones" of 31:14 should be identified as the angels of holiness. Cf. Angel, *Otherworldly*, 42.

[347] Dimant, "Men as Angels," 99.

[348] That the angels celebrate *Shavuot* and are circumcised contribute to this motif as well; see James M. Scott, *On Earth as It Is in Heaven: The Restoration of Sacred Time and Sacred Space in the Book of Jubilees* (JSJSup 91; Leiden: Brill, 2005), 1–8. The bulk of Scott's monograph focuses on how the themes of cultic cycles, chronology, and land are reflected "on earth as in heaven," but he begins by briefly highlighting instances of *imitatio angelorum*. Cf. Mach, *Entwicklungsstadien des jüdischen Engelglaubens*, 235, who puts the matter succinctly: "Israel hält den Sabbat, weil es en Engels gleicht."

gels of holiness] are by nature circumcised seems to imply that by fulfilling the covenant of circumcision, Jews become earthly replicas of God's celestial inner circle. On the other hand, the Gentiles did not receive such a command, for God "chose them not" (15:30) [emphasis mine].[349]

Jubilees is also clear that non-Jews cannot become part of the people of God, on even limited terms.[350] Thus, Jubilees' emphasis is on both Israel in its entirety and Israel exclusively,[351] and it should therefore come as no surprise that the notion of priestly holiness is extended to the entire nation,[352] whose special status is communicated, in part, via "plant" imagery (e.g., Jub 1:16; 16:26; 21:24 36:6; cf. Isa 60:21; 61:3; 1 En 10:16; 93:10).[353]

---

[349] Angel, *Otherworldly*, 38.

[350] See Hanneken, *The Subversion of the Apocalypses*, 88–104, who compares the stance of Jubilees to that of other texts.

[351] Hanneken, *The Subversion of the Apocalypses*, 97–104, 292, suggests that one of the reasons for this focus on the entire people of God is that Jubilees "presents itself as instruction for Israelites of all times and all classes," and therefore took issue with more narrowly defined notions of the faithful prevalent in other texts. As Hanneken also points out, this does not mean that Jubilees is completely without of language that could be interpreted as elitist (e.g., Michel Testuz, *Les idées religieuses du Livre des Jubilés* [Geneve: Droz, 1960], 33, proposed that Jub. 1:29, which speaks of "all the elect ones of Israel," was an early reference to the group that would become the Essenes) nor does it suggest that Jubilees is overly permissive when it comes to defining Israel (e.g., Segal, *The Book of Jubilees*, 241–245, highlights the strictness with which Jub. 15:26 mandates circumcision on the eighth day for membership in Israel, a contention which may be part of a polemical salvo against Jews who were less stringent on this issue). However, the overarching emphasis of Jubilees is that the entire nation is elect. Cf. Regev, "The Ram and Qumran," 193, who cites Jub. 23 as an example of a text, like the *Animal Apocalypse*, that showcases "religious elitism" and a "destiny" for ethnic Israel – yet "without sectarian withdrawal and separation."

[352] See the discussion of Angel, *Otherworldly*, 38–40, who notes, for example, that Jubilees' accounts of both the rape of Dinah by Shechem (30:1–25; cf. Gen 34:1–31) and the rape of Bilhah by Reuben (33:1–20; cf. Gen 35:21–22) denounce the incidents in sacerdotal terms. Cf. Segal, *The Book of Jubilees*, 10–11, who discusses the "priestly outlook" of Jubilees as one of the four main ideological and theological emphases of the work (the others being the giving of the laws prior to Sinai, a hepdatic chronological system, and angelology).

[353] On Jubilees' use of the plant imagery, see Tiller, "The Eternal Plant," 323–324, who observes that it emphasizes God's concern for "historical Israel," the presence of God among his people, and the nation's permanence. While Tiller also notes that the metaphor "does not imply that the people will be associated with the heavenly temple" as it does in some of the Qumran sectarian texts (see Chapter 5, below), his statement can be qualified insofar as one of the key ways Jubilees stresses that God is with Israel is through the ministry of the angel of the presence, who is apparently a being of an extraordinarily high rank due in part to his service before God in the celestial sanctuary (cf. 30:18; 31:14). Cf. VanderKam, *Jubilees 1–21*, 155, who observes that while other uses of the plant metaphor may suggest that "only a small part of the people" are in view (e.g., 1QS VIII, 4–6), "it is not so

A perhaps obvious corollary of Jubilees' emphasis on all Israel and its correspondence to the angelic realm is one that should not be overlooked: It is not merely Israel's priests that are represented by the angels of the presence and the angels of holiness; it is the entire nation that corresponds to the angelic priests (cf. 16:18). To be sure, Levi and his descendants are specifically compared to the angels of the presence and the angels of holiness, as quoted above (cf. 30:18; 31:14).[354] But as Himmelfarb points out, the comparison between the Levitical line and the angels is part of a larger correlation integral to the outlook of the book:

> As the heavenly observance of the Sabbath and the Feast of Weeks indicates, *Jubilees* understand not only priests but also the entire people of Israel to be the earthly counterparts of the angels; indeed, all Jews are the counterparts of the angels of presence and the holy ones, the very classes of angels to which Levi's descendants are compared, since these are the angels who observe the Sabbath with God from its creation.[355]

She goes on to suggest that the connection Jubilees posits between the entire nation and the highest-ranking angels should be seen in contrast to the presupposition of *BW* that only the extraordinarily righteous – as exemplified in Enoch – could attain an angel-like status and role.[356] While caution is warranted insofar as *BW* may describe a revelatory *experience*,[357] whereas the point under consideration here is Jubilees' implied *correspondence* between the people and the angels, Himmelfarb's point is invaluable in that it highlights a noteworthy feature of Jubilees among Second Temple period texts: its positing of a relationship of some kind between a generously-defined Israel and the angelic priests of the heavenly sanctuary.[358]

Given both the priestly connotations of the angels of the presence and the angels of holiness and what Jubilees has implied about the correspondence these beings have with Israel, perhaps it is only natural that the book portrays the nation as having an individual, angelic leader, who has a sacerdotal title: a well-known feature of Jubilees is a singular figure known as *the* angel of the presence.[359] The angel of the presence is not only responsible for serving as Jubilees' narrator but also presumably stands at the head of the previously

---

clear that the writer of Jubilees is making such a point here. At least he furnishes no explicit statement limiting the population of those who constitute the future plant."

[354] On these "competing conceptions of the priesthood" in Jubilees, see Angel, *Otherworldly*, 38–45; 73 n. 210.

[355] Himmelfarb, "The Book of Jubilees," 39–42.

[356] Himmelfarb, "The Book of Jubilees," 390; cf. eadem, *A Kingdom of Priests*, 53–84.

[357] And one that, ultimately, seems to be for the benefit of others; see my discussion of *BW*, above.

[358] It would be an overstatement, however, to suggest that Jubilees is the only Second Temple Period text to posit an analogous relationship between Israel and the angelic host, which, as we have seen, appears to be the picture operative in Dan 7–12.

[359] For a detailed study, see VanderKam, "The Angel of the Presence," 378–393.

mentioned angelic class of the same name.[360] In numerous instances, the angel of the presence includes himself in the actions of the comrades of his class of angels.[361] But quite often this figure singles himself out as having an especially important role in the life of God's people, not least when he speaks of his standing between the Israelites and the Egyptians at the Red Sea (48:13)[362] or his responsibilities in the dictation of the heavenly tablets to Moses (1:27–2:1) and in the writing of the Torah (50:2).[363] The Ethiopic title, *mal'aka gass*, literally means "the angel of the face," and a Jubilees manuscript from Qumran (4Q216 V, 5) reveals that the Hebrew title included the word הפנים; thus, the complete designation for the angelic class was most likely מלאכי הפנים[364] and מלאך הפנים for its leader, titles which, as we have seen, appear to have been partially derived from Isa 63:9, a verse situated in a passage referring to Israel's rescue during its flight from Egypt. In what may be a related interpretive move, the persona of the angel of the presence in Jubilees, while in addition to being the product of the author's exegetical reflection of certain מלאך יהוה and מלאך אלהים passages (cf. Gen 16:7–11; 21:17; 22:11–15; Exod 3:2),[365] seems particularly indebted to the angel of the exodus, who assists and protects Israel during their wanderings in the desert (cf. Exod 14:19; 23:20–23; 32:34).[366] The affinity between the two angels is perhaps most evident in their respective descriptions.

---

[360] Hannah, *Michael and Christ*, 49, n. 109, summarizes the matter as follows: "The author of *Jubilees* apparently believed in both a class of angels so named (2:2) and *the* angel of the presence who revealed the contents of *Jubilees* to Moses."

[361] As denoted by the use of the first-person plural. E.g., Jub. 2:17: "And [God] gave *us* the Sabbath day as a great sign so that *we* should perform work for six days and that *we* should keep Sabbath from all work on the seventh day. He told *us* – all the angels of the presence and all the angels of holiness (these two great kinds) – to keep Sabbath with him in heaven and on earth" (cf. Jub. 3:4, 9, 12, 15; 4:6, 23; 14:20; 19:3; 30:18, 41:24; 48:10, et al.).

[362] E.g., before mentioning an instance of the collective work of his class, Jub. 48:13 notes these words of the angel of the presence: "And *I* stood between the Egyptians and Israel, and *we* delivered Israel from his hand and from the hand of his people." *Contra* Hannah, *Michael and Christ*, 50, who suggests that the "we" of 48:13 refers to the angel of the presence and God.

[363] VanderKam, "The Angel of the Presence," 385, summarizes as follows: "The author of *Jubilees* made one of these elite angels the revealer of his annotated history of early biblical times."

[364] See VanderKam and Milik, DJD 13, 13–15.

[365] VanderKam, "The Angel of the Presence," 388–390.

[366] On the similarities of this angel to the angel of the Exodus, see VanderKam, "The Angel of the Presence," 385–388. The guardian-like role of this angel makes for an intriguing contrast with Jub 15:31–32 (cf. Sir 17:17), which echoes Deut 32:8–9 in that it implies that God is Israel's guardian: "For the Lord did not draw near to himself either Ishmael, his sons, his brothers, or Esau. He did not choose them (simply) because they were among Abraham's children, for he knew them. But he chose Israel to be his people. He

Table 5: Comparison of Exod 14:19 and Jub. 1:29[367]

Exod 14:19	מַלְאַךְ הָאֱלֹהִים הַהֹלֵךְ לִפְנֵי מַחֲנֵה יִשְׂרָאֵל
	The angel of God, who was going before the Israelite army
Jub. 1:29	*mal'aka gass za-yahawwer qedema ta'ayenihomu la-'esra'el*
	The angel of the presence, who went before the camp of Israel

The descriptions are nearly identical, and the word פנים is used in reference to Israel's angelic assistant in Exod 14:19 and in the other Exodus passages just referenced.[368] Moreover, the designation מלאך הפנים indicates that "such beings enter into the very presence of God himself,"[369] and thus the title is eminently appropriate for the head of a class of angels who serve as heavenly priests. Finally, in its depiction of the angel of the presence, Jubilees has borrowed from the biblical texts the concept of a high-ranking angel who speaks with God's authority.[370]

---

sanctified them and gathered (them) from all mankind. For there are many nations and many people and all belong to him. He made sprits rule over all in the order to lead them astray from following him. *But over Israel he made no angel or spirit rule because he alone is their ruler.* He will guard them and require them for himself from his angels, his spirits, and everyone, and all his powers so that he may guard them and bless them and so that they may be his and he theirs from now and forever [emphasis mine]." Attempts to explain this tension include Hanneken, *The Subversion of Apocalypses*, 69–88, 117–118, who argues that the unmediated governance suggested in Jub. 15:31–32 ensures that the sovereignty of God is not hindered, either by the wickedness of the Gentiles' angelic guardians or the limited abilities of Israel's angelic guardians, as is the case in many apocalyptic texts (e.g., Dan 10:21). This divine "hand's on" approach is an example of Jubilees' tendency to subvert features typical of apocalypses. Thus, the direct rule of God, in conjunction with the subversion of the Mastema-led angelic forces of evil (cf. Jub 10:11; 49:2), serves to emphasize that nothing can thwart the covenant God established with Israel at creation. Alternatively, Kugel, *A Walk Through Jubilees*, 256–259, has proposed that Jub 15:25–34 is one of approximately 30 interpolations inserted into the text (*contra* VanderKam, *Jubilees 1–21*, 25–28, who surveys various proposals and champions a single-author interpretation). If Kugel is correct, it may have been that the interpolator was at least partially motivated by a discomfort with the guardianship characteristics of the angel of the presence and, in deference to Deut 32:8–9, added the statement of Jub. 15:31–32, even if it resulted in tension with the text as it stood. However, it may simply be that Jub. 15:31–32 is emphasizing that Israel's guardianship is ultimately a prerogative of God himself – Israel's preeminent protector – who is frequently portrayed, in both the Hebrew Bible and Second Temple Period texts, as dispatching angelic assistance for the benefit of his people.

[367] Cf. VanderKam, "The Angel of the Presence," 385.

[368] VanderKam, "The Angel of the Presence," 386.

[369] VanderKam, "The Angel of the Presence," 382.

[370] A well-known feature of the מלאך יהוה – especially in early texts (e.g., Judg 6) – is that this figure is virtually indistinguishable from Yhwh. For recent discussion and bibli-

In light of the authority and stature of the angel of the presence, some commentators have suggested that this figure should be identified as the archangel Michael.[371] In support, Hannah points out the Michael-like role of the angel of the presence in going before the camp of Israel (1:29) and in delivering the nation from the hand of the wicked angel, Mastema (48:13).[372] Indeed, Mastema has been referred to as the evil counterpart of the angel of the presence (cf. 10:11; 17:15–16; 18:9),[373] even if the dualistic symmetry of Jubilees is not quite as exact as it is in other texts.[374] Intriguingly, a Greek fragment of Jubilees preserved in Syncellus' *Chronographia* (ca. late 8th or 9th cent. CE) testifies to a discrepancy when compared to the Ethiopic version: Instead of the plurality of angels who assist the descendants of Noah in the midst of their struggles with evil spirits/angels (10:1–14), the corresponding story in *Chronographia* (49:6–15) has Michael casting the evil spirits into the abyss. VanderKam has argued that there are periphrastic tendencies at work in *Chronographia's* citations of Jubilees and has therefore cautioned that the Michael identification may be the work of Syncellus himself.[375] Nevertheless, Hannah rightly notes the significance of at least one ancient reader equating Jubilees' narrator with Michael.[376]

In sum, the covenant marks of the angels of the presence and the angels of holiness signify that these angelic priests are closely associated with Israel, whose protection and value are underscored by the fact that their heavenly counterparts serve in closest proximity to God. Moreover, given the juxtapo-

---

ography on this point, see Michalak, *Angels as Warriors*, 35–36. Similarly, VanderKam, "The Angel of the Presence," 393, describes Jubilees' מלאך הפנים as follows: "For the sake of his own book, the writer has established its … unquestioned authority by tying it directly to the extraordinary angel of the presence. He is the one who dictates all the words of *Jub.* 2–50 to Moses. Yet, not only is the angel of the presence the authority behind these words; the writer further bolsters the authority of his book by picturing this angel as reading to Moses from the inscribed tablets of heaven and he does all of this by divine command. What could be more authoritative than a book written by Moses, dictated to him by an angel of the very face of God, based on the unimpeachable contents of the heavenly tablets, and mandated by God himself?" As Segal, *The Book of Jubilees*, 9, summarizes, "In certain instances, an angel or angels in *Jubilees* come in the place of God in the Pentateuch. The most conspicuous case of the replacement of God by an angel is the narrative frame of the entire book, in which the angel of the presence speaks to Moses at Sinai, and dictates to him from the Heavenly Tablets."

[371] So R. H. Charles, *The Book of Jubilees or the Little Genesis* (London: A. & C. Black, 1902), 9; followed by, e.g., Hannah, *Michael and Christ*, 49–50.

[372] A righteous angel battling with his wicked adversary is reminiscent of Dan 10, where Michael strives against the angelic princes of Greece and Persia; see Hannah, *Michael and Christ*, 48–49.

[373] VanderKam, *The Book of Jubilees*, 128. Cf. Michalak, *Angels as Warriors*, 85.

[374] Collins, *Seers, Sibyls, and Sages*, 271. Cf. Segal, *The Book of Jubilees*, 237.

[375] VanderKam, *Textual and Historical Studies*, 8.

[376] Hannah, *Michael and Christ*, 50.

sition of the title and role of the angel of the presence, Jubilees hints that at least some angels were envisioned as serving as both guardians and priests.

H. 4QInstruction

The composition known as *4QInstruction* (henceforth, *4QInstr*) is extant in several fragmentary manuscripts, the latest of which is dated paleographically to the middle or late Herodian period.[377] On historical and thematic grounds, however, the text is frequently judged to have been composed in the 2nd cent. BCE or even earlier.[378] Indeed, while the consensus is that *4QInstr* is a non-sectarian composition,[379] it is understandable why it seems to have been a valued part of the Qumran movement's library, as there are numerous parallels with sectarian thought and, as such, may have been influential or a point of departure for the convictions of the sect.[380]

More specifically, *4QInstr* is a text that juxtaposes Jewish wisdom and apocalyptic traditions:[381] though Proverbs-like in that it is a collection of

---

[377] For a convenient overview of the manuscripts (= 1Q26, 4Q415–418, and 4Q423), see Matthew J. Goff, *4QInstruction* (WLAW 2; Atlanta: SBL Press, 2013), 1–7, whose text, sigla, and translation are cited, here. For an earlier treatment, see John Strugnell and Daniel J. Harrington, S. J., eds., *Qumran Cave 4 XXIV: Sapiential Texts, Part 2: 4QInstruction (Musar le mevin): 4Q415ff with a Re-edition of 1Q26* (DJD 34; Oxford: Claredon Press, 1999). Additional major studies include John Kampen, *Wisdom Literature* (ECDSS; Grand Rapids: Eerdmans, 2011); Jean-Sébastien Rey, *4QInstruction: Sagesse et eschatologie* (STDJ 81; Leiden: Brill, 2009); Benjamin G. Wold, *Women, Men, and Angels: The Qumran Wisdom Document Musar LeMevin and its Allusions to Genesis Creation Traditions* (WUNT 2/201; Tübingen: Mohr Siebeck, 2005); Matthew J. Goff, *The Worldly and Heavenly Wisdom of 4QInstruction* (STDJ 50; Leiden: Brill, 2004); Eibert J. C. Tigchelaar, *To Increase Learning for the Understanding Ones: Reading and Reconstructing the Fragmentary Early Jewish Sapiential Text 4QInstruction* (STDJ 44; Leiden: Brill, 2001).

[378] *4QInstr's* affinities with apocalyptic texts strongly suggest a 2nd cent. BCE date of composition. The fact that the Maccabean revolt is not mentioned has prompted scholars to posit a pre-160s BCE date of composition, with some proposing a date as early as the Persian period. For discussion, see Elgvin, "The Mystery to Come," 130–131; Goff, *4QInstruction*, 28–29; Strugnell and Harrington, DJD 34, 21–22.

[379] On this point, see the survey of scholarship by Angel, *Otherworldly*, 63.

[380] This may also explain the relatively large number of copies of the work discovered among the Scrolls. On the similarities between this text and sectarian compositions, see Goff, *4QInstruction*, 28. E.g., it is often suggested that *The Hodayot* quotes *4QInstr* (cf. 1QH[a] XVIII, 29–30; 4Q418 55 10); see idem, "Reading Wisdom at Qumran: 4QInstruction and the Hodayot," *DSD* 11 (2004): 263–288; Elgvin, "The Mystery to Come," 116–117; Strugnell and Harrington, DJD 34, 21, 36.

[381] On the various ways scholars have understood the intersection of wisdom and apocalyptic genres and themes in the text, see the discussion of Goff, *The Worldly and Heavenly*

teachings without a narrative framework,[382] it emphasizes that this wisdom stems from special revelation, which the text's addressees are exhorted to study. As the recipients of revelation, they have knowledge of רז נהיה, "the mystery to come/that is to be" (e.g., 4Q416 2 III, 18; 4Q418 123 II, 4), which has a significant role in creation, history, and eschatological redemption.[383] Further underscoring this privilege is that the addressee of the text is frequently referred to as a מבין, "understanding one," a term used elsewhere to denote sages (cf. Prov 8:9; 17:10, 24; Dan 1:4; 8:27).[384] Moreover, the use of the plural מבינים indicates that the מבין was envisioned as part of a larger group who enjoyed divine favour.[385] The designation מטעת עו|לם, "eternal planting" (4Q418 81 13;[386] cf. 4Q423 1), is also employed, which, as noted earlier in this chapter, is similar to Third Isaiah's epithets for ethnic Israel (Isa 60:21; 61:3). The usage here has thus been considered another means by which the community behind *4QInstr* could claim that God had uniquely granted it an honoured standing (cf. 1 En 10:16; 93:10, 13; Jub 1:16; 16:26; 21:24; 36:6)[387] – and one that would even culminate in "eternal joy" (4Q417 2 I, 10–12).[388]

Wisdom, 24–27. More recently, see Davis Hankins, "4QInstruction's Mystery and the Mastery of Wisdom," *DSD* 23 (2016): 183–205.

[382] Goff, *4QInstruction*, 8.

[383] See Goff, *4QInstruction*, 14, 27, who notes that the same expression is used in the *Community Rule* to describe the revelation to which the Qumran movement was privy (e.g., 1QS XI, 3–4). Cf. Lange, "Sages and Scribes," 275–276; Wold, *Women, Men, and Angels*, 20–24; Elgvin, "The Mystery to Come," 132–139.

[384] Lange, "Sages and Scribes," 274.

[385] Cf. Goff, *4QInstruction*, 10–12; see further, below.

[386] On the numerous fragments associated with 4Q418 81 and the resultant nomenclature issues, see Goff, *4QInstruction*, 5–7, 239–262 who, e.g., refers to this important text as 4Q418 81 + 81A.

[387] For overviews of the use of the plant metaphor in *4QInstruction*, see Tiller, "The Eternal Planting," 324–326; Swarup, *The Self-Understanding*, 89–107. Goff, *4QInstruction*, 257, observes the similarities between this claim and the exclusivist claims made by the Qumran movement (e.g., 1QS VIII, 5–6; XI, 8). Cf. Angel, *Otherworldly*, 69 n. 190. Similarly, Elgvin, "The Mystery to Come," 127, suggests that "the community behind *4QInstruction* sees itself as the remnant and nucleus of Israel which represents a fulfilment of the prophesies in Isaiah 59–61," though, arguably, the descriptor "nucleus" may inadvertently dilute the exclusivist import of the text as it presupposes that others can join. As noted earlier, Stuckenbruck, "4QInstruction and the Possible Influence," 254, suggests that that the plant metaphor is appropriated more narrowly in *4QInstruction* than in 1 Enoch, insofar as it is less ambiguously "equivalent to a particular group within Israel" in the former. Alternatively, Strugnell and Harrington, DJD 34, 308–309, appeal to the use of the phrase in the Hebrew Bible to suggest that it "need not presuppose a dualistic or specifically sectarian theology" in *4QInstr*.

[388] On the exchange of mourning for joy as it pertains to the מבין, see Goff, *4QInstruction*, 17, 194–201.

For the purposes of this study, the most relevant conviction of *4QInstr* –
and perhaps the basis for those just listed – is the claim that the addressee has
a connection to the angels.[389] 4Q418 81 1–5 states that[390]

1 שפתיכה פתח מקור לברך קדושים ואתה כמקור עולם הלל [שמו כי]א הבדילכה מכול

2 רוח בשר ואתה הבדל מכול אשר שנא והנזר מכול תעבות נפֹשֹן כי]א הוא עשה כול

3 ויורישם איש נחלתו והוא חלקכה ונחלתכה בתוך בני אדם[ובנ]חֹלֹתו המשילֹכֹה ואתה

4 בזה כבדהו בהתקדשכה לו כאשר שמכה לקדוש קודשים[לכול בני]תֹבל ובכוֹל[

מ]לֹ[אכים]

5 הפיל גורלכה וכבודכה הרבה מאדה וישימכה לו בכור בֹן

1 Your lips he has opened as a spring to bless the holy ones. So you, as an eternal spring,
praise [his name, beca]use he has separated you from every
2 fleshly spirit. And you, separate yourself from all that he hates and keep away from all
abominations of the soul, [beca]use he has made everyone
3 and has bequeathed to each man his inheritance. He is your portion and your inheritance
among humankind, [and over] his [in]heritance he has given you dominion. So you
4 in this way glorify him, by making yourself holy to him, as he has established you as
most holy [of all the people of the] world. And among all the [a]n[gels]
5 he has cast your lot and your glory he has greatly magnified. He has established you for
himself as a firstborn son among …

The notion of being in a גורל with the angels (cf. 4Q416 2 III, 11–12) is one
of the most striking similarities *4QInstr* has with Qumran sectarian texts.
This does not mean, however, that exactly the same claims are being made.
As Goff suggests, the nature of the distinction between the addressee and
those not in his religious circle is "theological rather than physical."[391] That
is, while *4QInstr* may reveal that its composers were convinced that they had
more in common with the angels than they did with outsiders[392] – and as

---

[389] Cf. Goff, *4QInstruction*, 17: "Being like the angels allows the *mebin* two core benefits that humans cannot normally attain. First, this status provides an explanation as to
why heavenly revelation was disclosed to him. … Second, the addressee has the potential
to obtain a blessed afterlife."

[390] Cf. Strugnell and Harrington, DJD 34, 300; Goff, *4QInstruction*, 240–241.

[391] Goff, *4QInstruction*, 245.

[392] On this point, Wold, *Women, Men, and Angels*, 179–181, provides a thorough discussion of the connection between the addressee's affinity with the angels and the well-
known claim of 4Q417 1 I, 17, which states that "according to the likeness of the holy ones
he fashioned him." Wold writes: "If one reads 4Q417 1 I lines 15–18 as a description of
all humanity created in the likeness of God and the angels, and a segment losing revelation
later called 'spirit of flesh', some aspects of 4Q418 81 come into sharper focus. The column begins with a statement that the addressee has been separated from the spirit of flesh
(ll. 1–2). … A distinction is made in line 3 that the addressee has a different inheritance
(God) than others [*sic*] sons of Adam. The lot of the addressee is with the angels (ll. 4–5)
who possess and seek knowledge. The identity of the addressee, discussed in relation to
4Q417 1 I as spiritual, is based upon behavior and seeking knowledge. Metaphorically, the
addressee dwells within an Edenic garden (4Q423 1, 2 i) and partakes of its many wisdom

such, may have even applied the designation קדושים to angels and the addressees with deliberate ambiguity[393] – the text does not encourage piety-motivated self-removal from society for the purposes of cultivating this angelic affinity.[394] Moreover, though the addressee is exhorted to bless the angels (e.g., 4Q418 81 1),[395] there are no indications of ascent experiences or liturgical fellowship with the angels in the present time as there are in some of the texts composed by the Qumran movement,[396] even if there are hints that angelic communion was an anticipated feature of post-mortem existence akin to Dan 12:3 and 1 En. 104:2–6 (cf. 4Q417 2 I, 10–12; 4Q418 69 II, 12–14; 4Q418 126 II, 7–8).[397] Indeed, "the addressee of 4QInstruction does not

---

bearing trees. If the addressee's community is called an 'eternal planting' in line 13, it may relate to the imagery of being part of the faithful among humanity who continue to partake of trees of knowledge in the garden. Therefore, motifs of creation and the garden converge in 4Q418 81 that distinguish the addressee from the spirit of flesh and relate him to the holy ones." Cf. Fletcher-Louis, *All the Glory*, 114–122. For discussion of whether *4QInstr* envisions those with the wayward "spirit of flesh" as influenced by demons, see Wold, "Demonizing Sin? The Evil Inclination in 4QInstruction," 39–48.

[393] E.g., 4Q418 81 12, begins with a reference to angelic "holy ones" and may end with a reference to the elect human "holy ones"; see Stuckenbruck, "4QInstruction and the Possible Influence," 252; Goff, *4QInstruction*, 245. *Contra* Elgvin, "The Mystery to Come," 120, who understands both references in line 12 as referring to the human elect. Cf. Fletcher-Louis, *All the Glory*, 176–187, who, as part of his angelmorphic anthropology proposal, understands the קדושים of line 12 as human laity who are blessed by the addressee, who is a priestly figure.

[394] In fact, the opposite is in view, as the text repeatedly exhorts the addressees to live wisely, especially as it pertains to financial matters; see Goff, *4QInstruction*, 245–246.

[395] See Goff, *4QInstruction*, 244, 255, who rightly emphasizes that the addressee's praise of the angels is connected to the angels' (exemplary) praise of God, and that it is via his praise that the addressee grasps his affinity with the angels. Cf. Wold, *Women, Men, and Angels*, 181: "The angels in the document are worthy of blessings as subordinates to God." For further on "benedictive activity" directed to angels in *4QInstr* specifically and early Judaism more broadly, see Stuckenbruck, "'Angels' and 'God,'" 64–65; idem, *Angel Veneration and Christology. Contra* Fletcher-Louis, *All the Glory*, 177–178, 185–187, who claims that the notion of angel veneration is "hard to find" in early Jewish texts. I will return to this theme when I discuss *The Songs of the Sabbath Sacrifice* in Chapter 5.

[396] So Goff, *4QInstruction*, 16–17, 105, 251.

[397] On this point, see John J. Collins, "The Eschatologizing of Wisdom in the Dead Sea Scrolls," in *Sapiential Perspectives: Wisdom Literature in Light of the Dead Sea Scrolls: Proceedings of the Sixth International Symposium of the Orion Center for the Study of the Dead Sea Scrolls and Associated Literature, 20–22 May 2001* (eds., idem, Gregory E. Sterling, and Ruth A. Clements; STDJ 51; Leiden: Brill, 2004), 57–58. Cf. Angel, *Otherworldly*, 62, 77; Goff, *4QInstruction*, 17–18, 237–238. *Contra* Benjamin G. Wold, "Jesus Among Wisdom's Representatives: 4QInstruction," in *Enoch and the Synoptic Gospels: Reminiscences, Allusions, Intertextuality* (eds., Loren T. Stuckenbruck and Gabriele Boccaccini; EJL 44; Atlanta: SBL Press, 2016), 332–333, who proposes that 4Q418 81 envisions "present participation with the angels" and that the author "is not simply looking forward to a future and eschatological participation in another world … ."

obtain in this life all the rewards allotted to him ... . He is a student who needs to learn more and live uprightly in order to attain such rewards."[398]

Very little is said about the angels with whom an affinity was envisioned,[399] so the precise identity or vocation of these angels can only be inferred. However, several scholars have supported a reading of 4Q418 81 12 that charges the privileged human addressee to "open a fountain of all the holy ones."[400] Given that *4QInstr* elsewhere celebrates the fact that the priestly-titled מלאכי קודש, "angels of holiness" (cf. Jub. 2:2; 2:18) are said to "pursue after all the roots of understanding" (4Q418 55 8–9), it may be that this "fountain" is, at least in part, the knowledge of the heavenly priesthood and its wisdom revealed for the benefit of the faithful community the addressee represents.[401]

---

[398] Goff, *4QInstruction*, 105.

[399] E.g., Goff, *4QInstruction*, 17, observes that there are no named angels in the book.

[400] While Strugnell and Harrington, DJD 34, 303, 308, opt for פתח] [שׁיר כול קדוֹשים, "begin with a *song* for all the holy ones," they concede the possibility of פתח [מ]קוֹר כול קדוֹשים, "open a *fountain* ..." (cf. 4Q418 81 1). A strong case for מקור has been made by Stuckenbruck, "'Angels' and 'God,'" 65, who notes a resultant translational issue to sort out (and one which touches upon interpretive matters already discussed): "[I]f the fountain is to be opened *for* 'all his holy ones', then we may consider whether this watering metaphor extends to the 'plantation'. In this way, the fountain (perhaps referring to the instruction given to the addressee) would be that which feeds or waters the eternal planation (i.e., the human community of 'holy ones' called by God's name). In this case, the 'holy ones' to be honoured could be readily identified as the righteous congregation of the elect. If the fountain, however is *of* the holy ones, ... [it] would signify that the chosen community (the eternal plantation) is being allowed to receive or participate in the fountain which belongs to the angel[ic holy ones]." As Angel, *Otherworldly*, 75–76, rightly observes, one would expect a dative ל prefixed to כול if the intended sense was "*for* all the holy ones." Furthermore, the absence of any boasts of ascent experiences might suggest that the "fountain of all the holy ones" is the *reception* of heavenly wisdom – a theme which is emphasized repeatedly throughout *4QInstr* – rather than *participation with* the angels, though such a distinction may, admittedly, be difficult to parse. For further on the text-critical issues of line 12 and its interpretation, see Tigchelaar, *To Increase Learning*, 94–95; Wold, *Women, Men, and Angels,* 161–179; Goff, *4QInstruction*, 242, 255–256.

[401] Note the similar comments of Angel, *Otherworldly*, 76 n. 222: "The 'fountain' of the angels may refer to their superior knowledge of God's mysteries, especially if the word מקור refers to concealed wisdom here as it does in 1QS 11." Cf. Stuckenbruck, "4QInstruction and the Possible Influence," 252; Wold, *Women, Men, and Angels*, 178. This "fountain" may also include נס[תּרי מחשבתו, "the secrets of his plan" (4Q417 1 I, 11–12), a phrase which "conveys ... the status of supernatural revelation"; so Goff, *4QInstruction*, 153. Cf. Elgvin, "The Mystery to Come," 138, who notes similar language applied to revelation in foundational texts of the Qumran movement (cf. 1QS V, 11; XI, 16; CD III, 14). On the designation אל הדעות, "the God of knowledge" (cf. 4Q417 1 I, 8) as integral to the notion of revealed heavenly mysteries and knowledge in *4QInst*, see Goff, *The Worldly and Heavenly*, 64–67.

Caution is necessary, however, because the extent to which *4QInstr* is concerned with priestly matters is debated.[402] First, the reference to God as חלקכה ונחלתכה (4Q418 81 3) is clearly an allusion to Num 18:20, where it describes the allotment of the Aaronic priests,[403] though it has been countered that the usage here may simply be a way of emphasizing the election of the addressees.[404] Second, although it is possible לקדוש קודשים (4Q418 81 4) indicates that the addressees are being dubbed "holy of holies," with the phrase constituting a deliberate evocation of the temple[405] or even a priest-hood-laity distinction,[406] it has been suggested that the expression may be

---

[402] In brief, some of *4QInstr's* language and themes have prompted scholars to conclude that matters of the priesthood are central to the composition; see, e.g., Lange, "Sages and Scribes," 275: "this text expresses priestly concerns repeatedly." *Contra* Goff, *4QInstruction*, 26–27, who argues that priestly topics are relatively sparse and that the text gives numerous indications that the addressees are of a socio-economic standing too low to be priests. But also see Tigchelaar, *To Increase Learning,* 236, who has proposed that different sections of the text have different addressees, which could explain why some sections of *4QInstr* (e.g., 4Q418 81) contain priestly language and themes whereas many do not.

[403] As Strugnell and Harrington, DJD 34, 20, succinctly put it: "Is it literally an Aaronid status which is intended here …?" Those who have answered in the affirmative include Armin Lange, "Determination of Fate by the Oracle of the Lot," in *Sapiential, Liturgical and Poetical Texts from Qumran: Proceedings of the Third Meeting of the International Organization for Qumran Studies, Oslo, 1988: Published in Memory of Maurice Baillet* (eds., Daniel K. Falk, Florentino García Martínez, and Eileen M. Schuller; STDJ 35; Leiden: Brill, 2000), 39–48; Fletcher-Louis, *All the Glory*, 178–185.

[404] E.g., Goff, *4QInstruction*, 246–247: "The holiness of the *mebin* is indeed an important motif in 4Q418 81, and to this end priestly language is used. … There are references to cultic and halakhic issues in 4QInstruction. … If the *mebin* were a priest, one would expect much more of this kind of material. Ritual purity is not a major theme of 4QInstruction. The fact that the intended addressees include women (4Q415 2 ii) problematizes further the opinion that they are priests. The priestly traditions in 4Q418 are better understood as being invoked metaphorically, to explain the elect status of the addressee. The claim in Num 18:20 that God is the special portion of the priests signifies their authority over the temple and its sacrifices. In 4QInstruction this biblical claim is applied to the *mebin*, denoting the special inheritance that God has established for him: that the *raz nihyeh* has been disclosed to him, that he is in the lot of the angels …, and that he has the potential to attain eternal life." Others scholars who read the priestly language and prerogatives of *4QInstr* metaphorically or as a "democratization" of priestly themes include, Torleif Elgvin, "Priestly Sages? The Milieus of Origin of 4QMysteries and 4QInstruction," in *Sapiential Perspectives*, 67–87; Angel, *Otherworldly*, 68–73.

[405] E.g., Angel, *Otherworldly*, 69: "Thus there is reason to believe that the circle(s) behind 4QInstruction conceived of itself as a type of ideal temple." Cf. Church, *Hebrews and the Temple*, 108–110.

[406] E.g., Fletcher-Louis, *All the Glory*, 179, who understands line 4 and other elements of 4Q418 81 as making this distinction: "In the context of a text preserved in the Qumran Library the fact that an individual is place 'for the holy of holies' … must evoke the way in which the priesthood within the Qumran community are set up as the holy of holies over against the laity who are the holy ones. Not only does line 3 *cite* the privilege of the Aaronic priesthood, the whole of lines 3–4a seem to have in mind a distinction between the

functioning simply as a superlative, again underscoring the chosen status – and of course, holiness – of the מבין.[407] Third and as noted earlier in this chapter, מבינים is used in the Hebrew Bible to refer to the Levites in their role as teachers (cf. Ezra 8:12–16; 2 Chr 35:3),[408] yet it is seemingly learning rather than teaching that is the primary focus of *4QInstr*.[409]

---

position ('inheritance') of the righteous in general and the position of this particular individual: '*each* man has his inheritance, and God is *yours*'. ... In this case the addressee is a priest who, like the high priest in 1QSb 4:28, is set apart 'for the holy of holies' and given the divine privilege assigned to Aaron by the biblical text. The repeated reference to the 'holy ones' in 4Q418 81 is best taken, in this context, as a reference to the laity of Israel who are 'holy' whilst Aaron is a 'holy of holies' [emphases retained].

[407] A helpful overview of לקדוש קודשים is provided by Goff, *4QInstruction*, 248–249 (cf. idem, *The Worldly and Heavenly Wisdom*, 22–23), who does not interpret it as a reference to the temple, at least primarily, but as the superlative "most holy one." In response to readings that see a priesthood-laity distinction, see Wold, *Women, Men, and Angels*, 107, 162, 170–173, 178–179, here 179, who questions whether 4Q418 81 "truly warrants a division between an exalted priestly figure and the 'laity' of the community. An understanding of the these lines as fixedly defined, priestly verses [*sic*] laity, is not warranted by the evidence available. If the addressees of the document generally have in common access to רז נהיה and pursue and achieve knowledge to differing degrees (4Q418 55 10: 'Ac]cording to their knowledge they will honour a man more than his neighbor, and according to one's insight is his honour'), then such a clear division may not be applicable. While the relationship between addressee(s) and 'men of good pleasure' in 4Q418 81 could have expression in terms of an exalted figure and laity, such distinctions may be too strict. Rather, it may be best to conceive of 4Q418 81 as addressed to an elect community whose members have attained varying degrees of sanctity and who all hold the holy ones in esteem as superior models who should be emulated and revered." Cf. Tigchelaar, *To Increase Learning*, 231, who while sympathetic to the priestly import of 4Q418 81, nonetheless states that the "translation 'holy of holies' should perhaps be avoided since it may suggest that the addressee is appointed as a sanctuary." It should also be noted that the addressee's holiness and separation from a "spirit of flesh" are often compared to the priestly blessing Jacob pronounces on Levi in Jub. 31:14, cited above; see, e.g., Fletcher-Louis, *All the Glory*, 78–79. As observed, however, the Book of Jubilees not only compares Levi and his descendants to the angels of the presence and the angels of holiness but also suggests that the entire nation in some way corresponds to these angelic priests. Thus, any appeal to Jub. 31:14 to argue for a priesthood-laity distinction in 4Q418 81 should be done cautiously. On this point, see Angel, *Otherworldly*, 73 n. 210.

[408] See Lange, "Sages and Scribes," 274–275.

[409] This is not to say that didactic concerns are absent from the document, nor is its moniker "Instruction" undeserved. But it is the zeal the angels have for *learning* that distinguishes them from slothful humanity, and the addressees are therefore exhorted to emulate this angelic trait (cf. 4Q418 55 8–12; 69 II, 10–15). On emulation of the angels, see the comments of Strugnell and Harrington, DJD 34, 33; Tigchelaar, *To Increase Learning*, 220; Wold, *Women, Men, and Angels*, 157–161; Stuckenbruck, "4QInstruction and the Possible Influence," 252. *Contra* Fletcher-Louis, *All the Glory*, 119–120, who argues that humans are being described in exalted (angelmorphic) terms. On the *4QInstr's* emphasis on learning rather than teaching, see Matthew J. Goff, "Gardens of Knowledge: Teachers in Ben Sira, 4QInstruction, and the Hodayot," in *Pedagogy in Ancient Judaism and Early Christianity* (eds., Karina Martin Hogan, Matthew J. Goff, and Emma Wasserman; EJL 41;

Thus, while it is possible that the text asserts an affinity specifically with priestly angels for the purposes of attaining knowledge of the celestial priesthood, this is far from explicit. Instead, *4QInstr* is content to stress an angelic analogy without specifying all facets of the nature and purpose of this relationship. Arguably more than any other composition discussed in this chapter, *4QInstr's* exclusivity and the grandiosity of its claims,[410] including the notion that the addressees uniquely have an affinity with the angels, may indicate that its authors were part of a "sect."[411] However, the organization of this group does not appear to be as formal as that of the Qumran movement nor its boasts as grandiose or stringent,[412] even if some of *4QInstr's* motifs and assertions were apparently considered attractive enough to be adopted and modified by the sectarians whose library was discovered in the desert of Judah.

Atlanta: SBL Press, 2017), 180: "This Qumran text stresses not what the teacher provides but what the student does with it." On the relatively "unusual" portrayal of angels as learning rather than teaching in early Jewish literature, see idem, *4QInstruction*, 217–218, 235–238. But also see Wold, "Jesus Among Wisdom's Representatives," 317–336, here 332–333, who proposes that the didactic authority of the מבין in 4Q418 81 is connected to his relationship with the angels. Specifically, he explores the use of the designation משכיל – often translated "instructor" in Qumran sectarian texts (e.g., 1QS IX, 21; 1QHᵃ XX, 14) – and its relationship to מבין: "4Q418 frg. 81 contains instruction from a maskil about how a maven is to act in the role of maskil – just like him [see, e.g., line 17: "Improve greatly in understanding and from all of your teachers get ever more learning ..."]. Moreover, the *maskil* derives authority to teach about mysteries from his present participation with the angels, and when he teaches others how to act in this role, he exhorts them to bless and glorify the angels. The author is not simply looking forward to a future and eschatological participation in another world; in 4QInstruction the *maskilim* enjoy a relationship to the heavenly realm in the present insofar as they relate angelic beings when seeking רז נהיה."

[410] E.g., Strugnell and Harrington, DJD 34, 20: "And what does it signify that the sage's authority is no longer 'among the children of Israel' [as per Num 18:20] but 'among the sons of Adam/among mankind' [cf. 4Q418 81 3]? This *prima facie* remarkably bold claim to the universality of the maven's authority and to his authority in the international courts in which he is often described as serving – does this mean what on the surface it is saying? Nothing suggests a more minimalist interpretation." Intriguingly, Fletcher-Louis, *All the Glory*, 180, understands this re-reading of Num 18:20 to be evidence of "the cultic cosmology that we would expect from priestly traditions. The priest is set apart for the holy of holies which functions as sacred center of the whole cosmos instantiated in the cult where he and the rest of people of God embody the true Adam." *Contra* Angel, *Otherworldly*, 68, who argues that the "combination of priestly *and* royal expression in this passage indicates the use of symbolic language and decreases the probability that it is addressed to a real priest" [emphasis mine].

[411] So Goff, *4QInstruction*, 27.

[412] So, too, Goff, *4QInstruction*, 27. Cf. Elgvin, "The Mystery to Come," 117, 128; Strugnell and Harrington, DJD 34, 308–309. I would suggest that this is especially the case as it pertains to the issue of being the true Israel, which is not nearly as explicit here as it is in the compositions penned by the Qumran movement for whom this seems to have been a central theme.

I. Son of God Text (4Q246)

The *Aramaic Apocalypse* or *Apocryphon of Daniel* – which is commonly known as the *Son of God Text* (henceforth, *SGT*)[413] – is a single fragmentary manuscript (4Q246), dated on the basis of paleography to the Herodian period (ca. 25 BCE).[414] The text consists of two columns, the first of which is only partially extant; that there was at least a third column is suggested by the presence of a construct form in the last word of the second column. As for the content of the text, it appears that a seer is interpreting the visionary experience of a king who is troubled by what he has seen (4Q246 I, 1–3), namely the tribulations wrought by foreign oppressors (cf. I, 4–8; II, 2–3, 8–9). The most well-known and debated aspect of the vision is a figure referred to as ברה די אל, "the son of God" and בר עליון, "the son of the Most High" (II, 1). There have been several suggestions as to the identity of this figure and both his relationship to the tribulations witnessed by the king and how he is connected to the rise of the people, an event mentioned near the end of the extant document (cf. II, 4–6).[415]

In general, interpretations of this "son of God" fall into one of two categories: negative or positive.[416] Negative understandings include a pre-Christian antichrist-like figure or a historical king, with Alexander Balas and Antiochus Epiphanes having been proposed.[417] What these interpretations share in common is that the lofty epithets of divine sonship have been blasphemously

---

[413] The text was partially published by Joseph A. Fitzmyer, "The Contribution of Qumran Aramaic to the Study of the New Testament," *NTS* 20 (1974), 382–407. The first full publication was Emile Puech, "Fragment d'une Apocalypse en Arameen (4Q246 = pseudo-Dan[d]) et le 'Royaume de Dieu'," *RB* 99 (1992): 98–131; more recently, idem, "246. 4QApocryphe de Daniel ar," in *Qumran Cave 4:XVII: Parabiblical Texts, Part III* (eds. George J. Brooke et al.; DJD 22; Oxford: Oxford University Press, 1997), 165–184.

[414] See Puech, DJD 22, 166. The text's linguistic parallels with Daniel (see below) suggest a *terminus post quem* of the mid 2nd cent. BCE.

[415] See Florentino García Martínez, "The Eschatological Figure of 4Q246," in *Qumran and Apocalyptic: Studies on the Aramaic Texts from Qumran* (STDJ 9; Leiden: Brill, 1992), 168, who also notes that there is uncertainty as to the "historical or apocalyptical character of the description of the future evils narrated to the king."

[416] García Martínez, "The Eschatological Figure," 168.

[417] For the antichrist reading, see David Flusser, "The Hubris of the Antichrist in a Fragment from Qumran," *Imm* 10 (1980): 31–37. For the Balas interpretation, see Józef T. Milik, "Les modèles araméens du Livre d'Esther dans la Brotte 4 de Qumrân," *RevQ* 15 (1992): 383, who originally proposed this reading in a 1972 presentation at Harvard University. On the Antiochus interpretation, see Edward M. Cook, "4Q246," *BBR* 5 (1995): 43–66; also see Puech, who initially allowed this understanding (idem, "Fragment d'une Apocalypse," 98–131; idem, "Notes sur le fragment d'apocalypse 4Q246 – 'le fils de Dieu'," *RB* 101 [1994]: 533–558), then preferred it (idem, DJD 22, 165–184), but has recently stood behind a positive messianic understanding of the text (see Collins, *The Scepter and the Star*, 173 n. 13, who cites Puech's 2008 presentation on this subject).

usurped, and that rise of the people of God is understood to be indicative of the downfall of this oppressive figure's kingdom. The numerous linguistic affinities the text has with the Book of Daniel have been noted,[418] and Dunn has proposed that "the people of God" (II, 7) are intended to mirror the victorious fate of the Danielic "people of the Holy Ones of the Most High" and the "one like a son of man," whom he interprets as a collective symbol.[419] But like the interpretations mentioned above, Dunn understands "the son of God" to be a malevolent figure whose downfall results in the victory of God's people. Others, however, have proposed an individualistic interpretation that sees the son of God in a positive light, namely, as the Davidic messiah (cf. 4Q174 1 I, 7; Pss. Sol. 17:4, 32–42);[420] the very similar language used of Jesus in the Lukan infancy narrative (cf. Luke 1:32–33) is said to lend credence to this interpretation.[421] In light of the linguistic parallels with Dan 7, it has also been posited that the son of God figure may be an implicit, messianic reworking of the coming of the "one like a son of man."[422]

---

[418] For a convenient listing of the linguistic parallels 4Q246 has with the Book of Daniel, see Géza G. Xeravits, *King, Priest, Prophet: Positive Eschatological Protagonists of the Qumran Library* (STDJ 47; Leiden: Brill, 2003), 86.

[419] So Dunn, "'Son of God' as 'Son of Man,'" 198–210, who is strongly opposed to the angelic interpretation of Dan 7:13; for further on the collective interpretation of the "son of man," see my discussion of Daniel, above. Cf. Annette Steudel, "The Eternal Reign of the People of God – Collective Expectation in Qumran Texts (4Q246 and 1QM)," *RevQ* 17 (1996): 509–521, who also emphasizes the corporate character of 4Q246's hope.

[420] Cf., e.g., Collins, *The Scepter and the Star*, 171–214; idem, "The Background of the 'Son of God' Text," *BBR* 7 (1997): 54; idem, "The Son of God Text from Qumran," in *From Jesus to John: Essays on Jesus and New Testament Christology in Honor of Marinus de Jong* (ed. Martinus C. De Boer; JSNTSup 84; Sheffield: JSOT, 1993), 65–82; Frank Moore Cross, "The Structure of the Apocalypse of 'Son of God,'" in *Emanuel: Studies in Hebrew Bible, Septuagint, and Dead Sea Scrolls in Honor of Emanuel Tov* (eds., Shalom M. Paul et al.; Leiden: Brill, 2003), 151–158; Johannes Zimmermann, "Observations on 4Q246 – The 'Son of God,'" in *Qumran-Messianism* (eds., James H. Charlesworth, Hermann Lichtenberger, and Gerbern S. Oegema; Tübingen: Mohr Siebeck, 1998), 175–190. For a recent defense of the messianic interpretation, see Ferda S. Tucker, "Naming the Messiah: A Contribution to 4Q246 'Son of God' Debate," *DSD* 12 (2014): 150–175. Also see Joseph A. Fitzmyer, "4Q246: The 'Son of God' Document from Qumran," *Bib* 74 (1993): 153–174, who views the son of God as a "Davidic king" but objects to referring to this figure as a "messiah" (because this epithet is not found in the text).

[421] For comments on the relevance of 4Q246 for Historical Jesus studies, cf., e.g., Craig A. Evans, "Jesus and Dead Sea Scrolls from Qumran Cave 4," in *Eschatology, Messianism, and the Dead Sea Scrolls* (eds., idem and Peter W. Flint; SDSSRL; Grand Rapids: Eerdmans, 1997), 93; Cross, "The Structure of the Apocalypse," 153–154; Matthew L. Walsh, "Dead Sea Scrolls: Son of God Text (4Q246)" in *The Encyclopedia of the Historical Jesus* (ed., Craig A. Evans; New York: Routledge Press, 2008), 141–143.

[422] See Collins, *The Scepter and the Star*, 177–178. Cf. Karl A. Kuhn, "The 'One like a Son of Man' Becomes the Son of God," *CBQ* 69 (2007): 22–42; Seyoon Kim, *The 'Son of*

Two additional understandings of *SGT* – one positive and one negative, and not unrelated to those surveyed above – are especially relevant. The first belongs to García Martínez, who has argued that the son of God should be identified as a principal angel figure.[423] More recently, García Martínez has developed this proposal in that he views 4Q246's son of God as "human and heavenly at the same time."[424] Though he readily acknowledges that "the human character of the mysterious personage of 4Q246 is not emphasized,"[425] García Martínez is essentially 1.) combining the aforementioned messianic and collective interpretations of *SGT* with his own angelic interpretation;[426] and he does so by 2.) positing that the "son of God" has an earthly, messianic counterpart. Thus, the relationship between the "the son of God" (II, 1) and the rise of "the people of God" (II, 7) is seen to be analogous to that of the exaltation of Danielic "one like a son of man" and the reception of the kingdom by "the people of the holy ones of the Most High." Against this interpretation, it has been pointed out that "son of God" in the singular is not a title for a principal angel figure, though the idea of God as the "strength" of an angel is not far removed from other texts:[427] no matter their charge or potency, angels require God to intervene.[428]

A second interpretation of *SGT* especially relevant to the present study – and one which is effectively a counter to García Martínez's latest reading –

Man' as the Son of God (Tübingen: Mohr Siebeck, 1983); *contra* Dunn, "'Son of God' as 'Son of Man,'" 198–210. See further, below.

[423] García Martínez, "The Eschatological Figure," 172–179.

[424] See Florentino García Martínez, "Two Messianic Figures in the Qumran Texts," in *Qumranica Minora II* (STDJ 64; Leiden: Brill, 2007), 20–24, here 23.

[425] García Martínez, "Two Messianic Figures," 23.

[426] Though, strangely, he is reticent to retain the term "angelic" for "the son of God," which is made all the more surprising since he cites the angelic interpretation of the Danielic "one like a son of man" and the similar figure from the *Similitudes of Enoch* as parallels; see García Martínez, "Two Messianic Figures," 23–34, who prefers to use the adjective "superhuman." Though Collins, *The Scepter and the Star*, 183, opts for the messianic interpretation of 4Q246, he is open to an angelic understanding: "One other text should be considered in support of the angelic interpretation of the 'Son of God.' The *Similitudes* ... are not found at Qumran, and are probably the product of a different sect, although their apocalyptic worldview is similar in many respects to that of the community. A central role in this document is filled by a figure called 'that Son of Man,' who is patently meant to recall the 'one like a son of man' of Daniel 7." Cf. Nickelsburg and VanderKam, *1 Enoch 2*, 113–120.

[427] So Collins, *The Scepter and the Star*, 181–183. While the plural "sons of God" and similar appellations are commonly used as angelic designations, the closest parallel in the singular is perhaps Dan 3:25, though admittedly this is not a title as it is in 4Q246.

[428] As we will see in Chapter 4, both the *War Scroll* and *11QMelchizedek* present angels as divinely-commissioned eschatological agents of judgment who usher in reigns of peace for Israel (cf. 11Q13 II, 13–15; 1QM XVII, 5–8), making a similar reading of 4Q246's son of God a strong option; so García Martínez, "Two Messianic Figures," 20–24.

has been proposed by Segal, whose "literary-theological connection" between Deut 32, Ps 82, and Dan 7 was noted in Chapter 2.[429] Given 4Q246's use of Dan 7, Segal views the son of God as the Ps 82-inspired heavenly (i.e., angelic) counterpart of the fourth beast in Daniel's vision (cf. Dan 7:7–8), who has been recast in *SGT*. Segal's reading primarily stems from two factors: 1.) the nomenclature of the son of God, which he argues is ultimately drawn from the unjust and demoted אלהים and בני עליון of Ps 82:6–7, who, in Segal's evaluation, are cast as beasts in Dan 7; and 2.) a linear reading of *SGT*, which stresses that the son of God emerges in the midst of a period of upheaval and thus contributes to it.[430] In addition to being susceptible to the same critique as a positive angelic interpretation – that the son of God/Most High in the singular is not anywhere a title granted to an angel – the fragmentary condition of 4Q246 means that it is questionable whether a linear approach to *SGT* is correct. Citing the influence of Dan 7 and other apocalyptic texts, Collins has defended an oscillatory understanding of the text that allows for the mention of (a future) positive figure in an otherwise chaotic scene, and he thus does not deem it necessary to view the son of God as malevolent.[431]

Its fragmentary condition and variegated interpretive history render the study of 4Q246 particularly challenging and caution is warranted when drawing conclusions. Yet there is much to commend in García Martínez's latest reading of *SGT*: in keeping with the apparent influence of Dan 7, his emphasis on the relationship between celestial *and* earthly realities is important. And this is especially true of his interpretation of the son of God/Most High as "both human and heavenly at the same time," not least because of the messianic and angelic associations of these epithets. Interpreted in this way, 4Q246 is indicative of the belief that the עם אל (i.e., Israel) had an angelic guardian whose influence was connected to their eschatological "rise."[432]

---

[429] See Segal, "Who is the 'Son of God?'" 289–312.

[430] Segal, "Who is the 'Son of God?'" 301–304, outlines *SGT* as follows: a.) I, 1–8: negative era of strife under the king(s) of Assyria and Egypt; b.) I, 9–II, 2: uncertain content, though it is in this section that "the son of God/Most High" is mentioned; c.) II, 2–3: negative era of international conflict; d.) II, 4–9: positive era in which the people of God are victorious. Since the progression from Segal's section c.) to d.) is the only "clearly marked" transition from negative to positive, he considers the son of God to be responsible for the unrest prior to section d.).

[431] Though Collins, "The Background," 58–59, concedes that the "repetitions in Daniel 7 are occasioned by the process of interpretation, and this is not overtly the case in 4Q246." For a response to Collins, see Segal, "Who is the 'Son of God?'" 304.

[432] Conversely, if one assumes Segal's reading is correct, it is possible that the non-extant sections of the text referred to a righteous counterpart of the malevolent son of God, since hostile angelic figures akin to what Segal is proposing for 4Q246's son of God (e.g., Belial, the Angel of Darkness, etc.) often have a God-dispatched angelic opponent (cf. *BW*, *AA*, Jubilees, 1QS III–IV; *11QMelchizedek*; 1QM; et al.).

J. Summary

This chapter has focused on several Qumran non-sectarian compositions in which angels associated with Israel are prevalent. While angelic guardians are the focus of certain texts (Dan 7–12; perhaps *SGT*, depending on how it is interpreted), others either refer to both angelic guardians and priests or suggest that some angels served in a dual capacity. As it pertains to angelic guardians (e.g., Dan 7:13–14; 10:13, 21; 12:1; 1 En. 20:5; 90:14; 4Q544 1 14; Tob 5–12; Jub. 1:29; 48:13), at least two summary observations can be made. First, some texts advocate violent resistance (*AA*; *EE*), and others suggest that faithfulness is demonstrated through wise teaching, piety, or patient suffering (Dan 7–12; Tobit); in all cases, the knowledge of Israel's angelic guardianship, whether it occurs on earth or in heaven, would have been a profound encouragement for those to whom it was revealed.[433] It would also have served to remind faithful Jews of their connection to their heavenly counterparts, a bond that in some cases was envisioned as culminating in postmortem angelic fellowship and angel-like exaltation (e.g., Dan 12:3; 1 En. 104:2–6). Second, angelic guardians are never sufficient in and of themselves: despite a lofty rank or charge, these beings – and thus the nation – are ultimately dependent on the decisive support, intervention, or judgment of the God of Israel (e.g., Dan 7:22; 1 En. 1:9; 90:15; 100:4; *Bodl.* col. b 21–22).[434]

The existence and actions of angelic priests as depicted in these texts would have similarly encouraged those to whom this knowledge was revealed. In chaotic times, a temple in heaven would have functioned as reassurance that the corruption of some priests – angelic or human – ultimately does not negate the efficacy of the heavenly priesthood or its counterpart in Jerusalem (*BW*). Moreover, the intercession provided by the heavenly priests and their sin-purging incarceration of unrighteous spiritual beings (Dan 9–10; *BW*; *AA*; *EE;* Tob), were likely no small comforts in the minds of those who composed these texts. As with angelic guardians, high value is placed on the connection between Israel's priestly line and their angelic counterparts: some texts suggest that to be the ideal priesthood on earth is to emulate the heavenly priesthood because it is its basis for knowledge and teaching (*ALD*; *VA*); arguably, the culmination of such thinking is that it is not just Israel's priests but the entire nation that corresponds to the angels who minister in closest proximity to God (Jub.).

---

[433] Cf. Michalak, *Angels as Warriors*, 241, 245, who observes that in the late Second Temple Period literature angels either a.) fight in the heavenly equivalent of an earthly battle; or b.) intervene directly on the battlefield. I will return to this observation in my discussion of the *War Scroll*; see Chapter 4, below.

[434] As I noted in Chapter 1, Michalak, *Angels as Warriors*, 243, points out that even angels of high rank have "no independent power to initiate their own missions."

Finally, that action is undertaken and knowledge taught/conveyed by the most elite of angels (e.g., Dan 9; 1 En. 10:1–15, 24:6, 93:6; Tob 12:15; Jub. 1:27; possibly 4Q418 81) enhances the authority of what is revealed and the prestige of the protection afforded; revelatory confidence is also heightened by making ancient heroes like Enoch and Levi the "recipients" of this knowledge, which complements (yet sometimes seems to outshine) the Mosaic Torah. What is interesting to note, however, is that even if a patriarch is a stand-in for a given text's authors – who are thereby claiming special knowledge of the angelic realm, heavenly wisdom, etc. – it is difficult to describe the outlooks of many of the works discussed in this chapter as exclusivist, at least rigidly so. While many texts hint at a special role for its authors or evaluate fellow Jews more stringently than others (especially *EE; 4QInstr*), it is noteworthy that, in other texts, Israel is defined in a relatively generous manner (e.g., Dan 7–12; Jub.). Furthermore, all three of the Enochic works examined here have universalistic leanings. This does not mean that the authors of these texts did not consider themselves or their own circles privileged because of their knowledge of, connection to, and/or assistance from these angelic guardians and priests. But as we will see, in comparison to the sectarian works from Qumran, the texts discussed in this chapter are either 1.) not as rigidly or formally exclusivist; or 2.) seemingly open to a generously-defined understanding of Israel and, in some cases, not void of eschatological hope for even Gentiles, however puzzling or ambiguous such assertions may be.

Chapter 4

Angels Associated with Israel in the Sectarian Texts
Part I: Angelic Guardians

A. Introduction

In the preceding chapter, I examined angels associated with Israel in non-sectarian texts, noting how the revelation of the existence of these beings and the belief of a correspondence with them, as well as the hope of receiving their assistance and the anticipation of post-mortem angelic fellowship, were important facets of the works in which they are featured. Turning to texts of a sectarian provenance, I will highlight similar themes, but here my focus will be on the development and expansion of these motifs at Qumran, especially as it is manifested in the sect's well-known boasts of angelic fellowship,[1] which is more elaborate than the distinctly post-mortem privilege anticipated in texts like Dan 12 and 1 En. 104. Specifically, I will explore the relationship between angelic fellowship and the assertions of the sect to be the true Israel.

Scholars have observed, however, that there are different "forms" of this angelic communion. For example, Schäfer lists four types of fellowship: 1.) the *Hodayot* depict the community as intermingling with the angels *in heaven* as they praise God together (but he allows for the possibility that the sectarians thought the angels were present with them *on earth*); 2.) the first-person speaker of the so-called *Self-Glorification Hymn* boasts of his elevation among the angels *in heaven* and his superiority to any angel or human; 3.) *Songs of the Sabbath Sacrifice* is a different work in that the focus is not on humans but on the angelic priests, whom the sectarians invite to perform their liturgical and sacrificial duties in the heavenly sanctuary; 4.) the *War Scroll*, in which humans and angels are united *on earth* for the great eschatological battle.[2] That there is a coherence among Schäfer's categories can be seen in the similar ways[3] other scholars have classified angelic fellowship: Tuschling

---

[1] Dimant, "Men as Angels," 99, captures the provocative nature of the notion of this fellowship by referring to it as the "notorious" communion of the sect with the angels.

[2] Schäfer, *The Origins of Jewish Mysticism*, 151–152.

[3] Cf. Tuschling, *Angels and Orthodoxy*, 117; Kuhn, *Enderwartung*, 69; Moshe Weinfeld, *Normative and Sectarian Judaism in the Second Temple Period* (LSTS 54; London: T & T Clark, 2005), 48.

discusses the *Vorstellungskreise* proposed by Kuhn, including holy war and priestly communion; and these are akin to the kinds of angelic fellowship noted by Weinfeld: eschatological warfare, common praise, and eternal life.

In short, the organization of the remainder of this study is effectively a distillation of the categories of angelic fellowship just mentioned: liturgical communion with the (priestly) angels, which I will address in the next chapter, and the anticipation that the sectarian soldiers and the angelic guardians of Israel would fight together as a single army at the impending eschatological war. A significant section of this chapter will thus include a discussion of the *War Scroll*. But before doing so, I will examine two other texts, *The Treatise on the Two Spirits* from *The Community Rule* (1QS) and *11QMelchizedek* (11Q13), as both seem to contain the types of beliefs that could have been foundational or served as an impetus for the martial angelic fellowship of 1QM.

B. Setting the Stage for Martial Angelic Fellowship

I. The Treatise on the Two Spirits (1QS III, 13–IV, 26)

The lengthy dualistic theological statement known as the *Treatise on the Two Spirits* (henceforth, *TTS*) spans the second half of column three and the entirety of column four of the *Community Rule* from Cave 1.[4] *TTS* is of interest because its dualism includes the pitting of two angel-led contingents against one another. Due to the fact that 1QS was among the first texts discovered by the Bedouin but also because this early cache of manuscripts included a number of documents universally considered to be of sectarian provenance,[5] scholars have often concluded that the dualistic outlook of *TTS* was a foundational component of the Qumran movement's theology.[6] In other words, it

---

[4] See the early publication of 1QS in Millar Burrows, John C. Trevor, and William H. Brownlee, eds., *The Dead Sea Scrolls of St. Mark's Monastery. II.2, Plates and Transcription of the Manual of Discipline* (New Haven: ASOR, 1951). All text, sigla, and translations (with occasional minor adjustments of the latter) are based on the more recent edition of Elisha Qimron and James H. Charlesworth, "The Rule of the Community (1QS)," in *The Dead Sea Scrolls: Hebrew, Aramaic, and Greek Texts with English Translations, Vol. 1: Rule of the Community and Related Documents* (ed., J. H. Charlesworth et al.; PTSDSSP 1; Tübingen: Mohr Siebeck; Louisville: Westminster John Knox Press, 1994), 6–51.

[5] E.g., the *Hodayot* (1QH^a) and the *War Scroll* (1QM).

[6] Mladen Popovic, "Light and Darkness in the Treatise on the Two Spirits (1QS III 13–IV 26) and in 4Q186," in *Dualism in Qumran* (ed., Geza G. Xeravits; LSTS 76; London: Continuum, 2010), 148, remarks that *TTS* is often considered to be "a text of theological importance and the school example of the Qumran community's dualistic worldview." In the same volume as Popovic's essay, Charlotte Hempel, "The Treatise on the Two Spirits and the Literary History of the Rule of the Community," 102, implies that the dualistic

has been assumed that *TTS* is a sectarian composition and was an integral part of the *Community Rule* from its inception.

But the discovery and publication of shorter recensions of the *Community Rule* from Cave 4 – texts that lack *TTS* as well as other material – have complicated the matter.[7] What is certain is that *TTS* was "not invariably part of the of *Community Rule*."[8] The question, however, is whether 1QS testifies to a developmental expansion of the *Serekh* tradition or whether the shorter Cave 4 texts are an abbreviation of the tradition preserved in 1QS.[9] I consider the former view to offer the most explanatory power,[10] and in this scenario *TTS*

---

designation, the "Sons of Light," has been frequently employed in the secondary literature as a designation for those responsible for the scrolls with little or no qualification. Cf., e.g., André Dupont-Sommer, "L'instruction sur les deux Esprits dans le Manuel de Discipline," *RHR* 142 (1952): 5–35; Preben Wernberg-Møller, *The Manual of Discipline: Translated and Annotated with an Introduction* (STDJ 1; Leiden: Brill, 1957), 47; Jacob Licht, "An Analysis of the Treatise on the Two Spirits in DSD," ScrHier 4 (1965): 88–100; Alfred R. C. Leaney, *The Rule of Qumran and Its Meaning* (NTL; London: SCM Press, 1966), 143; Philip S. Alexander, "Predestination and Free Will in the Theology of the Dead Sea Scrolls," in *Divine and Human Agency in Paul and His Cultural Environment* (eds., John M. G. Barclay and Simon J. Gathercole; LNTS 335; London: T & T Clark, 2006), 27–49; Florentino García Martínez, *Qumranic Minora I: Qumran Origins and Apocalypticism* (STDJ 63; Leiden: Brill, 2007), 233; Claude Coulot, "L'instruction sur les deux esprits (1QS III, 13–IV, 26)," *RSR* 82 (2008): 147–160.

[7] E.g., both 4QS[d] and 4QS[e] begin at what is the equivalent of 1QS V. For the Cave 4 *Serekh* texts, see Philip S. Alexander and Geza Vermes, *Qumran Cave 4.XIX: 4QSerekh Ha-Yahad and Two Related Texts* (DJD 26; Oxford: Claredon, 1998). For a summary of Qumran fragments which share similarities to *TTS* or may be related to it, see Hempel, "The Treatise on the Two Spirits and the Literary History," 107–110.

[8] Collins, *The Scriptures and Sectarianism*, 188.

[9] 1QS is dated on basis of paleography to 100–75 BCE. Championing the developmental scenario is Sarianna Metso (*The Textual Development of the Qumran Community Rule* [STDJ 21; Leiden: Brill, 1997]; and more recently, "Phases of Textual Growth," in eadem, *The Serekh Texts* [LSTS 62; London: T & T Clark, 2007], 15–20), despite the fact that the paleography of the Cave 4 fragments has been judged to be later than that of 1QS. Conversely, Philip S. Alexander ("The Redaction History of the Serekh Ha-Yahad: A Proposal," *RevQ* 17 [1996]: 437–456; cf. idem, "The Recensional History of the Serekh ha-Yahad," in DJD 26, 9–12) has argued that the Cave 4 fragments are an abbreviation of the 1QS tradition. Also see Schofield, *From Qumran to the Yahad*.

[10] For a helpful overview of the issues, see Michael Knibb, "The Rule of the Community," *EDSS* 2:793–797, who summarizes as follows: "Alexander's stress on the importance of paleographical considerations has to be taken seriously. On the other hand, the view put forward by Metso better takes account of the indication within [1QS] itself that its text is composite, and that it acquired its present form by a process of evolution [e.g., the additions of *TTS* and quotations of scripture]." Most recently, see Jutta Jokiranta, "What is 'Serekh ha-Yahad (S)'? Thinking About Ancient Manuscripts as Information Processing," in *Sibyls, Scriptures, and Scrolls*, 611–635, who, in addition to providing an up-to-date summary,

was either 1.) composed by the sect and added to the *Community Rule* at a later time;[11] or 2.) a non-sectarian composition subsequently adopted by the sect and added to the *Community Rule*,[12] perhaps with additions to both components.[13] A second factor prompting scholars to question the provenance of *TTS* is its so-called universalistic perspective,[14] which stands in contrast to the Qumran movement's more exclusive claims.

Regardless of its origins, *TTS* occupies a prominent position in a quintessential sectarian document, and it is therefore not surprising that speculation has arisen as to why *TTS* may have been included.[15] I will return to this "why" question in greater detail, below. For now, it is sufficient to note that *TTS* uses dualism both to demarcate who is elect and to clarify the place of the elect in God's plan. While such observations may be "banal,"[16] they are im-

---

discusses the appropriateness of referring to "S" texts, given the discrepancies between the various manuscripts traditionally grouped together as *Serekh* texts.

[11] E.g., Collins, *The Scriptures and Sectarianism*, 193.

[12] A number of scholars have argued that *TTS* was inserted more or less wholesale into the *Serekh* tradition: cf., e.g., Licht, "An Analysis of the Treatise," 88–100; Jerome Murphy-O'Connor, "La genèse littéraire de la Règle de la Communauté," *RB* 76 (1969): 528–549; Hartmut Stegemann, *The Library of Qumran: On the Essenes, John the Baptist and Jesus* (Grand Rapids: Eerdmans, 1998), 110; Armin Lange, *Weisheit und Prädestination: Weisheitliche Urordnung und Prädestination in den Textfunden von Qumran* (STDJ 18; Leiden: Brill, 1995), 127–128; Jörg Frey, "Different Patterns of Dualistic Thought in the Qumran Library," in *Legal Texts and Legal Issues: Proceedings of the Second Meeting of the International Organization for Qumran Studies, Cambridge, 1995: Published in Honour of Joseph M. Baumgarten* (eds., Moshe Bernstein, Florentino García Martínez, and John Kampen; STDJ 23; Leiden: Brill, 1997), 289.

[13] See especially Hempel, "The Treatise on the Two Spirits and the Literary History," 113–119, who proposes how not just *TTS* but also the *Serekh* materials that surround it may have been modified to facilitate the union of the documents.

[14] Universalistic in the sense that there is nothing in *TTS per se* limiting the positive element of dualistic opposites such as האמת והעול, "truth and deceit," to the Qumran movement, and that it is only within the context of 1QS that such identifications can/must be made; so Jutta Leonhardt-Balzer, "Evil, Dualism and Community: Who/What Did the Yahad Not Want to Be?" in *Dualism in Qumran*, 134–136. Cf. Hempel, "The Treatise on the Two Spirits and the Literary History," 115; eadem, "Maskil(im) and Rabbim: From Daniel to Qumran," in *Biblical Traditions in Transmission: Essays in Honour of Michael A. Knibb* (eds., Charlotte Hempel and Judith Lieu; JSJSup 111; Leiden: Brill, 2006), 152–154; Newsom, *The Self as Symbolic Space*, 88.

[15] While it is possible that the removal of *TTS* from the tradition was prompted by a change in perspective, an abbreviated recension of the *Serekh* tradition does not demand the conclusion that *TTS* was thereby rejected by the Qumran movement (i.e., it simply may have been that a condensed version of the rules was desired).

[16] Leonhardt-Balzer, "Evil, Dualism and Community," 141, 146, concedes the banality of these observations, but she also suggests that *TTS* was important because it helped the sect decipher who they did *not* want to be: "others." Cf. Nickelsburg, "The We and the

portant if the goal is to understand the sectarians' self-identity. In order to comprehend fully the relationship the elect have with the aforementioned angel-led contingents, some comments on both the structure and content of *TTS*, as well as how *TTS* functions within 1QS, will be helpful.

My own demarcation of *TTS* is indebted to earlier proposals:[17]

Table 6: Outline of TTS

Section	1QS Reference	Themes
Introduction	III, 13–15a	Admonition for the *maskil* to teach the treatise and an introductory statement that its contents concern the nature of humanity and כול מיני רוחותם, "all their spiritual varieties"[18]
Overview of Divine Sovereignty		
1.	III, 15b–17a	Foundational statement on the sovereignty of God and his sustaining power over the created order
2.	III, 17b–19	Aspect #1 of God's Sovereignty: the two *inclinational* spirits at work within humankind
3.	III, 20–IV, 1	Aspect #2 of God's Sovereignty: the two *angelic* spirits influencing humankind
Practical Out-Workings of Divine Sovereignty		
4.	IV, 2–8 and IV, 9–14	The respective paths and eschatological rewards/punishments of those led by the spirit of truth and spirit of deceit
5.	IV, 15–26	Mechanics of the division and reiteration of the eschatological fates

A key to understanding *TTS* is that there is not just one form of dualism at work within it, but that the text simultaneously employs psychological (or inclinational) dualism, cosmic (or angelic) dualism, and ethical (or moral)

Other," 273, who rightly states that, from the perspective of *TTS* (and its placement in 1QS), non-members of the Qumran movement are the "epitome of the 'Other.'"

[17] Cf. Popovic, "Light and Darkness in the Treatise on the Two Spirits," 150–153; Frey, "Different Patterns," 290; Lange, *Weisheit und Prädestination*, 140–143; Jean Duhaime, "Cohérence structurelle et tensions internes dans l'Instruction sur les Deux Esprits (1QS III 13–IV 26)," in *Wisdom and Apocalypticism in the Dead Sea Scrolls and in the Biblical Tradition* (ed., Florentino García Martínez; BETL 168; Leuven: Peeters, 2003), 103–132; Licht, "An Analysis of the Treatise," 88–100.

[18] As per the translation of Florentino García Martínez and Eibert J. C. Tigchelaar, *DSSSE*, 1:75.

dualism.[19] The recognition that the various dualisms complement and interact with each other is particularly important in light of the fact that the word רוח, "spirit," is used somewhat confusingly to refer to both inclinational and angelic dualisms.[20] It is angelic dualism with which I am obviously most concerned, and since this form of dualism is showcased in what I have demarcated as *TTS's* third section (III, 20–IV, 1), my discussion will highlight these lines.

---

[19] On this point, see especially James H. Charlesworth, *John and the Dead Sea Scrolls* (ed., idem; New York: Crossroad, 1991), 76–106; Frey, "Different Patterns," 290–295; Popovic, "Light and Darkness," 153–165; Loren T. Stuckenbruck, "The Interiorization of Dualism within the Human Being in Second Temple Judaism: The Treatise of the Two Spirits (1QS III:13–IV:26) in its Tradition-Historical Context," in *Light Against Darkness: Dualism in Ancient Mediterranean Religion and the Contemporary World* (eds., Armin Lange et al.; JAJSup 2; Göttingen: Vandenhoeck & Ruprecht, 2011), 145–168. Additionally, the various dualisms have been a driving force for speculation on source-critical matters and the history of the formation of *TTS* itself. Cf., e.g., Peter Osten-Sacken, *Gott und Belial: traditionsgeschichtliche Untersuchungen zum Dualismus in den Texten aus Qumran* (SUNT 6; Göttingen: Vandenhoeck & Ruprecht, 1969), 17–28; Jean Duhaime, "L'Intruction sur les deux esprits et le interpolations dualistes a Qumrân (1QS III, 13–IV, 26)," *RB* 84 (1977): 566–594; idem, "Dualistic Reworking in the Scrolls from Qumran," *CBQ* 49 (1987): 40–43. However, proposals for how *TTS* came to attain its present shape and content are at least just as speculative as deciphering *TTS's* relationship to 1QS, and for this reason, Frey, "Different Patterns," 290, is right to emphasize the "compositional unity" of the text. On this issue, see Hempel, "The Treatise on the Two Spirits and the Literary History," 113, who comments that while some of the distinctive dualistic elements "may well have originated separately, it seems impossible to try to disentangle their current interconnection."

[20] *Contra* Preben Wernberg-Møller, "A Reconsideration of the Two Spirits in the Rule of the Community (1Q Serke 3:13–4:26)," *RevQ* (1961): 422, who understood רוח only in terms of psychology, mood, disposition, propensity, etc., and thus roughly equivalent to the rabbinic יֵצֶר distinctions. However, it is unnecessary to pit one form of dualism against another in *TTS*, and here John J. Collins, *Apocalypticism in the Dead Sea Scrolls* (New York: Routledge, 1997), 41, is instructive: "[*TTS*] clearly identifies the two spirits with the Prince of Light and the Angel of Darkness (3:20–1). The dualism is simultaneously psychological, moral, and cosmic. There is a synergism between the psychological realm and the agency of the supernatural angels or demons." On the use of רוח to refer to demons, see Philip S. Alexander, "The Demonology of the Dead Sea Scrolls," in *The Dead Sea Scrolls After Fifty Years: A Comprehensive Assessment* (2 vols.; eds., Peter W. Flint and James C. VanderKam; Leiden: Brill, 1999), 2:331. Cf. Frey, "Different Patterns," 291–293; Davidson, *Angels at Qumran*, 153–156; Arthur E. Sekki, *The Meaning of Ruah at Qumran* (SBLDS 110; Atlanta: Scholars Press, 1989), 7–67; Arnold A. Anderson, "The Use of 'Ruah' in 1QS, 1QH and 1QM," *JSS* 7 (1962): 293–303. For a recent and detailed discussion of the forms of dualism at work in *TTS* and their parallels in other Qumran texts, see Mladen Popovic, "Anthropology, Pneumatology, and Demonology in Early Judaism: The Two Spirits Treatise (1qs iii, 13–iv, 26) and Other Texts from the Dead Sea Scrolls," in *Dust of the Ground and Breath of Life*, 58–98.

Having already set out that two opposing inclinational spirits are at work *within* humankind in what I have demarcated as *TTS's* second section (1QS III, 17b–19), column III continues by announcing that humankind also has *outside* influences in the form of two opposing angels:

20 ביד שר אורים ממשלת כול בני צדק בדרכי אור יתהלכו וביד מלאך
21 חושך כול ממשלת בני עול ובדרכי חושך יתהלכו ...

20 And in the hand of the Prince of Lights (is) the dominion of all the Sons of Righteousness; in the ways of light they walk. But in the hand of the Angel of
21 Darkness (is) the complete dominion of the Sons of Deceit; and in the ways of darkness they walk ...

One immediately notices the interplay of angelic and ethical dualisms,[21] as well as the relative theological neatness of the above statements insofar as there are two distinct angelic leaders, peoples, and paths. However, the second half of line 21 and following makes things far less tidy theologically:[22]

21 ...   ובמלאך חושך תעות
22 כול בני צדק וכול חטאתם ועוונותם ואשמתם ופשעי מעשיהם בממשלתו

21 ... By the Angel of Darkness [comes] the aberration of
22 all the Sons of Righteousness; all their sins, their iniquities, their guilt, and their iniquitous works are under his dominion.

The section continues with the comment that the subordinates of the Angel of Darkness have a hand in making the Sons of Light stumble (III, 24a).[23] Therefore, the Angel of Darkness not only has sway over the Sons of Deceit (= those within whom are the inclinational spirit of deceit), but he and his comrades also negatively impact the Sons of Justice/Sons of Light (= those within whom is the inclinational spirit of truth).[24]

---

[21] I.e., these angelic "princes" are at least partially responsible for influencing the respective moral paths of those in their "hand." For the use of שר as an angelic designation, see the discussion of Dan 7–12 in Chapter 3, above.

[22] See the comments of Ceclia Wassén, "Good and Bad Angels in the Construction of Identity in the Qumran Movement," in *Gottesdienst und Engel*, 77, who summarizes as follows: "... the separation between the spheres is not as firm as it initially seems."

[23] Indeed, angelic subordinates over and through whom the Angel of Darkness rules likely constitute part of his ממשלה mentioned in line 22. Cf. 1QM XVII, 7–8, discussed later in this chapter. While there is no explicit indication that the Prince of Lights has a retinue, this is certainly possible; see the comments of Michalak, *Angels as Warriors*, 170; Frey, "Different Patterns," 292–293; Davidson, *Angels at Qumran*, 156; Anderson, "The Use of Ruach," 299.

[24] As Alexander, *Mystical Texts*, 24, summarizes: "The Qumran sect believed that the world is the theatre of a cosmic struggle between good and evil, fought out by proxies in both the material and spiritual realms." Cf. Dimant, "Men as Angels," 96: "Seeing themselves as part of the hosts of Light, the Qumranites viewed all their political conflicts and theological controversies in terms of [a] metaphysical struggle."

If *TTS* aided in the recognition of who is elect and who is not, the division of humankind into two opposing lots is surely a means to this end, as Leonhardt-Balzer points out. She also observes that *TTS* "maintains the awareness that even the sons of righteousness are fallible due to the influence of the Angel of Darkness. Thus there is a certain tension between the predestination of man through God and the influence of the Angel of Darkness on the Sons of Light."[25] To be sure, the tension is real, and it may be symptomatic of the more robust tension *TTS* has with Israelite/Jewish tradition – a tradition that heavily emphasized the freedom to choose or reject the covenant (e.g., Josh 24:15).[26] But to dwell on these tensions without due emphasis on the mitigation of the tensions advocated by *TTS* itself and its placement in 1QS would be unfortunate.

First, *TTS* is clear that every human heart is a battleground of sorts for the war between truth and injustice. Column IV continues with this:

23 ... עד הנה יריבו רוחי אמת ועול בלבב גבר

24 יתהלכו בחכמה ואולת ...

23 ... Until now the spirits of truth and deceit struggle in the hearts of humans,
24 they walk in wisdom or folly ...

TTS also suggests that what is determinative for one's actions and eschatological destiny is the measure of their inheritance/share in lots of truth or injustice. Column IV, 24b–25a reads:

---

[25] Leohardt-Balzer, "Evil, Dualism and Community," 141. Cf. Duhaime, "Dualistic Reworking," 42: "The idea that the sons of righteousness go astray is ... unexpected in a catechesis on the two ways which is concerned with a clear-cut separation between men according to their conduct."

[26] On this topic, see the influential essay of Karl Georg Kuhn, "Die Sektenschrift und die iranische Religion," *ZTK* 49 (1952): 296–316. Collins, *The Scriptures and Sectarianism*, 186–189, discusses the proposed Persian background of *TTS's* dualism and summarizes it vis-à-vis the canonical picture as follows: "The traditional covenant presupposed a vigorous doctrine of free will, by which the Israelites were to choose to obey the commandments or not, and were fully responsible for their actions. The suggestion that human beings are determined by angelic or demonic forces, and that their design is established in advance, departs radically from this view, and has very little precedent in the Hebrew Bible." *Contra* Paul Heger, *Challenges to Conventional Opinions on Qumran and Enoch Issues* (STDJ 100; Leiden: Brill, 2012), 227–310, who argues that Persian influence on *TTS* has been overstated. Whatever the possible influences, it is widely recognized that the dualism of *TTS* is not the "absolute" dualism of Zoroastrianism but more "moderate" in that God's sovereignty is never in question. On this point, see Popovic, "Light and Darkness," 151. For helpful discussions of the (in)appropriateness of using the term "dualism" in a Jewish/monotheistic context, see Stuckenbruck, "The Interiorization of Dualism," 145–168, esp. 146–148; Shaul Shaked, "Qumran and Iran: Further Considerations," *IOS* 2 (1972): 433–446.

24 ... וכפי נחלת איש באמת יצדק וכן ישנא עולה וכירשתו בגורל עול ירשע בו וכן
25 יתעב אמת כיא בד בבד שמן אל עד קץ נחרצה ועשות חדשה ...

24 ... According to a man's share in truth shall he be righteous and thus hate deceit, and
according to his inheritance in the lot of deceit he shall be evil through it, and thus
25 loathe truth. For God has sorted them into equal parts[27] until the appointed end and the
making of the new. ...

The fallibility of the righteous is thereby tempered by the knowledge that God
has the matter sorted out, with the implication being that time would reveal
that those responsible for 1QS are indeed the "Sons of Light," whose inheritance in the truth is greater than their shares in the lot of injustice.[28]

A second way the fallibility of the righteous is mitigated is, for the present
study, more important. I just noted the role of the Angel of Darkness and the
spirits of his lot; how *TTS* says this evil is countered is significant. Column
III reads:

24 ... ואל ישראל ומלאך אמתו עזר לכול
25 בני אור ...

24 ... But the God of Israel and his Angel of Truth help all
25 the Sons of Light.

Duhaime is convinced that this line is secondary to *TTS* and part of a larger,
multi-stage interpolation that runs from III, 18b–25a;[29] he further posits that
the cosmic/angelic dualism of this section was added in order to personalize
the inclinational spirits of light and darkness referred to earlier in *TTS*, as well

---

[27] Charlesworth translates בד בבד שמן as "set them apart," which is not as clear as
"sorted them into equal parts." For the latter translation, see García Martínez and Tigchelaar, *DSSSE*, 1:79.

[28] Duhaime, "Dualistic Reworking," 42: "The conflict will be resolved, it is assumed, at
the end; therefore, the tension between the present era and the end is an *eschatological*
dualism [emphasis retained]." Cf. Charlesworth, *John and the Dead Sea Scrolls*, 76–89;
Alexander, "Predestination and Freewill," 37–38; Collins, *The Scriptures and Sectarianism*,
189–190. On the possibility of a relationship between *TTS* and 4Q186, and whether the
latter may have been used to determine one's inheritance in the truth or injustice, see Popovic, "Light and Darkness," 148–165, esp. 156–163; cf. idem, *Reading the Human Body:
Physiognomics and Astrology in the Dead Sea Scrolls and Hellenistic-Early Roman Period
Judaism* (STDJ 67; Leiden: Brill, 2007).

[29] Duhaime, "Dualistic Reworking," 38–43, argues that there are several items suggesting that III, 18b–25a constitute an addition, including i.) "marginal ticks," which may indicate scribal recognition of a new section (e.g., III, 13 and IV, 26 = the beginning and end of
TTS, respectively; cf. IV, 2, 9, 15); ii.) the "double introduction" of spirits in 18b & 25b–
26a; iii.) the observation that III, 13–IV, 14 is a "coherent continuity" without III, 18b–25a.
Duhaime is expounding upon the arguments that 1QS III, 20–25 (give or take a few lines) is
a "digression" (so Licht, "An Analysis of the Treatise," 92) or a "modifizierende Anhang"
(so Ehrhard Kamiah, *Die Form der katalogischen Paränese im Neuen Testament* [WUNT 7;
Tübingen: Mohr Siebeck, 1964], 48 n. 6, 163–167).

as to "strengthen the sons of light by spelling out the aggression which they suffer and the help they are given."[30] Whatever the text's source-critical history, Duhaime is correct that III, 24–25 functions as *TTS's* response to the disturbing picture of evil announced in the preceding lines.

At the same time, the angelic dualism of III, 20–IV, 1 serves a much greater purpose than to personalize the inclinational spirits or to spell out the help granted to the Sons of Light. The statement at III, 24b–25a arguably serves as the climax of both what I have demarcated as the third section and the entire first half of *TTS*. Given the chiastic structure of my third section,[31] "God's Angel of Truth" is apparently another name for the Prince of Lights.[32] The use of a singular verb with a composite subject (i.e., God *and* his Angel of Truth) at III, 24 has perplexed interpreters, but likely the best solution is that עֶזְר be read as a noun rather than a verb.[33]

Intriguingly, this section contains the only occurrence of the word "Israel" in *TTS*. That the Sons of Light are assisted by "the God of *Israel* and his Angel of Truth" lends further support to the argument that the adoption of *TTS's* dualistic thought was not a rejection of the Mosaic covenant:[34] as Collins has argued, the dualism of *TTS* was at least partially attractive to the Qumran

---

[30] Duhaime, "Dualistic Reworking," 43.

[31] According to my outline, the first major section of *TTS* (III, 13–IV, 1) is comprised of three sub-sections, the last of which focuses on cosmic/angelic dualism. In turn, this last sub-section can be outlined according to the following chiastic structure: a. The Prince of Lights rules the Sons of Justice (III, 20a); b. The Angel of Darkness rules the Sons of Deceit (20b–21a); b.' The Angel of Darkness/his spirits cause the Sons of Justice to fall (21b–24a); a.' God and his Angel of Truth aid the Sons of Light (24b–25a).

[32] Collins, *Apocalypticism in the Dead Sea Scrolls*, 38–43; cf. idem, "Powers in Heaven," 17.

[33] This is the primary suggestion of Wernberg-Møller, *The Manual of Discipline*, 72 (i.e., "But the God of Israel and his Angel of Truth [are] *support* [עֶזְר] for all the Sons of Light ..."). This proposal makes good sense given that the same noun is used to describe the angelic succor of *11QMelchizedek* and the *War Scroll* (cf. 11Q13 II, 14; 1QM XVII, 6). Another possibility is that the singular verb is meant to emphasize a close correspondence between Yhwh and his agent, thus conveying that "God's Angel of Truth" is a being of extraordinary rank, ability, and commissioning. This is akin to the relationship between the God of Israel and the מלאך יהוה proposed by Heiser, "Should Elohim," 127; idem, "Co-Regency in Ancient Israel's Divine Council," 218–220. As previously noted, Heiser understands the מלאך יהוה to be God's "vice-regent," second only to Yhwh in the ranks of the divine council, and he points out that God and this angel are the subjects of a grammatically singular verb in the blessing of Gen 48:15–16. Elsewhere, Heiser posits God's Angel of Truth as the מלאך יהוה (see idem, "The Divine Council," §7.4). But unlike the well-known ambiguity of some of the Angel of Yhwh passages, it must be stressed that the God of Israel is clearly differentiated from his angelic agent in 1QS III. I will further comment on the identity of God's Angel of Truth in my discussion of 11Q13 in the following section of this chapter.

[34] Even if, as already discussed, the adoption of *TTS* resulted in some tension with biblical tradition; see Collins, *The Scriptures and Sectarianism*, 193–194.

movement due to its ability to explain the disobedience of other Jews.[35] Elsewhere, Collins has suggested that *TTS* was a way for the Qumran movement to enhance its assertions to be peerless on *halakhic* matters:

The dualism of light and darkness went hand in hand with the separation of the sect from the rest of Judaism. It is probably fruitless to argue whether the division or the myth came first. If we judge by 4QMMT, the separation of the sect was primarily due to legal disagreement, and so we might suppose that the doctrine of the two spirits was adopted secondarily[36] to provide a theological explanation of the social division.[37]

Moreover, *TTS* is situated within 1QS between the well-known covenant renewal ceremony (I, 16–III, 12) and detailed regulations for community life (V, 1–VII, 25 and VIII, 1–X, 8), sections which effectively assert the Qumran movement as Israel "as it ought to be."[38]

Excursus: The Qumran Movement as the True Israel

As a rejoinder to arguments that the *Community Rule* is not as exclusivist in its focus as the *Damascus Document*,[39] Collins observes:

1QS 5:8 states that members of the community bind themselves by oath "to return to the Torah of Moses, according to all which he has commanded." 5:22 speaks of "the multitude of Israel who dedicate themselves to return to his covenant through the community." The covenant renewal ceremony at the beginning of 1QS is clearly modeled on Deuteronomy, with its curses and blessings. The community is clearly imagined in the context of biblical Israel, and is in effect a re-constitution of Israel as it ought to be. It is in this ideal sense that 1QS 2:22 can refer to those who participate in the covenant ceremony as "every man of Israel."[40]

In the same essay, Collins is quick to point out that the sect hoped that the distinction between Israel and the Sons of Light would eventually collapse, that the separation of the sect from the rest of Judaism was likely envisioned

---

[35] Collins, "The Construction of Israel," 37.

[36] The view that *TTS* was secondarily adopted to bolster legal arguments is related to/complements the proposal discussed above that 1QS represents an expansion of the *Serekh* tradition.

[37] Collins, *The Scriptures and Sectarianism*, 193. Murphy-O'Connor, "La genèse littéraire de la Règle," 528–549, suggests that *TTS* was adopted and included for encouragement in the midst of crises. Cf. Hempel, "The Treatise on the Two Spirits and the Literary History," 107. Also see Tuschling, *Angels and Orthodoxy*, 137, who claims that "it is conformity to angelic behaviour that guarantees to the community that their praxis (*halakah*) is correct." I will address the Qumran movement's attempts live in imitation of the angels when I discuss the *Songs of the Sabbath Sacrifices* in Chapter 5.

[38] Collins, "The Construction of Israel," 33.

[39] For this view, see Ellen J. Christiansen, "The Consciousness of Belonging to God's Covenant and What It Entails According to the Damascus Document and the Community Rule," in *Qumran Between the Old and New Testaments*, 87.

[40] Collins, "The Construction of Israel," 32–33.

to be temporary, and hopes of a national restoration were never completely abandoned.[41] However, this relative optimism needs to be articulated with caution for one runs the risk of understating the boldness and uniqueness of sectarian claims – and, intriguingly, Collins, in a more recent discussion, has seemingly qualified his earlier statement:

> The Scrolls never deny that the covenant is intended for all Israel, and the authors were well aware that their movement was not identical with all Israel in the present. They hoped it would be so in the eschatological future, but even then the War Scroll acknowledged that "the violators of the covenant" would share the lot of the Kittim. In short, from the perspective of the sect, it is not true that all Israel has a share in the world to come.[42]

These assertions are echoed by numerous scholars in a variety of ways. For example, Schiffman writes that, "All in all, the authors of the various sectarian texts found at Qumran saw both the people and the Land of Israel in ideal terms. They expected that as the true Israel, separated from both errant Jews and from the non-Jewish world, they could live a life of perfect holiness and sanctity … ."[43] Moreover, the concept of the covenant is central to the claims of the sect, and as Bautch notes, "although the covenants described in the *Rule of the Community* and the *Damascus Document* have affinities with those made in the Hebrew Bible, in the scrolls the covenants do not indicate 'a relationship between God and ethnic Israel,' as covenant clearly does in [the Book of] Jubilees, and refer rather to 'a particularistic covenant relationship.'"[44]

---

[41] Collins, "The Construction of Israel," 38, 41–42.

[42] Collins, *The Scriptures and Sectarianism*, 181–182. Analogous comments are made by John S. Bergsma, "Qumran Self-Identity: 'Israel' or 'Judah'?" *DSD* 15 (2008): 178, who stresses that "the identification of the *Yahad* with 'Israel' in 1QS … is very strong," even if the Qumran movement hoped that wider Israel would recognize the error of their ways and acknowledge the sectarian covenant as the only legitimate religious foundation for the nation. Cf. Graham Harvey, *The True Israel: Uses of the Name Jew, Hebrew and Israel in Ancient Jewish and Early Christian Literature* (AGJU 35; Leiden: Brill, 1994), 191, 217, who notes various references to "Israel" in the Dead Sea Scrolls, including ethnic Israel as well as a sectarian self-designation. However, he draws the puzzling conclusion that the concept of the "True Israel" is absent from the sectarian compositions. I will return to the relationship between ethnic Israel and the sect in my discussion of 1QM, below.

[43] Lawrence H. Schiffman, "Israel," *EDSS* 1:390.

[44] Richard J. Bautch, *Glory and Power, Ritual and Relationship: The Sinai Covenant in the Post-Exilic Period* (LHBOTS 471; London: T & T Clark, 2009), 139–140, who has incorporated a quotation of Ellen J. Christiansen, *The Covenant in Judaism and Paul: A Study of Ritual Boundaries as Identity Markers* (AGJU 27; Leiden: Brill, 1995), 157. Cf. Metso, *The Serekh Texts*, 24: "[T]he community considered itself the only true keeper of the covenant, thus effectively excluding the rest of Israel." Also see the comments of Swarup, *The Self-Understanding*, 72, who examines the biblical "plant" and "house" metaphors used to assert the true Israel claims of the Qumran movement and whose conclusions are nearly identical to those of Bautch et al.: "The DSS community understood itself to be the 'elect' whom God had chosen and to whom he had given an eternal possession. They

For this reason, Talmon stresses the importance of the covenant renewal ceremony (1QS I, 16–III, 12), which itself elucidates the boldness of sectarian aspirations:

The thread of Israel's historical past, which had snapped when Jerusalem and the temple were destroyed [in 587 BCE], is retied with the establishment of the *Yahad's* "renewed covenant." The intrinsic community-signification of ברית comes to the fore in the induction rite of novices into the *Yahad*, when also the membership of veterans was presumably reaffirmed. This annually repeated ritual is palpably molded upon the "Blessing and Curse" ceremony, which the Pentateuchal tradition reports to have been enacted by Moses prior to Israel's enrootment in the land of Canaan (Deut 27–28). ... The *Yahad* members perceived the reenactment of the biblical ceremony in their induction ritual as the confirmation of their community's claim to be the only legitimate heir to biblical Israel.[45]

The contribution the dualism of 1QS III, 13–IV, 26 makes to these claims and themes is that it "absolutizes" them: as Nickelsburg explains, *TTS* "encompasses all of humanity in its scope," and from the perspective of the Qumran movement, "the rest of Israel – to say nothing of humanity – constitutes the Other, as darkness is other than light."[46] And regardless of its origins, *TTS* was deliberately situated in 1QS, a document whose writers considered themselves "to be exclusively Israel, the chosen of God."[47] Thus, *TTS's* prominent placement in 1QS affirms the obvious: the Sons of Light are the members of the Qumran movement,[48] the ones who constitute the true Israel.

---

were now keeping the obligations of the covenant and therefore fulfilling the purpose of the elect. However, the DSS community differed from other Jewish groups in their view of election. The community understood its election as an election of individuals rather than of the nation of Israel, and they perceived themselves to be the restored Israel. This is contrary to Second Temple expectation which hoped for a future re-establishment of Israel in which all Israel would be restored. The participation of other Israelites was only possible if they joined the community as individuals. Further, one could not be born into the sect. Entrants had to take an oath (1QS 5:8)." I will return to the metaphors of "house" and "plant" in my discussions of the *Hodayot* and the *Songs of the Sabbath Sacrifice* in Chapter 5.

[45] Shemaryahu Talmon, "The Community of the Renewed Covenant: Between Judaism and Christianity," in *The Community of the Renewed Covenant* (eds., Eugene Ulrich and James C. VanderKam; CJAS 10; Notre Dame: University of Notre Dame Press, 1994), 13–14.

[46] Nickelsburg, "The We and Others," 273. Similarly, Luca Arcari, "'Minority' as a Self-Definition Discourse," 347–348, observes that the Qumran movement, who polemically referred to themselves as "Israel," interpreted history in such a way that they were the faithful remnant while the rest of the nation were the "others" whom God punishes.

[47] Nickelsburg, "The We and Others," 273.

[48] The identification of the Sons of Light with the sectarians is bolstered by what Hempel, "The Treatise on the Two Spirits and the Literary History," 113–119, refers to as "thematic links" between *TTS* and other sections of 1QS: e.g., the opposition of האמת

Thus, the placement of 1QS III, 24b–25a means that at the heart of *TTS* is the affirmation that to be counted among the Sons of Light – that is, to be a member of the Qumran movement or the true Israel – is not simply to be on the righteous or winning side of the dualistic divide: it means that one's help in the midst of the cosmic struggle between good and evil is the God of Israel and his Angel of Truth, who is also known as the Prince of Lights.[49]

To be sure, sectarian boasts of martial fellowship with the angels (to be discussed later in this chapter) are bolder than the assertion of 1QS III, 24b–25a. But the fact that the Qumran movement claimed the God of Israel's Angel of Truth as *their* help is no small contention because it is the usurpation of the angelic assistance that was normally the hope of the entire nation. In the context of the *Community Rule*, this contention also seems to be considered an integral component of what it means to be the true Israel. The presupposition of a uniquely close relationship to an angelic guardian figure is central to another sectarian text, *11QMelchizedek*.

II. 11QMelchizedek (11Q13)

The document known as *11QMelchizedek* (henceforth, *11QMelch*) is a fragmentary,[50] thematic *pesher*[51] which outlines the career of its namesake,[52] a

---

והעול is prominent in both *TTS* and 1QS V–IX, and the latter instances make explicit what is implied in the former. In Hempel's own words, "Truth (אמת) and injustice (עולה and עול) occur very frequently in the *Treatise*. This polarity is also a central defining feature of the community in 1QS v–ix//4QS. Thus, according to 1QS v 2 the people of injustice emerge as the nemesis of the community which itself is referred to as a 'foundation of truth' (1QS v 5) and 'house of truth' (1QS v 6). ... A further particularly instructive example is found in 1QS vi 14f ... in the context of admission into the community, a process that is described in terms of being permitted by the official at the head of the many to enter 'the covenant to return to the truth and to turn away from all in justice.'" On the designation "people of injustice," see eadem, "The Community and Its Rivals According to the Community Rule from Caves 1 and 4," *RevQ* 18 (2003): 47–81. For more on *TTS's* placement within 1QS and the identification of the Sons of Light with the Qumran movement, cf. Leonhardt-Balzer, "Evil, Dualism, and Community," 134; eadem, "Evil at Qumran" in *Evil in Second Temple Judaism and Early Christianity*, 19; "Hans-Walter Huppenbauer, *Der Mensch zwischen zwei Welten: Der Dualismus der Texte von Qumran (Höhle I) und der Damaskusfragmente: Ein Beitrag zur Vorgeschichte des Evangeliums* (AthANT 32; Zürich: Zwingli Verlag, 1959), 22–26.

[49] Tuschling, *Angels and Orthodoxy*, 115, 136, notes the significance of the dualistic divide. Cf. Wassén, "Good and Bad Angels," 73–75, 89. Hannah, *Michael and Christ*, 75, rightly observes that the sect claimed Israel's angel succor as their own.

[50] While fourteen fragments and two columns of text (with vestiges of another) were discovered, the original length of the document is unknown. Only the extant second column is in relatively good condition, but even this section requires much restoration. The text has been dated on the basis of paleography to the 1st cent. BCE, but a quotation of Dan 9 suggests it may have been composed as early as the middle of the 2nd cent. BCE. Initially published by Adam S. Van der Woude, "Melchisedek als himmlische Erlösergestalt in den

figure of extraordinarily high rank and privilege. Melchizedek's lofty depiction has generated much discussion concerning his precise nature, but the most common identification of this eschatological protagonist – and the view accepted here – is that Melchizedek is an angelic benefactor of God's people and the leader of the spiritual beings who contend against the wicked angel Belial and his forces.

Recasting the year of jubilee (cf. Lev 25:13) in an eschatological framework, *11QMelch* describes the last days as the tenth of ten jubilees (II, 7).[53] During the final jubilee period, Melchizedek will liberate those who are captive and free them from their iniquities (II, 6); at the end of this jubilee will be

---

neugefundenen eschatologischen Midraschim aus Qumran Höhle XL," *OtSt* 14 (1965): 354–373, it has been more recently presented in Florentino García Martínéz, Eibert J. C. Tigchelaar, and Adam S. Van der Woude, eds., *Qumran Cave 11.II: 11QS-18, 11Q20–31* (DJD 23; Oxford: Claredon Press, 1998), 221–241, which will serve as the basis for the Hebrew text, sigla, and translations cited here (with occasional minor adjustments of the latter). For additional textual comments, see Emile Puech, "Notes sur le manuscript de 11Qmelkîsédek," *RevQ* 12 (1987): 483–513; Milik, "Milkî-sedeq et Milki-resa," 109–124.

[51] In addition to the so-called "continuous" *pesharim*, which are verse-by-verse interpretations of a particular work (e.g., the commentary on Habakkuk =1QpHab), the Qumran movement also approached biblical interpretation thematically by using a collection of scriptures to develop an idea. In the case of *11QMelch*, a wide-range of passages including Lev 25, Deut 15, Pss 7 and 82, and Isa 52 and 61 are employed to describe an eschatological scenario and its protagonist. Both the terms "continuous" (or "running") *pesher* and "thematic" *pesher* were coined by Jean Carmignac, "Le Document de Qumrân sur Melki-sédek," *RevQ* 7 (1970): 343–378. On the Qumran *pesharim*, see Shani Berrin, "Qumran Pesharim," in *Biblical Interpretation at Qumran* (ed., Matthias Henze; SDSSRL; Grand Rapids: Eerdmans, 2005), 110–133; Timothy H. Lim, "The Genre of Pesher: Definition and Categorization" in idem, *Pesharim* (CQS 3; London: Sheffield Press, 2002), 44–53.

[52] Though the human priest Melchizedek is only mentioned twice in the Hebrew Bible (and briefly at that; cf. Gen 14 and Ps 110), he was the impetus for much speculation in the Second Temple Period and beyond. On the various Melchizedek traditions of early Judaism and Christianity, see Eric F. Mason, "Melchizedek Traditions in Second Temple Judaism," in *The Dead Sea Scrolls in Context: Integrating the Dead Sea Scrolls in the Study of Ancient Texts, Languages, and Cultures* (eds., Armin Lange et al.; VTSup 140; Leiden: Brill, 2011), 345–360, which summarizes relevant portions of idem, *'You Are a Priest Forever': Second Temple Jewish Messianism and the Priestly Christology of the Epistle to the Hebrews* (STDJ 74; Leiden: Brill, 2008), 138–190. Cf. Annette Steudel, "Melchizedek," *EDSS* 535–537; Davila, "Melchizedek: King, Priest, and God," 217–234; idem, "Michael, Melchizedek and War in Heaven," 259–272; Kobelski, *Melchizedek and Melchiresha*; Fred L. Horton, *The Melchizedek Tradition: A Critical Examination of the Sources to the Fifth Century AD and in the Epistle to the Hebrews* (SNTSMS 30; Cambridge: Cambridge University Press, 1976); Marinus de Jonge and Adam S. van der Woude, "11Q Melchizedek and the New Testament," *NTS* 12 (1966): 301–326.

[53] On the early Jewish tradition of the eschaton as the last jubilee, cf. Dan 9; T. Levi 16–18, 1 En. 91, 93; see Xeravits, *King, Priest, Prophet*, 72.

a day of atonement for God's people (II, 6–7).[54] The reason given for these events is found in line 9:

9 הואה הקץ לשנת הרצון למלכי צדק ולצֿבֿ[א]יו עֿ[ם] קדושי אל לממשלת משפט...

9 it is the time for the year of the favour of Melchizedek, and of [his] arm[ies, the peop]le[55] [of] the holy ones of God, the administration of justice …

The statement uses the language of Isa 61:2 – a verse which proclaims the year of Yhwh's favour[56] – to announce the intervention of Melchizedek. The remarkable replacement of Melchizedek for Yhwh is a hallmark of *11QMelch*, and this feature sets Melchizedek apart as one who has been both commissioned to do God's will and as one who, in doing so, has been accorded privileges and descriptions that are normally the prerogatives of God himself. While another allusion to Isa 61 declares that Melchizedek will "carry out the vengeance of Go[d]'s judgments" (II, 13),[57] it is the text's use of Ps 82 that most elucidates the lofty stature and role of Melchizedek.

As discussed in Chapter 2, Ps 82 conveys the superiority of the God of Israel over all other celestial beings, some of whom God is asked to judge because of their negligence and malevolence. But whereas the psalm is clear that Yhwh is the אלהים[58] who "has taken his place in the divine council …," *11QMelch* reinterprets Ps 82:1 as a reference to Melchizedek[59] and his role as

---

[54] For a recent discussion of the eschatological timeline of the text, see Ariel Feldman, "New Light on the Ten Jubilees of 11QMelchizedek (11Q13)," *DSD* 25 (2018): 1–7.

[55] García Martinéz et al., DJD 23 has "nation"; see further, below.

[56] The first part of Isa 61:2 reads לקרא שנת־רצון ליהוה.

[57] While II, 13 says that Melchizedek will יקום נקם משפֿטֿי אֿ[ל, Isa 61:2 speaks of the יום נקם לאלהינו; also see the reference to השבויים, "captives," in II, 4, which may be the document's first allusion to Isa 61. On *11QMelch*'s use of expressions from Isa 61:1–3, see García Martinéz et al., DJD 23, 230, 232. Cf. Merrill P. Miller, "The Function of Isaiah 61:1–2 in 11QMelchizedek," *JBL* 88 (1969): 467–469.

[58] Tucshling, *Angels and Orthodoxy*, 132, entertains the possibility that the אלהים of Ps 82:1 originally referred to a "principal angel," which would mean that a "'high' angelology" was a central part of the mainstream cult and thus accepted by the Qumran community. However, she rightly states that there is no evidence for such a view and is quick to note the theological ingenuity of the interpretation of Melchizedek as אלהים.

[59] That the אלהים of the Ps 82:1 quotation in 11Q13 refers to Melchizedek is the consensus view, with which I concur; see, e.g., van der Woude, "Melchisedek als himmlische Erlösergestalt," 364, 367–368; Joseph A. Fitzmyer, "Further Light on Melchizedek from Qumran Cave 11," *JBL* 86 (1967): 37; Horton, *The Melchizedek Tradition*, 71, 75; Hannah, *Michael and Christ*, 70 n. 3; Xeravits, *King, Priest, Prophet*, 73; Mason, *'You Are a Priest Forever,'* 176–183. *Contra* Carmignac, "Le Document de Qumrân sur Melkisédek," 365–367, who opposed this identification on the basis of his conclusion that עליו at the beginning of II, 10 refers back not to Melchizedek but משפט in II, 9 (cf. García Martinéz et al., DJD 23, 231: "The suffix probably refers to Melchizedek although משפט [near the end of II, 9] could also be the antecedent"). However, Kobelski, *Melchzedek and Melchiresa*, 59–

heavenly judge (II, 10).[60] There are a number of examples of figures other than the God of Israel being called אלהים in the Hebrew Bible,[61] but the most pertinent for understanding *11QMelch* is found in Ps 82:6, where the אלהים are rebellious celestial beings. In the context of *11QMelch*'s use of Ps 82, these beings are the "spirits of Belial's lot" whom Melchizedek will judge (II, 11–12), and the stage is thus set for a showdown between the אלהים:[62] Melchizedek, aided by the righteous celestial beings,[63] will square-off against Belial and his forces. Analogous to Ps 82, *11QMelch* suggests that the wickedness of the spiritual realm somehow negatively impacts humanity, though the text is fragmentary at key points.[64]

60, is likely correct in his estimation: "whether the antecedent of *'lyw* is *mlky sdq* or *mspt*, 'judgment,' in no way affects the interpretation of *'lwhym* [as Melchizedek]."

[60] Ps 7:8–9 is quoted in II, 10b–11a to support the contention that it is Melchizedek who has been tasked with divine judgment. In this instance, however, אל is substituted for the psalm's יהוה. Just as עליו introduces the Ps 82:1 quotation at the beginning of line 10, עליו functions in the same capacity for the Ps 7 quotation near the end of line, so there is little doubt אל in some way refers to Melchizedek. Fitzmyer, "Further Light on Melchizedek," 33, 37, cites the reluctance to write the *tetragrammaton* at Qumran as the reason for this particular substitution. Horton, *The Melchizedek Tradition*, 77, takes it to mean that Melchizedek's judgments are synonymous with those of אל (i.e., God). In light of its proximity to the quotation of Ps 82:1, which locates the judgments of Melchizedek in the עדת אל, *11QMelch*'s use of אל in the Ps 7 quotation makes good sense. Cf. Kobelski, *Melchizedek and Melchiresa*, 62; van der Woude, "Melchisedek als himmlische Erlösergestalt," 365.

[61] Cf. Exod 4:16 (Moses); 1 Sam 28:13 (Samuel's ghost); 1 Kgs 18:24 (Baal); see Kobelski, *Melchizedek and Melchiresa*, 60 n. 35. For discussion of possible instances where אלהים refers to the beings of Yhwh's council, see Heiser, "Should Elohim," 123–136.

[62] Cf. Kobelski, *Melchzedek and Melchiresa*, 62; van der Woude, "Melchisedek als himmlische Erlösergestalt," 365.

[63] Line 14 reads: ובעזרו כול אלי [הצדק וה[ו]אה א]שר [כול בני אל והפן, "And all the gods [of justice] are to his help; [and h]e is (the one) wh[o   ] all the sons of God and he will … ." Though the poor condition of this line makes any interpretation of it tentative, most commentators understand the "gods" and "sons of god" to be references to the righteous celestial forces whom Melchizedek leads; see, e.g., Kobelski, *Melchizedek and Melchiresa*, 54, 71–72. *Contra* Carmignac, "Le Document de Qumrân sur Melkisédek," 366, who objects on the basis that Melchizedek seems to require help (עזר): "nous savon par al Règle de la Guerre et le reste de la literature qumrânienne que c'est toujours l'être supérieur qui vient en aide à l'être inférieur." In response, Xeravits, *King, Priest, Prophet*, 73–74, contends that, taken as a whole, *11QMelch*'s grandiose presentation of Melchizedek is hardly diminished by II, 14. Rather than constituting a negative feature, that Melchizedek is portrayed as having military forces under his command arguably serves to bolster his résumé. Cf. Dan 10:21–11:1, which mentions the martial support Michael provides his unnamed angelic comrade and, possibly, *vice versa*.

[64] Once again, the poor condition makes interpretation difficult, but Melchizedek's activity has been understood to include freeing "them" – presumably God's people – from the impact of the wickedness of Belial and his comrades: "the interpretation of it concerns Belial and the spirits of his lot wh[o   ], in [the]ir tur[ning] away from God's commandments to [commit evil]. And Melchizedek will carry out the vengeance of Go[d]'s judgments [and

It is thus clear that Ps 82 was considered to be a suitable template to describe the career of Melchizedek; and due to his roles as judge in the heavenly court, executor of divine vengeance, chief opponent of the rebellious heavenly beings, eschatological redeemer, and especially the way this is conveyed – through the substitution of the name of Melchizedek for the God of Israel in scripture quotations – it is understandable why a majority of commentators have identified Melchizedek as an extraordinarily high-ranking angel, perhaps Michael[65] or a figure of an even loftier standing.[66] However, the latter half of

---

on that day he will f]r[ee them from the hand of] Belial and from the hand of all the s[pirits of his lot]" (II, 12–13; cf. II, 25). The reconstruction/translation just cited from DJD 23 is similar to earlier proposals insofar as God's people on earth both suffer because of the actions of Belial and benefit from Melchizedek's celestial campaign against him. Cf. van der Woude, "Melchisedek al himmlische Erlösergestalt," 358; Fitzmyer, "Further Light on Melchizedek," 38; Milik, "Milkî-sedeq et Milki-resa," 106; Kobelski, *Melchzedek and Melchiresa*, 18–19; Puech, "Notes sur le manuscript de 11Qmelkîsédek," *RevQ* 12 (1987): 483–513. Also see Frans du Toit Laubscher, "God's Angel of Truth and Melchizedek," *JSJ* 3 (1972): 46–51, who on the basis of a parallel with 4QCatena[a] (= 4Q177) makes a strong case that the lacuna preceding "Belial" in II, 13 should be restored to ויעזור לכול בני אור מיד ב]ליעל, "And he (i.e., Melchizedek) will help all the sons of light from the hand of B]elial." In 4Q177, the subject of עזר is "the Angel of Truth," who is an important figure in 1QS III; see above.

[65] Steudel, "Melchizedek," *EDSS* 1:536, summarizes a common observation when she states that Melchizedek seems to be "almost identical" with the Prince of Light(s) and God's Angel of Truth from 1QS III, as well as Michael as portrayed in Dan 7–12 and 1QM XVII, 5–8 (see below). Indeed, many scholars have allowed that these are different names for the same figure; cf., e.g., García Martinéz et al., DJD 23, 222, 231; Davila, "Melchizedek: Priest, King, and God," 222; Kobelski, *Melchizedek and Melchiresha*, 58 n. 29, 71–74. Van der Woude, "Melchisedek al himmlische Erlösergestalt," 370–371, notes that the identification of Michael and Melchizedek is made in two medieval Rabbinic texts, but caution has been rightly urged in marshalling such late evidence for the interpretation of *11QMelch*; see Horton, *The Melchizedek Tradition*, 81–82; Mason, "Melchizedek Traditions," 356 n. 44. At the same time, one of the earliest extant texts among the Scrolls – *4QVisions of Amram* (=4Q543–548), discussed in Chapter 3, above – may have made the identification of Michael, Melchizedek, and the Prince of Light explicit, though the text is fragmentary. For the suggestion that the identification of Michael with the Prince of Light(s) et al. was a sectarian "secret," see Hannah, *Michael and Christ*, 67–75. It should also be noted that the Melchizedek of *11QMelch* is described in a priestly manner. On this issue, I am inclined to agree with Kobelski, *Melchizedek and Melchiresa*, 64–71, in that while the Melchizedek of extant *11QMelch* is "more of a warrior figure" than a priest, there are certainly hints of a priestly role (e.g., mention of the day of atonement). Moreover, we will see below that Melchizedek's name has been restored in the *Songs of the Sabbath Sacrifice*, where he may have been cast as the ranking angelic high priest. For recent treatments that emphasize the priestly aspects of Melchizedek's presentation in *11QMelch*, see Angel, *Otherworldly*, 152–165; Alexander, *Mystical Texts*, 70; Anders Aschim, "Melchizedek and Jesus: 11QMelchizedek and the Epistle to the Hebrews," in *The Jewish Roots of Christological Monotheism: Papers from the St. Andrews Conference on the Historical Origins of the Worship of Jesus* (eds., Carey C. Newman, James R. Davila, and Gladys S. Lewis; JSJSup

11QMelch's second column refers to an anointed messenger who is said to fulfill Second Isaiah's description of a peace-proclaiming herald (cf. Isa 52:7; 61:1; Dan 9:25–26),[67] and there is some ambiguity as to whether this herald and Melchizedek are one and the same (human) figure;[68] and since the two references to Melchizedek in the Hebrew Bible seem to refer to a priest (cf. Gen 14; Ps 110), this has been another reason offered for a human Melchizedek.[69] But such arguments are ultimately unsatisfactory. Not only would the

---

63; Leiden: Brill, 1999), 139–140. On the intriguing possibility that the relationship between Melchizedek and Michael is analogous to that of Enoch and the Son of Man in the Similitudes of Enoch and Metatron in 3 Enoch, see the discussion and bibliography provided by Orlov, *The Greatest Mirror*, 33–34.

[66] Heiser, "The Divine Council," §7.4, argues that an identification should be made between Melchizedek, the Prince of Light(s), God's Angel of Truth, the Angel of Yhwh, and the Danielic "one like a son of man" and the "Prince of the Host," which he suggests are various presentations of the "vice-regent" of the divine council. However, this vice-regent is to be differentiated from Michael, who is of a lower rank. For a similar interpretation, see Bampfylde, "The Prince of the Host," 129–134. Among the evidence Heiser marshals is that, unlike Melchizedek, the Second Temple Period literature never explicitly refers to Michael as an אלהים. As noted in Chapter 3, parsing the rank of Michael vis-à-vis the other angelic figures of Dan 7–12 is the subject of debate. But even if it is correct, in theory, that Michael holds a subordinate angelic rank, it is conceivable that he was envisioned as one of the gods/sons of God who is a "help" (עזר) to Melchziedek in II, 14. Cf. Dan 10:21–11:1, where Michael supports his unnamed angelic comrade. However, it was also previously mentioned that Michael's key role in Dan 12:1 is an obstacle to readings which ascribe him a subordinate status in the celestial hierarchy.

[67] Despite the poor condition of the text, it is virtually certain that Isa 52:7 is quoted in II, 15b–16, and the editors note the strong possibility of part of Dan 9:25–26 being quoted in II, 18, especially in light of the reading דני[א]ל. Isa 61:1, employed earlier in the second column, also refers to an anointed herald of God, and thus may be in view in line 19; see García Martinéz et al., DJD 23, 232.

[68] This was put forward as a possibility by Fitzmyer, "Further Light on Melchizedek," 40. Cf. Miller, "The Function of Isaiah 61:1–2," 467–469. Some have observed similarities between this herald and the eschatological prophet of 1QS IX, 11 and 4Q175 5–8; see the discussions of Angel, *Otherworldly*, 150–151; Horton, *The Melchizedek Tradition*, 68; van der Woude, "Melchisedek als himmlische Erlösergestalt," 376. On the very speculative proposal that the herald is the Teacher of Righteousness, see Puech, "Notes sur le manuscript," 513; Milik, "Milkî-sedeq et Milki-resa," 126. However, a *human* Melchizedek who is also the herald of the text has found little support; see further, below.

[69] Carmignac, "Le Document de Qumrân sur Melkisédek," 369, has argued that the figure of *11QMelch* is a purely human figure. Cf. Paul Rainbow, "Melchizedek as Messiah at Qumran," *BBR* 7 (1997): 179–194, who claims that Melchizedek is the Davidic Messiah. Fletcher-Louis, *All the Glory*, 216–221, argues that Melchizedek should *not* be viewed as "entirely suprahuman" (i.e., as an angel) but rather as a "divine human" (i.e., evidence of Fletcher-Louis' thesis that early Judaism testifies to an angelmorphic anthropology tradition). Also see Israel Knohl, "Melchizedek: A Model for the Union of Kingship and Priesthood in the Hebrew Bible, 11QMelchizedek, and the Epistle to the Hebrews" in *Text, Thought, and Practice in Qumran and Early Christianity: Proceedings of the Ninth Interna-*

enigmatic nature of Melchizedek in the Hebrew Bible have likely been ripe for imaginative Second Temple Period interpreters;[70] to understand the figure of *11QMelch* as human is to ignore the angelic symmetry of the text: Melchizedek is cast as the righteous opponent of Belial,[71] the leader of the wicked

---

tional Symposium of the Orion Center for the Study of the Dead Sea Scrolls and Associated Literature, Jointly Sponsored by the Hebrew University Center for the Study of Christianity, 11–13 January, 2004 (eds., Ruth A. Clements and Daniel R. Schwartz; STDJ 84; Leiden: Brill, 2009), 260, who objects to an angelic Melchizedek in 11Q13 because one of the foci of the *pesher* is Isa 61, which features a human prophet.

[70] As pointed out by Angel, *Otherworldly*, 151–152, who argues that "the author's dependence on Scripture clearly did not force him to comply with the 'literal' meaning of biblical traditions, especially as modern exegetes might understand it." Among those who follow a suggestion of David Flusser ("Melchizedek and the Son of Man [A Preliminary note on a new fragment from Qumran]," *Christian News from Israel* [April 1966)]: 26–27), Mason, *'You Are a Priest Forever,'* 171–172, proposes that Ps 110 was read in antiquity in such a way that it was addressed *to* Melchizedek (in heaven) rather than someone receiving a priesthood *like* Melchizedek's. In this reading, the author of *11QMelch* may have thought that the Melchizedek of Ps 110 was eternal, and the psalm's themes of heavenly privilege, dominion over enemies, and rendering judgment became a character sketch for a heavenly Melchizedek. Thus, the Melchizedek of *11QMelch* was influenced by a particular reading of Ps 110. Conversely, Anders Aschim, "Melchizedek the Liberator: An Early Interpretation of Genesis 14?" *SBLSP* 35 (1996): 43–58, proposes that the Melchizedek of Gen 14 may have been *understood* as Abram's heavenly patron who contends against the spiritual equivalents of Abram's enemies in the celestial realm, thus ensuring the patriarch's victory. But note the caution of Horton, *The Melchizedek Tradition*, 79: "We do not have enough of the document left to satisfy our curiosity about how the Melchizedek of Gen. xiv and Ps. cx could become such a figure or even to say ... that the Melchizedek of *11QMelchizedek* and the Melchizedek of Gen. xiv and Ps. cx were considered by the author to be one and the same."

[71] *Contra* Cargmignac, "Le Document de Qumrân sur Melkisédek," 369, who arrives at his conclusion that the figure of *11QMelch* is human by denying that Melchizedek is the subject of the quotations of Pss 7 and 82. Fletcher-Louis, *All the Glory*, 216–221, though he identifies Melchizedek as the subject of the psalms quotations, is dismissive of the close similarities Melchizedek shares with angels in the Qumran literature. But his contention that Melchizedek is a "divine human" does not sufficiently address Melchizedek's function as the righteous counterpart of Belial, a wicked angel. On Belial as a chief wicked angelic antagonist/Satan figure, see S. D. Sperling, "Belial בליעל," *DDD* 169–171; Michalak, *Angels as Warriors*, 170–181; Kobelski, *Melchizedek and Melchiresha*, 75–83; Francis Daoust, "Belial in the Dead Sea Scrolls: From Worthless to Stumbling Block to Archenemy," in *New Vistas on Early Judaism and Christianity From Enoch to Montreal and Back* (eds., Lorenzo DiTommaso and Gerbern S. Oegema; JCTC 22; London: Bloomsbury T&T Clark, 2016), 217–233; Ryan E. Stokes, "What is a Demon, What is an Evil Spirit, and What is a Satan?" in *Das Böse, der Teufel und Dämonen – Evil, the Devil, and Demons* (eds., Jan Dochhorn, Susanne Rudnig-Zelt, and Benjamin Wold; WUNT 2/412; Tübingen: Mohr Siebeck, 2017), 270–271. Fletcher-Louis also cites the ascent of the speaker of the *Self-Glorification Hymn* (see Chapter 5, below) – whom he also considers to be "divine human" – as a possible parallel to *11QMelch*. There is, however, no evidence of Melchize-

spiritual forces. Moreover, given the interpretation of Melchizedek as the אלהים of Ps 82:1, the text itself appears to differentiate between the herald and Melchizedek when it is announced – presumably by the herald, not Melchizedek himself – that "your God" is Melchizedek (II, 24–25).[72]

Other objections to an angelic interpretation of the figure of *11QMelch* are that Melchizedek is best understood as a divine hypostasis or perhaps even Yhwh himself.[73] But as already noted, II, 13 states that it is Melchizedek who carries out the vengeance of God's judgments, thus making a distinction between Yhwh and his agent. Indeed, that the herald deems it essential to comment on the identity of אלוהיך in II, 24 is redundant if "your God" is the God

---

dek's ascension in *11QMelch*, and Fletcher-Louis' argument that the language of *return* (cf. II, 10–11; Ps 7:8–9) functions as a description of how Melchizedek moves into his position of heavenly authority actually suggests the opposite: i.e., to *return* to a judgment role in the divine court presupposes that such a role has precedent, which would be a strange assertion to make of someone who is human. On the possibility that the verb in question is not שוב but a form of ישב, which may be more intelligible in the context of the psalm, see the comments of Fitzmyer, "Further Light on Melchizedek," 37, who notes the similarly problematic spelling of the word in the MT. Cf. Dahood, *Psalms 1*, 44.

[72] This is the main argument against equating a (human) herald with Melchizedek. More specifically, II, 23–25 returns to the language of Isa 52:7: "as is written about him (עליו): '[saying to Zi]on: your God is king'. [Zi]on i[s] [the congregation of all the Sons of Justice, who] establish the covenant, who avoid walking [on the p]ath of the people. And 'your G[o]d' (אל[ו]היך) is [... Melchizedek who will fr]ee them from the han]d of Belial." While it is true that the interpretation of אלוהיך at the end of II, 24 has not been preserved, most commentators consider the עליו of II, 23 to refer to Melchizedek rather than the herald of II, 18; it is therefore considered reasonable to expect our protagonist to be mentioned in II, 23–25, hence the restoration of Melchizedek, who is proclaimed by the herald as "your God." This view is especially persuasive in light of the role ascribed to אלוהיך, who rescues those in the clutches of Belial. The herald is thus not Melchizedek but the one who announces Melchizedek's eschatological career. Cf. García Martínez et al., DJD 23, 233; Mason, "Melchizedek Traditions," 358; Kobelski, *Melchizedek and Melchiresa*, 61. Alternatively, Heiser, "The Divine Council," §§4.2, 7.4, has made the intriguing suggestion that the herald should be equated with a *non-human* Melchizedek, in part because of 11Q13's use of Second Isaiah, the heralds of which have been understood to be members of the divine council. On the identify of Isaiah's heralds, see Christopher R. Seitz, "The Divine Council: Temporal Transition and New Prophecy in the Book of Isaiah," *JBL* 109 (1990): 229–247.

[73] On Melchizedek as a divine hypostasis, see Milik, "Milki-seqedk et Milki-resa," 125. On Melchizedek as Yhwh, see Franco Manzi, *Melchisedek e l'angelologica nellèpistola agli Ebrei e a Qumran* (AnBib 136; Rome: Pontifical Biblical Institute, 1997), 67–96; cf. Rick van de Water, "Michael or Yhwh? Toward Identifying Melchizedek in 11Q13," *JSP* 16 (2006): 75–86. For a survey and evaluation of additional understandings of Melchizedek, see Mason, *'You Are a Priest Forever'*, 185–190, who finds the angelic interpretation the "most convincing"; cf. idem, "Melchizedek Traditions," 357.

of Israel.[74]   By far the best explanation of Melchizedek's portrayal in *11QMelch* is the Second Temple Period interest in an angelic hierarchy in which God has granted lofty privileges to his righteous subordinates.[75]

This same trend likely influenced the designations *11QMelch* uses for God's people. First, II, 8 says that eschatological atonement will be for

8 ...כול בני [אור ו]אנש[י]גורל מל[כי]צדק[

8 ... all the Sons of [Light and for] the men of the lot of Mel[chi]zedek[.

The first lacuna requires the restoration of a key phrase. The line is frequently read with the word אור,[76] and the result is that the eschatological atonement and protection will benefit the "Sons of Light," the dualistic designation for members of the Qumran movement in 1QS and 1QM. Moreover, that "the men of the lot of Melchizedek" would then be parallel to the Sons of Light, which suggests that to be a sect member is, by definition, to be able to claim Melchizedek as angelic redeemer. Elsewhere in the Scrolls, the possession of a גורל is the exclusive privilege of either God himself or Belial (i.e., never a human prerogative),[77] an observation that both highlights the preeminence of Melchizedek in the mind of *11QMelch*'s author and underscores the close relationship the Qumran movement envisioned between themselves and their support in the heavenly realm. If the restoration at II, 9 is correct, an intimate connection with the angels may be further emphasized when the beneficiaries of Melchizedek's assistance are referred to as ע[ם קדושי אל, "the people of the holy ones of God." Similar to the phrase used in Dan 7:27, as well as the *War Scroll* (see below), it was argued in Chapter 3 that this language posits a

---

[74] So Horton, *The Melchizedek Tradition*, 75: "The author evidently thinks that the אלוהיך of Isa 52:7 [2:23] needs to be explained, something which would be unnecessary if אלוהיך were understood as 'God' (אל)." Cf. Kobelski, *Melchizedek and Melchiresa*, 72; Hannah, *Michael and Christ*, 71; Fitzmyer, "Further Light on Melchizedek," 30.

[75] So Angel, *Otherworldly*, 150. Cf. Davila, "Michael, Melchizedek, and War in Heaven," 270. For additional discussion, see Chapter 2.

[76] Puech, "Notes sur le manuscript de 11Qmelkîsédek," 483–513, claimed there was a trace of an aleph, but more recently this has been denied; see García Martinéz et al., DJD 23, 227, who nonetheless restores the text with אור. Cf., e.g., Horton, *The Melchizedek Tradition*, 70; Kobelski, *Melchizedek and Melchiresa*, 15. However, it is also quite common to allow that the text originally read "sons of אל"; cf. Milik, "Milkî-sedeq et Milki-resa," 98, who preferred this option. As Hannah, *Michael and Christ*, 70–71, observes, the attractiveness of the latter proposal is that Melchizedek would then be the head of a community comprised of both angels (sons of God) and humans (the lot of Melchizedek), which is a key feature of 1QM.

[77] So Kobelski, *Melchizedek and Melchiresha*, 60. Cf. Horton, *The Melchizedek Tradition*, 78; Angel, *Otherworldly*, 149.

genitival, possessive, or tutelary relationship between heaven and earth, which is an apt description of Melchizedek's function in *11QMelch*.[78]

The transfer of this divine prerogative to an angel and the resultant, tight-knit connection between the Qumran movement and their angelic succor may help to explain another designation by which God's people are known in *11QMelch*: "the inheritance of Melchizedek" (II, 5). The line as a whole is poorly preserved,[79] but it seems that נחלת מלכי צדק is a reference to those who will benefit from the eschatological jubilee that has just been announced (II, 2–4) and is about to be explained in detail (II, 6–25). Various passages from the Hebrew Bible are acknowledged as the background of this expression, all of which assert that Israel is the inheritance of Yhwh (e.g., 1 Sam 10:1; Isa 19:25, 47:6; Ps 78:71).[80] The most significant of these passages for my purposes is Deut 32:8–9, which was discussed in Chapter 2. By claiming that Israel is Melchizedek's נחלה, *11QMelch* is using the language of Deut 32:9 to assert something similar to *TTS*: that God has appointed an elite angel to watch over his people. The notion of inheritance in the Hebrew Bible is both familial and characterized by endurance,[81] and that *11QMelch* refers to the people as the נחלת מלכי צדק is more than a mere assignment for Melchizedek; he has been entrusted with something that ultimately belongs to God himself. Simultaneously, *11QMelch*, as a sectarian composition, equates "the men of the lot of Melchizedek" with the Sons of Light (as is it nearly universally restored in II, 8). It is unlikely then that the "inheritance of Mel-

---

[78] For the restoration, see García Martinéz et al., DJD 23, 227–231. Given that "the people of the holy ones of God" is seemingly in apposition to Melchizedek's "armies/host" (צבאיו) in II, 9, the noun עם may be indicating that the forces of Melchizedek include the sectarian soldiers. A less likely possibility here is that עם includes the angels and is an example of deliberate terminological ambiguity, which serves to emphasize the correspondence between the angelic guardians and the people they protect.

[79] It is likely this designation occurs 2x in line 5, but the later reading (נחלֹ[ת מלכי צ]דק) has to be restored; see García Martinéz et al., DJD 23, 230–231.

[80] The use of נחלה to describe Melchizedek's inheritance is in keeping with boldness of the *pesher* application of scripture quotations to the protagonist; see García Martinéz et al., DJD 23, 231, who grant נחלת מלכי צדק the lengthiest comment of any line in *11QMelch*.

[81] Israel is often described as a favoured son (e.g., Deut 32:6; Exod 4:22–23; Isa 63:13) not only to whom a נחלה has been given, especially land (cf. 1 Kgs 8:36; Ps 47:5[4]), but who are also themselves Yhwh's treasured נחלה, which when used in this figurative way stresses "the constant, enduring nature of its possession. The notion of permanent possession is in fact intimately associated with the concept of [נחלה], which constitutes a family's ancient property, an indispensable possession that could not be transferred from one clan to another"; so E. Lipinski, "נָחַל; נַחֲלָה," *TDOT* 9:328–331. As noted above, some see a priestly role for Melchizedek in *11QMelch*, and the priestly connotations of נחלה have been observed (cf. Num 18:20; Deut 10:9: 18:2; Josh 13:33). But it is normally God who is called the נחלה of the priests; see García Martinéz et al., DJD 23, 231.

chizedek" was thought to be Israel in a wider sense but rather the members of the sect, who have applied this designation to themselves.

In short, 11Q13 announces the career of Melchizedek, a figure with whom the authors and readers of this text claimed an intimate connection. As God's eschatological agent, Melchizedek is cast as an elite angelic guardian of the Sons of Light. As with the Prince of Lights/Angel of God's Truth from *TTS*, dependence on Melchizedek's superior protection was a key privilege of being a member of the Qumran movement, whose tutelary relationship with the angels may be further emphasized (if the reconstruction is accepted) by the designation "the people of the holy ones." Moreover, the *pesher* method employed throughout *11QMelch* not only results in the replacement of Yhwh with his elite agent, Melchizedek, but also strongly implies that it is sectarian-defined Israel that constitutes Melchizedek's inheritance. Thus again, included in the definition of what it means to be a member of the Qumran movement – and therefore part of the true Israel – is to have a privileged understanding of Israel's scriptures, which reveal that the sectarians alone were in the lot of the angel to whom the God of Israel has delegated great power and authority. But as extraordinary as these claims are, they are relatively modest in comparison to the lofty boasts of martial angelic fellowship found in the *War Scroll*.

C. The War Scroll and Related Texts

Not only has the relatively well-preserved *War Scroll* (henceforth, *WS*) from Cave 1 captured the attention of scholars from the initial days of Qumran studies,[82] it has also drawn comparisons to other sectarian documents from Cave 1, particularly because of *WS's* use of dualistic language.[83] As is the

---

[82] Dated on the basis of paleography to the second half of the 1st cent. BCE, 1QM comprises nineteen columns of extant text. Less than ten years after it was found, 1QM was published by Eleazar L. Sukenik, *The Dead Sea Scrolls of the Hebrew University* (Jerusalem: Magnes Press/The Hebrew University, 1955), 1–19, pls. 16–34, 47. Unless otherwise stated, I will cite the more recent critical edition of Jean Duhaime, "War Scroll," in *The Dead Sea Scrolls: Hebrew, Aramaic, and Greek Texts with English Translations: Volume 2: Damascus Document, War Scroll and Related Documents* (ed., J. H. Charlesworth et al.; PTSDSSP 2; Tübingen: Mohr Siebeck; Louisville: Westminster John Knox, 1995), 80–141, whose Hebrew text, sigla, and translations (with occasional adjustments of the latter) will be the basis for that cited in this chapter. It should be noted that it is Duhaime's general practice not to propose reconstructions where there are lacunae.

[83] Taken from the text's opening words, the longer name by which scholars sometimes refer to 1QM is *The Scroll of the War of the Sons of Light against the Sons of Darkness* (which served as the title of Yigael Yadin's commentary [trans. Batya and Chaim Rabin; Oxford: Oxford University Press, 1962]), and this terminology is characteristic of the dualistic language of certain sections of *WS*. As will be evident throughout my discussion, comparisons are often made between *WS* and other dualistic texts/passages from Qumran,

case with the *Community Rule*, related manuscripts from Cave 4 suggest that *WS* was the product of a complex literary development,[84] and I will address the relevance of source-critical proposals, below. For now, it is sufficient to state that, as it stands, 1QM espouses the common early Jewish expectation of eschatological angelic assistance for God's people, and that this hope is combined with sectarian claims of a uniquely close connection with their angelic guardians. The resulting fusion of these convictions amounts to a grandiose statement on the self-identity of the sectarians, who were convinced that they would fight in conjunction with the angels at the eschatological war.

My discussion of *WS* will be comprised of three parts. I will first highlight language that presupposes a close relationship between the human combatants and the angels. I will then examine statements that explicitly refer to the mingling of humans and angels as comrades in the eschatological war. Finally, I will look at references to Israel in light of source-critical scholarship on *WS* and demonstrate that, despite the use of what likely included non-sectarian/pan-Israel sources or traditions, the overall assertion of 1QM is that "Israel" is defined according to sectarian ideals.

I. Passages Presupposing a Close Human-Angel Relationship

A number of *WS* passages strongly suggest that a connection between the human warriors and the angelic realm is presupposed. More specifically, I noted earlier the readings that understand Dan 7:27 and 11Q13 II, 9 as positing a genitival, possessive, or tutelary relationship between the people and their angelic succor, and how this idea fits very well with the correspondence between heaven and earth envisioned in these texts.[85] A construction similar to those found in Daniel and *11QMelch* occurs in 1QM X, which is a prayer that begins by asking:

9 ומיא --------[86] כעמכה ישראל אשר בחרתה לכה מכול עמי הארצות

9 And who -------- is like your people Israel whom you have chosen for yourself among all the peoples of the lands?

Then, at the beginning of line 10, is the phrase עם קדושי ברית, which seems to explicate "your people Israel." Duhaime translates it as "the holy people of

---

especially 1QS's *TTS*. Cf. Davidson, *Angels at Qumran*, 213; Hannah, *Michael and Christ*, 62; Duhaime, *The War Texts*, 95–97.

[84] For the Cave 4 manuscripts, see Maurice Baillet, ed., *Qumrân Grotte 4.III (4Q482–4Q520)* (DJD 7; Oxford: Claredon Press, 1982), 12–72. Cf. Duhaime, "Cave IV Fragments Related to the War Scroll," in *The Dead Sea Scrolls*, 142–203.

[85] So Dequeker, "Saints of the Most High," 108–133, 179–187; followed by Collins, *Daniel*, 315–316, 319, 322.

[86] There is a horizontal scribal notation in this line; see Duhaime, "War Scroll," 116 n. 122.

the covenant." He thus understands קדושי as an attributive adjective.[87] But as per Dan 7:27, many scholars read קדושי as a substantive, resulting in the translation, "the people of the holy ones of the covenant."[88] Given the widespread recognition of the influence of Dan 7–8 on this line,[89] that X, 10 envisions a Daniel-like, tutelary correspondence between heaven and earth makes good sense. Admittedly, there is no Hebrew Bible precedent for referring to angels as holy ones *of the covenant*. There are, however, numerous early Jewish and Christian texts that point to the belief of angelic mediation at Sinai (cf. 1 En. 93:6; Jub. 1:27–29, 2:1; Josephus, *Ant.* 15.136; Acts 7:53; Gal 3:19; Heb 2:2). Moreover, how 1QM X elaborates upon עם קדושי ברית has a covenantal flavour: the passage continues by stating that the people of Israel were the privileged recipients of the law and angelic revelation.[90]

---

[87] Duhaime, "War Scroll," 117. Cf. Jean Carmignac, *La Règle de la Guerre des Fils de Lumière contre les Fils de Ténèbres: Texte Restauré, Traduit Commenté* (Paris: Letouzey et Ané, 1958), 145, whose translation ("Le people des saints de l'Alliance") is ambiguous but who seemingly understands the word as an attributive: "Ici l'auteur la complete en mettant directement en relation cette 'sainteté' avec l'Alliance." Elisha Qimron, *The Hebrew of the Dead Sea Scrolls* (HSS 29; Winona Lake: Eisenbrauns, 2008), 83 n. 63, cites 1QM X, 10 as one of approximately twenty examples from the Scrolls of the collective noun, עם, taking a plural concord. Also note the translation of Yadin, *The Scroll of the War*, 306, who adds two words (in italics): "a people of *men* holy *through* the covenant." In a section entitled "Angels in Our Midst: Human Angel Communities," Sullivan, *Wrestling with Angels*, 155–161, makes no mention of X, 10, and one is left to surmise that he takes קדושי as an attributive and thus not an angelic designation. Fletcher-Louis, *All the Glory*, 283, 428–429, concedes "the people of the holy ones of the covenant" as a viable option, but he prefers "the holy people of the covenant." But note 1QM XII, 1, where the *singular* קדוש (attributively) modifies עם, which may suggest that an attributive reading of קדושי at X, 10 is incorrect; see below.

[88] See especially the discussion of Collins, *Daniel*, 315. Cf. Dequeker, "Saints of the Most High," 155; Vermes, *CDSSE*, 175; Wise, Abegg, and Cook, *DSSANT*, 157; García Martínez and Tigchelaar, *DSSSE*, 1:129. Also see Robert D. Holmstedt and John Screnock, "Writing a Descriptive Grammar of the Syntax and Semantics of the War Scroll (1QM): The Noun Phrase as Proof of Concept," in *The War Scroll, Violence, War and Peace in the Dead Sea Scrolls and Related Literature: Essays in Honour of Martin G. Abegg on the Occasion of His 65th Birthday* (eds., Kipp Davis, Dorothy M. Peters, Kyung S. Baek, and Peter W. Flint; STDJ 115; Leiden: Brill, 2015), 82, who place the occurrence of קדושי in X, 10 in their list of *WS's* substantival adjectives. Intriguingly, Heiser, "The Divine Council," §7.3, renders the phrase "the people of the holy ones," but he understands "the holy ones" as a reference to humans.

[89] Even among those who translate עם קדושי ברית as "the holy people of the covenant"; see, e.g., Carmignac, *La Règle de la Guerre*, 145, who states that "Daniel (7, 27 et 8, 24) a créé l'expression 'le peuple des saints' et elle est passée dans le 'style' de Qumrân"; he also notes that there is similar language elsewhere in 1QM (see XII, 8, VI, 6, and XVI, 1).

[90] So Dequeker, "The Saints of the Most High," 157, who notes the "covenantal background" of lines 10–11. It has been rightly observed that column X continues by describing the warriors as those who "see the angels" (Michalak, *Angels as Warriors*, 152), were "ex-

Similar language is found in another prayer, this time at 1QM XII, 1–9; and like X, 10, the phrase at XII, 8 may have a tutelary sense:

8 ... כיא קדוש אדוני ומלך הכבוד אתנו עם קדושים

The translation of the first part of the line, "for holy is the Lord and the glorious king (is) with us," is relatively clear, but the next phrase, עם קדושים, is not. Duhaime translates it as *"together with* the holy ones," thus taking עַם as the preposition, עִם.[91] However, for two reasons it is better to read עם as עַם, "people," and in apposition to אתנו, "with us."[92] The first reason "the *people of* the holy ones" should be preferred over *"together with* the holy ones" is that it avoids the grammatically awkward construction of having two prepositions, אֶת and עִם, side by side.[93] Second and more significantly, עם קדושים is immediately followed by three parallel statements which give practical, wartime expression to the presupposition that the people have an intimate connection to the angels (cf. XII, 8–9).[94]

That both 1QM X, 10 and XII, 8 should be understood as referring to the "the people of the holy ones" is arguably reinforced by two occurrences of what Collins dubs the "reverse"[95] of the phrase. The first of these is found at VI, 6 and comes at the end of a rule for battalion formation and the descriptions of the inspirational words to be written on the javelins of those assembled for war. After stating that the warriors will use their weapons to enact the judgment of God on their enemies, the section concludes with this triumphant exclamation:

6 ... והיתה לאל ישראל המלוכה ובקדושי עמו יעשה חיל

6 ... And the kingship shall belong to the God of Israel and among the holy ones of his people he shall do worthily.

---

alted to see the angels" (Steudel, "The Eternal Reign," 522), or had a "special connection with the angels" (Sullivan, *Wrestling with Angels*, 159). Such statements are only complemented by understanding עם קדושים as "the people of the holy ones," but the significance of this reading is often overlooked.

[91] Duhaime, "War Scroll," 121. Cf., e.g., Jan van der Ploeg, *Le Rouleau de la Guerre: Traduit et Annoté avec une Introduction* (STDJ 2; Leiden: Brill, 1959), 47; Holmsteadt and Screnock, "Writing a Descriptive Grammar," 83. Also see 1QHª XI, 22–23; XIX, 14–15, where עַם is virtually certain.

[92] I.e., "For the Lord is holy, the king of glory is *with us, the people of the holy ones* ...";
see, e.g., the translations of Carmignac, *La Règle de la Guerre*, 178; Yadin, *The Scroll of the War*, 316; Dequeker, "The Saints of the Most High," 159. Fletcher-Louis, *All the Glory*, 435, prefers "holy people," as he does at X, 10.

[93] So Dequeker, "The Saints of the Most High," 159.

[94] I will address the content of the statements in XII, 8–9 later in the present chapter.

[95] Collins, *Daniel*, 315.

The second occurrence of the phrase is virtually identical to the first and is found in 1QM XVI, 1, functioning as the climax of a hortatory address the high priest is to recite to the soldiers:

1 ... אל ישראל קרא חרב על כול הגואים ובקדושי עמו יעשה גבורה

1 ... The God of Israel has summoned a sword against all the nations, and among the holy ones of his people he will do mightily.

The influence of Num 24:18 – which is quoted directly in 1QM XI, 5–7 – is recognized on both VI, 6 and XVI, 1,[96] but the relevance of the parallel has occasionally been misconstrued. For example, since 1QM modifies Num 24:18 by using "the holy ones of the people" rather than "Israel," some have suggested that "the holy ones" are the human warriors and that the focus of these passages is on the militaristic achievements of the people.[97] However, the context of Num 24 is emphatic that any triumph of Israel is God's doing,[98] an assertion shared by VI, 6 and XVI, 1.[99] Moreover, in keeping with the important roles angels have in *WS*, it is entirely appropriate that God is said to secure victory through his angelic holy ones.[100]

At the same time, the role of the human warriors at VI, 6 and XVI, 1 should not be understated, and the phrase "the holy ones *of the people*" assists in emphasizing this. While Dequeker contends that "the people of the holy ones" and "the holy ones of his people," are two sayings that "must have the same

---

[96] Num 24:18 (the end of which is relevant here) reads: הָיָה אֱדוֹם יְרֵשָׁה וְהָיָה יְרֵשָׁה שֵׂעִיר אֹיְבָיו וְיִשְׂרָאֵל עֹשֶׂה חָיִל, "Edom will become a possession, Seir a possession of its enemies, while *Israel* does valiantly."

[97] So Brekelmans, "The Saints of the Most High," 325; Sylvester Lamberigts, "Le Sens de *qdwsym* dans les texts de Qumrân," *ETL* 46 (1970): 32. Cf. Fletcher-Louis, *All the Glory*, 398, who states that "the holy ones" of VI, 1 and XVI, 1 "must refer to humans" without further argument. Also see Richard Bauckham, "The Early Jerusalem Church, Qumran, and the Essenes," in *The Dead Sea Scrolls as Background to Postbiblical Judaism and Early Christianity*, 80–81, who reads "the holy ones of his people" as a human designation at 1QM VI, 6; XVI, 1 (as well as at 4Q511 2 I, 6; for discussion of this text, see Chapter 5), though he does not explain his decision. But as Collins, *Daniel*, 315 n. 351, rightly notes, "1QM differs from the Numbers text precisely by the mention of holy ones, so the meaning of this phrase cannot be determined by the parallel." I discussed "holy ones" as an angelic designation in Chapter 3. On the term as a designation for angels specifically in *WS*, see, e.g., Yadin, *The Scroll of the War*, 231; Dequeker, "The Saints of the Most High," 153–159; Collins, *Daniel*, 315–316.

[98] Note the summary statement of Num 24:23: אוֹי מִי יִחְיֶה מִשֻּׂמוֹ אֵל, "Alas, who can live when *God* does this?"

[99] So Collins, *Daniel*, 315.

[100] As I will highlight at the end of this chapter, a similar theme of God achieving victory through his angels is operative in 1QM XVII; see Duhaime, "Dualistic Reworking," 51.

meaning,"[101] there may be an important nuance. If, as Dequeker maintains, "the people of the holy ones" is a tutelary genitive meaning something akin to "the people who belong to the holy ones,"[102] surely its reverse does not mean exactly the same thing: that is, the holy ones *of the people* may suggest that the holy ones belong to the people or that the people can lay claim to the angelic holy ones in some way. Given the grand and cosmic scale upon which the war is envisioned in 1QM,[103] it is conceivable that this phrase contributed to the rallying cry of the document and to the formation of *WS's* readers, the prospective human combatants. As Newsom has argued, even non-polemical sectarian compositions that share affinities with other late Second Temple Period texts were intended to be formative and can function polemically for the simple reason that "every act of formation is also an act of estrangement. Every act of discourse is also an act of counter-discourse. ... [the language of other texts] can appear faulty and defective or shallow and superficial."[104] How much more would the formational import be, then, if a phrase from the influential Book of Daniel[105] is effectively reversed and employed in an overtly polemical text like *WS*? The bold assertion that the angels in some way belong to the people functions well as a rationale for the presumptuous notion that I will examine shortly: that the human warriors expected the angels to be their war-time comrades.

Another *WS* passage that seems to presuppose a close relationship between angels and humans is found is the opening lines of column XII:

1 כיא רוב קדושים [א]לה בשמים וצבאות מלאכים בזבול קודשכה לה[ן]ודות אמת[]כה
ובחירי עם קודש
2 שמתה לכה ב ̊ [   ] ̊ פר שמות כול צבאם אתכה במעון קודשכה ומ[ן   ] ̊ ים בזבול
כבודכה

---

[101] Dequeker, "The Saints of the Most High," 155. Cf. Collins, *Daniel*, 315–316, who seems to follow Dequeker's assumption that the phrases have the same meaning yet, as already noted, he simultaneously refers to "the holy ones of the people" as the *reverse* of the Danielic phrase "the people of the holy ones."

[102] Dequeker, "The Saints of the Most High," 156.

[103] The Sons of Light saw themselves as God's decisive counterstrike against wickedness; see, e.g., Carmignac, *La Règle de la Guerre*, 92, who in reference to 1QM VI, 6, comments: "L'auteur conçoit la guerre des Fils de Lumière comme une juste punition qui rendra aux impies la rançon du mal qu'ils ont fait à Dieu et à son peuple ... ."

[104] Admittedly, these words of Newsom, *The Self as Symbolic Space*, 269, are written in reference to the *Hodayot's* function in shaping sectarian identity, but the principle is relevant, here.

[105] On the influence of Daniel in the Scrolls generally and *WS* specifically, see, e.g., Flint and Collins, eds., *The Book of Daniel: Composition and Reception*; Flint, "The Daniel Tradition at Qumran," in *Eschatology, Messianism, and the Dead Sea Scrolls*, 41–60; Duhaime, *The War Texts*, 65–71; Collins, *The Scriptures and Sectarianism*, 102–116.

3 וחסדי ברכו[תיכה] וברית שלומכה חרתה למו בחרט חיים למלוך °[ ]בכול מועדי
עולמים

1 For there is a multitude of holy ones in the heavens, and the hosts of angels (are) in your holy habitation to pr[aise] your [truth.] The elect ones of the holy people,
2 you have set for yourself *b* [...] *pr*. The names of all their hosts (are) with you in your holy dwelling; *wm* [...] *ym* in your glorious habitation.
3 The mercies of [your] blessing[s] and the covenant of your peace, you have engraved for them with a stylus of life, to reign [...] in all the appointed times forever, ...

In line 1, "holy ones" is synonymous with "the hosts of angels," thus referencing celestial beings who are on God's side.[106] "The elect ones of the holy people"[107] are most often considered to be the earthly complement of the holy ones/host of angels, namely the human warriors. Not only does this view accord well with the use of בחיר elsewhere in the Scrolls, where it carries the sense of righteous remnant of Israel;[108] it also anticipates the focus on the combined human-angel army later in column XII. The implication that the angels, as well as the people, are part of God's covenant (line 3) underscores this relationship.[109] Alternatively, it has been suggested that "the elect ones of the holy people" are not humans on earth but the souls of dead humans in heaven, who work in conjunction with the קדושים and צבאות מלאכים.[110]

---

[106] While it is sometimes allowed that the קדושים refers to humans here, the consensus view is that "the holy ones" of line 1 are angels because of their location (heaven) and the fact that they are parallel to "the host of angels," whose location is also in heaven (lit.: holy habitation); see, e.g., Bastiaan Jongeling, *Le Rouleau de la Guerre des Manuscrits de Qumran* (SSN 4; Assen: Van Gorcum, 1962), 274; Dequeker, "The Saints of the Most High," 158; Davidson, *Angels at Qumran*, 230. Objecting to this reading is Fletcher-Louis, *All the Glory*, 398, 423–425, who claims that the holy ones/host of angels is a reference to "the Israelites in their angelomorphic mode." But as Tuschling, *Angels and Orthodoxy*, 121–122, observes, Fletcher-Louis' angelmorphic reading (here and elsewhere) "squeezes out the angels almost entirely" and does so by violating "the obvious sense of the text." Cf. Michalak, *Angels as Warriors*, 163–164.

[107] Note that in the phrase, "the elect ones of the holy people," קודש is in the singular, which suggests it is attributively modifying עם; *contra* 1QM X, 10; XII, 8, discussed, above.

[108] See Philip R. Davies, *1QM, the War Scroll from Qumran: Its Structure and History* (BibOr 32; Rome: Biblical Institute Press, 1977), 100–101, who notes this "well-defined meaning" of בחיר in other Qumran texts; cf., e.g., CD IV, 3–4; 1QpHab IX, 12; X, 13; 4Q171 (=4QpPsᵃ) IV, 13–15. I will address the identity of "Israel" in *WS* later in the present chapter.

[109] Cf. Jub. 15:27–28, which speaks of the angels of the presence and the angels of holiness of whom Dimant, "Men as Angels," 99, writes: "they alone were created circumcised ... . A sign of the divine covenant, it marks them as partakers of this covenant, and as heavenly counterparts of earthly Israel." See Chapter 3, above.

[110] So Carmignac, *La Régle de la Guerre*, 170, 172; cf. Yadin, *The Scroll of the War*, 242. Davies, *1QM, the War Scroll*, 101 n. 30, is overstating when he says that Carmignac

Given the previously discussed early Jewish anticipation of an angel-like afterlife for the righteous (e.g., Dan 12:3; 1 En. 104:2–6),[111] understanding
בחירי עם קודש as the souls of deceased humans who have received the reward
of becoming associates of the angels merits serious consideration.[112] The likelihood of this view may be enhanced by lines 4–5:

4 ולפקוד צ°[ ]   ]יריכה° לאלפיהם ולרבואותם יחד עם קדושיכה[ ]מלאכיכה לרשות
יד

5 במלחמה[ ]   ]קמי ארץ בריב משפטיכה ועם בחירי שמים נוצ̇[חים [

4 and to muster s […] *yrykh* according to their thousands and their myriads, together with
your holy ones […] your angels, so that they have a mighty hand
5 in the battle […] the rebels of the earth in the strife of your judgments, and the people of
the elect ones of the heavens shall be victo[rious … .]

In line 4, it is common to restore צבאות as the first word of the initial lacuna,[113] with בחיריכה often proposed as the second word.[114] The resulting
phrase is thus "the host of your elect ones." As per line 1, the elect ones are
mentioned "together with"[115] "your holy ones" and "your angels";[116] this observation, in combination with the language used to describe the elect ones –

---

and Yadin understand "the chosen ones" as a class of angels (along with the קדושים and
צבאות מלאכים).

[111] On this topic, see Collins, "The Angelic Life," 291–295; and most recently, idem,
The Scriptures and Sectarianism, 195–211. For what seems to be the Qumran movement's
take on *post-mortem* angel-like honour and angelic fellowship, cf. 1QS IV, 6–8; 1QM I, 8–
9.

[112] Though caution is necessary because it seems that the rewards of angelic fellowship
and angel-like honour envisioned in Daniel and 1 Enoch occur at the resurrection/post-
eschatological judgment.

[113] Cf., e.g., Yadin, *The Scroll of the War*, 315; Carmignac, *La Régle de la Guerre*, 175;
van der Ploeg, *Le Rouleau*, 144; García Martínez and Tigchelaar, *DSSSE*, 1:132. *Contra*
André Dupont-Sommer, "Règlement de la Guerre des Fils de Lumière: traduction et notes,"
RHR 148.2 (1955): 162, who proposes צרים, "adversaries," a reading which is dependent
upon understanding that the verb פקד means "to chastise" (see "פקד," *HALOT* 3:957).
However, that פקד is followed by רשה, "to authorize/direct" (cf. the noun, רִשְׁיוֹן, "authori-
zation/empowerment"; e.g., Ezra 3:7), suggests that פקד is better translated as "mus-
ter/command" (see "פקד," *HALOT* 3:956).

[114] Since בחיר is found in lines 1 and 5, the near universal restoration of the legible
יריכה to יריכה[בח] is sound. *Contra* Carmignac, *La Régle de la Guerre*, 175, who opts for
בגוריכה.

[115] The phrase עם קדושיכה is preceded by the adverb, יחד, "together." The correct
reading therefore is "together with (עִם) your holy ones," not "the people (עַם) of your holy
ones" as in X, 10 and XII, 8.

[116] Each of these three groups have the 2nd person plural suffix, יכה, suggesting that they
are, in some sense, to be taken together (i.e., on the same side).

namely, "thousands" and "myriads"– only strengthens the understanding of this group as righteous human souls who are now associates of the angelic throng.[117] Moreover, line 5 refers to the victory of "the people of the elect ones of the heavens,"[118] a designation that not only specifies the celestial habitation of the elect ones but also differentiates the elect ones from the people. In the same way that the phrase "the people of the holy ones" may indicate a tutelary relationship between the angels and the people, "the people of the elect ones of the heavens" may suggest that the souls of the righteous, as part of the heavenly contingent and members of the covenant, have an intimate connection with the people on earth that will factor immensely in the upcoming eschatological war.

II. Humans and Angels: Comrades at the Eschatological War

While the statements from *WS* just surveyed suggest a close relationship between angels and humans, these statements are general in nature or merely hint at how this relationship will manifest itself during the eschatological war. In addition to mentioning that the names of the archangels were to be placed on their shields (IX, 14–16), a practice which seems to have served as a claim that the warriors identified with and had the leadership of these angels,[119] other assertions are more specific and reveal the presumptuous belief that the human warriors would uniquely fight in conjunction with the angels during the war at the end of days. This conviction is reiterated several times and in different ways throughout *WS*.

The first statement in this category occurs in *WS's* opening column and serves to set the tone for the rest of the document. After predicting the ultimate victory of the forces of the God of Israel in what is billed as the long-awaited and divinely-ordained eschatological battle, I, 10–11 describes the respective combatants:

10 ...   בו יתקרבו לנחשיר גדול עדת אלים וקהלת

11 אנשים בני אור וגורל חושך נלחמים יחד לגבורת אל בקול המון גדול ותרועת אלים ואנשים ליום הווה...

---

[117] For the use of אלף and רבוא to describe the angelic host quantitatively, see, e.g., Num 10:36; Ps 68:18; Dan 7:10.

[118] Once again, while עם could be taken as the preposition עִם (so, e.g., van der Ploeg, *La Rouleau*, 47), a majority of scholars prefer to read עַם.

[119] Davidson, *Angels at Qumran*, 228, comments that "the use of the archangels' names presumably expresses the sect's sense of identification with these angelic champions who are God's four leading attendants and Angels of the Presence. The names would serve as a reminder to all the troops that the holy angels were with them as mighty warriors." Cf. Yadin, *Scroll of the War*, 237. Also see Michalak, *Angels as Warri*ors, 158–161, who tentatively suggests an angelic understanding of the inscriptions on the trumpets (II, 15–III, 11).

10 ... On this (day) they shall clash in great carnage; the congregation of divine beings and the assembly of
11 men, the Sons of Light and the lot of darkness, shall fight each other to (disclose?) the might of God, with the uproar of a large multitude and the war cry of divine beings and men, on the day of calamity. ...

Here, we are informed of a key facet of the designation "Sons of Light" as well as of their opponents, the "lot/Sons of Darkness": these groups are comprised of both humans and angels.[120] In every sense, then, the war is cosmic in scope, an all-encompassing confrontation between good and evil.[121] Underscoring that the righteous warriors belong to the Sons of Light – and that membership in this group includes a powerful human-angelic union – are the words of a blessing to be recited by the priests found column XIII:

ובגורל אור הפלתנו ... 9

10 לאמתכה ושר מאור מאז פקדתה לעוזרנו וב˚[ ]]ק וכול רוחי אמת בממשלתו...

9 You have cast us in the lot of light
10 according to your truth. The Prince[122] of Light, long ago, you entrusted to our rescue wb [...]q; all the spirits of truth are under his dominion.

The "Prince of Light" has an analogous role in TTS,[123] and I have already noted that many scholars have identified this figure with Michael who is mentioned elsewhere in WS (cf. 1QM IX, 15–16; XVII, 7–8), though the Michael identification is not certain.[124] But whether the Prince of Light is a name for

---

[120] A detail not explicitly conveyed (though not excluded) by the use of the same terms in TTS and 11QMelch; cf. Davidson, Angels at Qumran, 214, 216, 229. Just as the war-cry of the angels likely encouraged the soldiers (so Yadin, The Scroll of the War, 87), Michalak, Angels as Warriors, 157, rightly stresses that the belief in the angelic presence in and of itself would have served the same function.

[121] Cf. Duhaime, "Dualistic Reworking," 55. On Belial's leadership of the Sons of Darkness in WS, see Davidson, Angels at Qumran, 217–221; Michalak, Angels as Warriors, 180; Daoust, "Belial in the Dead Sea Scrolls," 226–230.

[122] Duhaime, "War Scroll," 123, renders שר as "commander," which is a less common translation.

[123] In TTS, the title is the plural "Prince of Lights" (cf. CD V, 18), whereas in 1QM it is the singular "Prince of Light."

[124] The frequent suggestion that Michael, the Prince of Light(s), God's Angel of Truth, and Melchizedek represent different names for the same principal angel, as well as objections to Michael's inclusion in this identification, have already been noted. For additional discussion, see Yadin, The Scroll of the War, 235–236; Carmignac, La Règle, 114 n. 8. On the Prince of Light as a divine warrior, which seems to be his function here, see Michalak, Angels as Warriors, 165–166. The reading of Fletcher-Louis, All the Glory, 410–411, that Michael is "not simply Israel's principal guardian angel, but is her secret name, carrying in himself her vocation and privileged God-like-ness," is part of his larger angel-morphic/divine humanity proposal, which, as noted, has been criticized for minimizing the role and significance of angels.

Michael or an angelic superior who secures his victory, it is interesting that *WS* makes a point of emphasizing both Michael's exaltation and his association with Israel.[125] This is important because according to the Book of Daniel, Michael is the leader of the angelic holy ones who constitute the celestial counterparts of Israel (cf. Dan 10:13, 21; 12:1). Moreover, the reference to the Prince of Light is surrounded by comments on the role and ultimate downfall of the Prince of Light's adversary, Belial (see XIII, 2, 4, 11; cf. I, 1, 3, 5, 13, 15; IV, 2; XI, 8; XIV, 9; XV, 3, 17; XVI, 11; XVII, 15; XVIII, 1, 3, 16). As Collins notes, this

shows that the *War Scroll* is adapting the tradition of Daniel and attempting to correlate the dualism of the 'Treatise on the Two Spirits' with established Jewish traditions. The main difference over against Daniel is that Michael is now paired with Belial, the Prince of Darkness, rather than with the angelic princes of specific nations.[126]

The pitting of the Prince of Light/Michael against the chief wicked angel, Belial – as opposed to various national angels – further emphasizes the all-encompassing scope of the war and the mixed (i.e., angel-human) composition of the two camps. The latter point is perhaps best known from *WS's* assertion that the presence of the angels necessitated a heightened state of ceremonial cleanliness; 1QM VII, 3–6 states:

```
3 ...          וכול נער זעטוט ואשה לוא יבואו למחנותם בצאתם
4 מירושלים ללכת למלחמה עד שובם וכול פסח או עור או חגר או איש אשר מום עולם
   בבשרו או איש מנוגע בטמאת
5 בשרו כול אלה לוא ילכו אתם למלחמה כולם יהיו נדבת מלחמה ותמימי רוח ובשר
   ועתודים ליום נקם וכול
6 איש אשר לוא יהיה טהור ממקורו ביום המלחמה לוא ירד אתם כיא מלאכי קודש עם
   צבאותם יחד...
```

3 ... No young boy or woman shall enter their camps when they leave
4 Jerusalem to go to battle until their return. Neither lame, nor blind, nor crippled, nor a man in whose flesh there is a permanent blemish, nor a man stricken by some uncleanliness
5 in his flesh, none of them shall go to the battle with them. They shall all be volunteers for war, perfect ones of spirit and flesh, and ready for the Day of Vengeance. Any
6 man who is not purified from a (bodily) discharge on the day of the battle shall not go down with them, *for the holy angels are together with their armies* [emphasis mine]. ...[127]

---

[125] I will address this subject in greater detail, below.

[126] Collins, "Powers in Heaven," 17–18.

[127] Duhaime, "War Scroll," 111, renders צבאותם as "their 'host,'" which obscures the fact that the word refers to the human "armies," which is a more appropriate translation. Inexplicably, Davies, *1QM, the War Scroll*, 42, denies that *WS* speaks of angelic assistance on the battlefield. But see the critique of Jean Carmignac, "On Philip R. Davies, *1QM, the War Scroll from Qumran*," *RevQ* 9 (1978): 599–603. Cf. Michalak, *Angels as Warriors*, 157.

To be sure, the presence of the angels is a reason given for purity in the camp,[128] but *WS* seems to temper and even overshadow this humility by emphasizing that the human warriors have the angels as their "brothers in arms."[129] The presence of the angels is reiterated in the High Priest's pre-battle speech in column XV: after the exhortation in lines 6–12 for the (human) troops not to fear the enemy, line 14 states that "the h]eroes of the gods" and "the holy ones" – both angelic designations – are, respectively, "girding themselves for war" and "mustered for battle," descriptions which function to explain how God's hand is against "all the wic[ked] spirits."[130] Similarly, 1QM XII, 8–9 stresses the closeness[131] of the angels via three statements (indicated by the prepositions בְּ or עִם and the first-person plural suffix נוּ at the end of each line, italicized in translation); the statements are listed in parallel:

8 ... גבו] [צבא מלאכים בפקודינו
9 וגבור המלח[מה] בעדתנו
וצבא רוחיו עם צעדינו

8 *gbw* [...][132] the host of angels (is) *among our* numbered men,
9 and the mighty one of wa[r] (is) *in our* congregation,
and the host of his spirits (is) *with our* foot-soldiers ...

---

[128] For an overview of this topic and the "quixotic" purity ideals of *WS*, see Ian Werrett and Stephen Parker, "Purity in War: What is it Good for?" in *The War Scroll, Violence, War and Peace*, 295–316. Cf. Annette Steudel, "Biblical Warfare Legislation in the War Scroll (1QM VII:1–7 and X:1–8)," in *The Reception of Biblical War Legislation in Narrative Contexts* (ed., Christoph Berner and Harald Samuel; BZAW 460; Berlin: de Gruyter, 2015), 183–186, who highlights the priestly resonances of 1QM's camp organization and the regulations for inclusion in it (cf. Lev 21:17–21; Num 1–10). Also see Cecilia Wassén, "Women, Worship, Wilderness, and War: Celibacy and the Constructions of Identity in the Dead Sea Scrolls," in *Sibyls, Scriptures, and Scrolls*, 1377–1379, who emphasizes that war-time itself was a factor for the stringent purity/celibacy demands (cf. Deut 23:10–15; 1 Sam 21:2–7).

[129] Michalak, *Angels as Warriors*, 152, captures this well by noting in three successive comments that i.) the angels are "brothers in arms" with the human warriors; ii.) the presence of angels required ritual purity; and iii.) the people are those who "see the angels" (cf. 1QM X, 11). The influence of Deut 23:14 on this passage has been noted in that purity was demanded in the camp. But whereas Deuteronomy mentions Yhwh's presence, the focus of 1QM VII, 3–6 is on the presence of the angels. Cf. Davidson, *Angels at Qumran*, 231; Steudel, "Biblical Warfare Legislation," 185–186. That being said, even divinely commissioned angelic support never removes the need for God to intervene or secure victory. For further on this last point, see below.

[130] While not well-preserved, the end of column XV stresses the angelic dimension of the war, including Belial's eventual destruction.

[131] Davidson, *Angels at Qumran*, 230, describes 1QM XII, 6–8 as having "the angels actually involved with the sectarian army."

[132] Duhaime, "War Scroll," 121, does not attempt to restore the small tear between גבו and צבא, but see Carmignac, *La Régle de la Guerre*, 179, who proposes גבורות, which both carries the appropriate sense and adequately fills the space; i.e., "*the mighty deeds of* the host of angels are among our numbered men."

Though "the mighty one of war" may refer to God himself (cf. Exod 15:3; Ps 24:8),[133] if one takes into consideration the lofty descriptions and roles principal angel figures are granted in the sectarian texts including *WS* (cf. 1QM IX, 15–16; XIII, 10; XVII, 6–7; 11Q13 II, 9–13; 1QS III, 20–25), the Prince of Light/Michael may be in view. Regardless, that the angels are *with* the human warriors is an unmistakable conviction of *WS*.

Yet important questions remain unanswered: if the Sons of Light are a human-angel coterie, *in what sense* are the Prince of Light/Michael-led angels with the human warriors, and does the concept of *with* envisioned here differ from that found in the scenarios of other texts? To address these questions, a few observations are required. First, in an effort to better understand *WS*, Davidson has noted that angelic "participation"[134] in Israel's battles has biblical precedent. Such language, however, is plagued by the same lack of specificity that prompts my question in the first place in that it fails to describe *how* the angels participate. Though not specifically responding to Davidson, Michalak has recently defined angelic participation or assistance in the late Second Temple Period literature as follows: angels either a.) fight in the heavenly/angelic equivalent of earthly conflicts (e.g., Dan 7–12), or b.) intervene directly in human history/conflicts, with their intervention providing a significant psychological or morale boost for the earthly beneficiaries (e.g., 1 En. 1:9; 90:14–19).[135] While helpful to a degree, some texts straddle both of Michalak's categories,[136] and this is true when it comes to *WS*. For instance,

---

[133] If correct, this reading forms an alternating emphasis in XII, 8–9 between the presence of the angels and God himself, a point that both complements a similar pattern in the immediately preceding lines and underscores the idea that even divinely commissioned celestial forces are ultimately dependent on God. Cf. Yadin, *The Scroll of the War*, 317; Davidson, *Angels at Qumran*, 230; Steudel, "The Eternal Reign," 523. Also see Carmignac, *La Régle de la Guerre*, 179: "Pour obtenir une phrase bien cadencée, l'auteur, qui vient de mettre en scène Dieu, puis les anges, puis Dieu, se doit de revenir aux anges, et de fait il construit un nouveau membre bien parallèle: 'les puissances de l'armé des anges sont dans nos enrôlés ... l'armée de ses esprits est avec nos fantassins et nos cavaliers.'"

[134] See Davidson, *Angels at Qumran*, 230, who is surely correct when he points out that the eschatological scenario of *WS* and its angelic assistance is grander than the situations of "more limited significance" envisioned in the Hebrew Bible. Cf. Miller, *The Divine Warrior*, 143; Hannah, *Michael and Christ*, 60; Sullivan, *Wrestling with Angels*, 157; Duhaime, *The War Texts*, 103–116.

[135] Michalak, *Angels as Warriors*, 241, 245. Cf. Duhaime, "Dualistic Reworking," 49, who suggests that the angelic presence "toughens those standing on the 'firing line' by stressing that the group is living on the very day that God has chosen to humble the empire of ungodliness and to provide his lot with personified heavenly help, peace, blessing, and even dominion over the nations as well as the gods. One could say: The more severe the struggle, the closer the salvation and the greater the reward."

[136] Prime examples being the texts examined earlier in this chapter, as there is nothing about the angelic assistance described in *TTS* or *11QMelch* precluding it from either of

although *WS* never provides detailed descriptions of angel-to-angel combat and the focus is on the earthly battle,[137] it seems clear enough that the text presupposes a dualistic picture akin – though certainly not identical – to the angelic struggle between the angels associated with Israel and their wicked opponents in Dan 7–12;[138] after all, are we to assume that, despite the many references to righteous angels throughout *WS*, they do not in some way strive directly against the wicked Belial and the spirits of his lot? Additionally, knowledge of this angelic struggle could not help but be of significant psychological import to those involved in the earthly conflict,[139] and angel-versus-angel and heavenly components of the war by no means preclude the direct

---

Michalak's categories. Cf. John J. Collins, "Patterns of Eschatology at Qumran," in *Traditions in Transformation: Turning Points in Biblical Faith* (eds., Baruch Halpern and Jon D. Levenson; Winona Lake: Eisenbrauns, 1981), 353, who highlights the problems of trying to fit *WS* into the categories of Sigmund Mowinckel, *He That Cometh: The Messiah Concept in the Old Testament and Later Judaism* (Nashville: Abingdon Press, 1954), 281, namely, this-worldly or other-worldly. Also see Davidson, *Angels at Qumran*, 214.

[137] So Fletcher-Louis, *All the Glory*, 397–401, who presses this point too far in the service of his angelmorphic/divine humanity thesis with the result that the critique of Tuschling, *Angels and Orthodoxy*, 121–122, is again apropos: angels are being unjustifiably "squeezed out."

[138] Using terms that will be familiar from my discussion of *TTS*, Davidson, *Angels at Qumran*, 231–232, writes, "It is clear that dualistic concepts are essential to an understanding of the nature of the eschatological war. Cosmic dualism is important in that two camps of angelic beings are involved, with God also on the side of Michael. There is spatial dualism too, in that there are two worlds, the heavenly and the earthly. Our author does not actually discuss the conflict between the angels directly, for his concern is focused on the war on earth. But war between the angels is presupposed by the exaltation of Michael among the angels [1QM XVII, 6–8], by the fact that God defeats Belial and his spirits, and by the involvement of both people and angels in the battle (1QM I, 9–11). Although we do not find a description like that of the confrontation between Michael and the Prince of Persia, as described in Dan 10:13, 20–21, or the heavenly war of Rev 12:7–9, with Michael and his angels opposing the dragon, the conceptual framework is nevertheless similar. 1QM XII, 1–2 involves the same idea." Cf. John G. Gammie, "Spatial and Ethical Dualism in Jewish Wisdom and Apocalyptic Literature," *JBL* 93 (1974): 356–359, who suggests that the heaven/earth relationship – or "spatial dualism" – reaches "its apogee" in *WS*. More specifically, the correspondence between the realms constitutes an "analogical dualism"; as referenced in Duhaime, "Dualistic Reworking," 34, 48, who thus uses the term "analogical spatial dualism" to describe the worldview of *WS*. But also see the critique of Church, *Hebrews and the Temple*, 105–108, who objects to "spatial" as a descriptor of *WS's* dualism. Even if Church is overstating the matter insofar as he denies a heavenly component of the battle, he is right to note that the dualisms of Dan 7–12 and *WS* are not exactly the same. I would suggest the difference, however, is that while *WS* upholds the worldview of Daniel, it simultaneously widens it, and it is in this sense that spatial dualism reaches its "apogee" in *WS*, as per Gammie's observation.

[139] As per its function in Dan 7–12; cf., e.g., Collins, *The Apocalyptic Imagination*, 111.

intervention of angels in human skirmishes on the battlefield.[140] Thus, to in-
quire about the sense in which the Prince of Light-led angels are *with* the human warriors is, at the same time, to consider the uniqueness of *WS's* picture
of angelic assistance. While difficult to describe with precision, I would suggest there are two main differences: 1.) the attitude and posture of the human
warriors anticipating angelic assistance; which, in turn, is connected to 2.) the
role the warriors have in relation to the angels.[141]

I have already highlighted how *WS* presupposes a close relationship between the people and angels, and that this relationship may be conveyed not
only through the notion that the human warriors are "the people of the holy
ones" but also through what has been called the "reverse" of the expression,
"the holy ones of the people." The idea arguably inherent especially in the
latter designation – that the people lay claim to the angels – reveals a pre-
sumptuousness that exceeds the confident but comparatively modest sentiments of other texts, particularly non-sectarian compositions.[142] If correct, the
employment of both expressions[143] means that angels and humans belong to
each other, thereby underscoring the angel-human composition of the Sons of
Light. Simultaneously, this bold stance elucidates the uniqueness of the angelic presence envisioned in *WS*: if, to use Michalak's distinctions (and some
help from English prepositions), angels who fight in the heavenly equivalent
of an earthly conflict can be described as *for* humans, whereas angels who
intervene directly in human conflicts can be described as both *for* and *with*
humans, the impression given by *WS* is that its angelic assistance is excep-

---

[140] On the intervention of the angels in *WS*, see the comments of Michalak, *Angels as
Warriors*, 155–157; Davidson, *Angels at Qumran* 220; Osten-Sacken, *Gott und Belial*, 221.

[141] See the complementary observations of Richard Bauckham, *The Climax of Prophecy*
(Edinburgh: T & T Clark, 1993), 210–227, who notes two Holy War traditions: one in
which God and his angels act without human contribution (e.g., Exod 14:13–14; 2 Kgs
19:32–35) and another in which humans take on a more active role (e.g., 1 En. 90:19); in
Bauckham's estimation, a distinctive aspect of *WS* is the *extent* of the human contribution.
Cf. Rowland, *The Open Heaven*, 42. According to Fletcher-Louis, *All the Glory*, passim,
WS presents humans as angelmorphically transcending human ontology. However, I concur
with Sullivan, *Wrestling with Angels*, 159, 228, that human transformation is not a distinctive element of *WS*. Cf. O'Neill, "Review of Fletcher-Louis, *Luke-Acts*, 225–230, who
similarly concludes, "claims to ontological identity are simply a misunderstanding of the
Jewish evidence [as] there is a clear and consistently maintained difference in kind between
God and angels and human beings. On this point, also see Michalak, *Angels as Warriors*,
151, 156.

[142] E.g., the reference to Michael as "your prince" (Dan 10:21) or the implied correspondence between the people and the covenant-marked "angels of the presence" (cf. Jub.
2:2, 18, 30; 6:18; 15:27; 30:18; 31:14).

[143] As well as "the elect ones of the holy people" (XII, 1) and "the people of the elect
ones" (XII, 5).

tional insofar as the angels fight both *for* and *in conjunction with* humans.[144] Said a different way, the anticipation of, knowledge of, and/or first-hand experience of angelic assistance as depicted in other texts is modest in comparison to *WS*,[145] where it is implied not only that the angels fight *for* humans but also that the angels will fight *in conjunction with* humans. Thus, as it pertains to *WS*, Michalak's categories of either a.) an angelic/heavenly battle; or b.) angelic intervention on earth, not only introduce a false dichotomy (as they may in other texts), but also are unable to articulate fully the distinctiveness of *WS*:

Table 7: The Uniqueness of the *War Scroll's* Angelic Assistance

Type	Description: Angels fight _____ humans
Angelic equivalent of an earthly battle	*for*
Angelic intervention on earth	*for* and *with*
1QM	*for* and *in conjunction with*

Though the anticipation of the presence of the angels prompted a heightened attention to ritual purity, the extreme sensitivities of a text like Josh 5:13–15 have all but disappeared[146] in that *WS* depicts the righteous human warriors and God's angels as comrades; in fact, this comradeship and the presumptuous posture underlying it may suggest that those responsible for *WS* saw themselves as functional equals of the angels. In this sense, angelic "assistance," though not incorrect, is descriptively deficient, and *WS* is rightly cited as a martial example of the well-known sectarian concept of angelic *fellowship*.[147]

---

[144] To be clear, I am using the English prepositions "for" and "in conjunction with" to highlight *the sense conveyed* by various passages, and my use of these words does not necessarily indicate the Hebrew combination of יַחַד and עִם, which, it has been suggested, frequently expresses the notion of angelic communion in *WS*; see, e.g., Michalak, *Angels as Warriors*, 154; Osten-Sacken, *Gott und Belial*, 223. This is an overstatement, however, as the adverb יַחַד and the preposition עִם only occur in proximity to one another at 1QM VII, 6 and XII, 4 (cf. 11Q14 1 II, 14–15: "For God is with you [עמכם] and [his holy] angels [ar]e [standing] in your congregation [בעדתכם]; see García Martínez et al., DJD 23, 248).

[145] This includes 2 Maccabees: while the Maccabean texts were not found among the Scrolls and therefore are not treated here, the affinities 2 Macc's depictions of celestial assistance have with *WS* are often noted. Cf., e.g., Yadin, *The Scroll of the War*, 237; Davidson, *Angels at Qumran*, 225–226. However, the anticipation of angelic support in 2 Macc is markedly less confident and presumptuous than that of 1QM (cf. 2 Macc 3:22–26; 5:2–4; 10:29–30; 11:6–12; 15:22–24 = 1 Macc 7:41).

[146] In Chapter 2, above, I briefly discussed Josh 5:13–15, a passage which makes clear that Joshua and his fellow Israelites are the subordinate beneficiaries of the angelic army.

[147] Cf. the following comments on the interaction of angels and humans in *WS*: Schäfer, *The Origins of Jewish Mysticism*, 151–152, who uses the term "fellowship" with the angels; Tuschling, *Angels and Orthodoxy*, 119, who refers to "communion" with the angels; Han-

III. The Sons of Light: The Identity of the Human Warriors

Thus far in my discussion of *WS*, I have commented little on the specific identity of those portrayed as having fellowship with the angels: the human warriors. While the presence of dualistic terminology (e.g., the "Sons of Light" or
"Prince of Light") has traditionally led to the conclusion that the warriors are
sect members, source-critical scholarship on *WS* and the ways in which the
text refers to "Israel" complicate this identification.

The majority view, based on external and internal evidence, is that *WS* is a
composite text.[148] As briefly noted above, the Cave 4 discoveries (the external evidence) support the view that 1QM was the product of a complex literary development, with some fragments deemed to be copies, others recensions, and still others considered to be evidence of different compositions on a
related subject.[149] But even before the Cave 4 material was published, scholars recognized that different traditions have been brought together in *WS* (the
internal evidence).[150] The general consensus is that *WS* preserves two major
traditions: a day-long, "best-of-seven" war against the "Kittim"[151] and their
allies referenced in columns I and XV–XIX; and a forty-year conflict – the so-
called "war of divisions" – against a broad range of international enemies
found in columns II–IX; it is also common to view the priest-led prayers found
in columns X–XIV as a collection that was added to give *WS* a liturgical di-

---

nah, *Michael and Christ*, 59, who speaks of the soldiers' "companionship" with the angels;
Michalak, *Angels as Warriors*, 152, dubs the humans and angels as "brothers in arms";
Sullivan, *Wrestling with Angels*, 156 n. 44, contends that "the term 'utopian' might be appropriate … , insomuch as the War Scroll seems to describe a synergy between humans and
angels as the 'Sons of Light.'"

[148] Early scholarship on 1QM considered it the work of a single author; cf. Yadin, *The
Scroll of the War*, 3, 6, 14–17, 243; and especially Carmignac, *La Règle de la Guerre*, xi–
xiv. For a recent summary of the source-critical scholarship of *WS*, as well as a reading that
seeks to mitigate the need to rely upon redactional proposals, see Todd Scacewater, "The
Literary Unity of 1QM and its Three-Stage War," *RevQ* 27 (2015): 225–248.

[149] See Brian Schultz, *Conquering the World: The War Scroll (1QM) Reconsidered*
(STDJ 76; Leiden: Brill, 2009), 391, who classifies the manuscripts as follows: 4Q492,
4Q494, and 4Q495 are copies of 1QM; 4Q471, 4Q491, 4Q493, and 4Q496 are recensions of
1QM; and 4Q285 and 11Q14 are different compositions with similar (martial) subject matter. Also see Duhaime, *War Texts*, 50–53.

[150] Hence what Davidson, *Angels at Qumran*, 214, refers to as the "difficulties in ascer-
taining the actual course of the war"; see below.

[151] On the use of "Kittim" as an epithet for foreign antagonists in the Qumran texts, see
James E. Bowley, "Prophets, Kittim, and Divine Communication in the Dead Sea Scrolls:
Condemning the Enemy Without, Fighting the Enemy Within," in *Enemies and Friends of the
State: Ancient Prophecy in Context* (ed., Christopher A. Rollston; University Park: Ei-
senbrauns, 2018), 497–499.

mension.[152] While some scholars consider the first column of 1QM and its dualistic language to be the earliest or among the earliest part(s) of the document,[153] others have argued that the traditions preserved in columns II–IX – which have been said to be largely void of the dualism of column I – should be considered the oldest sections of *WS*, and that any dualistic language and sentiments were later added.[154] The question as to whether the dualism of 1QM is early or late is, of course, reminiscent of scholarly discussions of *TTS* and its relationship to 1QS, and while I concur with Sullivan that "there does not seem to be any specific set of angel beliefs related to any one level of redactional activity,"[155] each view potentially has implications for identifying the human warriors and their relationship to the angels.

A recent and detailed argument for the priority of column I is that of Schultz, who, in keeping with the consensus view that a source-critical distinction can be made between columns I and II, reads the redacted 1QM as outlining a two-stage war: the seven-stage battle against the Kittim in column I (which he considers the inspiration for columns XV–XIX), followed by the decades-long, international conflict in column II–IX. In support of this reading, he notes the precedence for two-stage conflicts in a variety of texts (cf. Mic 5:4–5; 1 En. 85–90; Pss. Sol. 17; 4QFlor).[156] Schultz then draws the following conclusion: whereas the protagonists of the initial battle are primarily

---

[152] On *WS* as a liturgical text, see Daniel F. Falk, "Prayer, Liturgy, and War," in *The War Scroll, Violence, War and Peace*, 275–294.

[153] For a helpful overview, see Duhaime, *The War Texts*, 44–48, who highlights the various articulations of this understanding: e.g., André Dupont-Somer, *The Essene Writings from Qumran* (trans. Geza Vermes; Oxford: Basil Blackwell, 1961), 166, viewed columns XV–XIX as an annex to columns I and II–XIV; van der Ploeg, *Le Rouleau de la Guerre*, 7–22, considered column I and XV–XIX as the earliest sections, noting the war therein is different from the decades-long conflict envisioned in column II; Osten-Sacken, *Gott und Belial*, 29–115, emphasized the influence of biblical passages and themes – especially Dan 11:40–45 – on column I, with the dualistic tone and language of I, 11–15 serving as the framework for columns XV–XIX, and the war tradition of columns II–VI subsequently added to this foundation. Also see Schultz, *Conquering the World*, 86–169, 391–402, who supports the priority of the dualistic first column and with whom I will interact, below.

[154] Cf. Davies, *1QM, the War Scroll*, 123; idem, "Dualism in the Qumran War Texts," in *Dualism in Qumran*, 8–19; Jean Duhaime, "La redaction de 1QM XIII et l'évolution du dualisme à Qumrân," *RB* 84 (1977): 210–238; idem, "Dualistic Reworking," 43–51.

[155] Sullivan, *Wrestling with Angels*, 156.

[156] A welcomed aspect of how Schultz, *Conquering the World*, 237, reads the text is his attempt to decipher the logic of 1QM as it stands (i.e., despite the various sources): "the focus on source and redaction criticisms has resulted in a lack of effort to seek out the text's inherent coherence, with the result that M has been labeled as being more disunified than it really is." Cf. Martin G. Abegg, Jr., Review of Brian Schultz, *Conquering the World: The War Scroll (1QM) Reconsidered*, *BBR* 22 (2012): 589: "[Schultz] brings a welcome sense of unity to the message of the text while at the same time allowing the inconsistencies a voice that sheds important light on the evolution and context of the work's creation."

sect members, a national "restoration" before the second stage means that Israel *en masse* will fight in the international campaign. A discrepancy between columns I and II serves as a main impetus for his reading: in column I, "the Sons of Light" are in some way associated with "the Sons of Levi, The Sons of Judah, and the Sons of Benjamin" (I, 1–4), who will fight against not only the Kittim but also apostate Jews dubbed "violators of the covenant" (I, 2);[157] in contrast, column II involves "all the tribes of Israel" (II, 7), hence the need for some kind of national restoration between the two stages of the war.

While Schultz's reading of *WS* is well-argued, I am convinced that some of his language can be nuanced. For example, he argues that the Sons of Light are comprised of not "just the sectarians,"[158] and that generic terms such as עם אל, "the people of God," support this contention.[159] Similarly, though Schultz notes instances in the Scrolls when עדה, "congregation," is employed as a sectarian self-designation in non-eschatological contexts, he suggests that the Qumran movement preferred to use this word in reference to a national resto-

---

[157] Traditionally, the three tribes mentioned at I, 2 have been understood as a sectarian self-designation (i.e., synonymous with the Sons of Light). Cf., e.g., Yadin, *The Scroll of the War*, 4, 212 n. 3; Harvey, *The True Israel*, 26; Alex P. Jassen, "Violent Imaginaries and Practical Violence in the War Scroll," in *The War Scroll, Violence, War and Peace*, 185. However, the grouping of Levi, Judah, and Benjamin is somewhat unusual (on this point, see Davies, *1QM, the War Scroll*, 114 n. 7, who observes that "Judah and Levi" are the norm), with the only instance of the three together in the Scrolls occurring in the non-sectarian text 4Q372 (see Eileen M. Schuller, "4Q372 I: A Prayer About Joseph," *RevQ* 14 [1990]: 349–376). Hanan Eshel, "The Prayer of Joseph from Qumran, a Papyrus from Masada and the Samaritan Temple on Mount Gerizim," *Zion* 56 [1991]: 125–136 [Hebrew], has suggested that the references to Levi, Judah, and Benjamin are unfavourable in both 4Q372 and 1QM, and thus the three tribes should not be understood as a sectarian appropriation but as a designation for the antagonists of the Qumran movement. Cf. John Screnock, "Word Order in the War Scroll (1QM) and Its Implications for Interpretation," *DSD* 18 (2011): 29–44, who finds syntactical support for Eshel's reading. Also see Bergsma, "Qumran Self-Identity," 179–186, who observes that "Judah" can sometimes be used to refer disparagingly to those whom the sect considered apostate (cf., e.g., 4Q171 II, 13–15). In a detailed response to Eshel's reading, Schultz, *Conquering the World*, 103–124, proposes that the three tribes encompass all Jews in Judea – sectarian and non-sectarian – who, unlike the wayward "violators of the covenant," had not aligned themselves with the king of the Kittim; see further, below.

[158] Schultz, *Conquering the World*, 123–124.

[159] In reference to the term עם אל, Schultz, *Conquering the World*, 124, states that "in the entire Qumran corpus, it is used only in M" (cf. 1QM I, 5; III, 13; 4Q496 10 4 [reconstructed]; but also see 4Q246 II, 4). Schultz further suggests that the usage of this phrase may stem from an early point in the history of the sect when members "would have allowed for the existence of others who, although not part of their movement, sought to remain faithful to God in contrast to those who were 'violators of the covenant.'" I will return to these issues later in this chapter. For now, it is sufficient to note that the use of a "generic" phrase in a sectarian document may not be indicative of openness to outsiders but rather sectarian appropriation/reduction of a broadly nationalistic source.

ration that would characterize the messianic age, particularly as delineated in the *Rule of the Congregation* (e.g., 1QSa I, 1).[160] However, Schultz relegates to a footnote the following key insight that should be granted much greater prominence: "the messianic age [is the period] during which *all Israel will have joined the sectarians* [emphasis mine]."[161] The reason this qualification is so crucial is that, if not granted its proper weight, both the uniqueness of the sectarian convictions and the confidence with which they were held are in danger of being undermined. In other words, to speak of a "restoration" of Israel in *WS* without due significance granted to the fact that *WS* either labels other Jews as "violators of the covenant" (I, 2) or shares the dualistic language of other sectarian texts (e.g., 1QS, *11QMelch*) – texts that effectively envision and prescribe the reconstitution of Israel or claim for the sect the privileged angelic assistance that was previously a prerogative of the Jewish people more broadly understood – may unintentionally suggest that a national restoration would come at the expense of conversion[162] to the ways and outlook of the Qumran movement.[163] In this sense, the comment of Sanders (quoted by Schultz) has the potential to be misleading: "the sect did not, at least very often, think of itself as 'Israel' *during the time of its historical existence* [emphasis retained]."[164] Indeed, the sect may not have ever claimed that in the

---

[160] Note the words of 1QSa I, 1: זה הסרך לכול עדת ישראל באחרית הימים, "And this is the rule for the entire congregation of Israel in the last days." But especially in its absolute form, Schultz, *Conquering the World*, 353–365, claims that the use of עדה in the sectarian scrolls often envisioned a unified Israel of the messianic age. In support, he observes that 1QS never uses "*the* congregation" to refer to the sectarians and all occurrences of the expression in 1QM are found in columns II–V, a section which he considers to be part of the post-restoration stage of the eschatological war. But even if correct in his observation that the absolute use of עדה has a special eschatological connotation, "*the* congregation" may simply refer to the coming together of various *sectarian* communities at the end of days, a point with which Schultz briefly interacts but implicitly dismisses in favour of emphasizing a national restoration scenario. More importantly, the language of restoration has the potential to detract from the stringency of the sectarian outlook; see below.

[161] Schultz, *Conquering the World*, 357 n. 93.

[162] I use "conversion" cautiously, cognizant that it is a problematic modern concept.

[163] The language of "restoration" may more appropriately describe the scenario envisioned near the conclusion of the *Animal Apocalypse* (cf. 1 En. 90:32–35); see Chapter 3, above.

[164] E. P. Sanders, *Paul and Palestinian Judaism: A Comparison of Patterns of Religion* (Minneapolis: Fortress, 1977), 254; as cited in Schultz, *Conquering the World*, 365, who on the same page (n. 120) quotes the relatively optimistic conclusions of Collins, "The Construction of Israel," 34, 38. However, as I have previously noted, Collins' more recent comments on the same subject (see idem, *The Scriptures and Sectarianism*, 181–182) rightly stresses the demands of the sectarian covenant and specifically cites 1QM I, 3 to make the point that the Qumran movement did not anticipate all Israel as having a place in the world to come. Cf. Martin G. Abegg, "The Covenant of the Qumran Sectarians," in *The Concept of Covenant in the Second Temple* (eds., Stanley E. Porter and Jacqueline C. de Roo; JSJSup 71; Leiden: Brill, 2003), 97, who also quotes Sanders and refers to the writer

present they were the *sum total* of Israel, and the specific instances of the Qumran movement referring to itself as "*the* congregation" may be primarily reserved for eschatological contexts. But these observations should not detract from the point that the sect envisioned itself as the *true* Israel[165] to which apostate Jews must join if they wanted to be considered part of God's legitimate people, and that "violators of the covenant," who have rejected the sectarian ways,[166] must accept their covenantal ideal.[167] Indeed, Schultz points out that there are instances elsewhere in the Qumran texts when "all Israel" is used as "an apologetic that God's covenant for the sect is intended for the entire nation" (cf. CD XV, 5; XVI, 1).[168] As Bautch comments, the sect does not envision

---

of 1QSa as presaging "a time when the need would no longer be only for a Rule of the Community ..., but rather for a Rule of the Congregation *of Israel*. ... At the end of the age, Israel would finally become coincident with the sectarian community [emphasis retained]." While Abegg's last statement, that Israel would "become coincident" with the sectarians, is clearer than the language of a "national restoration," he does not explicitly mention a conversion of ethnic Israel to the ways of the sect. Bergsma, "Qumran Self-Identity," 178–189, also uses the language of an eschatological "restoration" of the twelve tribes to describe the scenario envisioned by various sectarian texts (including *WS*; cf. 1QM III, 13; V, 1), but he simultaneously emphasizes that the Qumran movement envisioned themselves as "the vanguard" or "spearhead" of such hopes, strongly implying that the prophetic expectations of a unified "Israel" (cf. Isa 11:11–12; Jer 23:7–8; Ezek 37:19–22) could not be legitimately realized outside of the sectarian covenant.

[165] On the Qumran movement as "the true Israel," see the excursus earlier in the present chapter. Cf. Philip R. Davies, "The 'Damascus' Sect and Judaism," in *Pursuing the Texts: Studies in Honour of Ben Zion Wacholder* (eds., John C. Reeves and John Kampen; JSOTSup 184; Sheffield: JSOT Press, 1994), 75–77, whose comments admittedly pertain to another text (*Damascus Document*), but nonetheless articulate well how the sectarians viewed themselves vis-à-vis the rest of "Israel"/other Jews: "Did the sect regard itself as [the] true Israel? The answer is clearly 'yes', though the language of CD does not place radical stress on this. ... The name 'Israel' can ... be used not only of the nation of the past, but also the nation of the present. But we also find 'Israel' applying to the sect: 'cities of Israel' in 12.19, clearly referring to its dwellings (cf. the 'seed of Israel' in 12.22), and in 12.8 the חבור ישראל (cf. חבר in 14.16). In 3.13, too, the 'covenant with Israel' is that made with the sect. One should not make much of this ... . The sect is the real Israel, and is therefore Israel; but there is also a wider Israel, a false Israel, but still an Israel that cannot easily be called anything else. The wider Israel, according to CD, is misled by Belial .... It is to this Israel that the sect of CD basically opposes itself ... ."

[166] Cf. Davidson, *Angels at Qumran*, 216: "The 'offenders against the covenant' [see Dan 11:32] are apostate Jews, meaning those Jews not belonging to the sect."

[167] For discussion of this point and the role of 1QSa in articulating the relationship between the sect and ethnic Israel at the eschaton, see Bautch, *Glory and Power*, 139–153.

[168] While Schultz, *Conquering the World*, 364, mentions that most uses of "all Israel" occur in an eschatological context (i.e., his national restoration scenario at the eschaton), he does not comment on how an "apologetic" use of the phrase might be related to the eschatological occurrences he references.

a special destiny for the nation of Israel because it understands the future apocalyptically in terms of the group's own vindication and exaltation; events in the final age will bring the group itself to assume the role of Israel. One clear example of this is found in 1QSa, which begins with the sect referring to itself as עדת ישראל באחרית הימים, "the congregation of Israel in the final days." ... [T]he sectarian nature of the Jewish group responsible for the Dead Sea Scrolls shapes ... its understanding of Israel ... . [T]he "emphasis [is] on a covenantal obedience and a status of perfection rather than membership by birth."[169]

Thus, rather than saying that the Sons of Light of WS are not *just* the sectarians, I would suggest a more helpful way of summarizing the matter is to say that it was hoped that the Sons of Light would eventually encompass not just those who were *presently* sectarian and that any yearnings for eschatological unity would come via conversion.[170]

Not surprisingly, the discrepancy between WS's opening two columns has also been addressed by those who support the priority of column II. Davies, for example, argues that the tradition of the twelve tribes fighting against their enemies (II, 10) "has not been obliterated" in column I but has undergone a dualistic revision.[171] According to his reading, the reference to Levi, Judah, and Benjamin (I, 2) is a vestige of the "pan-Israelite" tradition of column II.[172] But rather than viewing the use of the three tribes as a way of distinguishing the sect from other Jews, Davies claims that it is an intra-sect distinction: the sons of Levi, Judah, and Benjamin, who are dubbed in I, 2 גולת המדבר, "the exiles of the wilderness/desert,"[173] will later be joined by other sectarians, fellow Sons of Light who are similarly dubbed exiles – but exiles from "the wilderness of the peoples/nations" (I, 3). In Davies' own words:

It seems that by the three tribes mentioned, something less than the whole of the Judean community is meant; only the "exiles of the wilderness" are to be understood. These await the return of others of their number from exile in the "wilderness of the nations." Since 1QM was discovered amongst the Qumran caves, and since other Qumran texts refer to "sons of light," we can fairly safely equate the "sons of light" with the Qumran sect. These men were not only from the tribes of Judah, Benjamin and Levi, but were also "exiles of the

---

[169] Bautch, *Glory and Power*, 139–140, who incorporates a quotation of Newsom, *The Self as Symbolic Space*, 117. I will reference similar readings, below.

[170] Cf. Sanders, *Paul and Palestinian Judaism*, 254, who, despite his previously cited contention that the Qumran movement did not frequently "think of itself as 'Israel' *during the time of its historical existence*," also states the following: "The [sectarian] community believed that eschatological Israel would be formed by the *conversion* of the rest of Israel to the way of the sect [emphasis mine]."

[171] Davies, "Dualism in the Qumran War Texts," 13, who further notes that this "dualistic revision of the entire scheme of the war in col. i, however dramatic its effect, does not therefore seek to obliterate the already existing non-dualistic scheme, but as far as possible to accommodate it. Obviously, only in this way was it feasible to reuse so much of the material already in existence."

[172] Davies, *1QM, the War Scroll*, 114–115.

[173] Presumably, the desert/wilderness *of Jerusalem* (I, 3), which is to be differentiated from the desert/wilderness *of the peoples or nations*; see below.

wilderness" inasmuch as they lived by the shore of the Dead Sea. Apparently, these men were awaiting the return of others of their number from the "wilderness of the nations."[174]

In sum, despite utilizing a source that originally espoused a pan-Israelite ideal, Davies argues that 1QM as it now stands is the product of a dualistic revision that restricts the earlier, nation-wide tradition to the sectarians.[175]   Correspondingly, Duhaime contends that even if the sources were non-sectarian, the redacted product contributed to the sectarian identity in that it consolidated a break with what was considered a perverted environment.[176]

Both of the views just surveyed have strengths and weaknesses. Although Schultz' emphasis on a large-scale national restoration helps to mitigate the problem of a small sect engaging in an international military campaign,[177] he favours an early date (mid 2nd cent. BCE) for at least column I,[178] a view that

---

[174] Davies, *1QM, the War Scroll*, 115.

[175] According to his reading of the text, Davies, *Dualism and the Qumran War Texts*, 19, explains that the editor of 1QM "did not clearly separate his own conception from that of the existing tradition" (e.g., Israel becomes the Sons of Light, and non-sectarian Jews and the nations become the Sons of Darkness). Also note Davidson, *Angels at Qumran*, 215: "Even the people of Israel, as 'offenders against the covenant' (1QM I, 3) are included in the catalogue of the sect's enemies." Hannah, *Michael and Christ*, 75: "[T]he sectarians define 'Israel' … narrowly." Collins, *The Scriptures and Sectarianism*, 192: "[The sectarians] rejected the notion that all Israel has a share in the world to come, even if they still tended to equate the Sons of Light with Israel in texts like the War Scroll that referred to the eschatological time. The division between the Sons of Light and Sons of Darkness was not universalistic – Gentiles were assumed to belong to the Sons of Darkness except for the poorly attested case of proselytes. But the covenantal community was no longer equated with ethnic Israel." Cf. Newsom, "Constructing 'We, You, and Others,'" 13.

[176] Jean Duhaime, "La règle de la guerre (1QM) et la construction de l'identité sectaire," in *Defining Identities*, 145: "Il ne fait cependant aucun doute que sa rédaction finale s'est faite dans un groupe à tendance sectaire forte et qu'elle a servi ses intérêts à l'époque tourmentée ou l'occupation romaine de la Palestine divisait la communaute juive."

[177] On this point, see Schultz, *Conquering the World*, 158–159 n. 247.

[178] Schultz, *Conquering the World*, 158–159, considers column I to have been composed before 63 BCE. He gives three reasons, the second and third of which are closely related: i.) The clear allusions to Dan 11:40–45 in column I (on this, see Osten-Sacken, *Gott und Belial*, 28–62; Davidson, *Angels at Qumran*, 222, 232) were likely attempts to address the fact that both the death of Antiochus Epiphanes (= king of the north in Dan 11:40) and the redemption that was supposed to follow Antiochus' death (Dan 12:1–3) did not happen as per Daniel. In the words of Schultz: "The fact that M's 'king of the Kittim' is standing in for Daniel's 'king of the north' and that the Qumranites never called the Roman leaders 'kings' supports the Seleucid identification of M's 'kittim of Assyria,' and confirms that at least column 1 of M was composed prior to Pompey's conquest of Jerusalem." ii.) Schultz is sympathetic to the view that the Teacher of Righteousness was the High Priest during the so-called *intersacredotium* (159–153 BCE). Thus, after the Teacher's priestly tenure, the sectarians would have been unsatisfied with the temple establishment and conceivably would have desired a war against such "violators of the covenant." That 1 Macc 9:23 speaks of "transgressors of the law" and "doers of unrighteousness" may lend credence to

stands in a degree of tension with the recent trend in Qumran scholarship that
sees the dualism of the sectarian texts as secondarily adopted and thus later.[179]
At the same time, caution is warranted if the presence or absence of dualism is
pressed too hard in the service of determining the date of a given section of
WS. As noted above, Davies considers columns II–IX to be the earliest tradition in *WS*, in part because of the lack of "dualistic language,"[180] and to be
sure, the *language* of light and darkness is largely absent[181] from these columns. But dualistic thought can be expressed beyond this characteristic terminology. Indeed, the dualism of *WS* – unlike *TTS* in 1QS – is not predomi-
nately confined to an easily distinguished block of material, as the notion of a
battle between opposing angelic forces permeates all sections of *WS*.[182] Thus,

---

the possibility that the sectarians would have found other Jews who shared their displeasure
with the Jerusalem priesthood. iii.) If 4QMMT was written to Jonathan before he became
High Priest (so Hanan Eshel, "4QMMT and the History of the Hasmonean Period," in
Reading 4QMMT: New Perspectives on Qumran Law and History [eds., John Kampen and
Moshe Bernstein; SBLSymS 2; Atlanta: Scholars Press, 1996], 62–63), it may have been,
according to Schultz, "at a point when [the sectarians] still hoped for broad endorsement of
their ideologies among the general population, that segment which in their estimation had
not yet disqualified itself from being part of the 'people of God.'"

[179] Precisely how much later, of course, depends on one's conclusions regarding the priority of the various traditions included in *WS* and when it is determined these traditions
were brought together as found in 1QM. While there is little agreement, scholars are relatively sure of the limits of *WS*: the references to Dan 11–12 indicate a *terminus a quo* of
164 BCE, and paleographical analysis of 1QM suggests a *terminus ad quem* of the mid 1st
cent. BCE. For a thorough treatment of the dating of the M tradition, see Duhaime, *The
War Texts*, 65–101. Davies, "Dualism in the Qumran War Texts," 12, allows that *WS* may
represent the earliest form of Qumran dualism, but he rejects the notion that *WS* is *ground-
ed* in dualism, as we have seen. I have also mentioned that Schultz, *Conquering the World*,
158 n. 247, is sympathetic to a mid 2nd cent. BCE dating of the dualistic column I, and that
he considers the hopeful tone of the contemporaneous 4QMMT to be indicative of an optimism that manifested itself in the outlook that there were still non-sectarian Jews who had
not yet disqualified themselves from being part of the people of God. Such optimism, as
discussed, coheres with what Schultz posits as a national restoration in the midst of *WS's*
two-stage eschatological war. Intriguingly, Collins, *Scriptures and Sectarianism*, 194,
employs 4QMMT to draw quite a different conclusion: MMT indicates that the sect's split
with other Jews was primarily for legal reasons and therefore dualism was likely "adopted
secondarily to provide a theological explanation of the social division." Collins' comments
are made specifically regarding *TTS* (see above), but they highlight the trend that sees dualism as a product of later redaction. Cf. Duhaime, "Dualistic Reworking," 35–36.

[180] Davies, "Dualism in the Qumran War Texts," 13.

[181] But see Davidson, *Angels at Qumran*, 225, who notes "Sons of Darkness" at III, 6, 9.

[182] As I have already highlighted; cf. Collins, *The Apocalyptic Imagination*, 168, who
makes this observation explicitly. It is, therefore, inaccurate for Davies, "Dualism in the
Qumran War Texts," 16–17, to describe the dualistic portrait of *WS* as "rather slight."

given the prominence of angelic dualism throughout *WS*, detailed text-critical proposals need not be hastily accepted.[183]

Given the difficulties surrounding *WS's* source-critical history and date of composition or compiling,[184] it is fortunate that sorting out the particulars is not demanded for my purposes. I am most concerned with the final form of the text, and what this discussion has highlighted is that when it comes to the identity of the human warriors, diverse appraisals of the source-critical history of *WS* arrive at roughly the same conclusion: whether through what Schultz refers to as a large-scale national, eschatological *restoration* – though I have suggested that *conversion* is a better term – or via the appropriation of pan-Israelite tradition (or a combination thereof), *WS* casts those who fight in conjunction with the angels as the true, sectarian-defined Israel.[185] This conclusion is in-keeping with the angelological convictions of *TTS* and *11QMelch* insofar as it is the unique privilege of the members of the Qumran movement to benefit from what was traditionally the assistance offered to the nation more generously defined. And again, it seems that an integral component of what it meant to be sectarian-defined Israel was to have access to this succor.

But as I have shown, *WS* speaks of the relationship between the humans and angels in an even loftier manner than *TTS* and *11QMelch*: a presumptuous mutuality is envisioned between the angels and the sectarian warriors, who together comprise the Sons of Light. Both this mutuality and the notion that privileged angelic succor is an integral component of what it means to be the

---

[183] This is especially the case if such proposals are prompted by a perceived tension between God's supremacy and a high-profile role for principal angel figures (see, e.g., Duhaime, "Dualistic Reworking," 43–46; cf. Davies, *1QM, the War Scroll*, 109), because even within texts that focus on angels, the sovereignty of the God of Israel is never in doubt. On this point, see Hannah, *Michael and Christ*, 63, who speaks of the "limited dualism" of the sect (e.g., 1QH[a] IX, 9–41) and God's superiority to all angels (cf. 1QH[a] XV, 31–32; XVIII, 8). Cf. Xeravits, "The Angel's Self-Revelation in Tobit 12," 1416.

[184] Cf. Duhaime, *War Texts*, 100–101: "All things considered, the date of the composition of 1QM as we have it remains quite elusive. Many indications point to the Hellenistic period … . In this hypothesis, 1QM 1 would have been written very early after Daniel 11–12 and the Kittim would be the Greeks; the weaponry and strategy would have been assembled within a very short period of time. But no argument for this dating seems really compelling, either; and the texts could be a late composition or reworking from the Roman period. In this case, the vision of Daniel 11–12 would have been reinterpreted to fit the expectations of a group under occupation by the Romans, the Kittim of the time, whose weapons and tactics could be observed almost on a daily basis. The document would have eventually incorporated early material and slightly updated it."

[185] See the comments of Robert A. Kugler, "The War Rule Texts and a New Theory of the People of the Dead Sea Scrolls: A Brief Thought Experiment," in *The War Scroll, Violence, War and Peace*, 170–171, who notes that those behind the later (dualistic) form of the document (especially columns XV–XIX) seem to have adopted a "one against all" mentality and "a radicalised view of themselves."

true Israel are best seen in an integral passage near the end of the extant document. 1QM XVII, 5–9 reads as follows:[186]

היום מועדו להכניע ולהשפיל שר ממשלת   5 ...

6 רשעה וישלח עזר עוֹלָמִים לגוֹרל |פ]דֹותו בנבורת מלאך האדיר למשרת מיכאל באור
עולמים

7 להאיר בשמחה בּרית ישראל[187] שלום וברכה לגורל אל להרים באלים משרת מיכאל
וממשלת

8 ישראל בכול בשר ישמח צדק בּמרומים וכול בני אמתו יגילו בדעת עולמים ואתם בני
בריתו

9 התחזקו במצרף אל עד יניף ידו וֹמִלֹא מצרפיו רזיו למעמדכם vacat

5 ... Today is His appointed time to subdue and to humble the Prince of the dominion of
6 wickedness. He will send eternal assistance to the lot to be redeemed by Him through the
might of an angel: He has magnified the authority of Michael in eternal light,
7 to light up in joy the covenant of Israel, peace and blessing to the lot of God, so as to raise
among the gods the authority of Michael and the dominion
8 of Israel over all flesh. Righteousness shall rejoice up on high, and all sons of His truth
shall be glad in eternal knowledge. But you, sons of his covenant,
9 be strong in God's crucible, until he shall lift up His hand and shall complete His testing
through his mysteries with regard to your standing vacat

It is helpful to view the beginning of this passage as answering a series of implied questions: How will God win the war and defeat the angelic leader of wickedness and his forces? By sending help to his redeemed lot. By what means will God help? Via the "might of an angel,"[188] who is frequently identified as Michael, though some have suggested that this is an even higher-ranking angel, whose lofty stature ensures the eminence of Michael and the forces he commands.[189] While there is merit to both interpretations, this an-

---

[186] The translation is from Yadin, *The Scroll of the War*, 340, with minor adjustments.

[187] On the restoration of ברית ישראל from fragments, see Duhaime, "War Scroll," 132.

[188] As noted, the reading adopted here is that of Yadin, *The Scroll of the War*, 340, who understands האדיר to be a verb (cf. Isa 42:21). However, the word is often considered to be an adjective modifying מלאך, resulting in the translation "majestic angel." While there are admittedly various valid translations of lines 6–7, reading האדיר as an adjective may not be the preferable option because it means that the clause following it is without a verb. Cf., e.g., Duhaime, "War Scroll," 133, who is forced to supply a verb, which is in parentheses: "He has sent an everlasting help to the lot whom he has redeemed through the might of the *majestic* angel. (He will set) the authority of Michael in everlasting light." Other translations understand למשרת מיכאל as continuing the construct chain; e.g., Wise, Abegg, and Cook, *DSSANT*, 165: "... by the power of the majestic angel *of* the authority of Michael"; Vermes, *CDSSE*, 183: "... by the might of the princely Angel *of* the kingdom of Michael."

[189] Heiser, "The Divine Council," §7.4, argues that this angel should be identified with others from the Hebrew Bible and the Qumran texts, including the Angel of Yhwh, the "one like a son of man," the Prince of the Host, the Prince of Light(s), God's Angel of Truth, and Melchizedek. As previously noted, Heiser interprets these figures to be various presentations of God's "vice-regent," second only to Yhwh in the hierarchy of the divine council.

gel's identity is not my primary concern, here. More significant for my purposes is that the answer to the third implied question – What are the results of this angelic help? – includes two references to "the authority of Michael." Thus, even if the מלאך of line 6 is not Michael, *WS* is seemingly at pains to underscore Michael's exaltation, which is similar to the outlook of the Book of Daniel (cf. Dan 12:1). Moreover, the full answer to the third implied question, which is showcased in lines 6–8, complements the close relationship between angels and humans discussed thus far:

Table 8: Parallelism of 1QM XVII, 6–8

להאיר בשמחה ברית ישראל	האדיר למשרת מיכאל באור עולמים
to light up in joy *the covenant of Israel*	He has magnified *the authority of Michael* in eternal light

שלום וברכה לגורל אל
Peace and blessing
to the lot of God

וממשלת ישראל בכול בשר	להרים באלים משרת מיכאל
and *the dominion of Israel* over all flesh	so as to raise among the gods *the authority of Michael*

Several items require comment. First, that there is an intimate connection between heaven and earth is indicated by two statements that parallel Michael

---

But Heiser does *not* consider Michael to be a figure who occupies this lofty standing. As it pertains to 1QM XVII, though Heiser follows Yadin in reading האדיר in line 6 as a verb, he interprets the phrase בגבורת מלאך as adverbially related to האדיר and thus deems the sense to be as follows: "*by the might of an angel* (i.e., Michael's superior) God has magnified the authority of Michael." While this reading perhaps makes it easier to posit a distinction between Michael and an angelic superior, it does not necessitate the interpretation of Michael as a subordinate. Instead, it may be that Michael himself is the מלאך through whom God magnifies "the authority of Michael," a designation which should be understood in a collective sense (i.e., the righteous angelic forces under Michael's command). Moreover, a challenge to viewing Michael as occupying a subordinate rank is that the exaltation of "the authority of Michael" is said to be "among the gods" (באלים), which may also complicate/undermine the emphasis Heiser's places on the fact that Michael is never explicitly referred to as a "god" in early Jewish texts. For other readings that understand the angel of line 6 as superior to Michael, see Bampfylde, "The Prince of the Host," 131–132; Helmer Ringrenn, *The Faith of Qumran: Theology of the Dead Sea Scrolls* (Philadelphia: Fortress, 1963), 82–83. Cf. Johannes P. Rohland, *Der Erzengel Michael* (BZRGG 19; Leiden: Brill, 1977), 16, who equates Michael with the Angel of Yhwh, whose jurisdiction is earth, while the angel of line 6 is Israel's advocate in heaven.

and Israel,[190] the first of which uses light/illumination (אור) imagery. Second, ברית ישראל is a clear reference to God's people,[191] but more curious is משרת מיכאל, which is obviously angelic, but in what sense? While it may be that משרה refers to the archangel's "authority"[192] in a literal sense, it more likely includes a collective character: that is, משרת מיכאל is a reference to the righteous angels Michael assists and those through and over whom he has sway.[193] The advantage of the latter understanding is that it better complements the collectivity of not only ברית ישראל in the first parallel but also ממשלת ישראל[194] in the second.

Thus, in this passage we have the leader of the angelic host,[195] the collective angelic host,[196] and the people,[197] which is the same three-fold distinction observed in the Book of Daniel.[198] Moreover, a connection between the angelic forces and Israel suggests that: 1.) the former represent heavenly Israel

---

[190] Again, *contra* Fletcher-Louis, *All the Glory*, 472, who does not see a spatial dualism but rather a way of emphasizing an angelmorphic understanding of Israel.

[191] Specifically, those who accept the sectarian reconstitution of Israel. On this point, see my discussion, above. Cf., Davidson, *Angels at Qumran*, 226, who in reference to 1QM XVII, 7–8 states that "Israel (the sect) will gain dominance over all flesh." Davies, *1QM, the War Scroll*, 81, also specifies the "true Israel." This identification is confirmed by the use of "absolutizing" dualistic terminology similar to that of 1QS; see further, below.

[192] Most scholars read משרת as the construct form of the noun מִשְׂרָה, "authority" (cf. Isa 9:5–6). *Contra* Dupont-Sommer, "Règlement de la Guerre," 175, who considers the word to be a participle of שׁרת (cf. André Caquot, "Les Service des Anges," *RevQ* 13 [1988]: 425–429; allowed by Duhaime, "War Scroll," 133 n. 76), with the result that Israel is dubbed "the servant of Michael." If correct, *WS* would be stating that Israel, as the servant of Michael, is being exalted over the divine beings, and given the text's lofty claims, it would be tempting to draw this conclusion. But note the critique of Carmignac, *La Régle*, 239, who more plausibly argues for reading משרת as a construct form of מִשְׂרָה, as it better complements ממשלה which is parallel to it in lines 7–8.

[193] Davidson, *Angels at Qumran*, 227. Cf. Cargmignac, *Le Régle*, 238.

[194] For a collective sense of ממשלה, see 1QS III, 20, where the "dominion" of the Prince of Light includes the בני צדק (cf. 2 Chr 32:9, where ממשלה refers to the "military forces" of Sennacherib). Davies, *1QM, the War Scroll*, 81, suggests that the ממשלה of XVII, 8 is that of the "true Israel," a statement followed by parenthetical references to Dan 7:22, 27. He offers no commentary, but the Danielic verses pertain to the possession of the kingdom by "the holy ones" (7:22) and "the people of the holy ones" (7:27), thus suggesting that Davies reads ממשלה collectively.

[195] I.e., "the angel" of line 6, who may be Michael or, alternatively, Michael's superior.

[196] I.e., "the authority of Michael," which is the angelic retinue under Michael's command, which was undoubtedly envisioned as including its leader and namesake.

[197] I.e., "the covenant/dominion of Israel," namely, the sectarian-defined people of God.

[198] Cf. Collins, *Daniel*, 318, who observes a three-fold distinction in Dan 7 between the "one like a son of man" (the leader of the host), "the holy ones of the Most High" (the collective host), and "the people of the Holy Ones of the Most High" (Israel).

in a manner reminiscent of Dan 7–12;[199] and 2.) the amalgam of heavenly Israel and earthly Israel into one eschatological army is a sectarian usurpation and widening of the apocalyptic notion that "earthly realities reflect and mirror heavenly ones."[200] Therefore, the mention of Michael, Israel's angelic guardian *par excellence*,[201] is no accident. Third, between the two Michael-Israel parallels, a blessing is pronounced on the גורל אל. While seemingly awkward or extraneous, its placement underscores the human-angel composition of the Sons of Light. In short, heavenly Israel and the true earthly Israel, *as a unit*, constitute "the lot of God"[202] – a fact immediately reinforced by the second Michael-Israel parallel. Fourth, various dualistic terms are used, including גורל (e.g., 1QM I, 5–14; 1QS III, 24; 11Q13 II, 8) and ממשלה (e.g., 1QM I, 6; 1QS III, 20–23; 11Q13 II, 9), as well as בני אמת (e.g., 1QS IV, 5–6) and פדות (e.g., 1QM I, 12).[203] Again, while these terms may be indicative of redaction,[204] more certain is that they reiterate the sect's usurpation of the authority of Michael – that is, Israel's angelic succor – for themselves. Indeed, *WS* can suitably be grouped with texts Tuschling has described as performing an "apologetic function, justifying the secession from mainstream Judaism."[205] The end result is a document, which in the words of Duhaime, makes the definitive statement that "those who do not stand with the right leaders and the cosmic powers behind them will suffer destruction by the wrath of God."[206]

---

[199] Also see Duhaime, "Dualistic Reworking," 51, who observes that *WS's* victory is "the exaltation of Michael over all gods, perhaps in the manner of the exaltation of the 'one like a son of man' in Daniel 7." On the angels as heavenly Israel, see Collins, *Daniel*, 318–319, who speaks of the "synergism" between the people and their heavenly counterparts.

[200] Hannah "Guardian Angels," 420.

[201] It is important to note that 4Q491 11 I has been controversially associated with 1QM, including lines which have been dubbed "the hymn of Michael." Due to the association of this text with the *Self-Glorification Hymn*, I will examine 4Q491 in Chapter 5, below.

[202] Though *WS* has the sectarians belonging to "the lot of God" rather than that of an angel (see Davidson, *Angels at Qumran*, 224–227), the significance of this observation could easily be overstated since 1QM envisions a high-ranking angel as the leader of God's lot.

[203] Davies, *1QM, the War Scroll*, 80–81.

[204] E.g., Duhaime, "Dualistic Reworking," 46–51, suggests that 1QM has taken what was originally a God vs. Belial scenario from 4Q491 11 II, 13–18 and turned it into a Michael vs. Belial scenario, albeit one that is ordained by God. Cf. Davidson, *Angels at Qumran*, 228: "It is noteworthy that the opposition does not lie between God and Belial directly, but instead between Michael and Belial. There is a sense in which God himself stands outside of the conflict." However, if the angelic battle is primary in *WS*, the text is clear that all facets of the conflict and its timing are determined by God.

[205] So Tuschling, *Angels and Orthodoxy*, 117. Cf. Collins, *The Scriptures and Sectarianism*, 193–194, who, as noted, suggests that cosmic/angelic dualism was secondarily adopted as way of emphasizing separation from other Jews for *halakhic* and social reasons.

[206] Duhaime, "Dualistic Reworking," 55.

D. Summary

As "the people of the holy ones" (cf. 1QM X, 10; XII, 8), the members of the Qumran movement were convinced that they had a special connection to the angelic succor that was previously available to the nation more broadly defined, and this assertion is made in different ways, not only in *WS* but also in *TTS* and *11QMelch*. Moreover, all three texts suggest that this close relationship to their celestial guardians was an integral component of what it meant to be the true Israel. However, the sectarians also referred to these same guardians as "the holy ones of the people" (cf. 1QM VI, 6; XVI, 1), which, as I have argued, may point to the presumptuous belief that they laid claim to these angels. The eschatological war-time expression of the sect's lofty convictions was not simply that the angels would be *for* and/or *with* them: the unique picture of *WS* is that the angels of heavenly Israel would fight *in conjunction with* the warriors of the true earthly Israel, namely, the sectarian soldiers, who together constitute "the lot of God."

As numerous commentators have observed, the redactional history of *WS* is complex. But even if it is likely that earlier, pan-Israel sources have been employed in 1QM, it does not negate the fact that the redacted document brilliantly conveys that a sectarian-defined Israel would emerge victorious at the eschaton. Finally, and most significantly, for a group that considered itself to be the nation "as it ought to be," there arguably would have been no better claim than to boast that fidelity to the sectarian covenant included martial fellowship with the army of heavenly Israel led by the nation's celebrated angelic guardian *par excellence*, Michael, who, if not foremost among his angelic fellows, at the very least was envisioned as exalted and supported by his celestial superior for the well-being and glory of the people he represents.

Chapter 5

Angels Associated with Israel in the Sectarian Texts
Part II: Angelic Priests

A. Introduction

The notion of a sectarian-angel army in 1QM is grandiose, but other texts reveal something loftier in that the Qumran movement apparently did not consider fellowship with the angels as an experience that would have to wait for the eschatological war. A feature of several statements in the *Hodayot*, for example, is that at least some measure of angelic fellowship was envisioned as a present reality.[1] More specifically, the texts I will discuss in this chapter juxtapose the sectarian notion of angelic fellowship and the aforementioned Second Temple Period belief that heaven includes a sanctuary served by an angelic priesthood. The synthesis of these convictions resulted in claims that the Qumran movement enjoyed present liturgical communion with the priestly angels associated with Israel.[2] As I will demonstrate, boasts of liturgical fellowship with the angelic priests were closely connected to and enhanced the identity of the sect as the true Israel.

The chapter will be organized as follows. I will first examine the boasts of angelic fellowship in the *Hodayot* and in the hymn found at the end of 1QS. Next, I will examine the *Songs of the Sabbath Sacrifice*,[3] a document which is often viewed as one of the ritual mechanisms for achieving liturgical communion with the angels at Qumran. I will then turn to brief statements regarding communion with the angels in 4Q181, *Songs of the Sage*, and the *Rule of Blessings*. Lastly, I will discuss the *Self-Glorification Hymn*, whose angelic fellowship sentiments are the loftiest and boldest of all the Qumran texts and will thus serve as an appropriate way to conclude the chapter.

---

[1] See, e.g., Schäfer, *The Origins of Jewish Mysticism*, 124, 151–152, who differentiates between the future angelic fellowship of the *War Scroll* and the present angelic fellowship of the *Hodayot*. This distinction is a somewhat controversial point among scholars, and I will return to it, below.

[2] Cf. Schäfer, *The Origins of Jewish Mysticism*, 151–152; Weinfeld, *Normative and Sectarian Judaism*, 48, who list common praise with the angels as a form of angelic fellowship.

[3] The provenance of the *Songs of the Sabbath Sacrifice* is disputed, and I will address this issue in my treatment of the text.

B. The Hodayot and Related Texts

My discussion of the *Hodayot* will be comprised of two parts. I will first highlight the pertinent angelic fellowship passages, noting the nature and function of angelic communion in this text. I will then explore how angelic fellowship in the *Hodayot* – as well as analogous sentiments in 1QS XI, 7–8[4] – contributed to sectarian claims to be the true Israel. I have addressed the sectarian provenance of 1QS above; the *Hodayot* have also been considered sectarian texts from the time of their discovery.[5] While at least one so-called

---

[4] Given the *Hodayot*-like qualities of 1QS XI, it has been proposed that the *Hodayot* existed at least as early as 1QS, which is dated on the basis of paleography to the early 1st cent. BCE. This suggestion is supported by one of the Cave 4 *Hodayot* manuscripts; see Emile Puech, "Hodayot," *EDSS* 1:366. Cf. Devorah Dimant, "The Composite Character of Qumran Sectarian Literature," in eadem, *History, Ideology, and Bible Interpretation in the Dead Sea Scrolls: Collected Studies* (FAT 90; Tübingen: Mohr Siebeck, 2014), 178.

[5] Terminological and thematic affinities with other sectarian texts (e.g., reference to the "Maskil," dualistic elements, angelic fellowship, etc.) have led to the conclusion that the *Hodayot* were composed, edited, and/or complied by the Qumran movement. On this issue, see the essays of Devorah Dimant, "The Qumran Manuscripts: Contents and Significance" and "The Vocabulary of Qumran Sectarian Texts," in eadem, *History, Ideology, and Bible Interpretation*, 27–56, 57–100. On the possibility that some of the hymns pre-date the sect, see Angela Kim Harkins, "A New Proposal for Thinking About 1QH[a] Sixty Years After Its Discovery," in *Qumran Cave 1 Revisited: Texts from Cave 1 Sixty Years after Their Discovery: Proceedings of the Sixth Meeting of the IOQS in Ljubljana* (eds., Daniel K. Falk and Eibert J. C. Tigchelaar; STDJ 91; Leiden: Brill, 2010), 102–134; cf. eadem, "The Community Hymns Classification: A Proposal for Further Differentiation," *DSD* 15 (2008): 121–154; eadem, "Observations on the Editorial Shaping of the So-Called Community Hymns from 1QH[a] and 4QH[a] (4Q427)," *DSD* 12 (2005): 233–256. Like the sectarian S and M traditions, *Hodayot* manuscripts were found in Cave 1 (1QH[a] and 1QH[b]) and Cave 4 (4QH[a–e] and 4QHpap[f] [= 4Q427–432]). Dated paleographically to the early Herodian period, 1QH[a] is the latest extant witness to the H tradition. The sequence and earlier paleography of the Cave 4 manuscripts may suggest that the sequence of psalms in 1QH[a] was initiated at an early point in the tradition, even if certain witnesses may have only contained specific blocks of psalms; see further below. Earlier work on the *Hodayot* followed the column and line numbering of Eleazar Sukenik, *Otzar ha-Megillot ha-Genuzot* (Jerusalem: Bialik, 1954); cf. idem, *The Dead Sea Scrolls of the Hebrew University* (Jerusalem: Magnes, 1955). However, subsequent material and paleographic analysis of the scroll led Hartmut Stegemann, "Rekonstruktion der Hodajot: Ursprüngliche Gestalt und kritisch bearbeiteter Text der Hymnenrolle aus Höhle 1 von Qumran" (Ph.D. diss.; University of Heidelberg, 1963); idem, "The Material Reconstruction of 1QHodayot," in *The Dead Sea Scrolls: Fifty Years after their Discovery. Proceedings of the Jerusalem Congress, July 20–25, 1997* (eds., Lawrence H. Schiffman and Emmanuel Tov; Jerusalem: Israel Exploration Society in cooperation with the Shrine of the Book, Israel Museum, 2000), 272–284, and Emile Peuch, "Quelques aspects de la restauration du Rouleau des Hymns (1QH)," *JJS* 39 (1988): 38–55, to conclude independently from one another that the fragments and columns of 1QH[a] had been

recension of the *Self-Glorification Hymn* is related to the *Hodayot*, its content, proposed use, and possible relationship to other texts warrant a separate discussion later in this chapter.

I. Angelic Fellowship in the Hodayot: Present and Liturgical

In various places, the *Hodayot* specify the honour God has bestowed upon the speaker(s)[6] or the security in which God has enabled him/them to walk (cf.

---

published by Sukenik in an order that was not that of the original document. The renumbering by Stegemann and Puech is thought to reflect the original order and has been adopted in the recent DJD volumes. As such, the Hebrew text, sigla, column and line numbering, and translations of the *Hodayot* cited here follow Stegemann, Schuller, and Newsom, DJD 40. For the Cave 4 manuscripts, see Eileen M. Schuller, "4Q427–432," in *Qumran Cave 4.XX: Poetical and Liturgical Texts, Part 2* (DJD 29; Oxford: Clarendon, 1999), 69–232. For helpful overviews of various topics in *Hodayot* scholarship with bibliography, see eadem, "Recent Scholarship on the Hodayot," 119–162; eadem and L. DiTommaso, "A Bibliography of the Hodayot, 1948–1996," *DSD* 4 (1997): 55–101. Also see Dimant, "The Composite Character," 177–179, who provides a concise summary of pertinent issues.

[6] Traditionally, the voice of individual psalms has been attributed to either the Teacher of Righteousness (i.e., the so-called "Teacher Hymns," variously delineated as running from 1QH[a] columns IX or X–XIX) or the larger sectarian community (i.e., the so-called "Community Hymns," which are found in 1QH[a] columns I–VIII or IX and XX–XXVIII); the block of Teacher Hymns (TH) is thus flanked by two blocks of Community Hymns (CH 1 and CH 2). On the history of these distinctions and the burgeoning interest in their (re)definition, see Schuller, "Recent Scholarship," 122, 137–146 (also see p. 270 n. 243 of the present chapter). Newsom, *The Self as Symbolic Space*, 196–198, 287–292, points out that current discussions have largely abandoned seeing a definitive connection between the historical Teacher of Righteousness and the Teacher Hymns, with Newsom herself being a prominent advocate of the view that the Teacher Hymns reflect the leadership of the sect more broadly. She also contends that even a leadership inspired-*hodayah* does not mean that it is void of significance for the "ordinary" sectarian insofar as these psalms may have promoted "ideal" sectarian ways. For further on the Teacher Hymns and their role in the leadership of the sect, see Judith H. Newman, "The Thanksgiving Hymns of 1QH[a] and the Construction of the Ideal Sage through Liturgical Performance," in *Sibyls, Scriptures, and Scrolls*, 940–957. While Harkins, "A New Proposal," 121–122, 133–134, has argued that angelic fellowship in the *Hodayot* is limited to TH and CH 2, as we will see below, there are (admittedly fragmentary) references in column VII and VIII; also see column III, which seems to refer to angelic fellowship in line 32, but the poor condition of the rest of the column means the context of the line is virtually impossible to decipher. As Esther G. Chazon, "Liturgical Function in the Cave 1 Hodayot Collection," in *Qumran Cave 1 Revisited*, 137, 149, observes, angelic fellowship is not limited to any one section of the *Hodayot*, and these important claims may even have been a unifying editorial feature. Cf. Emile Puech, *La Croyance des Esséniens en al vie future: Immoralité, resurrection, vie éternelle? Historie d'une croyance dans le judaïsme ancien* (2 vols; Paris: J. Gabalda, 1993), 417, who similarly does not detect any difference between the "eschatology" (the

1QHᵃ IV, 26–27; VII, 29–30; XV, 27; XX, 1). But these passages are modest in comparison with the extraordinary privileges boasted about elsewhere in the *Hodayot*. Two examples are frequently cited, the first of which is from column XI:[7]

20 *vacat*   אודכה אדוני כי פדיתה נפשי משחת ומשאול אבדון

21 העליתני לרום עולם ואתהלכה במישור לאין חקר ואדעה כיא יש מקוה לאשר

22 יצרתה מעפר לסוד עולם ורוח נעוה טהרתה מפשע רב להתיצב במעמד עם

23 צבא קדושים ולבוא ביחד עם עדת בני שמים ותפל לאיש גורל עולם עם רוחות

24 דעת להלל שמכה ביחד רנה ולספר נפלאותיכה לנגד כול מעשיכה

20 *vacat* I thank you, Lord, that you have redeemed my life form the pit, and that from Sheol-Abaddon

21 you have lifted me up to an eternal height, so that I walk about on a limitless plain. I know that there is hope for one whom

22 you have formed from the dust for an eternal council. And a perverted spirit you have purified from great sin that it might take its place with

23 the host of the holy ones and enter into community with the congregation of the children of heaven. And you cast for the man an eternal lot with the spirits

24 of knowledge, that he might praise your name in a common rejoicing and recount your wonderful acts before all your works. ...

---

category in which Puech places angelic fellowship) of the Teacher Hymns and the Community Hymns.

[7] These lines are part of a psalm that extends from XI, 20–37; see Stegemann, Schuller, and Newsom, DJD 40, 146. Since communal praise is a feature of the Community Hymns, this psalm has not infrequently been considered as such, despite its placement in the Teacher Hymn block: cf., e.g., Kuhn, *Enderwartung*, 70; Michael C. Douglas, "Power and Praise in the Hodayot: A Literary Critical Study of 1QH 9:1–18:14" (Ph.D. diss.; University of Chicago, 1998), 245, 254. Conversely, Sara J. Tanzer, "The Sages at Qumran: Wisdom in the 'Hodayot,'" (Ph.D. Diss.; Harvard University, 1986), 106, 122–127, discusses why she considers this psalm a Teacher Hymn (though a "hybrid" of sorts), including a close connection between it and the immediately preceding Teacher Hymn (XI, 6–19). On the relationship between this psalm and XI, 6–19, see Julie A. Hughes, *Scriptural Allusions in the Hodayot* (STDJ 59; Leiden: Brill, 2009), 228–229, who considers the Teacher/Community Hymn labels "inadequate" for XI, 20–37. Cf. Newsom, *The Self as Symbolic Space*, 256–261. Chazon, "Liturgical Function," 138–140, observes the use of two characteristics of the Teacher Hymns in XI, 20–37: the use of the אודכה אדוני incipit and rescue from the "pit." Moreover, in keeping with Newsom's comments mentioned in the preceding footnote, Chazon suggests that "although the author of the Teacher Hymn in 1QHᵃ XI, 20–37 writes from an individual perspective, the terms he employs for the shared station and joint praise with the angels and the similar usage of these terms in the Community Hymns strongly suggest that he also has his elect community in view – the earthly counterpart to the 'congregation of the sons of heaven.'"

Frequently noted for correspondences with XI, 20–24, the second well-known angelic fellowship passage is found in XIX, 13–17:[8]

13 ...   ולמען כבודכה טהרתה אנוש מפשע להתקדש
14 לכה מכול תועבות נדה ואשמת מעל להוחד עֿםֿ בני אמתך ובגורל עֿםֿ
15 קדושיכה להרים מעפר תולעת מתים לסוד אֿןֿמתכה] ומרוח נעוה לבינתכֿהֿ
16 ולהתיצֿבֿ במעמד לפניכה עם צבא עד ורוחו[ת עולמ] וֿלהתחדש עם כול הֿןֿווה]
17 וֿנֿהיה ועם ידעים ביחד רנה   vacat

13 ... For the sake of your glory you have purified a mortal from sin so that he may sanctify himself

14 for you from all impure abominations and from faithless guilt, so that he might be united with the children of your truth and in the lot with

15 your holy ones, so that a corpse infesting maggot might be raised up from the dust to the council of [your] t[ruth], and from a spirit of perversion to the understanding which comes from you,

16 and so that he may take (his) place before you with the everlasting host and the [eternal] spirit[s], and so that he may be renewed together with all that i[s]

17 and will be and with those who have knowledge in a common rejoicing. *vacat*

That the psalmists can celebrate being exalted by God to commune with the angels[9] is somewhat paradoxical, given that another prominent feature of the

---

[8] These lines are from a psalm that begins at XIX, 6 and possibly ends at XX, 6, though some consider XIX, 18 as commencing an entirely new psalm (i.e., not just a new section). For the various proposals, see Stegemann, Schuller, and Newsom, DJD 40, 242. On this psalm as a Community Hymn with strong wisdom elements, see Tanzer, "The Sages at Qumran," 23–24, 37–42. Hughes, *Scriptural Allusions*, 226, conveniently highlights the parallels between XI, 20–24 and XIX, 13–17, including purification from sin, mention of קדושים and צבא, being raised from the dust, reference to an eternal council, being cleansed from a perverted spirit, and the phrase "a community of rejoicing." In light of these affinities, Kuhn, *Enderwartung*, 80–85, considered the passage from column XIX to be a reworking of those from column XI.

[9] A number of angelic designations are used in these passages, and as Davidson, *Angels at Qumran*, 205, explains: "[T]he author(s) did not tire of rearranging the various epithets applying to angels, producing many combinations. This, of course, is consistent with the use of poetic form, but nevertheless does highlight the interest of the writer(s) in angels." For the use of "sons of heaven" as a designation for angels, see 1 En. 6:2; 13:8. For the use of "host of heaven" (or similar constructions), see 1 Kgs 22:19; 2 Macc 10:29–30; 1QM XII, 1–9. Though קדושים/צבא and רוחות may occasionally be applied to sect members and inclinational spirits, respectively, the context and parallel constructions confirm that "the host of holy ones" and "the sons of heaven" in XI, 23–24 as well as "the eternal host" and "the eternal spirits" in XIX, 16 refer to angelic beings. These statements are thus indicative of angelic communion; see Svend Holm-Nielsen, *Hodayot: Psalms at Qumran* (ATDan 2; Aarhus: Universitetsforlaget, 1960), 68; Menahem Monsoor, *The Thanksgiving Hymns: Translated and Annotated with an Introduction* (STDJ 3; Leiden: Brill, 1961), 117; Puech, *La Croyance*, 370; Bjorn Frennesson, *"In a Common Rejoicing": Liturgical Communion with Angels in Qumran* (SSU 14; Uppsala: Uppsala University Library, 1999), 49 n. 33; Sullivan, *Wrestling with Angels*, 162. However, scholars have rightly noted the קדושים of XIX, 14–15 are more difficult to interpret, in large part

Hodayot is their vigorous declarations of human depravity (cf. 1QH[a] V, 31–35; IX, 23–29; XI, 24–26; XIX, 22–25; 1QS XI, 9–10). However, these so-called "Niedrigkeitsdoxologien"[10] by no means cancel the exuberance of the claims of angelic fellowship but rather serve as a rhetorical foil[11] to

because the word is parallel with בני אמתך, a phrase which seems more naturally to be a reference to sect members; see, e.g., the discussion of Mathias Delcor, *Les Hymnes de Qumran (Hodayot): texte hébreu, introduction, traduction, commentaire* (Paris: Letouzey et Ané, 1962), 236–237, who highlights the ambiguity. If the "holy ones"/"sons of your truth" are sect members (i.e., synonymous parallelism), the sense would seem to be that the sectarians are, in turn, those who are raised to stand in the presence of the (angelic) eternal host/everlasting spirits as per line 16; so Holm-Nielsen, *Hodayot*, 187; Kuhn, *Enderwartung*, 82–83; Stephen F. Noll, "Angelology in the Qumran Texts," (Ph.D. diss; University of Manchester, 1979), 92; Tanzer, "Sages at Qumran," 37. Alternatively, the parallelism may not be synonymous but complementary: i.e., sons of your truth = sectarians, whereas the holy ones = angels; so Theodor Herzl Gaster, *The Dead Sea Scriptures* (rev. ed.; Garden City: Anchor Books, 1964), 178; Puech, *La Croyance*, 378; Frennesson, *"In a Common Rejoicing,"* 53 n. 73. While I am inclined to accept the former interpretation, it is clear that angelic fellowship is not ruled out in the passage even by the latter because of the statement of XIX, 16. I will address the possibility of word play in these lines, below.

[10] Kuhn, *Enderwartung*, 27, influentially dubbed the passages of intense humility, "Niedrigkeitsdoxologien." Cf. Holm-Nielsen, *Hodayot*, 274–282; Hermann Lichtenberger, *Studien zum Menschenbild in Texten der Qumrangeinde* (SUNT 15; Göttingen: Vandenhoeck & Ruprecht, 1980), 73–93. Frennesson, *"In a Common Rejoicing,"* 58, captures the paradox well when he says that the *Hodayot* move "within a span of great, not to say extreme humility, as well as great self-esteem and a sense of being elected ... ." On the biblical foundations of the *Niedrigkeitsdoxologien*, see Carol A. Newsom, "Deriving Negative Anthropology through Exegetical Activity," in *Is There a* Text, 258–274. On the role humility plays in the Teacher Hymns, see Newman, "The Thanksgiving Hymns," 944–950. For a recent reevaluation of the *Hodayot's* anthropological outlook, see Nicholas A. Meyer, *Adam's Dust and Adam's Glory in the Hodayot and the Letters of Paul: Rethinking Anthropology and Theology* (NovTSup 168; Leiden: Brill, 2016).

[11] A few observations are pertinent. First, Angela Kim Harkins, "Reading the Qumran Hodayot in Light of the Traditions Associated with Enoch" *Hen* 32 (2010): 400 (cf. eadem, "Elements of the Fallen Angels Traditions in the Qumran Hodayot," in *The Fallen Angels Traditions: Second Temple Period Developments and Reception History* [eds., eadem, Kelley Coblentz Bautch, and John C. Endres; CBQMS 53; Washington: Catholic Biblical Association, 2014], 8–24), rightly points out that the "awareness of wretchedness of the human condition emerges only after the human speaker is positioned in a heavenly congregation. ... With the proximity of the human to the heavenly, the experience of unworthiness is intensified." That being said, the understanding of the *Niedrigkeitsdoxologien* as a "foil" is helpful (see Kyle B. Wells, *Grace and Agency in Paul and Second Temple Judaism: Interpreting the Transformation of the Heart* [NovTSup 157; Leiden: Brill, 2015], 124), because the *Hodayot* to do not seem to "land" on the sentiments of the Niedrigkeitsdoxologien: i.e., precisely because lowliness is not the dominant impression conveyed by the *Hodayot*, Carol A. Newsom, "Religious Experience in the Dead Sea Scrolls: Two Case Studies," *Experientia, Volume 2: Linking Text and Experience* (eds., Colleen Shantz and Rodney Werline; EJL 35; Atlanta: Society of Biblical Literature,

emphasize that divine grace and election have more than countered the lowliness of those so chosen by God.[12] In fact, the extravagance of God's favour can be seen in different ways,[13] not least of which is the nature of angelic communion itself. It has been noted that 1QS IV, 6–8 and 1QM I, 8–9 anticipate an angel-like afterlife for sect members, and that the unique vision of the *War Scroll* is that the angels and sectarians would serve as comrades during the great eschatological conflict. But the perfect verbs[14] of 1QH[a] XI, 20–24 and XIX, 13–17 have been widely understood to mean that these lines speak of angelic fellowship as "a present reality," though this by no means rules out future implications.[15]

2012), 212, 215, suggests that the expression Neidrigkeitsdoxologie "puts the emphasis in the wrong place," opting for the designation, "'masochistic sublime,' since the experience of exalted and profound knowledge and moral capacity is intensified precisely by a repeated encounter with the nothingness that is the human on its own. ... The pleasure of seeing oneself constituted and destined for heavenly reward by means of the overwhelming power and mercy of God is experienced and even intensified by simultaneously expressing and experiencing one's natural human sinfulness and loathsomeness."

[12] Scholars have investigated the *Hodayot's* perplexing juxtaposition of penitential/self-deprecatory sentiments alongside determinist theology. E.g., Eileen M. Schuller, "Petitionary Prayer and the Religion of Qumran," in *Religion in the Dead Sea Scrolls*, 38, observes that the Neidrigkeitsdoxolgien "function to introduce praise of God's justice and mercy to such a wretched creation, and never as a petition for a change in the human condition." Similarly, Esther G. Chazon, "Low to Lofty: The Hodayot's Use of Liturgical Tradition to Shape Sectarian Identity," *RevQ* 26 (2013): 5–9, notes that "given its deterministic worldview and firm belief in its members' predestined election by grace, one would not expect the Qumran community to resort to petitionary prayer of any kind let alone for forgiveness of sin. ... [But h]ere it is important to distinguish between penitential prayers proper and generically different texts that avail themselves of penitential motifs for their own purposes. The *hodayot* fall into the latter category ... . The *hodayot's* formulation *per se* is then quite standard, the sectarian adaptation lying in the recontextualization into the context of thanksgiving for election by grace."

[13] E.g., repentance and knowledge – two things which, in theory, could be attributed to human effort or piety – are viewed by the *Hodayot* author(s) as gifts from God; see Newsom, "Religious Experience," 212.

[14] Specifically, both of the passages just cited display a series parallel lines consisting of perfect verbs followed by infinitives of purpose or result; e.g., 1QH[a] XI, 22–23: "a perverted spirit you have purified (טהרתה) from great sin that it might take (להתיצב) its place with the host of the holy ones and enter (לבוא) into community with the congregation of the children of heaven ... "; see Bonnie P. Kittel, *The Hymns of Qumran: Translation and Commentary* (SBLDS 50; Chico: Scholars Press, 1981), 60–63 (col. XI), 116 (col. XIX). On infinitives of purpose/result, see Paul A. Joüon, *A Grammar of Biblical Hebrew* (trans. and rev., Takamitsu Muraoka; 2 vols.; SubBi 14; Rome: Pontifical Biblical Institute, 1991), §124 *l*.

[15] See Collins, *The Scriptures and Sectarianism*, 199–200, who in reference to 1QH[a] XI and XIX says that "in these ... passages the fellowship with the angels promised to the

While Kuhn is well-known for advocating the present significance of these verbs,[16] and Puech the future or eschatological (he considers them examples of the "parfait prophétique"[17]), both of their views as well as those of most who weigh-in on this subject are nuanced, and it is not so much that scholars accept *in toto* one connotation over another than it is a matter of emphasis.[18] While I accept the majority opinion that these *Hodayot* passages claim a robust measure of angelic fellowship as a present reality for the sect,[19] the language used in attempting to strike a balance between this present reality and its future consummation has sometimes been problematic. For instance, context indeed suggests that the "eternal height" of XI, 20 "represents the new life in the sectarian covenant, characterized by רום and עולם, in contrast to life outside the covenant, which is Sheol and Abbaddon," but it is surely an exaggeration to say that XI, 20–24 "does not seem to concern the future life,"[20] especially given the eschatological focus of XI, 20–37 as a whole.[21] Conversely, it may not give due credit to the present implications of angelic fellowship to refer to these claims as a "foretaste"[22] of the eschaton. I would suggest, however, that Tuschling's articulation comes close to striking a helpful balance: "Present transcendence and eschatological fulfillment are not the same, although one leads to the other."[23]

---

righteous after death in [1 En. 104:2–6 and Dan 12:3] is claimed for members of the sectarian community" even if "the Scrolls do not envision a world fully redeemed."

[16] Kuhn, *Enderwartung*, 44–112.

[17] Puech, *La Croyance* 369–370.

[18] On this point, see Ken Penner, "Realized or Future Salvation in the Hodayot," *JBS* 5 (2002): 1–49.

[19] Cf., e.g., the views of Nickelsburg, *Resurrection*, 153–155; Rowland, *The Open Heaven*, 117–118; Davidson, *Angels at Qumran*, 193; Chazon, "Human and Angelic Prayer," 43–45; Dimant, "Men as Angels," 93–103; Frennesson, *"In a Common Rejoicing,"* 54; Schäfer, *The Origins of Jewish Mysticism*, 123, 198; Sullivan, *Wrestling with Angels*, 163; Hughes, *Scriptural Allusions*, 228; John J. Collins, "Metaphor and Eschatology: Life beyond Death in the Hodayot," in *Is There a Text*, 415–420.

[20] So Holm-Nielsen, *Hodayot*, 66, 68, 187, who makes similar comments regarding XIX, 16–17: just because the "probable thought here is of angels before the throne of God," and that "membership of the community is identical to fellowship with God," does not mean the passage is void of future eschatological significance. Cf. Delcor, *Les Hymnes*, 127, who calls attention to "une véritable communion mystique entre la communauté terrestre et la cour angélique céleste et point n'est besoin de comprendre tout notre texte au futur." But it is likely overstating the matter to suggest that the community is "vit déjà ici-bas comme si elle était dans l'au delà."

[21] On the eschatology of the end of the psalm, see Michalak, *Angels as Warriors*, 176–180. On how the present deliverance of the first part of the psalm and the eschatological deliverance of the end of the psalm work together, see Hughes, *Scriptural Allusions*, 228–229.

[22] So Alexander, *Mystical Texts*, 72.

[23] Tuschling, *Angels and Orthodoxy*, 118. That present transcendence leads to eschatological fulfillment is perhaps well-illustrated by the word גורל, which, as we have

More can be said regarding the nature of angelic fellowship in the *Hodayot*. Several psalms refer to angels as גבורים, "warriors" or "mighty ones" (cf. XI, 36; XIII, 23; XVI, 12; XVIII, 36),[24] yet it is clear that in at least

---

seen, occurs with some frequency in the sectarian texts (e.g., 1QS III, 24; IV, 24, 26; XI, 7; 1QM I, 1–15; XIII, 5–12; 1QHᵃ XI, 23; XIV, 16; XIX, 14; 11Q13 II, 8, 12, 13). On גורל specifically in the *Hodayot*, see Holm-Nielsen, *Psalms at Qumran*, 68; Schäfer, *The Origins of Jewish Mysticism*, 124–125. Though Puech, *La Croyance*, 370–371, has argued that גורל has only future implications in 1QHᵃ XI, 23 and XIX, 14, it is questionable whether גורל ever has such a strict definition. The word occurs over 75x in the Hebrew Bible, and even when it includes the figurative sense of "destiny," there are real implications for the present (cf., e.g., Jer 13:25; Ps 16:5–6). Moreover, *The Treatise on the Two Spirits* is clear that to be part of a "lot" is to have very present angelic succor that carries inherent eschatological relevance. Even in the future-oriented *11QMelchizedek* and *War Scroll*, there are no indications that being part of a "lot" is anything less than the eschatological outworking of present realities. Frennesson, *"In a Common Rejoicing,"* 49–50 (cf. Angel, *Otherworldly*, 93 n. 45), has suggested that the parallelism of 1QHᵃ XI, 22–23 supports the identification of membership in an angelic גורל with being stationed with "the host of the holy ones"/entering into community with "the congregation of the sons of heaven," since this identification conveys the idea of a "present reality and not just something that is 'vécu dans la foi et l'espérance'" (as per Puech, *La Croyance*, 372). In addition to the present force of the verbs, the analysis of Kittel, *The Hymns of Qumran*, 62–63, supports Frennesson's assertion. As briefly mentioned above, XI, 22–24 exhibits a pattern of perfect verbs followed by infinitives of purpose/result. The following is a more detailed presentation of Kittel's analysis:

טהרתה מפשע רב	verb 1
להתיצב במעמד עם צבא קדושים	infinitive a
ולבוא ביחד עם עדת בני שמים	infinitive b
ותפל לאיש גורל עולם עם רוחות דעת	verb 2
להלל שמכה ביחד רנה	infinitive a
ולספר נפלאותיכה לנגד כול מעשיכה	infinitive b

As Kittel highlights, "the first line states the action of God (the cleansing of man's spirit); the two infinitives phrases attached to this clause indicate the purpose or result of this action. It is done so that (ל) man can take his place in the assembly of the [angels]. The second independent clause of the stanza begins with a restatement of that result – God places man with the [angels] – and a new set of purposive or result clauses are attached to this statement. The whole stanza, then, is arranged not only with some attention to parallelism, but in an interlocking fashion." In light of this – and to further Frennesson's point – it is not just that a גורל with the angels is parallel to similar sentiments; it is that this claim was apparently deemed worthy of more forceful restatement via a perfect verb in its own independent clause.

[24] גבור is often used in the Hebrew Bible to refer to human warriors (e.g., Josh 1:14; Judg 6:12; Ps 33:16; 2 Chr 14:7), a usage echoed in the *Hodayot* (e.g., 1QHᵃ XI, 40; XIV, 33, 36; XVIII, 26). The word, however, is not infrequently employed as designation for supernatural beings including the *Nephilim* (e.g., Gen 6:4; see P. W. Coxon, "Gibborim גבורים," *DDD* 345–346), righteous angels (e.g., Ps 103:20; 1QM XV, 14), and the God of Israel (e.g., Isa 42:13; Jer 20:11; Ps 24:8). As noted above, it is uncertain whether the

two such instances the focus is not primarily eschatological or martial. In column VII we read:[25]

17 ... ואנחנו ביחד נועדֹ֗יֹם ועם ידעים נׄ֗וֹסׄ]רֹהׄ֗ל֗כׄ֗ונׄרׄ]נׄנה ברוב[

18 רחמיכֹ]ה ‏ ‏ ‏ ‏ ‏ ‏ ‏ ‏]ח עם גבוריכה ובהפלא נספרֹה יחד ברעֹ]ת אל]וֹעד]ׄ‏ ‏ [

19 בעדתׄ]ן ‏ ‏ ‏ ‏ ‏ ‏]ֹה וצאאצאינו הודעׄ]תה עֹ]ֹם בני איש בֹתׄוֹכׄ]ן בני]אדם [‏ ‏ [

17 And as for us, in the community of those gathered and with those who have knowledge we are inst[ruc]ted by you and we cry [out in the abundance of]
18 yo[ur] compassion [ ]h with your warriors. And when (you) act wondrously we will recount (it) together in the know[ledge of God] and until [ ]
19 in the assembly of[ ]h and our offspring [you] have caused to understand together with the children of men in the midst of[the children of] Adam [ ]

Analogous assertions are found in column VIII:[26]

‏ ‏ ‏ ‏] ולעׄצתׄך תקראׄנׄי ‏ ‏ ‏ ‏ ‏ ‏ ‏ ‏ ‏ וׄמׄקור אור פתֹחׄתֹהׄ]ן ‏ ‏ ‏ ... 14
להׄון]חֹד עם צֹבא ‏ ‏ ‏ 15 לֹהׄלל קֹוֹדֹשֹך מֹפי כל מעשֹׄיך כׄיֹא פעלתֹ]ה
16]גׄ]בׄוֹרׄי עֹוֹלם ...

14 ... A source of light you have opened [ ] and for your council you have called me
15 to praise your holiness by the mouth of all your creatures, for you have don[e to be un]ited with the host of
16 the eternal [wa]rriors ...

Certainty is ruled out by their fragmentary condition, but VII, 17–19 and VIII, 14–16, like XI, 20–24 and XIX, 14–16, would appear to be examples of present angelic communion, since the people are said to be "with those who have knowledge" (VII, 17),[27] "with [God's] warriors" (VII, 18),[28] and "united

---

"mighty one of war" (גבור המלחמה) in 1QM XII, 9 refers to an angel or God. For further discussion and references, see Davidson, *Angels at Qumran*, 197–198; Michalak, *Angels as Warriors*, 27, 89–90.

[25] In addition to its location in the CH 1 block, the first person plural pronoun suggests that this is a community hymn; see Frennesson, *"In a Common Rejoicing,"* 57; cf. Tanzer, "Sages at Qumran," 82. Column VII is poorly preserved, but by taking the Cave 4 manuscript evidence into consideration, Schuller has suggested that VII, 17–19 is part of a relatively short psalm that runs from VII, 12–20. For comments on the psalm and the reconstruction of the text, see Stegemann, Schuller, and Newsom, DJD 40, 37, 99–100.

[26] This psalm likely begins at VII, 21 and ends at VIII, 40–41; see Stegemann, Schuller, and Newsom, DJD 40, 110–111. Tanzer, "Sages at Qumran," 88, describes this psalm as a Community Hymn in which angelic fellowship is specified as a reward for the righteous.

[27] For "those with knowledge" as an angelic designation, see Frennesson, *"In a Common Rejoicing,"* 48 n. 27, 54 n. 79, 57. On the *Hodayot's* celebration of divinely revealed knowledge, see Bowley, "Prophets, Kittim, and Divine Communication," 492–493. On the *Hodayot's* author as "an interpreter of knowledge" (e.g., X, 15) as opposed to the sect's adversaries who are dubbed "deceitful interpreters" (e.g., XII, 8), see Devorah Dimant, "The Interpretation of Ezekiel in the Hodayot," in *HĀ-'ÎSH MŌSHE: Studies in Scriptural Interpretation in the Dead Sea Scrolls and Related Literature in Honor of*

with the host of eternal warriors" (VIII, 15–16).[29] Also like XI, 20–24 and XIX, 13–17, the angelic fellowship in columns VII and VIII is marked by the praise of God: רנן and הלל are widespread in liturgical passages of the Hebrew Bible (e.g., Deut 32:43; Isa 16:10; Pss 5:12; 95:1), with the Piel of ספר not infrequently employed in similar settings.[30] All three verbs or their cognates appear in the *Hodayot* passages listed above (cf. VII,17; VIII, 15–16, 18; XI, 24; XIX, 17). The ritual purity requisite for the proper praise of God in a cultic context may have driven the choice of the word מקוה in XI, 21: Fletcher-Louis notes that in a psalm that praises God for his forgiveness and purification, מקוה, which is universally translated "hope," is likely functioning as a double entendre, meaning both "hope" and "ritual bath."[31] Indeed, numerous commentators have noticed that a main purpose of fellowship with the angels is worship, which is succinctly summarized in the phrase ביחד רנה, "in a common rejoicing" (cf. 1QHᵃ XI, 24; XIX, 17).[32]

Moshe J. Bernstein (eds., Binyamin Goldstein, Michael Segal, and George J. Brooke; STDJ 122; Leiden: Brill, 2017), 80 n. 8. Also see Montgomery, "A Stream from Eden."

[28] Holm-Nielsen, *Hodayot*, 269, proposes "the people of your warriors" as a translation for עם גבוריכה, which is similar to the previously discussed designation "the people of the holy ones" (cf. Dan 7:27; 1QM X, 10; XII, 8; 11Q13 II, 9).

[29] I.e., there are no indications of this being a future-oriented togetherness. Moreover, VII, 17 has a Niphal participle of יעד, which in the Hebrew Bible frequently expresses the present-focused activities of God meeting Israel at the sanctuary before the mercy seat (cf. Exod 25:22; 29:43–46; 30:6, 36) and his assembling of the congregation for worship (cf. Num 10:3; 1 Kgs 8:5; 2 Chr 5:6); see J. P. Lewis, "יעד," *TWOT* 387.

[30] Cf. J. Kühlwein, "ספר," *TLOT* 2:810: "In the *piel* meaning ('to narrate'), *spr* has a specifically theological setting in the Psalms: in the vow of praise and in reports that people communicate God's mighty acts that they have experienced or heard of to others. … Objects of the narration are Yhwh's name (Pss 22:23; 102:22; cf. Exod 9:16), his wonders (Pss 9:2; 26:7; 40:6; 75:2), famous acts (Pss 9:15; 78:4; 79:13; cf. Isa 43:21) … ."

[31] Fletcher-Louis, *All the Glory*, 108–112. Cf. Harkins, "Reading the Qumran Hodayot," 38. For additional examples of double entendres in the *Hodayot*, see below. On ritual bathing in the Scrolls, see CD X, 11–12; 1QS III, 4–6.

[32] On "common rejoicing" as a purpose of angelic fellowship, see Chazon, "Liturgical Function," 137–148; Frenneson, *"In a Common Rejoicing,"* 57; Davidson, *Angels at Qumran*, 192. Cf. Schäfer, *The Origins of Jewish Mysticism*, 124–125, who comments on how these passages use the language of Job 38:7, but whereas the Joban line refers to angels joining together to praise God, the *Hodayot* speak of the liturgical communion of angels and humans. That human-angel worship is a purpose of angelic fellowship is emphasized by the fact that both occurrences of ביחד רנה are found in the infinitive lines of the aforementioned perfect verb/infinitive of purpose constructions; see Kittel, *The Hymns of Qumran*, 58, 60, 62, 111, 116. Earlier *Hodayot* scholarship proposed that 1QHᵃ XIX, 28–29 also referred to the joining together of humans and angels for worship, in part because the words יחד and רנה occur in close proximity to each other. But as Schuller has pointed out, the Cave 4 manuscripts help to restore a more general picture of all creation

The notion that the sectarians have somehow united with the angels in heaven for liturgical purposes is only enhanced by use of the nouns סוד and עדה. Both words are biblical designations for the divine assembly (cf. Jer 23:18–22; Pss 82:1; 89:6–9),[33] and though they can refer to human assemblies (cf. Exod 16:1; Lev 8:4; Ps 83:4; Prov 11:13),[34] the angelic terminology combined with the language of being lifted up or exalted[35] by God strongly suggest that סוד and עדה refer to the divine assembly in 1QH[a] VII, 19[36] and

---

joining together to praise God; see Stegemann, Schuller, and Newsom, DJD 40, 246–247; cf. Frenneson, *"In a Common Rejoicing,"* 55.

[33] On the divine council in the Hebrew Bible, see Chapter 2.

[34] I briefly discussed sectarian usage of עדה in Chapter 4.

[35] Hughes, *Scriptural Allusions*, 214, points out the "geographical" extremes (i.e., Sheol vs. Heaven) of the opening lines. Cf. Newsom, *The Self as Symbolic Space*, 256: "Significant verbal links between the conclusion of the preceding *hodayah* and the beginning of this one [1QH[a] XI, 19–37] point to the symbolic nexus on which this anxiety is focused – the claim of Sheol. Where the woman pregnant with a viper/nothingness was consigned to the Pit and Sheol at the conclusion of the earlier text, this prayer opens with thanks that 'you have redeemed my life from the Pit, and that from Sheol-Abaddon you have brought me up to an eternal height' (lines 19–20). Various polar terms are used to mark the transformation of the speaker's situation: low/high; dust/eternal council; perverted sprit/holy ones; and so forth (lines 19–23). The prayer would initially appear to build on the externalizing of the negative in the previous composition in order to consolidate a sense of the distinction between self and other, good and evil, saved and damned, and in so doing reinforce a relatively unified subjectivity." More can be said, however, on the nature or sense of these extremes or poles. Though some scholars see the angelic fellowship of the *Hodayot* as envisioning angelic descent or a heaven-on-earth experience (cf., e.g., Frennesson, *"In a Common Rejoicing,"* 11–13, 50; Tuschling, *Angels and Orthodoxy*, 119; Church, *Hebrews and the Temple*, 111), others view it as human ascent to heaven (cf., e.g., Chazon, "Human & Angelic Prayer," 43–45; Schäfer, *The Origins of Jewish Mysticism*, 151–152; Angel, *Otherworldly*, 84). While I think the latter interpretation best accounts for the *Hodayot's* exaltation language, an important observation is made by Alexander, *The Mystical Texts*, 118–119, who is sympathetic to the human ascent understanding: "The lack of explicit reference [to an actual ascent as there is in 1 Enoch] raises another intriguing possibility, namely that the Qumranites' view of heaven was more sophisticated than we might suppose. Heaven was not really 'up there': such spatial language is only symbolic and metaphorical. Rather the spiritual, heavenly world constitutes a parallel universe, another dimension. ... [T]his opens up the possibility of seeing the *yihud* with the angels in more psychological terms, as a more internal process than we might at first suppose."

[36] Whereas in XI, 23 God has enabled the psalmist to be part of the עדת בני שמים, the construct chain of VII, 19 is broken. Harkins, "A New Proposal," 114, states that the references to "children of men" and "children of Adam" later in line 19 point to a human congregation. However, Schuller has suggested that VII, 19 be restored to בעדת קדושים, which would likely refer to a heaven, especially if בדעת אל is corrected to בעדת אל as per 4QH[a] 8 I, 10; see Stegemann, Schuller, and Newsom, DJD 40, 102, 106.

XI, 22–23 (cf. XXV, 26, 32),[37] an assembly to which the sectarian worshipers have been granted access. This is further emphasized by the use of מעמד, "station" (cf. XI, 22; XIX, 16): the word is used in the Hebrew Bible to refer to priestly service in the Jerusalem temple (cf. 1 Chr 23:28; 2 Chr 35:15), but it also likely lies behind the words used elsewhere to describe the standing of the angelic throng in the throne room of the heavenly temple.[38]

This observation complements the significant angelic fellowship claim of column XIV not yet discussed:[39]

15 ...   וידעו כול גוים אמתכה וכול לאומים כבודכה כי הביאותֿהֿ ∘| [סודכה
16 לכול אנשי עצתכה ובגורל יחד עם מלאכי פנים ואין מליץ בנים לק[ן

15 ... Thus all the nations will acknowledge your truth and all the peoples your glory, for you have brought [ ] your secret counsel
16 to all the people of your council, and in a common lot with [or: in a lot together with] the angels of presence, without an intermediary between them *lq*[...

The fragmentary state of the text is again unfortunate, but it seems that line 16 is making a vital assertion about angelic fellowship.[40] The psalmist claims to be in a גורל with the angels, and that this human-angel lot denotes communion – as opposed to a pedestrian claim that both contingents happen to be on the same (righteous) side of the dualistic divide – is suggested by the

---

[37] Delcor, *Des Hymnes*, 126, notes the similarities between XI, 20–24 and Ps 89:6–7, verses which speak of the divine assembly. Cf. Davidson, *Angels at Qumran*, 167 n. 3; Hughes, *Scriptural Allusions*, 221. *Contra* Holm-Nielsen, *Hodayot*, 67, who states that "man's expectation of heavenly glory is realized in the existence of the community," and as such considers סוד עולם to a be "a fixed term for the community." I will address the perhaps deliberate ambiguity of סוד (as well as קדושים) in 1QH[a] XIX, 15, below.

[38] In my discussion of 1 En. 12:4, I noted the proposal that מעמד was translated by the Greek word στάσις to refer to the "station" of the priestly angels in the *Book of Watchers*; see Chapter 3. Chazon, "Human & Angelic Prayer," 44 (cf. eadem, "Liturgical Function," 139, 145), refers to מעמד as an angelic fellowship "motif" of the *Hodayot*. Alexander, *Mystical Texts*, 87 n. 4, similarly notes the "technical" sense of the word in Qumran mystical contexts. Cf. Frennesson, *"In a Common Rejoicing,"* 48; Harkins, "A New Proposal," 116. Jacob Licht, *The Thanksgiving Scroll* (Jerusalem: Bialik Institute, 1957), 84, 163 [Hebrew], observed that מעמד may stand behind the word used in the heavenly scene in the *Similitudes* (cf. 1 En. 60:2).

[39] These lines are part of a relatively long Teacher Hymn that runs from XIII, 22–XV, 8; see Stegemann, Schuller, and Newsom, DJD 40, 184. On the contribution XIV, 15–16 makes to the psalm, see Davidson, *Angels at Qumran*, 194, who notes that while the psalmist's opponents are characterized by unfaithfulness to the covenant, the righteous have communion with the angels as their reward.

[40] As Sullivan, *Wrestling with Angels*, 163, notes, the text's condition is "frustrating," but the notion of fellowship between angels and people is clear.

clarificatory statement that there is "no intermediary[41] between" the sectarians and the angels.[42] But this time, the angels with whom the sectarians are grouped are specified as the מלאכי פנים, a statement entirely appropriate in a document emphasizing liturgical fellowship with the angels. As discussed in Chapter 3, Jubilees and other texts suggest that "the angels of the presence" are among the elite celestial beings who serve before God as the priests of the heavenly sanctuary[43] and as the heavenly archetypes to whom Israel and its priesthood on earth correspond and ideally emulate (cf. Jub. 2:2, 18, 30; 6:18; 30:18; 31:14; 1 En. 40:1–9; Tob 12:15; T. Levi 3:7; T. Jud. 25:2).[44] Moreover, fellowship between the sectarians and the angels is here stated "in the boldest way possible,"[45] as it is a claim that being a

---

[41] On the nuances of מליץ, which can mean "mediator," "translator," or "interpreter," cf. Holm-Nielsen, *Hodayot*, 114; Frennesson, *"In a Common Rejoicing,"* 52 n. 56; Stegemann, Schuller, and Newsom, DJD 40, 187.

[42] The last two letters before the *vacat* in line 16 are לק, with Schuller proposing that לקדושים be restored, resulting in the following sense: "'and there is no need (or: there is no longer need) of an interpreter acting between both of them (אנשי עצתכה and מלאכי פנים) for your holy ones (the angels) do make answer according to the spirit'; that is, there is a [direct] relationship between men and angels in cultic language, so that the utterances of these human beings can be understood in the heavens without further help of angelic mediation." See Stegemann, Schuller, and Newsom, DJD 40, 187.

[43] Cf. Holm-Nielsen, *Hodayot*, 114; Chazon, "Liturgical Function," 137 n. 5; Michalak, *Angels as Warriors*, 65, 83. Tuschling, *Angels and Orthodoxy*, 117, understands communion with angels of the presence as stemming from the priestly character of the sect, which in turn is indebted to the Jubilees. Given the Qumran movement's apparent affinity for Jubilees – a work which says more about the angel(s) of the presence than any other extant text – Tuschling's observation should be taken seriously. Also see Schäfer, *The Origins of Jewish Mysticism*, 125–126.

[44] To reiterate, that these angels have been interpreted as archetypal can be seen in the ways scholars refer to them and/or their relationship with Israel/the sect: cf., e.g., Dimant, "Men as Angels," 99, 101, who speaks of the angels of presence as the "heavenly counterparts of earthly Israel," and the sectarians as those who "aimed at creating on earth a replica of the heavenly world"; Angel, *Otherworldly*, 38: "there is a direct parallel between the existence and action of [the angels of the presence] and those of their human counterparts on earth"; Frennesson, *"In a Common Rejoicing,"* 66: the sectarians "worshipped God in accordance with the heavenly model [provided by the angels]."

[45] Frennesson, *"In a Common Rejoicing,"* 52 (cf. Schäfer, *The Origins of Jewish Monotheism*, 125–126), who notes that a relationship to the elite angels of the presence means that the sectarians viewed themselves "as close to God as possible." This observation coheres with a proposal of Harkins, "Reading the Qumran Hodayot," 39, who suggests that as the reader moves along the individual psalms of 1QH[a], the speaker's proximity to God increases: whereas in XI, 20 the speaker (merely?) joins the angels, XIX, 16 specifies that the speaker can join the angels in standing *before* (לפני) God. Admittedly, the sentiment of XIX, 16 may be implicit in XI, 20. But if Harkins is correct in seeing a progression of sorts, XIV, 15–16 fits quite nicely: i.) XI, 20: with the angels = bold; ii.) XIV, 15–16: with the angels of presence = bolder; iii.) XIX, 16: before God with the angels = bolder still. Moreover, Harkins, "A New Proposal," 117, and Noll,

member of the Qumran movement entailed fellowship with the angels closest to God and heaven's priests. Given the boldness of the claims, it is important to understand how liturgical fellowship with these angels may have contributed to sectarian identity.

II. Angelic Fellowship as a Defining Sectarian Characteristic

I noted above that two passages from the *Hodayot* are especially well-known when it comes to angelic fellowship. A third passage, often cited alongside 1QH[a] XI, 20–24 and XIX, 13–17, is found in the psalm that concludes 1QS. The similarities these lines share with the *Hodayot* angelic fellowship passages will make their relevance readily apparent.[46] 1QS XI, 7–9 reads as follows:[47]

"Angelology in the Qumran Texts," 93 (cf. "Frennesson, "In a Common Rejoicing," 54 n. 76), have proposed, respectively, that the occurrences of לפניכה, "before you" in XV, 34 and XIX, 16 contribute to the notion of fellowship with the angels; i.e., just as the מלאכי פנים stand before (לפני) God, so too the sectarians, whom God has "stationed" (= Hiphil form of עמד; cf. XI, 22; XIX, 16 which, as already mentioned, refer to the מעמד of the sectarian worshippers with the angels).

[46] The psalm, a first-person hymn of the *Maskil*/Instructor, is found in 1QS X, 9–XI, 22. As is the case with the *Treatise on the Two Spirits*, not all extant S manuscripts preserve the psalm; scholars similarly disagree as to which tradition is earlier: the one containing the psalm (1QS and most 4QS witnesses) or 4QS[e], which ends with a calendrical (*Otot*) document. On the redaction of the psalm and the source-critical history of 1QS, see the works cited in Chapter 4, above; also see Murphy-O'Connor, "La genèse littéraire," 529– 532. On the role of the hymn in 1QS, see especially Newsom, *The Self as Symbolic Space*, 165–167, who argues that the "rhetorical shaping of the document, however, is quite different, depending on whether it concludes with the *Otot* or with the first-person hymn of the *Maskil*. With *Otot*, the focus on the figure of the *Maskil* is quickly subordinated to the content of his teaching. His presence in the document is no more vivid than that of the members described in the accounts of community procedure. The inclusion of the *Maskil's* first-person hymn, however, not only gives the *Maskil* a voice and presence but also provided the *Serek ha-Yahad* a much more forceful rhetorical structure and even something like a genuine conclusion. ... Although the *Maskil's* hymn deals with certain aspects of the responsibilities addressed in the instructions, much of its content does not have to do with those things that distinguish him from other members of the *Yahad*. In this regard the self-presentation of the *Maskil* provides a model of the ideal sectarian self. If one is properly shaped by the teaching and disciplines of the community, as they have been described in the *Serek ha-Yahad*, then this is the kind of voice with which one will speak." These comments are similar, of course, to those Newsom has made regarding the *Hodayot* Teacher Hymns (see above). On the affinities between 1QS X–XI and the *Hodayot*, cf. Frennesson, *"In a Common Rejoicing,"* 64; Stephen Hultgren, *From the Damascus Covenant to the Covenant of the Community: Literary, Historical, and Theological Studies in the Dead Sea Scrolls* (STDJ 66; Leiden: Brill, 2007), 426.

[47] Again, the Hebrew text, sigla, and translation cited here are based on that of Qimron and Charlesworth, "The Rule of the Community," 48–49. On the function of these lines in

לאש(ר) בחר אל נתנם לאוחזת עולם וינחי(ל)ם בגורל ... 7

8 קדושים ועם בני שמים חבר סודם לעצת יחד וסוד מבנית קודש למטעת עולם עם כול

9 קץ נהיה... ...

7 ... Those whom God has chosen he has set as an eternal possession. He has allowed them to inherit the lot of

8 the holy ones. With the sons of heaven he has joined together their assembly for the council of the community. (Their) assembly (is) a house of Holiness for the eternal plant during every

9 time to come. ...

Again, we are told that the sectarians are in a גורל with the angels, and once more this is qualified beyond the vague notion that they are on the same righteous team: God has actually joined "their assembly" – that is, the sectarian assembly[48] – with the angelic "sons of heaven" (cf. 1QH[a] XI, 23). Most telling is the purpose of this union, articulated here as לעצת יחד, "for[49] the council of the community," the technical term for the sectarians in the *Community Rule* (cf. 1QS III, 2; V, 7; VI, 3, 10, 14, 16; VII, 2, 22, 24; VIII, 1, 5, 22).[50] As I have highlighted already, 1QS effectively reconstitutes the sect and its covenant as the true Israel,[51] and the implication of juxtaposing this reconstitution with the notion of angelic fellowship is monumental: just as having the angelic guardians associated with Israel as comrades at the eschatological war seems to have been part of their definition of being the legitimate people of God, so too the notion of present liturgical fellowship with the nation's archetypal priests. There are numerous indications in both 1QS XI and the *Hodayot* that this was the case.

First, it is almost certain that the meaning of the term for "community," *Yahad* (יחד) – "union" (or adverbially, "together") – is related to the conviction that "togetherness with the angels [was] constitutive of the

---

the larger psalm, see Newsom, *The Self as Symbolic Space*, 169, who points out the *Hodayot*-like contrast between human sinfulness and God's gracious rescue of humans from their humble state – a rescue that includes angelic fellowship.

[48] The word for "assembly" used here is סוד, and in this instance an earthly "assembly" is in view, the relevance of which I will discuss, below; also see Frennesson, *"In a Common Rejoicing,"* 65–66, who stresses the present implications of angelic fellowship.

[49] Cf. Tyson L. Putthoff, *Ontological Aspects of Early Jewish* Anthropology (BRLJ 53; Leiden: Brill, 2016), 114, who notes that the *lamed* of purpose prefixed to עצה "signifies the reason for the human assembly's union with the celestial entourage"; he also observes that it is "[o]nly by uniting together do the two groups become the 'council of the *Yahad*.'"

[50] Cf. Collins, *The Scriptures and Sectarianism*, 200; Davidson, *Angels at Qumran*, 169. *Contra* Frennesson, *"In a Common Rejoicing,"* 66 n. 22, who prefers to read יחד as an adverb, though he acknowledges the possibility of the technical designation. For examples of the adverbial use of יחד, see below.

[51] See the excursus in Chapter 4.

covenant community on earth."[52] Evidence for this can be seen especially in 1QS XI, 8 and 1QH[a] VII, 17 and XI, 23, as in each of these lines the appearance of יחד as a reference to the community is immediately or closely followed by mention of angelic fellowship.[53] Moreover, the meaning of יחד may assist in explaining the otherwise perplexing choice of a non-biblical self-designation[54] for a group that considered itself peerless in matters of biblical interpretation and *halakha*: if "the *Yahad*" encapsulated what was deemed to be a central aspect of the sectarian worldview – namely, togetherness or union with the angels – the selection is quite appropriate.[55]

Second, there are instances when יחד seems to be part of a double entendre or word play,[56] which may have served to remind the reader/worshipper of the nature of the sectarian community. The phrase ביחד רנה (cf. 1QH[a] XI, 24; XIX, 17), mentioned above, is a case in point. Newsom translates it "a common rejoicing,"[57] which in context is a statement on the angel-human character of sectarian life. Given that "the *Yahad*" was the sectarians' preferred self-designation, if it is correct to read יחד as an adverb in XI, 24 and XIX, 17,[58] the choice can hardly be an accident. In a

---

[52] So Collins, *The Scriptures and Sectarianism*, 200; idem, "The Angelic Life," 297. Cf. Fletcher-Louis, *All the Glory*, 90; Schuller, "Recent Scholarship on the Hodayot," 151.

[53] Cf. Holm-Neilson, *Hodayot*, 68 n. 11: "to be taken into the community is the same as to be in fellowship with God, and therefore his hosts."

[54] So Douglas, "Power and Praise," 181 n. 94. Cf. Fletcher-Louis, *All the Glory*, 90. Also note the comments of Elior, *The Three Temples*, 171: "This at once visible and invisible [angelic] world was for them a divine source of authority, an eternal testimony, a cultic inspiration, a historical pledge; they sensed its presence as something palpable, a decisive mystical pattern endowed with divine meaning. Many of the works composed by the secessionist priests express this relationship between the community (or Council) of 'togetherness' (Heb. *yahad*) and the holy creatures in heaven. This was in fact the source of the name by which ... the members of the Community referred to themselves – the *yahad* – reflecting the assumed 'togetherness' of priests and angels. This is the clear import of [various passages in] the *Thanksgiving Hymns*."

[55] Cf. Chazon, "Human & Angelic Prayer," 43; eadem, "Liturgical Function," 139, who describes her third and highest category of human-angelic prayer/praise as "characterized by the *union* with the angels attained by human worshippers."

[56] On word plays as a frequently used rhetorical device in the *Hodayot*, see Stegemann, Schuller, and Newsom, DJD 40, 156. Cf. Harkins "Reading the Qumran Hodayot," 14, who focuses on the numerous word plays in 1QH[a] XI, 6–19, but as it pertains to XI, 20–37 notes only the previously mentioned word play of מקוה in line 21.

[57] See Stegemann, Schuller, and Newsom, DJD 40, 155, 248 (as per Vermes, *CDSSE*, 267, 294). Cf. Wise, Abegg, and Cook, *DSSANT*, 182, 196: "*together with* shouts of joy."

[58] The fact that יחד in 1QH[a] XI, 24 and XIX, 17 can be translated as a noun (i.e., a reference to the community) highlights the ambiguity that makes the word play possible: e.g., García Martínez and Tigchelaar, *DSSSE*, 1:167, 189: "in the *community* of jubilation"; Hughes, *Scriptural Allusions*, 215: "in a *community* of rejoicing"; Holm-Nielsen, *Hodayot*, 64, 185: "in *the choir* of rejoicing."

similar fashion, we have seen that 1QH[a] XIV, 16 states that the sectarians are בגורל יחד עם מלאכי פנים, "in a common lot with/in a lot together with the angels of the presence." What is intriguing about this example is that יחד, which is functioning as an adverb, is grammatically extraneous.[59] It is, however, the ideal word to emphasize the unmediated togetherness the sectarians share with God's angelic priests. Other word plays or double entendres involve the noun סוד. I noted above that סוד can refer to heavenly or earthly assemblies; in 1QS XI, 8 the latter is the primary meaning for both occurrences of the word. However, in light of biblical and sectarian precedent for using סוד to refer to the divine assembly, as well as the fact that the sectarian סוד is here being joined together with the angels, the word is likely functioning as a double entendre of sorts, calling further attention to the conviction that to be part of the sectarian סוד is to join the divine סוד.[60] A similar word play may be at work in 1QH[a] XIX, 14–16: in these lines, the angelic designation, קדושים, "holy ones," is parallel to "children of your truth." Since the latter is likely a reference to sect members, the same would be true of the "holy ones." To refer to the sectarians as "holy ones" is, in and of itself, a double entendre or perhaps more precisely, an example of deliberately ambiguous terminology.[61] But the children of your truth/holy ones are also said to be raised up from the dust "to the council of your truth"

---

[59] Cf. 1QH[a] XIX, 14–15, which has a similar construction and meaning yet lacks יחד (or any other adverb): בגורל עם קדושיכה, "in the lot with your holy ones." However, the omission of יחד may be due to the fact this phrase is part of an ellipsis, whose verb is יחד, "to unite," which itself may be a sectarian word play, given the subject matter of the lines (also see XXIII, 30).

[60] See Alexander, *Mystical Texts*, 56. Frennesson, *"In a Common Rejoicing,"* 66 n. 23, agrees that the human/earthly connotation is primary, but he rightly notes another possible meaning of סוד: "foundation." This meaning complements the reference to the Qumran movement as a "house of holiness," a designation upon which I will comment, below. Cf. Tiller, "The 'Eternal Planting,'" 329 n. 43, who recognizes the sentiment without specifying that it is a word play. Expounding on סוד as "foundation" is Putthoff, *Ontological Aspects*, 120–122, who emphasizes its use in the *Community Rule* as a way for the sectarians to assert themselves as God's "anthropomorphous" structure/place of worship, a practice he sees at work in similar building metaphors in other passages (e.g., 1QS VIII, 7–8).

[61] I will address additional examples of deliberate terminological ambiguity, below. Cf. Collins, *Daniel*, 314, 316, whose well-known comment more or less confirms what we have seen thus far: Despite some "inherent ambiguity in the use of the term at Qumran [e.g., 1QH[a] XIX, 16] ... the holy ones in the sectarian literature ... are normally angels or heavenly beings. Confusion arises because the human community is believed to mingle with the heavenly host in the eschatological war ... and in the community itself, and it can be called the people of the holy ones. There is no undisputed case in this literature, where the expression 'holy ones' in itself refers to human beings."

(לסוד אמתכה),[62] which is likely a reference to the sectarians. In light of the fact that סוד is used elsewhere as a designation for the divine assembly as well as the clear reference to angelic fellowship in XIX, 16, it would seem that another double entendre is intended here: to be part of the reconstituted Israel is to commune in an earthly סוד with fellow sectarian קדושים, who together commune with the angelic קדושים in a heavenly סוד. Lastly, a double entendre may help explain the use of מעמד: given that it is a word that describes the organization of the sectarian reconstitution of Israel (cf. 1QS II, 22–23; VI, 12), it is fitting that it is used as part of the claim that the sectarians have a *station* with the angels in heaven.[63]

For a third indication that present liturgical fellowship with the angels was part of the sectarian definition of being the legitimate people of God, I return to 1QS XI, 7–9. If, according to these lines, a purpose of God joining together the angels with the sectarian assembly (סוד) was "for the council of the community," the passage continues with a brief statement that further expounds this purpose: וסוד מבנית קודש למטעת עולם עם כול קץ נהיה, "(Their) assembly is a house of holiness for the eternal plant during every time to come" (cf. 1QS VIII, 5–8). Swarup's detailed study examines the metaphors of "house" (e.g., 2 Sam 7:10–14) and "plant(ing)" (e.g., Isa 60:21; 61:3), concluding that these biblical designations were appropriated by the Qumran movement to assert its "all encompassing role as 'a kingdom of priests and a holy nation'" as per Exod 19:5–6.[64] The sectarians could thus promote themselves as both the nation's righteous remnant and its undefiled priests. In other words, these terms constituted a powerful, two-pronged claim to be the true Israel. Swarup rightly concludes that sectarian use of these metaphors in 1QS is thereby distinguished from the less exclusivist use in the Hebrew Bible,[65] and it can also be differentiated from its application in texts such as 1 Enoch, Jubilees, and *4QInstruction*, which were discussed in

---

[62] On the restoration of אמתכה, see Stegemann, Schuller, and Newsom, DJD 40, 245.

[63] Frennesson, *"In a Common Rejoicing,"* 49, notes the dual use of the word, but does not refer to it as a word play.

[64] Cf. Swarup, *The Self-Understanding*, 193–196, who builds on the important yet brief study of Tiller, "The 'Eternal Planting,'" 268–294. The sect as "the true Israel" is widely noted in discussions of the "house" and "plant" metaphors; cf., e.g., Wernberg-Møller, *The Manual of Discipline*, 13–14; Davidson, *Angels at Qumran*, 166 n. 4; Frennesson, *"In a Common Rejoicing,"* 65. On the complementary idea that 1QS XI, 7–9 contributes to the Qumran movement's promotion of itself rather than the Jerusalem sanctuary as the legitimate temple, see Church, *Hebrews and the Temple*, 97–110; Stefan Beyerle, "Temples and Sanctuaries within Their Apocalyptic Setting," in *Various Aspects of Worship in Deuterocanonical and Cognate Literature* (eds., Géza G. Xeravits, József Zsengellér, and Ibolya Balla; DCLY; Berlin: De Gruyter, 2017), 48–49; Putthoff, *Ontological Aspects*, 103–138; Hilary Evans Kapfer, "The Relationship Between the Damascus Document and the Community Rule: Attitudes toward the Temple as a Test Case," *DSD* 14 (2007): 169.

[65] Swarup, *The Self-Understanding*, 70–73.

Chapter 3.[66] However, I would suggest that Swarup has understated the contribution angelic fellowship makes to the sectarian claims to be the true Israel. For example, the import of 1QS XI, 8 is surely more nuanced than the observation that "as much as the angels were in the presence of God, [the sectarians] too were now in the presence of God."[67] That is, if "house of holiness" and "eternal plant" are indicative of being God's legitimate people and Israel's undefiled priests, perhaps there is good reason why 1QS XI prefaces this assertion with a boast of angelic fellowship. I propose that 1QH[a] XIV, 16 hints at such a reason: there arguably would have been no better way for the sect to promote its identity as the true Israel than to claim to have fellowship with the angels of the presence, the very archetypes of the nation's priesthood. That 1QS XI, 7–9 envisions a connection with the heavenly priesthood finds support in the use of מבנית, a word which in the *Songs of the Sabbath Sacrifice* refers to the animate structures of the heavenly sanctuary (cf. 4Q403 1 I, 41, 44; 4Q405 14–15 I, 6; 11Q17 2–7).[68] More importantly, one of the two *Hodayot* passages examined by Swarup, 1QH[a]

---

[66] So Tiller, "The 'Eternal Planting,'" 313, who notes that the authors of 1QS and the 1QH[a] have "significantly narrowed" the application of the plant metaphor in comparison to its use in other early Jewish texts. While there is little doubt that *4QInstruction's* co-opting of the metaphor contributes to the exclusivist viewpoint of its authors, it has already been noted that the organization of the group responsible for that composition does not appear to be as formal as that of the Qumran movement nor its boasts as grandiose or stringent, especially in comparison to the emphasis the sectarians placed on being the true Israel. Cf. Jennifer Metten Pantoja, *The Metaphor of the Divine Planter: Stinking Grapes or Pleasant Planting?* (BibInt 155; Leiden: Brill, 2017), 191. Also see Bautch, *Glory and Power*, 139–140, who provides a helpful overview of the sectarian texts vis-à-vis the outlook of Jubilees.

[67] Situating 1QS XI, 7–9 in the context of the broader *Community Rule*, Swarup, *The Self-Understanding*, 72, emphasizes the exclusiveness of these lines, but he does not comment directly on the contribution angelic fellowship makes to the notion of the sect as the true Israel. Cf. Tiller, "The 'Eternal Plant,'" 329, who writes that "assimilation to the angels is connected with the 'eternal planting,'" but he does not elaborate as to the significance of this connection in 1QS XI, 7–9 other than noting that "a particular historical group of people within Israel are designated as the eternal planting because they also participate in the eschatological blessing of participation in heavenly activities with the angels." This is important, but Tiller does not explain *why* participation with the angels allows the sect to be designated as the eternal planting. Angel, *Otherworldly*, 77, observes the combination of the "plant" metaphor with angelic fellowship in 1QS XI, 7–9 as well as in 1QH[a] XIV, 15–18 (see below), but he does not comment on their functions in these texts. He is among many that suggest, however, that a possible background to these ideas is found in *4QInstruction*; see Chapter 3.

[68] I.e., this may be another word play alluding to the relationship between the sectarian "house" and the heavenly location of its angelic fellowship; see further, below.

XIV, 17–21,[69] is immediately preceded by the claim of fellowship with the angels of the presence in XIV, 16, which was just discussed. Beginning in line 17, the psalmist says of the sect that

17 ... ‏והם ישובו בפי כבודכה ויהיו שריכה בגור[ל עולם ונזע]ם
18 ‏פרח כציץ[ ] יציץ ל[ה]ור עולם לנ'ל נצר לעופי מטעת עולם ויצל צל על כול תב‎ל‎
‏וד[ן]ליותי[ו]
19 ‏עד שחק‎ים‎ ושרשיו עד תהום וכול נהרות עדן [ת]ל[]חלחנה ד[]ל[]י[]ותיו והיה לים‎ים‎ ל[אין]
20 ‏חקר וה‎ת‎אזרו על תבל לאין אפס וע‎ד‎ שאול [   ]   ‏ו[ה]יה מעין אור למקור
21 ‏עולם לאין חסר...

17 ... they repent because of your glorious command, so that they become your princes in the [eternal] lo[t and] their [shoot]
18 opens as a flower [blooms, for] everlasting fragrance, making a sprout grow into the branches of an eternal planting. And it will cast shade over all the world, and its br[anches]
19 will reach to the clouds, and its roots as far as the deep. All the rivers of Eden [make] its [br]an[ches m]oist and it will (extend) to the measure[less] seas,
20 and they move streaming over the world without end, and as far as Sheol [and] the spring of light will become an eternal
21 fountain, without lack. ...

In addition to the sectarians being referred to as שריכה, "your princes," which may be another example of deliberately ambiguous terminology and a way of asserting that "the lot and privileges ascribed to the community members are on a level with those of the angels,"[70] Swarup again points out that the plant metaphors – the original referents of which were Israel less stringently defined – have been reworked, actualized, and applied by the sectarians to themselves: they alone are the righteous remnant.[71] While there

---

[69] These lines are textually problematic. For discussion, cf. Swarup, *The Self-Understanding*, 16–34 (who follows Sukenik's line numbering); Stegemann, Schuller, and Newsom, DJD 40, 187–190.

[70] So Frennesson, *"In Common Rejoicing,"* 52, who rightly notes that this term is used of angels as well as high-ranking humans. Cf. Holm-Nielsen, *Hodayot*, 115. *Contra* Fletcher-Louis, *All the Glory*, 106, who views it as an example of exalted humanity in its "angelmorphic" or "divine" state.

[71] Swarup, *The Self-Understanding*, 23, 30–34. Cf. Devorah Dimant, "Qumran Sectarian Literature," in *Jewish Writings of the Second Temple Period* (ed., Michael E. Stone; Philadelphia: Fortress, 1984), 539. Abegg, "The Covenant of the Qumran Sectarians," 97, observes that the remnant concept also occurs earlier in column XIV, remarking that even if the Qumran movement was confident that the eschaton would mean that other Jews would accept the sectarian reconstitution of Israel, "in the evil meantime, the community saw themselves as the guardians of God's covenant until the time that all Israel would return. In the words of the sectarian hymnist [from 1QH[a] XIV, 11–12], '... You will raise up survivors among Your people and a remnant among Your inheritance. You will refine them so that they may be cleansed from guilt. For all their works are in Your truth, and in Your mercies You will judge them with abundant compassion and

is admittedly no mention of being a priestly "house of holiness" as there is in 1QS XI, 7–9,[72] such a boast would likely be redundant next to a claim stating that the sectarians enjoy an unmediated relationship with the priestly-titled angels of the presence. Thus, the assertion that the sect designated itself as the eternal planting because it experienced the eschatological blessings of angelic fellowship in the here and now is correct but insufficient:[73] the Qumran movement could claim (and simultaneously enhanced its claims) to be the true Israel in part because it had fellowship with the angels who were considered the archetypes of the nation's priesthood. Furthermore, we have seen that this fellowship has been specified as occurring with angels characterized by knowledge (cf. 1QH^a VII, 17; XI, 23–24; XIX, 17), a detail that not only complements the numerous claims of the sect to be the privileged recipients of heavenly insights[74] but may also assist in explaining 1QH^a XIV's use of מקור, which here and elsewhere may denote "the transmission of supernatural revelation."[75] It was argued in Chapter 3 that the charge to *4QInstruction*'s addressee, the מבין, to "open a fountain of all the holy ones," could be an exhortation to proclaim the revealed knowledge to his community, including the insights of the heavenly priesthood. Intriguingly, 1QH^a X, 20 announces in similar language that God grants understanding for this purpose: לפתוח מקור דעת לכול מבינים, "to open a fountain of knowledge for all who are able to understand." Both 1QH^a X, 20 and XIV, 21 have been described as having the "connotations of priestly praise

---

bountiful forgiveness; teaching them according to Your word.'" Moreover, that the sect claims to be the shoot/sprout that *grows into* an eternal plant may reveal confidence in the longevity, influence, and growth of the sect and/or conversion to sectarian ways (cf. Ezek 17:22–24; 31:2–14; Dan 4:9–12; Mark 4:32), though this should not be mistaken for blind optimism or quasi-universalism; see Chapter 4. Cf. Tiller, "The 'Eternal Planting,'" 329–331.

[72] Though notice that the sect *is* described as "the way of holiness" in 1QH^a XIV, 20–21 and as a "strong building" in XIV, 29.

[73] Tiller, "The 'Eternal Planting,'" 329–330, also understates the interplay of angelic fellowship and the exclusivist sentiments of the plant imagery when he says that the expansion of the sectarian shoot/plant "corresponds to" fellowship with the angels of the presence insofar as the growth of the sect even reaches up to heaven. But angelic fellowship is more than a matter of growth/influence – it is a matter of identity, especially given that an unmediated relationship with the angels of the presence is specified.

[74] E.g., 1QS IV, 22, which declares that God purifies the elect with this goal in mind: להבין ישרים בדעת עליון וחכמת בני שמים להשכיל תמימי דרך, "so that upright ones may have insight into the knowledge of the Most High and the wisdom of the sons of heaven, and the perfect in the Way may receive understanding." See Qimron and Charlesworth, "The Rule of the Community (1QS)," 19.

[75] So Goff, *4QInstruction*, 244, who observes the similar use of מקור in 1QS XI, 3. For other uses of "fountain" imagery in the *Hodayot*, see Strugnell and Harrington, DJD 34, 303. On the relationship between *4QInstruction* and the *Hodayot*, see Goff, "Reading Wisdom at Qumran," 263–288.

in the temple."[76]   It is thus conceivable that the authors of these psalms envisioned an integral relationship between communion with the angels of the presence, the revealed knowledge of heaven, and the teaching role of the sectarian priesthood and leadership.[77]

In short, if the sect was trying to convince its own members or to persuade outsiders that it constituted the true Israel,[78] what better way for a group with

---

[76] So Wold, *Women, Men, and Angels*, 164–165.

[77] It should be acknowledged, however, that מבין, which is only found at X, 20 in 1QH[a], is not strictly a priestly term; see Chapter 3. Cf. Lange, "Sages and Scribes," 274–277.

[78] The comments of Newsom, *The Self as Symbolic Space*, 343–344 (cf. eadem, "Kenneth Burke Meets the Teacher of Righteousness: Rhetorical Strategies in the Hodayot and the Serek Ha-Yahad," in *Of Scribes and Scrolls: Studies on the Hebrew Bible, Intertestamental Judaism, and Christian Origins: Presented to John Strugnell on the Occasion of his Sixtieth Birthday* [eds., John J. Collins, Harold W. Attridge, and Thomas H. Tobin; New York: University Press of America, 1990], 125–131) assist in bringing the angelic fellowship claims of 1QH[a] XIV, 15–16 into sharper focus. She highlights that a concern of the large psalm in which these lines are found (XIII, 22–XV, 8) is to address the defection, inner-community discord, and anti-leadership grumblings (XIII, 24–25) that may have been inevitable aspects of the confrontational nature of community life (cf. 1QS V, 24–VI, 1). Later in the hymn, the image of a fortified city is employed, likely to depict the covenanted community alone as a place of security and blessing (XIV, 29–38). Accordingly, Michael O. Wise, "The Concept of a New Covenant in the Teacher Hymns from Qumran (1QH[a] X–XVII)" in *The Concept of Covenant*, 126, argues that "entering and leaving the New Covenant of the Teacher of Righteousness were matters of eternal consequence. Utter destruction was the price one paid for making the wrong decision." While many no longer share Wise's confidence in seeing the Teacher Hymns as reflecting the voice of the historical מורה הצדק, it is difficult to object to his conclusion that the sectarian reconstitution of Israel's covenant was taken with utmost severity by the sect and its leadership. However, as much as angelic fellowship is set forth as both a benefit of fidelity to the sectarian covenant and something covenant rejecters would fail to experience (cf. Davidson, *Angels at Qumran*, 194; Newsom, *The Self as Symbolic Space*, 343; Michael O. Wise, *The First Messiah: Investigating the Messiah before Jesus* [San Francisco: Harper, 1999], 179; Hultgren, *From the Damascus Covenant*, 418–419), it is more than that: unmediated communion with the angels of the presence – the very beings who keep and bear the marks of the covenant in heaven (Jub. 2:18, 30; 6:18; 15:27–28) – would not only have served to legitimate the Teacher/sect as the correct interpreters and adherents to Israel's covenant; it would also have heightened the plausibility of the consequences for covenant rejection. Intriguingly, it has been suggested that one of the uses of the *Hodayot* and 1QS XI in sectarian life was their recitation in the well-known covenant renewal ceremony (cf. 1QS I, 16–III, 12). On the possibility that the psalms examined throughout this section and others were used for this purpose, see Davidson, *Angels at Qumran*, 188; Hughes, *Scriptural Allusions*, 227; Hultgren, *From the Damascus Covenant*, 429–431; Angela Kim Harkins, "The Performative Reading of the Hodayot: The Arousal of Emotions and the Exegetical Generation of Texts," *JSP* 21 (2011): 61; Newsom, *The Self as Symbolic Space*, 167; Judith H. Newman, "Covenant Renewal and Transformational Scripts in the Performance of the Hodayot and 2 Corinthians," in *Jesus, Paulus und die Texte von Qumran* (eds., Jörg Frey and Enno Edzard Popkes; WUNT 2/390; Tübingen: Mohr Siebeck, 2015), 298.

priestly concerns to do so than to announce that being members of the covenant community entailed worship with the angels who were the heavenly archetype and ideal of the nation's priesthood? Significantly, it is the celestial temple and the exemplary worship of its angelic priests that are the foci of the text to which I will now turn, the *Songs of the Sabbath Sacrifice*.

C. Songs of the Sabbath Sacrifice

Whereas the passages from the *Hodayot* and 1QS XI just examined were likely employed in liturgical settings and boast of common worship with the angels, the role these texts had in achieving this experience has traditionally not received much scholarly attention.[79] The same cannot be said of the *Songs of the Sabbath Sacrifice* (henceforth, *SSS*). While not the only proposed function of this work, here I accept readings of *SSS* that understand them as "one of the ritual mechanisms by which the Qumran community's belief in communion with the angels was actually experienced."[80]

My discussion of *SSS* will be comprised of two parts. I will first provide an overview of the contents of the document, highlighting its fascination with the heavenly temple and the angelic priests who minister in it. I will then examine the significance of *SSS* as it pertains to sectarian angelic fellowship claims, noting how the work's focus on the celestial sanctuary and the scholarly estimations of its function are eminently appropriate for a group that not only claimed fellowship with the angels but also was convinced that it was the true Israel. Although the provenance of *SSS* is debated, I will proceed under the assumption that it is a sectarian text.[81]

---

[79] But see the insightful recent work of Angela Kim Harkins, *Reading with an "I" to the Heavens: Looking at the Qumran Hodayot through the Lens of Visionary Traditions* (New York: de Gruyter, 2012), 267, who has proposed that the *Hodayot* "were read and experienced by the ancient community of covenanters within an on-going practice of performative prayer in which a reader sought to reenact the affective experiences that are described in them." Cf. Schäfer, *The Origins of Jewish Mysticism*, 151–152.

[80] Newsom, "Religious Experience," 216. On the use of *SSS* at Qumran, see below.

[81] Nine fragmentary copies of *SSS* were found at Qumran (4Q400–407 [= 4QShirot[a-h]] and 11Q17 [11QShirot]) and one at Masada (Mas1k), with paleographic estimations of the various manuscripts ranging from the late Hasmonean period to the late Herodian period. Treatments of the texts are found in the following: Cave 4 manuscripts: Carol A. Newsom, "Shirot 'Olat Hashabbat," in *Qumran Cave 4. VI: Poetical and Liturgical Texts, Part I* (eds., Esther Eshel et al.; DJD 11; Oxford: Claredon Press, 1998), 173–401; Cave 11 manuscript: Florentino García Martínez et al., "11QShirot 'Olat ha-Shabbat," in DJD 23, 259–304; Masada manuscript: Carol A. Newsom and Yigael Yadin, "The Masada Fragment of the Qumran Songs of the Sabbath Sacrifice," *IEJ* 34 (1984): 77–88. Cf. Newsom, *Songs of the Sabbath Sacrifice*, which was the first publication of all the relevant material. While establishing the provenance of *SSS* would be challenging even without the Masada discovery, Mas1k introduces an obvious difficulty in evaluating the origins of the

I. The Heavenly Temple and Angelic Priesthood of SSS

Even a cursory reading of *SSS* reveals that it is dominated by the heavenly temple and its angelic priesthood,[82] and scholars have highlighted how this

---

work: the presence of the document somewhere other than Qumran. The challenging nature of determining *SSS's* provenance can be seen in the successive evaluations of Newsom, who i.) initially considered *SSS* to be sectarian (cf. *Songs of the Sabbath Sacrifice*, 1–4; eadem, "He Has Established for Himself Priests," in *Archaeology and History in the Dead Sea Scrolls: The New York University Conference on the Dead Sea Scrolls* [ed., Lawrence H. Schiffman; JSPSup 8; JSOTMS 2; Sheffield: JSOT Press, 1990], 103); ii.) subsequently "experimented" with the notion of viewing *SSS* as an "adopted or naturalized text within the sectarian perspective of the Qumran community" (eadem, "'Sectually Explicit,'" 179–185); and iii.) eventually returned to her earlier conclusion of sectarian provenance (eadem, "Religious Experience," 205 n. 1). Arguments marshaled for *SSS* as a non-sectarian composition include the use of אלהים as a divine epithet (something rare in the acknowledged sectarian texts) and the non-polemical nature of the document. However, the sectarian *Songs of the Sage* (4Q510–511) employs אלהים with frequency (see below), and as Newsom, *The Self as Symbolic Space*, 269, has noted, even texts that are not explicitly polemical may function as such, especially in an environment of religious competition where the language of outsiders may be considered "faulty and defective or shallow and superficial." With this in mind, the grandiose revelatory claims implicit in *SSS's* detailed knowledge of the heavenly world only complement the angelic fellowship boasts of the sect. Moreover, it is not unreasonable to conclude that the Masada copy of *SSS* was brought there from Qumran, and scholars have also noted numerous similarities (both terminological and ideological) with sectarian texts such as the *Community Rule* and the *Hodayot,* not least of which is the use of the *Maskil* leader designation (see below). For discussion of these issues, see Daniel K. Falk, *Daily, Sabbath, and Festival Prayers in the Dead Sea Scrolls* (STDJ 27; Leiden: Brill, 1998), 127–130; Alexander, *Mystical Texts*, 51, 97; Tuschling, *Angels and Orthodoxy*, 124; Klawans, *Purity, Sacrifice, and the Temple*, 135; Henry W. M. Rietz, "Identifying Compositions and Traditions of the Qumran Community: The Songs of the Sabbath Sacrifice as a Test Case," in *Qumran Studies: New Approaches, New Questions* (eds., Michael T. Davis and Brent A. Strawn; Grand Rapids: Eerdmans, 2007), 29–52; Brent A. Strawn and Henry W. M. Rietz, "(More) Sectarian Terminology," in *Qumran Studies*, 53–64; Judith H. Newman, "Priestly Prophets at Qumran: Summoning Sinai through the Songs of the Sabbath Sacrifice," in *The Significance of Sinai: Traditions about Sinai and Divine Revelation in Judaism and Christianity* (eds., George J. Brooke, Hindy Najman, and Loren T. Stuckenbruck; TBN 12; Leiden: Brill, 2008), 43–46; Schäfer, *The Origins of Jewish Mysticism*, 130; Angel, *Otherworldly*, 85–87, 106; Noam Mizrahi, "Aspects of Poetic Stylization in Second Temple Hebrew: A Linguistic Comparison of the Songs of the Sabbath Sacrifice with Ancient Piyyut," in *Hebrew in the Second Temple Period: The Hebrew of the Dead Sea Scrolls and of Other Contemporary Sources: Proceedings of the Twelfth International Symposium of the Orion Center for the Study of the Dead Sea Scrolls and Associated Literature and the Fifth International Symposium on the Hebrew of the Dead Sea Scrolls and Ben Sira, Jointly Sponsored by the Eliezer Ben-Yehuda Center for the Study of the History of the Hebrew Language, 29–31 December, 2008* (eds., Stephen E. Fassberg, Moshe Bar-Asher, and Ruth A. Clements; STDJ 108; Leiden: Brill, 2013), 147.

[82] Cf. Klawans, *Purity, Sacrifice, and the Temple*, 135: "The extant portions of the *Songs of the Sabbath Sacrifice* seem to do little else but describe the celestial worship of God as carried out by the angels." The most vocal objections to a dualistic interpretation

composition is indebted to the exegetical traditions of certain Hebrew passages, including the תבנית of the earthly sanctuary (e.g., Exod 25:9), which I noted in Chapter 2.[83] In fact, the work has been called "the most detailed and explicit portrait of the angelic priesthood and the celestial temple

---

of *SSS* have been those of Fletcher-Louis, *All the Glory*, 252–394. As previously noted, he often understands angels not to be angels at all but humans (in this case, the Qumran sectarians) in their redeemed "angelmorphic," "angelic," or "divine" state, which is also its originally-intended "theological anthropology" (cf. Gen 1:26–28). For a detailed response to Fletcher-Louis' reading specifically as it pertains to *SSS*, see Alexander, *Mystical Texts*, 45–47, whose five main points of rebuttal echo objections to the application of Fletcher-Louis' angelmorphic anthropology approach to the *War Scroll* and the *Hodayot*; they can be summarized as follows. First, his thesis is counter-intuitive: it strains plausibility to argue, to the extent that Fletcher-Louis does, that references normally thought to refer to angels or heaven are actually references to humans and earth. Second, his reading does not sufficiently pay attention to the dualism of the text. Third, the notion of angelmorphism itself is far from clear, especially when the text's dualism is not appreciated: i.e., if figures traditionally understood to be angels are humans, it is difficult to understand what angelmorphism means. Fourth, the text is treated in an overly literal fashion insofar as it misconstrues the use of *anthropo*morphism as applied to angels. Fifth, the reading overemphasizes the realized aspects of the sect's eschatology. Fletcher-Louis has recently returned to the arguments of *All the Glory*, and while he no longer favours the term "angelmorphic" and acknowledges that some *SSS* passages refer to actual angels, he still firmly insists that the dualistic notion of a heavenly temple "up there" in ancient Judaism is "a modern scholarly myth"; see idem, "On Angels, Men and Priests," 141–166, here 143 n. 3, 151, 154, 161. However, even if as per Fletcher-Louis certain Second Temple Period texts portray the Jerusalem temple as microcosmic (e.g., Joseph, *B.J.* 5:212–213, 218; *Ant.* 3:123, 132, 146, 182, 179–187; Philo, *Spec.* 1:82–97; *QE* 2:51–124), I remain unconvinced that this observation bears the weight of the pervasive, anti-dualistic burden Fletcher-Louis places on it. This is especially true for texts like *SSS*, which are replete with designations which elsewhere refer to *celestial* beings – and are cogently and widely interpreted as such in *SSS*. For a proposal that is similar in some respects to that of Fletcher-Louis, see Newman, "Priestly Prophets," 31 n. 8, who does not consider *SSS* to be portraying a heavenly temple indwelt by angels but instead argues that "the material temple of men" should be "understood figuratively as the divine temple." Cf. Christopher R. A. Morray-Jones, "The Temple Within: The Embodied Divine Image and its Worship in the Dead Sea Scrolls and Other Early Jewish and Christian Sources," *SBL Seminar Papers, 1998* (SBLSP 37; Atlanta: Scholars Press, 1998), 400–431.

[83] For the use of תבנית in *SSS*, cf. 4Q403 1 I, 43–44; 4Q403 1 II, 3, 16; 4Q404 6 5; 4Q405 20–21–22 II, 8; 11Q17 8 3; 9 6; see Davila, "The Macrocosmic Temple," 1–19, here 18, who notes many such exegetical traditions and summarizes as follows: "biblical texts that describe the earthly Temple (or in the case of Ezekiel 40–48, a proposed blueprint for the earthly Temple) have been ransacked for details about the cosmic Temple and its angelic priesthood." Cf. Church, *Hebrews and the Temple*, 138; Jared C. Calaway, "Heavenly Sabbath, Heavenly Sanctuary: The Transformation of Priestly Sacred Space and Sacred Time in the Songs of the Sabbath Sacrifice and the Epistle to the Hebrews (Ph.D. diss; Columbia University, 2010), 167–170.

not only at Qumran, but in all of Second Temple Jewish literature."[84]   The content of *SSS* is intimately related to its thirteen-song structure,[85] which can be outlined as follows:[86] Songs 1–5 describe the establishment, arrangement, and responsibilities of the angelic priesthood, an initial account of the celestial temple, and fragmentary references to celestial warfare; Songs 6–8 speak of the praises of the seven chief angelic princes and their deputies as well as the animate temple itself; and in bewildering detail, Songs 9–13 provide a description of the celestial temple, which is inspired by the sanctuary of Ezek 40–48; there are also references to the throne chariot/*merkabah*, heavenly sacrifices, and the regalia of the angelic high priests.[87]

In addition to using common terms for angels such as "divine beings" (אלים), "gods" (אלוהים),[88] "holy ones" (קדושים), "spirits" (רוחות), and

---

[84] Angel, *Otherworldly*, 84. Cf. Klawans, *Purity, Sacrifice, and the Temple*, 112: "A well-developed angelology … is an absolute prerequisite for the notion of a heavenly temple."

[85] The introduction to each song is clear that the thirteen songs were used for at least the first thirteen Sabbaths of the year. Scholars disagree, however, as to whether the songs were only used for the opening quarter of the assumed 364-day calendar (so, e.g., Newsom, "He Has Established, 114) or whether the cycle of songs was repeated in the second, third, and fourth quarters (so, e.g., Alexander, *Mystical Texts*, 52). While this issue is not particularly relevant to my discussion, there may be symbolic significance to the fact that in the first quarter of the year Songs 12 and 13 would have occurred after *Shavuot*; see below.

[86] As per Newsom, "He Has Established," 103–120, whose overview is followed by a brief, song-by-song commentary. More detailed treatments are provided by eadem, *Songs of the Sabbath Sacrifice*; Alexander, *Mystical Texts*, 15–72; James R. Davila, *Liturgical Works* (ECDSS; Grand Rapids: Eerdmans, 2000), 97–167. For a convenient reconstructed presentation of *SSS* according to song, see Carol A. Newsom, ed., "Angelic Liturgy: The Songs of the Sabbath Sacrifice (4Q400–407, 11Q17, Mas1k): A Composite Text," in *The Dead Sea Scrolls: Hebrew, Aramaic, and Greek Texts with English Translations* (ed., J. H. Charlesworth et al.; PTSDSSP 4B; Tübingen: Mohr Siebeck; Louisville: Westminster John Knox Press, 1994), 138–189. I will return to the question of structure, below, when I briefly address where the climax of the text is located.

[87] Cf. Alexander, *Mystical Texts*, 17, who notes that the rather brief description of the temple in Song 1 anticipates the more detailed accounts found in the later songs.

[88] It is a stretch to say with Schäfer, *The Origins of Jewish Mysticism*, 133, that some of the angelic designations, especially those that have a variation of אל or אלהים as part of their name, blur the division between angels and God. While it is correct that *SSS* refers to certain angels as honoured by lesser angels and humans (cf. Song 2:20 [= 4Q401 14 I, 5), it is because of these angels' exemplary worship of God that they are so honoured. If Song 11 depicts the angels as "recoiling" (מהר) from God's voice, their subordinate status is further emphasized. Thus, even the most elite of the angelic priests are ontologically distinct from God and obedient to his will, which includes the revelation of divine knowledge. On these points, see Stuckenbruck, *Angel Veneration*, 157–164; Tuschling, *Angels and Orthodoxy*, 130; Alexander, *Mystical Texts*, 19, 21, 29, 39. On the subordinate status of the angels, see especially 4Q403 1 I, 35–36. For comments, see Davidson, *Angels*

numerous constructs based on these words,[89] a few other designations employed by *SSS* are noteworthy. As we have seen, the language of the Book of Jubilees, the *Hodayot*, and other texts suggests that certain angels had sacerdotal roles, and similar designations are employed here. For example, Song 1:4[90] (= 4Q400 1 I, 4) refers to the משרתי פנים, "ministers of the presence," a title that approximates the מלאכי פנים already discussed (e.g., Jub. 2:2, 18; 1QH^a XIV, 16).[91] Moreover, *SSS* is the earliest extent Jewish text to employ the word priest in reference to an angel:[92] כוהני קורב, "priests of the inner sanctum,"[93] is a designation seemingly in apposition to not only

---

at Qumran, 240, 245. Cf. Tuschling, *Angels and Orthodoxy*, 124, who mentions the "derivative holiness" of the angels.

[89] For a thorough discussion of angelic terminology and references, see Newsom, *Songs of the Sabbath Sacrifice*, 23–38; Davidson, *Angels at Qumran*, 236–237, 247–253, 338–342, who notes that this "rich inventory" of terminology may account for *SSS's* relatively infrequent use of מלאך, which perhaps was considered too mundane.

[90] Song 1:4 designates the fourth line of the first song. All such references, as well as the Hebrew text, sigla, and translation of *SSS* cited here are from the composite arrangement of Newsom, "Angelic Liturgy," 138–189.

[91] While the terms are obviously different – and thus the influence of Jubilees and its "angels of the presence" cannot be proven (so, e.g., Tuschling, *Angels and Orthodoxy*, 125; Newsom, *Songs of the Sabbath Sacrifice*, 36) – in light of Ps 103:21, which uses משרתיו as an angelic designation, there is no reason to think that משרתי פנים and מלאכי פנים are not synonymous; so Davidson, *Angels at Qumran*, 238–239, 249. Cf. Davila, "The Macrocosmic Temple," 12–17, who proposes that *SSS* employs various themes from Isa 63:7–14, including the designation מלאך פניו; see Chapter 2.

[92] Newsom, *Songs of the Sabbath Sacrifice*, 26. Cf. Davidson, *Angels at Qumran*, 248; Falk, *Daily, Sabbath, and Festival Prayers*, 136; Tuschling, *Angels and Orthodoxy*, 124. *Contra* Fletcher-Louis, "On Angels, Men and Priests," 164, who denies that angels are ever clearly referred to as priests in ancient Jewish texts. But the evidence of *SSS* does not support his objection. E.g., it is difficult *not* to read the string of epithets in Song 1:1–5 as referring to angelic priests: "Praise the God of … O godlike beings of all the Most Holy Ones … among the eternally holy, the Most Holy Ones. And they have become for him priests of the inner sanctum, ministers of the presence in his glorious inner room. In the congregation of all the divine beings of knowledge … ."

[93] The word קורב is often translated as "inner sanctum" (lit.: "nearness") and is thus read as an example of a noun which in Biblical Hebrew would follow the *qatl* or *qitl* pattern but in the Scrolls follows a *qutl* pattern. For discussion, see Qimron, *The Hebrew of the Dead Sea Scrolls*, 65; Newsom, *Songs of the Sabbath Sacrifice*, 36–37; Swarup, *The Self-Understanding*, 135. *Contra* Noam Mizrahi, "Aspects of Poetic Stylization," 155–156, who argues that קורב is not a noun that *SSS* uses interchangeably with דביר (discussed below) to refer to the celestial temple's holy of holies but a verbal noun/infinitive of קרב, and therefore describes the actions of the priest as those who approach or draw near to God (cf. Song 1:20 [= 4Q400 1 I, 20]; Ezek 40:46; 42:13; 43:16; 44:15; 45:4). Either way, the sense is the same: these angelic כוהנים have been accorded the highest of sacerdotal privileges in the celestial temple. Cf. Davila, *Liturgical Works*, 98, who suggests that interpretive reflection upon Exod 23:20–23 "in which God tells the Israelites that he is sending his angel before them and that they should obey this angel 'for

משרתי פנים but also קדושי קדושים, "Most Holy Ones" (e.g., Song 1:10),[94] and likely refers to the most elite/privileged of angelic priests. It would also seem that the seven נשיאי רוש, "chief princes,"[95] and נשיאי משנה, "deputy princes,"[96] who are respectively summoned to praise in Song 6 and Song 8, are alternative epithets for the angelic high priests and their most senior assistants. It may be that these seven chief princes correspond to the early Jewish tradition that envisioned seven (rather than four) archangels (cf. 1 En. 20:1–8),[97] though this is far from certain as there are factors that complicate decipherment of the work's angelic hierarchy. One such factor is that the notion of "seven" is a prominent feature of *SSS*.[98] Another complicating factor is the possible reference to Melchizedek in 4Q401 11 3, which Newsom locates somewhere between Songs 3–5 and restores as follows: מלכי]צדק כוהן בעד[ת אל, "Melchi]zedek, priest in the assemb[ly of God"; Newsom also proposes that 4Q401 22 3 be restored to מל[כי צדק, which is immediately preceded by reference to the priestly-consecratory idiom מלו ידיהם, "they fill their hands" (cf. Exod 29:9, 33, 35), even if she acknowledges that there are other possibilities (e.g., כוהני צדק).[99] Although

---

my name is in his midst' (כי שמי בקרבו). The composers of *Songs of the Sabbath Sacrifice* may have taken this phrase to mean 'for My name is in his (the angel's) interior (sanctuary),'" with Davila further suggesting that Melchizedek may have been the angel so envisioned; see below.

[94] Or "Holiest of Holy Ones," a designation which is an obvious allusion to the "Most Holy Place/Holiest of Holies" of the temple in which these angels serve; see Schäfer, *The Origins of Jewish Mysticism*, 132. I will return to the architecture of the heavenly temple, below. On the apposition of these designations in Song 1, see Davidson, *Angels at Qumran*, 239.

[95] As Newsom, *Songs of the Sabbath Sacrifice*, 27, points out, the word translated prince is not the common angelic epithet שר but rather נשיא, which is only elsewhere used as an angelic designation in *Sefer Ha-Razim* (ca. 4th cent. CE). Regardless, the notion of angelic "princes" is entirely appropriate given that God is most frequently referred to as "king" in *SSS*; see Alexander, *Mystical Texts*, 37.

[96] On the notion of deputy chief priests, see Alexander, *Mystical Texts*, 33–34. Cf. 2 Kgs 23:4; 25:18; 1QM II, 1. For examples in the Rabbinic Literature, see *m. Tamid* 7:3; *m. Yoma* 4:1; *b. Yoma 39a*.

[97] See, e.g., Davidson, *Angels at Qumran*, 249–251.

[98] If there were just seven priests (i.e., chief priest, deputy chief priest, and five others), interpretation would be relatively simple as each priest would be responsible for the seven psalms mentioned in Song 8; see Alexander, *Mystical Texts*, 33. However, the celestial temple itself also appears to be sevenfold, which complicates the matter. I will discuss this in greater detail, below. For discussion of various aspects of *SSS's* sevenfold character, see Christian Stettler, "Astronomische Vorstellungen in den Sabbatopferliedern," in *Gottesdienst und Engel*, 99–117.

[99] Newsom, *Songs of the Sabbath Sacrifice*, 133–134, 143–144. Also see Alexander, *Mystical Texts*, 22–25, 69–71, who discusses Melchizedek and the theme of cosmic warfare in Songs 3–5.

Tuschling is right to point out that "the conjectured mentions of Melchizedek [...] do not fit well with known schemes of archangels,"[100] her objection that there is nothing in SSS that suggests "a single chief angel over the seven chief princes" is the subject of debate. The fragmentary nature of SSS means all proposals are tentative. But Newsom and Alexander have both argued that SSS's rare singular כוהן at 4Q401 11 3 (cf. 4Q403 1 II, 24) may imply that Melchizedek is envisioned as the ranking high priest.[101] Elaborating on this interpretation, as well as the observation that fragment 11 has strong affinities with 11Q13 II, 10,[102] Davila has noted that 4Q402 4 7–10, which he places in the vicinity of Song 5, mentions the "war of God" (cf. 1QM XV, 12) and the "war of heavenly clouds" (cf. Rev 12:7);[103] what he considers a related fragment, 4Q402 2 4, refers to the inner-most part of the heavenly temple,[104] the place where only the most privileged of angels would be permitted to serve. Davila thus infers that Song 5 (and perhaps the songs that precede it)[105] depict Melchizedek as "the high-priestly, eschatological [angelic] redeemer, much the same as in 11QMelchizedek."[106] As previously noted, the

---

[100] As Tuschling, Angels and Orthodoxy, 125, observes, "It is tempting to equate the two highest ranks [i.e., the chief princes and their deputies] with the angels of the presence of the angels of sanctification in Jub 2 [...]. It is also tempting to equate the chief priests with the archangels, since this term is not used in the Songs, and in some traditions at least there are seven archangels (e.g., T. Levi 8). On the other hand, [...] in 11Q13 (11QMelch), Melchizedek is a single chief angel, comparable to Michael." Cf. Davidson, Angels at Qumran, 253–254, who refers of the difficulty of finding a "single leading angel" in SSS and urges caution in the acceptance of the Melchizedek reading.

[101] Cf. Newsom, Songs of the Sabbath Sacrifice, 134, 241; eadem, "He Has Established," 108. In the words of Alexander, Mystical Texts, 22, "כוה[ן]] here, without qualification, almost certainly means 'high priest,' as commonly in biblical Hebrew (1 Sam 23:9; 30:7; 2 Sam 15:27, 1 Kgs 1:8; 1 Chron 16:39)." Also see 1QM II, 1, which seemingly differentiates between human chief priests and the High Priest.

[102] Newsom, Songs of the Sabbath Sacrifice, 134.

[103] Davila, "Melchizedek, Michael, and War in Heaven," 263, additionally notes that 4Q402 1 3–4 refers to the (presumably angelic) designation גבורי עוז and eschatological judgment. On the issue of heaven rather than earth as the location of the war, see Davidson, Angels at Qumran, 246–247. Michalak, Angels as Warriors, 288, highlights the similarities with 1QHᵃ XI, 35–36.

[104] The extant phrase is בדביר מלך, "in the inner room of the king," the significance of which I will address, below. Cf. Newsom, Songs of the Sabbath Sacrifice, 151.

[105] I.e., Songs 3 and 4. Cf. Newsom, "He Has Established," 106, who similarly groups Songs 3–5 together thematically.

[106] Davila, "Melchizedek, Michael, and War in Heaven," 263. Cf. idem, Liturgical Works, 164–167; Tuschling, Angels and Orthodoxy, 131–132; Michalak, Angels as Warriors, 186–189; Mason, "Melchizedek Traditions," 354–355. Whereas extant 11QMelch emphasizes Melchizedek's role as an eschatological redeemer/warrior figure and only implicitly mentions his priestly status (so Kobelski, Melchizedek and Melchiresa, 64–71; see Chapter 4, above), perhaps a complete copy of SSS would reveal that it is the mirror image/complement of 11QMelch insofar as Melchizedek's priestly prerogatives are

name Melchizedek has found considerable support as a designation for
Michael,[107] though some scholars maintain a distinction between these
angels.[108]

While the "connection between priestly ordination in the celestial temple
and the final battle is not intuitively obvious,"[109] a number of observations
assist in explaining this curious juxtaposition. First, though it is clear that not
all angels are priests,[110] it would appear that at least some angels tasked with
priestly roles also have a martial role, namely Melchizedek and perhaps
others. Thus, the human boundary familiar from the *War Scroll* – that priests
bless and prepare the soldiers for battle but do not take part in the fighting –
has apparent exceptions in the angelic realm, a notion which we have seen at
work in other texts.[111] Second, establishing the proper credentials – and
thereby guaranteeing (or at least emphasizing) the requisite purity – is a

---

in the foreground but not completely to the exclusion of his eschatological redeem-
er/warrior status. Alexander, *Mystical Texts*, 24–25, rightly observes that the fragmentary
state of *SSS* makes it difficult to determine whether the cosmic warfare is eschatological or
already playing out.

[107] For Melchizedek as a name for Michael in discussions of *SSS*, cf. Davila,
"Melchizedek, Michael, and War in Heaven," 264; Alexander, *Mystical Texts*, 56.

[108] E.g., Heiser, "The Divine Council," §7.4, who not only understands Melchizedek to be
the "vice-regent" of God's council and thus a celestial being of a higher rank than Michael
but also cautiously proposes that epithets like מלך אלוהים, "king of the gods" (e.g., Song
12:33 [= 4Q405 23 I, 13]), and מלך מלכים לכול סודי עולמים, "king of kings for all the
eternal assemblies" (e.g., Song 7:5 [= 4Q403 1 I, 34]), may be references to this vice-
regent/Melchizedek. In support, Heiser appeals to the witness of the Ugaritic texts in which
El's subordinate, Baal, is designated "king of the gods." But without clear indications to the
contrary, such titles are most naturally understood as references to the God of Israel (cf. Ps
95:3; Dan 2:47; 1 En. 9:4); see Newsom, *Songs of the Sabbath Sacrifice*, 217, 323–331;
Davila, *Liturgical Works*, 123–125; Mizrahi, "The Cycle of Summons," 62–63; Alexander,
Mystical Texts, 37.

[109] So Davila, "Melchizedek, Michael, and War in Heaven," 263.

[110] On this point, see Alexander, *Mystical Texts*, 15–19, 46, who notes that Song 2:19–
20 mentions the priestly "Most Holy Ones," who are said to be honoured by – and thus
differentiated from – the regular angels, here referred to as "all the camps of the godlike
beings." Cf. Angel, *Otherworldly*, 88, who highlights that the very first Sabbath song
makes this distinction (see Song 1:3–4 [= 4Q400 1 II, 3–4]).

[111] In his discussion of Songs 12 and 13, Schäfer, *The Origins of Jewish Mysticism*,
139–140, posits that the angels who serve God as priests and the angels who come and go
from heaven in order to execute God's judgment and assist the righteous (cf. 4Q405 23 I,
1–14) are one and the same. As I noted in my discussion of non-sectarian texts, both
Michael in 1 Enoch and the angel of the presence in Jubilees have been interpreted as
combining the roles of chief warrior-guardian and high priest (cf. As. Mos. 10:2, where
Michael is arguably presented in a similar dual fashion; *contra* Angel, *Otherworldly*, 95 n.
60, who only sees a priestly role). On the possible martial connotations of some of the
priestly angelic designations in *SSS* (e.g., ראשים and נשיאים), see Michalak, *Angels as
Warriors*, 186–187.

matter of obvious importance when it comes to both priestly concerns and preparedness for battle, and it is therefore not surprising that angels would be depicted as appropriately qualified.[112] A third connection between priestly and martial tasks of the angels can be seen in *SSS's* framework, which has been described as built on the "praise of God":[113] in other words, even the martial duties of the angels, carried out in the strength of the Creator, are acts of worship bringing praise to the one who commissions and sustains them.

That worship is central to the text is witnessed not only in the sacrifices and many blessings the angels are said to offer to God but also in the architecture of the heavenly temple,[114] which is clearly not a physical building but an animate and mysterious spiritual house of worship which joins with the angels in their praise of God.[115] Contributing to the grandeur of the temple is the manner in which it is described. The temple is, on the one hand, relatively straightforward as it is said to comprise just two main

---

[112] Cf. 1QM VII, 3–6, which is clear that the soldiers must maintain a heightened level of purity and cleanliness because the angels were in their midst, a conviction presupposing the belief that the angelic warriors were pure; see Davila, "Melchizedek, Michael, and War in Heaven," 264. Cf. Newsom, "He Has Established," 1–6, who specifically mentions that Song 5's concern for purity among the angelic camps is reminiscent of the *War Scroll*.

[113] See Newsom, "Religious Experience," 217.

[114] For his recent objections to *SSS* as referring to a heavenly temple, see Fletcher-Louis, "On Angels, Men and Priests," 151–158, here 154, who argues instead that Songs 9–13 showcase "the notion that the roofed sanctuary of the [Jerusalem] temple was identified with heaven." The Jerusalem temple-as-microcosm claim figures prominently in his interpretation of *SSS's* priests as exalted humans, who are thus described with what have been traditionally understood to be angelic epithets. But to reiterate, just because some ancient Jewish texts uphold a microcosmic view of the Jerusalem temple does necessitate that other compositions deny a heavenly temple and priesthood, especially texts like *SSS*, whose "rich inventory" of angelic designations (so Davidson, *Angels at Qumran*, 248) makes it difficult to conclude that humans rather than celestial beings are in view.

[115] On the living and non-material nature of the temple, see Alexander, *Mystical Texts*, 30–34, who argues that the animation should not be taken as a figure of speech as it perhaps should in Ps 24:7–9. A case in point is the phrase תבנית אלוהים in 4Q403 1 II, 16, which plausibly refers to the *merkabah*, with Alexander translating it as "a structure of *elohim*" (i.e., a structure composed of *elohim* = angels). Newsom, *Songs of the Sabbath Sacrifice*, 229, renders the phrase "a divine structure," thus understanding אלוהים adjectivally. Both translations are possible, but the benefit of Alexander's is that it overcomes the problem of material furnishings in a heavenly/spiritual temple. Abusch, "Sevenfold Hymns in the Songs of the Sabbath Sacrifice and the Hekhalot Literature," 227, refers to the phenomenon of angelic décor as the "angelification of temple architecture." Also see the recent proposal of Putthoff, *Ontological Aspects*, 103–138, here 129, who has argued that the animate heavenly temple testifies to a "fusion" of sorts: "The ontological boundaries separating the sect from both the angels with whom they share a worshipping space and the actual space in which they worship have fully disappeared. Angels, humans and the celestial Temple have now become a single worshipping amalgam." According to Putthoff, it is in this quite literal sense that the community can thus refer to itself as a "house of holiness" as per 1QS VIII, 5–8.

sections: an outer nave called the אולם, which corresponds to the holy place of the Jerusalem temple, and an inner room called the דביר, which corresponds to the holy of holies.[116] On the other hand, *SSS's* fondness for the number seven complicates interpretation, as the temple itself is said to be sevenfold and is thus spatially ambiguous.[117] This of course meshes with the sevenfold priesthood mentioned above. But the most difficult aspect of *SSS's* spatiality is that there are seven דבירים with seven מרכבות. While it is possible that the multiple sanctuaries are meant to be understood concentrically or superimposed on each other, this does not solve the problem

---

[116] For helpful overviews of the structure of *SSS's* heavenly temple and the biblical background of its terminology, cf. Alexander, *Mystical Texts*, 34–35, 52–55; Collins, *The Scriptures and Sectarianism*, 202; Schäfer, *The Origins of Jewish Mysticism*, 136. Noam Mizrahi, "The Songs of the Sabbath Sacrifice and Biblical Priestly Literature: A Linguistic Reconsideration" *HTR* 104 (2011): 35–41, 56–57, points out that the word דביר does not occur in the so-called priestly material of the Hebrew Bible (i.e., the P-source of the Pentateuch and Ezekiel) but is found in non-priestly sources in reference to the holy of holies in Solomon's temple (see 1 Kgs 6:31; 1 Kgs 8:6 // 2 Chr 5:7 [cf. 1 Kgs 6:16; 7:50]; Ps 28:2) – observations which are problematic for the oft-repeated assumption that *SSS* was the product of the priestly tradition. Mizrahi thus concludes that "the author of the *Songs* had no special relation to the priestly literature because no such literature – as a distinct and recognizable body of texts – was ever available to him. He was influenced by the biblical literature, and this influence extends to various strata and sections of the Hebrew Bible." On the differences between the heavenly and earthly temples, see the concise remarks of Klawans, *Purity, Sacrifice, and the Temple*, 136, who notes that the main differences between the two lie in the celestial temple's animate and sevenfold natures. Cf. Newsom, "He Has Established," 110, who sees the engraved cherubim of Solomon's temple (1 Kgs 6; cf. Ezek 40–48) as the counterparts of the animate "engravings" on the vestibules of the heavenly temple mentioned in Song 9. Schäfer, *The Origins of Jewish Mysticism*, 135, specifically highlights the influence of Ezek 41:18 and 25 on Song 9, and he suggests that "the angels (paradoxically called *elohim hayyim*) turn into decorations of the heavenly Temple and, in order to become part of the praise of the Temple's architecture, are 'reanimated' again."

[117] Collins, *The Scriptures and Sectarianism*, 202, summarizes the matter well: "The heavenly temple is evidently imagined by analogy with the earthly temple, except that no attention is paid to any outer courts. The holy place is an *ulam*, while the holy of holies is the *debir*, which contains the *merkabah* throne. Everything is sevenfold, so there are apparently seven temples. It is not clear how they relate to each other. The text gives no indication of their spatial relationship, and there is no reason to correlate them with 7 heavens. The motif of 7 heavens only becomes common after the turn of the era." Cf. Alexander, *Mystical Texts*, 30–31, who notes the "impressionistic, mazy vision" of the temple that has been influenced by Dan 7, Isa 6, and especially Ezek 1 and 10. Davidson, *Angels at Qumran*, 238, points out that in contrast to the much later *3 Enoch*, the seven sanctuaries of *SSS* do not come with a spatial blueprint.

of having seven holy of holies housing seven throne-chariots.[118] In light of this quandary, the heaven-as-indescribable explanation is compelling:

The lack in [SSS] of a detailed cosmology that can be clearly imagined is almost certainly deliberate. Our author(s) would have completely agreed with the later Merkabah mystics that heaven is bewildering, awesome world, intrinsically unlike anything we know on earth, a place where terrestrial natural laws do not apply. The sevenfoldness may, therefore, be symbolic, and not meant to be taken literally. It is essentially a rhetorical device, which expresses the transcendent perfection and holiness of the celestial temple.[119]

Indeed, SSS's description of the heavenly temple and its angelic celebrants is an "experiential *tour de force*,"[120] and it is therefore not surprising that scholars have considered both its use and significance to be matters of no small importance in the liturgical life of the Qumran movement.

II. The Use and Significance of SSS: An Ideal Text for the True Israel

Newsom highlights the various proposals for the use of SSS at Qumran including the text as 1.) a substitute for the sacrifices the sectarians could not make in Jerusalem due to their dissatisfaction with the Jerusalem priests; 2.) an apocalyptic or apocalyptic-like text meant to convey detailed information of the heavens; or 3.) an instrument of ascent or mystical praxis.[121] As relevant as these proposals are, they do not exhaust the text's meaning or significance, and I concur with Newsom and others that the best way of viewing the contribution SSS made to sectarian life is to consider it a document that enhanced priestly self-understanding[122] – but also a liturgical text, the numinous and highly repetitive language of which contributed to a meditative experience of worship. Mizrahi captures the essence of this kind of reading:

The religious experience mediated in the Songs crucially depends on a profound correlation between human worship and its heavenly equivalent. Although the precise nature of this relation may be debated, the liturgical logic underlying the Songs obviously presumes that human prayer echoes the sublime songs of praise performed at the heavenly

---

[118] So Alexander, *Mystical Texts*, 53. Even if, as Newsom, "He Has Established," 109, 111, points out, each individual temple differentiates between multiple *merkavot* and *the merkabah* (i.e., that belonging to God), the seven-fold nature of the temple still presents an interpretive dilemma; see below.

[119] Alexander, *Mystical Texts*, 28–32, 53–57, who also explains that a figurative interpretation would mean that the seven chief princes and their deputies should not be taken literally either. These observations explain why there is not an exact correspondence between the celestial and terrestrial sanctuaries, even if a parallel relationship is assumed.

[120] So Newsom, "Religious Experience," 218.

[121] Newsom, "He Has Established," 114.

[122] Newsom, "He Has Established," 114, acknowledges that her priestly self-understanding viewpoint has been influenced by Maier, *Vom Kultus*, 133–135. For further comments on the priestly import of SSS, see Collins, *The Scriptures and Sectarianism*, 202.

temple. From this point of view, the detailed description of the heavenly songs establishes a liturgical model, which, in principle, can and should be emulated by human worshippers. This model, as repetitive as it may be, should still be manageable by lowly creatures of flesh and blood. Put differently, it should be a poetic model that can be realized in actual, liturgical practice.[123]

An objection to *SSS* as liturgy is that nowhere is the *content* of the angelic praises specified – it is simply said *that* the angels praise God.[124] Yet this objection misfires insofar as *SSS* frequently invites the angels to praise, an undertaking which arguably constitutes an act of worship and facilitates a worship experience (cf. Ps 148).[125] Moreover, it has been observed that the absence of the content of the praise of the angels seems to have been a deliberate move which draws attention to the primary focus of *SSS*: the angelic priests themselves.[126] *SSS's* near obsession with the angelic priests is of course a main reason why scholars consider the document to have contributed to the Qumran movement's priestly self-understanding – but *how* the text made this contribution is not explicitly articulated anywhere in *SSS*. In what follows I will interact with some of the scholarly proposals as to how

---

[123] See Noam Mizrahi, "Earthly Liturgy and Celestial Music: The Poetics of the Cycle of Praise of the Sixth Sabbath Song," in *Gottesdienst und Engel*, 127–128, who makes these comments in the course of proposing an antiphonal and prosodic reading of Song 6. For further on *SSS* as liturgy, see, e.g., idem, "Aspects of Poetic Stylization," 149–150; Chazon, "Human & Angelic, 42–43." On the language of *SSS* as intending to facilitate an experience of worship, see Newsom, "He Has Established," 103; cf. eadem, "Religious Experience," 218–220. Repetition is especially prominent in Songs 6–8. On the role of repetition in Jewish mysticism, Newsom cites Steven T. Katz, "Mystical Speech and Mystical Meaning," in *Mysticism and Language* (ed., idem; New York: Oxford University Press, 1992), 14–15. On the nominal and participial sentences and "baroque" construct chains of Songs 9–13 contributing to a lofty atmosphere of praise, see Newman, "Priestly Prophets," 61.

[124] I.e., if there is no liturgy to recite or emulate, how then is the document liturgical? Chazon, "Human & Angelic Prayer," 41–43; eadem, "Liturgical Communion," 98–102, suggests that the ontological-thus-qualitative divide between angels and humans is one reason why the actual content of the angelic praise is omitted from *SSS*. But this may place too much emphasis on the humility of Song 2; see below.

[125] Cf. Newsom, "Religious Experience," 217: "The recitation of a liturgical text that summons to praise is by definition a worship experience." *Contra* Schäfer, *The Origins of Jewish Mysticism*, 131, who specifically dubs *SSS* a "liturgical invitation" rather than liturgy proper. Sullivan, *Wrestling with Angels*, 150, makes the important point that the liturgical nature of the text may be one reason why not all angelological [and spatial?] questions are answered.

[126] The result is indeed bold, but that may be the point: if the content of the angels' praise was included, the focus would be on God rather than the angels; so Newsom, *Songs of the Sabbath Sacrifice*, 16. Cf. Tuschling, *Angels and Orthodoxy*, 125: "Omitting the actual words of the angelic praise is a means by which attention is turned to the angels rather than God."

SSS enhanced sectarian priestly identity, and I will then offer my own suggestions as to how *SSS* contributed not only to the sect's priestly identity but also to its claims to be the true Israel.

The clearest reference to human worshippers is in Song 2:17–26 (= 4Q401 14 I, 5–8; 4Q400 2 1–8), a section in which the first person plural speakers[127] compare their priesthood with that of heaven:

[כיא נכבדת ב] [אלי אלים לר]	17
[ ] שמי מלכות כב]וד[כה	18 לראשי ממשלות
	19 להלל כבודכה פלא באלי דעת ותשבוחות מלכותכה בקדושי קדושים
	20 המה נכבדים בכול מחני אלוהים ונוראים למוסדי אנשים פלא
	21 מאלוהים ואנשים יספרו הוד מלכותו כדעתם ורוממ[ן
	22 שמי מלכותו ובכול מרומי רום תהלי פלא לפי כול[
	23 כבוד מלך אלוהים יספרו במעוני עומדם ו[ן
	24 מה נתחשב [ב]ם וכוהנתנו מה במעוניהם וק[ו]דשנו
	25 קודש[י]הם [מה] תרומת לשון עפרנו בדעת אל[י]ם
	26 [ל]ר[נ]תנו נרוממה לאלוהי דעת[ן

17 [...] For you are honored among [...] the most godlike divine beings *lr* [...]
18 to the chiefs of the dominions [...] the heavens of your glor[ious] realm
19 to praise your glory wondrously with the divine beings of knowledge and the laud of your kingship among the Most Holy Ones.
20 They are honored among all the camps of godlike beings and revered by human assemblies. More wondrously
21 than godlike or human beings they declare the majesty of his kingship according to their knowledge and they exalt [...]
22 the heavens of his realm. And in all the highest heights wondrous psalms according to all [...]
23 glory of the king of godlike beings they declare in the dwellings (where they have) their stations. But [...]
24 how shall we be accounted [among] them? And how shall our priesthood (be accounted) in their dwellings? And [our] ho[liness ...]
25 their holines[s? What (is)] the offering of our tongue of dust (compared) with the knowledge of divine [beings? ...]
26 [...] for our [exu]ltation, let us exalt the God of knowledge [...]

This passage opens with references to the elite standing and peerless worship offered by the "Most Holy Ones," those angels which Song 1 also labels the "ministers of the presence" and the "priests of the inner sanctum." To be sure, part of the speakers' response to this angelic prowess is humility. But

---

[127] Note the numerous first person plurals in Song 2; see Newsom, "Angelic Liturgy," 144–147. Virtually all commentators understand these first-person speakers as referring to human worshippers, though Klawans, *Purity, Sacrifice, and the Temple*, 136, mentions the possibility that it is lesser angels who are voicing their unworthiness vis-à-vis elite angels.

in a *Hodayot*-like fashion,[128] these humble protestations are far from the final word on the matter, as the last extant statement of these human priests is a resolute call to worship: "Let us exult the God of knowledge" (2:26).[129] Collins has argued that *SSS* is "the main evidence that fellowship with the angels is focused on the heavenly temple,"[130] and with his comment in mind it is important to note that *SSS* – especially Song 2 – is not only reminiscent of the *Hodayot* but is also best read as complementing one of its most significant angelological claims: that the sectarians enjoyed liturgical fellowship with the angelic priests who served in closest proximity to God.[131]

How *SSS* may have facilitated this communion is spelled out by Alexander:

We are explicitly told that the Songs are to be recited by the Maskil. However, they imply that the Maskil does not recite them on his own, but in the presence of others. These are the "we" referred to in Song 2, whose priesthood is compared with the priesthood of the angels in heaven. These are also presumably the human community who are the recipients of angelic blessings in Songs 6 and 8. In other words, we have here a public liturgy, in which a prayer-leader leads a congregation, who may join him in reciting in whole or in part the words of the hymns. That congregation exhorts the angels in heaven to perform their priestly duties in the celestial temple, and somehow through this liturgical act it feels drawn into union with the angels in worshipping God. ... The worshippers' consciousness that they were surrounded by hostile, evil forces would have been psychologically important for their act of worship, reinforcing their sense of unity, and heightening their feeling of reassurance and privilege at having access to such august celestial beings. The whole liturgy turns on a dualism between earth and heaven, between the worshipping congregation below and the worshipping congregation above, and on the attempts of the earthly congregation to overcome this dichotomy.[132]

---

[128] On the similarities between the humility of Song 2 and the Niedrigkeitsdoxologien of the *Hodayot*, see the comments of Newman, "Priestly Prophets," 46; Angel, *Otherworldly*, 96–97.

[129] *SSS* is also filled with imperative summons to the angels to worship (ostensibly recited by the *Maskil* and other sectarians); see below.

[130] Collins, *The Scriptures and Sectarianism*, 202.

[131] On the quietness, stillness, silence, etc., of the angels' worship in *SSS* (particularly in Song 11) and the influence of 1 Kgs 19:12, see Dale C. Allison, "The Silence of the Angels: Reflections on the Songs of the Sabbath Sacrifice," *RevQ* 13 (1988): 189–197. Cf. Tuschling, *Angels and Orthodoxy*, 127; Schäfer, *The Origins of Jewish Mysticism*, 138; Newsom, "Religious Experience," 219. Also see Alexander, *Mystical Texts*, 39, who notes the contradiction this silence introduces given the implied exuberance of *SSS's* other descriptions of angelic worship. But this is likely another effectively employed example of the heaven-as-indescribable motif. As Newman, "Priestly Prophets," 63, points out, the reference to the Elijah narrative also heightens the Sinai and prophetic (i.e., *SSS* as revelation) motifs at work in the text; see further, below.

[132] Alexander, *Mystical Texts*, 44–47, advocates an interpretation similar to that of Newsom, "He Has Established," 106, 113–118 (cf. eadem, *Songs of the Sabbath Sacrifice*, 71–72; "Religious Experience," 221), who emphasizes the importance of Song 2 when it

As we have seen, one of the ways the *Hodayot* and 1QS XI express the notion of angelic fellowship is to say that the sectarian סוד has been joined together with the divine סוד; it is thus noteworthy that *SSS* refers to the heavenly location where the sectarians have "access to such august celestial beings" (to use Alexander's turn of phrase) as a סוד, which is where God has יסד, "established," for himself an angelic priesthood (cf. Song 1:11, 30; 7:35).[133] Other examples of terminological affinity with previously discussed sectarian texts include מעמד and מבנית. *SSS* employs מעמד to refer to the "stations" of the magnificently garbed priestly angels who serve before God (cf. Song 13:18–24 [= 4Q405 23 II, 7–12]), a use which complements the heavenly "station" the sectarians have with the angels according to the *Hodayot* (cf. 1QH[a] XI, 22).[134] Whereas *SSS* uses מבנית to refer to the animate heavenly temple (cf. Song 7:12, 15 [= 4Q403 1 I, 41, 44; 4Q405 14–15 I, 6]; Song 13:32 [= 11Q17 2–1–9 7]), the *Community Rule* employs this word as a sectarian self-designation (cf. 1QS XI, 8; see also 1QS VII, 5–10) and may hint at the relationship between the sectarian priestly "house" and the location of its privileged fellowship with heaven's angelic priests.[135]

---

comes to understanding the purpose/function of the text. See also Collins, *The Scriptures and Sectarianism*, 202, who supports the interpretation of Newsom and Alexander. Cf. Hannah, *Michael and Christ*, 60, who notes the "implicit confirmation" of angelic fellowship provided by Song 2. While Schäfer, *The Origins of Jewish Mysticism*, 144, does not see in the *Songs* "the idea of a liturgical communion of angels and humans that is so dominant in the unquestionably Qumranic texts," he concedes that they could have been read in the context of worship in order for the Qumran movement to participate with the angels in their liturgy.

[133] Newman, "Priestly Prophets," 44–45, highlights the use of Hebrew roots in individual songs or clusters thereof, observing the "ambiguity attached to the precise meaning of the word, which may have more than one referential value." In comments that are analogous to those I made in reference to the *Hodayot*, Newman intriguingly points out that one of these roots is יסד, from which סוד is derived. Describing the use of this word in Song 1, Newman writes that סוד/יסד indicates "the establishment of the priesthood but suggestive already of another foundation, the groundwork that is laid for the construction of the animate temple to come in the seventh song, building up from the *shovei pesha'*, who constitute the *Yahad* or some segment of it" (cf. 1QS III, 26; IV, 6; VIII, 4b–13; CD X, 6; XIX, 4). Cf. Alexander, *Mystical Texts*, 56.

[134] Cf. Newsom, "He Has Established," 117–118, who cites 1QH[a] XI, 22–24, noting that "whether or not the author the *Hodayot* was referring specifically to his experience in the liturgy of the *Sabbath Shirot*, the spirituality is much the same. Newman, "Priestly Prophets," 70, similarly suggests that this *Hodayot* passage "encapsulates in brief the liturgical movement of the *Songs*."

[135] On this reading, see Davidson, *Angels at Qumran*, 168; Schäfer, *The Origins of Jewish Mysticism*, 128; Frennesson, *"In a Common Rejoicing,"* 66; Fletcher-Louis, *All the Glory*, 302; Torleif Elgvin, "Priests on Earth as in Heaven: Jewish Light on the Book of Revelation," in *Echoes from the Caves: Qumran and the New Testament* (ed. Florentino García Martínez; STDJ 85; Leiden: Brill, 2009), 268–269; Angel, *Otherworldly*, 90. On

Comparison of *SSS* with other sectarian texts has uncovered additional fascinating similarities – similarities that indicate that the Qumran movement's angelic fellowship experiences may have prompted them to strive to make sectarian community life as angel-like as possible. Dimant has highlighted the "striking resemblances" between angelic activities (as outlined in *SSS*) and sectarian activities (as outlined in the *Community Rule, Hodayot, Habakkuk Pesher,* and *Damascus Document*) including:[136] the formation of a special community (cf. 4Q400 1 I, 2–6; 1QS I, 1–15; VIII, 5–16), a covenant with God (cf. 4Q400 1 I, 2–7; 1QM XII, 3; 1QS I, 8; II, 26; III, 11–12; IV, 22; V, 8–9; CD XX, 10–12),[137] the reception of special laws (cf. 4Q400 1 I, 15; 4Q405 23 I, 10–12; 1QS V, 11; VIII, 11–13; CD III, 14; VI, 2–11), bloodless offerings and expiation (cf. 4Q403 1 II, 26; 4Q405 23 II, 11–12; 1QS VIII, 9–10; IX, 4–5),[138] purity (cf. 4Q400 1 I, 14–15; 1QS III, 4–10), the absence of evil/sin in their midst (cf. 4Q511 1 6–7; 1QS I, 16–28; CD XVI, 7; XX, 30–32), the praise of God (cf. 1QM XII, 1–2; 4Q511 35 5; 1QS I, 21–22; XI, 15; 1QH^a IX, 28–32; XI, 24; 4Q504 1–2 VII, 1–13), the possession of divine wisdom (cf. 4Q401 17 4; 4Q402 4 2; 4Q403 1 I, 36, 39; 1QpHab II, 7–10; 1QH^a IX, 21; 1QS IV, 22; XI, 3), and a teaching role (cf. 4Q400 1 I, 17; 1QS III, 13). I will address the significance of some of these activities later in this chapter. For now, it is important to understand that the sectarians were engaging in *imitatio angelorum,* thereby portraying themselves as the faithful counterparts and fellow worshippers with the archetypes of Israel's priesthood.[139]

---

the use of מבנית in the *SSS*, see Newsom, *The Songs of the Sabbath Sacrifice,* 213, 284, 377. Also see Putthoff, *Ontological Aspects,* 128–134, who, as noted, has proposed that the animate structures of the celestial temple in *SSS* are more than just a creative depiction of heaven's architecture: the uses of מבנית in *SSS* and 1QS XI, 9, indicate that "[the sect members, together with the angels] now participate not merely in the angelic worship but in the actual construction of the celestial Temple itself. The sectarians, in other words, are the Temple." Cf. 4Q286 (= *4QBerakhot*^{a}) 1 II, 7, which uses the related word, מבנה, in reference to the heavenly temple; also see Ezek 40:2, which uses מבנה to refer to Ezekiel's famous temple blueprint.

[136] See Dimant, "Men as Angels," 100–101.

[137] It should be noted that 4Q400 1 I, 2–7 does not use the word ברית, though the concept of a unique relationship between God and the angels is arguably present in this passage; Dimant also contends that the "covenant of peace" mentioned in 1QM XII, 3 includes the angels; see eadem, "Men as Angels," 100 n. 31.

[138] Song 1:16 states that the priestly angels atone for the repentant; cf. Davidson, *Angels at Qumran,* 240–241; Newsom, *Songs of the Sabbath Sacrifice,* 104–105.

[139] On the concept of *imitatio angelorum* generally, Klawans, *Purity, Sacrifice, and the Temple,* 113, explains that "priestly concerns with ritual purity are often explicitly understood as efforts to imitate the nature of the angels." On angelic imitation as a key to understanding *SSS,* see Newsom, "He Has Established," 115, who states that the text "invites an analogy between the angelic and human priests. Cf. *Alexander, Mystical Texts,*

Taking these insights into consideration, Dimant observes that while Jubilees draws a parallel between the angels closest to God and all Israel, the witness of *SSS* and other sectarian texts is that the Qumran movement has appropriated the nation's prerogative for itself[140]– so much so that they were convinced they should imitate the priestly angels with whom they claimed to have fellowship.[141] Scholars have not given due consideration to Dimant's observation, and this can be demonstrated by looking at the significance attributed to *SSS*. While proposals stressing that *SSS* would have facilitated an "experiential validation" of the sect's claims to be the true priesthood are persuasive and undoubtedly part of the picture, they do not sufficiently address the archetypal import of the text.[142] Scholars have rightly emphasized the "priority of heaven"[143] and that the Qumran movement "drew its vitality precisely from the envisioning of the community as a model of the imaginal temple."[144] But these important observations still fall short of specifying a simple yet profound facet of this vitality, thereby not fully appreciating the exclusivist implications of Dimant's observation: to boast of fellowship with and to imitate the archetypes of Israel's priesthood would have been a powerful way for the Qumran movement to enhance its claims to

---

15–16, who writes that "the economy of heaven mirrors the economy of earth, a theme that runs like a purple thread through the whole of the Sabbath songs."

[140] Dimant, "Men as Angels," 101: "The analogy between men and angels is already present in Jubilees. But here it is drawn between the angels and Israel. In the sectarian writings this parallel is applied to the community itself."

[141] Dimant, "Men as Angels," 101, understands the imitation of/analogy with the angels to constitute fellowship with the angels; see further, below.

[142] While Newsom, *Songs of the Sabbath Sacrifice*, 71–72, also refers to *SSS* as the "model and image of the Qumran priesthood," she does not elaborate on this point but emphasizes the experiential import of the text. Cf. eadem, "'Sectually' Explicit," 180; Swarup, *The Self-Understanding*, 133; Frennesson, *"In a Common Rejoicing,"* 96.

[143] So Alexander, *Mystical Texts*, 42, 47 61, who in addition to speaking of the "almost platonic" and "more real world" of heaven envisioned in *SSS*, notes that "The Sabbath Songs project onto heaven the polity and practices of earthly Israel in order to reflect this image back to earth to validate what is happening here. This is probably not very consciously done: it is an outsider's view of the process. The author(s) of the Songs would have believed unquestioningly in the priority of the celestial priesthood, and seen the earthly priesthood as engaged in imitation of it."

[144] So Angel, *Otherworldly*, 101–106, 298, here 105, who makes an excellent case for the archetypal significance of the text. Particularly influenced by the work of Henry Corbin (*Temple and Contemplation* [London: KPI, 1986], 267–303) and Elliot R. Wolfson ("Seven Mysteries of Knowledge: Qumran E/Soterism Recovered," in *The Idea of Biblical Interpretation: Essays in Honor of James L. Kugel* [eds., Hindy Najman and Judith H. Newman; JSJSup 83; Leiden: Brill, 2003], 177–213), Angel warns against reductionism and understatement, emphasizing that the celestial temple was not imaginary/fictional in the minds of *SSS*'s author(s) but envisioned as real and paradigmatic and the basis for liturgical fellowship with the angels (cf. 1QH[a] XI, 22–24, which Angel cites in support).

be the true Israel. Indeed, Newman is right to stress that any reading of *SSS* should do justice to the "zealous, ascetic sectarians whose writings and practices reflect a vivid concern for political and material matters in the here and now."[145] More specifically, if one of the purposes of the heavenly sanctuary and its angelic celebrants was to safeguard the human priesthood as "Israel's God-appointed spiritual leaders,"[146] there likely would have been no better way for the sectarians – a group whose priestly preoccupations are showcased in lofty self-designations such as "a holy house for Israel, and a foundation of the holy of holies for Aaron" (1QS VIII, 5–6) – to underscore that their reconstitution of Israel's covenant was correct than to claim fellowship with and to emulate meticulously those angels whose priesthood was considered to be the very model for that of Israel.[147] It is also likely that the dissolution of the dualistic boundary between heaven and earth, which other texts anticipate as occurring at the eschaton,[148] is here envisioned as being at least partially realized via angelic fellowship.

Moreover, *SSS*'s conclusion, which provides a detailed description of the angelic high priests and their regalia,[149] is an apt exclamation point not just to

---

[145] Newman, "Priestly Prophets," 30, makes this statement in reference to readings of *SSS* that focus primarily on its experiential or mystical significance, thereby hoping to broaden the scope of what was considered to be its envisioned relevance, use, etc.

[146] So Alexander, *Mystical Texts*, 19.

[147] This is especially true if the celestial temple-as-archetype was as important as Angel, *Otherworldly*, 298, suggests it was (see above). On the connection between elitist/ideal sentiments and reciting the angelic liturgy of *SSS*, cf. Newman, "Priestly Prophets," 57; Steven Fraade, "Ascetical Aspects of Ancient Judaism," in *Jewish Spirituality from the Bible to the Middle Ages* (ed., Arthur Green; New York: Crossroad, 1986), 269.

[148] As noted in Chapter 3, Dyma, "Tempel, Raum, und Zeit," 45, discusses proximity to God in the eschatological scenario of the *Animal Apocalypse* (cf. 1 En. 90:28–38) as a resolution of the tension prompted by a polluted Jerusalem temple, though admittedly there is debate as to whether the new Jerusalem ("the house") of this scene specifically refers to a temple. However, *SSS's* detailed depiction of heaven, considered alongside of the angelic fellowship claims of the *Hodayot* and other sectarian texts, point to the conviction that the Qumran movement understood their worship as a unique coming-together of the heavenly and earthly realms, effectively constituting a down-payment of the hope to which Dyma refers as the eschatological dissolution of the realms.

[149] For comments on the relevant portions of Song 13, see Newsom, *Songs of the Sabbath Sacrifice*, 371–373. On the terminology of the various components of the regalia, see Schäfer, *The Origins of Jewish Mysticism*, 140–141. On the importance of the regalia (the breastplate, in particular) to Song 13, see Fetcher-Louis, *All the Glory*, 356–391, especially 386–387. On the (male) authority represented by the regalia/breastplate, see Jennifer Zilm, "Multi-Coloured Like Woven Works: Gender, Ritual Clothing and Praying with the Angels in the Dead Sea Scrolls and the Testament of Job," in *Prayer and Poetry in the Dead Sea Scrolls and Related Literature: Essays in Honor of Eileen Schuller on the Occasion of Her 65th Birthday* (eds., Jeremy Penner, Ken M. Penner, and Cecilia Wassén; STDJ 98; Leiden: Brill, 2012), 435–449. Alexander, *Mystical Texts*, 50, has proposed that

the rest of *SSS* but also to the *Hodayot's* claim that the sect enjoyed fellowship with the priestly angels of the presence (cf. 1QH[a] XIV, 16). Song 13:18–23 (= 4Q405 23 II, 7–12) states that:

18 ... במעמד פלאיהם רוחות רוקמה כמעשי אורג פתוחי צורות הדר
19 בתוך כבוד מראי שני צבעי אור רוח קודש קדשים מחזקות מעמד קודשם לפני
20 מ|לכ רוחי צבעין טוהר |בתוך מראי חור ודמות רוח כבוד כמעשי אופירים מאירי
21 או|ר וכול מחשביהם ממולח טוהר חשב כמעשי אורג אלה ראשי לבושי פלא לשרת
22 ראשי ממלכות ממלכות קדושים למלך הקודש בכול מרומי מקדשי מלכות
23 כבודו בראשי תרומות לשוני דעת[ן ו]ברכו לאלוהי דעת בכול מעשי כבודו

18 In their wondrous station (are) spirits of mingled colors like woven work, engraved with images of splendor.
19 In the midst of the glorious appearance of scarlet are (garments) dyed with a light of a spirit of holiest holiness, those who stand fast (in) their holy station before
20 (the) [k]ing, spirits of [brightly] dyed stuffs in the midst of the appearance of whiteness. And the likeness of (the) glorious spirit (is) like fine gold work, shedding
21 [ligh]t. And all their decoration is brightly blended, an artistry like woven works. These are the chiefs of those wondrously arrayed for service,
22 the chiefs of the kingdoms of kingdoms, Holy Ones of the king of holiness in all the heights of the sanctuaries of his glorious
23 realm. In the chiefs of offerings (are) tongues of knowledge [and] they bless the God of knowledge (together) with all his glorious works.

In concert with the focus *SSS* has on the angels themselves rather than the content of their praises and other areas of interest, this picture of the high-priestly angels vividly accentuates the Qumran movement's conviction that they communed with the heavenly realm's most elite, here dubbed "the chiefs of those wondrously arrayed for service." An important reason why this connection with the angelic priests would have muted the anxiety of the sect's lack of clout in Jerusalem[150] was that it constituted communion with Israel's archetypal high priesthood, enabling the sectarians to persuade themselves of the following: their present rejection of the human temple authorities did not mean that they were cut off from the nation's God-ordained celebrant(s)-in-chief, and their common rejoicing with the ranking

---

Song 13 may mark the high point in the use of *SSS* as a liturgical text: the sectarian worshippers or, more likely, the leader thereof (i.e., the "mystic") "dons the celestial priestly robes, and serves in the temple, and it is this enrobement that marks the climax of his experience." Cf. Fletcher-Louis, "Angels, Men and Priests," 142–143, who understands such interpretations as approaching his own but suggests that they are nevertheless "reluctant" in that they still unwilling to jettison the notion of a heavenly temple served by an angelic priesthood.

[150] So Newsom, "He Has Established," 115–117, who also mentions the muting of the more general anxiety inherent in the comparison of the human priesthood with the angelic.

priests of the "more real world of heaven"[151] would thus have made a forceful contribution to the conviction that the sect was the true Israel.

That there was a relationship between high priestly fellowship and the sect's aspirations to be the true Israel may be indicated not just by Song 13's content but also by its placement in the cycle: the thirteenth song arguably functions as one of the climaxes of the text,[152] and it is also one of the two songs following the festival of *Shavuot*, which would have occurred on the day after the eleventh Sabbath Song.[153] *Shavuot* is associated with one of Israel's foundational religious events: the revelation of God's presence and Torah at Sinai; this remembrance was also the occasion of the Qumran movement's annual covenant renewal ceremony, an event that seems to have included the evaluation of current sect members and the initiation of new ones (cf. 1QS I, 16–III, 12),[154] and the symbolic significance of this

---

[151] So Alexander, *Mystical Texts*, 61.

[152] The question of where the climax of *SSS* should be located has perplexed scholars and has generated some debate. For a review of the options, see Angel, *Otherworldly*, 97 n. 70. Newsom, *Songs of the Sabbath Sacrifice*, 13–21, views the 13-song text as exhibiting a pyramidal structure, with the central seventh song's angel and animate temple praise constituting the apex. Alexander, *Mystical Texts*, 49, sees the *merkabah* vision of Song 12 as the climax but then is puzzled as to why Song 13, which he considers to be anti-climactic, should serve as the conclusion. An alternative reading has been advocated by Morray-Jones, "The Temple Within," 400–431, who views Song 12 as the true climax, dubbing Song 7 a sort of "secondary [or perhaps better: preliminary] crescendo." However, Song 13 as at least one of the high points should not be too hastily dismissed. Schäfer, *The Origins of Jewish Mysticism*, 142, sees the angelic sacrifices as being offered on behalf of the true/faithful Israel and thus it would be "somewhat rash" not to consider Song 12 or 13 as *SSS's* "dramatic peak." But as Newsom, "He Has Established," 113, has argued, the sacrifices offered by the angels only receive limited attention before the focus is, once again, on the angels, especially the vivid depiction of the high priestly vestments: "That the thirteenth and final Sabbath song should contain such encomium of the angelic high priests is really not surprising. From the first Sabbath song, with its account of the establishment of the angelic priesthood, through the central songs with their formulaic accounts of the praises of these seven priestly councils, to the final thirteenth song, the subject of chief interest in the *Sabbath Shirot* is the angelic priesthood itself." Cf. Fletcher-Louis, *All the Glory*, 386–387, who considers Song 13 to be the climax of *SSS* because it showcases what he deems to be the zenith of priestly angelmorphism.

[153] Since *SSS* states that its cycle begins on the first Sabbath of the year (cf. Song 1:1), *Shavuot*, which is observed on the fifteenth day of the third month, would have fallen on the day after the eleventh Sabbath (as per the 364-day solar year assumed by the text); see Newman, "Priestly Prophets," 61.

[154] On the requirements for new members in 1QS, see Metso, *The Serekh Texts*, 8–10, 28–30. On the importance of *Shavuot* at Qumran, see Newman, "Priestly Prophets," 61–71, here 62, who highlights that initiates of the sectarian covenant were required to study the Torah of Moses "according to everything which has been revealed from it" (1QS V, 8). This is suggestive to Newman of "an esoteric dimension of instruction, or at least a knowledge of Mosaic torah with a sectarian inflection." At Qumran, *Shavuot* was therefore a celebration of divine revelation, which was appropriately lauded by Songs 11,

progression should not be overlooked: it would only be after recommitment or initial admittance to the sectarian reconstitution of Israel that the attentions of the sect members would be turned to *SSS's* most detailed depictions of the attendant angels of the *debir/merkabah* (Song 12) and its most extravagant presentation of the angelic high priests and their regalia (Song 13).[155] It is also important to mention that, according to Song 1, the priestly angels atone for כול שבי פשע, "all those who repent of transgression" (Song 1:16; cf. T. Levi 3:5).[156] In other sectarian texts, this phrase serves as a quasi-technical

---

12, and 13, due not only to their emphasis on the *debir* and *merkabah* (i.e., where God resides, thus the source of revelation) but also because of their numerous allusions to Sinai (e.g., ממולח טוהר; cf. Exod 30:35; 4Q405 19 4 et al.; see Newsom, *Songs of the Sabbath Sacrifice*, 297–298) and themes from the prophetic tradition (e.g., קול דממת שקט, "still voice"; cf. 1 Kgs 19:12 [which is set at Sinai]; 4Q405 19 7). A collection of fragmentary sectarian texts that shares similarities with *SSS* and which has also been associated with the covenant renewal ceremony is *Berakhot* (4Q286–290), the manuscripts of which are dated paleographically to the early 1st cent. CE. For text and translation, see Bilhah Nitzan, "286. 4QBerakhot[a]," through "290. 4QBerakhot[e]," in DJD 11, 7–74. On the significance of *Berakhot* for the covenant renewal ceremony, see eadem, "4QBerakhot[a-e] (4Q286–290): A Covenant Renewal Ceremony in Light of the Related Texts," *RevQ* 16 (1995): 487–506. For helpful overview of the angelological significance of the text, see Church, *Hebrews and the Temple*, 116–121. For comments on the how *Berakhot* fuses the exclusivist sentiments of the covenant renewal ceremony as it is known in 1QS and the union between the sectarians and the angels, see Alexander, *Mystical Texts*, 63.

[155] Cf. Davila, *Liturgical Works*, 90; Alexander, *Mystical Texts*, 49, 63 who stress the importance of the *merkabah* visions of Songs 11 and 12 flanking *Shavuot*. But in typical *SSS* fashion, Song 12 and Song 13 which follow *Shavuot* ultimately devote more attention to the priestly angels than to the subject matter with which each song begins: the *merkabah* and heavenly sacrifices, respectively. As Newsom, "He Has Established," 112, points out, "While the [throne chariot in Song 12] is obviously of great significance in the cycle of the *Sabbath Shirot*, one must note that it does not appear, in and of itself, to constitute the goal of the experience provided by this work. The description of the *merkabah* does not occur in the final song but at the beginning of the penultimate song. It forms part of a large descriptive complex, encompassing both the twelfth and thirteenth Sabbath songs. Its function in the *Sabbath Shirot* may be clarified by looking at the material that follows," which is a description of angelic worship in "the ideal temple." *Contra* Schäfer, *The Origins of Jewish Mysticism*, 144–145, who considers the most valuable aspect of the text not to be the angels or liturgical communion with them but *SSS's* depiction of the angelic sacrifices: "The sacrifice on earth has become corrupt, and it is only the angels in heaven who are still able to perform this ritual so crucial to the existence and well-being of the earthly community (until it becomes fully united with the angels)." But the way Song 13 reverts its focus to the angels themselves does not support Schafer's reading.

[156] The comment of Tuschling, *Angels and Orthodoxy*, 127, that the sacrifices of Song 13 may be interpreted as either the counterpart of the earthly sacrifices or allegorical highlights the difficulty in determining the precise nature of these angelic offerings. Davidson, *Angels at Qumran*, 236 n. 8, summarizes the opinion of many in viewing the offerings as "sacrifices of praise," and thus "at least by analogy with the earthly system, the angels were thought to offer sacrifices, even though no particular sacrifice as practiced

term for the community (cf. 1QH^a X, 11–12; XIV, 9; 1QS X, 20; CD II, 5), and its use in *SSS* suggests that the Qumran movement viewed itself as uniquely benefiting from the angelic sacrifices and the atonement afforded by them – benefits which included God's goodwill/favour (רצון).[157] If the angelic sacrifices should be understood as an offering of praise, atonement and/or its benefits may include the revelation of what constitutes the ideal worship of God.[158] That the angels are revealers of the things of heaven is undoubtedly related to designations that highlight them as possessing דעת,[159] which is likely also connected to the angels' teaching role. השמיעו נסתרות,

---

in Judaism might have been in the author's mind." Cf. Dimant, "Men as Angels," 102. For discussions of the language used in Song 12 (= 4Q405 23 I, 5) and Song 13 (= 11Q17 21–22 4–5) to describe the angelic sacrifices, cf. Schäfer, *The Origins of Jewish Mysticism*, 140; Church, *Hebrews and the Temple*, 140–142. On the notion of praise as a substitute for offerings at Qumran, see Lawrence H. Schiffman, "The Dead Sea Scrolls and the Early History of Jewish Liturgy," in *The Synagogue in Late Antiquity* (ed., Lee I. Levine; Philadelphia: American Schools of Oriental Research, 1987), 33–48; Angel, *Otherworldly*, 241. Cf. 1QS IX, 3–6; see also Heb 13:15; Rev 5:8. *Contra* Falk, *Daily, Sabbath, and Festival Prayers*, 136, who argues for a literal heavenly sacrifice, citing T. Levi 3:5–6, Rev. 6:9 and 8:3–5 as suggestive of heaven having animal sacrifices (following Gray, *Sacrifice in the Old Testament*, 159, who contends that the altar depicted in T. Levi. 3:5–6 "corresponds to the altar of burnt-offering, not to the golden altar or altar of incense in the earthly temple"). However, the propitiatory sacrifices of heaven in T. Levi. 3:5–6 are "rational and bloodless," as Falk himself concedes. Cf. Dimant, "Men as Angels," 100 n. 32, who specifically cites T. Levi 3:5–6 in arguing that *SSS* implies bloodless angelic sacrifices. Davidson, *Angels at Qumran*, 245, highlights that "chiefs of the realm of the holy ones" in Song 13:22–23 (= 4Q405 23 II, 11–12) are the "chiefs of the 'praise offerings' (תרומות)." Cf. Newsom, *Songs of the Sabbath Sacrifice*, 339.

[157] In addition to my brief comments above, see Davidson, *Angels at Qumran*, 240–241; and especially Newsom, *Songs of the Sabbath Sacrifice*, 104–105. Cf. Newman, "Priestly Prophets," 44–45.

[158] Cf. Alexander, *Mystical Texts*, 42–43: "How [the] Sabbath Songs conceives of the relationship between the celestial and terrestrial cults is an important question. There can be little doubt that in its view it is the heavenly offerings that are ultimately efficacious: heaven is the place of 'knowledge' and perfection; earth the place of ignorance, deficiency and sin. But what then is the purpose of the earthly cult? It is a sacramental re-enactment of the heavenly cult, which atones only insofar as it follows the true celestial pattern? Might the apparent emphasis on the 'odour' (*reiah*) of the sacrifices at 11Q17 21–22 4–5 be significant? Is the thought that the angelic praises are the 'odour' of the earthly sacrifices? If the earthly cult is in tune with the heavenly, then the earthly sacrifices get caught up and presented to God in the praise of the angels."

[159] E.g., אלי דעת in Song 2:19 (= 4Q400 2 1); cf. 1QH^a VII, 17; XI, 23–24; XIV, 15–16; XIX, 16–17. On this point, see Alexander, *Mystical Texts*, 19: "For our author, true worship has to be founded on knowledge, and the greater the knowledge the truer the worship." Cf. Newsom, "He Has Established," 116: "adequate praise can only be expressed by those who have knowledge of the wonderful mysteries of God." On the influence of the revelatory role of Jubilees' angel of the presence, see Dimant, "Men as Angels," 102; Newman, "Priestly Prophets," 62.

"those who make known hidden things" (Song 2:40 [= 4Q401 14 II, 7]) are presumably the priestly angels because their nearness to God has equipped them to reveal such heavenly mysteries and knowledge to humanity, though it may be that lesser angels (or both angels and humans) are the envisioned recipients.[160]   But given that the sectarian priests are said to have a teaching/revelatory role (cf. 1QS VI, 3–8; 1QM X–XII; CD XIII, 2–7), readings of the text that understand the priestly angels as serving as the model for the teaching responsibilities of the sect's priesthood make good sense.[161] Moreover, Deut 29:28 specifically contrasts the נסתרות of God with the Torah that had been revealed to all of Israel. The "hidden things" revealed by the priestly angels to the sectarians therefore seem to serve as a statement marking the distinction between the privileged members of the Qumran movement, who form a coterie with the priestly angels, and outsiders, who do not share this privilege (cf. 1QS IX, 16–17). The use of נסתרות in CD III, 10–16 as well as 1QS V, 11 would indicate this reading is correct.[162]

---

[160] So Newsom, *Songs of the Sabbath Sacrifice*, 30, 139.

[161] See, e.g., Davidson, *Angels at Qumran*, 241. On the teaching role of the sectarian priests, see Florentino García Martínez, "Priestly Functions in a Community without Temple," in *Gemeinde ohne Temple: zur Substituierung und Transformation des Jerusalemer Temples und seines Kults im Alten Testament, antiken Judentum und frühen Christentum* (eds., Beate Ego et al.; WUNT 118; Tübingen: Mohr Siebeck, 1999), 309–311.   On the authority the angelic connection and modeling conferred, cf. Newman, "Priestly Prophets," 39; Russell C. D. Arnold, *The Social Role of Liturgy in the Religion of the Qumran Community* (STDJ 60; Leiden: Brill, 2006), 146–148.

[162] On the knowledge of angels as having priestly/cultic significance, see Tuschling, *Angels and Orthodoxy*, 124; Newsom, *Songs of the Sabbath Sacrifice*, 139.   Alexander, *Mystical Texts*, 21, comments as follows on the influence of Deut 29:28: "In light of [CD III, 10–16], it is reasonable to take the Qumran community as the recipients of the revelation of secrets mentioned at 4Q401 14 II, 7. If the priestly angels, as is likely, are the subject of השמיעו ('they have made known'), then the thought would be just as the first Torah was given at the hand of angels, so also was the new Torah. This may explain the community's confidence in offering up to God its terrestrial liturgy, despite its deep sense of unworthiness, when compared with the glorious angels. The terrestrial liturgy is based on revelation. The new utterance of God's mouth, conveyed first to the priestly angels, and then by them to the community, has embraced heaven and earth, and realigned the earthly and heavenly liturgies. It is this that gives the community confidence to approach God. It is surely no accident that it is liturgical matters that head the list of the content of 'hidden things' in CD III, 14." Also, it has been recently re-proposed that the sectarians offered sacrifices at Qumran.   See, e.g., Jodi Magness, "Were Sacrifices Offered at Qumran?   The Animal Bone Deposits Reconsidered," *JAJ* 7 (2016): 5–34 (*contra* Lawrence H. Schiffman, "A Qumran Temple: The Literary Evidence," *JAJ* 7 [2016]: 71–85).   Even if it is allowed that the sectarians offered such sacrifices, any knowledge revealed by heaven's priests, in conjunction with their experiences of liturgical fellowship in the celestial temple as facilitated by *SSS*, would have bolstered confidence that these offerings – likely considered provisional, at best – were being conducted as legitimately as possible.

On the subject of knowledge, it should be noted that Song 1:6 (= 4Q400 1 I, 6) has the intriguing phrase עם בינות כבודי, which has been variously interpreted. While Newsom and Davila have adopted Qimron's suggestion that כבודי is a Qal passive participle in construct with the noun אלוהים which follows it (i.e., "the people of discernment, *glorified [by]* God"), this form of כבד is elsewhere unattested.[163] However, Newsom initially read כבודי as an adjective (i.e., "the people [who possess] *his glorious* insight"), taking אלוהים to be part of the next phrase, even though there is *vacat* following אלוהים. Either way, a plain reading might suggest humans are in view, in which case it could be understood as a positive sectarian "spin" on a phrase that in other contexts is a term of derision for Qumran movement's enemies who are dubbed those "*without* insight" (cf. CD V, 16; 1QH[a] X, 19; Isa 27:11). But the context is strongly indicative of the phrase being an angelic epithet, as it seems to be in apposition to אלוהים, which is just one of the numerous other designations for angels in Song 1. Newsom cited 1QM XII, 8 as the lone example of עם referring angels,[164] but as I argued previously, the עם קדושים of that line likely refers to the people who have a tutelary relationship to the angelic holy ones (cf. Dan 7:27; 1QM X, 10). Fletcher-Louis reads עם בינות כבודי as a human designation and he understands אלוהים as appositionally connected, offering the phrase as corroboration of his "divine" theological anthropology proposal and citing a similar string of epithets in the *Songs of the Sage* in support.[165] Another possibility, which I consider the strongest option, is that עם בינות כבודי is deliberately ambiguous as per the use of קדושים and שר in 1QH[a] (cf. 4Q418 81 12). Thus, referring to angels as "the *people* of his glorious insight" underscores the tight-knit angel-human fellowship and its benefits – including angelically revealed knowledge – which *SSS* celebrates and facilitates.[166]

Finally, *SSS* hints at the posture with which angelic fellowship was experienced and emulation of the angels was undertaken. In my discussion of the *War Scroll* (see Chapter 4), I highlighted the document's boldness insofar as it envisions a presumptuous mutuality between the sectarians and angelic warriors. *SSS* similarly hints at a self-assured reciprocity between the sectarian worshippers and angelic priests. While it is true that Song 2 emphasizes that part of the emotional response of the first person plural speakers is humility, the question of how the heavenly and angelic

---

[163] Elisha Qimron, "A Review Article of the *Songs of the Sabbath Sacrifice: A Critical Edtion*, by Carol Newsom," *HTR* 79 (1986): 358–359. Cf. Newsom, "Angelic Liturgy," 139; Davila, *Liturgical Works*, 98.

[164] Newsom, *Songs of the Sabbath Sacrifice*, 99.

[165] Fletcher-Louis, *All the Glory*, 283, 298–299. On *Songs of the Sage*, see below.

[166] See Angel, *Otherworldly*, 95. I noted that something similar may be at work in *11QMelch* (cf. 11Q13 II, 9); see Chapter 4. I will return to this subject, below.

priesthoods can be reckoned together is, as we have seen, not met with despair or even silence but a resolute cohortative: "Let us exult the God of knowledge" (Song 2:26 [= 4Q400 2 8]). In Newsom's words, the second song conveys "a tone of wonder ..., but also a sense of analogy with the angelic priesthood."[167] That a sense of analogy rather than just humble awe is at work can be seen in the formulaic introduction to the thirteen songs, each of which includes an imperative summons to praise, ostensibly recited by the *Maskil*[168] and other sectarian worshippers. A prime example is the relatively well-preserved Song 7:1–3 (= 4Q404 2 12; 4Q404 3 1–3; 4Q403 1 I, 30–32):

1 למשכיל שיר עולת השבת השביעית בשש עשר לחודש השני[169] הללו אלוהי מרומים הרמים בכול

2 אלי דעת יגדילו[170] קדושי אלוהים למלך הכבוד המקדיש בקודשו[171] לכול קדושו ראשי תושבחות

3 כול אלוהים שבחו לאלוהי ת[ן]שבחות הוד ...

---

[167] Newsom, "He Has Established," 115: "[In the second Sabbath song], the human community briefly contemplates its inadequacy in comparison with the angelic worshippers, but then proceeds to offer its praise." Cf. Davidson, *Angels at Qumran*, 245: "The sectarian community praises God in association with the angels (4Q400 2 1–8), even though their praise is impoverished by comparison (4Q400 2 6–7)." Newman, "Priestly Prophets," 49: "the repetition of the angelic 'tongues' in the sixth and eighth songs picks up the theme introduced in the [second] song in which the human participants ask how the offering of their tongues of dust might be compared with those of the angels. The implied answer is that the human offering should somehow rival that of the angels ... ." *Contra* Schäfer, *The Origins of Jewish Mysticism*, 132, who speaks of the inferiority of humans vis-à-vis angels and reads the humility of Song 2 as a statement that the human priesthood is "nothing compared to the angelic priesthood in heaven." Cf. Chazon, "Human & Angelic Prayer," 41–43; eadem, "Liturgical Communion," 98–102. See also Noam Mizrahi, "The Cycle of Summons: A Hymn form the Seventh Song of the Sabbath Sacrifice (4Q403 1i 31–30)," *DSD* 22 (2015): 63, who makes similar comments in reference to Song 7: "The theological unease embedded in the very idea that God's kingship depends on acknowledgement from lesser beings is significantly attenuated if words of performative praise are put not in the mouths of mortals – whose conception and death are immersed in impurity – but rather in the mouths of celestial and spiritual beings that are intimately related to the deity." But again, this emphasis on human unworthiness may miss the boldness of the sectarian worshippers and what they are claiming via the use of *SSS*.

[168] On the *Maskil* as worship/prayer leader, the community's senior (high) priest and possible successor to the Teacher of Righteousness, see Alexander, *Mystical Texts*, 49.

[169] This word is not extant in 4Q403, but is supplied on the basis of the formula preserved in the other Songs; see Newsom, "Angelic Liturgy," 162 n. 5.

[170] The נ has been restored from a ק, which was likely a spelling error; see Newsom, "Angelic Liturgy," 162 n. 7.

[171] The ש has been restored from an ע, which may have been the result of either scribal error or manuscript deterioration; see Newsom, "Angelic Liturgy," 162 n. 8. Cf. Mizrahi, "The Cycle of Summons," 47.

1 For the Master [lit: Maskil]. Song of the sacrifice of the seventh Sabbath on the sixteenth of the <second> month. Praise the God of the exalted heights, O exalted ones among all the
2 divine beings of knowledge. Let the Holy Ones of the godlike beings ma<g>nify the king of glory who sanctifies by his holine<ss> all his holy ones. O chiefs of the lauding of
3 all the godlike beings, laud the majestically [l]audworthy Go[d] ...

The summons to worship God is addressed to the angels, who are referred to using a variety of designations, but Song 7 extends this call beyond the post-introduction הללו familiar from the other songs, as imperatives and jussives are frequent throughout lines 2–12. Another instance of *SSS* envisioning a self-assured relationship with the angels may be present in Songs 6 and 8. As briefly noted above, these songs mention the blessings offered by the angelic chief princes and their deputies, but the language used to describe the recipients of these blessings is ambiguous and may not refer to the exemplary priestly angels but to the human community that worships with them:

The phrases which allude to the moral qualities of those blessed (e.g., לכול תמימי דרך) certainly need not be taken as referring to human worshippers. The Sabbath Shirot refers to statutes promulgated for the angels through which they attain to purity and holiness (4Q400 1 I, 5, 15) and describes the angels as obedient (4Q405 23 I, 10–11). It is possible, however, that just as the human community joins with the angels in the praise of God (4Q400 2 6–8) they are also considered to be recipients of the blessings of the chief princes, along with the [other] angelic worshippers.[172]

Though the designations used throughout the songs may indicate that angels rather than humans are the recipients of these blessings, alternatively, the very cooperation between heaven and earth under discussion could either mean that references to humans and angels are interspersed or a deliberate terminological ambiguity akin to what was proposed for Song 1:6 has been employed.[173] If this interpretation is correct, it is further confirmation of the

---

[172] Newsom, *Songs of the Sabbath Sacrifice*, 196. Cf. Alexander, *Mystical Texts*, 44: "[The 'we' of Song 2] are presumably the humanity community who are the recipients of the angelic blessings in Songs 6 and 8."

[173] Again, it may be that *SSS* has applied designations to angels that are more frequently associated with humans (e.g., עם, נשיא, and perhaps כול תמימי דרך) to emphasize that the sectarians were honoured members of a human-angel coterie. Alexander, *Mystical Texts*, 17, sees such terminological ambiguity as indicative of "the parallelism between Israel on earth and the angels in heaven." For further, see the comments of Church, *Hebrews and the Temple*, 134–135; Davidson, *Angels at Qumran*, 243–244; Swarup, *The Self-Understanding*, 142; Davila, *Liturgical Works*, 104. On the difficulties such terminological ambiguity introduces to making a distinction between angels and humans, see Sullivan, *Wrestling with Angels*, 152–155. For an instructive discussion on the topic, see Angel, *Otherworldly*, 93–95, who concedes the ease with which many of the epithets can be read as references to angels but at the same time recognizes that not entertaining a human reading of some of the designations may sometimes undermine a document's intended complexity. However, the notion that members of the Qumran movement could occasionally be described with angelic designations – or angels with human ones – in order

presumptuous posture with which the sect approached its relationship with the angelic priests, as they viewed themselves as worthy of being blessed by the angels whom they exhorted to praise God. Thus, the sectarian boasts were not only that they enjoyed fellowship with and meticulously emulated

---

to emphasize their privileged lot needs to be differentiated from Fletcher-Louis' thesis that angels are not angels but actually "angelmorphic" or "divine" humans. This observation, in turn, is just one part of the larger debate as to whether *SSS* and other texts envision humans as undergoing some kind of (ontological) transformation. For an overview, see Zilm, "Multi-Coloured," 436–439, who articulates two scholarly poles: i.) interpretations which blur the ontological lines between angels and humans (cf., e.g., Tushling, *Angels and Orthodoxy*, 118; Newman, "Priestly Prophets," 31 n. 8; Putthoff, *Ontological Aspects*, 103–138); and ii.) more "conservative" approaches which maintain an ontological distinction between humans and angels (cf., e.g., Klawans, *Purity, Sacrifice, and the Temple*, 136; Chazon, "Human & Angelic," 41–43; Dimant, "Men as Angels," 101; Angel, *Otherworldly*, 96, 105). Zilm's approach is a "middle-ground" of sorts, postulating that the human worshippers became progressively "angel-like" as the cycle moves from the humility of Song 2 to its climax in Song 13 (on this point, cf. Newman, "Priestly Prophets," 71). On the key distinction between *ontological transformation to* an angel as opposed to becoming/acting angel-*like*, cf. Sullivan, *Wrestling with Angels*, 165, 228; 236; Chazon, "Liturgical Communion," 101, 105. While I am closer to the pole that sees an ontological distinction between humans and angels, I would suggest that fellow "conservative" readers (to use Zilm's descriptor) may, on occasion, unnecessarily restrict the notion of angelic fellowship. For instance, in the articles just cited, Chazon places *SSS* in her second category of religious experience, "two choirs: praying like the angels" rather than her third, "one congregation: joining the angels"; and Dimant understands angelic fellowship as analogical rather than actual. Both viewpoints do not allow for the possibility that the question of the sectarian priests in Song 2:24 – "how shall our priesthood (be accounted) in their dwellings?" – expects and, indeed, *has* a positive and resolute outcome just two lines later (= "Let us exult the God of knowledge"). Moreover, in light of *SSS's* detailed descriptions of the heavenly temple, I do not think that praying "like" the angels or an analogical understanding of angelic fellowship grants sufficient consideration to the imperatival call to worship of each song as constituting a worship experience that was boldly conceived of as occurring with the angelic priests. For these reasons, I find compelling the reading of Alexander, *Mystical Texts*, 44–46, who reads *SSS* as advocating an ontological distinction between angels and humans – but at the same time upholds the idea that it testifies to actual fellowship with the angels (though see his discussion of the *Self-Glorification Hymn* in ibid., 90, where he references the speaker's "angelification"). Cf. Newsom, *Songs of the Sabbath Sacrifice*, 71–72, whose well-known quotation begins by stating that *SSS* facilitated "a mystical communion with the angels. The priests of the Qumran community understood themselves as alone representing the true and faithful priesthood, בני צדוק and בני צדק. Yet physical realties seemed to contradict their claim. They did not have authority in the temple; they could not conduct its sacrificial service; they possessed neither the sacred vestments nor utensils. ... What was specifically needed at Qumran, however, were not merely arguments couched in visionary form to demonstrate the authenticity of the claims of the group but rather some form of experiential validation of their claims. ... That the Sabbath songs functioned primarily to form the identity and confirm the legitimacy of the priestly community is also reflected in the fact that the work does not find its climax in the description of the divine merkabah but rather in the glorious appearance of the celestial high priests in their ceremonial vestments, [the] model and image of the Qumran priesthood."

those angels whose priesthood was thought to be the model for that of the nation of Israel; the Qumran movement also confidently considered their community to have, in some sense, a standing on par with these heavenly priests.

D. 4Q181, 4Q511, 1QSb & The Self-Glorification Hymn

Several sectarian documents contain brief yet similar examples to the texts discussed above, and in this section I will present a sampling of such works. Lastly, I will examine the so-called *Self-Glorification Hymn* which in many respects surpasses the loftiness of all other sectarian texts and will thus serve as an appropriate way to bring this chapter to a close.

I. Pesher on the Periods B/Ages of Creation B (4Q181)

4Q181[174] states that the benefits of angelic fellowship belong to God's elect, with a portion of the second column of fragment 1 reading as follows:

3 ...   הגיש מבני תבל   *vacat*   להתחשב עמו בע[ו]דת]

4 [א]ל[ים לעדת קודש במעמד לחיי עולם ובגורל עם קדושיו ...

3 ... he brought near some of the sons of the world *vacat* to be reckoned with him in a con[gregation of]
4 the [d]ivine beings for a holy congregation in a station of everlasting life and in a lot with his holy ones. ...

---

[174] For the *editio princeps*, see John M. Allegro, ed., *Qumran Cave 4.1 (4Q158–4Q186)* (DJD 5; Oxford: Claredon, 1968), 79, who published his text without commentary. 4Q181, which is dated on the basis of paleography to the Herodian period, was initially grouped with 4Q180 and together were dubbed the *Pesher on the Periods* (or *Ages of Creation) A and B*, due to both the genre/content of 4Q180 and the similarities 4Q180 shares with fragment 2 of 4Q481; see Milik, "Milki-sedeq et Milkiresa," 112–124. However, there is some discussion as to the relationship between the texts: Devorah Dimant, "The 'Pesher on the Periods' (4Q180) and 4Q181," *IOS* 9 (1979): 77–102, has argued that these are two different compositions. Alternatively, C. Ariel, A. E. Yuditsky, and Elisha Qimron, "The Pesher on the Periods A–B (4Q180–4Q181): Editing, Language, and Interpretation," *Meghillot* 11 (2014): 3–40 [Hebrew], have proposed that 4Q180 and 4Q181 are two versions of the same work, the longer of which is preserved in 4Q181. For a detailed treatment of the text with translation, commentary, and bibliography, see Devorah Dimant, "On Righteous and Sinners: 4Q181 Reconsidered," in *Manières de penser danls l'antiquité méditerranéenne et orientale: Mélanges offerts à Francis Schmidt par ses elves, ses collègues et ses amis* (eds., Christophe Batsch and Madalina Vartejanu-Joubert; JSJSup 134; Leiden: Brill, 2009): 61–85. The Hebrew text, sigla, and translations of 4Q181 cited here are those of Dimant (with occasional minor translational adjustments).

In addition to the passage making better sense if עם קדושיו is rendered "*with his holy ones*" rather than "*the people* of his holy ones" (cf. Dan 7:27; 1QM X, 10; XII, 8; 11Q13 II, 9), that the former is the correct understanding can be highlighted by looking at the parallelism. Specifically, the placement of the prepositions (which are italicized in translation) suggests that עִם is עַם not the noun עַם:

Table 9: Parallelism of Prepositional Phrases in 4Q181 1 II, 3–4

Prepositional Phrase	Infinitive
	להתחשב עמו
	to be reckoned with him
בעדת אלים לעדת קודש	
in a congregation of the divine beings *for* a holy congregation	
במעמד לחיי עולם	
in a station *of/for* everlasting life	
ובגורל עם קדושיו	
and *in* a lot *with* his holy ones	

The language is similar to that of the *Hodayot*, 1QS, and *SSS*,[175] and the use of מעמד may indicate that the fellowship envisioned here was with the angelic priests (cf. 1 Chr 23:28; 2 Chr 35:15; 1QH[a] XI, 22; XIX, 16; *SSS* 13:18–24 [= 4Q405 23 II, 7–12]). It would seem that there is a present sense to this station with the angels,[176] although 4Q181 is the clearest exemplar in the sectarian texts of the wider early Jewish belief that angelic fellowship will also be a hallmark of "eternal life" (cf. 1QS IV, 6–8; 1QM I, 8–9; Dan 12:3; 1

---

[175] Terminology employed in other angelic fellowship passages includes חשב (cf. *SSS* 2:24 [= 4Q400 2 6]; this word also appears in a similar context in both recensions of the *Self-Glorification Hymn*: cf. 4Q491 11 I, 14, 18; 4Q471b 1 1); עדה (cf. 1QH[a] VII, 19; XI, 22–23); קדושים (cf. 1QH[a] XI, 23; 1QS XI, 8; *SSS* 1:10 [= 4Q400 1 I, 10]); אלים (cf. *SSS* 2:17 [= 4Q401 14 I, 5]); גורל (cf. 1QH[a] XI, 23; XIV, 16; XIX, 14, 16; 1QS XI, 7; 1QM XVII, 7). A comparison of 1QS XI, 8 and 4Q181 1 II, 2 reveals that an additional facet of the language of 4Q181 is this: while the former is a positive reference to the Qumran movement, the latter uses similar language to describe the sect's evil celestial and human counterparts, which are dubbed "a community of wickedness"). Thus, the opposing human-angel coteries have once again been delineated; see Ariel, Yuditsky, and Qimron, "The Pesher on the Periods, 3–40; Dimant, "On Righteous and Sinner," 79.

[176] The perfect verb that governs the statement (Hiphil of נגש) suggests that the communion envisioned is not only for the future; cf. Davidson, *Angels at Qumran*, 275, who claims that the passage "mentions the present experience of the Qumran community as being one of sharing fellowship with the angels."

En. 104:2–6).[177] Moreover, while the text mentions "Israel" (cf. 4Q181 2 3), the dualistic tone of the document suggests that Israel is a sectarian appropriation, and thus 4Q181 makes a clear distinction between the members of Qumran movement and everyone else, here dubbed "the sons of the world."[178] But the text has also been rightly described as encapsulating a key conviction of the sect in that adherence to their reconstituted covenant meant being in a "single assembly with the angels, thus earning eternal life."[179] 4Q181 therefore corroborates what we have witnessed in the sectarian texts thus far: having a (priestly) station before God with the angels is intimately connected to the sect's consideration of themselves as the true Israel.

II. Songs of the Sage (4Q511)

The *Songs of the Sage* (henceforth, *SSage*) are hymns of praise and thanks, to be led by the *Maskil*,[180] sung to protect the sectarians from the influence of evil spirits. In addition to mentioning the establishment of the angelic priesthood (cf. 4Q511 35 2–5),[181] *SSage* reinforces the notion that there is a

---

[177] Dimant, "On Righteous and Sinner," 79.

[178] In addition to using גורל in a dualistic/predeterministic sense in lines 4–5 (cf. 1QS III, 24; IV, 24–26; 1QM XVII, 7) and contrasting the impurities of the wicked with the mercy bestowed upon the elect (cf. 4Q181 1 II, 3; 1QS IV, 2–14), the partitive prefixing of מן to בני in line 3 conveys that the sectarians are elect and thus the true Israel; see Dimant, "On Righteous and Sinners," 77–78. Cf. Davidson, *Angels at Qumran*, 272–273.

[179] Dimant, "On Righteous and Sinner," 78.

[180] As indicated by numerous occurrences of למשכיל, from which the English translation "Sage" stems. For the Hebrew text and sigla cited below, as well as notes on the affinities *SSage* has with other sectarian texts, see Baillet, DJD 7, 215–262, who dated the manuscripts on the basis of paleography to the last quarter of the 1st cent. BCE. Translations cited here are based on García Martínez and Tigchelaar, *DSSSE*, 2:1026–1037. For important discussions of *SSage*, including the למשכיל heading and the text's sectarian provenance, see Newsom, "'Sectually' Explicit," 183–184; Bilhah Nitzan, "Hymns from Qumran," *The Dead Sea Scrolls: Forty Years of Research* (eds., Devorah Dimant, Uriel Rappaport, and Yad Yitshak Ben-Tsvei; STDJ 10; Leiden: Brill, 1992), 53–63; eadem, *Qumran Prayer and Religious Poetry* (STDJ 12; Leiden: Brill, 1994), 227–272; Angel, *Otherworldly*, 92, 124–132; idem "Maskil, Community, and Religious Experience in the *Songs of the Sage* (4Q510–511)," *DSD* 19 (2012): 1–27. For a recent attempt to reorganize the numerous fragments of 4Q511 into a more coherent order, see idem, "The Material Reconstruction of 4QSongs of the Sage[b] (4Q511)," *RevQ* 27 (2015): 25–82. On the important point that *SSage* were not for the *Maskil's* benefit alone but intended to be "recited aloud as part of a communal ritual," see idem, "Reading the Songs of the Sage in Sequence: Preliminary Observations and Questions," in *Functions of Psalms and Prayers in the Late Second Temple Period* (eds., Mike S. Pajunen and Jeremy Penner; BZAW 486; Berlin: de Gruyter, 2017), 187.

[181] In this respect, *SSage* are reminiscent of *SSS* 1 (cf. 4Q400 1 I, 1–20); see Alexander, *Mystical Texts*, 69.

union between the angelic priests and the sect members, and it does this primarily in two ways. First, the text states outright that God has brought both the angels and the sectarians – who, significantly, are designated as "Israel" – into one lot. 4Q511 2 I, 7–10 exclaims that:

7 [אלוה]ים הנבונה שם [י]שראל [בש]נים עשר מחנות קד̇ו̇ש̇ן]ה לו̇
8 [   ]גורל אלוהים עם מל̇א̇ו̇כי]מאורות כבודו בשמו ת̇[ש]ב̇ו̇חת
9 [   ]ה̇ם תכן למועדי שנה [ומ]משלת יחד להתהל̇ל̇ו̇ן̇ ב[גורל
10 [אלוהים]ל̇פ̇י כבוד[ו ו]לשרתו בגורל̇ עם כסאו כיא אלוהי

7 By [Go]d's perceptive knowled[ge] he placed [I]srael [in t]welve camps of *his*[182] holy ones *in order to walk*
8 *and to enter the* lot of God with the ange[ls of] his glorious luminaries. On his name the pr[ai]se of
9 their [...] he instituted according to the feasts of the year, [and] the [do]minion of the Yahad, so that they would walk [in] the lot of
10 [God] according to [his] glory, [and] serve him in the lot of the people of his throne. For God is ...

The *War Scroll* also describes the sectarian-angel union as the "lot of God,"[183] but here the designation ממשלת יחד, "dominion of the Yahad,"[184] gives the angelic fellowship[185] a distinctly sectarian flavour. Though line 9 is fragmentary, the sense seems to be that sectarian feast-commemoration was

---

[182] For discussion of the translation of the end of line 7/beginning of line 8 and the proposed reconstructions on which they are based, including קדושיו, see Nitzan, *Qumran Prayer*, 260–261. Cf. Angel, *Otherworldly*, 126–127.

[183] Cf. 1QM XVII, 7, which has the phrase גורל אל.

[184] For translations that read יחד as the community's self-designation (rather than adjectivally), see, e.g., Baillet, DJD 7, 221–222; Wise, Abegg, and Cook, *DSSANT*, 528. Cf. Newsom, "'Sectually' Explicit," 184 n. 11, who lists numerous examples of when יחד does not have the definite article yet is used to refer to the sectarian community (cf. 1QS III, 2, 12; IX, 6; XI, 8; 1QSa I, 26; 1QSb IV, 26). Even if the intended sense is "communal dominion" (e.g., García Martínez and Tigchelaar, *DSSSE*, 2:1031), יחד is likely meant to evoke the *Yahad* via double entendre. It should be noted that ממשלה is applied to "Israel" in 1QM XVII, 7 which is a passage that also emphasizes the sectarian-angel composition of God's lot (see above). Cf. Ps 114:2, where the idea of a priestly kingdom is conveyed: "Judah became God's sanctuary (קדש), Israel his dominion (ממשלה)." For another example of sectarian-angel union in *SSage*, see 4Q511 10 11: "[God] judges in the council (סוד) of gods and men" (cf. 1QHa XI, 22; XIX, 15; 1QS XI, 7–9).

[185] The reference to the divine throne (כסא) in line 10 may be further indication that the angels with whom the sectarians have fellowship are the (priestly) angels closest to God. Note, however, that Elisha Qimron has suggested that the word is צבאו rather than כסאו, a reading which by no means diminishes the connection between the people and the angels (i.e., "in the lot of the people of his host"; cf. Dan 7:27; 1QM X, 10; XII, 8; 11Q13 II, 9); see idem, *The Dead Sea Scrolls: The Hebrew Writings, Volume 2* (Jerusalem: Yad Ben-Zvi Press, 2013), 318 [Hebrew].

so that the sectarians could be part of the angel-human lot of God/dominion of the *Yahad*.[186]

The second way the sectarian-angel lot is emphasized has affinities with the *Hodayot* and *SSS*, which, as argued above, employ deliberate terminological ambiguity by referring to humans with designations usually reserved for angels and *vice versa*. This can be seen in 4Q511 35 4, which refers to the heavenly priesthood using the following string of designations: כוהנים עם צדקו צבאו ומשרתים מלאכי כבודו, "priests, his righteous people, his army and servants, the angels of his glory." While any usage of the word עַם in reference to angels is puzzling at first glance,[187] we encountered this phenomena in *SSS* (Song 1:6 [= 4Q400 1 I, 6]; cf. 11Q13 II, 9), and an interpretation similar to what was put forward there is offered again here: the ambiguity of using עַם to refer to angels in what is already a "list of intentionally inclusive epithets [is] meant to underscore the unity of the heavenly and earthly groups in a single community."[188]   Angel has also cautiously proposed that fragment 35, which includes brief, first-person boasts/qualifications of the *Maskil* (lines 6–8), originally preceded fragment 18, a portion of text that contains more boastful content from the *Maskil*. If correct, this placement connects in a more substantial way the "intentionally inclusive epithets" of fragment 35 3–4 with the confident assertions of the

---

[186] So Alexander, *Mystical Texts*, 69. If this interpretation is correct, it complements what I suggested was a symbolic significance of Sabbath Songs 12 and 13 occurring post-*Shavuot*/covenant renewal ceremony: it was only *after* first-time admittance or recommitment to the reconstituted covenant of Israel that the attentions of the sect members are turned to *SSS's* most detailed depictions of the attendant angels of the *debir*/*merkabah* (Song 12) and its most extravagant presentation of the angelic high priests and their regalia (Song 13).

[187] Baillet, DJD 7, 237, rather than viewing the five designations in apposition to one another, saw four because he read משרתים as a construct, resulting in the translation "ministres des anges de Sa gloire." But as Angel, *Otherworldly*, 129, notes, if the goal of Baillet's reading was to mitigate "an unsettling description of human priests as the angels of God's glory," it does not work for at least two reasons: i.) משרתים is not a construct form; and ii.) even if one were to disregard משרתים, the word צבא is more naturally read as an angelic epithet in this context.   For further discussion on translational and interpretive issues of this passage, see Davidson, *Angels at Qumran*, 283–284; Fletcher-Louis, *All the Glory*, 164–165.

[188] See Angel, *Otherworldly*, 131, whose larger discussion references additional examples of this deliberate terminological ambiguity. It should be noted that the phrase of 4Q511 2 I, 10 just cited, בגורל עם כסאו, "in the lot of the *people* of his throne," may also be a deliberately ambiguous angelic designation, though it is less plausible that עם includes angels if Qimron's reading of בגורל עם צבאו is accepted, as the latter is arguably better understood as a reference to humans, perhaps specifying their tutelary relationship with the angelic host: i.e., "in the lot of the people *of* [= protected by] his host" (cf. Dan 7:27; 1QM X, 10; XII, 8).

Maskil. In other words, the sect's station with the angels is buttressed by the privileges and piety of the sectarian leadership.[189]

Lastly, a hint at the posture with which the author(s) of *SSage* approached the relationship between the sectarians and the angelic priests may be revealed in a poorly preserved section of fragment 2 of 4Q511. In line 5 of the first column, God's lot is variously referred to as "Jacob's best," his "inheritance," and "Israel";[190] line 6 then dubs the people:

6 שומ[רי דרך אלוהים ומסל[ת ק[ו]דשו לקדושי עמו ...

6 those who [kee]p the way of God[191] and his [h]oly path for the holy ones of his people.

Two words from this line, דרך and מסלה, occur in 1QS VIII, 14, which is a quotation of Isa 40:3 used to exclaim the sect's Torah-centric *raison d'être*; earlier in the same column, the verb שמר is employed to stress the faithful "keeping" of the Law that was to characterize sectarian life (VIII, 3). The implication that the sectarians alone are the ones who keep "God's way and his holy path" is bold in and of itself. But perhaps bolder still is the end of the line that specifies that this endeavor is לקדושי עמו. Admittedly, the meaning of the expression is difficult to ascertain.[192] I commented on the significance of nearly identical phrases in my discussion of the *War Scroll* (cf. 1QM VI, 6; XVI, 1),[193] where I argued that the genitive has a possessive sense. If a similar reading is accepted here, the implication is that the righteous path kept by the sectarians is also that of the angelic holy ones, who in some manner belong or pertain to God's people, the members of the Qumran movement. The sense would then be something like this: "those who keep the way of God and His holy path [which is the also that] *of*[194] the holy ones of his people." In the context of a passage that describes the sectarians in exalted terms (see line 5, cited above) and a document that is

---

[189] Angel, "The Material Reconstruction," 64–66, notes that the "content [of fragments 18 and 35] appears to flow very well," though he does not specifically mention a correlation between the credentials of the *Maskil* and angelic fellowship.

[190] See Angel, "Reading the Songs of the Sage in Sequence," 196, who notes that the scholars have seen the influence of Deut 32:9 on line 5.

[191] On *SSage* as a sectarian document despite the use of אלוהים as a name for God, see Newsom, "'Sectually' Explicit," 183–184.

[192] See, e.g., Angel, "Maskil, Community, and Religious Experience," 19–20, who cites the phrase as another example of deliberate terminological ambiguity in order to engender "the image of a liturgical community, including people and angels." While it is possible that this is the case (i.e., the usual angelic "holy ones" refers to people in this instance [cf. 1QHª XIX, 14–15]), I am not convinced this is the best interpretation, here.

[193] Cf. Baillet, DJD 7, 222, who cites 1QM VI, 6 and XVI, 1 as parallels.

[194] I.e., The ל of לקדושי עמו thus carries a genitival sense. Cf. "ל," *HALOT* 2:509; Kautzsch, *Gesenius' Hebrew Grammar*, §129; Bruce K. Waltke and M. O'Connor, *An Introduction to Biblical Hebrew Syntax* (Winona Lake: Eisenbrauns, 1988), 209–210; Qimron, *The Hebrew of the Dead Sea Scrolls*, 82.

focused on presenting the sectarians and the angels as God's united lot, reading line 6 this way is appropriate.[195]

Thus, the impression given by *SSage* is that even if the Qumran movement humbly offered prayers to God for protection from malevolent spiritual beings, there was a sense that they, as the true Israel, could also presume a fellowship and mutuality with the angelic priests of the heavenly sanctuary, which, in turn, would have enhanced their self-perception as God's legitimate people.

III. The Rule of Blessings (1QSb)

The Rule of Blessings is a collection of benedictions to be pronounced by the *Maskil* over various leaders of the Qumran movement.[196] Space precludes a full treatment of the many possible topics,[197] including the time period for which these benedictions were composed: the eschatological future, the eschaton as the present, or an amalgam that reads them proleptically.[198] The

---

[195] That the sectarians and angels are a unified lot finds an intriguing counterpoint in an observation of Angel, "Reading the Songs of the Sage in Sequence," 194–195. He notes that two separate *SSage* passages – while sharing the goal of the *Maskil*-led praise bringing about terror (פחד) for enemies of the sect – have different opponents in view: "spirits of the ravaging angels" in column 11, lines 13–14 (= 4Q511 1 4–5) and human covenant violators in column 15, lines 4–5 (= 4Q511 63–64 III, 4–5]). As Angel summarizes: "Thus, both stylistic continuity and an ironic shift in perspective are detected as one moves from columns 11 to 15. Whereas in the earlier passage the potentially frightening demons are terrified by the words of the *maskil*, in the later passage the words of the *maskil* function as a source of terror for wayward [i.e., non-sectarian] Jews, who are implicitly associated with the demons. It is striking that this shift in perspective, the counterpoising of the liturgical community with the accursed outsider who are linked with the wicked spirits appears only at the end of the scroll, and may well reflect a distinctive feature of the concluding hymn of the composition." Angel continues by noting the proposal of Esther Eshel, "Apotropaic Prayers in the Second Temple Period," in *Liturgical Perspectives*, 83–84, who has suggested that the hymns of *SSage* were used in the aforementioned covenant renewal ceremony, which would only reinforce outsiders as belonging to the lot of Belial (cf. 1QS II, 5–9).

[196] 1QSb is the second of two appendices (the first being *The Rule of the Congregation* [= 1QSa]) to 1QS and written in the same early 1st cent. BCE hand. The *editio princeps* was published by Józef T. Milik, "28b. Recueil des Bénédictions (1QSb)," in *Qumran Cave 1* (eds., idem and D. Barthélemy; DJD 1; Oxford: Claredon Press, 1955), 118–130. For a more recent edition, see James H. Charlesworth and Loren T. Stuckenbruck, "Blessings (1QSb)," in *The Dead Sea Scrolls*, 119–131, whose text, sigla, and translation, are cited, here.

[197] For an overview of the text and some of its interpretive issues with bibliography, see Charlesworth and Stuckenbruck, "Blessings," 119–121; Angel, *Otherworldly*, 107–123.

[198] On the various ways the text has been divided according to the intended recipients of the various benedictions, see the helpful summary of Wayne Baxter, "1QSb: Old Divisions Made New," *RevQ* 21 (2004): 615–629. On the future-eschatological significance of

view supported here is that the text looks forward toward the eschaton but that its proleptic significance should not be overlooked. I will highlight two relevant passages, the first of which is found in column III:

22 דברי ברכה למנ]שכיל לברך] את בני צדוק הכוהנים אשר

23 בחר במ אל לחזק בריתו ֹ] [חֹון כול משפטיו בתוך עמו ולהֹורותם

24 כאשר צוה ויקימו באמתֹן] ובצדק פקדו כול חוקיו ויתהלכו כאשֹן]ר

25 בחר יברככה אדוני מנ]מעון קונ]דשו וישימכה מכֹלול הדר בתונ]ך

26 קדושים וברית כהונתֹ]עולם יחֹ]דש לכה ויתנכה]]מקומֹכֹה]במעון[¹⁹⁹

27 קודש...

22 Words of blessing for the M[askil to bless] the Sons of Zadok, the priests whom
23 God chose to restore his covenant [...]*hwn* all his precepts in the midst of his people, and to instruct them
24 as he commanded. And they rose up in truth [...] and with righteousness watched over all his statutes and walked according [as]
25 he chose. May the Lord bless you from his [ho]ly [abode]. May he set you as a perfected ornament in the mids[t of]
26 the holy ones, and [may he r]enew for you the covenant of the [eternal] priesthood, and may he give you [...] your place [in the
27 holy [abode] ...

Significantly, the sectarian priests – here referred to as the Sons of Zadok,²⁰⁰ and thus portrayed as Israel's legitimate celebrants²⁰¹ – are honoured because

---

1QSb, see Lawrence H. Schiffman, *The Eschatological Community of the Dead Sea Scrolls: A Study of the Rule of the Congregation* (SBLMS 38; Atlanta: Scholars Press, 1989), 72–76. For readings that understand the text's references to the "last days" as the present time, see Hartmut Stegemann, "Some Remarks to 1QSa, to 1QSb, and to Qumran Messianism," *RevQ* 17 (1996): 479–505; Annette Steudel, "אחרית הימים" in the Texts from Qumran," *RevQ* 16 (1993): 225–246; Charlotte Hempel, "The Earthly Essene Nucleus of 1QSa," *DSD* 2 (1996): 253–269, esp. 255. For proleptic readings of the text, see Charlesworth and Stuckenbruck, "Rule of the Community," 2 n. 9; Johannes Zimmermann, *Messianische Texte aus Qumran: Königliche, priesterliche und prophetische Messiasvorstellungen in den Schriftfunden von Qumran* (WUNT 2/104; Tübingen: Mohr Siebeck, 1998), 284; Martin G. Abegg, Jr., "1QSb and the Elusive High Priest," in *Emanuel*, 3–16.

¹⁹⁹ במעון] קודש] is supplied by Milik, DJD 1, 124; cf. 1QSb IV, 25, cited below, which has the same expression. The space is left blank by Charlesworth and Stuckenbruck.

²⁰⁰ For an overview of priestly designations in the sectarian texts, see Kugler, "Priesthood at Qumran," 94–109. Baxter, "1QSb: Old Divisions," 624–625, notes the "exclusive grasp" that the Sons of Zadok came to have on the history of Israel's priesthood (cf. 1 Kgs 4:1–2; 1 Chr 29:22; Ezek 40:46), and while it is obvious that the recipients of the blessings in III, 22ff are considered Zadokite priests (cf., e.g., Milik, "28b. Recueil des Bénédictions," 118–130; Jacob Licht, *The Rule Scroll* [Jerusalem: Bialik Institute, 1965], 277–289; Abegg, "1QSb and the Elusive High Priest," 3–16), there is debate over the high priest's inclusion in these blessings. Whereas Licht and Abegg suggest that the high priest receives a separate blessing beginning at IV, 22, Baxter argues that the high priest should

they have faithfully taught the people as per the priestly mandate in Ezekiel.[202] If the reconstructions of lines 25–26 are accepted, this honour is bestowed from and (eventually?) in the presence of the angelic holy ones who reside with God in his מעון קודש, which elsewhere is a celestial reference (cf. Deut 26:15; Jer 25:30; 2 Chr 30:27). Angelic fellowship in heaven is presumably the focus, with the exaltation of the sectarian priests seemingly on par or perhaps even greater than that of the holy ones with whom they commune. Moreover, a reward of proximity to the angels, who elsewhere are characterized by knowledge (e.g., 1QH^a VII, 17; *SSS* 2:19 [= 4Q400 2 1]), is eminently appropriate for the Qumran movement's priests whose teachings almost certainly included that which, as noted earlier, was obtained via angelic revelation (e.g., *SSS* 2:40 [= 4Q401 14 II, 7]).

The honorific benedictions continue in column IV, but the fragmentary nature of the text has led to disagreement as to who receives this blessing: as noted, Baxter opts for the Zadokite priests in their entirety (including the high priest),[203] but others have argued that the high priest alone is envisioned, beginning at IV, 22.[204] I provisionally accept the latter view, which, if

---

be included with the Zadokites and that these blessings conclude at V, 19, just before the royal messiah's blessing, which commences in line 20. Prompted by the rare phrase "eternal covenant of the priesthood" in III, 26, Chang, *Phinehas, The Sons of Zadok, and Melchizedek*, 120–126, has proposed that, just as Ben Sira supported the Zadokite priest Simeon by developing a specifically "Aaronic priestly covenant ideology" (cf. Num 25:13; Sir 45:6–25; 51:1–24), the author of 1QSb may have similarly "wanted to build a priestly covenant ideology for a particular priestly group, namely the 'sons of Zadok,'" even if earlier in its history the sect had reasons for emphasizing other traditions. For further discussion on the relationship between priestly designations, see Charlotte Hempel, "Do the Scrolls Suggest Rivalry Between the Sons of Aaron and the Sons of Zadok and If So was it Mutual?" *RevQ* 24 (2009): 135–193; cf. eadem, "The Sons of Aaron in the Dead Sea Scrolls," in *Flores Florentino*, 207–224. But also see the cautionary note of George J. Brooke, "Patterns of Priesthood, Priestliness, and Priestly Function in Some Second Temple Period Texts," *JAAJ* 4 (2016): 14: "[N]ot every priestly term has to be understood as referring to a specific group. The authors and editors of texts use much terminology ideologically with reference to ideal or imagined realities."

[201] Whatever other connotations or specificities the term may have carried for Qumran movement, Baxter, "1QSb: Old Divisions," 627, is surely correct when he summarizes III, 22 as follows: "the community had the true heirs of Israel's high priesthood in their midst – the sons of Zadok."

[202] Chang, *Phinehas, The Sons of Zadok, and Mechizedek*, 122, notes terminological affinities between Ezek 44:23–24 and 1QSb III, 23–25, including ירה and משפט.

[203] Baxter, "1QSb: Old Divisions," 624–628.

[204] E.g., Abegg, "1QSb and the Elusive High Priest," 3–16, who argues that the presence of singular verbs and pronouns suggest that an individual recipient is intended. Cf. Licht, *The Rule Scroll*, 277–289.

correct, means that the high priest is singled-out for a Jubilees-like comparison near the end of column IV:[205]

ואתה	... 24
ת[ה]יה סביב משרת בהיכל	25 כמלאך פנים במעון קודש לכבוד אלוהי צבא[ו]ת
ל[ע]ת עולם ולכול קצי נצח ...	26 מלכות ומפיל גורל עם מלאכי פנים ועצת יחד[ן

24 ... And (may) you (be)
25 like an angel of the presence in the abode of holiness, for the glory of the God of
[H]ost[s   May] you be round about serving in the temple of
26 the kingdom and may you cast lot with the angels of the presence and the council of the community[for] eternal time, and for all glorious Endtime. ...

While it is noteworthy that the sectarian high priest is likened[206] to the priestly angels who serve in closest proximity to God, it is significant that this honour is envisioned as bestowed in the celestial sanctuary, which is indicated by the designation מעון קודש and היכל מלכות.[207] The statement that the high priest "casts the lot" (i.e., determines fate)[208] with both the angels of the presence and "the council of the *Yahad*" (עצת יחד)[209] clarifies that the high priest's position and privilege benefit the sectarian communi-

---

[205] We witnessed in Chapter 3 that Jub. 31:14 describes Jacob's blessing of Levi, which includes the prayer that his son would serve God in the Jerusalem temple "like the angels of the presence and the holy ones" (who serve God in the heavenly sanctuary). 1QSb IV, 24–26 thus appears to be a sectarian appropriation of this idea.

[206] *Contra* Fletcher-Louis, *All the Glory*, 152–158, who argues that that the priest *is* an angel of the presence. But as Sullivan, *Wrestling with Angels*, 165, rightly notes, "[the preposition כ] makes a comparison (like or as), not an equation."

[207] The biblical references to מעון קודש as God's celestial abode are cited above; the parallel term, היכל מלכות, though similar to the description of the Jerusalem temple in Sir 50:7 (היכל מלך), has analogous designations in *SSS* where it most plausibly refers to the celestial sanctuary (cf. 4Q400 1 I, 13, which has היכלי מלך; and 4Q405 23 II, 11, which has מקדשי מלכות). For discussion of this and other similarities to *SSS* and 1QSb, see Angel, *Otherworldly*, 117–123, who stresses the teaching and knowledge of the angelic priesthood and the concomitant responsibility of the sectarian priests in imparting this revelation (see especially, 1QSb IV, 22–23, 27). Cf. Frennesson, *"In a Common Rejoicing,"* 83–87.

[208] The exact sense of מפיל גורל is uncertain, but commentators have taken it as a reference to the divine prerogative to determine destiny/fate (cf. 1QS IV, 26), which is here granted to the high priest. For a discussion of the use of this language elsewhere in the Scrolls, see Lange, "Determination of Fate," 39–43. For a translation that reflects this, see Wise, Abegg, and Cook, *DSSANT*, 143: "ordering destiny with the angels of presence ... ." Cf. Frennesson, *"In a Common Rejoicing,"* 87; Schäfer, *The Origins of Jewish Mysticism*, 129, who propose that the expression may include an eschatological judging role for the sectarian-angel lot.

[209] The more common spelling is עצת היחד. For instances of the phrase as a community reference without the definite article, cf. 1QS III, 2; XI, 8; 1QSa I, 26; 4Q511 2 I, 9; see Angel, *Otherworldly*, 118 n. 46.

ty.[210] Additionally, the fact that the high priest casts the lot *with* (עִם) the angels of the presence and the community may suggest that they, too, have a destiny-determining role.

IV. Self-Glorification Hymn

The so-called *Self-Glorification Hymn* (henceforth, *SGH*) has a first-person speaker boasting that he has been exalted above even the angels, which is followed by an imperative summons to the community to praise God. There are multiple textual witnesses to *SGH*, and the general consensus is that there are two extant recensions: the unquestionably *Hodayot*-related "Recension A" (cf. 1QH[a] XXV, 34–XXVII, 3; 4Q427 [= 4QH[a]] 7; 4Q471b 1a–d [= 4Q431 or 4QH[e]]) and "Recension B" (cf. 4Q491 11 I, 8–18 [= 4Q491c]),[211] which has been controversially associated with the *War Scroll*.[212] While the

---

[210] So Angel, *Otherworldly*, 118. This may corroborate the fragmentary 1QSb I, 1–5, which hints that יראי אל, "those who fear God" (i.e., the wider community) are blessed "in the congregation of the holy ones" (בעדת קדושים), which is almost certainly a celestial reference. The consensus is that 1QSb I, 5 is part of a section that refers to the general membership of the sectarian community; see, e.g., Schiffmann, *The Eschatological Community*, 72; Baxter, "1QSb: Old Divisions," 616.

[211] The designations Recension A and Recension B have been very influential and were first used by Esther Eshel, "4Q471b: A Self-Glorification Hymn," *RevQ* 17 (1996): 175–203, who also coined the term "Self-Glorification Hymn." For the texts of the Recension A witnesses, see Stegemann, Schuller, and Newsom, DJD 40, 290–309 (for 1QH[a] XXV, 34-XXVII, 3); Schuller, DJD 29, 96–108 (for 4Q427 7); Schuller, DJD 29, 199–208 (for 4Q431); Eshel, "471b.," in DJD 29, 421–432 (for 4Q471b). For the text of the Recension B witness (4Q491 11), see Baillet, DJD 7, 26–30. For a discussion of all the relevant texts and their relationship to each other, see Michael O. Wise, "מי כמוני באלים: A Study of 4Q491c, 4Q471b, 4Q427 7, and 1QH[a] 25:35–26:10," *DSD* 7 (2000): 173–219; cf. Eileen M. Schuller, "A Hymn from a Cave Four *Hodayot* Manuscript: 4Q427 7 i + ii," *JBL* 113 (1993): 626; John J. Collins and Devorah Dimant, "A Thrice-Told Hymn: A Response to Eileen Schuller," *JQR* 85 (1994): 151–155; Devorah Dimant, "A Synoptic Comparison of Parallel Sections in 4Q427 7, 4Q491 11 and 4Q471B," *JQR* 85 (1994): 157–159.

[212] 4Q491 in its entirety was originally considered to be part of the Cave 4 *War Scroll* fragments published by Baillet, DJD 7, 12–44. But the relationship between the M tradition and 4Q491 was challenged by Martin G. Abegg, Jr., "Who Ascended to Heaven? 4Q491, 4Q427, and the Teacher of Righteousness," in *Eschatology, Messianism, and the Dead Sea Scrolls*, 61–73 (cf. idem, "4Q471: A Case of Mistaken Identity?" in *Pursuing the Text*, 137), who, on the basis of physical manuscript discrepancies, as well as paleographic, orthographic, and literary differences, divided 4Q491 into three separate "manuscripts." In his estimation, only two of these manuscripts are related to the *War Scroll*: while the first (= 4Q491a) shares common text with various material in 1QM, and the second (= 4Q491b) has echoes of 1QM, the third section (= 4Q491c) he deemed to have no relationship to the *War Scroll*. Given the parallels with the *Hodayot* texts, Abegg speaks of "clear generic relationship" between 4Q491c and the *Thanksgiving Hymns*. Although Abegg's proposal has been widely accepted, Florentino García Martínez, "Old Texts and Modern Mirages:

impetus for using the term "recension" is the obvious thematic and linguistic similarities among the extant witnesses, there have been some recent objections to this classification, as scholars have noted that the discrepancies are sufficient to question the term's appropriateness.[213] Complicating the issue is that the different literary settings have resulted in different attributions of identity for the "I" voice: a human voice as per those of the other *Hodayot* for Recension A[214] and the voice of an angel prompted by the *War Scroll's* reference to Michael (cf. 1QM XVII, 6–7) for Recension B.[215] An exhaustive treatment of these text-critical and interpretive issues is well beyond the parameters of the present study, but some brief comments are necessary. First, a *War Scroll* setting for this text does not demand that the "I" voice be angelic.[216] In fact, most scholars are convinced that the first-person speaker of 4Q491c is human (the view accepted here)[217] and, as such,

---

the 'I' of Two Qumran Hymns," in idem, *Qumranica Minora I*, 105–125, has objected to Abegg's separation of 4Q491 into three manuscripts, arguing that 4Q491c should thus be read in light of the echoes of the *War Scroll* of 4Q491b. Cf. Kipp Davis, "'There and Back Again': Reconstruction and Reconciliation of the War Text 4QMilhama[a] (4Q491[a–c])," in *The War Scroll, Violence, War and* Peace, 125–146, esp. 128–137, who supports Baillet's judgment that 4Q491 constitutes one manuscript. Also see Angel, *Otherworldly*, 136 n. 111, who references personal communication with Abegg, who has more recently expressed that he is "no longer convinced by some of his original arguments for dividing 4Q491 into three manuscripts."

[213] So García Martínez, "Old Texts," 115–116, who contends that "an analysis of the common elements – the shared phraseology and related expressions in both compositions – but also of their obvious differences, does not allow us to conclude that we are dealing with two genetically related compositions. Neither can be explained by the other. Nor can either be explained by an assumed common ancestor. The 'recension' idea cannot be applied in this case, at least not if we give it the meaning the word carries in the disciplines of textual and literary criticism where it originated." Cf. Stegemann, Schuller, and Newsom, DJD 40, 301 n. 10. It should be noted that if the recension terminology is retained, it is obviously problematic to speak of a *singular SGH*.

[214] For specific reasons why most scholars have concluded that the "I" voice of both recensions is human, see below.

[215] As discussed in the previous chapter, the general consensus is that 1QM incorporated pre-existent prayer/hymnic material. Given Baillet's assumptions that 4Q491 11 I, 8–18 was both hymnic and related to the *War Scroll*, he dubbed it "cantique de Michel" due to the reference to the archangel in 1QM XVII. I will return to the interpretation of the "I" voice, below.

[216] Although Collins, *The Scepter and the Star*, 151, rightly allows that "even a different recension may have had a different literary setting and be understood in a different way," his reading 4Q491c's "I" voice as human demonstrates that different settings do not demand different understandings of the same referent.

[217] Few scholars have supported Baillet's Michael interpretation. For discussion and bibliography, see Angel, *Otherworldly*, 137–138, who also provides a convenient list of arguments for a human interpretation. For a recent defense of the Michael interpretation, see García Martínez, "Old Texts," 122–124. The objection to the speaker as Michael is

the claims of both 4Q491c and the *SGH* texts more confidently associated with the *Hodayot* are the loftiest angelic fellowship boasts in all of the Scrolls. Thus, any understanding of communion with the angels and the contribution it made to sectarian identity would be incomplete without taking *SGH* into consideration. I will now highlight the most important claims of the texts.

As the longest *SGH* witness, 4Q491 11 I, 8–18 contains the greatest number of relevant statements. The extant first person singulars commence at the end of line 12, and the passage combines grandiose exclamations with rhetorical questions expecting a negative answer, which together function to assert the speaker's perseverance and resolve in the face of persecution (lines 15–16), as well as his matchless eloquence, teaching, and judgments (lines 16–17). Moreover, claims of angelic fellowship are on display in lines 14 and 18:[218]

14 ... אני עם אלים אתחשב ומכוני בעדת קודש ...

14 ... I am reckoned with the gods, my habitation is in the holy council ...

18 ... כ]יא אניא עם אלים מֹעֹמֹ[דֹי וכ]בֹודֹיֹٴ עם בני המלך ...

18 ... for my station is with the gods, and my glory abides with the sons of the king ...

---

due in large part to the influential observations made by Morton Smith, "Ascent to the Heavens and Deification in 4QM[a]," in *Archaeology and History*, 181–188 (cf. idem, "Two Ascended to Heaven," in *Jesus and the Dead Sea Scrolls* [ed., James H. Charlesworth; ABRL; New York: Doubleday, 1990], 290–301), who argued that someone of the archangel's stature would hardly need to boast of his exalted position, nor would he compare himself to earthly kings or have to be "reckoned" (חשב) with the gods (i.e., no angel would ever imply that he was not "originally at home in the heavens"). The same word in the Niphal plays a role in describing the (very human) contempt that the speaker has had to endure (4Q491 11 I, 15; cf. 1QH[a] XII, 23; Isa 53:3). On the language associated with the speaker's instruction as being more appropriate for a human than an angel, see Dimant, "A Synoptic Comparison," 161, who points out that מזל שפתי, "flow of my lips" (4Q491 11 I, 17) is used elsewhere in the sectarian texts as an expression for human praise/teaching (cf. 1QH[a] XIX, 5; 1QSb III, 27; 4Q511 63–64 II, 4). Another phrase that has been judged to be strange were it to stem from angelic lips is לוא כבשר תאוֹ[תי, "[My] desi[re] is not of the flesh" (4Q491 11 I, 14), as the speaker seems to be emphasizing his "inability to be tempted like ordinary mortals"; see Eshel, DJD 29, 423 n. 12; cf. eadem, "The Identification of the 'Speaker' of the Self-Glorification Hymn," in *The Provo International Conference on the Dead Sea Scrolls: Technological Innovations, New Texts, and Reformulated Issues* (eds., Donald W. Parry and Eugene Ulrich; STDJ 30; Leiden: Brill, 1999), 626. These and other arguments have prompted the vast majority of scholars to read the "I" voice as human, even in 4Q491c. However, it would be misleading to refer to this as *the* human interpretation since there is no consensus on the specific identity of the human speaker; see below.

[218] Text, sigla, and translations (with occasional minor adjustments of the latter) of 4Q491 are based on those of Wise, "מי כמוני באלים," 182–183; line numbers correspond to those of Baillet, DJD 7, 26–27.

It is possible that the reference to a throne in the middle of line 12 is further indication of the speaker's exaltation,[219] but perhaps the loftiest claims are found at the end of line 12 and continue into line 13:

לו]א דומי   ... 12

13 |ל|כבודי לוא {{ידמה}} ולוא ירומם זולתי ולוא יבוא ביא ...

12 ... No]ne can compare
13 [to] my glory, none have been exalted save myself, and none can oppose me ...

These boasts are not limited to 4Q491c. The *Hodayot*-associated witnesses make analogous and perhaps the best-known claims of the *SGH* texts. Here, I cite 4Q427 7 I, 8, 10–11:[220]

8 |ומי ישוה לי   מי כמוני |באלים[221]

10 | ידיד המ[ל]ך רע לקדושים ולוא יבא[222]

11 | ולכבו]די לוא ידמה כ[י]א̊ אני עם אלים מעמ̊ד̊[י]

---

[219] While the fragmentary state of the text precludes definitive identification of the speaker as the occupier of the throne, both the proximity of this reference to the "I" voice and the fact that the speaker says that "I sit in [... hea]ven" (line 13) alleviates some of the doubt that the throne belongs to him – but admittedly, ישב could mean "dwell" and a restoration is required to read "heaven." For discussion, see Joseph L. Angel, "The Liturgical-Eschatological Priest of the Self-Glorification Hymn," *RevQ* 24 (2010): 591 n. 29; Wise, "מי כמוני באלים," 180. On the relationship between a heavenly throne and exaltation in early Judaism, see Collins, *The Scepter and the Star*, 160–163. On the possibility that a throne indicates a rank above the angels, who are *not* privileged to sit, see Alexander, *Mystical Texts*, 86. For a highly speculative interpretation, which understands *SGH's* throne as a symbol of royal/Messianic investiture and which tentatively proposes that the speaker is "Menahem the Essene" (cf. Josephus, *Ant* 15:372–379), see Israel Knohl, *The Messiah Before Jesus: The Suffering Servant of the Dead Sea Scrolls* (Berkeley: University of California, 2000), who has more recently claimed that the fragmentary stone inscription referred to as the "Vision of Gabriel" supports his reading of *SGH*; see idem, *Messiahs and Resurrections in 'The Gabriel Revelation'* (London: Continuum, 2009). For critiques of Knoll's reading of *SGH* and objections to his corroborative use of the "Vision of Gabriel" stone, see John J. Collins, "Review of *The Messiah Before Jesus*," *JQR* 91 (2000): 185–190; idem, *The Scepter and the Star*, 164–170, who also references Aaron Yuditsky and Elisha Qimron, "Notes on the Inscription, 'The Vision of Gabriel,'" *Cathedra* 133 (2009): 133–144 [Hebrew]; Ronald Hendel, "The Messiah Son of Joseph: Simply 'Sign,'" *BAR* 35 (2009): 8. For studies on the Gabriel Stone more generally, see A. Yardeni and B. Elitzur, "Document: A First Century BCE Prophetic Text Written on Stone: First Publication," *Cathedra* 123 (2007): 55–66; Moshe Bar-Asher, "On the Language of 'The Vision of Gabriel,'" *RevQ* 23 (2008): 491–524.

[220] Text, sigla, and translation of 4Q427 7 are from Schuller, DJD 29, 96–108.

[221] Restored as per 4Q431 1: מִ֗י יִשׁ֗וֹ[ה לי (line 3); מִ֗י כמוני באלים (line 4); see Schuller, DJD 29, 203.

[222] Restored as per 4Q431 1: ידיד המלך (line 6); see Schuller, DJD 29, 203.

8 [and who will compare to me   and who is like me]among the heavenly beings?
10 [beloved of the ki]ng, a companion to the holy ones, and it will not come
11 [and to] my [glo]ry it will not be comparable; a[s f]or me, [my] station is with the
heavenly beings

An intriguing possibility with all of these quotations is not just that angelic communion is in view:[223] what is remarkable about both so-called recensions of *SGH* is that the speaker may be exalting himself above the angels with whom he is claiming fellowship.   Admittedly, there is uncertainty as to whether the speaker includes angels in his boasts of an incomparable status, especially in Recension B.[224]   But less ambiguous is Recension A, which, as we just saw, has the bold rhetorical question, "who is like me] *among the heavenly beings?*" (cf. 4Q427 7 I, 8; 4Q431 1 I, 4).[225]

As mentioned above, my reading of the texts is line with the majority view insofar as the nature of the references to the speaker's teaching, his hardships, and his opposition are strongly indicative of a human "I" voice for Recensions A and B.   But precisely which human may be claiming that he has been exalted above the angels is, as I also mentioned, another debated point.[226]   Specific proposals as to the identity of the human speaker include an ancient biblical hero,[227] the Teacher of Righteousness,[228] the current leader or *Maskil* of the Qumran movement,[229] or the eschatological high priest.[230]   I

---

[223] On *SGH* as an example of angelic fellowship akin to that discussed earlier in this chapter, see the comments of Schuller, DJD 29, 100–102; Chazon, "Liturgical Function," 145; Alexander, *Mystical Texts*, 86.   Note especially the terminological affinities between *SGH* and other angelic fellowship passages, including: the notion of being עם, "with," the angels (cf. 1QHᵃ VII, 17–19; XI, 22; XIX, 16–17); מעמד (cf. 1QHᵃ XI, 22; XIX, 16; *SSS* 13:18–24 [= 4Q405 23 II, 7–12]; 4Q181 1 II, 4); עדה (cf. 1QHᵃ VII, 19; XI, 22–23; 4Q181 1 II, 3–4); קדושים (cf. 1QHᵃ XI, 23; 1QS XI, 8; *SSS* 1:10 [= 4Q400 1 I, 10]; 4Q181 1 II, 4); אלים (cf. *SSS* 2:17 [= 4Q401 14 I, 5]; 4Q181 1 II, 4).

[224] I.e., does "none can compare" in 4Q491 11 I, 12–13 refer to other humans *and* angels or only other humans?

[225] Cf. Fletcher-Louis, "On Angels, Men and Priests," 161, who makes the intriguing claim that the exalted status of *SGH's* speaker is "the very thing we expect to happen" vis-à-vis the declaration of humanity as the pinnacle of creation in Gen 1:26–28.   However, it is far from certain that *SGH* and Gen 1 envision the same kind of dominion and prestige.

[226] For helpful summaries, cf. Schuller, DJD 29, 102 n. 37; Puech, *La Croyance*, 2:494; Angel, *Otherworldly*, 138; Collins, *The Scepter and the Star*, 155–160.

[227] E.g., Eric Miller, "The Self-Glorification Hymn Reexamined," *Hen* 31 (2009): 307–324, who emphasizes the importance of the Enoch tradition at Qumran, and thus surmises that *SGH* may be sectarian reflection upon their ante-diluvian hero.

[228] E.g., Abegg, "Who Has Ascended?" 72–73, who notes that "it is also possible that such a claim was made *on behalf of* the Teacher of Righteousness by the author(s) of the [*SGH*] texts … [emphasis retained]."

[229] E.g., Alexander, *Mystical Texts*, 89, who ties the origins of *SGH* to the Teacher of Righteousness but sees an ongoing leadership appropriation of the text: "If we assume that

think that there is much to commend in the view that, even if *SGH* was penned or inspired by the historical Teacher,[231] these texts had a significant and ongoing role for the priestly and liturgical leadership of the sect. But it would be a mistake to conclude that *SGH* is only concerned with leadership, as various factors seem to indicate a deliberate connection between the "I" voice of the leader figure and the wider community. With these things in mind, I will comment on each recension individually.

When it comes to Recension B, even if one accepts the recent objections to the division of 4Q491c from the *War Scroll*-related 4Q491b, and it is therefore tentatively allowed that there was once a connection between *SGH* and the *War Scroll*,[232] Schultz has demonstrated that this connection would have been short-lived.[233] However, I am not convinced that the contents of

---

the original [*SGH*] was composed by the Teacher of Righteousness, who, in the manner of his ancestor Levi, established his priestly and prophetic credentials within the community by ascent to heaven, then it would make sense to see each successive *Maskil* as reaffirming the Teacher's experience, and as demonstrating ... his fitness to lead the community."

[230] E.g., Eshel, DJD 29, 422–427; eadem, "4Q471b," 201–202, who emphasizes the similarities between the speaker and the eschatological priestly figure of 1QSb. Cf. Angel, "The Liturgical-Eschatological Priest," 591–599; idem, *Otherworldly*, 141–146, who provides a helpful list of the speaker's priestly characteristics (e.g., "separation from flesh" [i.e., special distinction], a teaching role, glory, and a standing among the angels), but he stresses the present involvement of this figure in the life of the sect: "In my opinion, the speaker should be understood as a member of the Qumran community who should be considered 'eschatological' only inasmuch as the liturgical experience allowed him to repeatedly escape linear historical time and be together with the angels." Also see Fletcher-Louis, *All the Glory*, 204–216, who interprets the speaker as a present "exalted priestly figure" – but one who has undergone angelmorphic transformation

[231] Cf., e.g., Eshel, DJD 29, 426, who, while ultimately preferring the eschatological high priest interpretation (see preceding note), writes the following: "There is no doubt that the Teacher of Righteousness played a major role in the life of the Qumran sect, and his death was a tragic event in their eyes. One may assume that a scribe, coping with the death of the Teacher of Righteousness, composed the Self-Glorification Hymn thinking of the Teacher of Righteousness while describing the eschatological high priests."

[232] For material arguments against dividing 4Q491c from the *War Scroll*-related 4Q491b, see García-Martinéz, "Old Texts," 111–114; Davis, "'There and Back Again,'" 128–137. Cf. Angel, *Otherworldly*, 136 n. 111, who, as noted, mentions Abegg's recent uncertainty regarding his earlier conclusions as published in "Who Ascended to Heaven?"

[233] As Schultz, *Conquering the World*, 30 n. 67, contends, "García-Martinéz, who rejects the suggestion that 4Q491c is a different composition than 4Q491b, consequently believes that both 4Q471b and 4Q491b do in fact relate to M. ... Yet even he concedes that the Hymn in question does not attribute to its protagonist any 'military function' ..., and that it was 'inserted into the context of materials related to the eschatological war.' ... Should García-Martinéz's assumption be correct, it must also be pointed out that the Hymn was then duly removed from such a war context very soon thereafter. It is nowhere to be found in M's extant text, nor is it likely that it was once part of the end which has been lost. ... Thus, while García-Martínez may well be right in that this *Self-Glorification Hymn*

SGH "are out of character with the rest of the extant M material."[234] That the *War Scroll* stresses a non-combatant yet prominent role for priests – in both battle formation and the pre-battle exhortation and prayers (cf., e.g., 1QM VII, 9–18; X, 2–8) – is clear. On the high priest's role in 1QM, Smith has (inadvertently) made an observation that may assist us in making sense of a *War Scroll* setting for *SGH*:

Just after the wicked have gained their one permitted victory, the Head Priest, trying to cheer up the righteous, promises that [God] will send Michael to help Israel (17:6f). A worse place for a victory hymn could not be found in the text. … Michael never appears in person, so 1QM provides no occasion for attributing to him the speech we have here.[235]

The point, of course, is that Smith does not consider it a viable option to interpret Michael as the "I" voice of 4Q491c. But to use Smith's own words, a human priest "trying to cheer up" the troops by boasting of his fellowship with (or exaltation above) the angels is a suitable complement not only to 1QM XVII[236] but also to what I argued was a key facet of the *War Scroll's* worldview: the bold and unique mutuality with which the Qumran movement envisioned its relationship with the angels associated with Israel. Indeed, the claims made in *SGH* are far from out of place in a document that not only boasts that the sectarians would fight in conjunction with the angels but also may presumptuously refer to these angels as the "holy ones *of the people*" (cf. 1QM VI, 6; XVI, 1). A *War Scroll* setting for *SGH* would have permitted the priest to bolster the confidence and presumption of the army by reminding them of his own exalted status "in the glory of the holy dwelling" (cf. lines 14–15).[237] Moreover, scholars have noted a "special affinity"[238] between the

---

… is not related to H as is currently thought, its relationship to M, if there ever was any, would have been short lived." Cf. Angel, *Otherworldly*, 136 n. 111, who cites Schultz.

[234] Angel, "The Liturgical-Eschatological Priest," 590, who is summarizing Schultz, *Conquering the World*, 30 n. 67.

[235] Smith, "Ascent to Heaven," 185.

[236] On the priestly "encouragement" offered in this section of 1QM, see the comments of Schultz, *Conquering the World*, 318; Dongshin Don Chang, "Priestly Covenant in 1QM and 1QSb," in *The War Scroll, Violence, War and Peace*, 157.

[237] What I am proposing as a possible function for *SGH* in a *War Scroll* setting has similarities with a comment found in the first edition of John J. Collins, *The Scepter and the Star: The Messiahs of the Dead Sea Scrolls and Other Ancient Literature* (ABRL; New York: Doubleday, 1994), 148–149: "Baillet placed 4Q491 11 in the War Rule, before the account of the battle corresponding to 1QM 16–17. It should be noted that 1QM 15 contains an exhortation to be spoken by the High Priest, and the end of column 16 contains the introduction to another exhortation on his part. The High Priest of the War Scroll is *de facto* the eschatological High Priest or Messiah of Aaron. While our canticle was not necessarily composed for this context, this placement is highly compatible with the view that the implied speaker is the eschatological priest/teacher. The claim that he has a throne in heaven is a validation of his authority, and serves the purpose of exhortation in the face of tribulation of the eschatological battle." For a complementary viewpoint, see the recent

speaker and the recipients of the second person plural imperatives in lines 20–23, which Baillet dubbed "cantique des justes" on the basis of the opening vocative (צדיקים).[239] Those addressed by the speaker are ostensibly the sectarian community – or in the context of the *War Scroll*, the soldiers of the sect – who are exhorted to praise God "in the holy dwelling" (line 20). The language thus matches that used to describe the speaker's exaltation, and as Alexander notes, "There is a large correspondence between the hymn of boasting and the exhortation: the speaker exhorts his audience to replicate to some degree his own experience and to join with the angels in heaven in worshipping God."[240] What is interesting about a possible *SGH-War Scroll* connection is that it may imply that the speaker and, by extension, the rest of the sectarian troops do not simply have Israel's angelic guardians as comrades but that they perceived themselves as outranking them in some way as well.[241] If there was ever a connection between the texts, why *SGH* was ultimately not incorporated into 1QM remains uncertain; perhaps the first-person mode of address was judged to be incongruent with the rest of the document. Regardless, if a decision not to include *SGH* in 1QM was made at some point, I am not convinced that it was because the boasts of *SGH* were considered too bold or inappropriate.

Turning to Recension A, a similar boldness is present, but here we have more to work with when discussing the literary setting, the identity of the speaker, and the significance of the boasts. Two observations are key. First, *SGH's* location among the *Community Hymns* of 1QH[a] needs to be taken

---

comments of Davis, "'There and Back Again,'" 144, who notes that 4Q491c and the priest-led statements of 1QM XVI–XVII share important commonalities: "The two hymns of 4Q491 frg. 11 i extol the speaker and the recipients as members of the divine council amid a period of adversity. The combination forms a declaration of divinely wrought victory and celebration in times of naturally manifest human distress. ... Baillet made the mistake of aligning frg. 11 with the mention of Michael in 1QM 17 and on the posited connection this formed with the self-glorification hymns in the preceding column. It is important to note that there is no mention of Michael at any point in 4Q491, and no reason to expect his appearance in any of the lacunae between either column. Baillet's title, *cantique du Michel*, was at best anachronistic, nevertheless it was partially correct by way of this allusion: the hymns of adversity and exultation in frg. 11 i quite nicely complement the description of military struggle and victory in [1QM II, which served as the inspiration for 1QM XIV–XIX], and both are comparatively constructed around the theme of cooperation between mortal pietists and the heavenly hosts."

[238] Angel, "The Liturgical-Eschatological Priest," 597.

[239] Baillet, DJD 7, 26–27. This section is marked off by an over-sized *lamed* (ל).

[240] Alexander, *Mystical Texts*, 86. Cf. Angel, "The Liturgical-Eschatological Priest," 597, who notes the affinities between the speaker and the community in the Recension A texts, as well; see below.

[241] Outranking of the angels is arguably a feature of the Recension A texts; see below.

seriously.[242] As Schuller has argued, "Whoever the referent may be in 4Q491 11 i, in the recension of this psalm that is found in the *Hodayot* manuscripts, the 'I' is to be understood in relationship to the 'I' voice we hear speaking in the other psalms, particularly the other Hymns of the Community."[243] Again, while it is possible or even likely that the claims and/or experience of a priestly leader figure such as the Teacher of Righteousness lie behind *SGH*, its placement in 1QH[a] suggests that the speaker's elevated status is something available to the community at large, perhaps even normative.[244] As with Recension B, the communal import of Recension A is further indicated by the affinities between the speaker and the references to the community in the surrounding material. In addition to the speaker denoting both himself and the community as "beloved" (cf. 4Q427 7 I, 10, 13),[245] and an implied

---

[242] Since the fragmentary remains of *SGH* are located between 1QH[a] XXV, 34 and XXVII, 3, this situates the text at the end of the second block of *Community Hymns* (CH2).

[243] Schuller, DJD 29, 102. *Contra* Collins and Dimant, "A Thrice-Told Hymn," 154–155, who on the basis of its lofty content simultaneously object to the classification of *SGH* as a *Community Hymn* and argue that it surpasses anything in the *Teacher Hymns*. While *SGH* does indeed stand out among the *Hodayot*, there are affinities with the TH: e.g., angelic fellowship, acknowledgement of God's salvation, and the weakness of the human condition; see Schuller, DJD 29, 100. Moreover, one still must account for *SGH's* placement in the CH2 block, and as mentioned above, Newsom, *The Self as Symbolic Space*, 196–198, 287–292, has made a strong case for viewing even *Teacher Hymns* as not being void of significance for the "ordinary" sectarian insofar as these psalms promoted "ideal" sectarian ways. Due its recentness, I can only make brief mention of the fresh proposal of Newsom that the *Community Hymns* are better viewed as "Maskil Hymns." Even if it necessitates the reevaluation of traditional categories, Newsom's reading may strengthen the connection between the spiritual experiences of the sectarian leadership and its promotion of theological identity formation/best practices for the wider membership; see eadem, "A Farewell to the Community Hymns?" (paper presented at the Triennial Meeting of the IOQS, Aberdeen, Scotland, 8 August 2019).

[244] This has been proposed in various ways. E.g., Chazon, "Angelic & Human Prayer," 45: "It is not impossible that the speaker, whether the Teacher of Righteousness or a similarly exalted leader of the *Yahad*, projected his own spiritual, perhaps even mystical, experience onto all members of his community or conversely, that the *Yahad* projected onto itself the Teacher's achievements and experiences" (cf. eadem, "Liturgical Function," 148, who stresses the liturgical – and thus communal – nature of *SGH's* setting in 1QH[a]). Alexander, *Mystical Texts*, 86: "There is a strong correspondence between the hymn of boasting and the exhortation: the speaker exhorts his audience to replicate to some degree his own experience and to join with the angels in heaven in worshipping God" (also see idem, "Qumran and the Genealogy," 227, who makes the plausible suggestion that *SGH* "may have served as a sort of introit to the Sabbath Songs. In this scenario, the *Maskil*, having recited his credentials to lead the congregation [by identifying with the lofty claims of the first-person speaker of *SGH*], then exhorts them to follow his example of uniting with the angels in their worship of God"). Cf. Wise, "מי כמוני באלים," 218.

[245] As Wise, "מי כמוני באלים," 218, states, "This is no mere coincidence. The repetition of the term is an intentional element of the melding process that was the

teaching-learning relationship (cf. 4Q471b 1a–d 3–4; 4Q427 7 I, 18–20),[246] the "I" voice claims to have a station "with the gods" (cf. 4Q427 7 I, 11, cited above), which is very similar to the language used to describe the lot of the community, here called "the poor" (cf. 4Q427 7 II, 8–9).[247] Moreover, the speaker-community relationship is integral to the liturgical focus of the surrounding text, as can be seen in the use of the second person plural imperatives (e.g., שירו, זמרו, etc.) issued by the speaker to the community (cf. 4Q427 7 I, 13–23). As Chazon notes, the speaker's fellowship with the angels, as well as the implication that he joins the angels in praising God, suggests that his exhortation to the "beloved ones" to offer praise means that he is "making a similar claim for all members of his community."[248]

This brings me to the second key observation for Recension A: the boasts of *SGH* should be considered in light of the other angelic fellowship claims of the *Hodayot*, especially that of 1QH[a] XIV, 16, which specifies that the sectarians enjoyed unmediated communion with the priestly angels of the presence. Taken together, the two observations suggest that the Qumran movement thought of itself not only as having liturgical fellowship with Israel's archetypal and model priests[249] but that they may also have been convinced that there was a sense in which they outranked these angels.

There is, however, a curious reticence among scholars to grant the full force of this speaker-community affinity to the sect members, even from those who have highlighted the importance of this relationship.[250] But in

---

Hodayot redaction. ידידים makes no appearance in the 4Q491c parallel, where the term is צדיקים (4Q491c 13)." Schuller, DJD 29, 103, allows for the possibility that ידידים is an angelic designation but concludes that "here it is probably all the members of the *Yahad* who are summoned to give praise … ." Also note Chazon, "Liturgical Function," 145: "An analogy between these 'beloved ones' … and the 'beloved of the king' … in the *Self-Glorification Hymn* is drawn by the very juxtaposition of these two passages and their use of the same nomenclature." *Contra* Davila, *Liturgical Works*, 117, who prefers the angelic interpretation of "the beloved ones."

[246] Angel, "The Liturgical-Eschatological Priest," 598.

[247] Cf. Schuller, DJD 29, 107; Chazon, "Liturgical Function," 146; Angel, "The Liturgical-Eschatological Priest," 597. Note also the affinities in language and sentiment 4Q427 7 II, 8–9 has with previously examined passages: "he lifts up the poor from the dust to the eternal height, and to the clouds he magnifies him in stature, and (he is) with the heavenly beings in the assembly of the community …" (cf. 1QH[a] XI, 20–24; XIX, 13–17).

[248] Chazon, "Angelic & Human Prayer," 45. Cf. Angel, "The Liturgical-Eschatological Priest," 598: "The identity of the speaker in the *Self-Glorification Hymn* thus appears to be inseparable from the liturgical community which he summons to worship."

[249] Another indication that the fellowship may have been envisioned as occurring with angelic priests is the use of the noun מעמד in 4Q427 7 I, 11, which is also employed in Recension B and in the other texts discussed in this chapter.

[250] E.g., Chazon, "Liturgical Function," 148, who, while stating that the speaker-community analogy "could be taken as … the promise of the most exalted state to which an individual might aspire," also says: "[T]he bold claims of the self-glorified speaker are

light of what scholars have referred to as *SGH's* correspondence, analogy, etc., between the speaker and his community, I do not see why the speaker's status as exceeding the angels would not also be true for other sect members, at least potentially so. Instructive on this point is Alexander, who, after entertaining the idea that the speaker is referring only to himself, concludes that his exaltation belongs to the community as well:

The speaker implies that in some way or other he is elevated even above the angels. ... The strong individuality of this voice is unmistakable: the "I" here, surely, is not, as elsewhere, a generic "I". The ascension of the speaker is cited to underscore his authority within the earthly community (the "beloved" whom he proceeds to address), and this only works if this experience is unusual or unique. If it is shared by all, then all can claim equal authority. This is astonishing and deeply puzzling. However, in the last analysis, it is unlikely that the destiny of this individual could be qualitatively different from that of the other members of his community.[251]

To be sure, Alexander also notes that exaltation may have been envisioned as tiered, insofar as one's standing in heaven corresponded to one's place in the sect's hierarchy. At minimum, this suggests that sectarians were thought to be on par with various angelic ranks, while the lofty summit noted in *SGH* was reserved for their leadership. But Alexander also allows for the possibility that *SGH*, like later *Hekhalot* literature, which considered "all Israel as equal before God's throne,"[252] imagined the speaker and those he exhorts as sharing the same superlative rank.

Moreover, recent scholarship has enhanced our understanding of the H tradition's development by noting the liturgical nature of various manuscripts, as well as the pride of place 1QHᵃ gives to the *Community Hymns*.[253] That *SGH* is located near the end of the second block of *Community Hymns* (and thus 1QHᵃ in its entirety) and integrated with liturgical exhortations are different reasons why *SGH* can aptly be described as the "crescendo" or "powerful culmination"[254] of the *Hodayot*. This

---

unique. He alone claims to be a companion to the angels ... and even the highest among them in that famous line, 'Who is like me among the heavenly beings?'" Cf. Harkins, "A New Proposal," 118, 132, who says that the speaker "has exceeded his angelic counterparts," and that *SGH's* "extraordinary claims serve as a powerful culmination of the human and angelic prayers throughout the TH and CH II material" – yet she does not elaborate on the relationship between the community and the speaker.

[251] Alexander, *Mystical Texts*, 90, 109.

[252] Alexander, *Mystical Texts*, 109–110 n. 15.

[253] On the liturgical orientation of 4Q427 and that it may only have contained *Community Hymns*, see Schuller, DJD 29, 86–87. On the liturgical nature of 1QHᵃ, see Chazon, "Liturgical Function," 135–149. On 4Q428 as a foundation for what would later become the collection of hymns in 1QHᵃ, see Harkins, "A New Proposal," 101–134.

[254] Harkins, "A New Proposal," 132, 134 n. 63. However, the *SGH* witnesses are found in various places in other manuscripts; see Schuller, DJD 29, 86, 96, 202–203.

placement stresses the correspondence between the speaker and those he is exhorting – a correspondence which may have served to imply that the sectarian community, spurred on by the experiences and piety of their leader, had joined him in achieving a glory and rank above even the loftiest angels.

E. Summary

The texts discussed in this chapter indicate that angelic fellowship was a cherished facet of sectarian life.   While 4Q181 and 1QSb emphasize communion with the angels as a hallmark of the impending eschatological age, the *Hodayot*, *SSS*, and *SSage*, as well as 4Q181 – and 1QSb, if read proleptically – are understood by scholars as advocating a robust measure of liturgical fellowship with the angels as a present benefit of membership in the Qumran movement.   But the key observation for my purposes is that this form of fellowship is implicitly or even explicitly stated as being with the angelic priests, which means that the envisioned communion was with the priesthood that served as the very archetype and ideal of the nation's priesthood.   For a group that considered itself to be the true Israel – its righteous remnant and undefiled priests – this privileged relationship with the God-ordained celebrants-in-chief would have been a powerful claim.   The passages that most explicitly juxtapose "true Israel" sentiments with liturgical angelic fellowship are 1QH^a XIV and 1QS XI.   But it is interesting that in 4Q181, 4Q511, 1QSb III–IV, and throughout the *Hodayot*, angelic communion is mentioned in close proximity to statements that point to the Qumran movement alone as the legitimate people of God.   Thus, what I highlighted as a feature of martial angelic fellowship is also on display in this chapter: an integral component of what it meant to be the true Israel was present liturgical fellowship with the angelic priests associated with Israel.

   With these things in mind, one can understand why it is apposite to describe *SSS* as an ideal text at Qumran: first, for its *tour de force* treatment of the heavenly temple, and, second, because of its proposed function as a liturgical text in facilitating common worship with the angelic priests.   *SSS* therefore helped, at least in part, to compensate for the sect's separation from Jerusalem by providing access to a pure temple and priesthood.   Yet it would be a misstep to think that the significance of this access is exhausted simply by the fact that the sectarians could worship in a functioning and undefiled sanctuary.   More profoundly, access to the celestial temple meant that the sectarian priesthood could indeed be reckoned with the angelic priesthood (cf. 4Q400 2 6), whose revelatory teaching (cf. 4Q400 1 I, 17; 4Q400 2 1; 4Q401 14 II, 7; 1QH^a XIV, 15–16) seems to have informed and served as the model for the teaching role of the sect (cf. 1QS III, 13; VI, 3–8; XI, 1; 1QSb II, 22–24; IV, 27; 1QM X–XII; CD XIII, 2–7), which considered itself to be the exclusive recipients of heavenly knowledge (cf. 1QH^a VII, 17; X, 20; XI, 23–24; XIX, 16–17; 1QS IV, 22; V, 11; CD III, 10–16).

But whereas the *Hodayot*, *SSS*, and other texts suggest that the sectarians considered themselves to be equal in rank to the angels, laid claim to the angels, or occasionally hint that they surpassed the angels in some sense, at least one recension of the *SGH* seems to take these lofty estimations a presumptuous step further in that the priestly leader of the sect boasts that his glory, knowledge, teaching, and rank surpass that of any angel; it is also possible that, by extension, the sect members, who were exhorted by this leader, were envisioned as sharing in his exaltation. For those who believed themselves to be the true Israel, there is perhaps only one claim that would have been more identity-shaping and identity-asserting than to claim fellowship with Israel's archetypal and ideal priests, and the implied answer to *SGH's* rhetorical question, מי כמוני באלים, contains this very boast: that the group who had reconstituted Israel's covenant was led by someone who had attained a glory and rank that surpassed all the divine beings. Indeed, what better way for the priestly-oriented sectarians to promote themselves as the true Israel than to suggest that their leadership – and perhaps even its general membership – had exceeded the heavenly archetype and ideal of the nation's priesthood?

Chapter 6

Conclusions and Expanding the Scope

A. Conclusions

I. Overview

I commenced this study by noting the Second Temple Period conviction that certain angels were closely associated with Israel, and that angels could be placed in at least two categories – guardians and priests – though in some cases angels served in more than one capacity. Chapter 1 continued with a history of research, which included numerous observations scholars have made about angels in the Dead Sea Scrolls and sectarian identity at Qumran as well as suggestions as to how scholarship might be advanced. From that survey, several points emerged as especially pertinent to my investigation: 1.) the importance of ancient apocalyptic worldviews, which envisioned a correspondence, connection, parallel, etc., between Israel and the angels; 2.) the priority of the heavenly realm, which constituted the archetypal or "more real" world; 3.) the fact that the Qumran movement considered itself to be the true Israel; 4.) the call for a more thorough study of the intersection of angelology and sectarian identity; and 5.) the proposal that a comparison of the sectarian angelic fellowship passages might reveal what they share in common. Bringing these points together, I have endeavored to show that the sectarian notion of angelic fellowship went beyond the relatively widespread idea that Israel corresponded to the angels or had some kind of connection with them. More specifically, I have argued that since the angelic guardians and priests with whom the sectarians were claiming fellowship were viewed as Israel's heavenly counterparts and even archetypal, boasts of angelic fellowship would have enhanced the Qumran movement's estimation of itself as the true Israel. Indeed, a commonality among the angelic fellowship texts is that they make important contributions to the sectarian conviction that they alone were the legitimate people of God.

II. Conceptual Foundations of Angels Associated with Israel

In order to discuss angels associated with Israel in as comprehensive a manner as possible, Chapter 2 reviewed the conceptual foundations of angelic guardians and priests in the Canaanite texts and in pre-exilic, exilic, and early post-exilic passages of the Hebrew Bible. Though the Canaanite literature can portray the terrestrial temple as the counterpart of a god's heavenly abode, the Hebrew Bible does not explicitly depict the wilderness tabernacle or the Jerusalem sanctuary as a mirror of Yhwh's heavenly dwelling, though there are instances of enthronement language and temple imagery in a celestial context (cf. Deut 26:15; 1 Kgs 22:19–21; Isa 6:1–13; Jer 25:30; Ezek 1:1–28; Ps 11:4; 2 Chr 30:27), and some have allowed that תַּבְנִית (cf. Exod 25:9, 40; 26:30; 27:8; 1 Chr 28:19) refers to a heavenly "archetype" and not merely a "blueprint." Similarly, there are only hints of the existence of the beings who might officiate in a heavenly temple, namely, the priest-like garb of the angels in Ezek 9:2–10:7 (cf. Exod 39:28; Lev 6:10; 16:4–34) or the phraseology of Mal 2:4–7 and Isa 63:9, with the latter passage likely serving as inspiration for the priestly angelic class known as "the angels of the presence" (cf. Jub. 1:27, 29; 2:1–2, 18, 30; 6:18; 15:27; 30:18; 31:14; 1QH^a XIV, 16; 1QSb IV, 25–26; also see T. Levi 3:7; T. Jud. 25:2; Matt 18:11).

While comparatively speaking, there is more material to consider when it comes to deciphering the background of angelic guardians, again only an outline of their development is possible. I highlighted both the Canaanite conception of the divine council, which depicts the high god, El, presiding over the assembly, and how this Canaanite type-scene has influenced Deut 32:8–9 and Ps 82. Moreover, I underscored the importance of Deut 32:8–9, which portrays the gods of the nations as ontologically distinct from and inferior to Yhwh but in a moral sense, relatively neutral. Conversely, Ps 82 and Isa 24:21–23 depict the gods of the nations as unambiguously wicked and hostile to Yhwh; these gods also impact the actions of humans, thus testifying to the belief that what happens in the heavenly realm is somehow connected to what happens on earth. This, suggests in part that the angels associated with the Gentile nations as depicted in Second Temple Period compositions (e.g., Dan 10) – as well as hostile trans-national, spiritual beings such as the Angel of Darkness and Belial (e.g., 1QS; 1QM) – are likely indebted conceptually to the gods of the nations.

But even a cursory comparison of pre-exilic, exilic, and early post-exilic Hebrew Bible passages with mid and late Second Temple Period compositions extant at Qumran reveals a curious tension: whereas the former frequently testify to the "hands-on" guardianship of Yhwh, the latter point to the belief that the God of Israel had consigned a significant role to other celestial beings. That is, despite the statement of Deut 32:8–9 – and the occasional echo of it in early Jewish literature (cf. Jub. 15:31–32; Sir 17:17) – a more elaborate arrangement was envisioned in that Israel now had high-profile angelic guardians to whom God had granted a more individuated role vis-à-vis the portrayal of angels in earlier texts. It was argued, however, that this should not be understood as detracting from grandeur of God but rather the opposite: the existence of these angels underscored the fact that God, as Israel's guardian-in-chief, had the prerogative to dispatch elite subordinates who obediently fulfill their mandates yet were ultimately still dependent on God's decisive judgment and support. Also, references to a celestial sanctuary serviced by angelic priests suggests an increasing comfort with and interest in this concept among Second Temple Period Jews when compared to the vague-at-best evidence of the Hebrew Bible.

III. Affinities between Non-Sectarian and Sectarian Texts

Given that non-sectarian texts constituted part of the "ancestral patrimony"[1] of the Qumran movement, it is hardly surprising that there are numerous affinities between texts of a non-sectarian provenance (Chapter 3) and sectarian compositions (Chapters 4–5). First, virtually all of the texts discussed in these chapters point to the belief that there was some sort of connection between Israel and its angelic guardians, and that a hallmark of this relationship was protection: I noted that an envisioned tutelary correspondence between Israel and the angels may be responsible for the genitival construction "the people of the holy ones" (Dan 7:27; 1QM X, 10; XII, 8), and other texts are clear that the nation's angelic succor is ready, willing, and able to protect the people of God when they are confronted by hostile angelic forces. It is also implied that this angelic succor serves as a reward for those who take seriously *halakhic* matters and devotion to Torah (Tob 12:12; 1QS III, 20–25). An important practical out-working of this protection was the conviction that angels aid Israel by intervening in both terrestrial battles (e.g., 1 En. 90:14) and celestial confrontations which may be related to strife on earth (e.g., Dan 7–12; 1 En. 10:1–15; 4Q402 4 7–10); it was also anticipated that angels would have a significant role in God's definitive eschatological judgment (e.g., 1 En. 1:9; *11QMelch*; 1QM). Unquestionably, the revealed knowledge that the faithful had such angelic guardianship would have served as a profound encouragement to Jews struggling on earth.

Another commonality non-sectarian and sectarian texts have is that it is not only Israel's angelic guardians who were thought to have a connection to the people: the angelic priests of the celestial sanctuary were envisioned as having a special relationship with Israel. Despite the corruption of some angelic or human priests, the revelations of and from a glorious and functioning heavenly temple would have confirmed its own efficacy and undergirded, at least in theory, the importance of the Jerusalem temple (e.g., 1 En. 14:8–23; *Songs of the Sabbath Sacrifice*). The knowledge of the angelic priests' intercessory role (e.g., 1 En. 8:4–10:22; 14:22; 93:6; 97:5; 99:3; 104:1; Tob 12:12–15) would have been an additional source of encouragement, and suggestions of a connection Israel's priests shared with the angelic priests implies that sacerdotal practice on earth was both ideally informed and en-

---

[1] So Wacholder, "The Ancient Judaeo-Aramaic," 271, who, as cited earlier, is referring specifically to the texts composed in Aramaic, though his comment equally applies to the non-sectarian works composed in Hebrew.

hanced by the revealed mysteries of its heavenly archetype (e.g., *Bodl.* col. a
9; b 21–22; 4Q213b 2 [cf. T. Levi 8:1]; 4Q545 4 16; 4Q401 14 II, 7). That
the priests who serve in the innermost part of the heavenly sanctuary are the
ones who have been commissioned to disclose heavenly secrets likely served
to heighten the confidence of the human recipients (e.g., Dan 9; 1 En. 10:1–
15, 24:6, 93:6; Tob 12:15; Jub. 1:27; 4Q418 81; 1QH^a VII, 17; XIX, 17;
4Q400 2 1; 4Q401 14 II, 7). Thus, the highest aspiration and loftiest prayer
that could be offered for Israel's priests and their leadership was that they
would be like the priestly "angels of the presence," who serve in closest proximity to God (e.g., Jub. 30:18; 31:14; 1QSb IV, 24–26). Lastly, numerous
passages suggest that the longed-for culmination of a relationship with the
angels was post-mortem angelic fellowship and angel-like glorification (e.g.,
Dan 12:3; 1 En. 104:2–6; 4Q417 2 I, 10–12; 4Q418 69 II, 12–14; 4Q418 126
II, 7–8; 4Q181 1 II, 3–4; 1QSb I, 5; III, 22–27; IV, 24–26).

IV. The Uniqueness of the Sectarian Outlook

However, the commonalities between non-sectarian and sectarian texts are
overshadowed by crucial differences. First, whereas non-sectarian texts imply definitions of Israel that either are relatively generous (e.g., Dan 7–12;
Jubilees) or contain exclusivist sentiments yet are paradoxically tempered by
universalistic statements (e.g., 1 En. 10:21; 90:36; 91:14), we have seen that
the Qumran movement is very clear that it considered itself alone to be the
legitimate people of God (cf. 1QS I, 16–III, 12; V, 20–22). The sect emphasized this via the appropriation of dualistic self-designations such as the
"Sons of Light" (e.g., 1QS III, 13–IV, 26; 11Q13 II, 8–9; 1QM I, 1; XVII, 7),
or biblical epithets for Israel such as "house of holiness" and "eternal planting" (cf. 1QS XI, 7–9; 1QH^a XIV, 17–21); and while the authors of a non-
sectarian text like *4QInstruction* can similarly use the plant metaphor to distance their own circle from outsiders (4Q418 81 13), their overall outlook
does not seem to be as rigidly or formally "sectarian," especially as it pertains
to the notion being the true Israel, which is not as explicit in this text as it is
in the compositions penned by the Qumran movement. Tellingly, other Jews
who reject the sectarian reconstitution of Israel are dubbed "violators of the
covenant" (1QM II, 1). A second difference – and what might be viewed as
an angelological implication of the first – is that sectarian texts evince the
belief that Israel's angelic guardians had a unique connection to the Qumran
movement, who had effectively usurped for themselves the privileges that
were formerly those of the nation more generously defined. That an exclusive relationship with the angels was an integral component of what it meant
to be the true Israel can be seen in both the *Community Rule's* placement of
the *Treatise on the Two Spirits*, which itself gives pride of place to the theme
of angelic guardianship (1QS III, 20–25), and the way the sectarians referred

to themselves as Melchizedek's "inheritance" (נחלה) (11Q13 II, 5), a designation which elsewhere is used to denote ethnic Israel as belonging to Yhwh (Deut 32:8–9). But the most profound difference between the non-sectarian and sectarian texts is this: whereas the former texts are confident that angelic guardians and priests had important roles to play in the life of God's people, the latter texts boast of communion with these angels prior to death.

I highlighted the *War Scroll's* claims that the impeding eschatological war would be characterized by the sectarians fighting side-by-side with the angels (cf. 1QM VII, 6; XII, 8–9), arguing that the outlook of the text is not simply that the angels will be *for* and *with* the soldiers as they are in other texts: the distinctive picture of the *War Scroll* is that the angels, led by Michael – who may have been known by various names including Melchizedek, the Angel of (God's) Truth, and the Prince of Light – would fight *in conjunction with* the warriors of true, earthly Israel, the sectarian soldiers, who are together referred to as "the lot of God" (1QM XVII, 8). A connection between the Michael-led angels and sectarian-defined Israel suggests that the former constitute heavenly Israel as per Dan 7–12, and the amalgam of heavenly Israel and earthly Israel into one eschatological army suggests that the sectarians had widened the apocalyptic notion that what happens on earth is a reflection of heavenly realities. Thus, the *War Scroll* resembles yet exceeds even the *Treatise on the Two Spirits* and *11QMelchizedek*, and the Qumran movement's unique relationship with their angelic guardians was thought to be an integral component of what it meant to be the true Israel. The *War Scroll* is therefore also expressing more than angelic "assistance" and is rightly described as containing a martial/eschatological example of angelic fellowship. That a presumptuous, angel-human mutuality was the foundation for these convictions is arguably suggested by the following observation: the *War Scroll* not only echoes the Book of Daniel in that it uses the tutelary genitival construction "the people of the holy ones" (cf. 1QM X, 10; XII, 8; Dan 7:27), it also employs the reverse phrase, "the holy ones of the people" (cf. 1QM VI, 6; XVI, 1; also see 4Q511 2 I, 6), which may imply that the sectarians felt that they could lay claim to their heavenly comrades. Such presumption is enhanced if the *War Scroll* was once connected to Recension B of the *Self-Glorification Hymn,* since the boasts of the priestly "I" voice suggest that the speaker and, by extension, the sectarian troops he is presumably exhorting, are "reckoned with the gods" and that, at the very least, no other human "can compare" to him/them (4Q491 11 I, 8, 14).

My examination of the *Hodayot's* angelic fellowship passages highlighted boasts of liturgical fellowship as a present benefit of membership in the covenant community (cf. 1QH[a] VII, 17–19; VIII, 14–16; XI, 20–24; XIX, 13–17), and that the fellowship so envisioned is with the priestly "angels of the presence" (1QH[a] XIV, 16). This articulation of present liturgical fellowship is corroborated by passages in the *Songs of the Sabbath Sacrifice* (passim), the *Community Rule* (1QS XI, 7–9), the *Pesher on the Periods B* (4Q181 1 II, 3–4), *Songs of the Sage* (cf. 4Q511 2 I, 7–10; 35 3–4), the *Self-Glorification Hymn* (cf. 4Q491 11 I, 14, 18; 4Q427 7 I, 10–11), and (if read proleptically) the *Rule of Blessings* (1QSb III–IV). Double entendres serve to emphasize that to have a מעמד in the sectarian סוד is to have a מעמד with the angels in a heavenly סוד (cf. 1QHᵃ XI, 22; XIX, 16; 1QS II, 22–23; VI, 12; XI, 8); that the sectarians, who referred to themselves as the *Yahad* (היחד), articulate a main purpose of angelic fellowship as the praise of God "in a common rejoicing" (ביחד רנה) is perhaps the most identity-defining example of this kind of word-play (cf. 1QHᵃ XI, 24; XIX, 17). Similarly, it is possible that deliberate terminological ambiguity – the application of angelic designations to humans and *vice versa* (e.g., שרים, קדושים, and עם) – may have served to underscore the extent to which angelic fellowship was considered a hallmark of sectarian life (cf. 1QHᵃ XIV, 17; XIX, 14–16; 4Q400 1 I, 6; 4Q511 2 I, 10; 35 3–4).

More importantly, the significance of the fact that angelic fellowship is specified as occurring with the priests of the heavenly temple is that the sectarians are thereby boasting of a unique relationship with the very archetypes and ideal of Israel's priesthood. Given that the Qumran movement asserted itself as the true Israel, fellowship with the God-ordained celebrants-in-chief of the heavenly sanctuary would have made a powerful contribution to their claims. The juxtaposition of angelic fellowship boasts and the use of the epithets "eternal plant(ing)" and "house of holiness" (cf. 1QHᵃ XIV, 16–21; 1QS XI, 7–9), as well as the use of מבנית to refer to both the sectarian "house" and the heavenly temple (cf. 1QS XI, 8; 4Q403 1 I, 41, 44; 4Q405 14–15 I, 6; 11Q17 2–1–9 7), suggest that the sect saw a correlation between angelic fellowship and its conviction that it was the true Israel. Additional support for this correlation is found in the proposals that texts showcasing angelic fellowship were recited as part of the Qumran movement's annual covenant renewal ceremony on *Shavuot*. Especially noteworthy in this regard are the *Songs of the Sabbath Sacrifice*, as the arrangement of this text indicates that it would have been post-*Shavuot* – that is, only after initial admittance and recommitment to the sectarian reconstitution of Israel – that the attentions of the sect members would have been turned to the most detailed depictions of the attendant angels of the *debir* and *merkavah* (Song 12) and the angelic high priests and their regalia (Song 13). While it is common to view the *Songs of the Sabbath Sacrifice* as one of the ritual mechanisms that afforded the Qumran movement access to a functioning and undefiled sanctuary, the significance of this access was not just that it compensated for their separation from Jerusalem: access to the celestial temple meant that the priestly sectarians could indeed be reckoned with Israel's archetypal priests (4Q400 2 6–7), whom the Qumran movement also strove to emulate. As with the *War Scroll*, the *Songs of the Sabbath Sacrifice* reveal that the posture adopted by the sectarians was presumptuous insofar as the they respond to

their own brief expressions of unworthiness vis-à-vis the angels with a resolute cohortative of praise (4Q400 2 8); the sectarians also address the angels
with numerous imperatival calls to worship, and the Qumran movement may
even have been convinced that, due to their exemplary worship of God, they
were the recipients of the blessings of the angelic high priests (Songs 6 and
8). Thus, life in the sectarian covenant not only included angelic fellowship
but also seems to have promoted the grandiose self-estimation that the members of the Qumran movement were, in some sense, equal to the angels associated with Israel. But as lofty as these claims are, at least one recension of
the *Self-Glorification Hymn* testifies to a much loftier boast, when the speaker
of Recension A asks: "Who is like me among the heavenly beings?" (cf.
4Q427 7 I, 8; 4Q431 1 4). The implied answer, of course, is that the speaker
views himself as peerless, even among the angels. It is also possible that this
superlative status has been obtained by the wider sectarian community whom
the speaker represents.

We are now in a better position to see the uniqueness of the sectarian texts
vis-à-vis the non-sectarian texts. To be sure, the idea encountered in some
non-sectarian texts – that authority is drawn from the pseudepigraphical attribution to an ancient hero, who has been granted a privileged, revelatory
experience, and who is likely a stand-in for a given work's author(s) – is
bold. However, this is rather unexceptional in comparison to the Qumran
movement openly claiming that they (will) have fellowship with the angels in
this life and implying that they are either 1.) equal to the angels in some
sense; or 2.) that its leadership and maybe even its general membership have
attained a rank and glory higher than the angels. To reiterate Newsom's
point, all claims made at Qumran were, in part, counter claims to those made
by other Second Temple Period Jews.[2] For those who were convinced that
the sectarian reconstitution of Israel's covenant was the only legitimate expression of the people of God, there would have been no better way to promote the Qumran movement as such than to boast that the sect members were
equal to – and perhaps even outranked – the guardians and priests who served
as Israel's heavenly counterparts. While scholars have not infrequently disa-
greed as to the precise meaning of sectarian angelic fellowship claims,[3] the
present study has demonstrated that at least part of the meaning is to be found
in the contributions these claims make to the identity of the sect as the true
Israel.

---

[2] Newsom, *The Self as Symbolic Space*, 3.
[3] See Schuller, "Recent Scholarship on the Hodayot," 151.

B. Expanding the Scope

The focus of this study has been angels associated with Israel, using the heuristic categories of guardians and priests. It may be fruitful, however, to explore other angelic roles to determine what contribution they make to the texts in which they are found, especially as it pertains to identity of the people of God or the concept of "Israel" operative within a given composition. Alternatively, there may be angelic activities not considered here that could conceivably be considered those of guardians or priests. For example, how should the angels in charge of the luminaries in the Enochic *Astronomical Book* (cf. 1 En. 72–82) be categorized?

A related line of inquiry concerns how angels are presented as priests, namely, that in some passages this is explicit (e.g., 1QH[a] XIV,16) while in others it is implicit (e.g., 1QH[a] XI, 20–24; XIX, 13–17). Investigating the possible reasons for this and its potential for illuminating the development of Hodayot traditions and collections could be promising avenues of research.[4]

The preceding pages have been exclusively devoted to compositions extant at Qumran, but a logical next step is to compare the sectarian texts to a wider array of early Jewish writings. The *Similitudes of Enoch* (cf. 1 En. 37–71) would be an ideal place to start, particularly because of its well-known "Son of Man" figure, who is cast as both the God-ordained champion of the people and a celestial being who seemingly outranks even the archangels, including Israel's traditional patron, Michael.[5] What might this say about the community for whom the *Similitudes* were written and how they viewed themselves vis-à-vis other Jews? There may also be value in comparing angelic functions in the Dead Sea Scrolls to those in compositions decidedly more open to outsiders like Joseph and Aseneth.[6]

Expanding the scope of this study to incorporate early Christian texts will also likely pay dividends.[7] Trebilco's monograph on the self-designations of early Christ-followers includes a detailed discussion of the epithet οἱ ἅγιοι

---

[4] I thank Dr. Joseph Angel of Yeshiva University for this suggestion.

[5] Cf. Collins, *The Apocalyptic Imagination*, 186–187.

[6] Cf. Jill Hicks-Keaton, *Arguing with Aseneth: Gentile Access to Israel's Living God in Jewish Antiquity* (Oxford: Oxford University Press, 2018).

[7] For a recent discussion of the relevance of topics such as the divine council for understanding the New Testament, see Michael S. Heiser, *The Unseen Realm: Recovering the Supernatural Worldview of the Bible* (Bellingham: Lexham Press, 2015), though it needs to be emphasized that Heiser's study is most accurately classified as a work of Christian theology. See the balance of appreciation and insightful critique of David B. Sloan, review of Michael S. Heiser, *The Unseen Realm: Recovering the Supernatural Worldview of the Bible*, *RBL* (2018).

(literally, "the holy ones"),[8] which is frequently translated "the saints" in the New Testament. He argues that the appropriation of οἱ ἅγιοι by the early Jerusalem church – and later made famous by the apostle Paul (e.g., 1 Cor 1:2; Phil 1:1; Rom 1:7) – is indebted to Jesus' self-referential use of the "one like a son of man" (Dan 7:13–14). In short, Trebilco contends that reflection upon Dan 7, which, as we have seen, depicts "the holy ones of the Most High" as represented by the "one like a son of man," prompted Christians to refer to themselves as "the holy ones." This is effectively the usurpation of an angelic appellation, and I have already begun to explore how the benefits Trebilco claims are conveyed by this Christian use of "holy ones" – namely, privilege, holiness, and unity – may be reinforced by more robust comparisons with the uses of קדושים in the Dead Sea Scrolls, including the notion of deliberate terminological ambiguity.[9]

---

[8] Paul Trebilco, *Self-designations and Group Identity in the New Testament* (Cambridge: Cambridge University Press, 2012), 122–163.

[9] Cf. Matthew L. Walsh, "'The Holy Ones' as a Christian Self-Designation: A Contextual Comparison of the Dead Sea Scrolls and the Pauline Corpus," (paper presented at the Annual Meeting of the IBR, Denver, CO, 16 November 2018).

Bibliography

A. Primary Literature

Alexander, Philip S. and Géza Vermes, eds. *Qumran Cave 4.XIX: 4QSerekh Ha-Yahad and Two Related Texts.* DJD 26. Oxford: Claredon, 1998.

Allegro, John M., ed. *Qumran Cave 4.I (4Q158–4Q186).* DJD 5. Oxford: Claredon, 1968.

Attridge, Harold W. and Robert A. Oden, Jr. *Philo of Byblos the Phoenician History: Introduction, Critical Text, Translation, Notes.* CBQMS 9. Washington: Catholic Biblical Association of America, 1981.

Attridge, Harold W. et al., eds. *Qumran Cave 4.VIII: Parabiblical Texts, Part 1.* DJD 13. Oxford: Clarendon Press, 1994.

Baillet, Maurice, ed. *Qumrân Grotte 4.III (4Q482–4Q520).* DJD 7. Oxford: Claredon Press, 1982.

Baillet, Maurice, Józef T. Milik, and Roland de Vaux, eds. *Les petites grottes de Qumran.* DJD 3. Oxford: Calrendon, 1962.

Barthélemy Dominique and Józef T. Milik, eds. *Qumran Cave 1.* DJD 1. Oxford: Clarendon, 1955.

Black, Matthew. *Apocalypsis Heni Graece.* PVTG 3. Leiden: Brill, 1970.

Brooke, George J. et al., eds. *Qumran Cave 4: XVII: Parabiblical Texts, Part 3.* DJD 22. Oxford: Oxford University Press, 1997.

Broshi, Magen et al., eds. *Qumran Cave 4 XIV: Parabiblical Texts, Part 2.* DJD 19. Oxford: Clarendon Press, 1995.

Burrows, Millar, John C. Trevor, and William H. Brownlee, eds. *The Dead Sea Scrolls of St. Mark's Monastery. II.2, Plates and Transcription of the Manual of Discipline.* New Haven: American School of Oriental Research, 1951.

Charlesworth, James H. and Loren T. Stuckenbruck. "Blessings (1QSb)." Pages 119–131 in *The Dead Sea Scrolls: Hebrew Aramaic, and Greek Texts with English Translations: Rule of the Community and Related Documents.* Edited by J. H. Charlesworth et al. PTSDSSP 1. Tübingen: Mohr Siebeck; Louisville: Westminster John Knox Press, 1994.

Charlesworth, James, H., ed. *The Old Testament Pseudepigrapha.* 2 volumes. ABRL. New York: Doubleday, 1983, 1985.

Chazon, Esther G. et al., eds. *Qumran Cave 4.XX: Poetical and Liturgical Texts, Part 2.* DJD 29. Oxford: Clarendon, 1999.

De Jonge, Marinus. *The Testaments of the Twelve Patriarchs: A Critical Edition of the Greek Text.* PVTG 1. Leiden: Brill, 1978.

Duhaime, Jean. "War Scroll." Pages 80–141 in *The Dead Sea Scrolls: Hebrew, Aramaic, and Greek Texts with English Translations: Volume 2: Damascus Document, War Scroll and Related Documents.* Edited by J. H. Charlesworth et al. PTSDSSP 2. Tübingen: Mohr Siebeck; Louisville: Westminster John Knox Press, 1995.

Ellliger, Karl, William Rudolph and H. P. Rüger, eds. *Biblia Hebraica Stuttgartensia*. Stuttgart: Deutsche Bibelgesellschaft, 1984.

Eshel, Esther et al., eds. *Qumran Cave 4. VI: Poetical and Liturgical Texts, Part I*. DJD 11. Oxford: Claredon Press, 1998.

García Martínez, Florentino et al., eds. *Qumran Cave 11.II: 11Q2–18, 11Q20–31*. DJD 23. Oxford: Claredon Press, 1998.

Hanhart, Robert. *Tobit*. SVTG 8/5. Göttingen: Vandenhoeck & Ruprecht, 1983.

Knibb, Michael A. *The Ethiopic Book of Enoch*. 2 volumes. Oxford: Claredon, 1978.

Milik, Józef T. *The Books of Enoch: Aramaic Fragments of Qumran Cave 4*. Oxford: Clarendon, 1976.

Newsom, Carol A. "Angelic Liturgy: The Songs of the Sabbath Sacrifice (4Q400–407, 11Q17, Mas1k): A Composite Text." Pages 138–189 in *The Dead Sea Scrolls: Hebrew, Aramaic, and Greek Texts with English Translations*. Edited by J. H. Charlesworth et al. PTSDSSP 4B. Tübingen: Mohr Siebeck; Louisville: Westminster John Knox Press, 1994.

–. *The Songs of the Sabbath Sacrifice: A Critical Edition*. HSM 27. Atlanta: Scholars Press, 1985.

Nougayrol Jean et al., eds. *Ugaritica V*. Paris: Imprimerie Nationale, 1968.

Pfann, Stephen J. et al., eds. *Cryptic Texts and Miscellanea, Part 1: Qumran Cave 4.XXVI*. DJD 36. Oxford: Clarendon, 2000.

Puech, Emile, ed. *Qumran Grotte 4.XXII: Textes araméens, première partie: 4Q529–549*. DJD 31. Oxford: Clarendon, 2001.

Qimron, Elisha and James H. Charlesworth. "The Rule of the Community (1QS)." Pages 5–51 in *The Dead Sea Scrolls: Hebrew, Aramaic, and Greek Texts with English Translations, Vol. 1: Rule of the Community and Related Documents*. Edited by J. H. Charlesworth et al. PTSDSSP 1. Tübingen: Mohr Siebeck; Louisville: Westminster John Knox Press, 1994.

Stegemann, Hartmut, Eileen M. Schuller, and Carol A. Newsom, eds. *1QHodayot^a with Incorporation of 1QHodayot^b and 4QHodayot^(a-f)*. DJD 40. Oxford: Clarendon, 2009.

Strugnell, John and Daniel J. Harrington, S. J., eds. *Qumran Cave 4 XXIV: Sapiential Texts, Part 2: 4QInstruction (Musar le mevin): 4Q415ff with a Re-edition of 1Q26*. DJD 34. Oxford: Clarendon Press, 1999.

Tov, Emmanuel et al., eds. *The Texts from the Judaean Desert: Indices and an Introduction to the Discoveries in the Judaean Desert Series*. DJD 39. Oxford: Clarendon, 2002.

Ulrich, Eugene et al., eds. *Qumran Cave 4. IX: Deuteronomy, Joshua, Judges, Kings*. DJD 14. Oxford: Claredon Press, 1995.

VanderKam, James C. *The Book of Jubilees: A Critical Text*. CSCO 510–511. SAT 87–88. Louvain: Peeters, 1989.

Wevers, John William, ed. *Deuteronomium*. SVTG 3/2. Göttingen: Vandenhoeck and Ruprecht, 1977.

Ziegler, Joseph, ed. *Isaias*. SVTG 14. Göttingen: Vandenhoeck & Ruprecht, 1983.

B. Secondary Literature

Abegg, Jr., Martin G. "1QSb and the Elusive High Priest." Pages 3–16 in *Emmanuel: Studies in Hebrew Bible, Septuagint, and Dead Sea Scrolls in Honor of Emmanuel Tov*. Edited by Shalom M. Paul et al. VTSup 94. Leiden: Brill, 2003.

–. "4Q471: A Case of Mistaken Identity?" Pages 208–242 in *Pursuing the Text: Studies in Honor of Ben Zion Wacholder on the Occasion of his Seventieth Birthday*. Edited by John C. Reeves and John Kampen. JSOTSup 184. Sheffield: Sheffield Academic Press, 1994.

–. Review of Brian Schultz, *Conquering the World: The War Scroll (1QM) Reconsidered. BBR* 22 (2012): 588–589.

–. "The Covenant of the Qumran Sectarians." Pages 81–97 in *The Concept of Covenant in the Second Temple*. Edited by Stanley E. Porter and Jacqueline C. de Roo. JSJSup 71. Leiden: Brill, 2003.

–. "Who Ascended to Heaven? 4Q491, 4Q427, and the Teacher of Righteousness." Pages 61–73 in *Eschatology, Messianism, and the Dead Sea Scrolls*. Edited by Craig A. Evans and Peter W. Flint. SDSSRL. Grand Rapids: Eerdmans, 1997.

Abusch, Ra'anan. "Sevenfold Hymns in the Songs of the Sabbath Sacrifice and the Hekhalot Literature: Formalism, Hierarchy and the Limits of Human Participation." Pages 220–247 in *The Dead Sea Scrolls as Background to Postbiblical Judaism and Early Christianity: Papers from an International Conference at St. Andrews in 2001*. Edited by James R. Davila. STDJ 46. Leiden: Brill, 2003.

Albertz, Rainer. "The Social Setting of the Aramaic and Hebrew Book of Daniel." Pages 171–204 in *The Book of Daniel: Composition and Reception*. Edited by John J. Collins and Peter W. Flint. VTSup 83.1. Leiden: Brill, 2001.

Albright, William F. "Some Remarks on the Song of Moses." *VT* 9 (1959): 339–346.

Alexander, Philip S. *Mystical Texts: Songs of the Sabbath Sacrifice and Related Manuscripts*. LSTS 61. London: T & T Clark, 2006.

–. "Predestination and Free Will in the Theology of the Dead Sea Scrolls." Pages 27–49 in *Divine and Human Agency in Paul and His Cultural Environment*. Edited by John M. G. Barclay and Simon J. Gathercole. LNTS. London: T & T Clark, 2006.

–. "Qumran and the Genealogy of Western Mysticism." Pages 213–245 in *New Perspectives on Old Texts: Proceedings of the Tenth International Symposium of the Orion Center for the Study of the Dead Sea Scrolls and Associated Literature, 9–11 January, 2005*. Edited by Esther G. Chazon and Betsy Halpern-Amaru. STDJ 88. Leiden: Brill, 2010.

–. "The Demonology of the Dead Sea Scrolls." Pages 332–353 in *The Dead Sea Scrolls After Fifty Years: A Comprehensive Assessment*. Edited by Peter W. Flint and James C. VanderKam. Leiden: Brill, 1999.

–. "The Reaction History of the Serekh Ha-Yahad: A Proposal." *RevQ* 17 (1996): 437–456.

Allison, Jr. Dale C. "The Silence of the Angels: Reflections on the Songs of the Sabbath Sacrifice." *RevQ* 13 (1988): 189–197.

Anderson, Arnold A. "The Use of 'Ruah' in 1QS, 1QH and 1QM." *JSS* 7 (1962): 293–303.

Angel, Joseph L. "Maskil, Community, and Religious Experience in the *Songs of the Sage* (4Q510–511)." *DSD* 19 (2012): 1–27.

–. *Otherworldly and Eschatological Priesthood in the Dead Sea Scrolls*. STDJ 86. Leiden: Brill, 2010.

–. "Reading the Songs of the Sage in Sequence: Preliminary Observations and Questions."
    Pages 185–211 in *Functions of Psalms and Prayers in the Late Second Temple Period.*
    Edited by Mike S. Pajunen and Jeremy Penner. BZAW 486. Berlin: de Gruyter, 2017.
–. "The Divine Courtroom Scenes of Daniel 7 and the Qumran Book of Giants: A Textual
    and Contextual Comparison." Pages 25–48 in *The Divine Courtroom in Comparative
    Perspective.* Edited by Ari Mermelstein and Shalom E. Holtz. Leiden: Brill, 2014.
–. "The Liturgical-Eschatological Priest of the Self-Glorification Hymn." *RevQ* 24 (2010):
    585–605.
–. "The Material Reconstruction of 4QSongs of the Sage[b] (4Q511)." *RevQ* 27 (2015): 25–
    82.
Arcari, Luca. "'Minority' as a Self-Definition Discourse in Second Temple Judaism."
    SMSR 83 (2017): 343–356.
Argall, Randall A. *1 Enoch and Sirach: A Comparative Literary and Conceptual Analysis
    of the Themes of Revelation, Creation, and Judgment.* Atlanta: Scholars Press, 1995.
Ariel, C., A. E. Yuditsky, and Elisha Qimron. "The Pesher on the Periods A–B (4Q180–
    4Q181): Editing, Language, and Interpretation." *Meghillot* 11 (2014): 3–40.
Arnold, Russell C. D. *The Social Role of Liturgy in the Religion of the Qumran Community.*
    STDJ 60. Leiden: Brill, 2006.
Aschim, Anders. "Melchizedek and Jesus: 11QMelchizedek and the Epistle to the He-
    brews." Pages 129–147 in *The Jewish Roots of Christological Monotheism: Papers from
    the St. Andrews Conference on the Historical Origins of the Worship of Jesus.* Edited by
    Carey C. Newman, James R. Davila, Gladys S. Lewis. JSJSup 63. Leiden: Brill, 1999.
–. "Melchizedek and Levi." Pages 773–788 in *The Dead Sea Scrolls Fifty Years After Their
    Discovery: Proceedings of the Jerusalem Congress, July 20–25, 1997.* Edited by Law-
    rence H. Schiffman and Emmauel Tov. Jerusalem: Israel Exploration Society, 2000.
–. "Melchizedek the Liberator: An Early Interpretation of Genesis 14?" Pages 43–58 in
    SBL Seminar Papers, 1996. SBLSP 35. Atlanta: Scholars Press, 1996.
Assmann, Jan. *Die Mosaische Unterscheidung: Oder der Preis des Monotheismus.* Mün-
    chen: C. Hanser, 2003.
–. *Moses the Egyptian: The Memory of Egypt in Western Monotheism.* Cambridge: Harvard
    University Press, 1997.
Attridge, Harold W. *The Epistle to the Hebrews: A Commentary on the Epistle to the He-
    brews.* Hermeneia. Philadelphia: Fortress Press, 1989.
Bampfylde, Gillian. "The Prince of the Host in the Book of Daniel and the Dead Sea
    Scrolls." *JSJ* 14 (1983): 129–134.
Bar-Asher, Moshe. "On the Language of 'The Vision of Gabriel.'" *RevQ* 23 (2008): 491–
    524.
Barbel, Joseph. *Christos Angelos: Die Anschauung von Christus als Bote und Engel in der
    gelehrten und volkstümlichen Literatur des christlichen Altertums.* Bonn: Hanstien,
    1941.
Barker, Margaret. *The Gate of Heaven: The History and Symbolism of the Temple in Jerusalem.*
    Sheffield: Sheffield Phoenix Press, 2008.
Bartelmus, Rüdiger. *Heroentum in Israel und seiner Umwelt.* ATANT 65. Zurich: Theol-
    ogischer Verlag, 1979.
Bauckham, Richard. *The Climax of Prophecy.* Edinburgh: T & T Clark, 1993.
–. "The Book of Revelation as a Christian War Scroll." *Neot* 22 (1988): 17–40.
–. "The Early Jerusalem Church, Qumran, and the Essenes." Pages 63–89 in *The Dead Sea
    Scrolls as Background to Postbiblical Judaism and Early Christianity: Papers from an*

International Conference at St. Andrews in 2001. Edited by James R. Davila. STDJ 46. Leiden: Brill, 2003.

Baumgarten, Albert I. *The Phoenician History of Philo of Byblos: A Commentary.* EPRO. Leiden: Brill, 1981.

–. "Who Cares and Why Does It Matter? Qumran and the Essenes Once Again!" *DSD* 11 (2004): 174–190.

Bautch, Richard J. *Glory and Power, Ritual and Relationship: The Sinai Covenant in the Post-Exilic Period.* LHBOTS 471. London: T & T Clark, 2009.

Baxter, Wayne. "1QSb: Old Divisions Made New." *RevQ* 21 (2004): 615–629.

Beek, Martinus A. *Das Danielbuch: Sein Historischer Hintergrund und seine literarische Entwicklung.* Leiden: Bringsberg, 1935.

Bergsma, John S. "Qumran Self-Identity: 'Israel' or 'Judah'?" *DSD* 15 (2008): 172–189.

Berner, Christoph. "The Four (or Seven) Archangels in the First Book of Enoch and Early Jewish Writings of the Second Temple Period." Pages 395–409 in *Angels: The Concept of Celestial Beings – Origins, Development and Reception.* Edited by Friedrich V. Reiterer, Tobias Nicklas, and Karen Schöpflin. DCLY. New York: de Gruyter, 2007.

Berrin, Shani. "Qumran Pesharim." Pages 110–133 in *Biblical Interpretation at Qumran.* Edited by Matthias Henze. SDSSRL. Grand Rapids: Eerdmans, 2005.

Bertram, G. "παρίστημι." *TDNT* 5:837–841.

Beyerle, Stefan. "Temples and Sanctuaries within Their Apocalyptic Setting." Pages 41–62 in *Various Aspects of Worship in Deuterocanonical and Cognate Literature.* Edited by Géza G. Xeravits, József Zsengellér, and Ibolya Balla. DCLY. Berlin: De Gruyter, 2017.

–. "The 'God of Heaven' in the Persian and Hellenistic Periods." Pages 17–36 in *Other Worlds and Their Relation to This World: Early Jewish and Ancient Christian Traditions.* Edited by Tobias Nicklas et al. JSJSup 143. Leiden: Brill, 2010.

Bickerman, Elias J. *The Jews in the Greek Age.* Cambridge: Harvard University Press, 1988.

Bietenhard, Hans. *Die himmlische Welt im Urchristentum und Spätjudentum.* WUNT 2. Tübingen: Mohr Siebeck, 1951.

Boatterweck, G. Johannes, Helmer Ringgren, and Heinz-Josef Fabry. *Theological Dictionary of the Old Testament.* Translated by David E. Green and Douglas W. Scott. 16 volumes. Grand Rapids: Eerdmans, 1974–2018.

Boccaccini, Gabriele. *Beyond the Essene Hypothesis: The Parting of the Ways between Qumran and Enochic Judaism.* Grand Rapids: Eerdmans, 1998.

Boecker, Hans-Jochen. *Redeformen des Rechtslebens im Alten Testament.* Second Edition. WMANT 14. Neukirchen-Vluyn: Neukirchener Verlag, 1970.

Bowley, James E. "Prophets, Kittim, and Divine Communication in the Dead Sea Scrolls: Condemning the Enemy Without, Fighting the Enemy Within." Pages 487–512 in *Enemies and Friends of the State: Ancient Prophecy in Context.* Edited by Christopher A. Rollston. University Park: Eisenbrauns, 2018.

Brekelmans, C. W. "The Saints of the Most High and Their Kingdom." *OtSt* 14 (1965): 305–329.

Brooke, George J. "Patterns of Priesthood, Priestliness, and Priestly Function in Some Second Temple Period Texts." *JAAJ* 4 (2016): 1–21.

–. *The Dead Sea Scrolls and the New Testament.* Minneapolis: Fortress, 2005.

–. "The Pesharim and the Origins of the Dead Sea Scrolls." Pages 34–42 in *Methods of Investigation of the Dead Sea Scrolls and the Khirbet Qumran Site: Present Realities and*

Future Prospects. Edited by Michael O. Wise et al. ANYAS 722. New York: The New York Academy of Sciences, 1994.

Caird, George. *Principalities and Powers: A Study in Pauline Theology*. Oxford: Claredon Press, 1956.

Calaway, Jared C. "Heavenly Sabbath, Heavenly Sanctuary: The Transformation of Priestly Sacred Space and Sacred Time in the Songs of the Sabbath Sacrifice and the Epistle to the Hebrews." Ph.D. diss., Columbia University, 2010.

Caquot, André. "Les Service des Anges." *RevQ* 13 (1988): 421–429.

Caragounis, Chrys C. *The Son of Man: Vision and Interpretation*. WUNT 38. Tübingen: Mohr Siebeck, 1986.

Carmignac, Jean. *La Règle de la Guerre des Fils de Lumière contre les Fils de Ténèbres: Texte Restauré, Traduit Commenté*. Paris: Letouzey et Ané, 1958.

–. "Le Document de Qumrân sur Melkisédek." *RevQ* 7 (1970): 343–378.

–. "On Philip R. Davies, *1QM, the War Scroll from Qumran*." *RevQ* 9 (1978): 599–603.

Carrell, Peter R. *Jesus and the Angels: Angelology and the Christology of the Apocalypse of John*. SNTSMS 95. New York: Cambridge University Press, 1997.

Casey, Maurice. *Son of Man: The Interpretation and Influence of Daniel 7*. London: SPCK, 1979.

Chang, Dongshin Don. *Phinehas, The Sons of Zadok, and Melchizedek: Priestly Covenant in Late Second Temple Texts*. LSTS 90. London: Bloomsbury T & T Clark, 2016.

–. "Priestly Covenant in 1QM and 1QSb." Pages 147–162 in *The War Scroll, Violence, War and Peace in the Dead Sea Scrolls and Related Literature: Essays in Honour of Martin G. Abegg on the Occasion of His 65th Birthday*. Edited by Kipp Davis et al. STDJ 115. Leiden: Brill, 2015.

Charles, R. H. *A Critical and Exegetical Commentary on the Book of Daniel*. Oxford: Clarendon, 1929.

–, ed. *The Apocrypha and Pseudepigrapha of the Old Testament*. 2 volumes. Oxford: Claredon, 1913.

–. *The Book of Enoch, or 1 Enoch*. Oxford: Clarendon, 1912.

–. *The Book of Jubilees or the Little Genesis*. London: A. & C. Black, 1902.

Charlesworth, James H. "A Critical Comparison of the Dualism in 1QS 3:13–4:26 and the 'Dualism' Contained in the Gospel of John." *NTS* 15 (1968–69): 389–418.

–. *John and the Dead Sea Scrolls*. New York: Crossroad, 1991.

–. "The Portrayal of Righteous as an Angel." Pages 135–151 in *Ideal Figures in Ancient Judaism: Profiles and Paradigms*. Edited by George W. E. Nickelsburg et al. SCS 12. Missoula: Scholars Press, 1980.

Chazon, Esther G. "Human and Angelic Prayer in Light of the Dead Sea Scrolls." Pages 37–45 in *Liturgical Perspectives: Prayer and Poetry in Dead Sea Scrolls: Proceedings of the Fifth International Symposium of the Orion Center for the Study of the Dead Sea Scrolls and Associated Literature*. Edited by Esther G. Chazon. STDJ 48. Leiden: Brill, 2003.

–. "Liturgical Function in the Cave 1 Hodayot Collection." Pages 135–149 in *Qumran Cave 1 Revisited: Texts from Cave 1 Sixty Years after Their Discovery: Proceedings of the Sixth Meeting of the IOQS in Ljubljana*. Edited by Daniel K. Falk and Eibert J. C. Tigchelaar. STDJ 91. Leiden: Brill, 2010.

–. "Low to Lofty: The Hodayot's Use of Liturgical Tradition to Shape Sectarian Identity." *RevQ* 26 (2013): 3–19.

Chilton, Bruce D. *The Targum of Isaiah*. ArBib 11. Wilmington: Michael Glazier, 1987.

Christensen, Duane L. *Deuteronomy 21:10–34:12*. WBC 6B. Nashville: Thomas Nelson, 2002.

Christiansen, Ellen J. "The Consciousness of Belonging to God's Covenant and What It Entails According to the Damascus Document and the Community Rule." Pages 71–85 in *Qumran Between the Old and New Testaments*. Edited by Frederick H. Cryer and Thomas L. Thompson. JSOTSup 290. Sheffield: Sheffield Academic Press, 1998.

–. *The Covenant in Judaism and Paul: A Study of Ritual Boundaries as Identity Markers.* AGJU 27. Leiden: Brill, 1995.

Church, Philip. *Hebrews and the Temple: Attitudes to the Temple in Second Temple Judaism and in Hebrews*. NovTSup 171. Leiden: Brill, 2017.

Clifford, Richard J. *The Cosmic Mountain in Canaan and the Old Testament*. HSM 4. Cambridge: Harvard University Press, 1972.

Coblentz Bautch, Kelley. "The Heavenly Temple, the Prison in the Void, and the Uninhabited Paradise: Otherworldly Sites in the Book of Watchers." Pages 37–53 in *Other Worlds and Their Relation to This World: Early Jewish and Ancient Christian Traditions*. Edited by Tobias Nicklas et al. JSJSup 143. Leiden: Brill, 2010.

Cogan, Mordechai and Hayim Tadmor. *II Kings: A New Translation with Introduction and Commentary*. AB 11. New York: Doubleday, 1988.

Cohen, Shaye J. D. "From the Bible to the Talmud: The Prohibition of Intermarriage." *HAR* 7 (1983): 23–39.

Collins, John J. "Apocalyptic Eschatology as the Transcendence of Death." *CBQ* 36 (1974): 21–43.

–. *Apocalypticism in the Dead Sea Scrolls*. Literature of the Dead Sea Scrolls. New York: Routledge, 1997.

–. *Beyond the Qumran Community: The Sectarian Movement of the Dead Sea Scrolls*. Grand Rapids: Eerdmans, 2010.

–. *Daniel: A Commentary on the Book of Daniel*. Hermeneia. Minneapolis: Fortress, 1993.

–. "Metaphor and Eschatology: Life beyond Death in the Hodayot." Pages 438–458 in *Is There a Text in this Cave? Studies in the Textuality of the Dead Sea Scrolls in Honour of George J. Brooke*. Edited by Ariel Feldman, Maria Cioată, and Charlotte Hempel. STDJ 119. Leiden: Brill, 2017.

–. "Patterns of Eschatology at Qumran." Pages 351–375 in *Traditions in Transformation: Turning Points in Biblical Faith*. Edited by Baruch Halpern, Jon D. Levenson, and Frank Moore Cross. Winona Lake: Eisenbrauns, 1981.

–. "Powers in Heaven: God, Gods, and Angels in the Dead Sea Scrolls." Pages 9–28 in *Religion in the Dead Sea Scrolls*. Edited by John J. Collins and Robert A. Kugler. SDSSRL. Grand Rapids: Eerdmans, 2000.

–. "Prince שׂר." *DDD* 662–664.

–. Review of Israel Knohl, *The Messiah Before Jesus*. *JQR* 91 (2000): 185–190.

–. Review of Michael Mach, *Entwicklungsstadien des jüdischen Engelglaubens in vorrabbinsicher Zeit*. *JBL* 119 (1994): 140–141.

–. "Stirring Up the Great Sea: The Religio-Historical Background of Daniel 7." Pages 121–136 in *The Book of Daniel in the Light of New Findings*. Edited by Adam S. van der Woude. BETL 106. Leuven: Leuven University Press, 1993.

–. "The Angelic Life." Pages 291–310 in *Metamorphoses: Resurrection, Body, and Transformative Practices in Early Christianity*. Edited by Turid Karlsen Seim and Jorunn Økland. Berlin: de Gruyter, 2009.

–. *The Apocalyptic Imagination: An Introduction to Jewish Apocalyptic Literature*. Second Edition. Grand Rapids: Eerdmans, 1998.

–. *The Apocalyptic Vision of the Book of Daniel.* HSM 16. Missoula: Scholars Press, 1977.

–. "The Background of the 'Son of God' Text." *BBR* 7 (1997): 51–62.

–. "The Construction of Israel in the Sectarian Rule Books." Pages 25–42 in *Judaism in Late Antiquity, Part 5: The Judaisms of Qumran: A Systematic Reading of the Dead Sea Scrolls, Vol. 1: Theory of Israel.* Edited by Alan J. Avery-Peck, Jacob Neusner, and Bruce D. Chilton. HdO 58. Leiden: Brill, 2001.

–. "The Eschatologizing of Wisdom in the Dead Sea Scrolls." Pages 49–61 in *Sapiential Perspectives: Wisdom Literature in Light of the Dead Sea Scrolls: Proceedings of the Sixth International Symposium of the Orion Center for the Study of the Dead Sea Scrolls and Associated Literature, 20–22 May 2001.* Edited by John J. Collins, Gregory E. Sterling, and Ruth A. Clements. STDJ 51. Leiden: Brill, 2004.

–. "The Heavenly Representative: The 'Son of Man' in the Similitudes of Enoch." Pages 111–133 in *Ideal Figures in Ancient Judaism: Profiles and Paradigms.* Edited by George W. E. Nickelsburg and John J. Collins. SCS 12. Missoula: Scholars Press, 1980.

–. "The Legacy of Canaan in Ancient Israel and Early Christianity." Pages 71–84 in *Biblical Essays in Honor of Daniel J. Harrington, S. J., and Richard J. Clifford, S. J.: Opportunity for No Little Instruction.* Edited by Christopher G. Frechette and Christopher R. Matthews. New York: Paulist Press, 2014.

–. "The Mythology of Holy War in Daniel and the Qumran War Scroll: A Point of Translation in Jewish Apocalyptic." *VT* 25 (1975): 596–612.

–. "The Otherworld in the Dead Sea Scrolls." Pages 95–116 in *Other Worlds and Their Relation to This World: Early Jewish and Ancient Christian Traditions.* Edited by Tobias Nicklas et al. JSJSup 143. Leiden: Brill, 2010.

–. *The Scepter and the Star: Messianism in Light of the Dead Sea Scrolls.* Second Edition. Grand Rapids: Eerdmans, 2010.

–. *The Scepter and the Star: The Messiahs of the Dead Sea Scrolls and Other Ancient Literature.* ABRL. New York: Doubleday, 1994.

–. *The Scriptures and Sectarianism: Essays on the Dead Sea Scrolls.* WUNT 332. Tübingen: Mohr Siebeck, 2014.

–. "The Son of God Text from Qumran." Pages 65–82 in *From Jesus to John: Essays on Jesus and New Testament Christology in Honor of Marinus de Jong.* Edited by Martinus C. de Boer. JSNTSup 84. Sheffield: JSOT, 1993.

–. "The Son of Man and the Saints of the Most High in the Book of Daniel." *JBL* 93 (1973): 50–66.

Collins, John J. and Devorah Dimant. "A Thrice-Told Hymn: A Response to Eileen Schuller." *JQR* 85 (1994): 151–155.

Cook, Edward M. "4Q246." *BBR* 5 (1995): 43–66.

Corbin, Henry. *Temple and Contemplation.* London: KPI, 1986.

Coulot, Claude. "L'instruction sur les deux esprits (1QS III,13–IV,26)." *RSR* 82 (2008): 147–160.

Coxon, P. W. "Gibborim גבורים." *DDD* 345–346.

Craig, Kenneth M. "Psalm 82." *Int* 49 (1995): 281–284.

Craigie, Peter C. *Deuteronomy.* NICOT. Grand Rapids: Eerdmans, 1976.

Cross, Frank Moore. *Canaanite Myth and Hebrew Epic: Essays in the History of the Religion of Israel.* Cambridge: Harvard University Press, 1973.

–. *The Ancient Library of Qumran: Revised and Expanded Edition.* Minneapolis: Fortress, 2004. Reprint of *The Ancient Library of Qumran.* New York: Doubleday, 1958.

B. Secondary Literature

293

–. "The Structure of the Apocalypse of 'Son of God.'" Pages 151–158 in *Emanuel: Studies in Hebrew Bible, Septuagint, and Dead Sea Scrolls in Honor of Emanuel Tov*. Edited by Shalom M. Paul et al. VTSup 94. Leiden: Brill, 2003.

Culianu, I. P. "The Angels of the Nations and the Origins of Gnostic Dualism." Pages 78–91 in *Studies in Gnosticism and Hellenistic Religions: Presented to Gilles Quispel on the Occasion of His 65th Birthday*. Edited by R. van den Broek and M. J. Vermaseren. Leiden: Brill, 1981.

Dahood, Mitchell J. *Psalms I: A New Translation with Introduction and Commentary*. AB 16. New York: Doubleday, 1964.

–. *Psalms II: A New Translation with Introduction and Commentary*. AB 17. Garden City: Doubleday, 1966.

Daoust, Francis. "Belial in the Dead Sea Scrolls: From Worthless to Stumbling Block to Archenemy." Pages 217–233 in *New Vistas on Early Judaism and Christianity From Enoch to Montreal and Back*. Edited by Lorenzo DiTommaso and Gerbern S. Oegema. JCTC 22. London: Bloomsbury T&T Clark, 2016.

Davidson, Maxwell J. *Angels at Qumran: A Comparative Study of 1 Enoch 1–36, 72–108 and Sectarian Writings from Qumran*. JSPSup 11. Sheffield: JSOT Press, 1992.

Davies, Philip R. *1QM, the War Scroll from Qumran: Its Structure and History*. BibOr 32. Rome: Biblical Institute Press, 1977.

–. "Redaction and Sectarianism in the Qumran Scrolls." Pages 152–163 in *The Scriptures and the Scrolls: Studies in Honour of A. S. van der Woude on the Occasion of his 65th Birthday*. Edited by Florentino García-Martínez, Anthony Hilhorst, and C. J. Labuschagne. VTSup 49. Leiden: Brill, 1992.

–. "The 'Damascus' Sect and Judaism." Pages 70–84 in *Pursuing the Texts: Studies in Honour of Ben Zion Wacholder*. Edited by John C. Reeves and John Kampen. JSOTSup 184. Sheffield: JSOT Press, 1994.

Davila, James R. *Liturgical Works*. ECDSS. Grand Rapids: Eerdmans, 2000.

–. "Melchizedek, Michael, and War in Heaven." Pages 259–272 in *SBL Seminar Papers, 1996*. SBLSP 35. Atlanta: Scholars Press, 1996.

–. "Melchizedek: King, Priest, and God." Pages 217–234 in *The Seductiveness of Jewish Myth. Challenge or Response?* Edited by S. Daniel Breslauer. Albany: State University of New York, 1997.

–. "The Macrocosmic Temple, Scriptural Exegesis, and Songs of the Sabbath Sacrifice." *DSD* 9 (2002): 1–19.

Davis Bledsoe, Amanda M. "Throne Theophanies, Dream Visions, and Righteous(?) Seers: Daniel, the Book of Giants, and 1 Enoch Reconsidered." Pages 81–96 in *Ancient Tales of Giants from Qumran and Turfan: Contexts, Traditions, and Influences*. Edited by Matthew Goff, Loren T. Stuckenbruck, and Enrico Morano. WUNT 360. Tübingen: Mohr Siebeck, 2016.

Davis, Kipp. "'There and Back Again': Reconstruction and Reconciliation of the War Text 4QMilhamaa (4Q491a–c)." Pages 125–146 in *The War Scroll, Violence, War and Peace in the Dead Sea Scrolls and Related Literature: Essays in Honour of Martin G. Abegg on the Occasion of His 65th Birthday*. Edited by Kipp Davis et al. STDJ 115. Leiden: Brill, 2015.

Davis, Philip G. "Divine Agents, Mediators, and New Testament Christology." *JTS* 45 (1994): 479–503.

Day, John. *God's Conflict with the Sea: Echoes of a Canaanite Myth in the Old Testament*. Cambridge: Cambridge University Press, 1985.

–. *Yahweh and the Gods and Goddesses of Canaan.* JSOTSup 265. Sheffield: Sheffield Academic Press, 2000.

De Jonge, Marinus and Adam S. van der Woude. "11Q Melchizedek and the New Testament." *NTS* 12 (1966): 301–326.

De Jonge, Marinus. "Levi, the Sons of Levi and the Law in Testament of Levi X, XIV–XV and XVI." Pages 180–190 in *Jewish Eschatology, Early Christian Christology and the Testaments of the Twelve Patriarchs: Collected Essays of Marinus de Jonge.* VTSup 63. Leiden: Brill, 1991.

–. "The Testament of Levi and 'Aramaic Levi.'" *RevQ* 13 (1988): 376–385.

De Moor, Johannes C. *The Rise of Yahwism.* Second Edition. BETL 91. Leuven: Leuven University Press, 1997.

De Vaux, Roland. *Archaeology and the Dead Sea Scrolls.* London: Oxford University Press, 1973.

Deissler, Alfons. *Die Psalmen.* Düsseldorf: Patmos, 1964.

Delcor, Matthias. *Le Livre de Daniel.* SB. Paris: Gabalda, 1971.

–. *Les Hymnes de Qumran (Hodayot): texte hébreu, introduction, traduction, commentaire.* Paris: Letouzey et Ané, 1962.

–. "The Apocrypha and Pseudepigrapha of the Hellenistic Period: Tobit." Pages 409–503 in *The Cambridge History of Judaism: Volume 2, The Hellenistic Age.* 2 volumes. Edited by W. D. Davies and Louis Finkelstein. Cambridge: Cambridge University Press, 1989.

Dequeker, L. "The Saints of the Most High." *OtSt* 18 (1973): 133–162.

Dijkstra, Meindert. "El, Yhwh and their Asherah: On Continuity and Discountinuity in Canaanite and Ancient Israelite Religion." Pages 43–74 in *Ugarit: Ein ostmediterranes Kulturzentrum im Alten Orient. Ergebnisse und Perspektiven der Forschung. Band I: Ugarit und seine altorientalische Umwelt.* Edited by Manfred Dietrich and Oswald Loretz. Abhandlungen zur Literatur Alt-Syrien-Palästinas 7. Münster: Ugarit Verlag, 1995.

Dimant, Devorah. "1 Enoch 6–11: A Methodological Perspective." Pages 323–339 in *SBL Seminar Papers, 1978.* SBLSP 1. Missoula: Scholars Press, 1978.

–. "A Synoptic Comparison of Parallel Sections in 4Q427 7, 4Q491 11 and 4Q471B." *JQR* 85 (1994): 157–161.

–. "Between Sectarian and non-Sectarian: The Case of the Apocryphon of Joshua." Pages 105–134 in *Reworking the Bible: Apocryphal and Related Texts at Qumran: Proceedings of a Joint Symposium by the Orion Center for the Study of the Dead Sea Scrolls and Associated Literature and the Hebrew University Institute for Advanced Studies Research Group on Qumran, 15–17 January, 2002.* Edited by Esther G. Chazon, Devorah Dimant, and Ruth A. Clements. STDJ 58. Leiden: Brill, 2005.

–. *History, Ideology, and Bible Interpretation in the Dead Sea Scrolls: Collected Studies.* FAT 90. Tübingen: Mohr Siebeck, 2014.

–. "Men as Angels: The Self-Image of the Qumran Community." Pages 93–103 in *Religion and Politics in the Ancient Near East.* Edited by Adele Berlin. Bethesda: University of Maryland Press, 1996.

–. "On Righteous and Sinners: 4Q181 Reconsidered." Pages 61–85 in *Manières de penser danls l'antiquité méditerranéenne et orientale: Mélanges offerts à Francis Schmidt par ses elves, ses collègues et ses amis.* Edited by Christophe Batsch and Madalina Vartejanu-Joubert. JSJSup 134. Leiden: Brill, 2009.

–. "Qumran Sectarian Literature." Pages 483–550 in *Jewish Writings of the Second Temple Period.* Edited by Michael E. Stone. Philadelphia: Fortress, 1984.

–. "Sectarian and Non-Sectarian Texts from Qumran: The Pertinence and Usage of a Taxonomy." *RevQ* 24 (2009): 7–18.
–. "The 'Pesher on the Periods' (4Q180) and 4Q181." *IOS* 9 (1979): 77–102.
–. "The Interpretation of Ezekiel in the Hodayot." Pages 78–95 in *HĀ-'ÎSH MŌSHE: Studies in Scriptural Interpretation in the Dead Sea Scrolls and Related Literature in Honor of Moshe J. Bernstein*. Edited by Binyamin Goldstein, Michael Segal, and George J. Brooke. STDJ 122. Leiden: Brill, 2017.
–. "The Qumran Aramaic Texts and the Qumran Community." Pages 197–205 in *Flores Florentino: Dead Sea Scrolls and Other Early Jewish Studies in Honour of Florentino García Martínez*. Edited by Anthony Hilhorst, Emile Puech, Eibert J. C. Tigchelaar. JSJSup 122. Leiden: Brill, 2007.
–. "The Qumran Manuscripts: Contents and Significance." Pages 23–58 in *Time to Prepare a Way in the Wilderness: Papers on the Qumran Scrolls by Fellows of the Institute for Advanced Studies of the Hebrew University, Jerusalem, 1989–1990*. Edited by Devorah Dimant and Lawrence H. Schiffman. STDJ 16. Leiden: Brill, 1995.
–. "Tobit and the Qumran Aramaic Texts." Pages 385–406 in *Is There a Text in This Cave? Studies in the Textuality of the Dead Sea Scrolls in Honour of George J. Brooke*. Edited by Ariel Feldman, Maria Cioată, and Charlotte Hempel. STDJ 119. Leiden: Brill, 2017.
Douglas, Michael C. "Power and Praise in the Hodayot: A Literary Critical Study of 1QH 9:1–18:14." Ph.D. diss., University of Chicago, 1998.
Drawnel, Henryk. *An Aramaic Wisdom Text from Qumran: A New Interpretation of the Levi Document*. JSJSup 86. Leiden: Brill, 2004.
Driver, S. R. *Deuteronomy*. Third Edition. ICC. Edinburgh: T & T Clark, 1973.
Du Toit Laubscher, Frans. "God's Angel of Truth and Melchizedek." *JSJ* 3 (1972): 46–51.
Duhaime, Jean. "Cohérence structurelle et tensions internes dans l'Instruction sur les Deux Esprits (1QS III 13 – IV 26)." Pages 103–131 in *Wisdom and Apocalypticism in the Dead Sea Scrolls and in the Biblical Tradition*. Edited by Florentíno García Martínez. BETL 168. Leuven: Peeters, 2003.
–. "Dualistic Reworking in the Scrolls from Qumran." *CBQ* 49 (1987): 32–56.
–. "L'Intruction sur les deux esprits et le interpolations dualistes a Qumrân (1QS III,13–IV,26)." *RB* 84 (1977): 566 594.
–. "La redaction de 1QM XIII et l'évolution du dualisme à Qumrân." *RB* 84 (1977): 210–238.
–. "La règle de la guerre (1QM) et la construction de l'identité sectaire." Pages 131–145 in *Defining Identities: We, You, and the Other in the Dead Sea Scrolls: Proceedings of the Fifth Meeting of the IOQS in Groningen*. Edited by Florentíno García Martínez et al. STDJ 70. Leiden: Brill, 2008.
–. *The War Texts: 1QM and Related Manuscripts*. CQS 6. London: T & T Clark, 2006.
Duke, Robert R. *The Social Location of the Visions of Amram (4Q543–547)*. StBibLit 135. New York: Peter Lang, 2010.
Dunn, James D. G. "'Son of God' as 'Son of Man' in the Dead Sea Scrolls? A Response to John Collins on 4Q246." Pages 198–210 in *The Scrolls and the Scriptures: Qumran Fifty Years After*. Edited by Stanley E. Porter and Craig A. Evans. JSPSup 26. Sheffield: Sheffield Academic Press, 1997.
Dupont-Sommer, André. "L'instruction sur les deux Esprits dans le Manuel de Discipline." *RHR* 142 (1952): 5–35.
–. "Règlement de la Guerre des Fils de Lumière: traduction et notes." *RHR* 148 (1955): 141–180.

–. *The Essene Writings from Qumran.* Translated by Géza Vermes. Oxford: Basil Black-well, 1961.

Dyma, Oliver. "Tempel, Raum, und Zeit in apokalyptischen Erwartungen." Pages in 33–48 *In memoriam Wolfgang Richter.* Edited by Hans Rechenmacher. ATSAT 100. St. Ottilien: Eos Verlag Erzabtei St. Ottilien, 2016.

Ego, Beate. "The Figure of the Angel Raphael According to His Farewell Address in Tob 12:6–20." Pages 239–253 in *Angels: The Concept of Celestial Beings – Origins, Development and Reception.* Edited by Friedrich V. Reiterer, Tobias Nicklas, and Karen Schöpflin. DCLY. New York: de Gruyter, 2007.

Eissfeldt, Otto. "El and Yahweh." *JSS* 1 (1956): 25–37.

–. *Das Lied Moses, Deuternomomium 32:1–43 und das Lehrgedicht Asaphs samt einer Analyse der Umgebung des Mose-Liedes.* Berlin, Akademie-Verlag, 1958.

–. *The Old Testament: An Introduction.* Oxford: Blackwell, 1964.

Elgvin, Torleif, ed. *Gleanings from the Caves: Dead Sea Scrolls and Artifacts from the Schøyen* Collection. LSTS 71. London: Continuum, 2016.

–. "Priestly Sages? The Milieus of Origin of 4QMysteries and 4QInstruction." Pages 67–87 in *Sapiential Perspectives: Wisdom Literature in Light of the Dead Sea Scrolls: Proceedings of the Sixth International Symposium of the Orion Center for the Study of the Dead Sea Scrolls and Associated Literature, 20–22 May 2001.* Edited by John J. Collins, Gregory E. Sterling, and Ruth A. Clements. STDJ 51. Leiden: Brill, 2004.

–. "Priests on Earth as in Heaven: Jewish Light on the Book of Revelation." Pages 268–269 in *Echoes from the Caves: Qumran and the New Testament.* Edited by Florentíno García Martínez. STDJ 85. Leiden: Brill, 2009.

–. "The Mystery to Come: Early Essene Theology of Revelation." Pages 113–150 in *Qumran between the Old and New Testaments.* Edited by Frederick H. Cryer and Thomas L. Thompson. JSOTSup 290. Sheffield: Sheffield Academic Press, 1998.

Eliade, Mircea. *The Myth of the Eternal Return or Cosmos and History.* Princeton: Princeton University Press, 1974.

Elior, Rachel. *The Three Temples: On the Emergence of Jewish Mysticism.* Oxford: Littman Library of Jewish Civilization, 2004.

Emerton, John A. "The Origins of the Son of Man Imagery." *JTS* 9 (1958): 225–242.

Eshel, Esther. "4Q471b: A Self-Glorification Hymn." *RevQ* 17 (1996): 175–203.

–. "Apotropaic Prayers in the Second Temple Period." Pages 69–88 in *Liturgical Perspectives: Prayer and Poetry in Dead Sea Scrolls: Proceedings of the Fifth International Symposium of the Orion Center for the Study of the Dead Sea Scrolls* and Associated Literature. Edited by Esther G. Chazon. STDJ 48. Leiden: Brill, 2003.

–. "The Identification of the 'Speaker' of the Self-Glorification Hymn." Pages 619–635 in *The Provo International Conference on the Dead Sea Scrolls: Technological Innovations, New Texts, and Reformulated Issues.* Edited by Donald W. Parry and Eugene Ulrich. STDJ 30. Leiden: Brill, 1999.

Eshel, Hanan. "4QMMT and the History of the Hasmonean Period." Pages 53–65 in *Reading 4QMMT: New Perspectives on Qumran Law and History.* Edited by John Kampen and Moshe Bernstein. SBLSymS 2. Atlanta: Scholars Press, 1996.

–. "The Prayer of Joseph from Qumran, a Papyrus from Masada and the Samaritan Temple on Mount Gerizim." *Zion* 56 (1991): 125–136.

Esler, Philip F. *God's Court and Courtiers in the Book of Watchers: Re-Interpreting Heaven in 1 Enoch 1–36.* Eugene: Cascade Books, 2017.

Evans Kapfer, Hilary. "The Relationship Between the Damascus Document and the Community Rule: Attitudes toward the Temple as a Test Case." *DSD* 14 (2007): 152–177.

Evans, Craig A. "Jesus and Dead Sea Scrolls from Qumran Cave 4." Pages 91–100 in *Eschatology, Messianism, and the Dead Sea Scrolls.* Edited by idem and Peter W. Flint. SDSSRL. Grand Rapids: Eerdmans, 1997.

Falk, Daniel K. *Daily, Sabbath, and Festival Prayers in the Dead Sea Scrolls.* STDJ 27. Leiden: Brill, 1998.

–. "Prayer, Liturgy, and War." Pages 275–294 in *The War Scroll, Violence, War and Peace in the Dead Sea Scrolls and Related Literature: Essays in Honour of Martin G. Abegg on the Occasion of His 65ᵗʰ Birthday.* Edited by Kipp Davis et al. STDJ 115. Leiden: Brill, 2015.

Feldman, Ariel. "New Light on the Ten Jubilees of 11QMelchizedek (11Q13)." *DSD* 25 (2018): 1–7.

Ferch, Arthur J. *The Apocalyptic Son of Man in Daniel 7.* AUSDDS 6. Berrien Springs: Andrews University Press, 1979.

Fitzmyer, Joseph A. "4Q246: The 'Son of God' Document from Qumran." *Bib* 74 (1993): 153–174.

–. *A Wandering Aramean: Collected Aramaic Essays.* Atlanta: Scholars Press, 1979.

–. "Further Light on Melchizedek from Qumran Cave 11." *JBL* 86 (1967): 25–41.

–. "The Contribution of Qumran Aramaic to the Study of the New Testament." *NTS* 20 (1974): 382–407.

–. *Tobit.* CEJL. Berlin: de Gruyter, 2003.

Fletcher-Louis, Crispin H. T. *All the Glory of Adam: Liturgical Anthropology in the Dead Sea Scrolls.* STDJ 42. Leiden: Brill, 2003.

–. "Further Reflections on a Divine and Angelic Humanity in the Dead Sea Scrolls." Pages 183–198 in *New Perspectives on Old Texts: Proceedings of the Tenth International Symposium of the Orion Center for the Study of the Dead Sea Scrolls and Associated Literature, 9–11 January, 2005.* Edited by Esther G. Chazon, Betsy Halpern-Amaru, and Ruth A. Clements. STDJ 88. Leiden: Brill, 2010.

–. *Luke-Acts: Angels, Christology, and Soteriology.* Tübingen: Mohr Siebeck, 1997.

–. "On Angels, Men and Priests (Ben Sira), the Qumran Sabbath Songs and the Yom Kippur Avodah." Pages 141–166 in *Gottesdienst und Engel im antiken Judentum und frühen Christentum.* Edited by Jörg Frey and Michael R. Jost. WUNT 2/446. Tübingen: Mohr Siebeck, 2017.

Flint, Peter W. "The Daniel Tradition at Qumran." Pages 329–367 in *The Book of Daniel: Composition and Reception.* Edited by John J. Collins and Peter W. Flint. VTSup 83.2. Leiden: Brill, 2001.

Flusser, David. "Melchizedek and the Son of Man (A Preliminary note on a new fragment from Qumran)." *Christian News from Israel* (April 1966): 26–27.

–. "The Hubris of the Antichrist in a Fragment from Qumran." *Imm* 10 (1980): 31–37.

Fraade, Steven. "Ascetical Aspects of Ancient Judaism." Pages 253–288 in *Jewish Spirituality from the Bible to the Middle Ages.* Edited by Arthur Green. New York: Crossroad, 1986.

Frankel, David. "El as the Speaking Voice in Ps 82:6–7." *JHebS* 10 (2010): 1–24.

Freedman, David Noel. "A Temple Without Hands." Pages 21–30 in *Temples and High Places in Biblical Times: Proceedings of the Colloquium in Honor of the Centennial of Hebrew Union College–Jewish Institute of Religion, Jerusalem, 14–16 March 1977.* Edited by A. Biran. Jerusalem: Hebrew Union College-Jewish Institute of Religion, 1981.

–, ed. *The Anchor Bible Dictionary.* 6 volumes. New York: Doubleday: 1992.

Frennesson, Bjorn. *"In a Common Rejoicing": Liturgical Communion with Angels in Qumran.* SSU 14. Uppsala: Uppsala University Library, 1999.

Frey, Jörg. "Different Patterns of Dualistic Thought in the Qumran Library." Pages 275–335 in *Legal Texts and Legal Issues: Proceedings of the Second Meeting of the International Organization for Qumran Studies, Cambridge, 1995: Published in Honour of Joseph M. Baumgarten.* Edited by Moshe Bernstein, Florentino García Martínez, and John Kampen. STDJ 23. Leiden: Brill, 1997.

Gammie, John G. "Spatial and Ethical Dualism in Jewish Wisdom and Apocalyptic Literature." *JBL* 93 (1974): 356–385.

García Martínez, Florentino and Adam S. van der Woude. "A 'Groningen' Hypothesis of Qumran Origins and Early History." *RevQ* 14 (1990): 521–541.

García Martínez, Florentino and Mladen Popovic, eds. *Defining Identities: We, You, and the Other in the Dead Sea Scrolls: Proceedings of the Fifth Meeting of the IOQS in Groningen.* STDJ 70. Leiden: Brill, 2008.

García Martínez, Florentino. "Aramaica Qumranica Apocalyptica?" Pages 435–447 in *Aramaica Qumranica: Proceedings of the Conference on the Aramaic texts from Qumran at Aix-en-Provence 30 June–2 July 2008.* Edited by Katell Berthelot and Daniel Stökl Ben Ezra. STDJ 94. Leiden: Brill, 2010.

–. "Priestly Functions in a Community without Temple." Pages 303–319 in *Gemeinde ohne Temple: zur Substituierung und Transformation des Jerusalemer Temples und seines Kults im Alten Testament, antiken Judentum und frühen Christentum.* Edited by Beate Ego et al. WUNT 118. Tübingen: Mohr Siebeck, 1999.

–. *Qumran and Apocalyptic: Studies on the Aramaic Texts from Qumran.* STDJ 9. Leiden: Brill, 1992.

–. "Qumran Origins and Early History: A Groningen Hypothesis." *FO* 25 (1988): 113–136.

–. *Qumranic Minora I: Qumran Origins and Apocalypticism.* STDJ 63. Leiden: Brill, 2007.

–. *Qumranica Minora II.* STDJ 64. Leiden: Brill, 2007.

–. "Scribal Practices in the Aramaic Literary Texts from Qumran." Pages in 329–341 in *Myths, Martyrs, and Modernity: Studies in the History of Religion in Honour of Jan N. Bremmer.* Edited by Jitse Dijkstra, Justin Kroesen, Jme Kuiper. Leiden: Brill, 2010.

–. "¿Sectario, no-sectario, o qué? Problems de una taxonomía correcta de los textos qumránicos." *RevQ* 23 (2008): 383–394.

–. "The Groningen Hypothesis Revisited." Pages 17–30 in *The Dead Sea Scrolls and Contemporary Culture: Proceedings of the International Conference at the Israel Museum, July 6–8, 2008.* Edited by Adolfo D. Roitman, Lawrence H. Schiffman, and Shani Tzoref. STDJ 93. Leiden: Brill, 2011.

Gaster, Theodor Herzl. *The Dead Sea Scriptures.* Revised Edition. Garden City: Anchor Books, 1964.

Gieschen, Charles A. *Angelmorphic Christology: Antecedents and Early Evidence.* AGJU 42. Leiden: Brill, 1998.

Goff, Matthew J. *4QInstruction.* WLAW 2. Atlanta: SBL Press, 2013.

–. "A Blessed Rage for Order: Apocalypticism, Esoteric Revelation, and the Cultural Politics of Knowledge in the Hellenistic Age." *HBAI* 5 (2016): 193–211.

–. "Gardens of Knowledge: Teachers in Ben Sira, 4QInstruction, and the Hodayot." Pages 171–194 in *Pedagogy in Ancient Judaism and Early Christianity.* Edited by Karina Martin Hogan, Matthew J. Goff, and Emma Wasserman. EJL. Atlanta: SBL Press, 2017.

–. "Reading Wisdom at Qumran: 4QInstruction and the Hodayot." *DSD* 11 (2004): 263–288.

–. *The Worldly and Heavenly Wisdom of 4QInstruction.* STDJ 50. Leiden: Brill, 2004.

Golb, Norman. "Who Hid the Dead Scrolls?" *BA* 48 (1985): 68–82.

–. *Who Wrote the Dead Sea Scrolls? The Search for the Secret of Qumran.* New York: Scribner, 1995.

Goldingay, John E. *Daniel.* WBC 30. Dallas: Word Books, 1989.

–. "Holy Ones on High." *JBL* 107 (1988): 495–497.

–. *Psalms: Volume 2: Psalms 42–89.* BCOTWP. Grand Rapids: Baker, 2007.

Goldman, Liora. "Dualism in the Visions of Amram." *RevQ* 24 (2010): 421–432.

Goldstein, Ronnie. "A New Look at Deuteronomy 32:8–9 and 43 in Light of Akkadian Sources." *Tarbiz* 79 (2009): 5–21.

Gonzales, A. "Le Psaume lxxxii." *VT* 13 (1969): 78–80.

Goodman, Martin. "A Note on the Qumran Sectarians, the Essenes and Josephus." *JJS* 46 (1995): 161–166.

Goppelt, L. "τύπος." *TDNT* 8:256–257.

Gordon, Cyrus H. "אלהים in Its Reputed Meaning of Rulers, Judges." *JBL* 54 (1935): 139–144.

–. "History of Religion in Psalm 82." Pages 129–131 in *Biblical and Near Eastern Studies: Essays in Honor of William Sanford LaSor.* Edited by G. A. Tuttle. Grand Rapids: Eerdmans, 1978.

Goulder, Michael D. *The Psalms of Asaph and the Pentateuch.* JSOTSup 20. Sheffield: Sheffield Academic Press, 1996.

Gray, George Buchanan. *Sacrifice in the Old Testament: Its Theory and Practice.* Second Edition. New York: KTAV Publishing House, 1971.

Greenfield, Jonas C., Michael E. Stone, and Esther Eshel. *The Aramaic Levi Document: Edition, Translation, Commentary.* SVTP 19. Leiden: Brill, 2004.

Gunkel, Hermann. *Schöpfung und Chaos in Urzeit und Endzeit: Eine religionsgeschichtliche Untersuchung über Gen 1 und Ap Joh 12.* Göttingen: Vadenhooeck & Ruprect, 1895.

Haag, E. "Der Menschensohn und die Hieligen (des) Höchsten. Eine literar-, form-, und traditionsgeschichtliche Studie zu Daniel 7." Pages 137–186 in *The Book of Daniel in the Light of New Findings.* Edited by Adam S. van der Woude. BETL 106. Leuven: Leuven University Press, 1993.

Hallermayer, Michaela. *Text und Überlieferung des Buches Tobit.* DCLS 3. Berlin: de Gruyter, 2008.

Halperin, David J. *The Faces of the Chariot: Early Jewish Responses to Ezekiel's Vision.* Tübingen: Mohr Siebeck, 1988.

Hamacher, Elisabeth. "Die Sabbatopferlieder im Streit um Ursrung und Anfänge der jüdischen Mystik." *JJS* 27 (1996): 119–154.

Handy, Lowell K. *Among the Host of Heaven: The Syro-Palestinian Pantheon as Bureaucracy.* Winona Lake: Eisenbrauns, 1994.

Hanhart, Robert. *Hebräische Wortforschung.* VTSup 16. Leiden: Brill, 1967.

–. *Tobit.* SVTG 8/5. Göttingen: Vandenhoeck & Ruprecht, 1983.

Hankins, Davis. "4QInstruction's Mystery and the Mastery of Wisdom." *DSD* 23 (2016): 183–205.

Hannah, Darrell D. "Guardian Angels and Angelic National Patrons in Second Temple Judaism and Early Christianity." Pages 413–435 in *Angels: The Concept of Celestial Beings – Origins, Development and Reception.* Edited by Friedrich V. Reiterer, Tobias Nicklas, and Karen Schöpflin. DCLY. New York: de Gruyter, 2007.

–. *Michael and Christ: Michael Traditions and Angel Christology in Early Christianity.* WUNT 2/109. Tübingen: Mohr Siebeck, 1999.

Hanneken, Todd R. *The Subversion of the Apocalypses in the Book of Jubilees*. EJL 34. Atlanta: Society of Biblical Literature, 2012.

Hanson, Paul D. "Rebellion in Heaven, Azazel, and Euhemeristic Heroes in 1 Enoch 6–11." *JBL* 96 (1977): 220–226.

–. *The Dawn of Apocalyptic: The Historical and Sociological Roots of Jewish Apocalyptic Eschatology*. Revised Edition. Philadelphia: Fortress Press, 1979.

Harlow, Daniel C. et al., eds. *The "Other" in Second Temple Period Judaism: Essays in Honor of John J. Collins*. Grand Rapids: Eerdmans, 2011.

Harrington, Hannah K. "Keeping Outsiders Out: Impurity at Qumran." Pages 187–204 in *Defining Identities: We, You, and the Other in the Dead Sea Scrolls: Proceedings of the Fifth Meeting of the IOQS in Groningen*. Edited by Florentino García Martínez and Mladen Popovic. STDJ 70. Leiden: Brill, 2008.

Harris, R. Laird, Gleason L. Archer, Jr., and Bruce K. Waltke, eds. *Theological Wordbook of the Old Testament*. 2 volumes. Chicago: The Moody Bible Institute, 1980.

Hartman, Lars. *Asking for a Meaning: A Study of 1 Enoch 1–5*. Lund: Gleerup, 1979.

Hartman, Louis F. and Alexander A. DiLella. *The Book of Daniel*. AB 23. Garden City: Doubleday, 1978.

Harvey, Graham. *The True Israel: Uses of the Name Jew, Hebrew and Israel in Ancient Jewish and Early Christian Literature*. AGJU 35. Leiden: Brill, 1994.

Hayes, Christine E. *Gentile Impurities and Jewish Identities: Intermarriage and Conversion from the Bible to the Talmud*. Oxford: Oxford University Press, 2002.

Heger, Paul. *Challenges to Conventional Opinions on Qumran and Enoch Issues*. STDJ 100. Leiden: Brill, 2012.

Heiser, Michael S. "Are Yahweh and El Distinct Deities in Deut. 32:8–9 and Psalm 82?" *HIPHIL* 3 (2006): 1–9. https://see-j.net/index.php/hiphil/article/view/29/26.

–. "Co-regency in Ancient Israel's Divine Council as the Conceptual Backdrop to Ancient Jewish Binitarian Monotheism." *BBR* 26 (2015): 195–225.

–. "Deuteronomy 32 and the Sons of God." *BibSac* 158 (2001): 52–74.

–. "Does Divine Plurality in the Hebrew Bible Demonstrate an Evolution from Polytheism to Monotheism in Israelite Religion?" *JESOT* 1 (2012): 1–24.

–. "Monotheism and the Language of Divine Plurality in the Hebrew Bible and the Dead Sea Scrolls." *TynBul* 65 (2014): 85–100.

–. "Monotheism, Polytheism, Monolatry, or Henotheism? Toward an Assessment of Divine Plurality in the Hebrew Bible." *BBR* 18 (2008): 1–30.

–. "Should אלהים (Elohim) with Plural Predication be Translated 'Gods'?" *BT* 61 (2010): 123–136.

–. "The Divine Council in Late Canonical and Non-Canonical Second Temple Jewish Literature. Ph.D. diss., University of Wisconsin–Madison, 2004.

Hempel, Charlotte. "Do the Scrolls Suggest Rivarly Betweeen the Sons of Aaron and the Sons of Zadok and If So was it Mutual?" *RevQ* 24 (2009): 135–193.

–. "Maskil(im) and Rabbim: From Daniel to Qumran." Pages 133–156 in *Biblical Traditions in Transmission: Essays in Honour of Michael A. Knibb*. Edited by Charlotte Hempel and Judith Lieu. JSJSup 111. Ledien: Brill, 2006.

–. "The Community and Its Rivals According to the Community Rule from Caves 1 and 4." *RevQ* 18 (2003): 47–81.

–. "The Earthly Essene Nucleus of 1QSa." *DSD* 2 (1996): 253–269.

–. *The Qumran Rule Texts: Collected Essays*. TSAJ 154. Tübingen: Mohr Seibeck, 2013.

–. "The Sons of Aaron in the Dead Sea Scrolls." Pages 207–224 in *Flores Florentino: Dead Sea Scrolls and Other Early Jewish Studies in Honour of Florentino García Martínez*. Edited by A. Hilhorst et al. JSJSup 122. Leiden: Brill, 2007.

–. "The Treatise on the Two Spirits and the Literary History of the Rule of the Community." Pages 102–120 in *Dualism in Qumran*. Edited by Geza G. Xeravits. LSTS 76. London: Continuum, 2010.

Hendel, Ronald. *Remembering Abraham: Culture Memory, and the History of the Hebrew Bible*. Oxford: Oxford University Press, 2005.

–. "The Messiah Son of Joseph: Simply 'Sign.'" *BAR* 35 (2009): 8.

Hicks-Keaton, Jill. *Arguing with Aseneth: Gentile Access to Israel's Living God in Jewish Antiquity*. Oxford: Oxford University Press, 2018.

Himmelfarb, Martha. *A Kingdom of Priests: Ancestry and Merit in Ancient Judaism*. Philadelphia: University of Pennsylvania Press, 2006.

–. *Ascent to Heaven in Jewish and Christian Apocalypses*. New York: Oxford University Press, 1993.

–. "Merkavah Mysticism since Scholem: Rachel Elior's *The Three Temples*." Pages 19–36 in *Mystical Approaches to God: Judaism, Christianity, Islam*. Edited by Peter Schäfer. München: R. Oldenbourg Verlag, 2006.

–. "The Book of Jubilees and Early Jewish Mysticism." Pages in 384–394 in *Enoch and Mosaic Torah: The Evidence of Jubilees*. Edited by Gabriele Boccaccini and Giovanni Ibba. Grand Rapids: Eerdmans, 2009.

Hollander, Harm W. and Marinus de Jonge. *The Testaments of the Twelve Patriarchs: A Commentary*. SVTP 8. Leiden: Brill, 1985.

Holm-Nielsen, Svend. *Hodayot: Psalms at Qumran*. ATDan 2. Aarhus: Universitetsforlaget, 1960.

Holmstedt, Robert D. and John Screnock. "Writing a Descriptive Grammar of the Syntax and Semantics of the War Scroll (1QM): The Noun Phrase as Proof of Concept." Pages 67–106 in *The War Scroll, Violence, War and Peace in the Dead Sea Scrolls and Related Literature: Essays in Honour of Martin G. Abegg on the Occasion of His 65th Birthday*. Edited by Kipp Davis et al. STDJ 115. Leiden: Brill, 2015.

Hölscher, Gustav. "Die Entstehung des Buches Daniel." *TSK* 92 (1919): 113–138.

Horbury, William. "Messianic Associations of the Son of Man." *JTS* 36 (1985): 34–55.

Horton, Fred L. *The Melchizedek Tradition: A Critical Examination of the Sources to the Fifth Century AD and in the Epistle to the Hebrews*. SNTSMS 30. Cambridge: Cambridge University Press, 1976.

Hossfeld, Frank-Lothar and Erich Zenger. *Psalms 2: A Commentary on Psalms 51–100*. Hermeneia. Minneapolis: Fortress, 2005.

Hughes, Julie A. *Scriptural Allusions in the Hodayot*. STDJ 59. Leiden: Brill, 2009.

Hultgren, Stephen. *From the Damascus Covenant to the Covenant of the Community: Literary, Historical, and Theological Studies in the Dead Sea Scrolls*. STDJ 66. Leiden: Brill, 2007.

Huppenbauer, Hans-Walter. *Der Mensch zwischen zwei Welten: Der Dualismus der Texte von Qumran (Höhle I) und der Damaskusfragmente: Ein Beitrag zur Vorgeschichte des Evangeliums*. ATANT 32. Zürich: Zwingli Verlag, 1959.

Hurtado, Larry W. "Monotheism, Principal Angels, and the Background of Christology." Pages 146–154 in *The Oxford Handbook of the Dead Sea Scrolls*. Edited by Timothy H. Lim and John J. Collins. Oxford: Oxford University Press, 2010.

–. *One God, One Lord: Early Christian Devotion and Ancient Jewish Monotheism*. Second Edition. Edinburgh: T & T Clark, 1998.

Japhet, Sara. *I & II Chronicles*. OTL. Louisville: Westminster John Knox Press, 1993.

Jassen, Alex P. "Violent Imaginaries and Practical Violence in the War Scroll." Pages 175–203 in *The War Scroll, Violence, War and Peace in the Dead Sea Scrolls and Related Literature: Essays in Honour of Martin G. Abegg on the Occasion of His 65th Birthday*. Edited by Kipp Davis et al. STDJ 115. Leiden: Brill, 2015.

Jenni, Ernst and Claus Westermann, eds. *Theological Lexicon of the Old Testament*. Translated by M. E. Biddle. 3 volumes. Peabody: Hendrickson, 1997.

Jokiranta, Jutta. *Social Identity and Sectarianism in the Qumran Movement*. STDJ 105. Leiden: Brill, 2013.

–. "What is "Serekh ha-Yahad (S)"? Thinking About Ancient Manuscripts as Information Processing." Pages 611–635 in *Sibyls, Scriptures, and Scrolls: John Collins at Seventy*. Joel Baden, Hindy Najman, and Eibert Tigchelaar. JSJSup 175. Leiden: Brill, 2016.

Jongeling, Bastiaan. *Le Rouleau de la Guerre des Manuscrits de Qumran*. SSN 4. Assen: Van Gorcum, 1962.

Joüon, Paul A. *A Grammar of Biblical Hebrew*. Translated and revised by Takamitsu Muraoka. 2 volumes. SubBi 14. Rome: Pontifical Biblical Institute, 1991.

Jurgens, Blake A. "Reassessing the Dream-Vision of the Vision of Amram (4Q543–547)." *JSP* 24 (2014): 3–42.

Kaiser, Otto. *Isaiah 13–39: A Commentary*. OTL. Philadelphia: Westminster, 1974.

Kamiah, Ehrhard. *Die Form der katalogischen Paränese im Neuen Testament*. WUNT 7. Tübingen: Mohr Siebeck, 1964.

Kampen, John. *Wisdom Literature*. ECDSS. Grand Rapids: Eerdmans, 2011.

Katz, Steven T. "Mystical Speech and Mystical Meaning." Pages 3–41 in *Mysticism and Language*. Edited by Steven T. Katz. New York: Oxford University Press, 1992.

Kautzsch, E., ed. *Gesenius' Hebrew Grammar*. Translated by A. E. Cowley. Mineola: Dover Publications, 2006.

Kim Harkins, Angela. "A New Proposal for Thinking About 1QHª Sixty Years After Its Discovery." Pages 101–134 in *Qumran Cave 1 Revisited: Texts from Cave 1 Sixty Years after Their Discovery: Proceedings of the Sixth Meeting of the IOQS in Ljubljana*. Edited by Daniel K. Falk and Eibert J. C. Tigchelaar. STDJ 91. Leiden: Brill, 2010.

–. "Elements of the Fallen Angels Traditions in the Qumran Hodayot." Pages 8–24 in *The Fallen Angels Traditions: Second Temple Period Developments and Reception History*. Edited by Angela Kim Harkins, Kelley Coblentz Bautch, and John C. Endres. CBQMS 53. Washington: Catholic Biblical Association, 2014.

–. "Observations on the Editorial Shaping of the So-Called Community Hymns from 1QHª and 4QHª (4Q427)." *DSD* 12 (2005): 233–256.

–. "Reading the Qumran Hodayot in Light of the Traditions Associated with Enoch" *Hen* 32 (2010): 359–400.

–. *Reading with an "I" to the Heavens: Looking at the Qumran Hodayot through the Lens of Visionary Traditions*. New York: de Gruyter, 2012.

–. "The Community Hymns Classification: A Proposal for Further Differentiation." *DSD* 15 (2008) 121–154.

–. "The Performative Reading of the Hodayot: The Arousal of Emotions and the Exegetical Generation of Texts." *JSP* 21 (2011): 55–71.

Kim, Seyoon. *The 'Son of Man' as the Son of God*. Tübingen: Mohr Siebeck, 1983.

Kittel, Bonnie P. *The Hymns of Qumran: Translation and Commentary*. SBLDS 50. Chico: Scholars Press, 1981.

Kittel, Gerhard and Gerhard Friedrich, eds. *Theological Dictionary of the New Testament.* Translated by Geoffrey W. Bromiley. 10 volumes. Grand Rapids: Eerdmans, 1964–1976.

Klawans, Jonathan. *Purity, Sacrifice, and the Temple: Symbolism and Supersessionism in the Study of Ancient Judaism.* New York: Oxford University Press, 2006.

Knohl, Israel. "Melchizedek: A Model for the Union of Kingship and Priesthood in the Hebrew Bible, 11QMelchizedek, and the Epistle to the Hebrews." Pages 255–266 in *Text, Thought, and Practice in Qumran and Early Christianity: Proceedings of the Ninth International Symposium of the Orion Center for the Study of the Dead Sea Scrolls and Associated Literature, Jointly Sponsored by the Hebrew University Center for the Study of Christianity, 11–13 January, 2004.* Edited by Ruth A. Clements and Daniel R. Schwartz. STDJ 84. Leiden: Brill, 2009.

–. *Messiahs and Resurrections in 'The Gabriel Revelation.'* London: Continuum, 2009.

–. *The Messiah Before Jesus: The Suffering Servant of the Dead Sea Scrolls* (Berkeley: University of California, 2000.

Kobelski, Paul J. *Melchizedek and Melchiresa.* CBQMS 10. Washington: Catholic Biblical Society of America, 1981.

Koch, Klaus. *Das Buch Daniel.* Darmstad: Wissenschaftliche Buchgesellschaft, 1980.

–. *Der Gott Israels und die Götter des Orients.* Göttingen: Vandenhoeck & Ruprecht, 2006.

Koehler, Ludwig, Walter Baumgartner, and Johann Jackob Stamm, eds. *The Hebrew and Aramaic Lexicon of the Old Testament.* Translated and edited under the supervision of M. E. J. Richardson. 4 volumes. Leiden: Brill, 1994–1999.

Korner, Ralph J. "The 'Exilic' Prophecy of Daniel 7: Does it Reflect Late Pre-Maccabean or Early Hellenistic Historiography?" Pages 333–353 in *Prophets, Prophecy, and Ancient Israelite Historiography.* Edited by Mark J. Boda et al. Winona Lake: Eisenbrauns, 2013.

Kratz, Reinhard G. *Translatio Imperii: Untersuchungen zu den aramäischen Danielerzählungen und ihrem theologiegeschichtlichen Umfeld.* WMANT 63. Neukrichen-Vluyn: Neukirchener Verlag, 1991.

Kraus, Hans-Joachim. *Psalms 60–150.* CC. Minneapolis: Augsburg, 1993.

Kugel, James L. *A Walk Through Jubilees: Studies in the Book of Jubilees and the World of its Creation.* JSJSup 156. Leiden: Brill, 2012.

–. "Levi's Elevation to the Priesthood in Second Temple Writings." *HTR* 86 (1993): 1–64.

Kugler, Robert A. *From Patriarch to Priest: The Levi-Priestly Tradition from Aramaic Levi to the Testament of Levi.* EJL 9. Atlanta: Scholars Press, 1996.

–. "Priesthood at Qumran." Pages 93–116 in *The Dead Sea Scrolls After Fifty Years:* A *Comprehensive Assessment: Volume 2.* Edited by Peter W. Flint and James C. VanderKam. Leiden: Brill, 1999.

–. *The Testaments of the Twelve Patriarchs.* GAP. Sheffield: Sheffield Academic Press, 2001.

–. "The War Rule Texts and a New Theory of the People of the Dead Sea Scrolls: A Brief Thought Experiment." Pages 163–172 in *The War Scroll, Violence, War and Peace in the Dead Sea Scrolls and Related Literature: Essays in Honour of Martin G. Abegg on the Occasion of His 65th Birthday.* Edited by Kipp Davis et al. STDJ 115. Leiden: Brill, 2015.

Kuhn, Heinz-Wolfgang. *Enderwartung und gegenwärtiges Heil: Untersuchungen zu den Gemeindeliedern von Qumran mit einem Anhang über Eschatologie und Gegenwart in der Verkündigung Jesu.* SUNT 4. Göttingen: Vandenhoeck and Ruprecht, 1966.

Kuhn, Karl A. "The 'One like a Son of Man' Becomes the Son of God." *CBQ* 69 (2007): 22–42.

Kuhn, Karl Georg. "Die Sektenschrift und die iranische Religion." *ZTK* 49 (1952): 296–316.

Kvanvig, Helge S. *Roots of Apocalyptic: The Mesopotamian Background of the Enoch Figure and of the Son of Man.* WMANT 61. Neukirchen-Vluyn: Neukirchener Verlag, 1988.

L'Heuruex, Conrad E. *Rank Among the Canaanite Gods: El, Baal, and the Rephaim.* HSM 21. Missoula: Scholars Press, 1979.

Laato, Antti. "The Chronology in the Animal Apocalypse of *1 Enoch* 85–90." *JSP* 26 (2016): 3–19.

Lacocque, André. "Allusions to Creation in Daniel 7." Pages 114–131 in *The Book of Daniel: Composition and Reception.* Edited by John J. Collins and Peter W. Flint. VTSup 83.1. Leiden: Brill, 2001.

–. *The Book of Daniel.* Translated by D. Pellauer. Atlanta: John Knox Press, 1979.

Lamberigts, Sylvester. "Le Sens de *qdwsym* dans les texts de Qumrân." *ETL* 46 (1970): 24–39.

Lange, Armin. "Considerations Concerning the 'Spirits of Impurity' in Zech 13.2." Pages 254–268 in *Die Dämonen – Demons.* Edited by Hermann Lichtenberger, Armin Lange, Diethard Römhelf. Tübingen: Mohr Seibeck 2003.

–. "Determination of Fate by the Oracle of the Lot." Pages 39–48 in *Sapiential, Liturgical and Poetical Texts from Qumran: Proceedings of the Third Meeting of the International Organization for Qumran Studies, Oslo, 1988: Published in Memory of Maurice* Baillet. Edited by Daniel K. Falk, Florentino García Martínez, and Eileen M. Schuller. STDJ 35. Leiden: Brill, 2000.

–. "Determination of Fate by the Oracle of the Lot." Pages 39–48 in *Sapiential, Liturgical and Poetical Texts from Qumran: Proceedings of the Third Meeting of the International Organization for Qumran Studies, Oslo, 1988: Published in Memory of Maurice Baillet.* Edited by Daniel K. Falk, Florentino García Martínez, and Eileen M. Schuller. STDJ 35. Leiden: Brill, 2000.

–. "Sages and Scribes in the Qumran Literature." Pages 217–293 in *Scribes, Sages, and Seers in the Eastern Mediterranean World.* Edited by Leo G. Perdue. Göttingen: Vandenhoeck and Ruprecht, 2008.

–. *Weisheit and Prädestination: Weisheitliche Urordnung and Prädestination in den Textfunden von Qumran.* STDJ 18. Leiden: Brill, 1995.

Leaney, Alfred R. C. *The Rule of Qumran and Its Meaning.* NTL. London: SCM Press, 1966.

Lenglet, Adrien. "La Structure littéraire de Daniel 2–7." *Bib* 53 (1972): 169–190.

Leonhardt-Balzer, Jutta. "Evil at Qumran." Pages 17–33 in *Evil in Second Temple Judaism and Early Christianity.* Edited by Chris Keith and Loren T. Stuckenbruck. WUNT 2/417. Tübingen: Mohr Siebeck, 2016.

–. "Evil, Dualism and Community: Who/What Did the Yahad Not Want to Be?" Pages 121–147 in *Dualism in Qumran.* Edited by Geza G. Xeravits. LSTS 76. London: Continuum, 2010.

Licht, Jacob. "An Analysis of the Treatise on the Two Spirits in DSD." *ScrHier* 4 (1965): 88–100.

–. *The Thanksgiving Scroll.* Jerusalem: Bialik Institute, 1957.

Lichtenberger, Hermann. *Studien zum Menschenbild in Texten der Qumrangeinde.* SUNT 15. Göttingen: Vandenhoeck & Ruprecht, 1980.

Lim, Timothy H. *Pesharim*. CQS 3. London: Sheffield Press, 2002.

Lioy, Dan. *Axis of Glory: A Biblical and Theological Analysis of the Temple Motif in Scripture*. StBibLit 138. New York: Peter Lang, 2010.

Lipinski, E. "נָחַל. נַחֲלָה." *TDOT* 9:328–331.

Littman, Robert J. *Tobit: The Book of Tobit in Codex Sinaiticus*. Sepuagint Commentary Series 9. Leiden: Brill, 2008.

Loretz, Oswald. *Psalmstudien*. BZAW 309. Berlin: de Gruyter, 2002.

Lueken, Wilhelm. *Michael: Eine Darstellung und Vergleichung der jüdischen und der morgenländisch-christlichen Tradition vom Erzenglel Michael*. Göttingen: Vandenhoeck & Ruprecht, 1898.

Mach, Michael. *Entwicklungsstadien des jüdischen Engelglaubens in vorrabbinischer Zeit*. TSAJ 34. Tübingen: Mohr Siebeck, 1992.

Machiela, Daniel A. "Aramaic Writings of the Second Temple Period and the Growth of Apocalyptic Thought." *JAAJ* 2 (2014): 113–134.

–. "Once More, with Feeling: Rewritten Scripture in Ancient Judaism – A Review of Recent Developments." *JSJ* 51 (2010): 308–320.

–. "Situating the Aramaic Texts from Qumran: Reconsidering Their Language and Socio-Historical Settings." Pages 88–109 in *Apocalyptic Thinking in Early Judaism: Engaging with John Collins' The Apocalyptic Imagination*. Edited by Cecilia Wassén and Sidnie White Crawford. JSJSup 182. Leiden: Brill, 2018.

Machiela, Daniel A. and Andrew B. Perrin. "Tobit and the Genesis Apocryphon: Towards a Family Portrait." *JBL* 133 (2014): 111–132.

Magness, Jodi. *The Archaeology of Qumran and the Dead Sea Scrolls*. SDSSRL. Grand Rapids: Eerdmans, 2002.

–. "Were Sacrifices Offered at Qumran? The Animal Bone Deposits Reconsidered." *JAJ* 7 (2016): 5–34.

Maier, Johann. *Vom Kultus zur Gnosis*. Salzburg: Otto Müller, 1964.

Manzi, Franco. *Melchisedek e l'angelologica nellèpistola agli Ebrei e a Qumran*. AnBib 136. Rome: Pontifical Biblical Institute, 1997.

Mason, Eric F. "Melchizedek Traditions in Second Temple Judaism." Pages 345–360 in *The Dead Sea Scrolls in Context. Integrating the Dead Sea Scrolls in the Study of Ancient Texts, Languages, and Cultures*. Edited by Armin Lange et al. VTSup 140. Leiden: Brill, 2011.

–. *'You Are a Priest Forever': Second Temple Jewish Messianism and the Priestly Christology of the Epistle to the Hebrews*. STDJ 74. Leiden: Brill, 2008.

Meier, S. A. "Angel of Yahweh יהוה מלאך." *DDD* 53–59.

Meinhold, Johannes. *Die Composition des Buches Daniel*. Greifswald: Abel, 1884.

Metso, Sarianna. *The Serekh Texts*. LSTS 62. London: T & T Clark, 2007.

–. *The Textual Development of the Qumran Community Rule*. STDJ 21. Leiden: Brill, 1997.

Meyer, Nicholas A. *Adam's Dust and Adam's Glory in the Hodayot and the Letters of Paul: Rethinking Anthropology and Theology*. NovTSup 168. Leiden: Brill, 2016.

Meyers, Carol. *Exodus*. NCBC. Cambridge: Cambridge University Press, 2005.

Michaelis, Wilhelm. *Zur Engelchristologie im Urchristentum: Abbau der Konstruktion Martin Werners*. Basel: Heinrich Majer, 1942.

Michalak, Aleksander R. *Angels as Warriors in Late Second Temple Period Literature*. WUNT 2/330. Tübingen: Mohr Siebeck, 2012.

Milik, Józef T. "4QVisions d'Amram et une citation d'Origene." *RB* 79 (1972): 777–92.

–. "Les modèles araméens du Livre d'Esther dans la Brotte 4 de Qumrân." *RevQ* 15 (1992): 321–406.
–. "Milkî-sedek et Milkî-resha' dans les anciens écrits juifs et chrétiens." *JJS* 23 (1972): 95–144.
Milik, Józef T. *Ten Years of Discovery in the Wilderness of Judaea.* SBT 26. London: SCM, 1959.
Miller, Eric. "The Self-Glorification Hymn Reexamined." *Hen* 31 (2009): 307–324.
Miller, Jr., Patrick D. "The Divine Council and the Prophetic Call to War." *VT* 18 (1968): 100–107.
–. *The Divine Warrior in Early Israel.* HSM 5. Cambridge: Harvard University Press, 1973.
Miller, Merrill P. "The Function of Isaiah 61:1–2 in *11QMelchizedek.*" *JBL* 88 (1969): 467–469.
Mizrahi, Noam. "Aspects of Poetic Stylization in Second Temple Hebrew: A Linguistic Comparison of the Songs of the Sabbath Sacrifice with Ancient Piyyut." Pages 147–163 in *Hebrew in the Second Temple Period: The Hebrew of the Dead Sea Scrolls and of Other Contemporary Sources: Proceedings of the Twelfth International Symposium of the Orion Center for the Study of the Dead Sea Scrolls and Associated Literature and the Fifth International Symposium on the Hebrew of the Dead Sea Scrolls and Ben Sira, Jointly Sponsored by the Eliezer Ben-Yehuda Center for the Study of the History of the Hebrew Language, 29–31 December, 2008.* Edited by Stephen E. Fassberg, Moshe Bar-Asher, and Ruth A. Clements. STDJ 108. Leiden: Brill, 2013.
–. "Earthly Liturgy and Celestial Music: The Poetics of the Cycle of Praise of the Sixth Sabbath Song." Pages 119–139 in *Gottesdienst und Engel im antiken Judentum und frühen Christentum.* Edited by Jörg Frey and Michael R. Jost. WUNT 2/446. Tübingen: Mohr Siebeck, 2017.
–. "The Cycle of Summons: A Hymn form the Seventh Song of the Sabbath Sacrifice (4Q403 1i 31–40)." *DSD* 22 (2015): 43–67.
–. "The Songs of the Sabbath Sacrifice and the Biblical Priestly Literature: A Linguistic Reconsideration." *HTR* 104 (2011): 33–57.
Monsoor, Menahem. *The Thanksgiving Hymns: Translated and Annotated with an Introduction.* STDJ 3. Leiden: Brill, 1961.
Montgomery, Eric. "A Stream from Eden: The Nature and Development of a Revelatory Tradition in the Dead Sea Scrolls." Ph.D. diss., McMaster University, 2013.
Montgomery, James A. *A Critical and Exegetical Commentary on the Book of Daniel.* ICC. Edinburgh: Clark, 1927.
Moore, Carey A. *Tobit: A New Translation with Introduction and Commentary.* AB 40A. New York: Doubleday, 1996.
Morgenstern, Julian. "The Mythological Background of Psalm 82." *HUCA* 14 (1939): 119–121.
Morray-Jones, Christopher R. A. "The Temple Within: The Embodied Divine Image and its Worship in the Dead Sea Scrolls and Other Early Jewish and Christian Sources." Pages 400–431 in *SBL Seminar Papers, 1998.* SBLSP 37. Atlanta: Scholars Press, 1998.
Mosca, Paul G. "Once Again the Heavenly Witness of Psalm 89:38." *JBL* 105 (1986): 27–37.
–. "Ugarit and Daniel 7: A Missing Link." *Bib* 67 (1986): 496–517.
Mowinckel, Sigmund. *He That Cometh: The Messiah Concept in the Old Testament and Later Judaism.* New York: Abingdon, 1955.

Mullen, Jr., E. Theodore. *The Assembly of the Gods: The Divine Council in Canaanite and Early Hebrew Literature.* HSM 24. Chico: Scholars Press, 1980.

Müller, Ulrich B. *Messias und Menschensohn in jüdischen Apokalypsen und in der Offen barung des Johannes.* Studien zum Neuen Testament 6. Gütersloh: Mohn, 1972.

Murphy-O'Connor, Jerome. "La genèse littéraire de la Règle de la Communauté." *RB* 76 (1969): 528–549.

–. "The Essenes and their History." *RB* 81 (1974): 215–244.

Murray, Robert P. R. "The Origin of the Aramaic *'ir*, angel." *Or* 53.2 (1984): 303–317.

Najman, Hindy. *Seconding Sinai: The Development of Mosaic Discourse in Second Temple Judaism.* JSJSup 77. Leiden: Brill, 2003.

Newman, Judith H. "Covenant Renewal and Transformational Scripts in the Performance of the Hodayot and 2 Corinthians." Pages 292–327 in *Jesus, Paulus und die Texte von Qumran.* Edited by Jörg Frey and Enno Edzard Popkes. WUNT 2/390. Tübingen: Mohr Siebeck, 2015.

–. "Priestly Prophets at Qumran: Summoning Sinai through the Songs of the Sabbath Sacrifice." Pages 177–213 in *The Significance of Sinai: Traditions about Sinai and Divine Revelation in Judaism and Christianity.* Edited by George J. Brooke, Hindy Najman, and Loren T. Stuckenbruck. TBN 12. Leiden: Brill, 2008.

–. "The Thanksgiving Hymns of 1QH^a and the Construction of the Ideal Sage through Liturgical Performance." Pages 940–957 in *Sibyls, Scriptures, and Scrolls: John Collins at Seventy.* Joel Baden, Hindy Najman, and Eibert Tigchelaar. JSJSup 175. Leiden: Brill, 2016.

Newsom, Carol A. "A Farewell to the Community Hymns?" Paper presented at the Triennial Meeting of the IOQS, Aberdeen, Scotland, 8 August 2019.

–. "Constructing 'We, You, and Others' though Non-Polemical Discourse." Pages 13–22 in *Defining Identities: We, You, and the Other in the Dead Sea Scrolls: Proceedings of the Fifth Meeting of the IOQS in Groningen.* Edited by Florentino García Martínez and Mladen Popovic. STDJ 70. Leiden: Brill, 2008.

–. "Deriving Negative Anthropology through Exegetical Activity." Pages 258–274 in *Is There a Text in this Cave? Studies in the Textuality of the Dead Sea Scrolls in Honour of George J. Brooke.* Edited by Ariel Feldman, Maria Cioatǎ, and Charlotte Hempel. STDJ 119. Leiden: Brill, 2017.

–. "He Has Established for Himself Priests." Pages 101–120 in *Archaeology and History in the Dead Sea Scrolls: The New York University Conference on the Dead Sea Scrolls.* Edited by Lawrence H. Schiffman. JSPSup 8. JSOTSup 2. Sheffield: JSOT Press, 1990.

–. "Kenneth Burke Meets the Teacher of Righteousness: Rhetorical Strategies in the Hodayot and the Serek Ha-Yahad." Pages 121–131 in *Of Scribes and Scrolls: Studies on the Hebrew Bible, Intertestamental Judaism, and Christian Origins: Presented to John Strugnell on the Occasion of his Sixtieth Birthday.* Edited by John J. Collins, Harold W. Attridge, and Thomas H. Tobin. New York: University Press of America, 1990.

–. "Religious Experience in the Dead Sea Scrolls: Two Case Studies." Pages 205–222 in *Experientia, Volume 2: Linking Text and Experience.* Edited by Colleen Shantz and Rodney Werline. EJL 35. Atlanta: Society of Biblical Literature, 2012.

–. Review of Crispin H. T. Fletcher-Louis, *All the Glory of Adam: Liturgical Anthropology in the Dead Sea Scrolls. DSD* 10 (2003): 431–435.

–. "'Sectually Explicit' Literature from Qumran." Pages 167–187 in *The Hebrew Bible and Its Interpreters.* Edited by William H. Propp, Baruch Halpern, and David Noel Freedman. Winona Lake: Eisenbrauns, 1990.

–. "The Reuse of Ugaritic Mythology in Daniel 7: An Optical Illusion?" Pages 85–100 in *Biblical Essays in Honor of Daniel J. Harrington, S. J., and Richard J. Clifford, S. J.: Opportunity for No Little Instruction.* Edited by Christopher G. Frechette and Christopher R. Matthews. New York: Paulist Press, 2014.

–. *The Self as Symbolic Space: Constructing Identity at Qumran.* STDJ 52. Leiden: Brill, 2004.

Newsom, Carol A. and Yigael Yadin. "The Masada Fragment of the Qumran Songs of the Sabbath Sacrifice." *IEJ* 34 (1984): 77–88.

Newsom, Carol A. with Brennan W. Breed. *Daniel: A Commentary.* OTL. Louisville: Westminster John Knox Press, 2014.

Nickelsburg, George W. E. *1 Enoch 1: A Commentary on the Book of 1 Enoch, Chapters 1–36, 81–108.* Hermeneia. Minneapolis: Fortress Press, 2001.

–. "Apocalyptic and Myth in 1 Enoch 6–11." *JBL* 96 (1977): 383–405.

–. "Enoch, Levi, and Peter: Recipients of Revelation in Upper Galilee." *JBL* 100 (1981): 575–600.

–. *Jewish Literature Between the Bible and the Mishnah*: *A Historical and Literary Introduction.* Minneapolis: Fortress, 1981.

–. *Resurrection, Immortality and Eternal Life in Intertestamental Judaism.* HTS 26. Cambridge: Harvard University Press, 1972.

–. "Revealed Wisdom as a Criterion for Inclusion and Exclusion: From Jewish Sectarianism to Early Christianity." Pages 74–91 in *To See Ourselves as Others See Us: Christians, Jews, and "Others" in Late Antiquity.* Edited by Jacob Neusner and Ernest S. Frerichs. Chico: Scholars Press, 1985.

–. "Seeking the Origin of the Two Ways Tradition in Jewish and Christian Ethical Texts." Pages 95–108 in *A Multiform Heritage: Studies on Early Judaism and Christianity in Honor of Robert A. Kraft.* Edited by Benjamin G. Wright. Atlanta: Scholars Press, 1999.

–. "The We and the Other in the Worldview of 1 Enoch, the Dead Sea Scrolls, and Other Early Jewish Texts." Pages 262–279 in *The "Other" in Second Temple Judaism: Essays in Honour of John J. Collins.* Edited by Daniel C. Harlow et al. Grand Rapids: Eerdmans, 2011.

Nickelsburg, George W. E. and James C. VanderKam. *1 Enoch 2: A Commentary on the Book of 1 Enoch Chapters 37–82.* Hermeneia. Minneapolis: Fortress, 2011.

Niditch, Susan. *Judges: A Commentary.* OTL. Louisville: Westminster John Knox, 2008.

–. *The Symbolic Vision in Biblical Tradition.* HSM 30. Missoula: Scholars Press, 1983.

Niehr, Herbert. "Götter oder Menschen – eine falsche Alternative: Bemerkungen zu Ps 82." *ZAW* 99 (1987): 94–98.

Nitzan, Bilhah. "4QBerakhot[a–e] (4Q286–290): A Covenant Renewal Ceremony in Light of the Related Texts." *RevQ* 16 (1995): 487–506.

–. "Harmonic and Mystical Characteristics in Poetic and Liturgical Writings from Qumran." *JQR* 85 1–2 (1994): 163–186.

–. "Hymns from Qumran." Pages 53–63 in *The Dead Sea Scrolls: Forty Years of Research.* Edited by Devorah Dimant, Uriel Rappaport, and Yad Yitshak Ben-Tsvei. STDJ 10. Leiden: Brill, 1992.

–. *Qumran Prayer and Religious Poetry.* STDJ 12. Leiden: Brill, 1994.

Noll, Stephen F. "Angelology in the Qumran Texts." Ph.D. diss., University of Manchester, 1979.

Noth, Martin. *The Laws in the Pentateuch and Other Essays.* London: Oliver and Boyd, 1966. Reprinted by London: SCM, 1984.

Novick, Tzvi. "Wisdom's Wandering Wandering: On the Evolution of a Motif." *Hen* 30 (2008): 104–118.

O'Neill, J. Review of Crispin H. T. Fletcher-Louis, *Luke-Acts: Angels, Christology, and Soteriology*. Tübingen: Mohr Siebeck, 1997. *JTS* 50 (1999): 225–230.

Oldenburg, Ulf. *The Conflict Between El and Baal in Canaanite Religion*. Leiden: Brill, 1969.

Olson, Daniel C. *A New Reading of the Animal Apocalypse of 1 Enoch: 'All Nations Shall Be Blessed.'* SVTP 24. Leiden: Brill, 2013.

Olyan, Saul M. *A Thousand Thousands Served Him: Exegesis and the Naming of Angels in Ancient Judaism*. TSAJ 36. Tübingen: Mohr Siebeck, 1993.

Orlov, Andrei A. *The Greatest Mirror: Heavenly Counterparts in the Jewish Pseudepigrapha*. Albany: SUNY Press, 2017.

Osten-Sacken, Peter. *Gott und Belial: traditionsgeschichtliche Untersuchungen zum Dualismus in den Texten aus Qumran*. SUNT 6. Göttingen: Vandenhoeck & Ruprecht, 1969.

Oswalt, John N. *The Book of Isaiah: Chapters 1–39*. NICOT. Grand Rapids: Eerdmans, 1986.

Owens, J. Edward. "Asmodeus: A Less Than Minor Character in the Book of Tobit: A Narrative-Critical Study." Pages 277–290 in *Angels: The Concept of Celestial Beings – Origins, Development and Reception*. Edited by Friedrich V. Reiterer, Tobias Nicklas, and Karen Schöpflin. DCLY. New York: de Gruyter, 2007.

Palmer, Carmen. *Converts in the Dead Sea Scrolls: Gēr and Mutable* Ethnicity. STDJ 126. Leiden: Brill, 2018.

Pantoja, Jennifer Metten. *The Metaphor of the Divine Planter: Stinking Grapes or Pleasant Planting?* BibInt 155. Leiden: Brill, 2017.

Penner, Ken M. "Realized or Future Salvation in the Hodayot." *JBS* 5 (2002): 1–49.

Perrin, Andrew B. "An Almanac of Tobit Studies: 2000–2014." *CurBR* 13 (2014): 107–142.

–. "Another Look at Dualism in *4QVisions of Amram*." *Hen* 36 (2014): 106–117.

–. "From Lingua Franca to Lingua Sacra: The Scripuralization of Tobit in 4QTobᵉ." *VT* 66 (2016): 117–132.

–. *The Dynamics of Dream-Vision Revelations in the Aramaic Dead Sea Scrolls*. JAJSup 19. Göttingen: Vandenhoeck & Ruprecht, 2015.

–. "The Textual Forms of Aramaic Levi Document at Qumran." Pages 431–452 in *Reading the Bible in Ancient Traditions and Modern Editions: Studies in Memory of Peter W. Flint*. Edited by idem, Kyung S. Baek, and Daniel K. Falk. EJL 47. Atlanta: SBL Press, 2017.

–. "Tobit's Contexts and Contacts in the Qumran Aramaic Anthology." *JSP* 25 (2015): 23–51.

Pope, Marvin H. *El in the Ugaritic Texts*. VTSup 2. Leiden: Brill, 1955.

Popovic, Mladen. "Anthropology, Pneumatology, and Demonology in Early Judaism: The Two Spirits Treatise (1qs iii, 13–iv, 26) and Other Texts from the Dead Sea Scrolls." Pages 58–98 in *Dust of the Ground and Breath of Life (Gen 2:7) – The Problem of a Dualistic Anthropology in Early Judaism and Christianity*. Edited by Jacques T.A.G.M. van Ruiten and George H. van Kooten. TBN 20. Leiden: Brill, 2016.

–. "Light and Darkness in the Treatise on the Two Spirits (1QS III 13–IV 26) and in 4Q186." Pages 148–165 in *Dualism in Qumran*. Edited by Geza G. Xeravits. LSTS 76. London: Continuum, 2010.

–. *Reading the Human Body: Physiognomics and Astrology in the Dead Sea Scrolls and Hellenistic-Early Roman Period Judaism*. STDJ 67. Leiden: Brill, 2007.

Porter, Paul A. *Metaphors and Monsters: A Literary-Critical Study of Daniel 7 and 8*. CB. Lund: C. W. K. Gleerup, 1983.

Poythress, Vern S. "The Holy Ones of the Most High in Daniel VII." *VT* 26 (1976): 208–213.

Pritchard, James B., ed. *Ancient Near Eastern Texts Relating to the Old Testament*. Third Edition. Princeton: Princeton University Press, 1969.

Puech, Emile. "Fragment d'une Apocalypse en Arameen (4Q246 = pseudo-Dan[d]) et le 'Royaume de Dieu.'" *RB* 99 (1992): 98–131.

–. *La Croyance des Esséniens en al vie future: Immoralité, resurrection, vie éternelle? Historie d'une croyance dans le judaïsme ancien*. 2 volumes. Paris: J. Gabalda, 1993.

–. "Notes sur le fragment d'apocalypse 4Q246 – 'le fils de Dieu'." *RB* 101 (1994): 533–558.

–. "Notes sur le manuscript de 11Qmelkîsédek." *RevQ* 12 (1987): 483–513.

–. "Quelques aspects de la restauration du Rouleau des Hymns (1QH)." *JJS* 39 (1988): 38–55.

Putthoff, Tyson L. *Ontological Aspects of Early Jewish Anthropology*. BRLJ 53. Leiden: Brill, 2016.

Qimchi, David. *Tehillim* in *Miqraot Gedolot*. Reprinted with partial English translation in A. J. Rosenberg, *Psalms*. 3 volumes. New York: Judaica, 1991.

Qimron, Elisha. "A Review Article of the *Songs of the Sabbath Sacrifice: A Critical Edition*, by Carol Newsom." *HTR* 79 (1986): 349–371.

–. *The Dead Sea Scrolls: The Hebrew Writings, Volume 2*. Jerusalem: Yad Ben-Zvi Press, 2013.

–. *The Hebrew of the Dead Sea Scrolls*. HSS 29. Cambridge: Harvard University Press, 1986. Reprinted by Winona Lake: Eisenbrauns, 2008.

Rainbow, Paul. "Melchizedek as Messiah at Qumran." *BBR* 7 (1997): 179–194.

Reed, Annette Yoshiko. *Fallen Angels and the History of Judaism and Christianity: The Reception of the Enochic Literature*. New York: Cambridge University Press, 2005.

Regev, Eyal. "The Ram and Qumran: The Eschatological Character of the Ram in the Animal Apocalypse (1 En. 90:1–13)." Pages 181–195 in *Apocalyptic Thinking in Early Judaism: Engaging with John Collins' The Apocalyptic Imagination*. Edited by Cecilia Wassén and Sidnie White Crawford. JSJSup 182. Leiden: Brill, 2018.

Rey, Jean-Sébastien. *4QInstruction: Sagesse et eschatologie*. STDJ 81. Leiden: Brill, 2009.

Richardson, H. Neil. "The Book of Tobit." Pages 526–534 in *The Interpreter's One-Volume Commentary on the Bible*. Edited by Charles M. Laymon. Nashville: Abingdon, 1971.

Rietz, Henry W. Morisada. "Identifying Compositions and Traditions of the Qumran Community: The Songs of the Sabbath Sacrifice as a Test Case." Pages 29–52 in *Qumran Studies: New Approaches, New Questions*. Edited by Michael T. Davis and Brent A. Strawn. Grand Rapids: Eerdmans, 2007.

Ringrenn, Helmer. *The Faith of Qumran: Theology of the Dead Sea Scrolls*. Philadelphia: Fortress, 1963.

Rofé, Alexander. *Angels in the Bible: Israelite Belief as Evidence by Biblical Traditions*. Second Edition: Jerusalem: Carmel, 2012, xii.

–. "The End of the Song of Moses (Deuteronomy 32:43)." Pages 164–172 in *Liebe und Gebot: Studien zum Deuteronomium*. Edited by Reinhard G. Kratz et al. Göttingen: Vandenhoeck & Ruprecht, 2000.

Roggia, R. G. "Alcune osservationioni sul culto di El a Ras-Samra." *Aevum* 15 (1941): 559–575.

Rohland, Johannes P. *Der Erzengel Michael*. BZRGG 19. Leiden: Brill, 1977.

Rokay, Zoltan. "Vom Stadttor zu den Verhöfen." *ZKT* 116 (1994): 457–63.

Rowland, Christoper. *The Open Heaven: A Study of Apocalyptic in Judaism and Early Christianity*. London: SPCK, 1982.

Russell, D. S. *The Method and Message of Jewish Apocalyptic: 200 BC–100 AD*. OTL. Louisville: Westminster, 1964.

Sanders, E. P. *Paul and Palestinian Judaism: A Comparison of Patterns of Religion*. Minneapolis: Fortress, 1977.

Sanders, Paul. *The Provenance of Deuteronomy 32*. OTS 37. Leiden: Brill, 1996.

Scacewater, Todd. "The Literary Unity of 1QM and its Three-Stage War." *RevQ* 27 (2015): 225–248.

Schäfer, Peter. *The Origins of Jewish Mysticism*. Tübingen: Mohr Siebeck, 2009.

Schiffman, Lawrence H. "A Qumran Temple: The Literary Evidence." *JAJ* 7 (2016): 71–85.

–. *Halakah at Qumran*. SJLA 16. Leiden: Brill, 1975.

–. "The Dead Sea Scrolls and the Early History of Jewish Liturgy." Pages 33–48 in *The Synagogue in Late Antiquity*. Edited by Lee I. Levine. Philadelphia: American Schools of Oriental Research, 1987.

–. *The Eschatological Community of the Dead Sea Scrolls: A Study of the Rule of the Congregation*. SBLMS 38. Atlanta: Scholars Press, 1989.

Schiffman, Lawrence H. and James C. VanderKam, eds. *The Encyclopedia of the Dead Sea Scrolls*. 2 volumes. Leiden: Brill, 2001.

Schmidt, N. "The Son of Man in the Book of Daniel." *JBL* 19 (1900): 22–28.

Schnabel, Eckhard J. Review of Gabriele Boccaccini, *Beyond the Essene Hypothesis*. *RBL* (2000).

Schofield, Alison. *From Qumran to the Yahad: A New Paradigm of Textual Development for The Community Rule*. STDJ 77. Leiden: Brill, 2009.

Scholem, Gershom G. *Jewish Gnosticism, Merkavah Mysticism, and Talmudic Tradition*. New York: Jewish Theological Seminary, 1960.

–. Gershom G. *Major Trends in Jewish Mysticism*. New York: Schocken Books, 1954.

Scholen, J. D. "The Exile of Disinherited Kin in *KTU* 1.12 and *KTU* 1.23." *JNES* 52 (1993): 209–220.

Schuller, Eileen M. "4Q372 I: A Prayer About Joseph." *RevQ* 14 (1990): 349–376.

–. "A Hymn from a Cave Four *Hodayot* Manuscript: 4Q427 7 i + ii." *JBL* 113 (1993): 605–628.

–. "Petitionary Prayer and the Religion of Qumran." Pages 29–45 in *Religion in the Dead Sea Scrolls*. Edited by John J. Collins and Robert A. Kugler. SDSSRL. Grand Rapids: Eerdmans, 2000.

–. "Recent Scholarship on the Hodayot." *CurBR* 10 (2011): 119–162.

Schuller, Eileen M. and Lorenzo DiTammaso. "A Bibliography of the Hodayot, 1948–1996." *DSD* 4 (1997): 55–101.

Schultz, Brian. *Conquering the World: The War Scroll (1QM) Reconsidered*. STDJ 76. Leiden: Brill, 2009.

Scott, James M. *On Earth as It Is in Heaven: The Restoration of Sacred Time and Sacred Space in the Book of Jubilees*. JSJSup 91. Leiden: Brill, 2005.

Screnock, John. "Word Order in the War Scroll (1QM) and Its Implications for Interpretation." *DSD* 18 (2011): 29–44.

Segal, Michael. *Dreams, Riddles, and Visions: Textual, Contextual, and Intertextual Approaches to the Book of Daniel*. BZAW 455. Berlin: DeGruyter, 2016.

–. "Monotheism and Angelology in Daniel." Pages 405–420 in *One God – One Cult – One Nation: Archaeology and Biblical Perspectives*. Edited by Reinhard G. Kratz and Hermann Spieckmann. BZAW 405. Berlin: de Gruyter, 2010.

–. *The Book of Jubilees: Rewritten Bible, Redaction, Ideology, and Theology*. JSJSup 177. Leiden: Brill, 2007.

–. "Who is the 'Son of God' in 4Q246? An Overlooked Example of Early Biblical Interpretation." *DSD* 21 (2014): 289–312.

Seitz, Christopher R. "The Divine Council: Temporal Transition and New Prophecy in the Book of Isaiah." *JBL* 109 (1990): 229–247.

–. *Zion's Final Destiny: The Development of the Book of Isaiah: A Reassessment of Isaiah 36–39*. Minneapolis: Fortress, 1991.

Sekki, Arthur E. *The Meaning of Ruah at Qumran*. SBLDS 110. Atlanta: Scholars Press, 1989.

Seow, C. L. "Face פנים." *DDD* 322–325.

Seybold, Klaus. *Das Gebet des Kranken im Alten Testament: Untersuchungen zur Bestimmung und Zuordnung der Krankheits – und Heilungspsalmen*. BWANT 19. Stuttgart: Kohlhammer, 1973.

Shaked, Shaul. "Qumran and Iran: Further Considerations." *IOS* 2 (1972): 433–446.

Sloan, David B. Review of Michael S. Heiser, *The Unseen Realm: Recovering the Supernatural Worldview of the Bible*, *RBL* (2018).

Smith, Mark S. and Wayne T. Pitard. *The Ugaritic Baal Cycle: Volume II: Introduction with Text, Translation and Commentary of KTU/CAT 1.3–1.4*. VTSup 114. Leiden: Brill, 2009.

Smith, Mark S. *God in Translation: Deities in Cross-Cultural Discourse in the Biblical Word* (Grand Rapids: Eerdmans, 2008.

–. *The Early History of God: Yahweh and the Other Deities in Ancient Israel*. Second Edition. Grand Rapids: Eerdmans, 2002.

–. *The Origins of Biblical Monotheism: Israel's Polytheistic Background and the Ugaritic Texts*. New York: Oxford University Press, 2000.

–. *The Ugaritic Baal Cycle: Volume I: Introduction with Texts, Translation and Commentary of KTU 1.1–1.2*. VTSup 55. Leiden: Brill, 1994.

Smith, Morton. "Ascent to the Heavens and Deification in 4QM[a]." Pages 181–188 in *Archaeology and History in the Dead Sea Scrolls: The New York University Conference in the Memory of Yigael Yadin*. Edited by Lawrence H. Schiffman. JSOT/ASORMS 2. JSPSup 8. Sheffield: JSOT Press, 1990.

–. "Two Ascended to Heaven." Pages 290–301 in *Jesus and the Dead Sea Scrolls*. Edited by James H. Charlesworth. ABRL. New York: Doubleday, 1990.

Soggin, J. Alberto. "The Conquest of Jericho through Battle." *EI* 16 (1982): 216.

Sperling, S. D. "Belial בליעל." *DDD* 169–171.

Stegemann, Hartmut. "Rekonstruktion der Hodajot: Ursprüngliche Gestalt und kritisch bearbeiteter Text der Hymnenrolle aus Höhle 1 von Qumran. Ph.D. dissertation. University of Heidelberg, 1963.

–. "Some Remarks to 1QSa, to 1QSb, and to Qumran Messianism." *RevQ* 17 (1996): 479–505.

–. *The Library of Qumran: On the Essenes, John the Baptist and Jesus*. Grand Rapids: Eerdmans, 1998.

–. "The Material Reconstruction of 1QHodayot." Pages 272–284 in *The Dead Sea Scrolls: Fifty Years after their Discovery. Proceedings of the Jerusalem Congress, July 20–25,*

1997. Edited by Lawrence H. Schiffman and Emmaunel Tov. Jerusalem: Israel Exploration Society in cooperation with the Shrine of the Book, Israel Museum, 2000.

Stettler, Christian. "Astronomische Vorstellungen in den Sabbatopferliedern." Pages 99–117 in *Gottesdienst und Engel im antiken Judentum und frühen Christentum*. Edited by Jörg Frey and Michael R. Jost. WUNT 2/446. Tübingen: Mohr Siebeck, 2017.

Steudel, Annette. "אחרית הימים" in the Texts from Qumran." *RevQ* 16 (1993): 225–246.

–. "Biblical Warfare Legislation in the War Scroll (1QM VII:1–7 and X:1–8)." Pages 183–192 in *The Reception of Biblical War Legislation in Narrative Contexts*. Edited by Christoph Berner and Harald Samuel. BZAW 460. Berlin: De Gruyter, 2015.

–. "The Eternal Reign of the People of God – Collective Expectation in Qumran Texts (4Q246 and 1QM)." *RevQ* 17 (1996): 509–521.

Stokes, Ryan E. "The Throne Visions of Daniel 7, *1 Enoch* 14, the Qumran *Book of Giants* (4Q530): An Analysis of their Literary Relationship." *DSD* 15 (2008): 340–358.

–. "What is a Demon, What is an Evil Spirit, and What is a Satan?" Pages 259–272 in *Das Böse, der Teufel und Dämonen – Evil, the Devil, and Demons*. Edited by Jan Dochhorn, Susanne Rudnig-Zelt, and Benjamin Wold. Pages 259–272. WUNT 2/412. Tübingen: Mohr Siebeck, 2017.

Stone, Michael E. "Enoch, Aramaic Levi, and Sectarian Origins." *JSJ* 19 (1988): 159–170.

–. "Enoch and the Fall of the Angels." *DSD* 22 (2015): 342–357.

Strawn, Brent A. and Henry W. Morisada Rietz. "(More) Sectarian Terminology." Pages 53–64 in *Qumran Studies: New Approaches, New Questions*. Edited by Michael T. Davis and Brent A. Strawn. Grand Rapids: Eerdmans, 2007.

Stuckenbruck, Loren T. *1 Enoch 91–108*. CEJL. New York: de Gruyter, 2007.

–. "4QInstruction and the Possible Influence of Early Enochic Traditions: An Evaluation." Pages 246–261 in *The Wisdom Texts from Qumran and the Development of Sapiential Thought*. Edited by Charlotte Hempel, Armin Lange, and Herman Lichtenberger. BETL 69. Leuven: Leuven University Press, 2002.

–. *Angel Veneration and Christology: A Study in Early Judaism and in the Christology of the Apocalypse of John*. WUNT 2/70. Tübingen: Mohr Siebeck, 1995.

–. "'Angels' and 'God': Exploring the Limits of Early Jewish Monotheism." Pages 45–70 in *Early Jewish and Christian Monotheism*. Edited by Loren T. Stuckenbruck and Wendy E. S. North. JSNTSup 263. London: T & T Clark, 2005.

–. "Coping with Alienating Experience: Four Strategies in Second Temple Texts." Pages 57–83 in *Rejection: God's Refugees in Biblical and Contemporary Perspective*. Edited by Stanley E. Porter. Eugene: Pickwick Publications, 2015.

–. "Daniel and Early Enoch Traditions in the Dead Sea Scrolls." Pages 368–386 in *The Book of Daniel: Composition and Reception*. Edited by John J. Collins and Peter W. Flint. VTSup 83.2. Leiden: Brill, 2001.

–. "'One like a Son of Man as the Ancient of Days' in the Old Greek Recension of Daniel 7, 13: Scribal Error or Theological Translation?" *ZNW* 86 (1995): 268–276.

–. "The Interiorization of Dualism within the Human Being in Second Temple Judaism: The Treatise of the Two Spirits (1QS III:13-IV:26) in its Tradition-Historical Context." Pages 145–168 in *Light Against Darkness: Dualism in Ancient Mediterranean Religion and the Contemporary World*. Edited by Armin Lange et al. JAJSup 2. Göttingen: Vandenhoeck & Ruprecht, 2011.

–. "The 'Otherworld' and the Epistle of Enoch." Pages 79–94 in *Other Worlds and Their Relation to This World: Early Jewish and Ancient Christian Traditions*. Edited by Tobias Nicklas et al. JSJSup 143. Leiden: Brill, 2010.

–. "Theological Anthropology and the Enochic Book of Watchers (1 En. 6–16)." Pages 16–35 in *Dust of the Ground and Breath of Life (Gen 2:7) – The Problem of a Dualistic Anthropology in Early Judaism and* Christianity. Edited by Jacques T.A.G.M. van Ruiten and George H. van Kooten. TBN 20. Leiden: Brill, 2016.

Sukenik, Eleazar. *Otzar ha-Megillot ha-Genuzot*. Jerusalem: Bialik, 1954.

–. *The Dead Sea Scrolls of the Hebrew University*. Jerusalem: Magnes Press/The Hebrew University, 1955.

Sullivan, Kevin P. *Wrestling with Angels: A Study of the Relationship between Angels and Humans in Ancient Jewish Literature and the New Testament*. AJEC 55. Leiden: Brill, 2004.

Suter, David. "Fallen Angel, Fallen Priest: The Problem of Family Purity in 1 Enoch 6–16." *HUCA* 50 (1979): 115–135.

Swartz, Michael D. "The Dead Sea Scrolls and Later Jewish Magic and Mysticism." *DSD* 8 (2001): 182–190.

Swarup, Paul. *The Self-Understanding of the Dead Sea Scrolls Community: An Eternal Planting, A House of Holiness*. LSTS 59. London: T & T Clark, 2006.

Sweeny, Marvin A. *I & II Kings: A Commentary*. OTL. Louisville: Westminster John Knox, 2007.

–. *Isaiah 1–39 with an Introduction to Prophetic Literature*. FOTL 16. Grand Rapids: Eerdmans, 1996.

Talmon, Shemaryahu. "The Community of the Renewed Covenant: Between Judaism and Christianity." Pages 3–24 in *The Community of the Renewed Covenant*. Edited by Eugene Ulrich and James C. VanderKam. CJAS 10. Notre Dame: University of Notre Dame Press, 1994.

Tanzer, Sara J. "The Sages at Qumran: Wisdom in the 'Hodayot.'" Ph.D. diss., Harvard University, 1986.

Terrien, Samuel. *The Psalms*. Grand Rapids: Eerdmans, 2002.

Tervanotko, Hanna. "A Trilogy of Testaments? The Status of the Testament of Qahat Versus Texts Attributed to Levi and Amram." Pages 41–59 in *Old Testament Pseudepigrapha and the Scriptures*. Edited by Eibert J. C. Tigchelaar. BETL 270. Leuven: Peeters, 2014.

–. "Visions, Otherworldly Journeys and Divine Beings." Pages 210–240 in *Crossing Imaginary Boundaries: The Dead Sea Scrolls in the Context of Second Temple* Judaism. Edited by Mika Pajunen and Hanna Tervanotko. Helsinki: The Finnish Exegetical Society, 2015.

Testuz, Michel. *Les idées religieuses du Livre des Jubilés*. Geneve: Droz, 1960.

Tigay, Jeffrey. *Deuteronomy: The Traditional Hebrew Text with the New JPS Translation*. JPSTC. Philadelphia: Jewish Publication Society, 1996.

Tigchelaar, Eibert J. C. "The Imaginal Context and the Visionary of the Aramaic New Jerusalem." Pages 257–270 in *Flores Florentino: Dead Sea Scrolls and Other Early Jewish Studies in Honour of Florentino García Martínez*. Edited by A. Hilhorst et al. JSJSup 122. Leiden: Brill, 2007.

–. *To Increase Learning for the Understanding Ones: Reading and Reconstructing the Fragmentary Early Jewish Sapiential Text 4QInstruction*. STDJ 44. Leiden: Brill, 2001.

Tiller, Paul A. *The Animal Apocalypse of 1 Enoch: A Commentary on the Animal Apocalypse of 1 Enoch*. EJL 4. Atlanta: Scholars Press, 1993.

–. "The 'Eternal Planting' in the Dead Sea Scrolls." *DSD* 4 (1997): 312–335.

Torrey, C. C. "Alexander Jannaeus and the Archangel Michael." *VT* 4 (1954): 208–211.

Tov, Emmanuel. *Textual Criticism of the Hebrew Bible*. Third Edition. Minneapolis: Augsburg Fortress Press, 2012.

Trotter, Jonathan R. "The Tradition of the Throne Vision in the Second Temple Period: Daniel 7:9–10, *1 Enoch* 14:18–23, and the *Book of Giants* (4Q530)." *RevQ* 25 (2012): 451–466.

Tsevat, Matitiahu. "God and the Gods in Assembly." *HUCA* 40–41 (1969–70): 129–130.

Tucker, Ferda S. "Naming the Messiah: A Contribution to 4Q246 'Son of God' Debate." *DSD* 12 (2014): 150–175.

Tuschling, R. M. M. *Angels and Orthodoxy: A Study of the Development in Syria and Palestine from the Qumran Texts to Ephrem the Syrian*. STAC 40. Tübingen: Mohr Siebeck, 2007.

Ulrich, Eugene. "The Text of Daniel in the Qumran Scrolls." Pages 573–585 in *The Book of Daniel: Composition and Reception*. Edited by John J Collins and Peter W. Flint. VTSup 83.2. Leiden: Brill, 2001.

Van de Water, Rick. "Michael or Yhwh? Toward Identifying Melchizedek in 11Q13." *JSP* 16 (2006): 75–86.

Van der Kooij, A. "Ancient Emendations in MT." Pages 152–159 in *L'Ecrit et L'Espirit: Etudes d'histoire du texte et de théologie biblique en homage a Adrian Schenker*. Edited by Dieter Böhler, I. Imbaza, and P. Hugo. Göttingen: Vandenhoeck & Ruprecht, 2005.

Van der Ploeg, Jan. *Le Rouleau de la Guerre: Traduit et Annoté avec une Introduction*. STDJ 2. Leiden: Brill, 1959.

Van der Toorn, Karel, Bob Becking, and Pieter W. van der Horst, eds. *Dictionary of Deities and Demons in the Bible*. Second Edition, Extensively Revised. Leiden: Brill, 1999.

Van der Woude, Adam S. "Melchisedek als himmlische Erlösergestalt in den neugefundenen eschatologischen Midraschim aus Qumran Höhle XL." *OtSt* 14 (1965): 354–373.

Van Ruiten, Jan Jacques T.A.G.M. "Angels and Demons in the Book of Jubilees." Pages 585–609 in *Angels: The Concept of Celestial Beings: Origins, Development and Reception*. Edited by Friedrich V. Reiterer, Tobias Nicklas, and Karen Schöpflin. DCLY. New York: de Gruyter, 2007.

VanderKam, James C. *Enoch and the Growth of an Apocalyptic Tradition*. CBQMS 16. Washington: The Catholic Biblical Association of America, 1984.

–. *Jubilees 1–21: A Commentary on the Book of Jubilees Chapters 1–21*. Hermeneia. Minneapolis: Fortress Press, 2018.

–. *Jubilees 22–50: A Commentary on Jubilees Chapters 22–50*. Hermeneia. Minneapolis: Fortress, 2018.

–. "The Angel of the Presence in the Book of Jubilees." *DSD* 7 (2000): 378–393.

–. *The Book of Jubilees*. GAP. Sheffield: Sheffield Academic Press, 2001.

–. *The Dead Sea Scrolls Today*. Second Edition. Grand Rapids: Eerdmans, 2010.

–. "The Theophany of 1 Enoch 1:3b–7, 9." *VT* 23 (1973): 136–38.

Vermes, Géza. *Les manuscrits du desert de Juda*. Paris: Desclée, 1954.

Von Rad, Gerhard. *Deuteronomy*. Second Revised Edition. OTL. Atlanta: Westminster, 1966.

Wacholder, Ben Zion. "The Ancient Judaeo-Aramaic Literature (500–164 BCE): A Classification of Pre-Qumranic Texts." Pages 257–281 in *Archaeology and History in the Dead Sea Scrolls: The New York University Conference in the Memory of Yigael Yadin*. Edited by Lawrence H. Schiffman. JSOT/ASORMS 2. JSPSup 8. Sheffield: JSOT Press, 1990.

Walsh, Matthew L. "Dead Sea Scrolls: Son of God Text (4Q246)." Pages 141–143 in *The Encyclopedia of the Historical Jesus*. Edited by Craig A. Evans. New York: Routledge Press, 2008.

–. "'The Holy Ones' as a Christian Self-Designation: A Contextual Comparison of the Dead Sea Scrolls and the Pauline Corpus." Paper presented at the Annual Meeting of the IBR, Denver, CO, 16 November 2018.

Waltke, Bruce K. and M. O'Connor. *An Introduction to Biblical Hebrew Syntax.* Winona Lake: Eisenbrauns, 1988.

Wassén, Cecilia. "Angels in the Dead Sea Scrolls." Pages 499–523 in *Angels: The Concept of Celestial Beings: Origins, Development and Reception.* Edited by Friedrich V. Reiterer, Tobias Nicklas, and Karen Schöpflin. DCLY. New York: de Gruyter, 2007.

–. "Good and Bad Angels in the Construction of Identity in the Qumran Movement. Pages 71–97 in *Gottesdienst und Engel im antiken Judentum und frühen Christentum.* Edited by Jörg Frey and Michael R. Jost. WUNT 2/446. Tübingen: Mohr Siebeck, 2017.

–. "Women, Worship, Wilderness, and War: Celibacy and the Constructions of Identity in the Dead Sea Scrolls." Pages 1361–1385 in *Sibyls, Scriptures, and Scrolls: John Collins at Seventy.* Edited by Joel Baden, Hindy Najman, Eibert Tigchelaar. JSJSup 175. Leiden: Brill, 2016.

Weinfeld, Moshe. *Deuteronomy 1–11: A New Translation with Introduction and Commentary.* AB 5. New York: Doubleday, 1995.

–. *Normative and Sectarian Judaism in the Second Temple Period.* LSTS 54. London: T & T Clark, 2005.

Wells, Kyle B. *Grace and Agency in Paul and Second Temple Judaism: Interpreting the Transformation of the Heart.* VTSup 157. Leiden: Brill, 2015.

Wernberg-Møller, Preben. "A Reconsideration of the Two Spirits in the Rule of the Community (1Q Serke 3:13–4:26)." *RevQ* (1961): 413–431.

–. *The Manual of Discipline: Translated and Annotated with an Introduction.* STDJ 1. Leiden: Brill, 1957.

Werner, Martin. *Die Entstehung des christlichen Dogma.* Tübingen: Katzmann, 1941.

Werrett, Ian and Stephen Parker. "Purity in War: What is it Good for?" Pages 275–294 in *The War Scroll, Violence, War and Peace in the Dead Sea Scrolls and Related Literature: Essays in Honour of Martin G. Abegg on the Occasion of His 65th Birthday.* Edited by Kipp Davis et al. STDJ 115. Leiden: Brill, 2015.

White Crawford, Sidnie and Cecilia Wassén, eds. *The Dead Sea Scrolls at Qumran and the Concept of a Library.* STDJ 116. Leiden: Brill, 2015.

White, Ellen. *Yahweh's Council: Its Structure and Membership.* FAT 2/65. Tübingen: Mohr Siebeck, 2014.

Wifall, Walter. "The Status of 'Man' as Resurrection." *ZAW* 90 (1978): 382–394.

Wildberger, Hans. *Isaiah 13–27.* CC. Minneapolis: Fortress Press, 1997.

Wise, Michael O. "מי כמוני באלים: A Study of 4Q491c, 4Q471b, 4Q427 7, and 1QH[a] 25:35–26:10." *DSD* 7 (2000): 173–219.

–. "The Concept of a New Covenant in the Teacher Hymns from Qumran (1QH[a] X–XVII)." Pages 99–128 in *The Concept of Covenant in the Second Temple.* Edited by Stanley E. Porter and Jacqueline C. de Roo. JSJSup 71. Leiden: Brill, 2003.

–. *The First Messiah: Investigating the Messiah before Jesus.* San Francisco: Harper, 1999.

Wold, Benjamin G. "Demonizing Sin? The Evil Inclination in 4QInstruction." Pages 34–48 in *Evil in Second Temple Judaism and Early* Christianity. Edited by Chris Keith and Loren T. Stuckenbruck. WUNT 2/417. Tübingen: Mohr Siebeck, 2016.

–. "Jesus Among Wisdom's Representatives: 4QInstruction." Pages 317–335 in *Enoch and the Synoptic Gospels: Reminiscences, Allusions, Intertextuality.* Edited by Loren T. Stuckenbruck and Gabriele Boccaccini. EJL 44. Atlanta: SBL Press, 2016.

–. *Women, Men, and Angels: The Qumran Wisdom Document Musar LeMevin and its Allusions to Genesis Creation* Traditions. WUNT 2/201. Tübingen: Mohr Siebeck, 2005.

Wolfson, Elliot R. "Mysticism and the Poetic-Liturgical Compositions from Qumran: A Response to Bilhah Nitzan." *JQR* 85 (1994): 185–202.

–. "Seven Mysteries of Knowledge: Qumran E/Soterism Recovered." Pages 177–213 in *The Idea of Biblical Interpretation: Essays in Honor of James L. Kugel*. Edited by Hindy Najman and Judith H. Newman. JSJSup 83. Leiden: Brill, 2003.

Xeravits, Geza G. *King, Priest, Prophet: Positive Eschatological Protagonists of the Qumran Library*. STDJ 47. Leiden: Brill, 2003.

–. "The Angel's Self-Revelation in Tobit 12." Pages 1399–1417 in *Sibyls, Scriptures, and Scrolls: John Collins at Seventy*. Edited by Joel Baden, Hindy Najman, and Eibert Tigchelaar. JSJSup 175. Leiden: Brill, 2016.

Yadin, Yigael. *The Scroll of the War of the Sons of Light against the Sons of Darkness*. Translated by Batya and Chaim Rabin. Oxford: Oxford University Press, 1962.

Yardeni, A. and B. Elitzur. "Document: A First Century BCE Prophetic Text Written on Stone: First Publication." *Cathedra* 123 (2007): 55–66.

Yuditsky A. and Elisha Qimron. "Notes on the Inscription, 'The Vision of Gabriel." *Cathedra* 133 (2009): 133–144.

Zacharias, H. Daniel. "Old Greek Daniel 7:13–14 and Matthew's Son of Man." *BBR* 21 (2011): 453–461.

Zehnder, Markus. "Why the Danielic 'Son of Man' Is a Divine Being." *BBR* 24 (2014): 331–347.

Zevit, Ziony. "The Exegetical Implications of Daniel viii 1, ix 21." *VT* 28 (1978): 488–492.

–. "The Structure and Individual elements of Daniel 7." *ZAW* 80 (1960): 394–396.

Zilm, Jennifer. "Multi-Coloured Like Woven Works: Gender, Ritual Clothing and Praying with the Angels in the Dead Sea Scrolls and the Testament of Job." Pages 435–449 in *Prayer and Poetry in the Dead Sea Scrolls and Related Literature: Essays in Honor of Eileen Schuller on the Occasion of Her 65th Birthday*. Edited by Jeremy Penner, Ken M. Penner, and Cecilia Wassén. STDJ 98. Leiden: Brill, 2012.

Zimmermann, Johannes. *Messianische Texte aus Qumran: Königliche, priesterliche und prophetische Messiasvorstellungen in den Schriftfunden von Qumran*. WUNT 2/104. Tübingen: Mohr Siebeck, 1998.

–. "Observations on 4Q246 – The 'Son of God.'" Pages 175–190 in *Qumran-Messianism*. Edited by James H. Charlesworth, Hermann Lichtenberger, and Gerbern S. Oegema. Tübingen: Mohr Siebeck, 1998.

Index of Ancient Sources

ANE and Other Texts

Hebrew Bible and LXX

20:8 (LXX)	87	33:5	46
29:11 (LXX)	89, 112	35:3	78, 141
30:16 (LXX)	87	35:10 (LXX)	87
30:22	78	35:15	214, 253
30:27	51, 260, 276		
32:9	199, 257		

Apocrypha/Deuterocanonical Writings

1 Maccabees

		Sirach	
1:37	87	7:30	112
2:42	15	17:17	48, 80, 86, 132, 276
4:30–35	101	45:6–25	260
5	127	50:7	261
7:13	15	50:14	108
7:41	187	51:1–24	260
9:23	194		
		Tobit	
2 Maccabees		3:16	124
3:22–26	187	3:17	124
5:2–4	187	5–12	147
10:29–30	187, 206	6:16–17	124
11:6–12	101, 187	7:11–13	124
14:6	15	8:3	123
15:22–24	187	11:14	6
		12:12–15	124–125, 277
		12:15	148, 215, 278
4 Ezra		13:15–17	125
13:26	65		

Pseudepigrapha

1 Enoch

		9:1–11	87
1–5	97	9:4	87, 232
1–36	83, 84–97	9:17	106
1:1–9	92, 93, 97	10	95, 99
1:4	92	10:1–15	116, 123, 148, 277, 278
1:9	147, 184, 277	10:4–15	92
6–16	63, 92, 96	10:11–11:2	88
6:2	206	10:16	95, 96, 108, 130, 136
6:3–8:3	84		
6:7	86	10:20	96
8:4–10:22	124, 277	10:21	96, 278
9–10	102	12–16	91, 97
9–16	87	12:1–2	84
9:1	84, 86–88		

Dead Sea Scrolls

IX, 9–41	196
IX, 21	240
IX, 23	210
IX, 23–29	207
IX, 28–32	240
X–XIX	204
X, 11–12	246
X, 15	211
X, 19	248
X, 20	223, 224, 273
XI, 6–19	205, 218
XI, 19–37	213
XI, 20	209, 215
XI, 20–24	3, 22, 66, 205, 208, 209, 211, 212, 214, 216, 271, 279, 282
XI, 20–37	205, 209
XI, 21	212
XI, 22	214, 239, 253, 255, 266, 280
XI, 22–23	66, 175, 208, 210, 214, 253, 266
XI, 22–24	210, 239, 241
XI, 23	217, 218, 253
XI, 23–24	206, 223, 246, 273
XI, 24	212, 218, 240, 280
XI, 24–26	207
XI, 35–36	231
XI, 36	210
XI, 40	210
XII, 8	211
XII, 23	264
XIII, 22–XV, 8	214, 224
XIII, 23	210
XIII, 24–25	224
XIV, 9	246
XIV, 11–12	222
XIV, 15–16	214, 215, 224, 246, 273
XIV, 15–18	221
XIV, 16	54, 210, 219, 221, 222, 229, 243, 253, 271, 276, 279, 282
XIV, 16–21	280
XIV, 17	280
XIV, 17–21	222, 278
XIV, 20–21	223
XIV, 21	223
XIV, 29	223

XIV, 29–38	224
XIV, 33	210
XIV, 36	210
XV, 27	205
XV, 31–32	196
XVI, 12	210
XVIII, 8	196
XVIII, 10	74
XVIII, 26	210
XVIII, 29–30	135
XVIII, 36	210
XIX, 5	264
XIX, 6	206
XIX, 13–17	3, 22, 66, 206, 208, 212, 216, 271, 279, 282
XIX, 14	210
XIX, 14–15	175, 206, 219, 257
XIX, 14–16	211, 219, 280
XIX, 15	214, 255
XIX, 16	206, 207, 214, 215, 219, 220, 253, 280
XIX, 16–17	209, 246, 266, 273
XIX, 17	212, 218, 223, 278, 280
XIX, 18	206
XIX, 22–25	207
XIX, 28–29	212
XX–XXVIII	204
XX, 1	205
XX, 6	206
XX, 14	142
XXIII, 30	219
XXV, 26	214
XXV, 32	214
XXV, 34–XXVII, 3	262, 270

1QM (War Scroll)

	210, 277
I	188, 189, 194, 196
I, 1	182, 278
I, 1–4	190
I, 1–15	210
I, 2	190, 191, 193
I, 3	182, 191, 193, 194
I, 5	182, 190
I, 5–14	200
I, 6	200
I, 8–9	179, 208, 253

Josephus

Philo

Pliny the Elder

New Testament

Eusebius

Rabbinic Literature

Index of Modern Authors

Index of Subjects

Wissenschaftliche Untersuchungen zum Neuen Testament

Edited by Jörg Frey (Zürich)

Associate Editors:

Markus Bockmuehl (Oxford) · James A. Kelhoffer (Uppsala)
Tobias Nicklas (Regensburg) · Janet Spittler (Charlottesville, VA)
J. Ross Wagner (Durham, NC)

WUNT I is an international series dealing with the entire field of early Christianity and its Jewish and Graeco-Roman environment. Its historical-philological profile and interdisciplinary outlook, which its long-term editor Martin Hengel was instrumental in establishing, is maintained by an international team of editors representing a wide range of the traditions and themes of New Testament scholarship. The sole criteria for acceptance to the series are the scholarly quality and lasting merit of the work being submitted. Apart from the specialist monographs of experienced researchers, some of which may be habilitations, *WUNT I* features collections of essays by renowned scholars, source material collections and editions as well as conference proceedings in the form of a handbook on themes central to the discipline.

WUNT II complements the first series by offering a publishing platform in paperback for outstanding writing by up-and-coming young researchers. Dissertations and monographs are presented alongside innovative conference volumes on fundamental themes of New Testament research. Like Series I, it is marked by a historical-philological character and an international orientation that transcends exegetical schools and subject boundaries. The academic quality of Series II is overseen by the same team of editors.

WUNT I:
ISSN: 0512-1604
Suggested citation: WUNT I
All available volumes can be found at
www.mohrsiebeck.com/wunt1

WUNT II:
ISSN: 0340-9570
Suggested citation: WUNT II
All available volumes can be found
at *www.mohrsiebeck.com/wunt2*

Mohr Siebeck
www.mohrsiebeck.com